ARTIST'S
WATERCOLOUR
TECHNIQUES

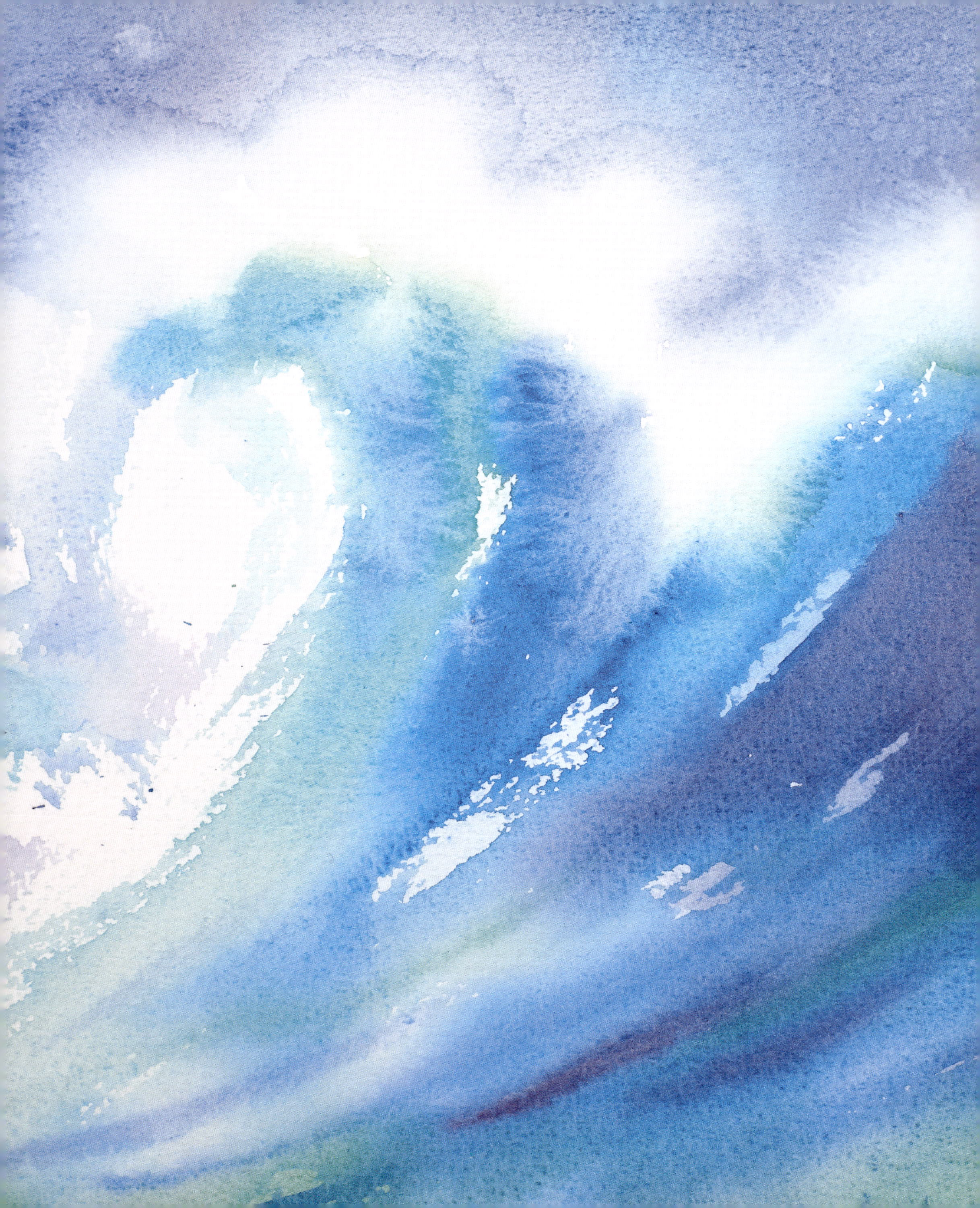

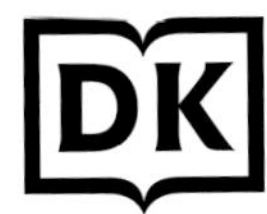

ARTIST'S **WATERCOLOUR** TECHNIQUES

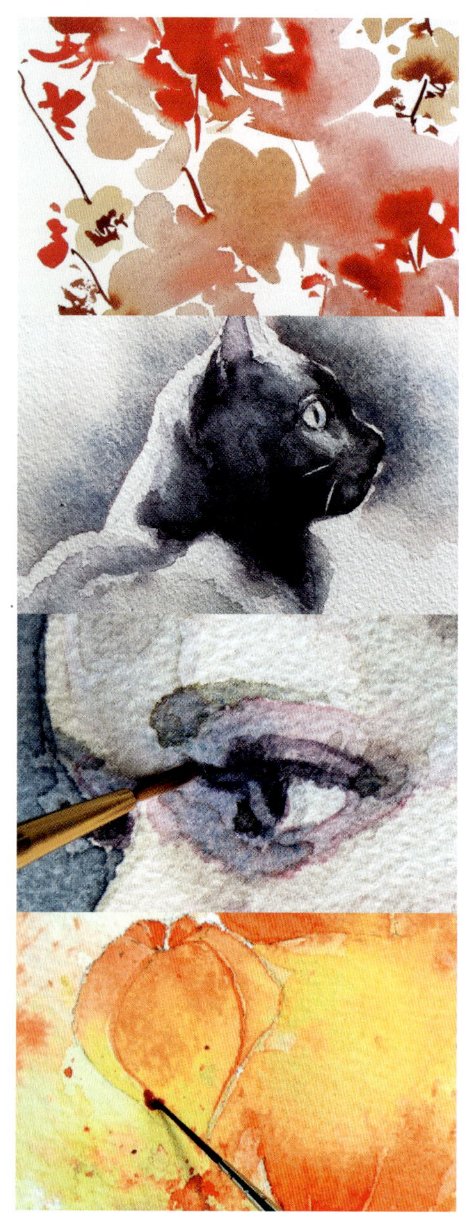

Contents

The basics

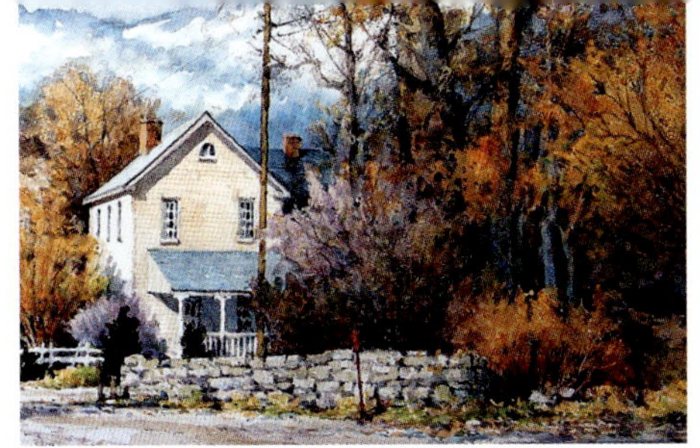

Techniques

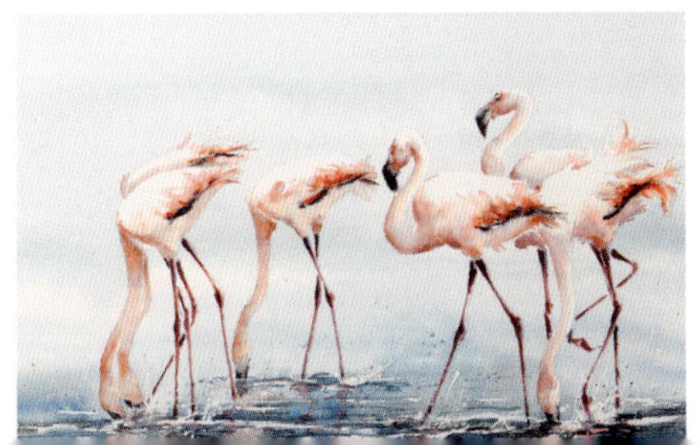

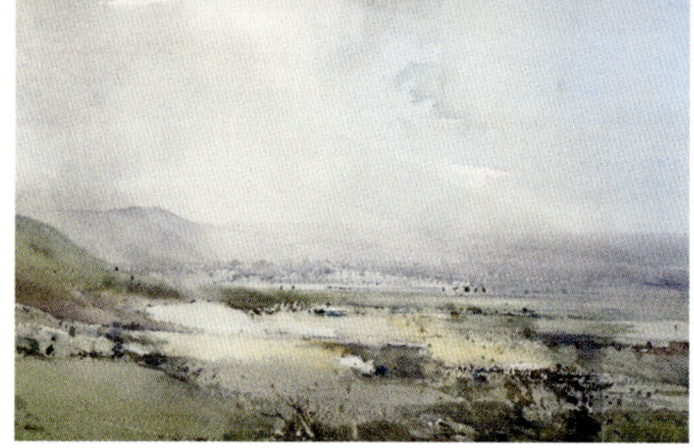

Subjects

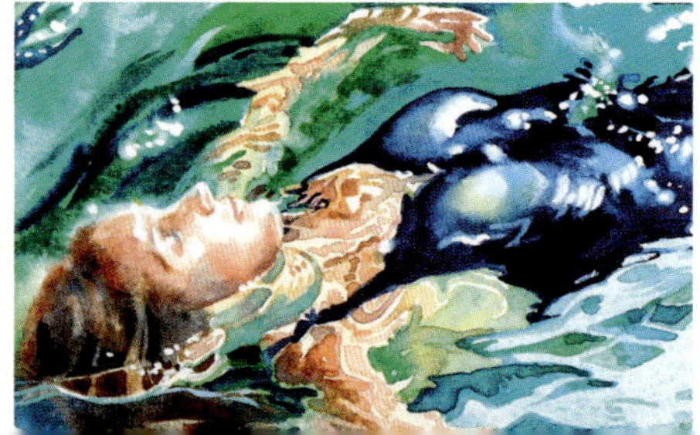

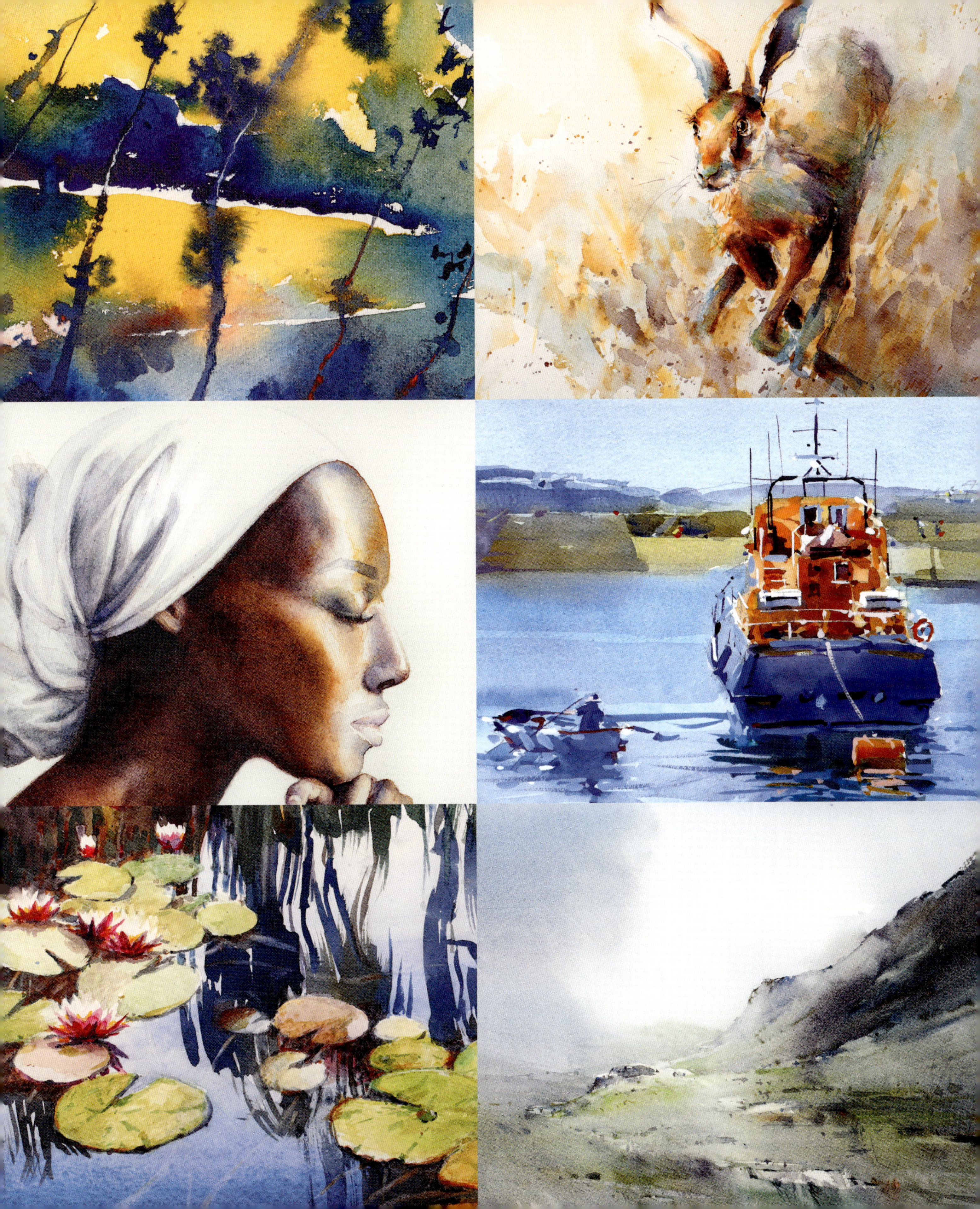

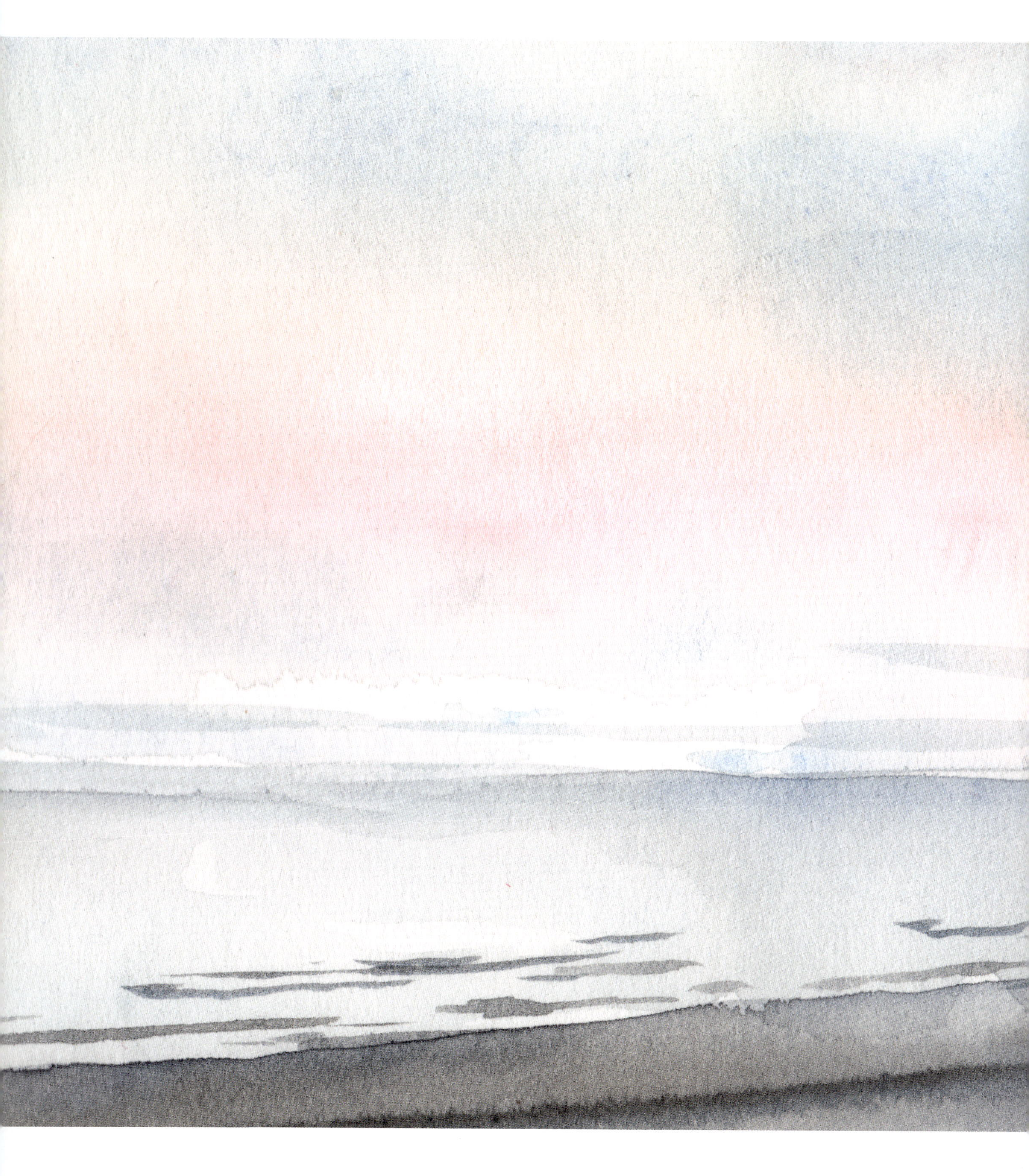

The basics

Why watercolour

DISCOVER A WATERY WORLD OF COLOUR

Watercolour has existed for thousands of years but artists are still enjoying experimenting with techniques and exploring new ways of using this medium. Discover how something as simple as a mix of pigment and water can give so much pleasure and delight when wielding a brush. Learn from other artists to develop your unique style.

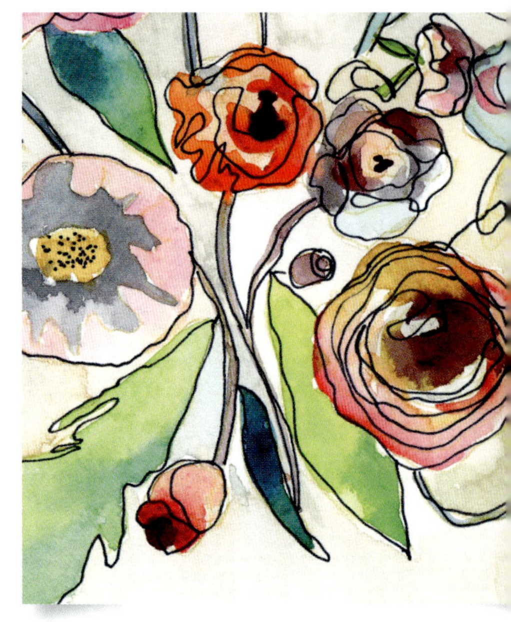

Watercolour creates transparent layers of colour that result in a freshness, clarity, and glow that no other medium can match. Watercolour also offers an immediacy to the artist as well as a certain amount of unpredictability – often watercolours are best when allowed to go their own way, creating beautiful and unexpected subtle blends.

The appeal of watercolour

Watercolour painting is incredibly accessible since it's the simplest medium to use in terms of the materials needed: a few paints, a couple of brushes, a sketchbook, and you are good to go. Compared with oil paints or acrylics, watercolours are cheap, easy to use, portable, and dry in minutes. They use exactly the same pigments as oils or pastels, which gives the paints rich and reliable colour, but with a unique luminosity.

Some people perceive watercolour purely as a sketching medium, but this idea could not be further from the truth. Many of history's finest artists, in fact, have used watercolour palettes to create paintings that are every bit as exciting and enduring as those in other media. And, as you'll see from the range of examples across the book, contemporary artists and illustrators continue to experiment, explore, and utilize watercolour to produce artworks in an inspirational variety of painting styles and effects.

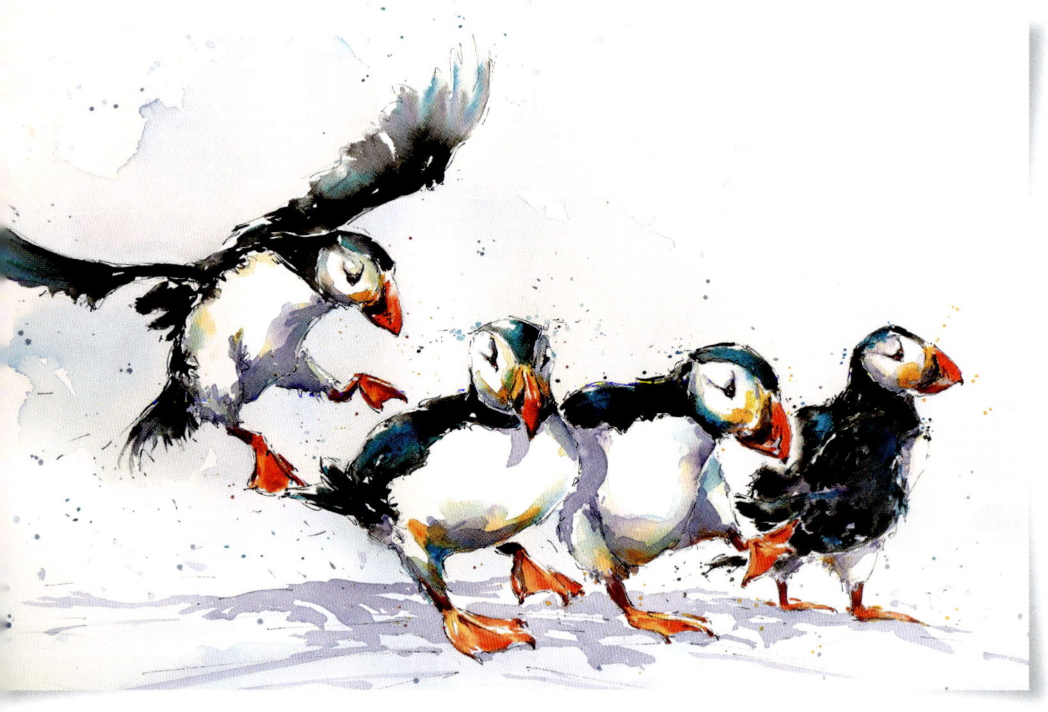

Capturing wildlife
Some subjects are never still, and the fluidity of watercolour is perfect for conveying energy and movement. This painting captures a moment in time as the birds come in to land and settle.

Colourful illustration

A contemporary take on a still life with flowers, this line-and-wash painting simply pops out of the page with its dynamic, expressive lines and intense colours.

Architectural scene

Watercolour allows for a loose, impressionistic style that is ideal for complex subjects, such as St Mark's Basilica in Venice, Italy.

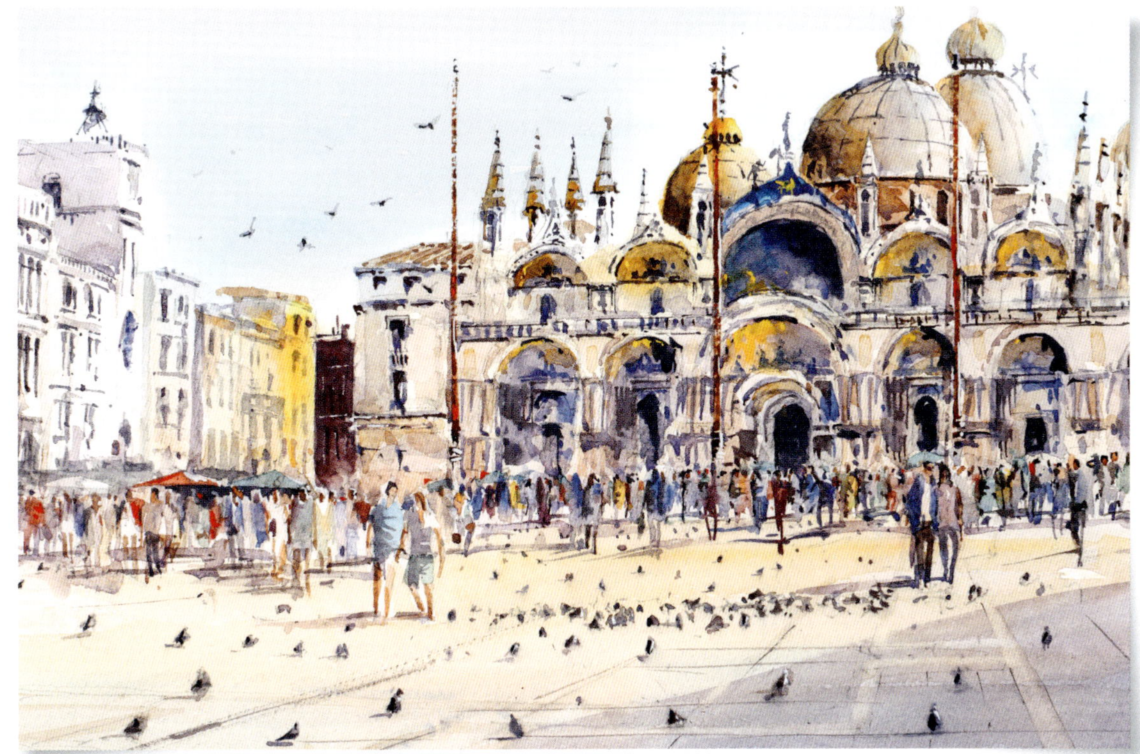

Building confidence

The techniques explored within this book show you what is possible with watercolours – from capturing crashing waves and portraying skin tones effectively, to fitting figures into a scene and experimenting with abstraction – but it is only with practice that you will develop the confidence to get the most from them. This is not the confidence that what you paint will be perfect, rather the confidence that it won't matter when it is not.

The pleasures of painting in watercolours range from manipulating loose, vibrant washes of colour to using precise and energetic brushwork.

What's more, no subject matter is out of bounds – the more traditional landscapes, seascapes, and buildings remain popular, but so, too, are still lifes, portraits, and animals.

Getting started

From kitting yourself out with the basics (and not buying too much) to learning a few essential "rules" that will reinforce the authenticity of your paintings, this first chapter holds your hand while you take your initial steps along what will probably be a lifelong journey of pleasure and discovery. Enjoy!

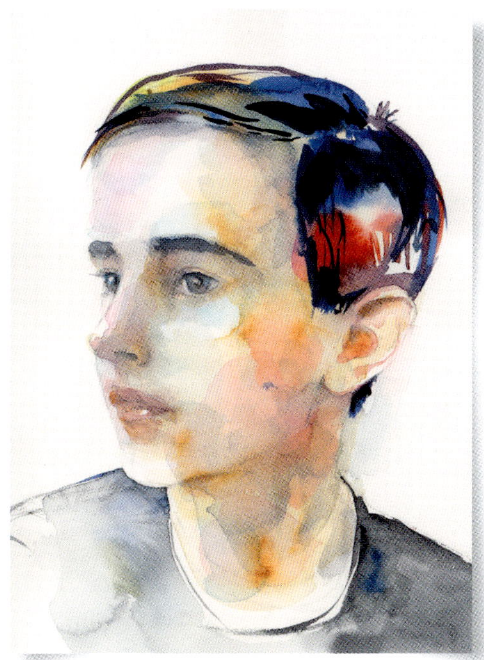

Contemporary portrait

Layers of colour create a dramatic but convincing portrayal of a person in this portrait. Colours can be abstract but still look harmonious in the final piece.

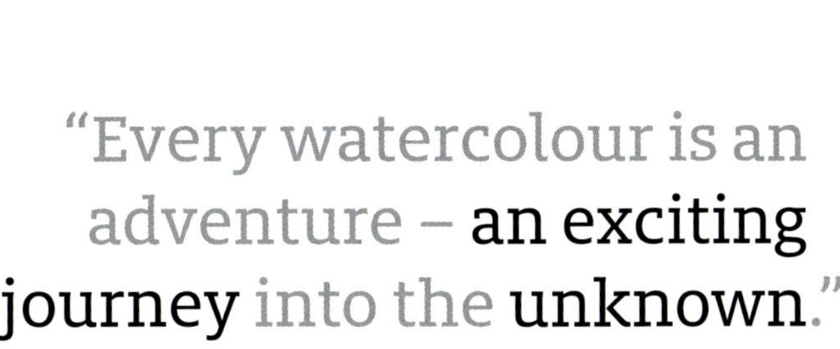

"Every watercolour is an adventure – **an exciting journey** into the **unknown.**"

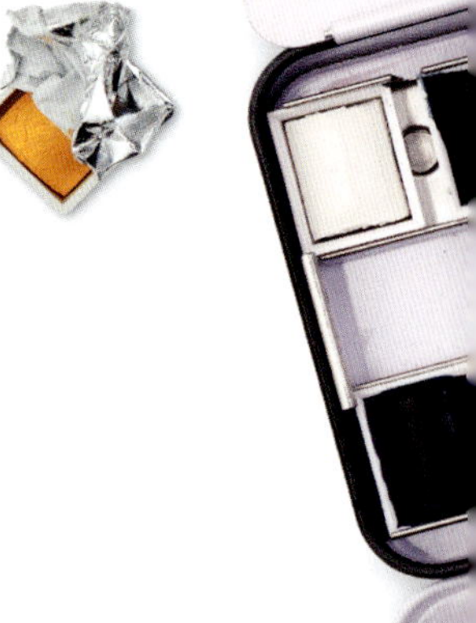

Watercolour paint

GETTING TO KNOW YOUR PIGMENTS

Watercolour paint is arguably the oldest painting medium. Natural earth pigments mixed with water were used to produce crude but effective painted images that, in some cases, have lasted for thousands of years. Earth pigments are still used today, but modern chemistry has given rise to a vast array of reliable, synthetic watercolour pigments that give consistent results for contemporary artists to add to their palettes.

What is watercolour?

Watercolour paint manufacture is a complex process and involves mixing colour pigment and water with other ingredients that include gum arabic, glycerine, and sugar syrups, such as honey. Gum arabic is a binder that holds everything in suspension, ensuring the pigment particles give an even spread of colour instead of clumping together. Glycerine prevents the dried paint from cracking, allowing easier mixing and re-wetting. Sugar syrups act as a moisture retainer that prevents the concentrated paint from drying out too much. Some people think that fillers are added as an economy, but the filler actually helps to create the buttery texture of tube watercolour paint, and ensures the consistency of the paint across a range.

Pans vs tubes

Traditional watercolour is available in tubes or as semi-hard cakes known as pans. They share identical pigments, are used in a similar way, and can be mixed together, but most artists prefer tubes.

Moist tube paint makes it easier and quicker to create mixes, particularly very dark or intense washes. To use tube paint, simply squeeze into the wells of a palette or paintbox and add to water to achieve the desired intensity of colour. Tube paint left on a palette will dry and harden, but can be re-wetted. You can use tubes to replenish depleted pans in this way.

The pigment numbering system

Watercolour paint is labelled with pigment numbers. This is a standard system used worldwide and allows you to check which pigments and how many are in a particular paint. Confusingly,

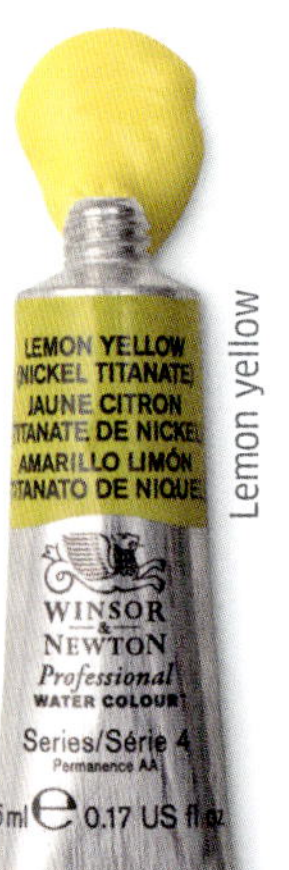

Lemon yellow

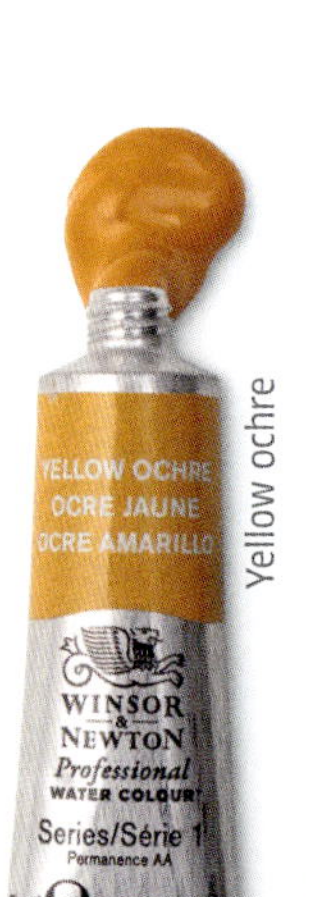

Yellow ochre

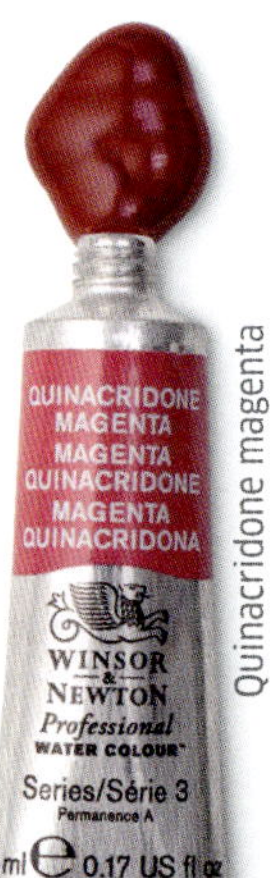

Quinacridone magenta

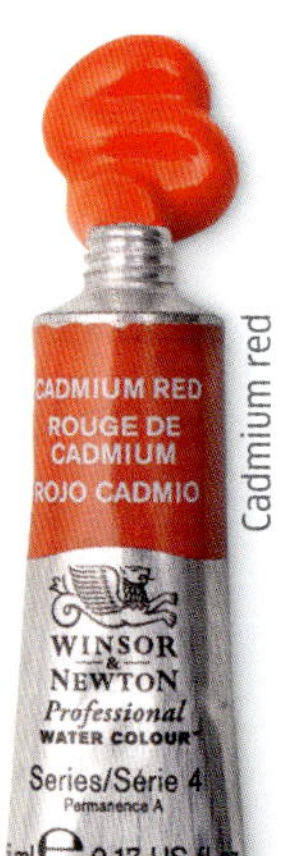

Cadmium red

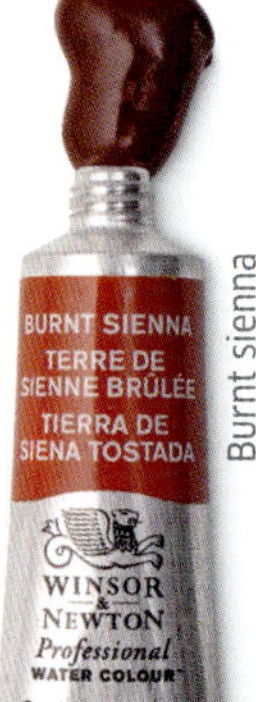

Burnt sienna

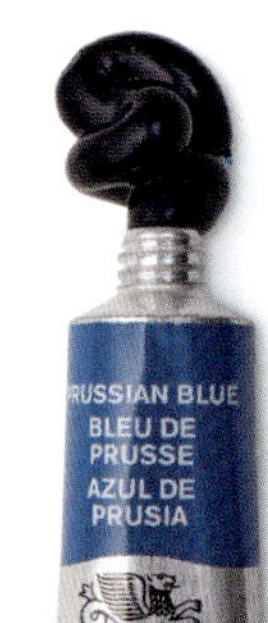

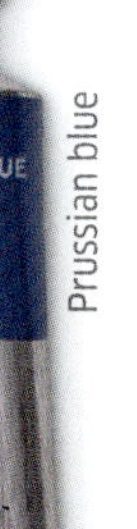

Prussian blue

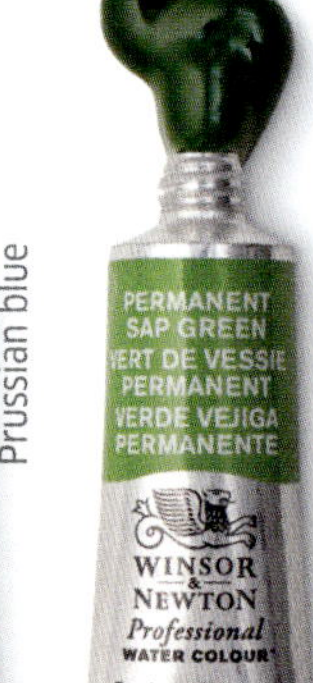

Sap green

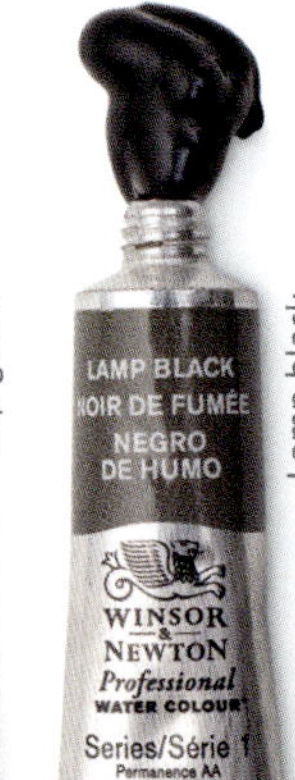

Lamp black

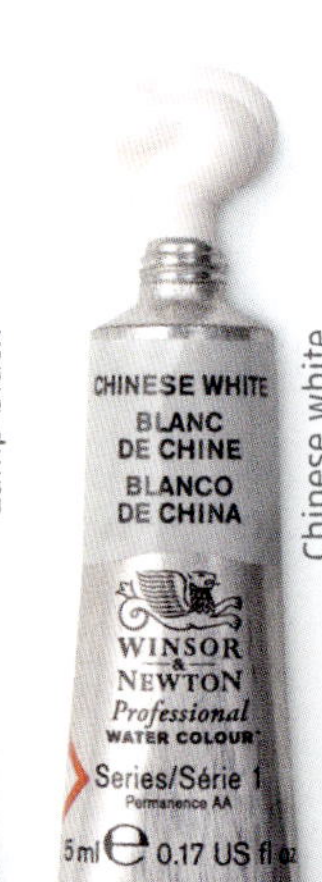

Chinese white

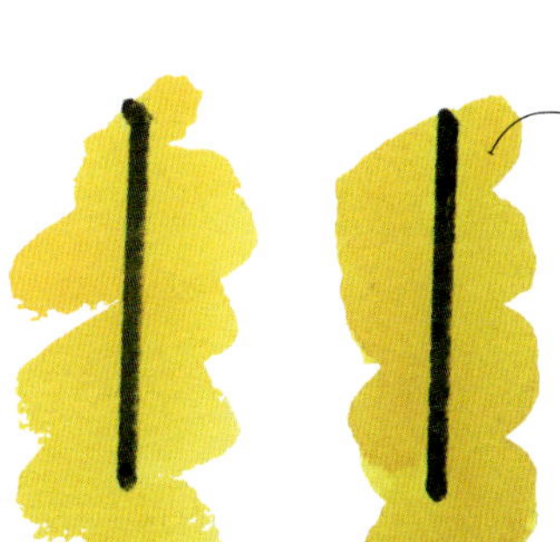

Pans
Pans are compact and convenient, and are ideal for a travelling paintbox.

different manufacturers can use different pigments for a paint with the same name, and similar pigments for paints with different names. PB15:3, for example, is known as Winsor blue green shade (GS), phthalo blue, primary blue, phthalocyanine blue, intense blue, and manganese blue hue depending on the paint manufacturer.

is labelled with "hue" after its name. This means that the paint has been formulated to match the colour of the named paint, usually a historically important pigment – for instance, "cobalt blue hue" rather than the pricier "cobalt blue". There are many reasons for not using the original pigment – there may be a safety concern, the original pigment may not be lightfast, or it may simply be too costly.

Pure colours and hues

Hue is simply another word for colour, but has another meaning when a paint

Student vs artist quality
The swatch on the right is student-quality cadmium yellow hue. On the left is artist's quality cadmium yellow. The difference is minimal, although the pure, artist's colour is perhaps a little fresher.

Tubes
Tubes are generally available in a greater variety of colours than pans. The moist paint makes mixing colour washes really quick and easy.

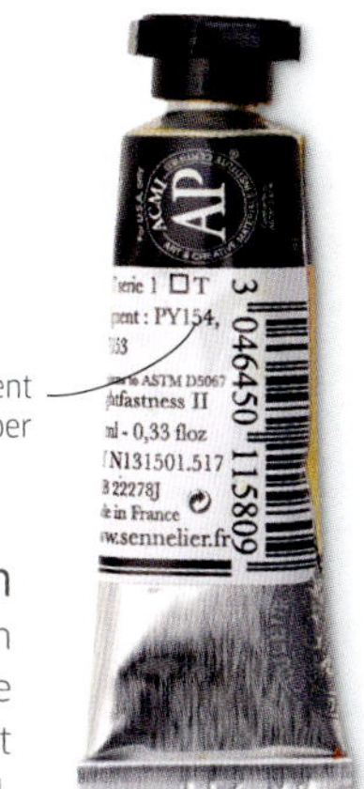
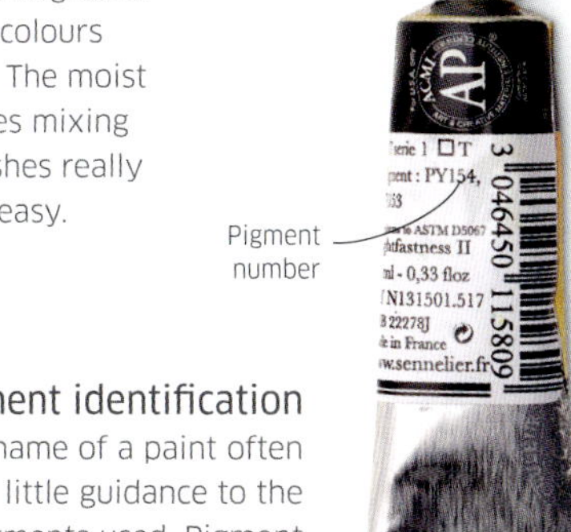

Pigment number

Pigment identification
The name of a paint often gives little guidance to the pigments used. Pigment numbers are standard.

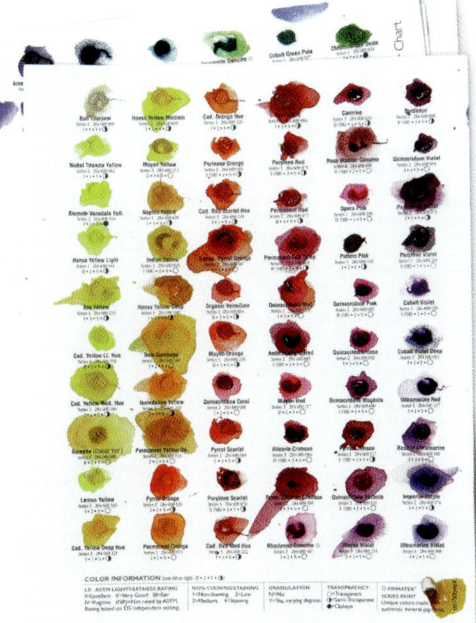

Colour cards
These cards, produced by some paint companies, contain small samples of the actual paints by a manufacturer, allowing an artist to compare many different paints at a modest cost.

Other water-based media

DIFFERENT WAYS OF APPLYING COLOUR

Traditional watercolour paints are not the only types of water-based media available. From liquid watercolours and acrylic inks to watercolour pens, markers, crayons, and pencils, there is an ever-increasing array of water-based possibilities and effects. Gouache is opaque watercolour that can be mixed with traditional transparent watercolour.

Inks and liquid watercolours

These intensely coloured liquids provide an instant hit of pure colour. Liquid watercolours and inks can be freely intermixed and diluted with water. The vibrancy of their colour makes them popular with illustrators, and you can choose between pigment-based lightfast ink or a dye-based ink that will fade. Similarly, water-soluble drawing inks can be used to create washes or for adding calligraphic marks when used with dip pens. Indian ink is mixed with a shellac binder and is unsuitable for use with fountain pens. It can be diluted and leaves a lightfast, waterproof mark. Acrylic inks are also an option but, unlike watercolour, they dry to a water-resistant finish that can't be lifted from the paper (or a palette).

Watercolour pencils and crayons

Unlike regular pencils and crayons that leave hard lines, watercolour pencils and crayons react with water to offer a softer effect when washed over. If you do not like to see drawn pencil lines in a finished painting, consider using either a watercolour pencil or a water-soluble graphite pencil instead, as either will blend with your watercolour as you paint. Watercolour pencils can be used dry and then washed over, or on wet paper they will produce a diffused line.

Use a pencil sharpener or file to create dust from a pencil and allow this to drop onto wet paper to give an unusual soft, speckled effect. Although watercolour pencils are not ideal for large washes, they can be used alongside conventional watercolours. Many urban sketchers simply use watercolour pencils and a water brush (see p.19) with their sketchbook as a convenient

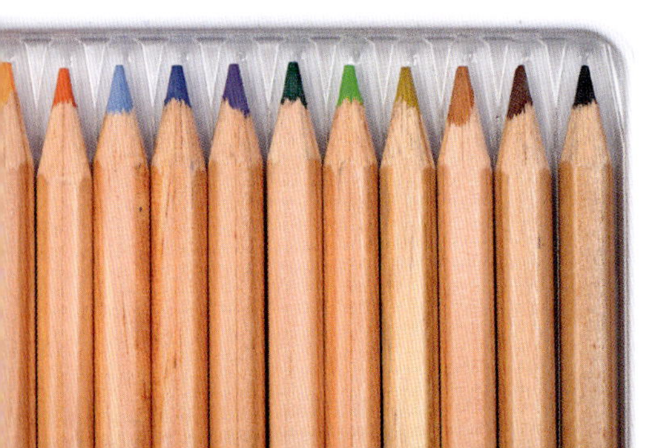

Watercolour pencils
You can sketch, draw, and lay colour as normal with watercolour pencils.

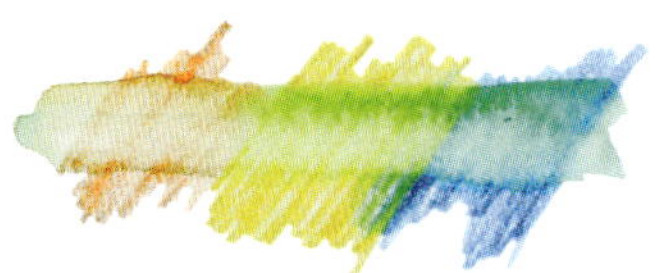

Washing over pencil
When water is brushed over the lines of watercolour pencil, it creates a wash. The wash will never be as pure as watercolour paint wash and some remnant of the pencil lines will still be visible.

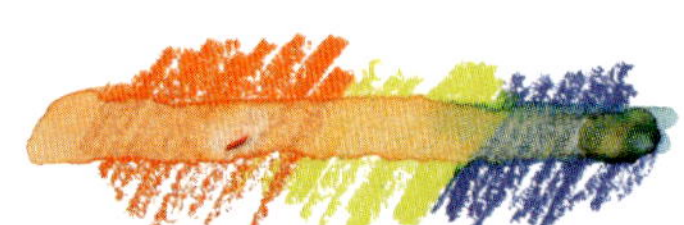

Washing over crayon
Washing water over the watercolour crayons releases the underlying colour. As with the pencils (see left) there may still be a suggestion of crayon lines remaining.

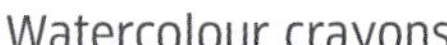

Watercolour crayons
A soft, waxy crayon means you can lay large areas of colour with broad strokes.

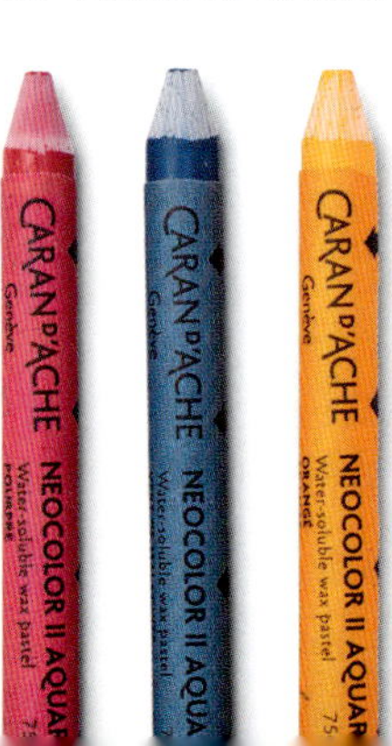

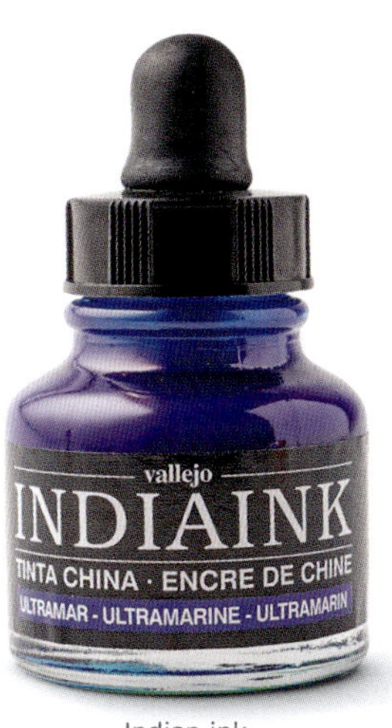
Indian ink

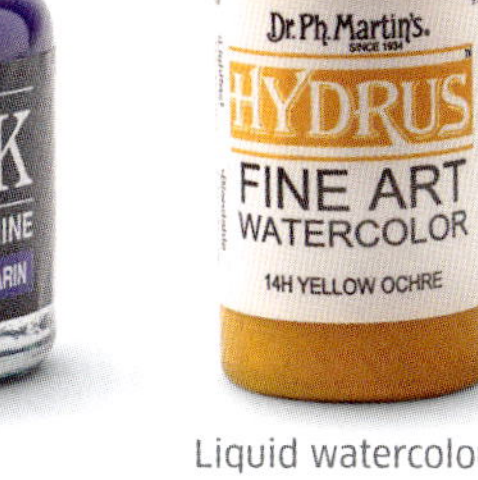
Liquid watercolour

Mixing ink and watercolour
Both liquid watercolours and acrylic inks will mix with watercolour but often in a slightly different way. Above, Indian ink repels the watercolour, pushing out to form an interesting edge.

sketching kit. Watercolour sticks and marker pens are a relatively recent innovation and both have high pigment loads ideal for producing swathes of dramatic colour.

Gouache paint
Unlike conventional transparent watercolour paint, gouache is an opaque watercolour. Gouache paint contains larger, more tightly packed pigment particles, which is what creates its opacity. The opaque nature of this paint offers the ability to paint light over dark, unlike watercolour.

White gouache straight from the tube is perfect for adding bright highlights in the final stages of your painting. What's more, it can also be mixed with conventional watercolour and water to produce interesting semi-opaque washes.

Some watercolour traditionalists abhor the use of gouache, but they may be surprised to find that certain watercolours, such as lilac, pink, Naples yellow, and lavender, all contain white paint in their formulation. Gouache was also included in the palettes of great watercolourists, like JMW Turner.

Watercolour marker pens
Use watercolour marker pens to create a variety of lines using different nibs, from fine to brush.

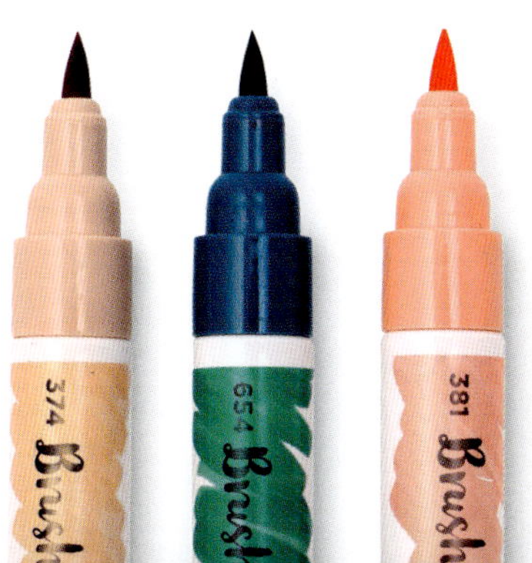

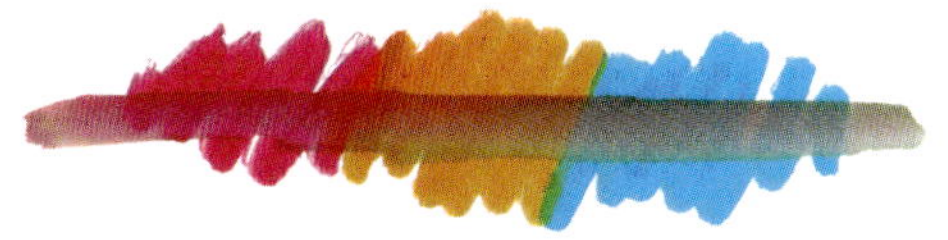

Washing over marker pen
Containing highly pigmented ink, marks from a watercolour marker pen will retain their vibrancy when washed. Use for subjects where bold colours are desired.

Uses of gouache
An alternative name for gouache is "body colour", which perfectly describes the opaque effect produced when white gouache is mixed with water and conventional watercolour. The resulting wash is ideal where you feel the paint needs more substance. It is perfect for painting cloudy skies and to capture the warm, rich sky colour at dawn and sunset.

Tube of gouache
Gouache looks very similar to watercolour, but the pigment is modified to produce opacity when the paint is used neat.

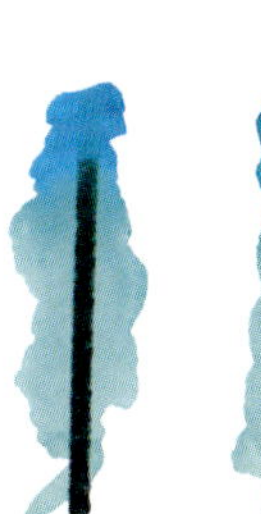
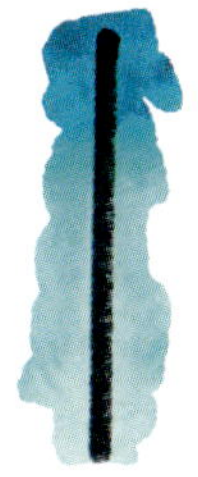
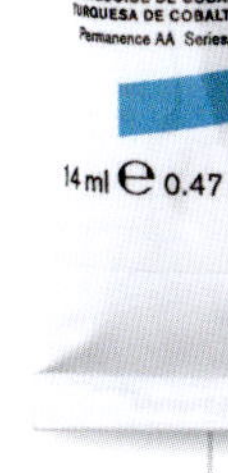

Gouache   Watercolour

Diluting gouache
Its opacity reduces dramatically when water is added. Diluted gouache (above, left) becomes almost as transparent as the watercolour on the right.

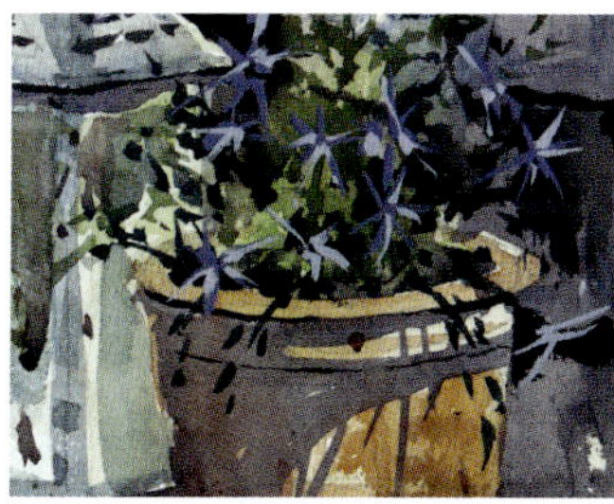

Using white gouache
Watercolour mixed with varying amounts of opaque white gouache has been used to paint the flowers, allowing the petals to be rendered with freshness and freedom.

Paper and other supports

THE CHOICE OF SURFACES

Almost all watercolour painting uses paper as its primary support. Watercolour paper has been specially treated to control the absorption of the paint, hence the choice of paper, more than anything else, will influence the appearance of your final painting. Other more unusual supports are also becoming available for use in watercolour art.

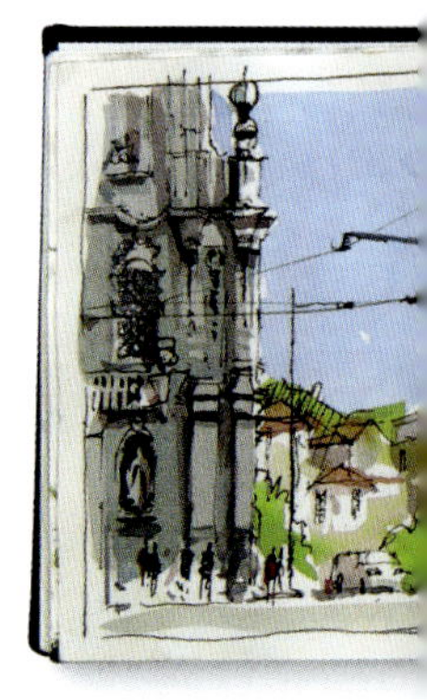

What is watercolour paper?

Paper is essentially a pressed, dried mat of plant fibres. The most expensive watercolour papers are made using 100 per cent cotton fibres or a mix of cotton and linen. Although some handmade paper is still manufactured, popular papers, such as Saunders, are nowadays made by machine.

Less expensive papers are made from cellulose pulp derived from wood with the lignin removed, which prevents the paper from yellowing. Watercolour papers also undergo a process known as "sizing", which controls how much of the watercolour wash is absorbed into the paper, as well as adding surface strength. All paper from high-quality paper mills is designed to last for hundreds of years without discolouring or falling apart.

Surface texture

You can choose from three basic textures of watercolour paper: smooth, rough, and something in between.

Hot-pressed paper has a beautifully smooth surface created by passing the paper through heated steel rollers. Such paper is popular with illustrators because of how well such a surface takes a pen line, but colour washes are a little more difficult to apply.

Rough papers have an uneven surface texture created by pressing the paper between woollen felts, rather than heated steel rollers. This surface will often be chosen by the loose impressionistic painter where detail may not be such an issue.

Passing rough paper through cold steel rollers removes some but not all of the textural surface, to produce cold-pressed (CP) paper or NOT paper (NOT means NOT hot-pressed). NOT

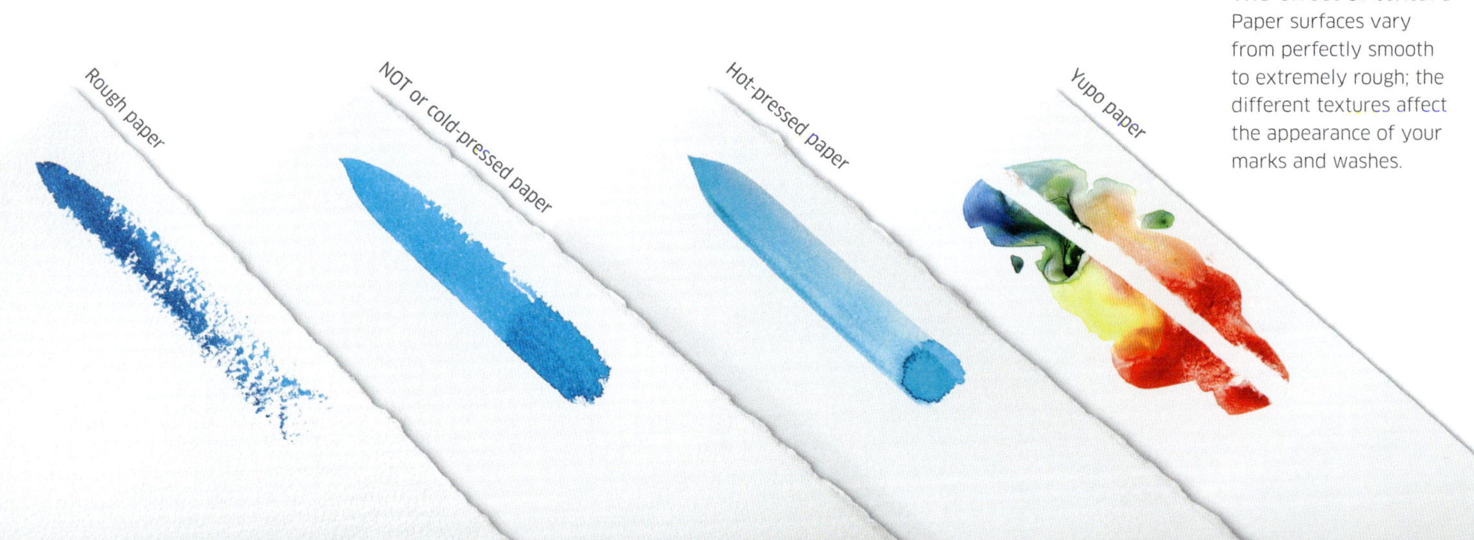

The effect of texture

Paper surfaces vary from perfectly smooth to extremely rough; the different textures affect the appearance of your marks and washes.

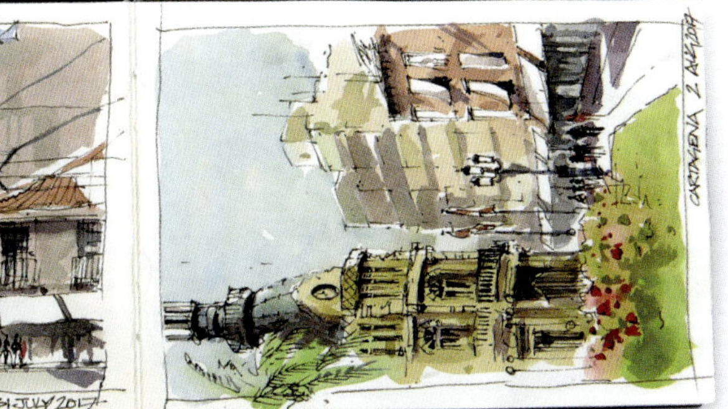

Sketchbooks

Ordinary cartridge paper sketchbooks can be used for watercolour. Paint economically as overly wet areas will degrade the paper.

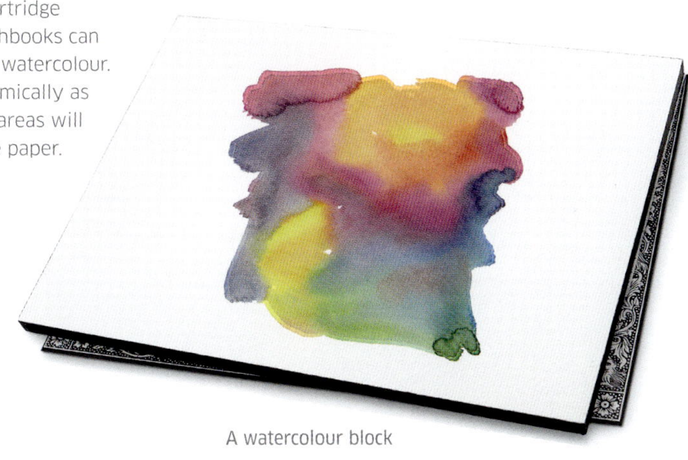

A watercolour block

paper has a texture in between hot-pressed and rough, and is probably the most common paper chosen by watercolour artists.

A paper's weight

The weight of paper is expressed as grams per square metre (gsm) or as weight in pounds per 500 imperial sheets (lb) and ranges from 190gsm (90lb) to 640gsm (300lb). The heavier the weight, the thicker the paper. Lighter papers under 300gsm (140lb) will need stretching first (see below) to prevent them from cockling when wet.

Watercolour blocks

As well as cut sheets of paper, you can also buy watercolour paper as rolls and in more expensive pads or blocks. Blocks are glued all round and although the paper will cockle when wet, it will dry perfectly flat as long as it is not removed from the block until it is dry.

Sketchbooks

A huge variety of paper from watercolour paper to cartridge paper and even kraft (brown) paper, can be bound up as a sketchbook. All are suitable for wet painting but papers other than watercolour paper will be more easily damaged and are more likely to exhibit "bleed through" and so are best used for quick studies only.

Yupo

This synthetic paper is made from polypropylene plastic. It produces effects akin to hot-pressed paper and is ideal for experimental techniques as, uniquely, the paint is not absorbed. This gives time to manipulate the paint and, if the effect is not to your liking, colour can be completely removed even when dry; simply wipe off and start again.

Stretching paper

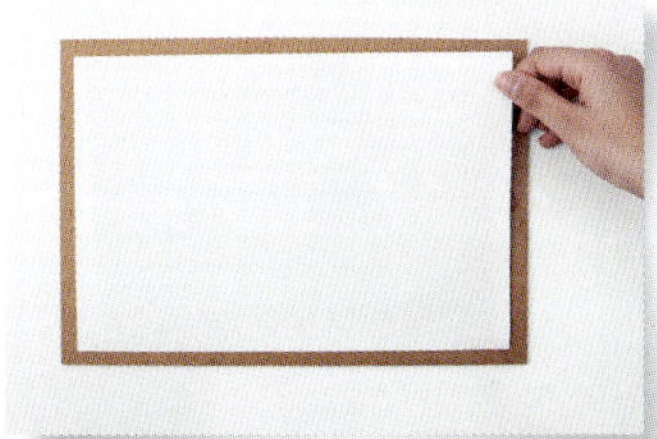

Step 1
Submerge a whole sheet of paper under water. For 300gsm (140lb) paper, soak for 15 minutes; less for lighter papers. Lift out and drain.

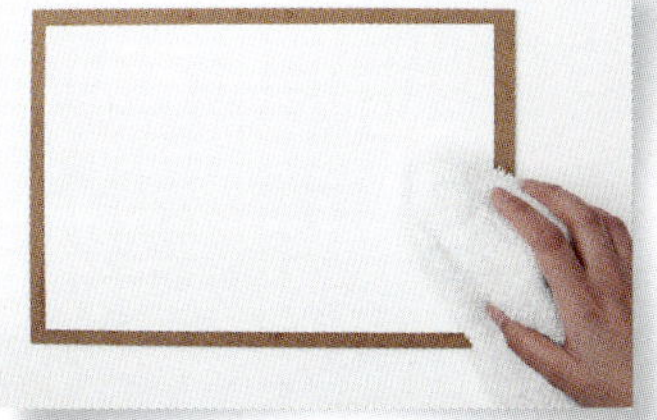

Step 2
Place the paper on a flat wooden board. Towel-dry the excess water from the edges; if the edges are too wet, the tape will not stick.

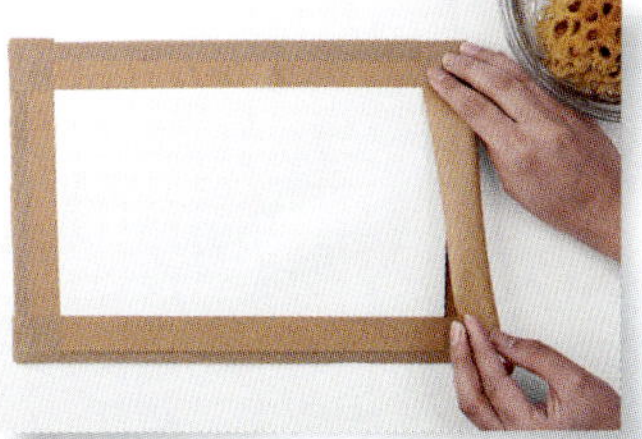

Step 3
Dampen some gummed paper tape and immediately place it along the edge of the paper, allowing at least 10mm (⅓in) overlap.

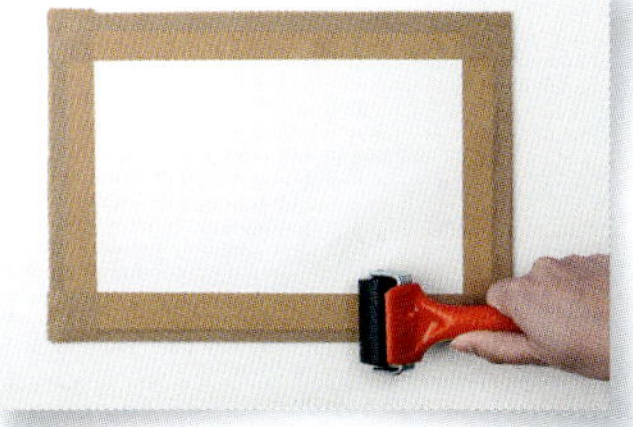

Step 4
Roll a rubber roller over the edges to make sure the tape is well pressed down. Then, leave in a horizontal position until dry.

Brushes

YOUR CHOICE OF TOOLS

Brushes are by far the most common way of applying paint to paper. They come in a huge variety of sizes and hair types. Although the most common are round or flat soft-hair brushes, there are also a number of shaped brushes designed for particular tasks. You don't need to spend a great deal on brushes – most experienced artists use only a few.

Brush shapes

The shape of a brush will largely determine the shape of the mark produced on the paper (see pp.20–21 for examples of mark-making with different shapes of brush). Artists generally use round brushes, flat brushes, or a mixture of both for almost all of their painting.

You may prefer to use a flat brush where you want to make a specific angular mark, whereas the marks produced by round brushes are less characteristic and perhaps more suited to general work. The chisel edge of a flat brush is good for creating straight lines, while the point of a round brush is perfect for fine, undulating lines (see also below and below right for specific brushes for achieving fine lines and other painterly effects).

Hair used for brushes

Traditionally sable was and is used for the best-quality and most expensive brushes. Sable hair brushes have a good balance of softness and spring, as well as holding a huge amount of paint mix for their size and releasing it in a smooth, consistent way.

Squirrel hair, too, is extremely fine and many artists favour squirrel mop brushes for their carrying capacity for laying large washes, as well as for their fine points. The hair is much softer than sable with virtually no spring.

Modern synthetic brushes are becoming extremely popular, partly on environmental and ethical grounds, and the quality and results of these synthetic brushes are improving all the time, with the best now rivalling natural hair. Older

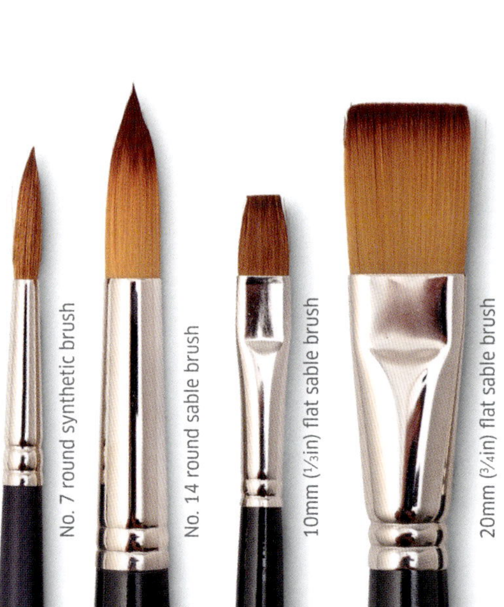

Round or flat?
By far the most common brush shapes are rounds and flats. These are made from a wide variety of hair types, both natural and synthetic.

Fine-line brushes
Some brushes are made specifically to produce fine lines. A rigger is a standard small, round brush with extra-long hairs. The reservoir brush is a fine sable rigger surrounded by a squirrel reservoir. The unusual-looking swordliner is designed with a long tapering point.

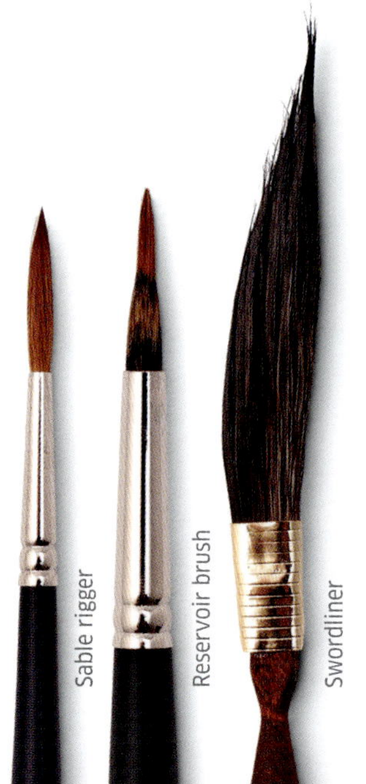

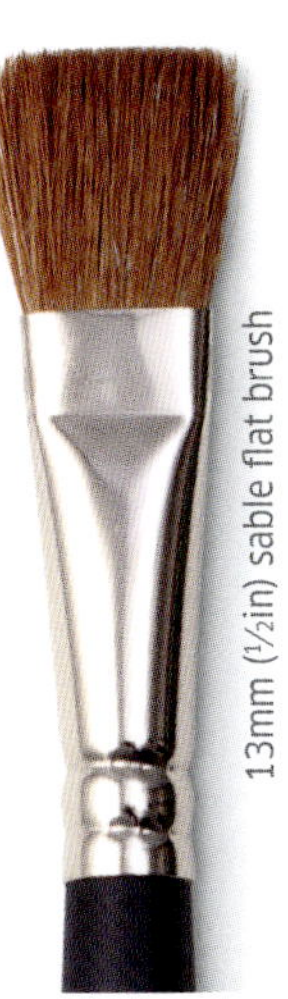

Types of hair
The three most common hairs used for brushmaking are sable, squirrel, and synthetic.

13mm (½in) sable flat brush

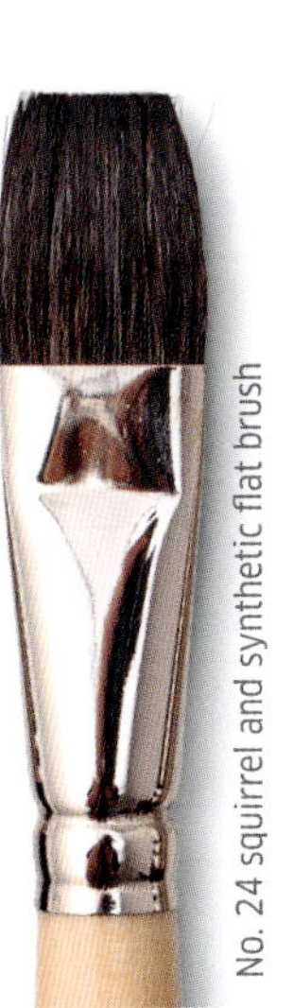

No. 24 squirrel and synthetic flat brush

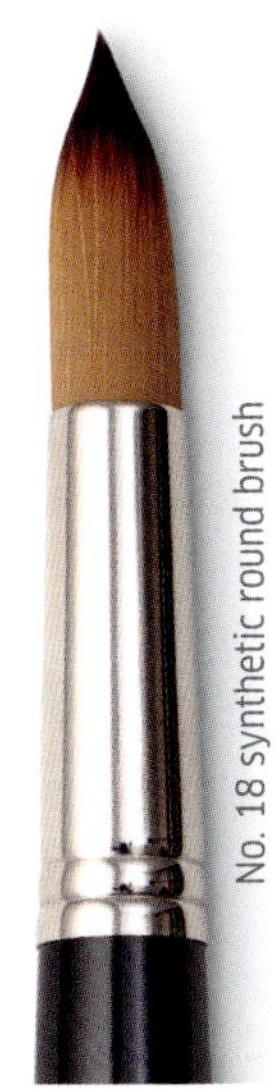

No. 18 synthetic round brush

> "No matter what **shape or size**, a brush must be able to **lay watercolour** on to paper **gently and smoothly.**"

synthetic brushes had a rather unnatural strong spring but the more recent types seem to have been designed to control this.

Unfortunately, all brushes (even expensive sable ones) will eventually wear out, particularly the fine points on round brushes. You can increase their life span by looking after your brushes, washing them well after each use, and storing them upright so that the hairs are not bent. If the hairs on natural brushes do become bent they will often straighten if they are dipped into very hot water for a couple of seconds and then left to dry.

Which size of brush?

In general, flat brushes and mops are sized according to their diameter, but round brushes have no standard sizing method except that larger brushes have larger numbers, and vice versa. In general, a round brush in the range of size 10–14 will suit most painters for most parts of their painting, with a smaller one in the 4–7 range for completing the more detailed parts.

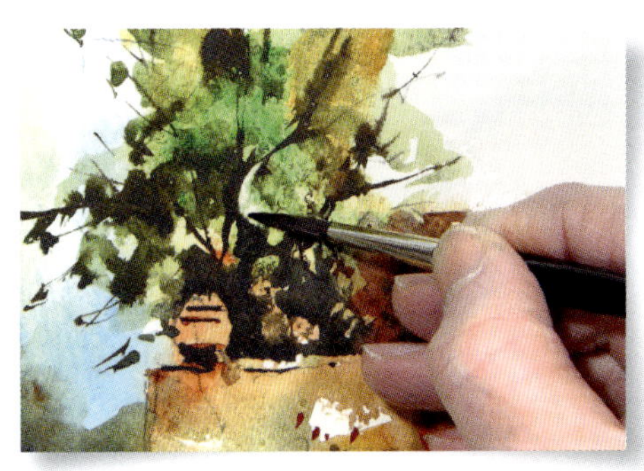

Lifting out colour
Highlights can be lifted from a watercolour by scrubbing gently with a brush. Sable or synthetic are best as a certain spring is required. Hog brushes are often recommended but can, in fact, damage lighter papers.

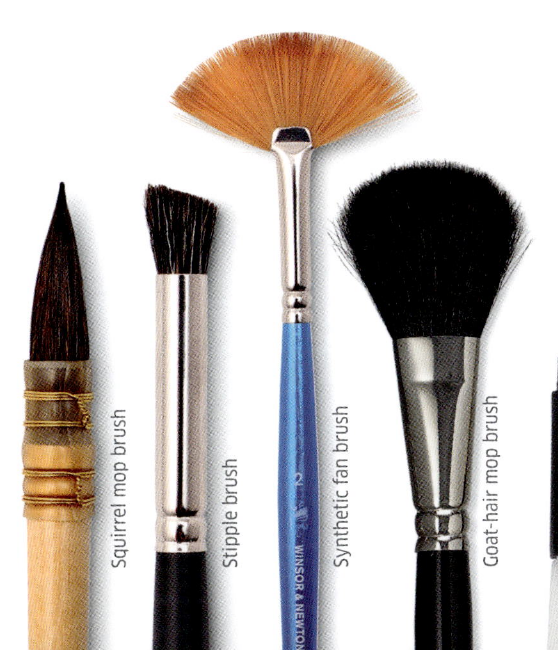

An array of brushes
Mop brushes can hold a lot of water for easy coverage on paper. Fan brushes can produce convincing grasses and fur, while stipplers are great for foliage. Water brushes are handy as they hold water within a squeezable cavity. Chinese brushes hold good points, and the Japanese hake brush is a versatile mark-maker.

Squirrel mop brush

Stipple brush

Synthetic fan brush

Goat-hair mop brush

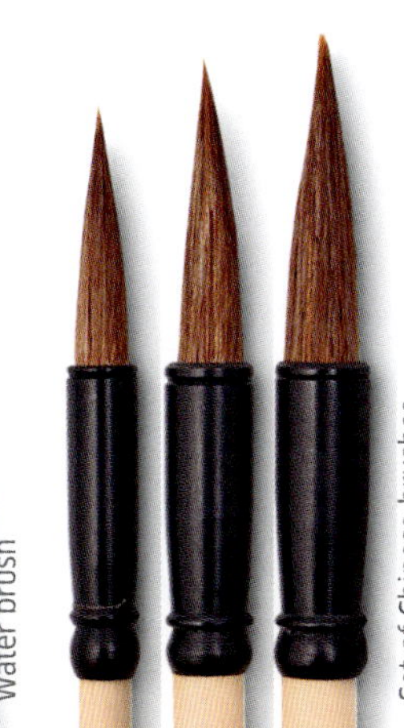

Water brush

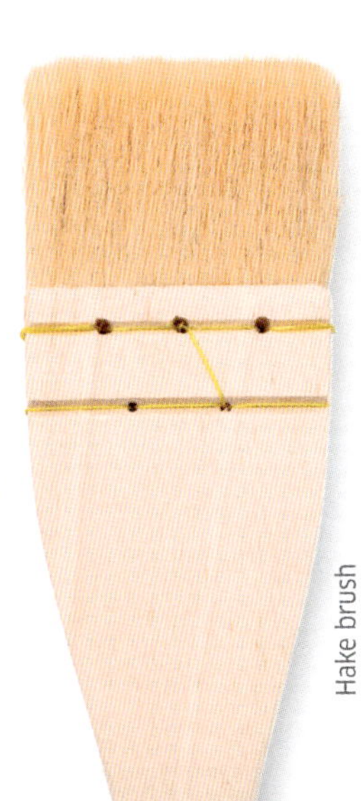

Set of Chinese brushes

Hake brush

Applying paint

EXPLORING PAINT EFFECTS

For the most part, applying paint to paper means using paintbrushes. But you can experiment and try out other alternatives to brushstrokes that offer a better likeness of a texture or add some randomness or dynamism. Almost anything goes. If something works for you (and the painting), there's no need to be concerned that it might not be the usual way of doing things.

■ Brushstrokes

Each brush produces a different type of mark – from the delicate, broken marks of a fan brush to flat, solid strokes of differing widths. Use the largest brush suitable for the effect you wish to achieve, then you'll need to use fewer strokes. Practise mark-making by holding the brush at different angles.

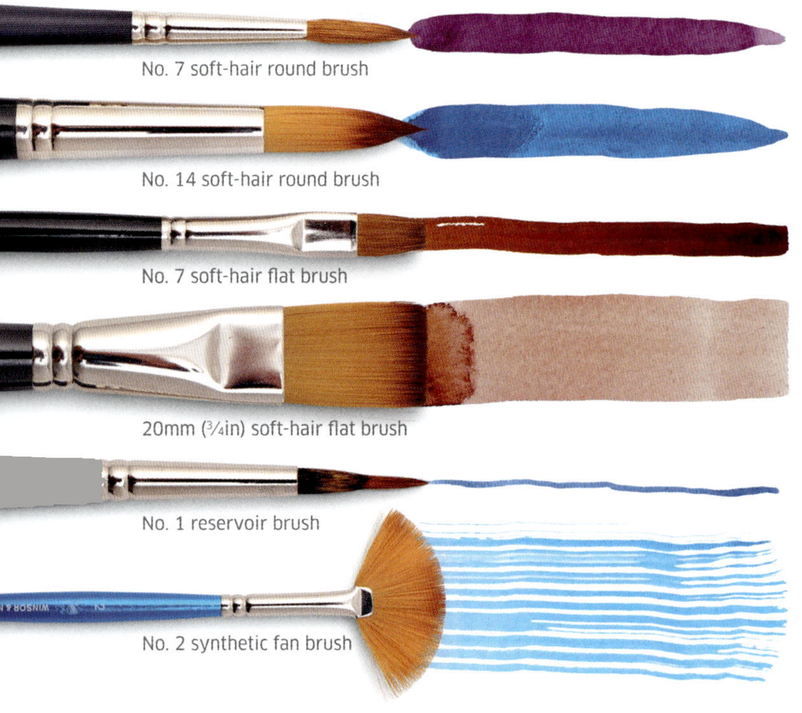

No. 7 soft-hair round brush

No. 14 soft-hair round brush

No. 7 soft-hair flat brush

20mm (¾in) soft-hair flat brush

No. 1 reservoir brush

No. 2 synthetic fan brush

STAMPING AND SPONGING

Widening your painting arsenal from just brushes (see pp.18–19) gives you access to a world of textures and shapes that would be hard to achieve otherwise. Use a variety of stamping tools to apply paint directly to paper – no brush required! Enjoy experimenting with an out-of-date credit card, plastic comb, or cardboard.

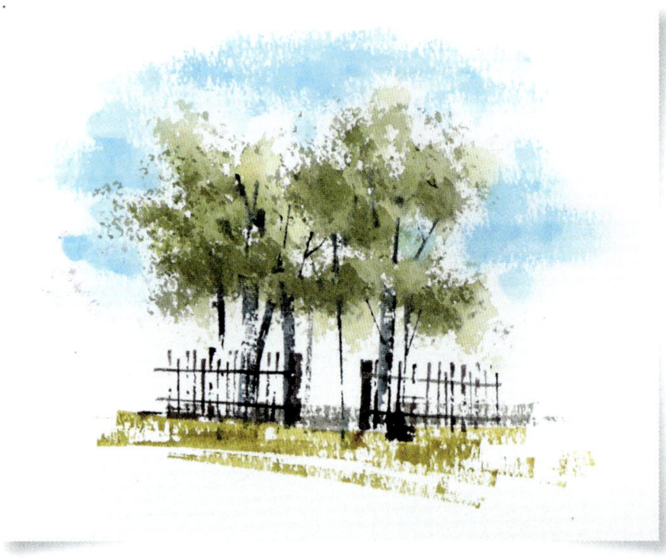

A "no brush" watercolour painting
Explore the world of mark-making and create a painting without lifting a brush. Here, edges of mount card were used to convey the tree trunks, fence, and foreground, while sponging with a natural sponge gives just the right impression for the tree canopies, and cotton wool created the cloudy sky.

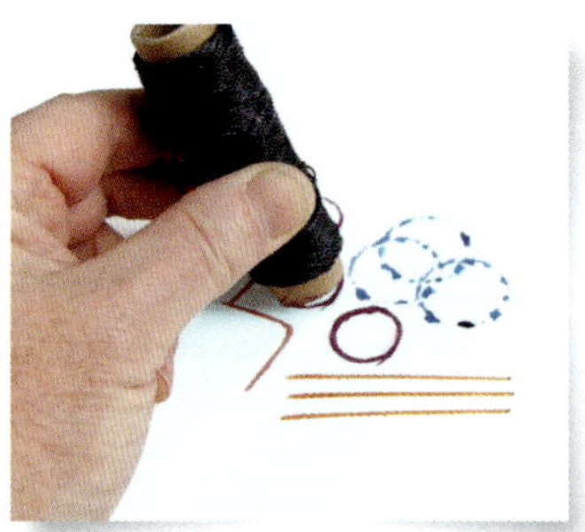

Watercolour stamping
Do-it-yourself stamping tools – bottle bases and wine corks, for instance – are all around you. Non- or less absorbent stamps will require a paint mix with less water.

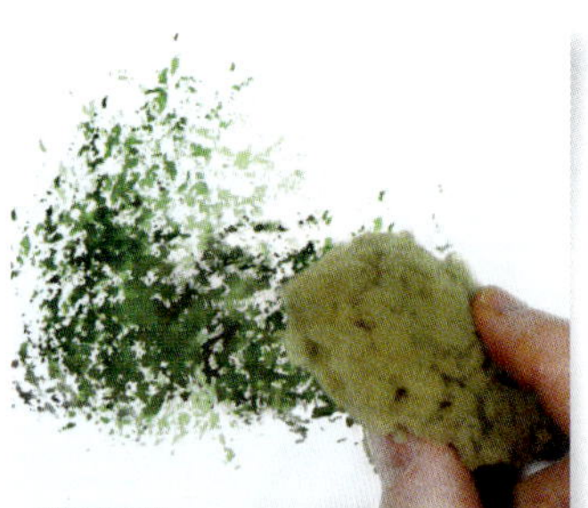

Textural sponging
Natural sponge, cotton wool, and scrunched-up paper all describe great textures. Use two or three paint mixes for variety and use sparingly to avoid overly "spongy" marks.

CONSISTENT LINES

When only lines of a consistent width will do, get to know how to use a ruling pen. This tool is highly adjustable and uses watercolour paint rather than ink.

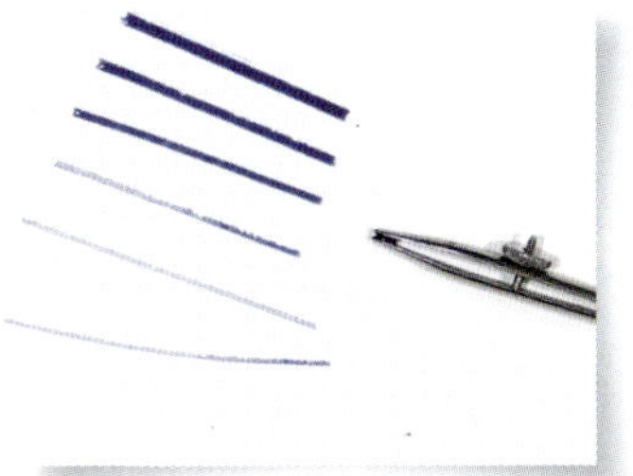

All widths of lines
A ruling pen is excellent for producing consistent lines of an even width. The width of the line can be adjusted by turning the knurled wheel.

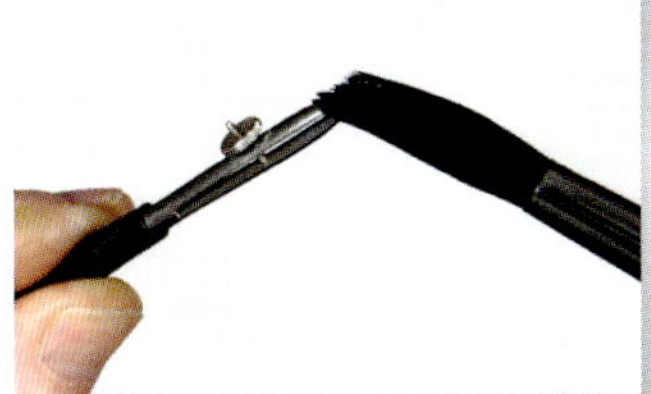

A simple refill
Unlike a pencil or pen, using a ruling pen allows you to stay within the realms of watercolour. Simply stroke a full brush against the edge of the blade to refill.

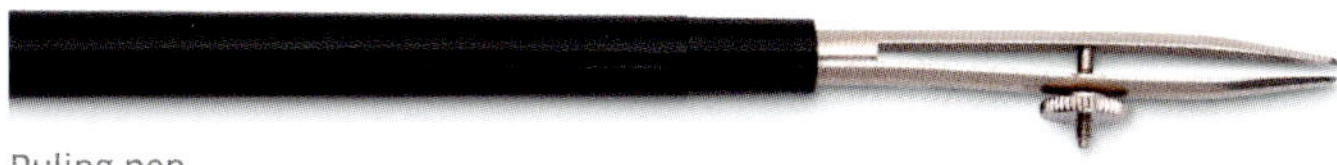

Ruling pen

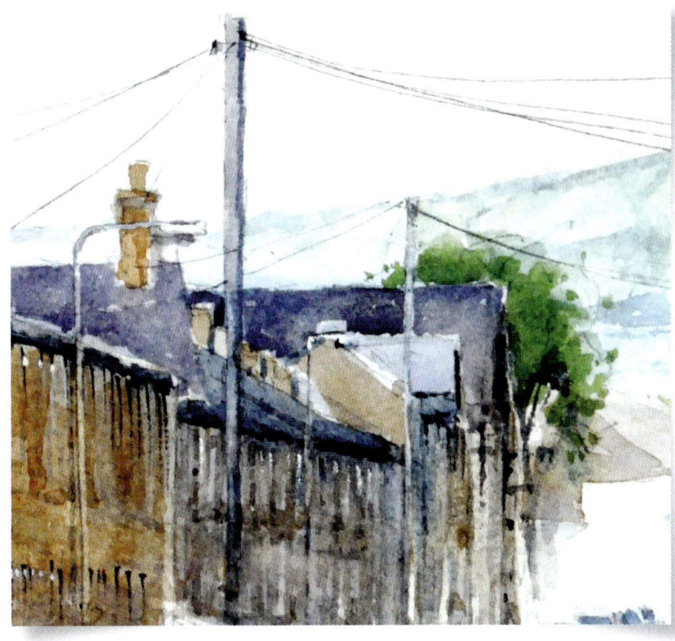

Street scene
Vertical telegraph poles punctuate a run of terraced houses in this scene of an everyday street. Here, a ruling pen was used to draw the convincing telephone wires.

SPLATTER AND SPATTER

Flicking paint onto the paper without touching it adds a sense of playful energy to your work. Splatter (large blobs) and spatter (tiny speckles) create a certain randomness and texture in a painting.

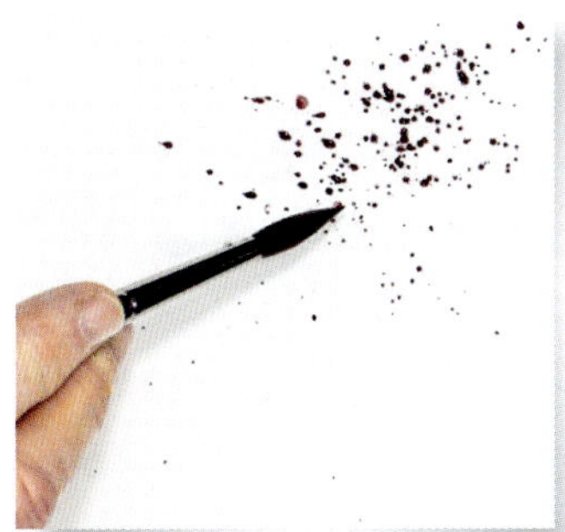

Paintbrush splatter
Use a regular paintbrush to create random arrays of paint blobs; the size of the brush will determine the rough size of the splatter. Experiment on a separate piece of paper to judge the effect before you work on your painting.

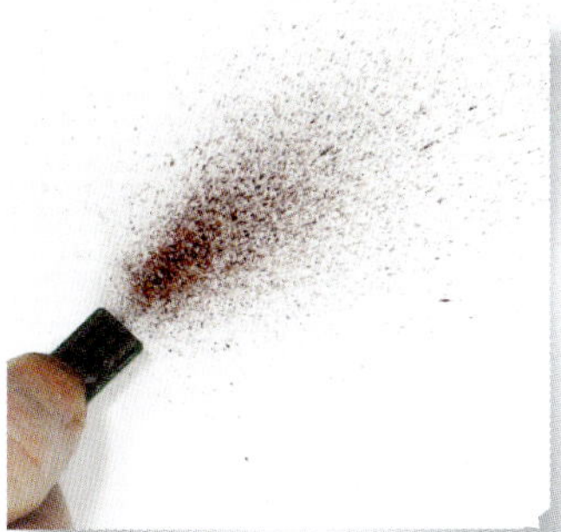

Toothbrush spatter
A toothbrush rubbed with a finger creates a very fine spatter – much finer than the splatter of paintbrush blobs. You can use such tiny particles of colour for describing intricate textures, such as sand on a beach.

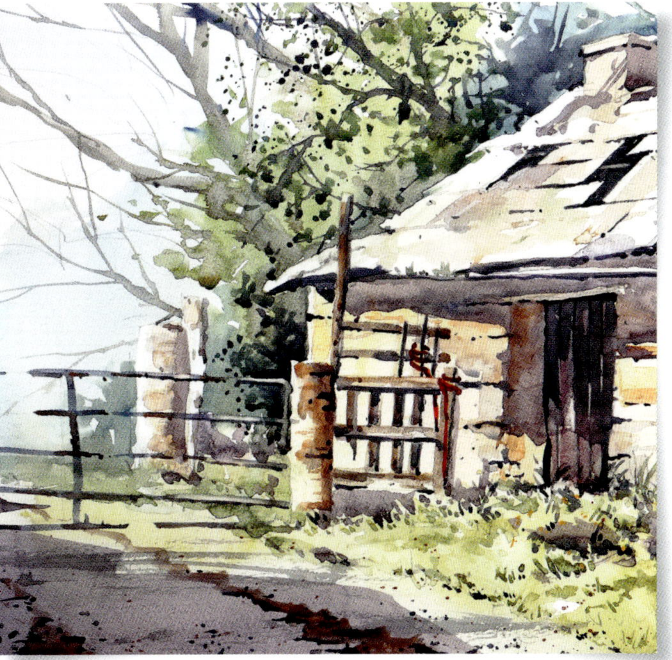

Using splatter effects
Splatter can be very useful in suggesting random arrangements of objects. In this painting, leaves, stones on the lane, and grass are all partly applied by splatter, which gives a more natural appearance as well as being much quicker to apply than individual marks.

Pencils, pens, and mediums

MAKING MARKS, ADDING EFFECTS

Pens and pencils are primarily used for the preparatory sketch before painting, although many artists also use them as an integral part of the finished work. Pen and wash is a traditional approach, where the pen forms the main structure of the painting and the watercolour washes are used to add colour and decoration to the drawing.

Pencils

A pencil drawing is by far the most common start to a watercolour. The purpose of the sketch is really more to plan where to put the washes and so normally the drawing is fairly simple. It is important to use a pencil that feels comfortable in your hand as well as creating the type of marks you want.

The traditional wooden pencil comes in a range of hardness levels, but requires constant sharpening with a sharpener or sharp knife; if you sharpen with a knife, you can vary the lead length. Many artists prefer a carpenter's pencil with its flat lead for producing a greater variety of lines while others favour a solid graphite stick.

Clutch pencils are convenient, requiring only the press of a button to advance the lead. Again, there is a good range of hardness but just as useful is the variety of lead diameters available. Each pencil is made for only one lead diameter. There is no "ideal" diameter; an artist will have their own preference. Diameters range from 0.2mm to 5.6mm; 0.9mm is a good choice. Anything below this size breaks very easily and anything above requires sharpening, either with the built-in sharpener that many of these pencils have, or with a separate lead sharpener.

Pens

A pen drawing goes superbly well with watercolour. A disposable or technical pen is convenient and you can find one that suits your needs since they come in a wide range of nib widths. They suit precise drawing but the nib can feel a little unresponsive.

A pen with a traditional metal nib gives a beautiful variety of line. The simplest of these pens is the dip pen,

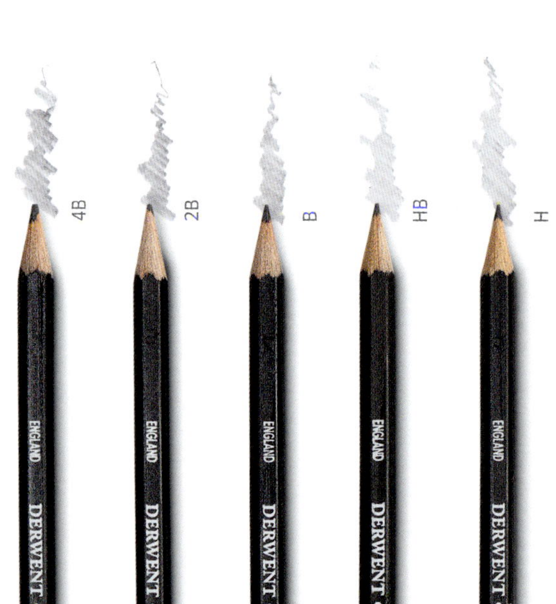

Graphite grades
Graphite comes in several degrees of hardness, represented by H = hard and B = black. HB would be considered average hardness and blackness, but most artists prefer 2B or 3B – soft enough not to dent the paper but not so soft that the graphite smudges to a large extent.

Graphite drawing tools
Graphite is usually used for the preliminary drawing ahead of the painting. Choose from a wide variety of hardnesses and widths, with options ranging from the thick graphite stick that produces broad strokes, to a clutch pencil that gives a fine, constant line.

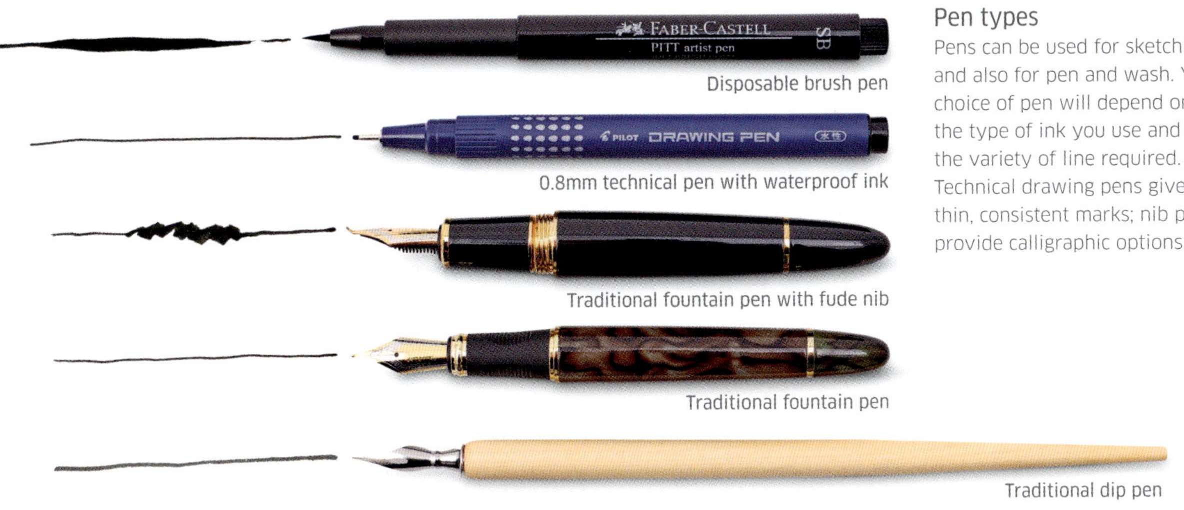

Pen types

Pens can be used for sketching and also for pen and wash. Your choice of pen will depend on the type of ink you use and the variety of line required. Technical drawing pens give thin, consistent marks; nib pens provide calligraphic options.

Disposable brush pen

0.8mm technical pen with waterproof ink

Traditional fountain pen with fude nib

Traditional fountain pen

Traditional dip pen

which is available with interchangeable nibs so that you can vary the width of the line. Its only disadvantage is the need to constantly dip into the ink. This is the only pen that can be used with Indian or any other shellac-based ink. These inks may be beautiful but will quickly destroy a fountain pen.

For those wanting to draw with a fountain pen, water-soluble inks, or special inks that are water soluble in the pen but dry water resistant, are the best choice. A special nib with an upward bend known as a fude nib gives the ultimate variety of line.

Watercolour mediums

Specially designed watercolour mediums are great for experimentation. Primer mediums, or ground, allow watercolour to be painted on almost any surface (such as canvas) and can be used to add opaque whites for texture. Binding mediums, including gum arabic (see box below), work with the paint to create a glossy appearance, add shimmer, and enhance luminosity. Granulating medium encourages the paint to separate and clump, creating a speckled effect; some artists use granulation to bring delicate textures and variety to washes.

Water-soluble graphite

Use these pencils to create drawings with a simple wash. Their lines disappear in the finished watercolour, so are popular with artists who don't want the pencil to remain.

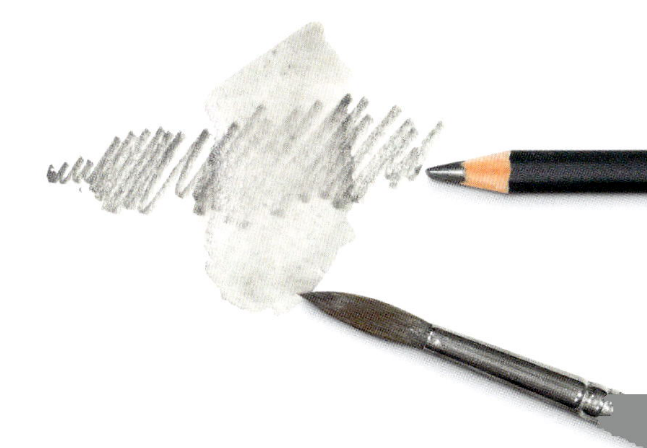

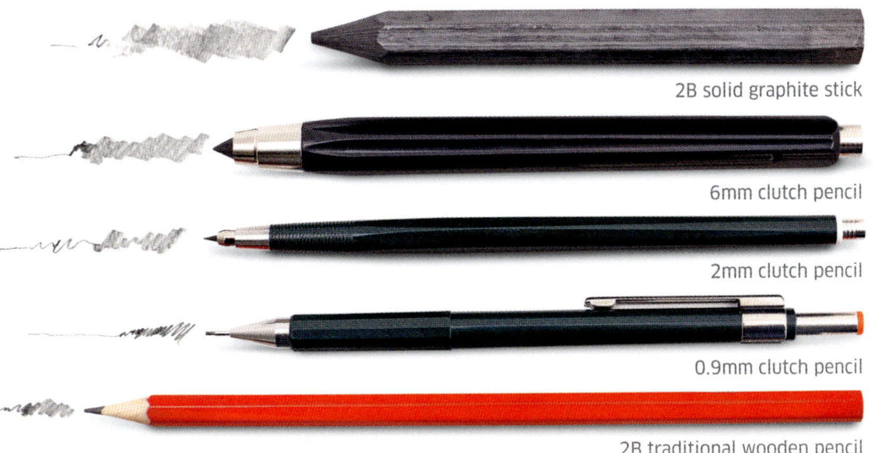

2B solid graphite stick

6mm clutch pencil

2mm clutch pencil

0.9mm clutch pencil

2B traditional wooden pencil

Using gum arabic

Gum arabic is a popular binding medium that limits the flow and bleed of colours, keeps a painting wetter for longer (extending your work time), and enhances the transparency and vibrancy of the colours. You can paint it neat onto damp paper, mix it in a 1:1 ratio with water and apply that as a wash, or mix it with the paint itself, depending on the effects you're after.

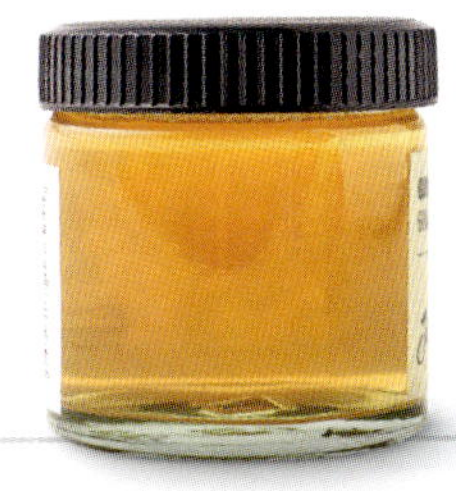

Observational skills

THE ART OF SEEING WHAT WORKS AS A PAINTING

Developing a painterly vision is not the same as simply opening your eyes and looking around you. Observing with a painter's eye means learning to see what elements make a good painting, a skill that becomes easier with practice. As an artist, you have the freedom to interpret what you see and express it in your own way.

Find the interest
The striking shapes of these windmills in Mykonos, Greece, instantly attract attention. But this view has a lot of distracting details that pull the focus away from the windmills.

Select a viewpoint
Getting up much closer to the windmills affords a view with a more interesting interaction between the buildings and a better overall composition (see also pp.26–27).

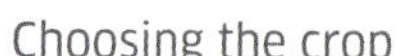

Choosing the crop
You are in complete control of what you paint; you get to decide what to move, omit, or emphasize for the best painting.

The dashed line is the chosen crop for the painting below

Noticing key elements
When you learn to really look at a potential subject – weighing up its tones and shapes, considering its colour scheme, and thinking about which parts to include and which to crop out – you'll start noticing the detail in everything around you. Whether you're capturing the reflections on a vintage car in the sunshine, architectural flourishes on buildings, the myriad of colours in a fruit still life, or clouds scudding across a stormy sky – all such details will help you decide whether the subject merits a sheet of watercolour paper.

Avoid the beginner pitfall of looking for a "pretty" subject. A subject can be pretty but this should play only a small part in your considerations. A pretty

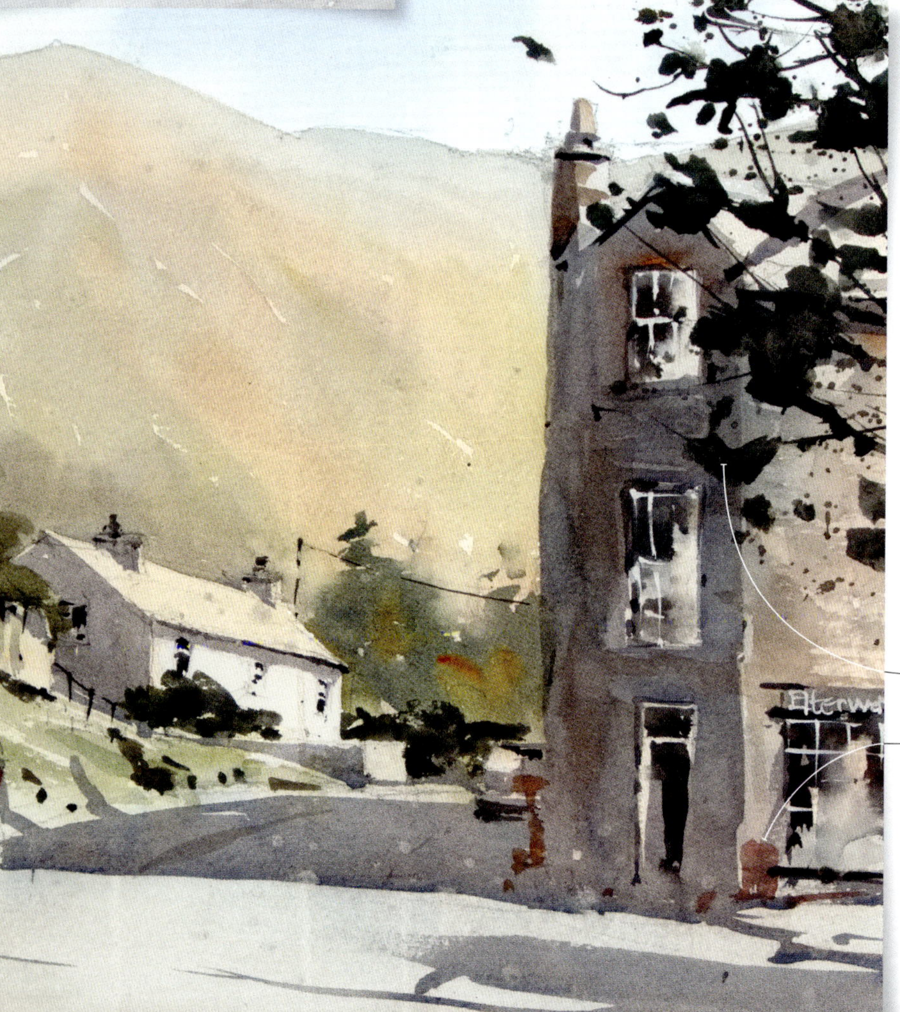

The tree now extends into the painted scene

The car from the original scene is cropped out

Your artistic licence
As well as cropping out distracting details (such as road signs) to create an interesting composition, you can play with any details that enhance and evoke the right atmosphere for your painting.

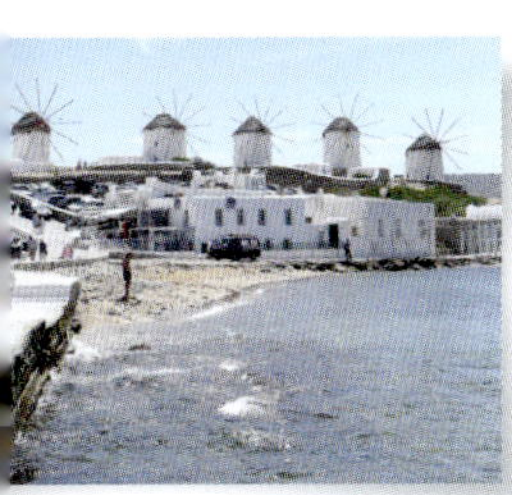

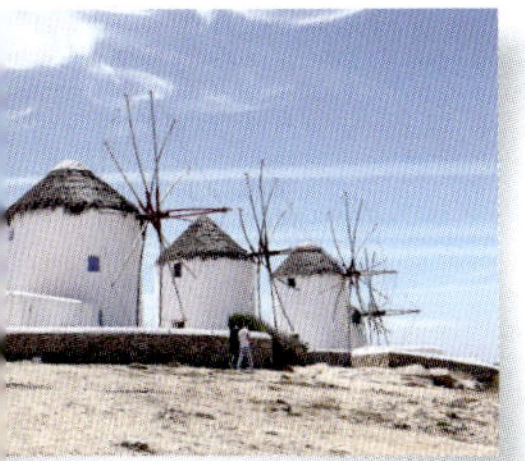

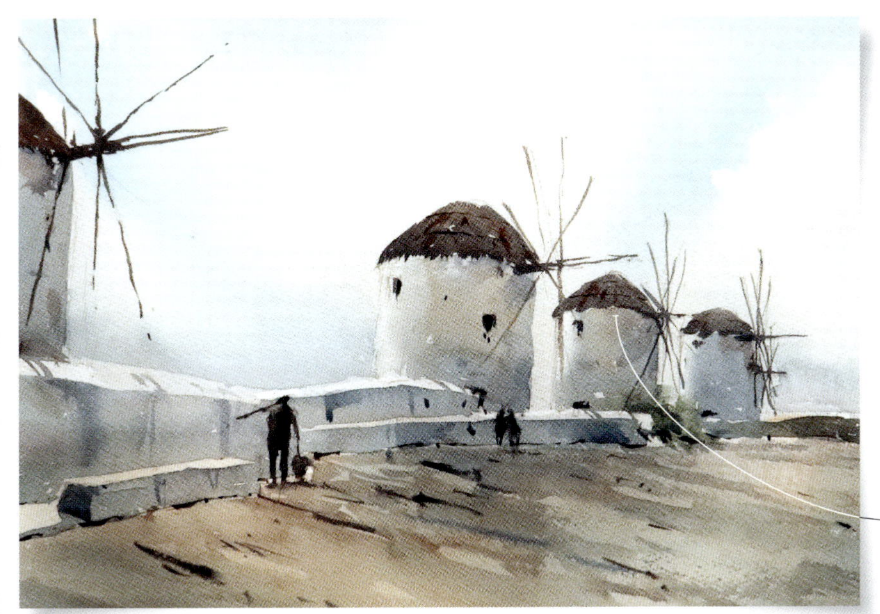

Look for shapes
The compositional beauty of this painting lies in the stark, bold shapes presented by the windmills. A simple way to find the main shapes is to squint your eyes, which blurs the detail so that the shapes are revealed.

The rounded shapes of the windmills stand out against the clear sky

subject will not necessarily result in a good painting. Instead, you must learn to look for other attributes that will excite you as you paint and add visual power to the finished piece.

Shapes and viewpoint
Unusual or dramatic shapes make for intriguing and powerful paintings, so look for those in your subject. A subject may not be obvious at first glance; investigating angles and heights of viewpoints can completely change how you see a subject and reveal the most pleasing shapes.

View a potential subject from all angles before settling on the one that you consider to be the most impactful and interesting. A still-life scene gives you ultimate control; arrange all the elements from different viewpoints, and adjust the lighting to achieve a pleasing composition of tonal shapes.

Tonal range and colour
With few exceptions it is the contrast of tones – the light and darkness – that gives a painting structure, impact, and excitement. Look for a subject with a simple array of a few interesting tonal shapes, ranging from very light to very dark. Adjust the lighting of your set-up, or your orientation to the subject if outdoors, until you manage to capture the best tonal contrast.

Colour helps create atmosphere but don't try to copy colours from real life. Instead use your imagination to adjust colours to suit the mood.

A tonal study
This painting captures a wide range of interesting tonal shapes. And the unidirectional light reveals great tonal contrast.

Dramatic lighting creates a great contrast between the darks and the lights

Look differently
Shapes, not things, create a painting. Here, the hand connects to the face to give one large overall shape with interesting edges. The lighting emphasizes the tonal differences.

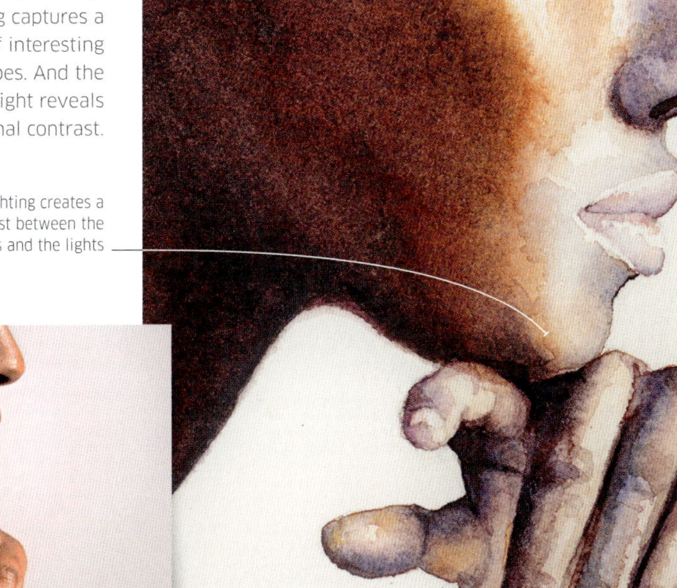

Perspective and composition

PORTRAYING THREE-DIMENSIONAL SPACE

Knowing the key points of composition and perspective will help your pieces have balance and a sense of reality. Linear perspective – how parallel lines appear to converge in the distance – is key to creating depth and distance in a painting. Composition, the arrangement of objects and shapes in a pleasing way, also has some easy-to-understand "rules" that you can employ.

PERSPECTIVE

The rules of linear perspective can be observed in many subjects, and are especially useful in landscapes along with those of aerial perspective. Linear perspective can be a little challenging but following the rules makes accurate drawing easier; extending horizontal lines to converge at a point on the horizon – the vanishing point – is key.

> "Emulating aerial perspective can help to add the dimension of depth to your painting."

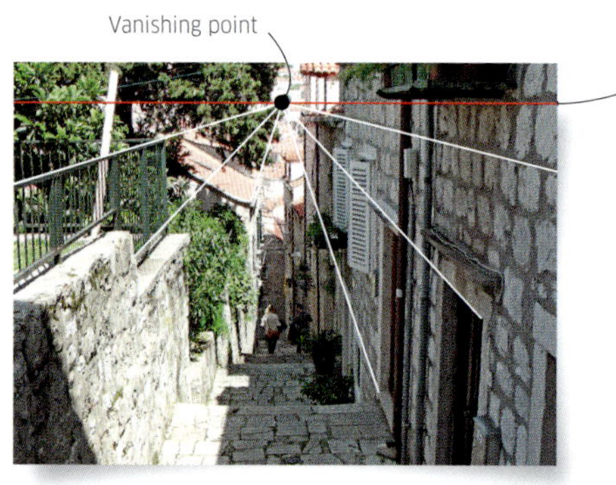

One-point perspective
In this view down a flight of steps, horizontals from the walls, railings, and houses all converge at one vanishing point.

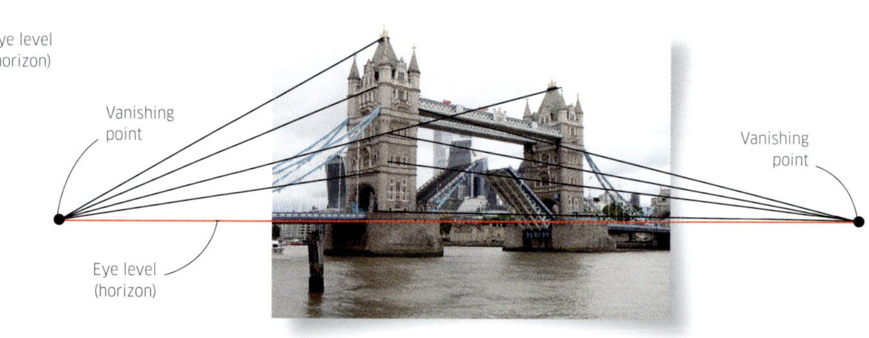

Two-point perspective
As the bridge in this photo is at an angle to the viewer, both sides are affected by perspective and so there are two vanishing points on the horizon. To help place them, remember that the horizon line always relates to the eye level of the viewer.

Aerial perspective
Another way of indicating perspective in a landscape is to imitate the effect of atmosphere on distant objects. The haze of the atmosphere makes objects appear less detailed, less colourful, and less tonal the further away they are.

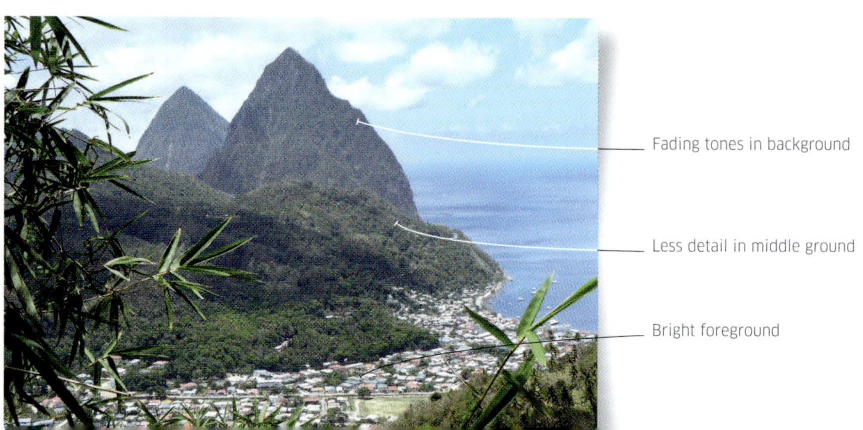

COMPOSITION

How you compose a scene or still life can spell success or disappointment for the finished piece. There are a few pieces of advice or "rules" that can shape a good composition, working alongside a sense of depth from perspective. There may be occasions when such rules can be broken, but if you understand them first you will be in a better position to decide if or when to break them.

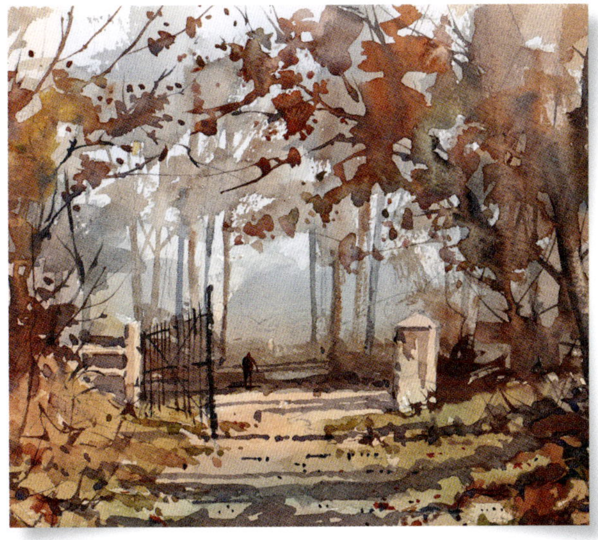

Focal point

Many paintings are created with the idea of a single focal point – a figure in the distance, as here. You can emphasize a focal point by having the strongest dark and lightest light or perhaps a strong colour contrast there. You can also have a series of focal points on a path (see below).

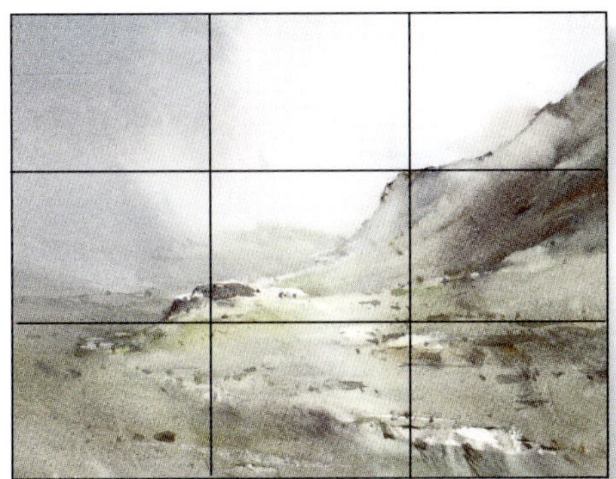

The rule of thirds

This useful compositional aid divides a subject into thirds both vertically and horizontally so that you end up with four lines and four crossing points. The main parts of a composition should be located around the lines, with the crossing points being the strongest focal points.

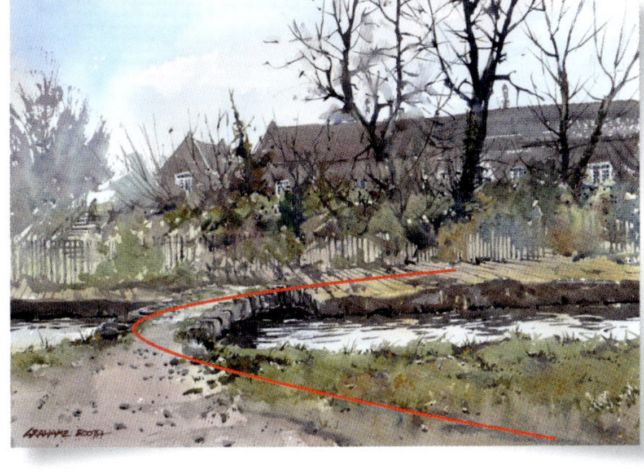

C-shaped path of focal points

Here, the "C" shape draws the eye along the foreground, across the bridge and along to the main tree. The tree is positioned at the intersection of thirds (see left), as is the gable of the building to the left of the tree and the bridge itself.

Path of focal points

Ideally, the different focal points of a painting should follow a path rather than be placed in a random way. Paths in the shape of C, L, U, S, and Z (and their mirror images) are considered to be good compositionally. Such shapes allow the eye to gently explore a painting. Elements of the painting itself can also direct the eye to a focal point, such as the branch of a tree, a ripple on the water, or a road.

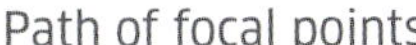

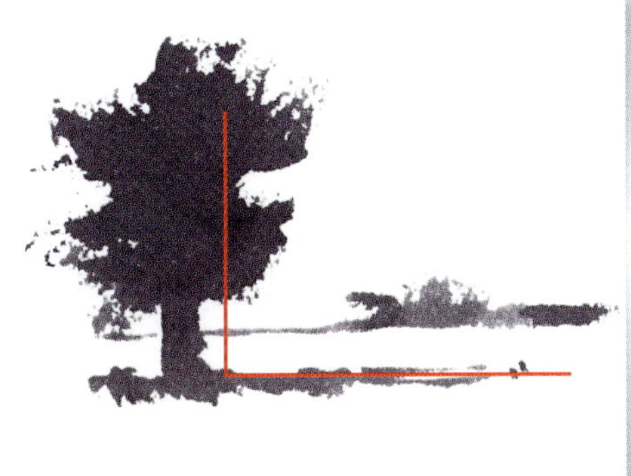

"L" shape

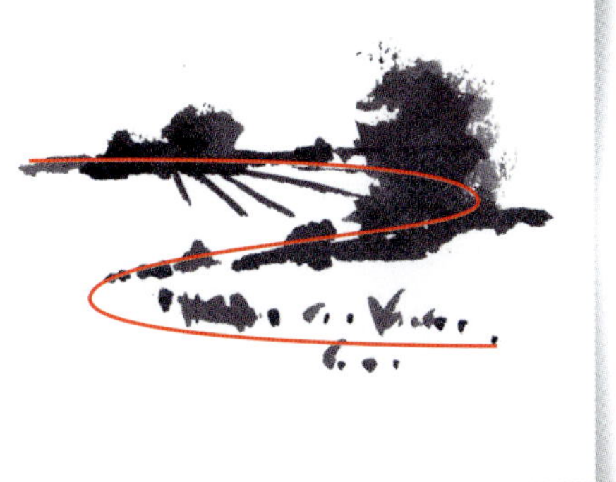

"S" shape

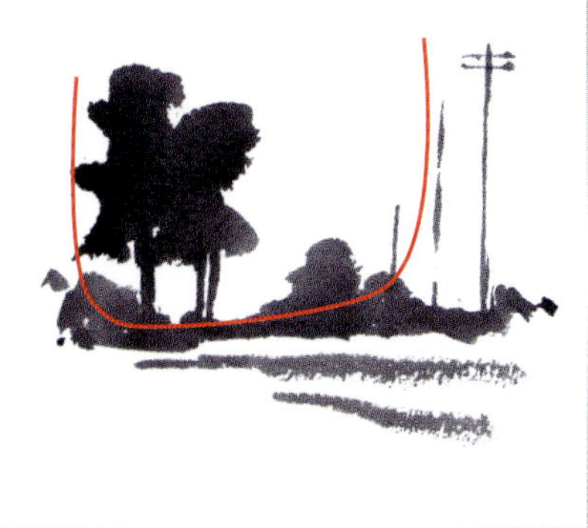

"U" shape

Drawing basics

PORTRAYING SCALE AND PROPORTIONS

If you can write your name or trace an image then you can draw. You can learn to produce a perfectly adequate drawing for reference and as the base of a painting. Accuracy is only part of the process, of course, as a good drawing will always convey something of the elusive "feel" of the subject.

▣ Measuring from life

Learning to use a pencil to measure is key for accurate drawing. Hold a pencil at arm's length and at eye level (note, a bent arm will skew measurements). Close one eye, look along your arm, lining up one end of the pencil with one end of the subject. Slide your thumb along the pencil to mark off the length and then transfer this to your paper.

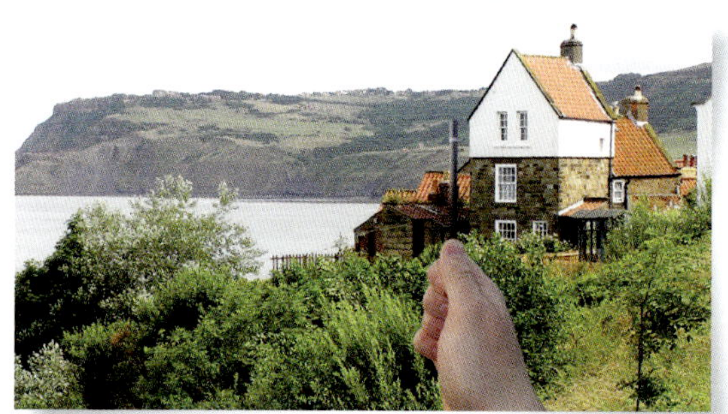

Look for key lines and angles

You want to get down enough information so that you know where to put the paint. Focus on the main parts of the subject; it's best to avoid too much detail.

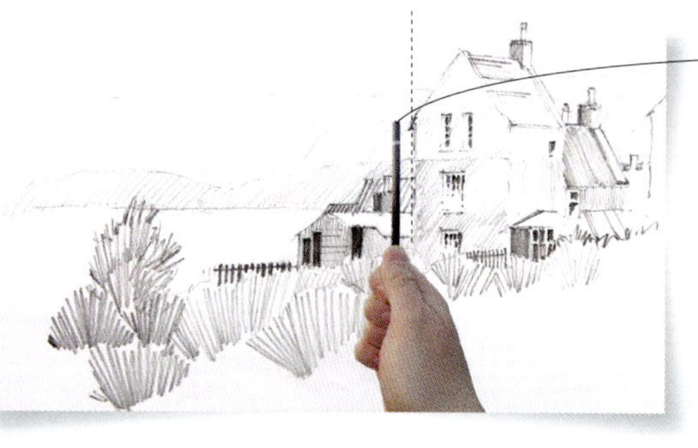

Transfer this length to your sketch once you've measured

Measuring lines

Choose one line to use as the base of the drawing. You can build a sketch in the right proportions by measuring how other lengths relate to this.

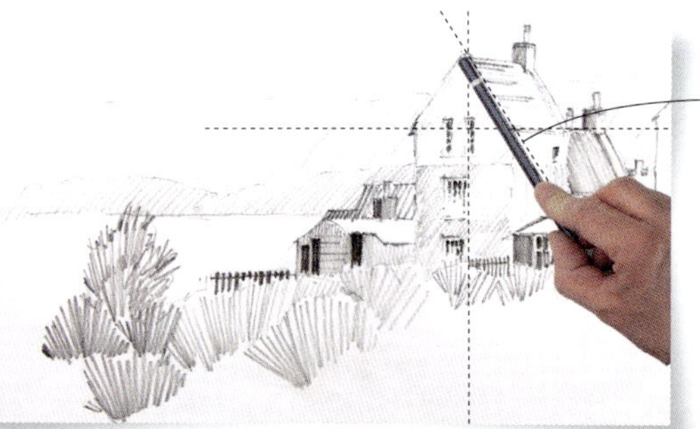

Measure angles by comparing against verticals and horizontals

Measuring angles

Hold your pencil as above while turning your hand to line up with the angled line in the scene, so you can draw it in the sketch.

▣ Measuring figures

Hold your pencil and use it as a measuring tool as described (see left). Measure the head and use this length to plot the height of a person and where the limbs start and end. Becoming practised in measuring people in this way will also allow you to check how they fit in a scene – you don't want people taller than doorways, for instance.

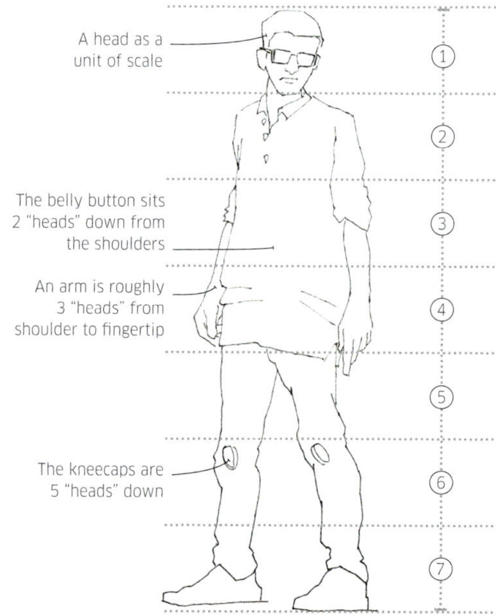

Using the head as a unit

The head can be a really useful unit of scale when drawing people to get a body's proportions right. Knowing that a standing person measures 7-8 heads tall, as well as a few key lengths (above), can mean your figures' limbs and torsos are in proportion.

■ Looking for relationships

When you observe a subject it is crucial to look at relationships within an individual object and between different objects. Look for these even before putting pencil to paper.

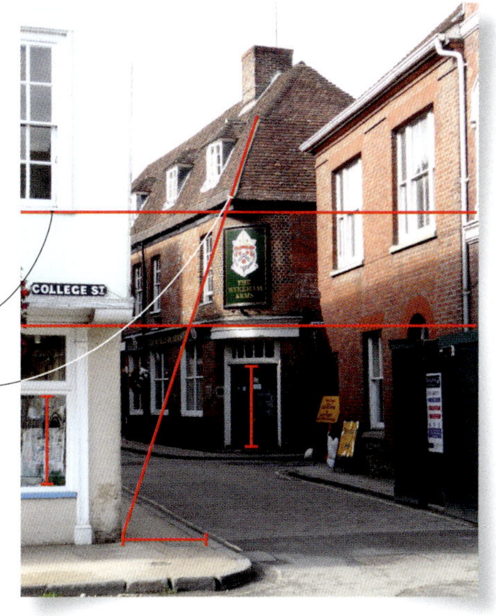
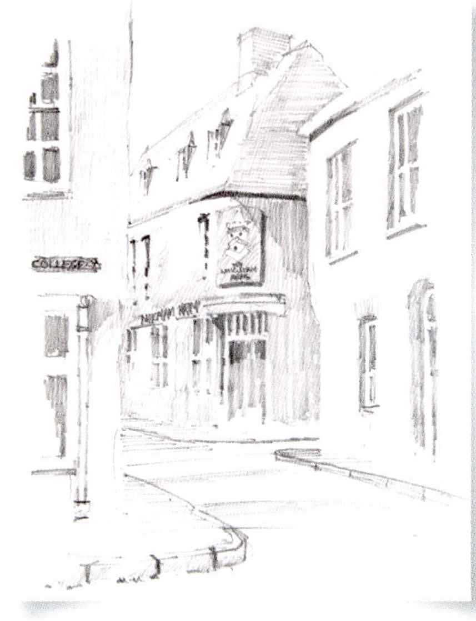

The bottom of the window is almost in line with the bottom of the pub's roof

Diagonal relationships are useful – see how the angle of the roof relates to the street corner

Useful heights and angles
Look at this scene. Can you see how the height of the pub door is the same as the height of the shop window? With practice, you notice all kinds of useful relationships.

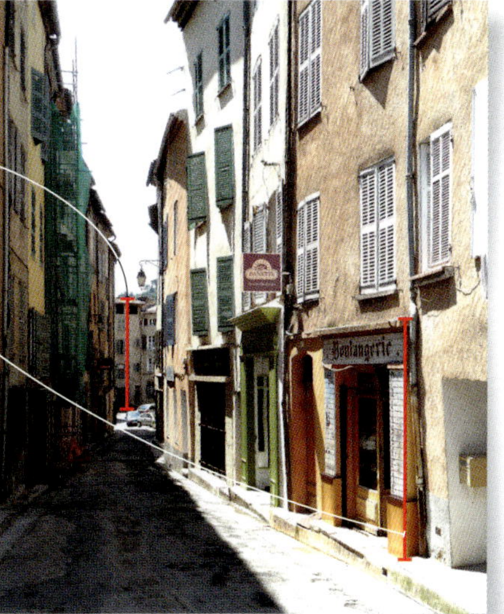
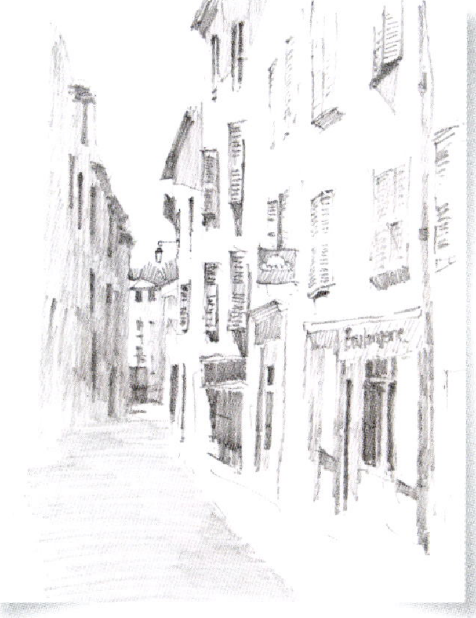

Compare this measurement to that in the foreground

Measuring shows that the shop front is twice the height of building at the end of the street

Dealing with depth
Always measure to check proportions. In this street scene, the height of the shop front and the building at the end of the street appear about the same to the eye. However, when measured (see the red lines), you can see that this isn't the case.

Contour drawing

Being able to see the main shapes of a scene helps improve your drawing. In contour drawing you keep your pencil on the paper and follow edges rather than objects. Where one object touches another, continue along the edge of the combined shape rather than completing the object.

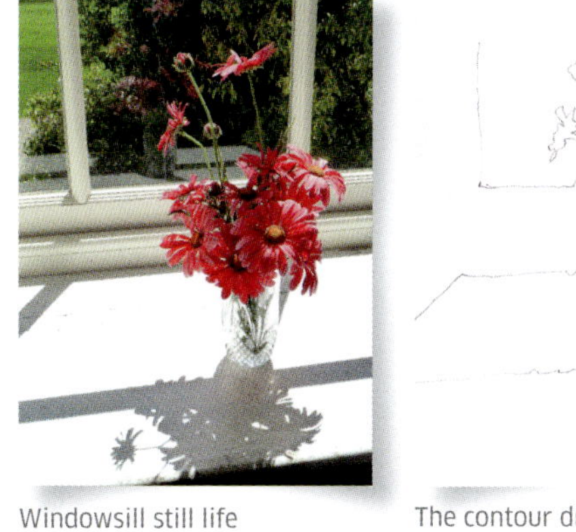

Windowsill still life

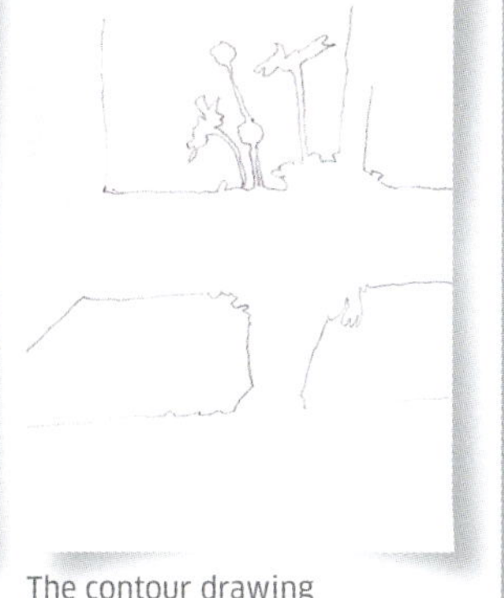

The contour drawing

> "With a little practice, **contour drawing** is generally more accurate and helps us to **see the subject as shapes.**"

Sketching and planning

HOW TO WORK BEST WITH YOUR REFERENCE MATERIAL

Many visual artists always carry a sketchbook, since you never know when the perfect subject may present itself. Once you've captured a quick sketch, dashed down any colour suggestions, and taken any supporting photos, it's time to sketch out, plan, and execute your painting.

■ Sketching on the move

Being able to dash down quick sketches is a great skill to develop and one that will improve with practice. It's surprising to see just how much you can leave out and still capture the essence of the subject. Limit your time to force speed of working, or try sketching looking out from a bus or train.

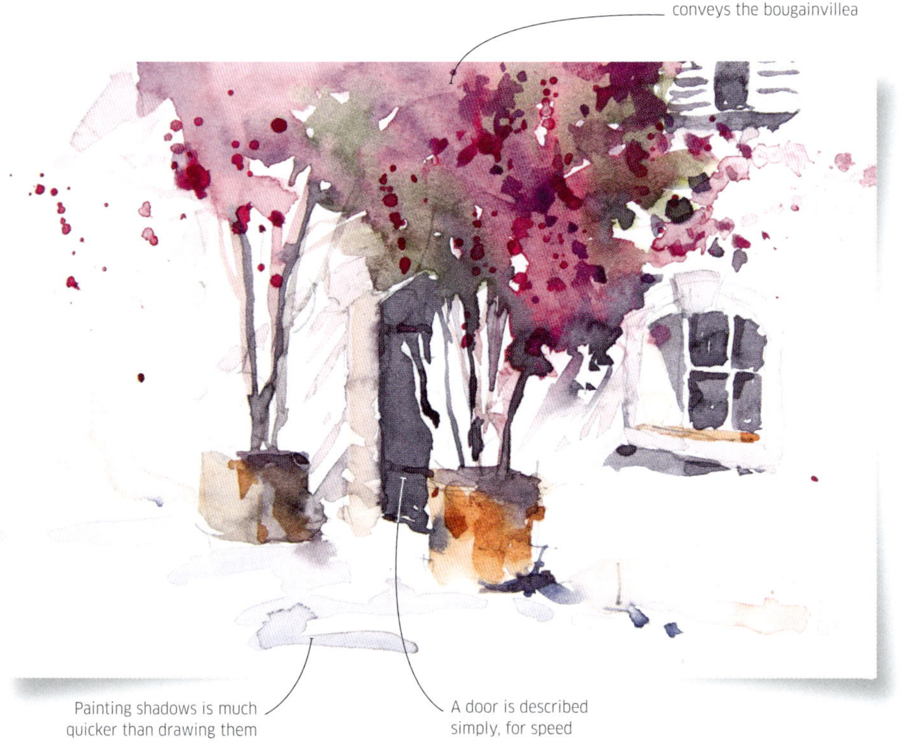

Recording things quickly
This sketch of bougainvillea took 10 minutes and doesn't include every detail – it doesn't need to. A splash of magenta records the main colour and replaces a multitude of pencil marks. The result is both quicker to do and more descriptive.

■ From real life to a painting

Watercolour is a spontaneous medium and the process is easier if you have an indication of where to place your paint. Creating a tonal study will help you plan a successful painting. When it is time to paint, your preparatory sketch should map out only the main features of your subject or, even better, the main tonal shapes. Avoid shading and use a soft pencil (2B or softer) so as not to dent the paper's surface.

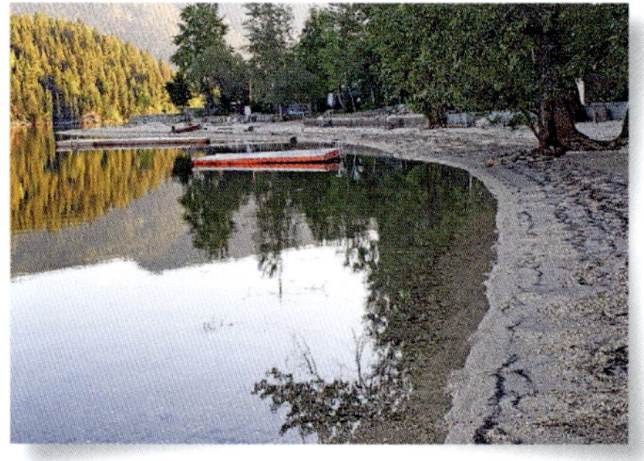

1 Observing the subject
Painting is all about the effects of light. Look for a good range of tonal variety and strong compositional elements. A photo can provide extra information for your painting.

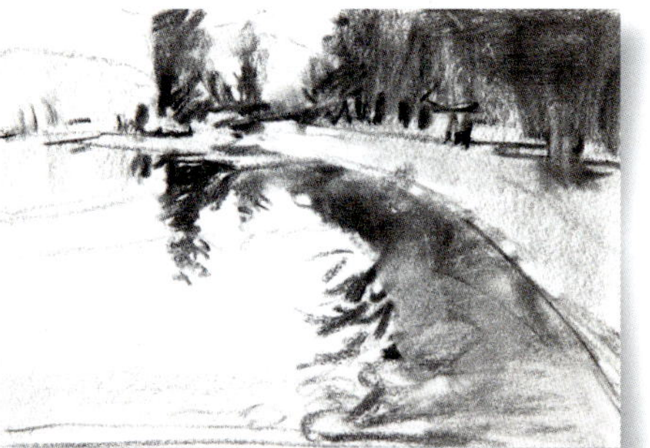

2 A tonal (value) study
This type of sketch helps plan the areas of light and shade you will paint. Draw or paint this quickly; do not focus on details. Aim for a few big interesting tonal shapes.

Photos – the whole picture

While it is useful to take a photograph of your subject (using a smartphone or a compact camera is fine), rarely does one photo offer enough to render a successful painting. Painters need more information, so take photos from different viewpoints as well as wide-angle and zoomed-in detail shots. However, a photograph cannot substitute the information you will gain from sketching.

Taking and using photos

PROS
- Is quick and simple
- Provides accuracy and detail
- May be the only option if the viewpoint is awkward or dangerous

CONS
- Cannot filter which elements of a scene excited you most
- Is poor at indicating depth
- Is no substitute for careful observation

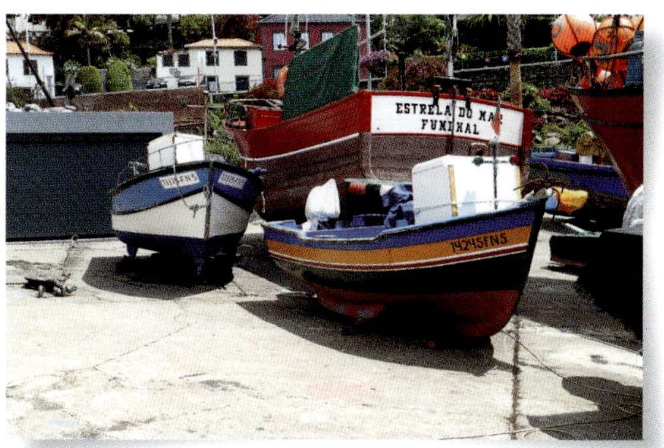

1 Take some photos
The pattern of these three boats and their sharp shadows in the sunshine is sure to appeal to many. While the buildings in the background appear equally bright in the photograph, the eye is drawn more to the boats.

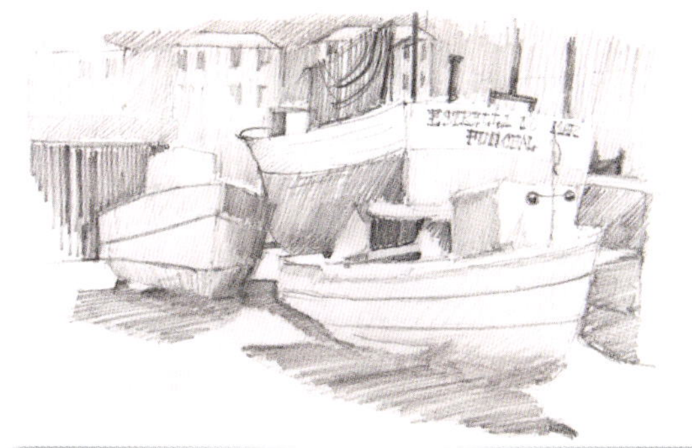

2 Sketch tonal areas
While the camera records everything, in a sketch you can focus on what catches your eye. Now is the time to decide what is the main focus, what to omit, and adjust accordingly. Quickly record the tones that will inform your painting.

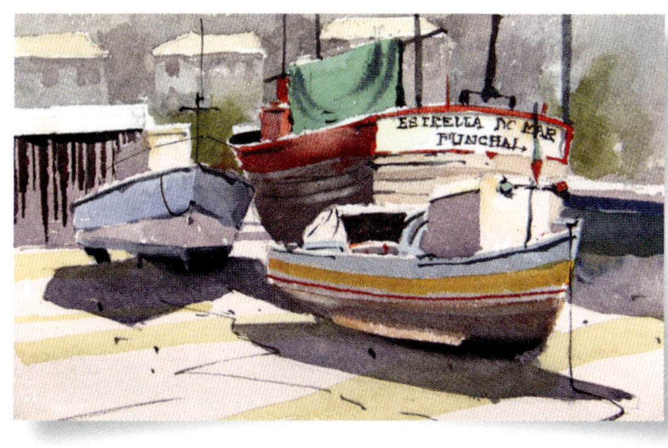

3 Refer to all sources
Working from your sketch helps to keep the painting simple, but it's good to have the photograph to refer to for colour information, to check relationships of objects within the scene, and to ensure the shapes are properly rendered.

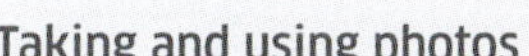

3 Preparatory sketch
Before applying paint, lightly draw the boundaries of the painted areas. It is best to leave a few scribbles rather than risk erasing and possibly damaging the watercolour paper.

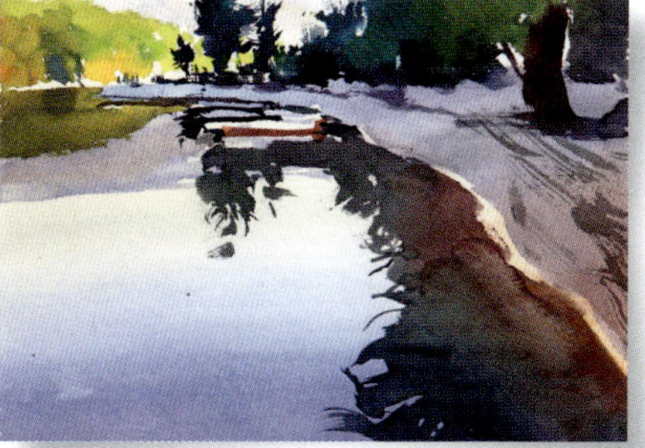

4 The final painting
Notice how this finished painting closely mirrors the tones in the tonal study. Tone is your most powerful weapon in constructing a painting. Details come far behind.

"You will **learn more** from **a single sketch** than from taking **a hundred photographs.**"

Colour theory

UNDERSTANDING COLOUR RELATIONSHIPS AND TONE

When it comes to painting, the three primary colours are red, yellow, and blue. In theory, all other colours could be mixed from the three primaries, but in practice additional colours are often used to extend the possible range.

◼ The painter's colour wheel

The traditional painter's colour wheel is based on one designed by Isaac Newton and its purpose is to show a logical relationship between the different colours of the painter's spectrum. The colour wheel is a representation of how any colour interacts with others. Only 12 colours are shown, when in reality, of course, there will be almost infinite subtle variations. The more colours that are added the duller a mixture gets.

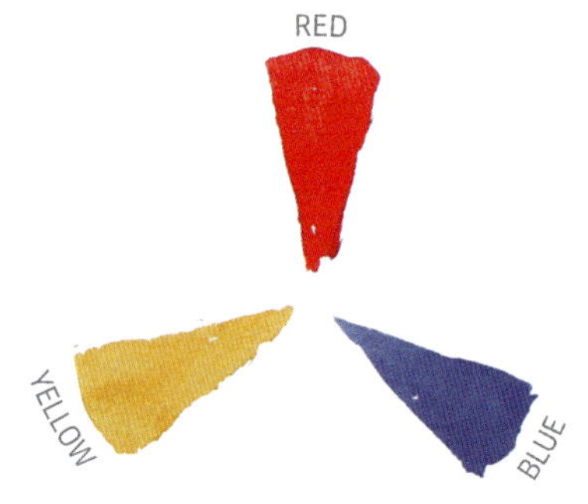

Primary colours
Red, yellow, and blue are primary colours. You cannot create primary colours using any other colours.

Secondary colours
If you mix two primary colours (such as red and yellow) you create a secondary colour (orange). These sit between primary colours.

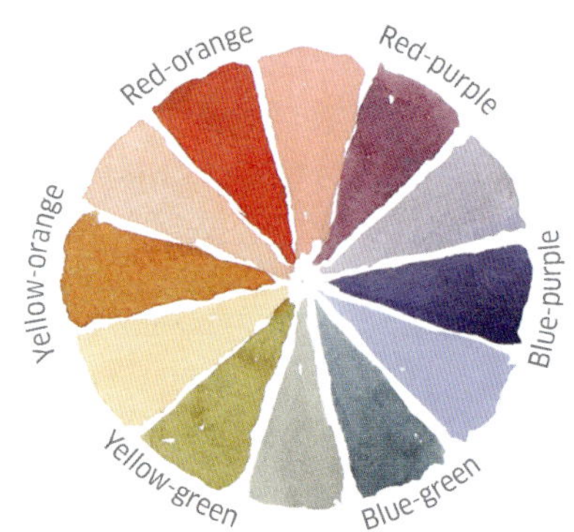

Tertiary colours
If you mix a secondary colour (such as purple) with an adjacent primary colour (say, blue), you create the tertiary colour blue-purple.

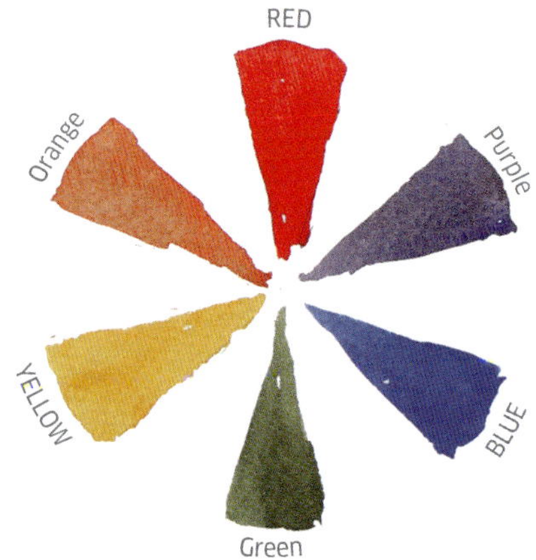

Complementary colours
Colours that sit opposite one another on the colour wheel – red and green, say – are known as complementary. They brighten each other when placed alongside but dull each other on mixing.

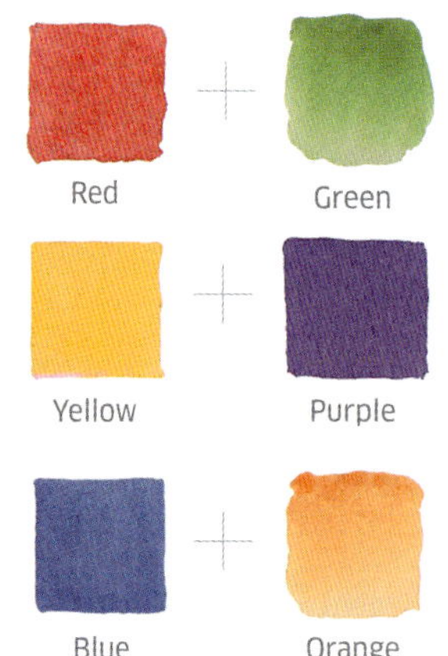

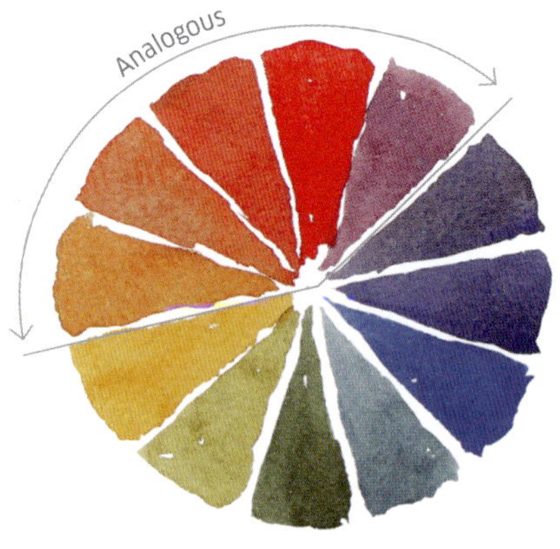

Analogous colours
Colours that sit next to one another in groups of three to five are said to be analogous. They create harmonious colour schemes.

The tone of a colour

Tone (also known as value) refers to the measure of the lightness or darkness of a colour. A good range of tone makes for a realistic representation of light and 3D form. The range of tones you can mix using watercolour is much less than what you see in nature. Effectively the darkest tone of any colour is a pure dark (black) and the lightest tone is pure light (white).

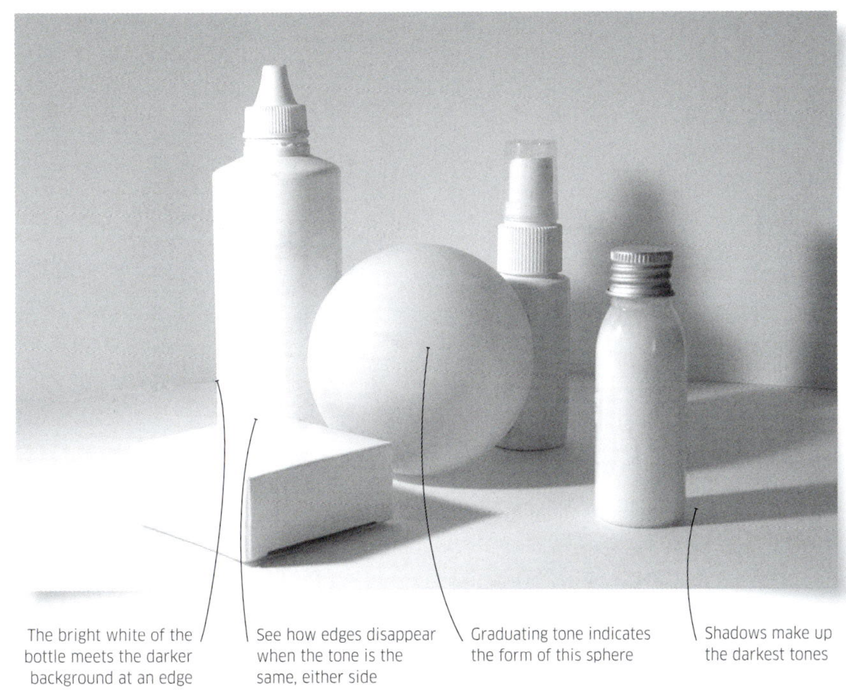

A range of tones

All of these objects are white, but under this controlled lighting a full range of tone is evident. Your eyes see their 3D forms as varying tones; in this monochrome scene these go from white to dark grey.

Tone 1 – light	Tone 2 – medium	Tone 3 – dark	Tone 4 – black

Tonal map to recreate the scene

For this tonal exercise, first draw the connected tonal shapes - lights, mediums, and darks - while ignoring the boundaries of objects. Paint all areas with a light wash (1); next paint areas 2 with a medium wash, then apply a dark wash to areas 3. Finally, add black for the darkest darks (4).

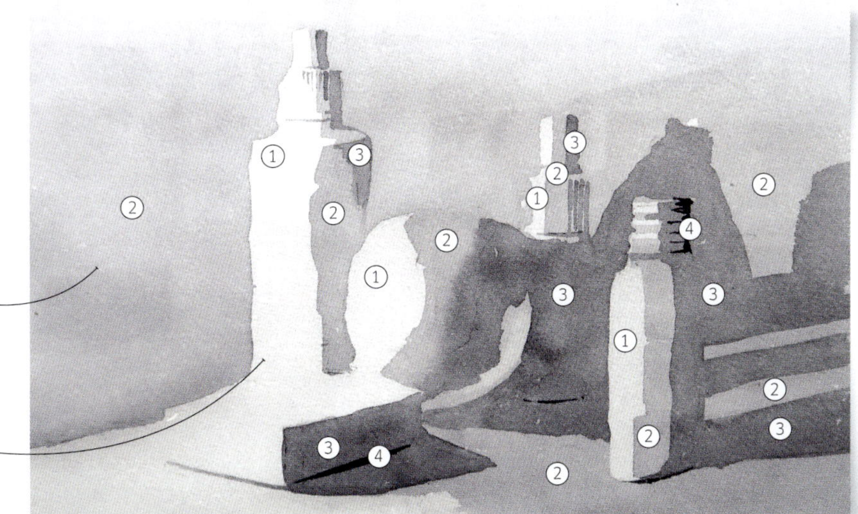

Adjusting the tonal value

Adjusting the lightness or darkness of a colour, either by altering the saturation or adding a darker hue, alters its tone or tonal value. The exercise above uses only a small range of values yet the forms are perfectly described through just four variations of one colour.

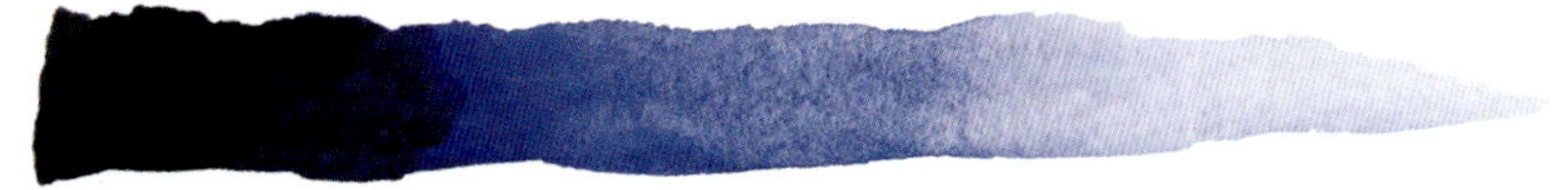

Darkening a colour

We can extend the range of tones available by adding a dark to the pure colour. When the colour is darkened, its tonal value is lowered.

Lightening a colour

In watercolour, rather than adding white to lighten a colour (as with other paints), water is used to produce a graduation of strength of colour (saturation).

Properties of colour

LEARNING MORE ABOUT HOW COLOURS WORK

Playing with colour can be a little like modern alchemy. Each pigment has specific characteristics that will affect how it mixes with water and how it flows on the paper. When different pigments blend the results can be spectacular – with new colours and beautiful effects, such as granulation.

■ Colour temperature and bias

Colours have "temperature": those within the red, yellow, and orange spectrum are generally referred to as "warm" while those spanning purple, blue, and green are "cool" (see pp.120–21).

In addition, there are warm and cool versions of a colour – a cool lemon yellow vs a warm cadmium yellow. In this respect, warm and cool refer to "colour bias". A blue biased towards purple is deemed as warm, whereas a blue biased towards green seems cool.

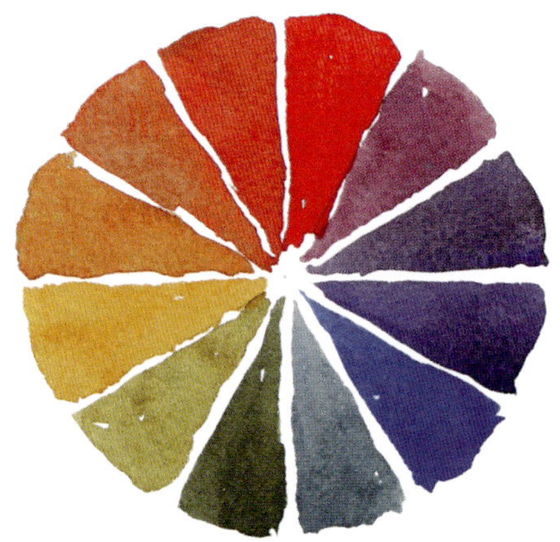

Warm colour wheel
This traditional colour wheel, made from a warm red, a warm yellow, and a warm blue, produces colours that are rich and warm. Warm colours appear to advance in a painting.

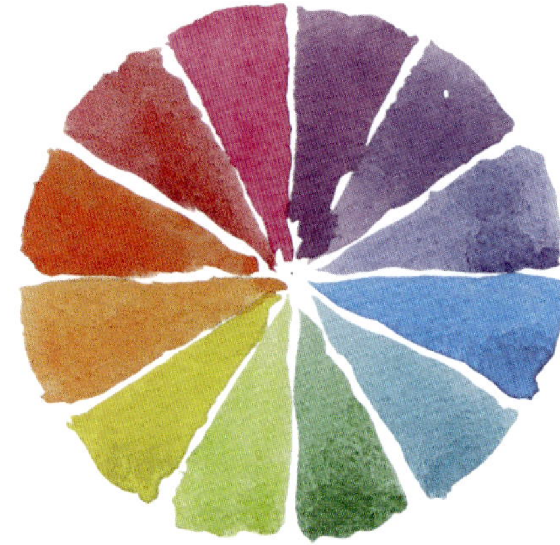

Cool colour wheel
This modern colour wheel results from mixing cool versions of red, yellow, and blue. The mixed colours are bright and cool. Cool colours appear to recede in a painting.

■ Colour harmony

You can enhance paintings no end by the colours you choose to use. With a little thought, you can create some brilliant colour relationships in your work. It's a good idea to start thinking about your colour scheme beforehand and try out various combinations; once you've settled on a palette, stick with it and don't start adding colours as you paint. Various approaches, shown on the right, help artists to make a painting more harmonious.

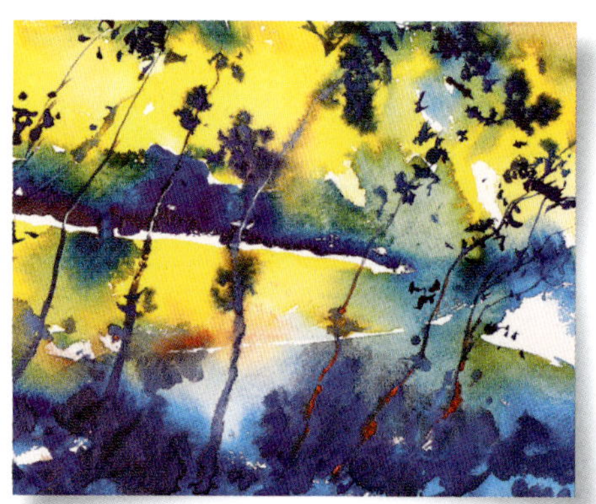

A limited palette
Painting with a limited palette of just a few colours results in mixes that have a common basis, producing works with great harmony.

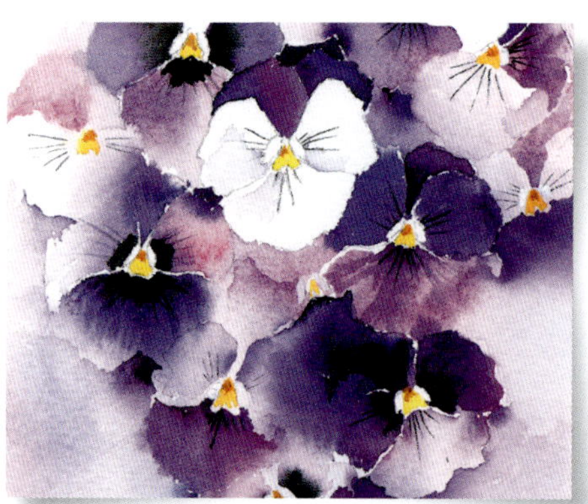

An analogous colour scheme
Evoke a gentle feel by choosing colours (the purples above) that are adjacent on the colour wheel; the yellow pop offers a strong contrast.

Pigment properties

There are certain pigment characteristics to consider when choosing colours that affect how they adhere to the paper and their strength. They are either staining (leave pigment when lifted out) or non-staining, and appear transparent, semi-transparent, semi-opaque, or opaque. Some pigments tend to granulate – a feature that can be exploited to add texture to a sky, for instance.

Also consider the issue of permanence. Some pigments, such as alizarin crimson, fade in light; others, such as aureolin, darken. Hue versions are more permanent.

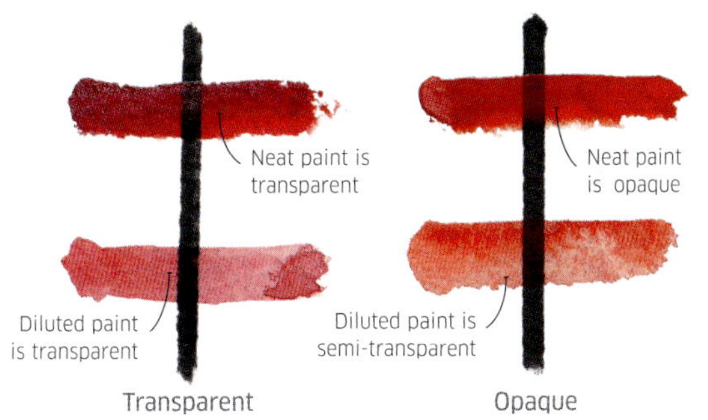

Transparency and opacity
Some pigments, such as alizarin crimson (far left), are transparent even when used straight from the tube, while others are opaque, such as cadmium red (left), which is opaque enough to cover black when neat but not when diluted.

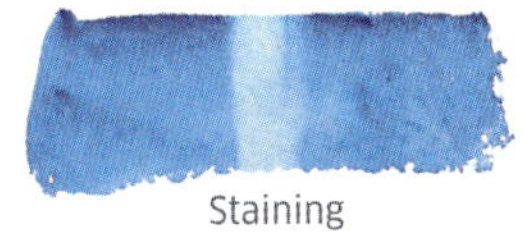
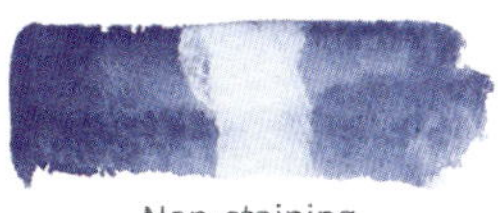

Staining power
It's good to know how staining a pigment is when choosing a colour scheme in case you want to lift out highlights. Phthalo blue (far left), for instance, is staining while French ultramarine (left) is non-staining.

Ability to merge
Generally pigments will merge depending on their relative mix strengths. Colour mixes of equal water content will tend to just blend (far left), but a mix with more water will tend to bloom into a mix with less water (left).

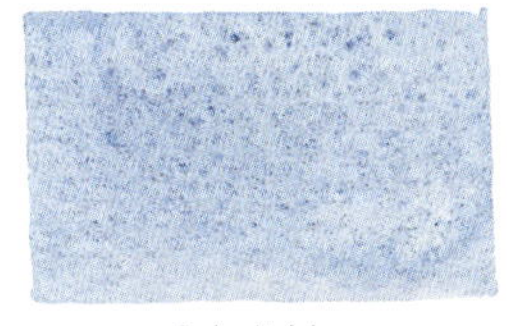

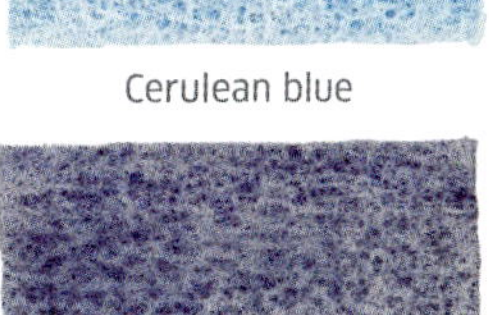

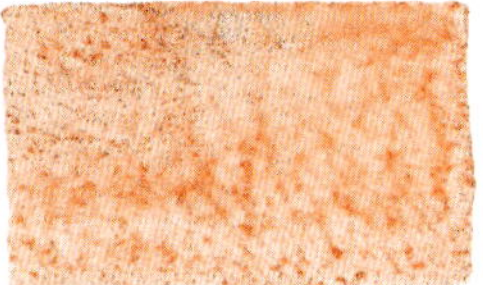

Granulation potential
Watercolour paint is a mixture of pigment and binder, such as gum arabic. Some pigments will separate from their binder and water, creating a grainy texture when dry. Certain pigments (see left) readily granulate.

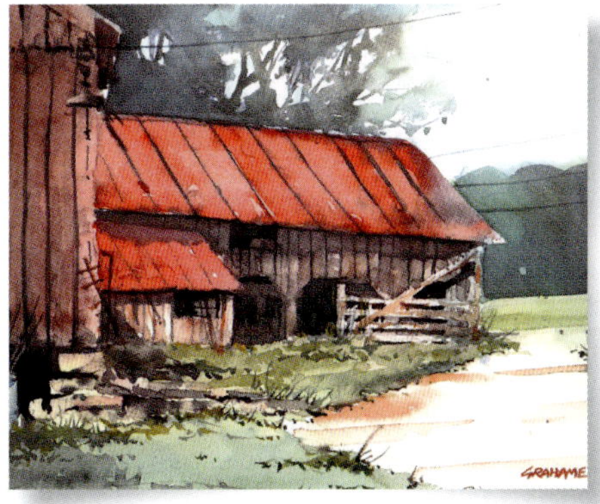

A complementary colour scheme
Complementaries sit opposite each other on the colour wheel (the red and green above) and produce vibrancy when side by side.

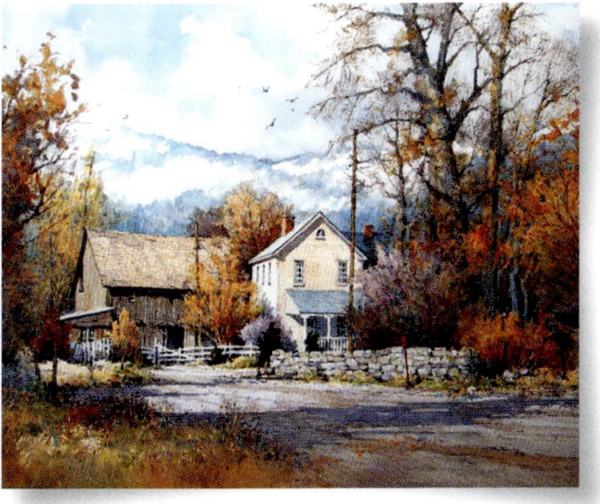

A warm atmosphere
Painting with predominantly warm colours creates warmth. To avoid too much coldness, use warm colours when painting a cool subject.

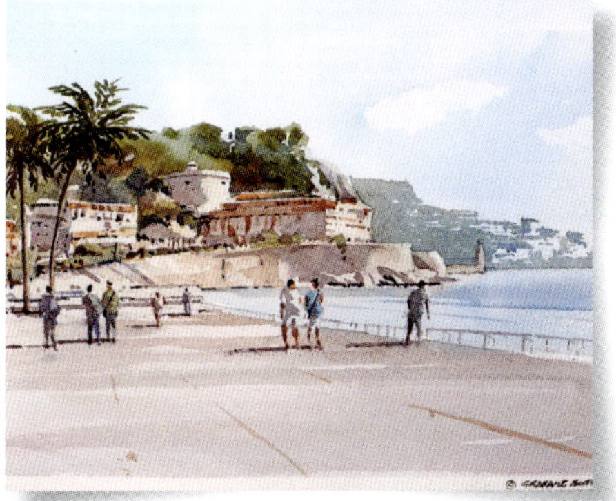

Repeated colours
Repeating colours in different parts of a painting creates harmony. Conversely, using an isolated colour will draw attention.

Colour mixing

USING COLOUR THEORY TO MIX PAINTS

You can create an almost infinite variety of hues from just a few basic colours. Using a limited palette to mix your own colours will help give your painting a harmonious, coherent feel. Watercolour dries lighter than the wet colour on the paper, so make your mixes slightly stronger to compensate.

Wet mixing methods

These two common methods will produce a smooth or a variegated colour. Don't rinse your brush between picking up colours, which can dilute the mix too much.

Mixing in a palette
This is the general method, and produces an evenly mixed colour.

Mixing on paper
This method creates more interesting but less controllable results.

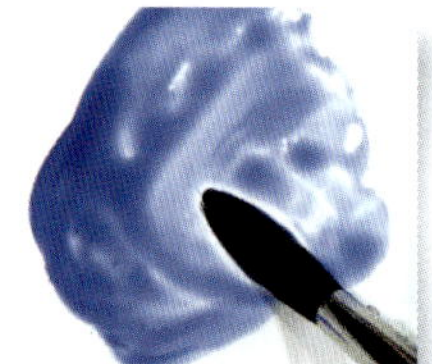

1 - Blend paint with water

1 - Apply first colour

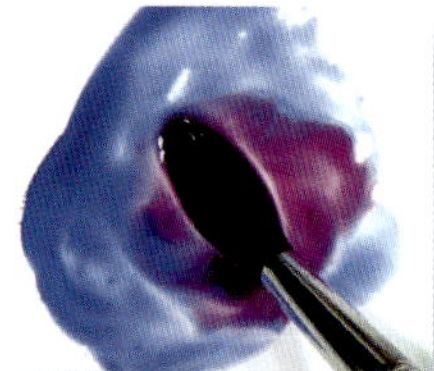

2 - Add second colour

2 - Add second colour

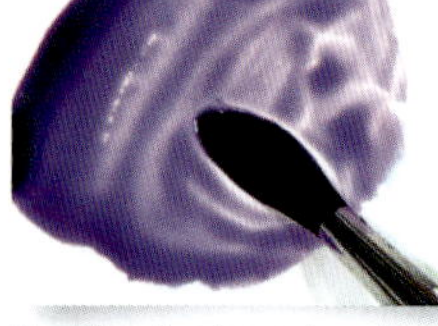

3 - Blend colours together

3 - Blend wet colours

Even colour

Variegated colour

◼ Accounting for colour bias

All colours have variations in undertone, known as colour bias. We describe these biases as "warm" or "cool", depending on whether they lean towards the warm or cool half of the colour wheel (see pp.120–21). For example, a warm blue is biased towards purple, whereas a cool blue is biased towards green. Colour bias will affect your mixes, so include a warm and cool version of each primary colour in your palette for versatility.

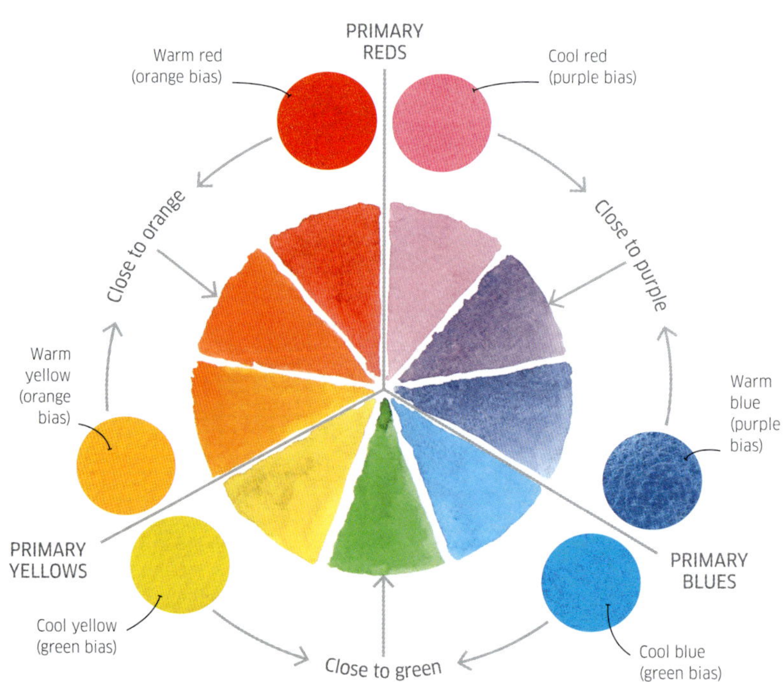

Twin primary system
This colour wheel shows a warm and cool "twin" for each primary colour. Each is placed near the secondary colour it is biased towards. Using six primary colours will allow you to mix both bright and muted secondaries.

Mixing bright secondary colours

Combining two primary colours that are biased towards the same secondary colour creates vibrant hues. For example, a blue with a green bias and a yellow with a green bias will make a bright clear green, often needed for flowers, still lifes, or sunny landscapes.

Cadmium red (orange bias)
+
Indian yellow (orange bias)
Bright orange

Phthalo blue (green bias)
+
Azo yellow (green bias)
Bright green

Quinacridone magenta (purple bias)
+
Ultramarine (purple bias)
Bright purple

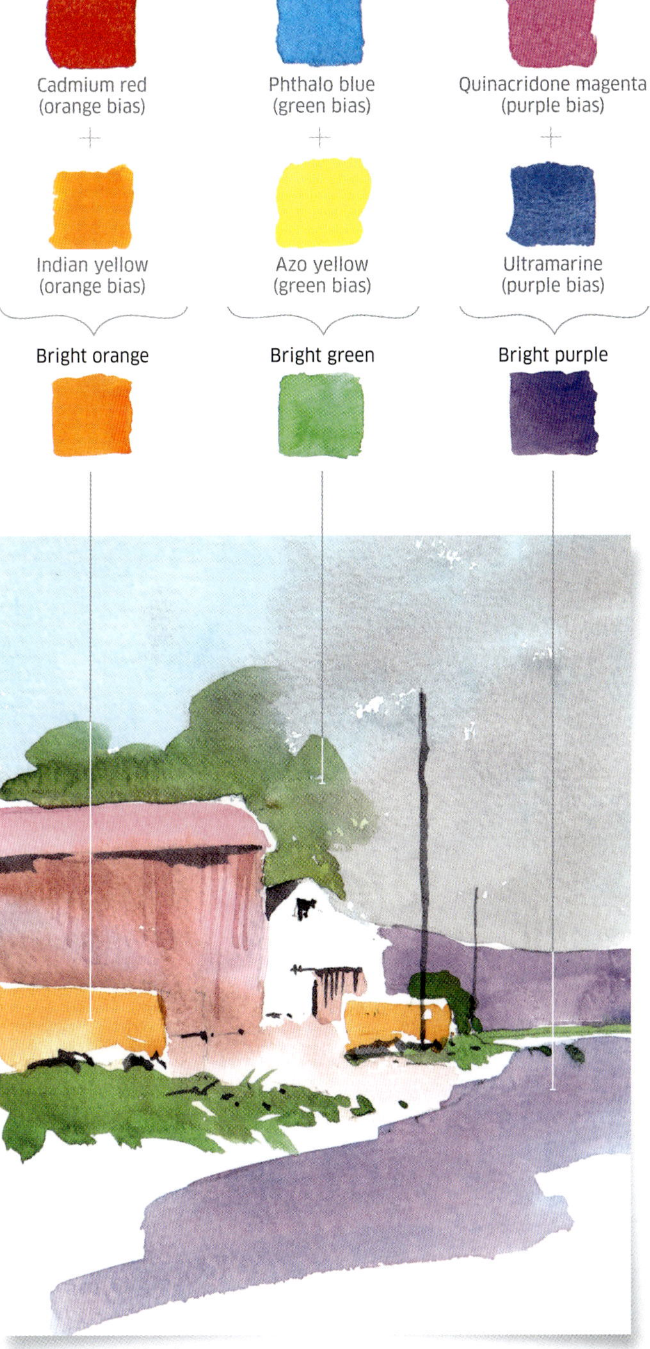

Brightly coloured landscape

Mixing muted secondary colours

If you mix two primaries that do not have the same bias you will create muted secondary colours. These colours are often useful for naturalistic landscapes. For example, a blue with a purple bias and a yellow with an orange bias will produce a soft, dull green.

Quinacridone magenta (purple bias)
+
Azo yellow (green bias)
Muted orange

Ultramarine (purple bias)
+
Indian yellow (orange bias)
Muted green

Cadmium red (orange bias)
+
Phthalo blue (green bias)
Muted purple

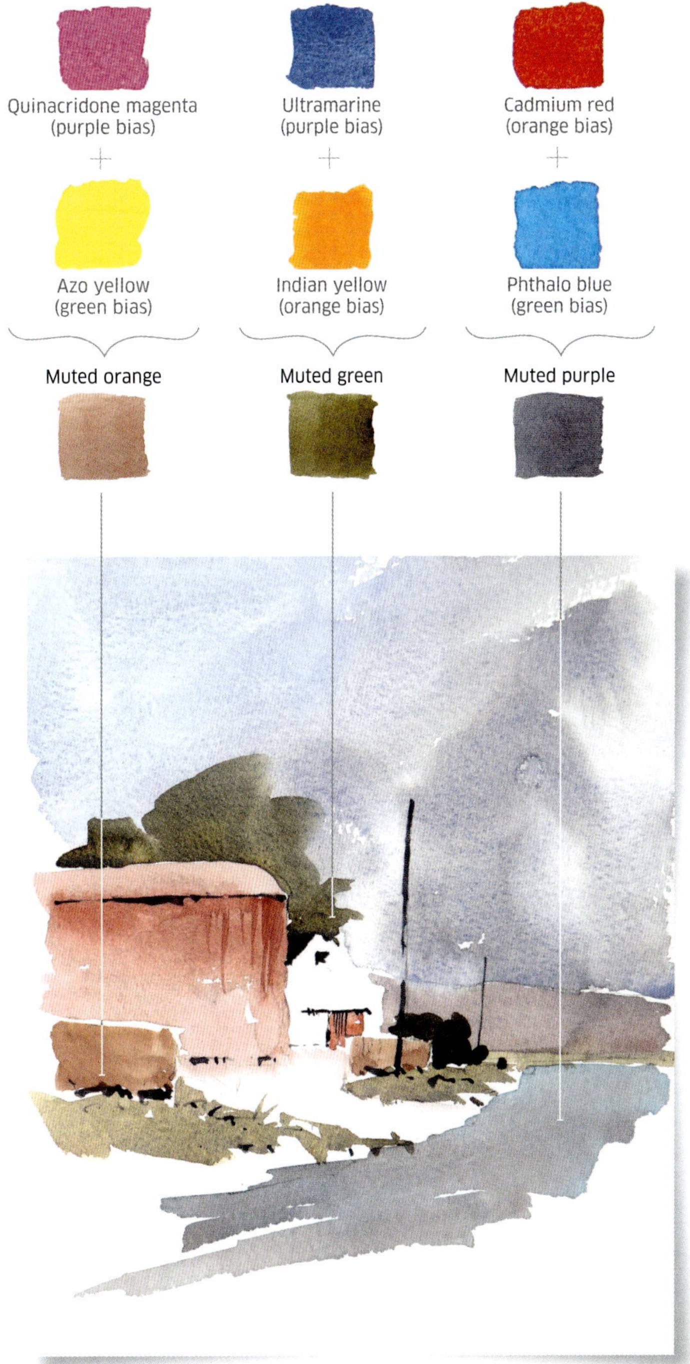

Muted landscape

Mixing neutrals and darks

Neutral and dark colours are essential in a well-balanced painting. Without dark colours and tones your painting will lack impact, and many colours in real-life subjects are actually quite muted and neutral.

Greys and blacks that you can buy premixed can sometimes look flat and boring, whereas neutrals and darks that you mix yourself will have undertones of other colours. A grey with a colour bias always looks much more natural in a painting.

There are two ways to create neutrals and darks: by mixing complementary colours (see p.32) or by mixing three primaries together. To neutralize any colour, simply add its complementary colour. For example, adding a touch of red to a bright green will dull it; the more you add, the more grey the colour becomes. Mixing three primaries will create a huge range of neutral hues – any primaries can be used. Adding more paint to the mix makes it darker and stronger, but there are also some quicker mixes for strong darks.

> ## "Mixing colour is the closest an artist gets to magic."

Lively neutrals

Mixing three primaries together produces various shades of grey. Depending on the chosen primaries and the amounts of each in the mix, these greys can have hints of warm red or brown, cool purple or green, and other colours, as shown in the examples below.

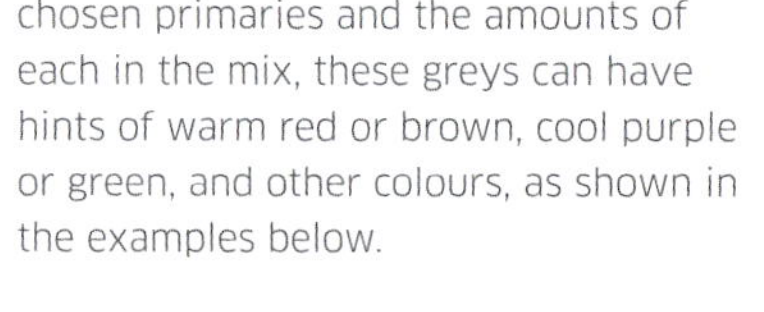

Cadmium red + Ultramarine + Indian yellow

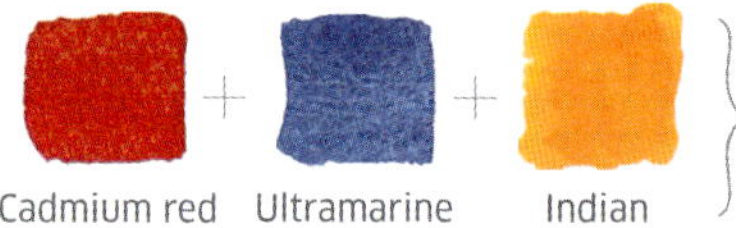

Quinacridone magenta + Azo yellow + Ultramarine

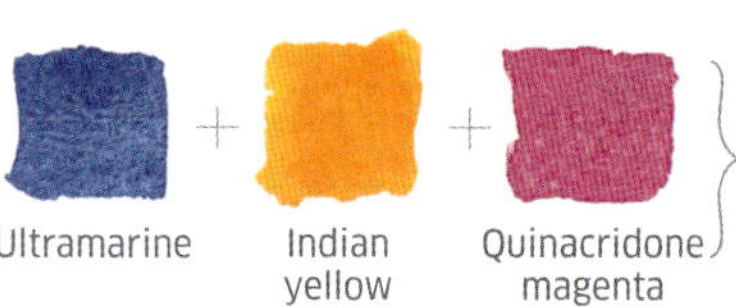

Ultramarine + Indian yellow + Quinacridone magenta

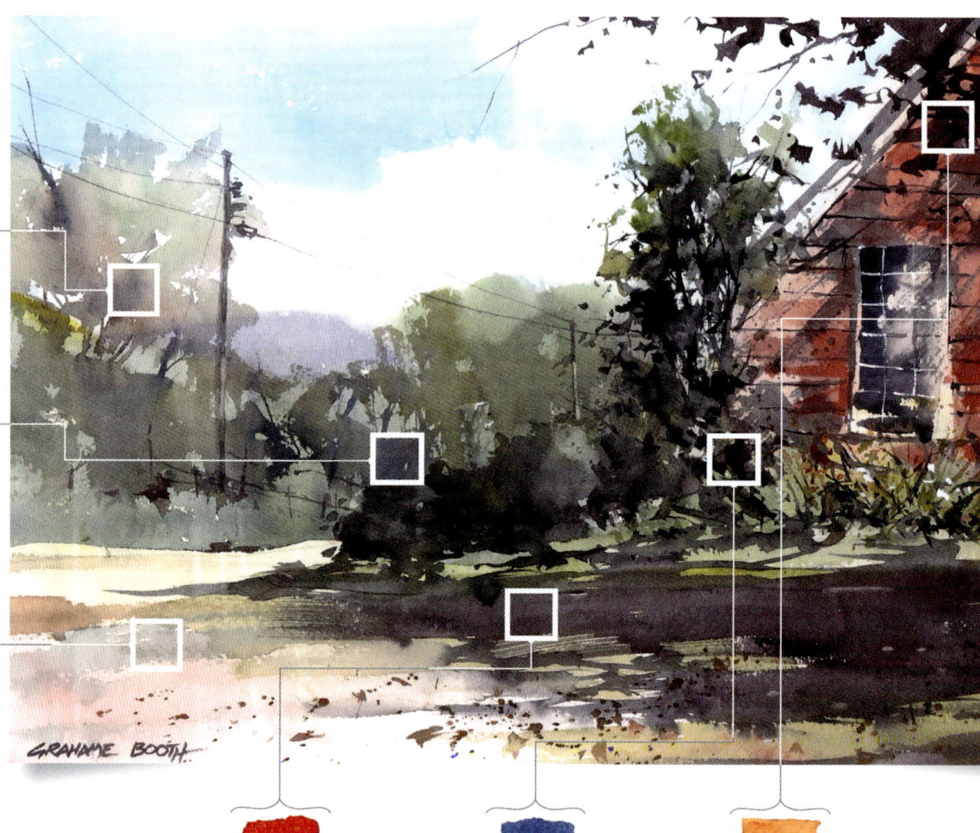

GRAHAME BOOTH

Vibrant darks

There are several two-colour combinations that readily create strong, useful darks. Here, phthalo blue's strong green bias neutralizes cadmium red, and makes an extremely dark green with burnt sienna. Ultramarine (a blue) and burnt sienna (an orange) gives the most neutral mix.

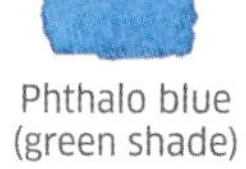

Cadmium red
+
Phthalo blue
(green shade)

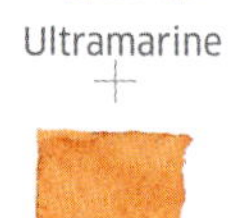

Ultramarine
+
Burnt sienna

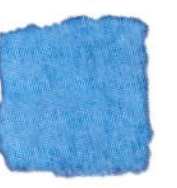

Burnt sienna
+
Phthalo blue
(green shade)

Colour reference charts

Painting colour charts is an excellent way to practise how to make specific hues. This involves painting your mixes on a grid to record the results, which you can keep and refer to later. You may be surprised to see that adding even small amounts of another colour can change the original completely.

Pairing primaries

One useful scheme for a chart is to explore the variety of bright and muted secondary hues we can mix from six twin primary colours (see also p.37). Don't feel you must use these specific colours; every artist has their own particular choice of colours.

1 Make a chart
Draw a grid on a piece of watercolour paper, allowing 10 squares per row.

2 Plot first colour
Working from the left of the row, paint a strong, pure mix of the first colour. Add increasing amounts of a second colour to the mix to paint the next four squares.

3 Plot second colour
Then working from the right of the row, repeat the process with the second colour, adding the first colour in increasing amounts. This will give you 10 colours mixed from just two paints.

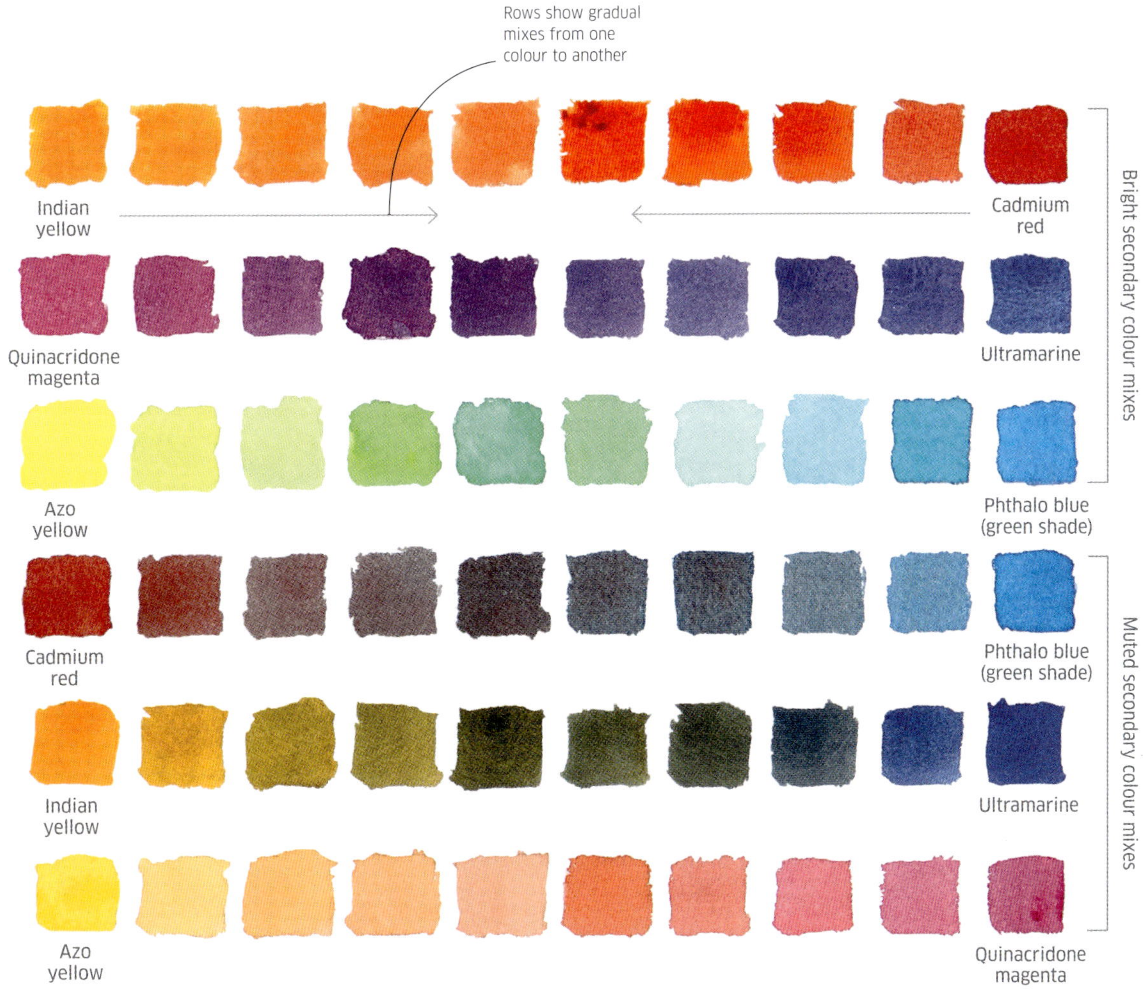

Optical colour mixing

Layering colours wet-on-dry creates a different type of colour mixing. The original colours remain intact (unlike with physical mixes) and the white paper also shines through. The eye registers all the layers at once to create an optical colour mix, much like how it perceives the dots of colour used in printing.

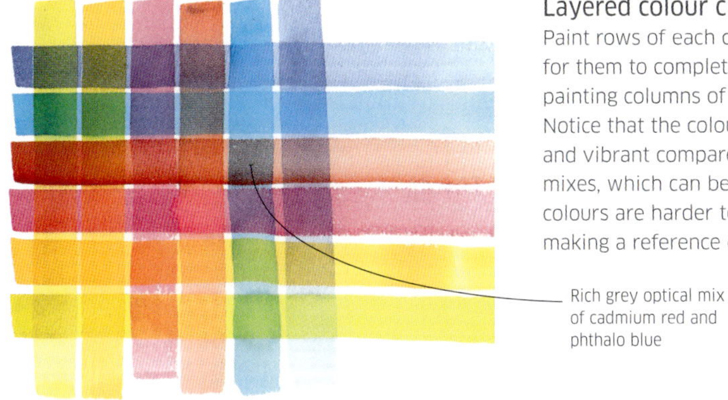

Layered colour chart

Paint rows of each colour, then wait for them to completely dry before painting columns of colour on top. Notice that the colours appear clear and vibrant compared to physical mixes, which can be duller. Layered colours are harder to predict, so making a reference chart is useful.

Rich grey optical mix of cadmium red and phthalo blue

Choosing a palette

HOW TO SELECT AND WORK WITH COLOURS FOR YOUR NEEDS

The term "palette" can refer to the actual choice of paints – such as a palette of blues – as well as to the physical container you use to store and mix your watercolour paints (also called a paintbox). With more than 250 different hues available, there is no shortage of choice in watercolour, so consider and research what you need before you start buying.

■ Your basic colour palette

A considered, core palette of primary colours can make your life as a painter easier because it will enable you to mix a huge range of hues. You can create many types of painting using primary colours as your foundation, as shown in the examples below. (See also pp.32–39.)

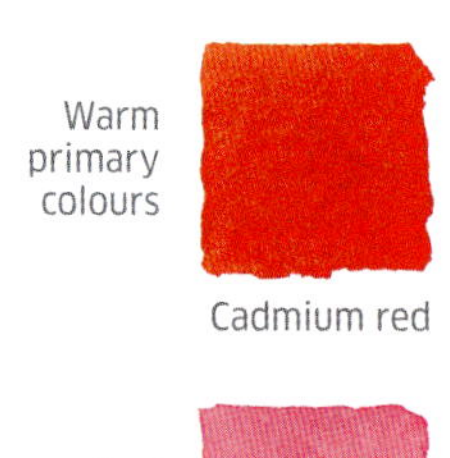

Core primary colours

With this set of warm and cool primary colours you can mix almost any hue imaginable. Other primary colours that are similar in hue to this selection will also be suitable. When choosing paints, do check for permanence or their likelihood to fade.

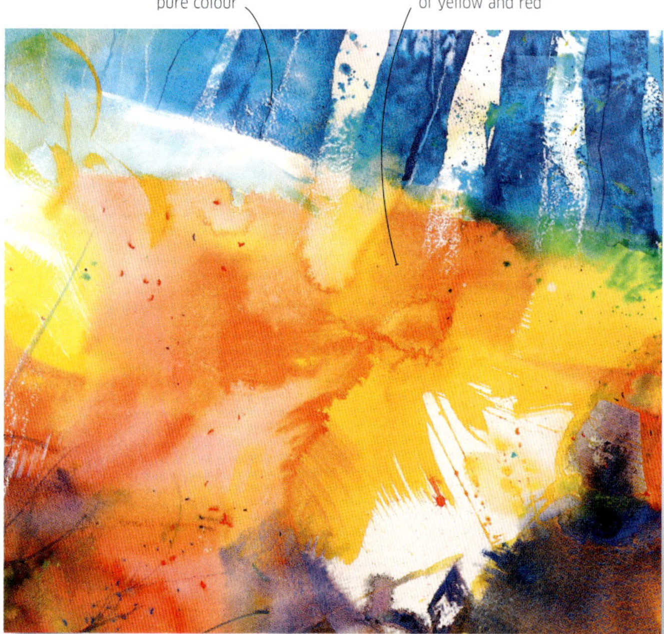

Pure primaries and secondary mixes

This abstract piece uses a bold limited palette of warm primary colours for impact. Cadmium yellow, cadmium red, and azure blue are applied wet-in-wet to create vibrant secondary colours.

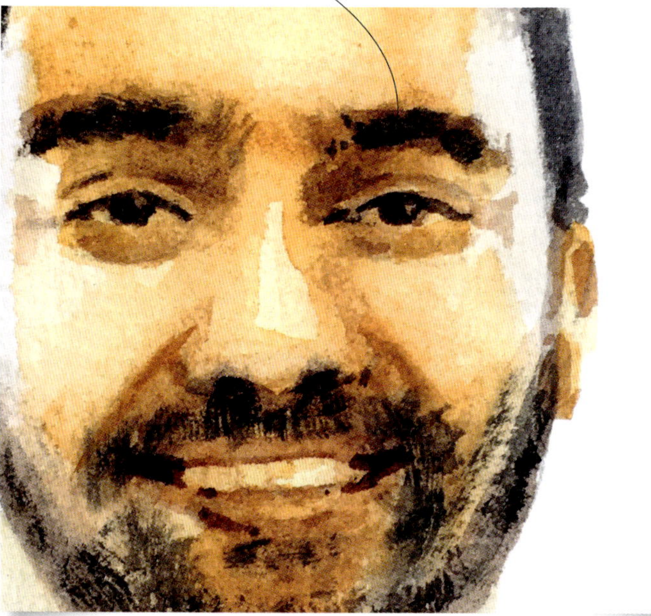

Neutrals mixed from primaries

Here, warm yellow raw sienna, cool alizarin crimson, and warm ultramarine blue are combined with touches of burnt sienna and burnt umber to mix a full range of skin tones for a realistic portrait.

Useful additional colours

While you can mix similar versions of popular colours such as burnt sienna, having premixed colours in your palette can be more convenient. Neutral tint (a strong dark) and titanium white gouache for highlights are both useful. You may also favour certain types of colour depending on your preferred subjects.

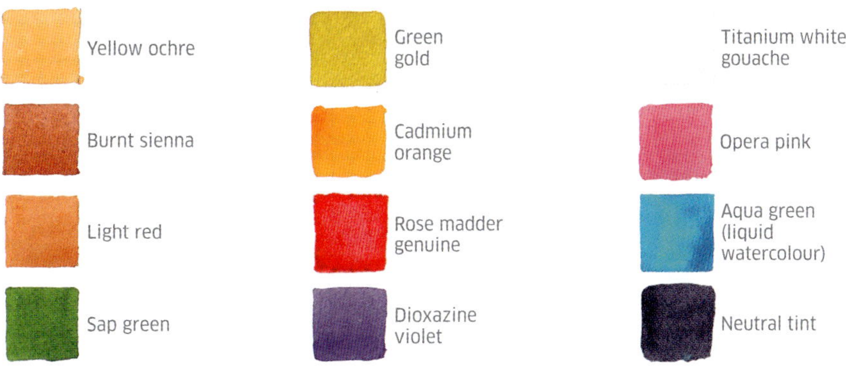

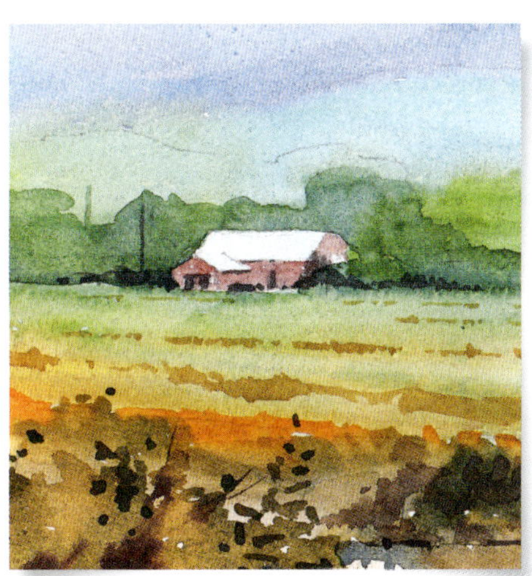

Useful colours for landscapes

As you would expect, muted, slightly dull earth colours are a worthwhile addition for a landscape palette. Pigments such as ochres and siennas were originally literally made from the earth.

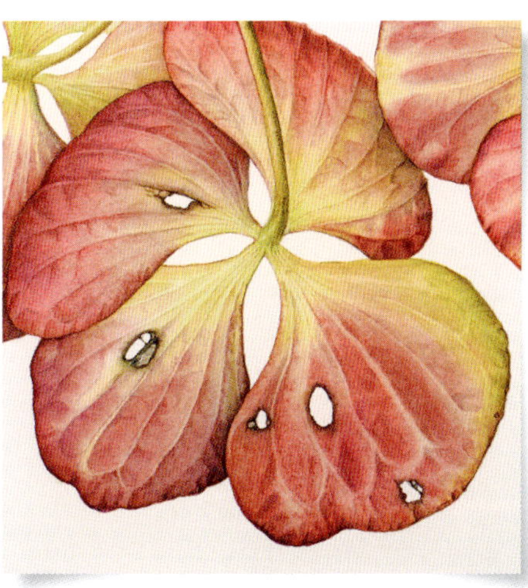

Useful colours for flowers

To encapsulate nature's vivid colour schemes, still-life painters often favour the freshest and brightest colours and will also include secondary colours in their palette. Painters tend to form firm favourites.

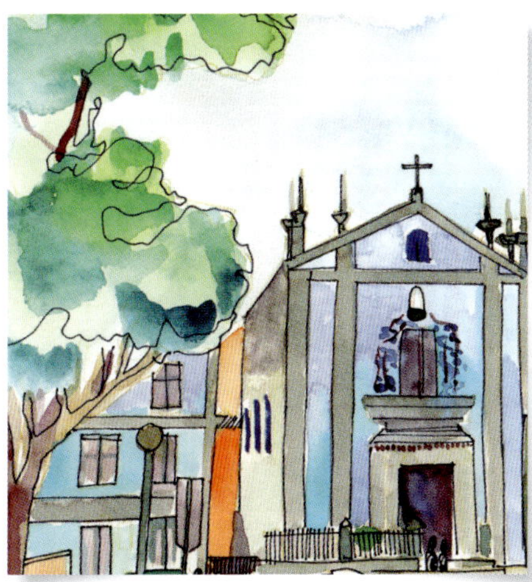

Useful colours for illustration

For illustration, black and white are useful additions to reinforce bright spots and shadows. Liquid watercolours, such as aqua green, provide illustrators with concentrated pigments for an immediate hit of colour.

Container choices

For ease of working, choose a paintbox or palette that can both store your squeezed paint or pans and provide good mixing areas. Palettes vary dramatically in price and construction, so choose something that fits your needs and your budget. All palettes should have deep paint wells to fit a full pan, or the equivalent in squeezed paint. There should also be a number of deep mixing areas that will hold at least 15ml (½fl oz) of mixed paint.

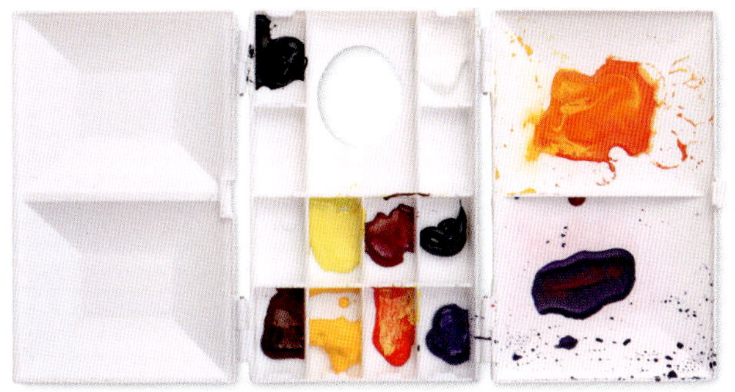

A versatile palette

This palette is convenient and easy to store and transport – ideal for *plein air* painting. Its generous paint-holding wells can be filled and topped up as needed, without waste.

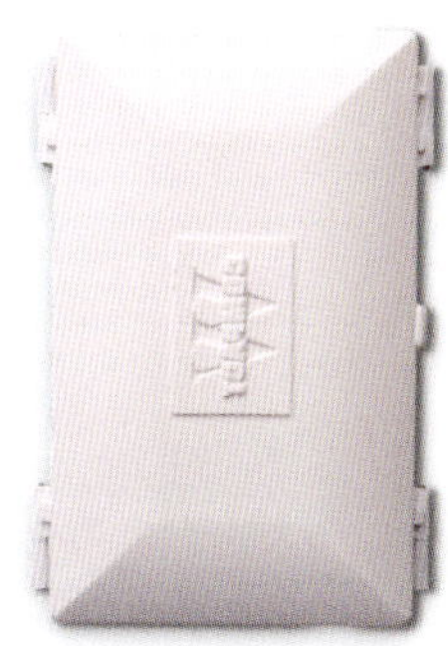

Closed palette

Your painting set-up

THE RIGHT EQUIPMENT WHEREVER YOU PAINT

Some artists prefer to practise their skills in the comfort of their own home or studio, surrounded by secondary sources and reference photos; others will attest that there is nothing like painting *en plein air* in front of a subject to help capture the depth that's easier to see in real life. Whichever location you prefer, be sure to make painting easier with the right set-up.

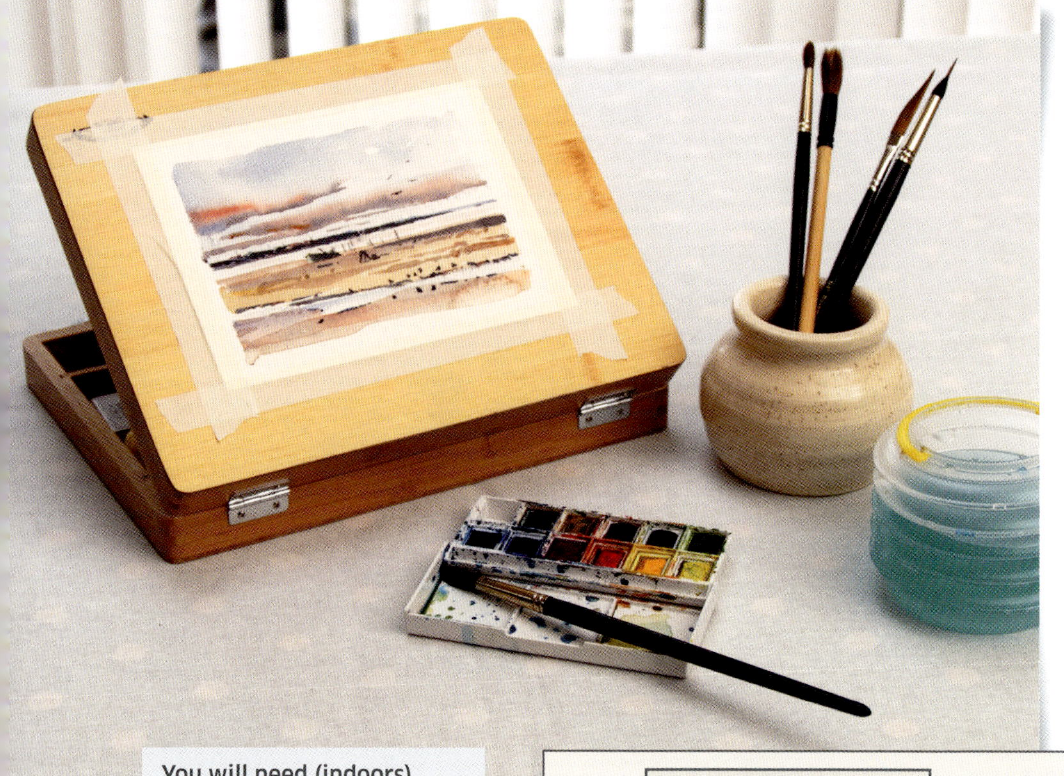

Painting indoors

There's no need for a dedicated studio space for indoor painting. Watercolour paint is easily removed from hard surfaces and has no smell, so many painters happily work at the kitchen table. What is important is to make sure you have everything you need within reach and to set up your workspace in exactly the same way every time (see below for an example set-up). You don't want to be searching for anything in the middle of an important wash.

A table-top easel is a useful addition to your painting kit: as well as holding your paper securely, it allows you to adjust its tilt, vital in directing the flow of washes down the paper. Wherever you set up your indoor workspace, choose somewhere with good natural

You will need (indoors)

- Container of water
- Paper towel
- Watercolour paper
- Board for holding paper
- Tape or clips to fix paper to board
- Watercolour paints and palette
- Selection of brushes
- Table-top easel (optional)
- Spray bottle (optional)

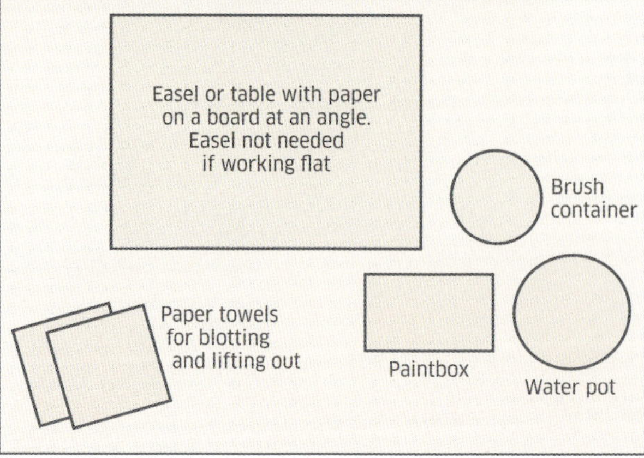

A right-handed set-up

It is natural to go from water to paint to paper. Such direction of work avoids the common problem of dripping water on to a painting! Always arrange paints in the same way in your palette, so you know exactly where the colours are.

Using a tripod as an easel

If you have a camera tripod already, there's no need to buy a field easel to enable your *en plein air* painting. Follow these steps to modify what you have.

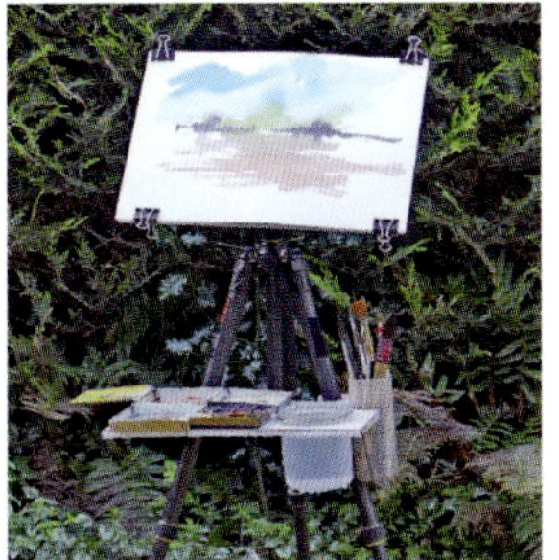

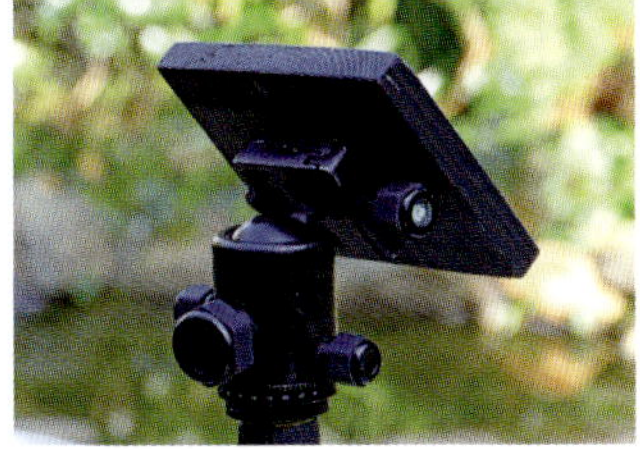

1 Adapting the tripod plate Screw the existing tripod plate to an 11cm (4½in) square of wood. Stick four strips of self-adhesive Velcro to the other side of the wood, and reinforce the strips with staples.

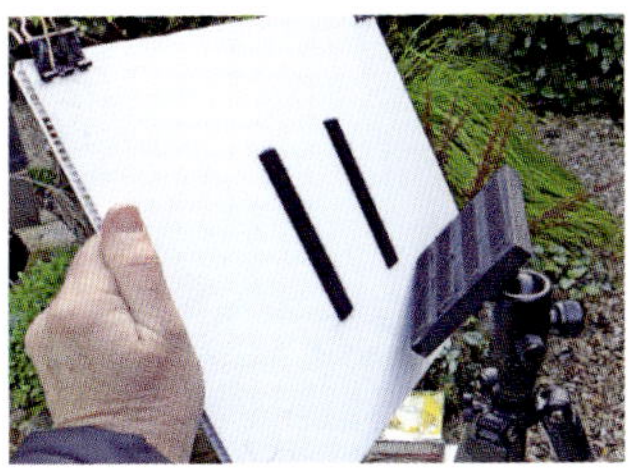

2 Fixing the board For the painting board, use a piece of 10mm (⅓in) corrugated plastic. Two strips of Velcro are enough to hold it firmly on the tripod, yet allow it to be easily removed when needed.

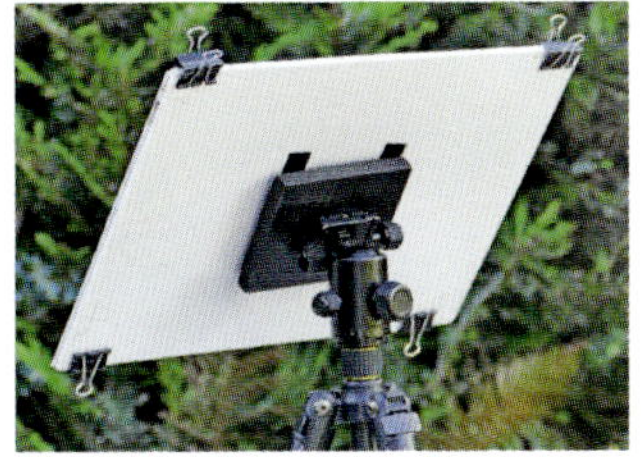

3 Ready for paper This painting board is sized for a quarter-sheet of paper, but the wooden holder on the tripod will work just as well with a half-sheet size. Clips are handy to secure the paper to the board.

daylight, if possible, but avoid the sun shining directly on to your paper as the glare can be tiring to the eyes. There are now inexpensive daylight bulbs and LED lamps available that provide a strong and even light, enabling you to paint anytime.

Working flat or at an angle?

Every artist will have a preferred angle for painting. Working flat is often preferred for wet-in-wet painting (see pp.52–55) as this allows paint to flood and merge easily. Working at an angle encourages washes down the paper, resulting in a fresh and even colour; a very steep angle allows drippy runs.

Outdoor painting

Plein air painting is made much easier when you have the right equipment; and exactly what that is depends upon what suits you as a painter. There's no need to rush out to buy all manner of specialist kit. As long as you can hold your paper steady, have all your paints and brushes to hand, and a source of water, you have all you need for a productive painting session. Over time and repeated sessions of painting outdoors, you'll refine what you take and source lightweight versions, as necessary. It's a good idea to carry all you need, and the bag itself can steady the set-up.

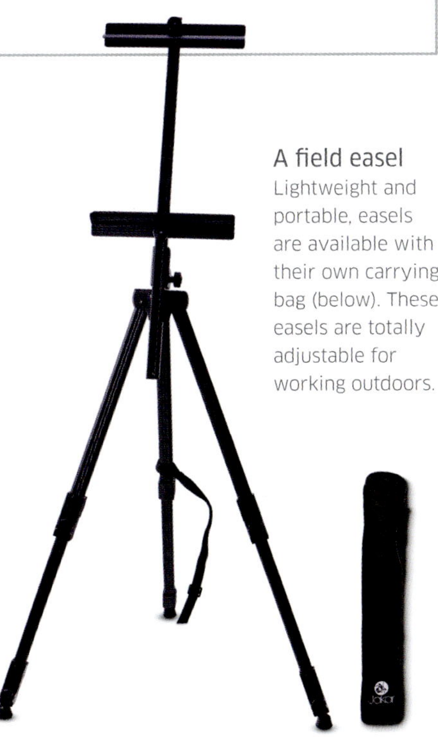

A field easel Lightweight and portable, easels are available with their own carrying bag (below). These easels are totally adjustable for working outdoors.

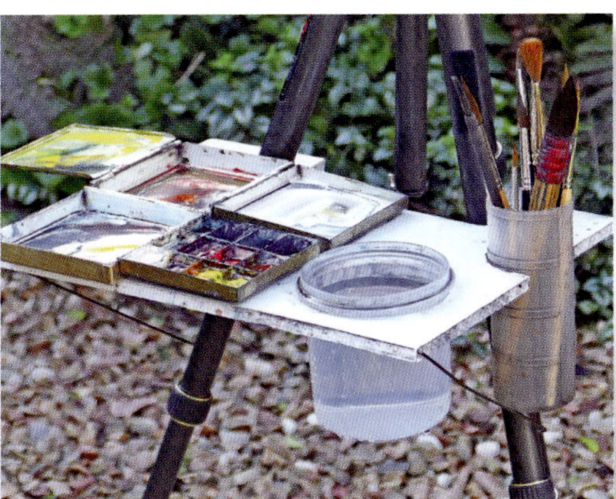

A customized outdoor set-up This plastic tray has cut-outs for a water container and brush case with space for the palette. A straightened-out wire coat hanger underneath adds stability. You don't have to buy an expensive easel set-up; make practical adjustments to a basic set-up over time.

You will need (outdoors)

- Field easel or modified tripod
- Container of water that can be fixed to your easel and a source of more clean water
- Watercolour paper
- Lightweight board to hold paper
- Tape or clips to fix paper to board
- Watercolour paints and palette
- Selection of brushes in a pot
- Paper towel
- Spray bottle

Displaying your paintings

HOW BEST TO PRESENT YOUR WORK

A painting almost always looks better and more impressive when well presented with a mount within a quality frame. The opposite holds true, unfortunately, when work is shoddily mounted or poorly framed. To celebrate the fruits of your labour, take some time to consider exactly how you want to present your watercolour paintings.

The difference a mount makes

The traditional method of framing a watercolour is first to mount it within a bevelled cut-out mount card. To give the painting enough space, use a minimum mount width of at least 8cm (3⅛in), even for small paintings. With larger pieces of, say, half-sheet size (38 x 56cm/15 x 22in), at least a 10cm (4in) width would be needed.

Mounts are cut using a special cutting machine that maintains the 45-degree angle of cut and ensures there is no overcutting or undercutting. Even the simplest of these machines is an expensive investment and most painters will use their local framing shop or online service to ensure a perfect and professional-looking result.

A double mount uses two mount cards with offset cut-outs to show a 5–10mm (⅕–⅖in) step and leads the viewer's eye into the painting; triple mounts are also available. The best card is whitecore mount card. Although the centre of all mount card is white when cut, only whitecore stays white.

Choosing the right frame

A picture frame is constructed from material known as "moulding". Such moulding comes in a vast range of colours, widths, and materials. Any frame should enhance rather than compete with your watercolour painting, and so the most popular mouldings are fairly simple shapes in natural wood; these can be finished, painted, or stained in a white or light colour. Other classic mouldings are brown and black, and a gilt finish appeals to many artists.

Be aware that some mouldings are more prone to damage, so if you plan to reuse frames (a sustainable approach), a natural hardwood frame in oak or ash is less likely to show the odd knock.

Glass or acrylic?

Keep your painting fresh with clear picture glass or, ideally, glass with a UV coating to stop fading; most framers can offer both. Quality, clear museum glass is non-reflective and absorbs UV light, but is more expensive. Acrylic – often supplied with frames bought online – is very light but also prone to scratching.

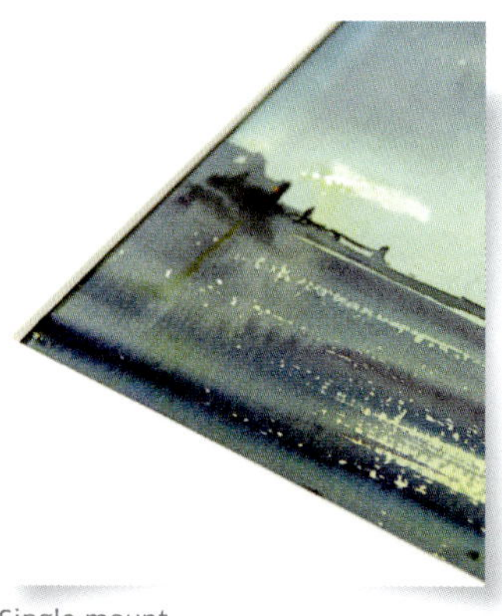

Single mount

Double mount

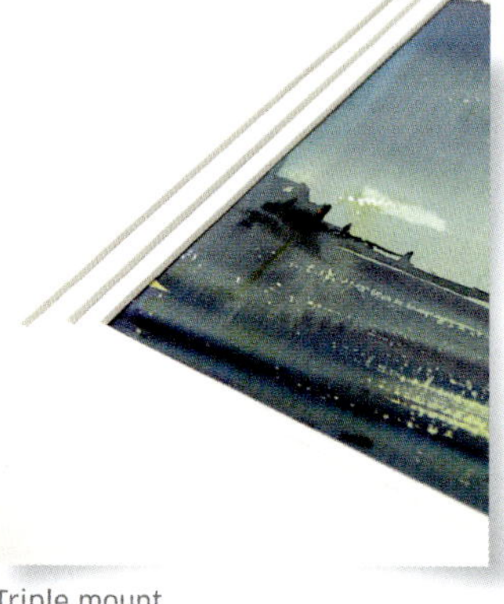

Triple mount

Picture mounts

Picture mounts are generally single, double, or more rarely, triple. As well as creating a gentle space around the painting, the mount also prevents the painting touching the glass, which could cause damage.

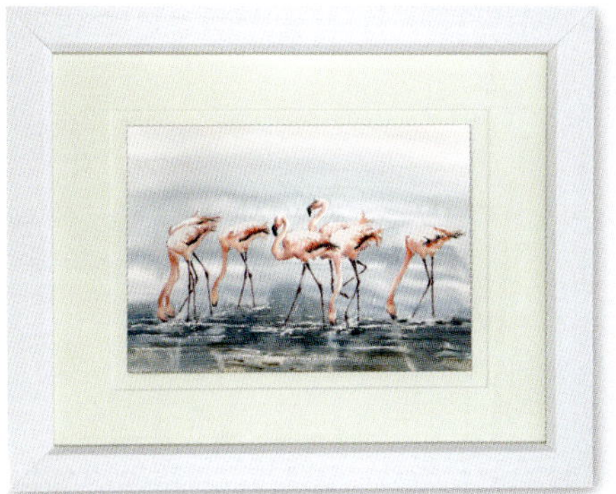

Wet-in-wet (see pp.52–55)

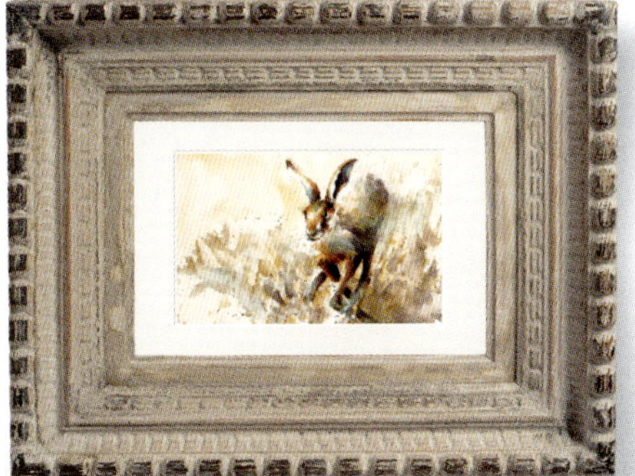

Creatures in motion (see pp.240–43)

A frame gallery

Watercolour paintings often work best within a simple frame. Here are a few examples to give you an idea of how to frame your next masterpiece.

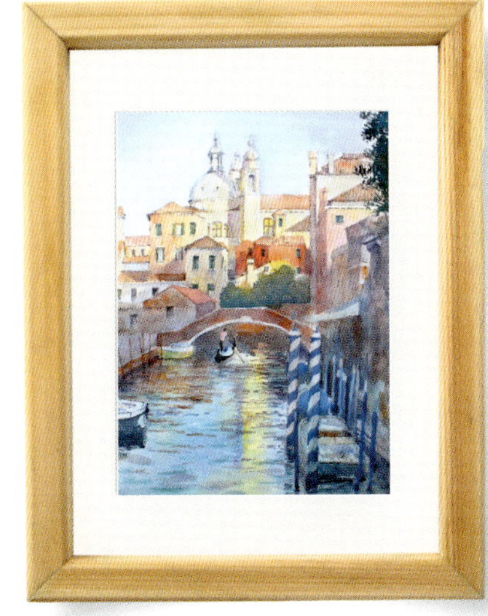

Still water (see pp.182–85)

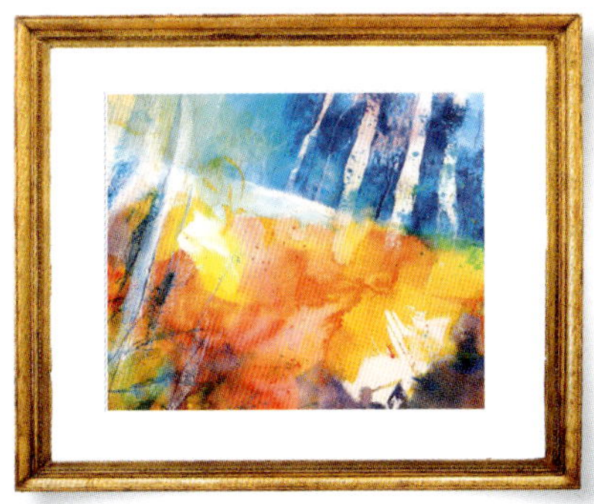

Towards abstraction (see pp.162–65)

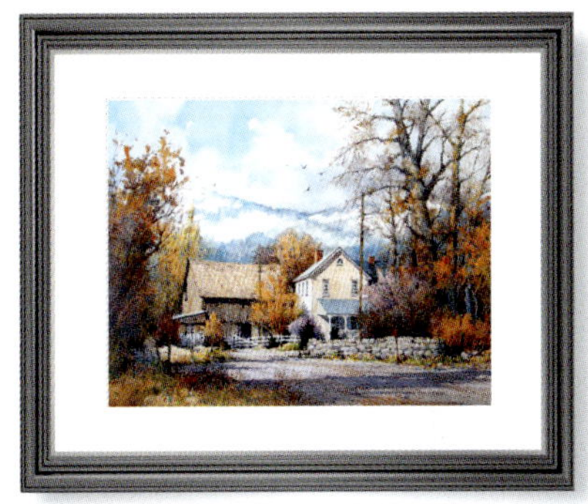

Showcase painting (see pp.142–43)

Floating mount

A painting can be made to appear as if it is "floating" above the mount by fixing it first to foamboard. The frame needs an inset to keep the mount and painting away from the glass.

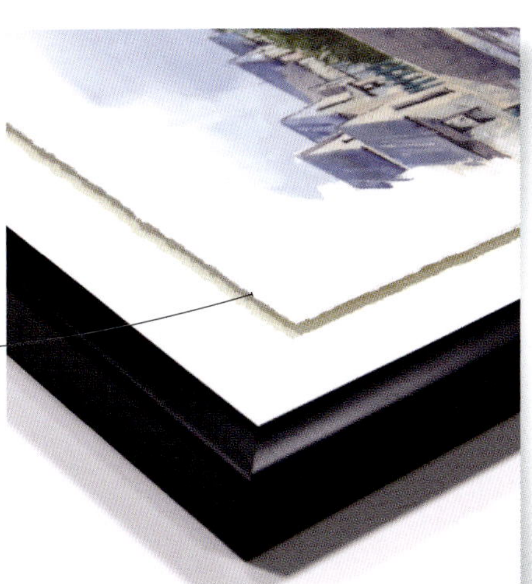

Edge of painting raised above the mount

Cutting a mount

It is hard to make a bevelled cut without specialist mount-cutting equipment; even then, proficiency requires a lot of practice.

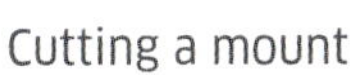

Deckled edges

Float-mounting often looks best when the painting has a deckled edge. Turn the painting over and simply tear off the edge of the paper by pulling it up against a steel ruler, or use an inexpensive deckle edge ripper.

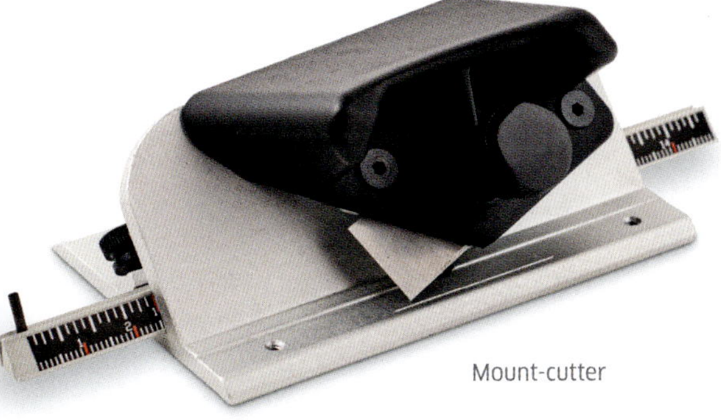

Mount-cutter

"**Don't skimp** on framing. Nothing will **hurt your painting** more than a **poor frame.**"

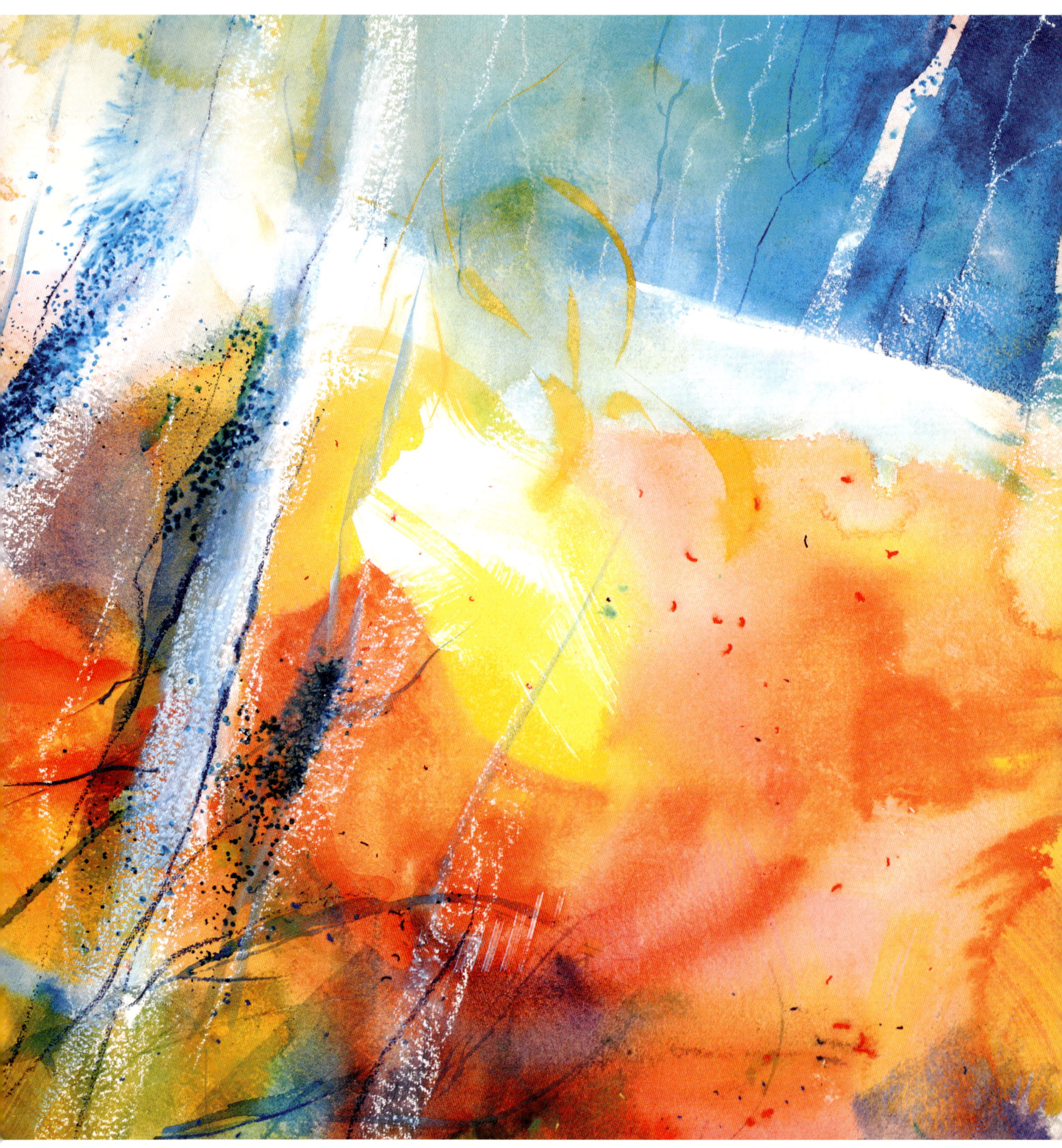

Techniques

Watercolour **techniques**

As a medium, watercolour is incredibly versatile, taking you from simple flat washes to mixed media and textured surfaces that suit many painting styles and subjects. The fluid, transparent nature of the paint makes it easy to apply with expressive strokes, producing paintings where colours blend and merge seamlessly with sparkling luminosity.

On the following pages, you will find 45 techniques to practise and develop your skills. They are grouped into three sections designed to build your repertoire and hone your style, from core techniques such as layering washes in the beginner section, to using theories of colour and composition in the intermediate section, to experimenting with mixed media in the advanced section. Showcase paintings in each section bring numerous techniques together.

1 Beginner techniques

■ See pp.50–89

The first section explains how to lay your base washes, working from light to dark in either wet-in-wet or wet-on-dry applications, along with tips on how to remedy mistakes.

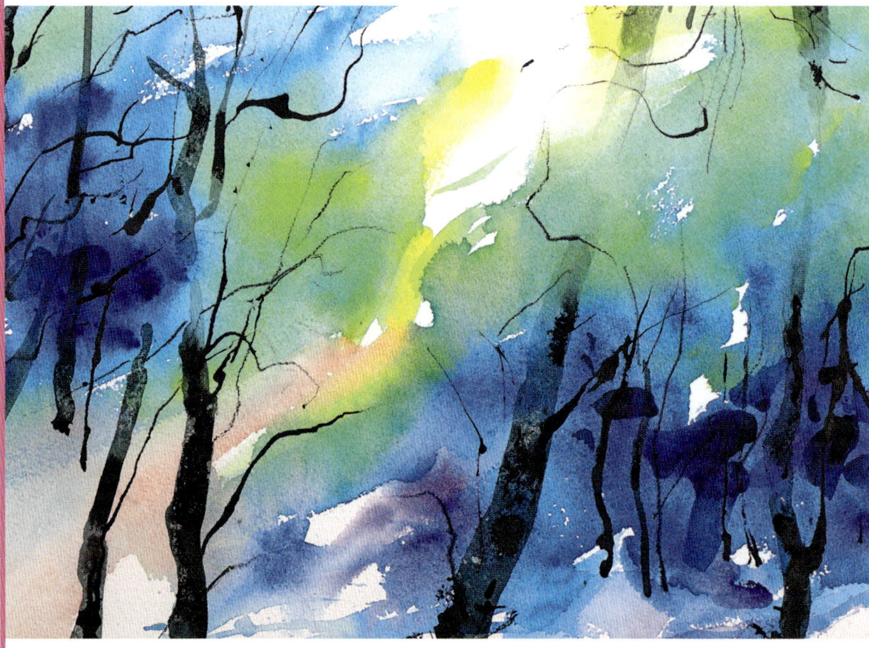

Beginner showcase painting (see pp.64–65)

2 Intermediate techniques

■ See pp.90–127

In the second section, develop an understanding of colour theory to use warm and cool colours, aerial perspective, complementary and analogous colours to best effect, with techniques such as glazing.

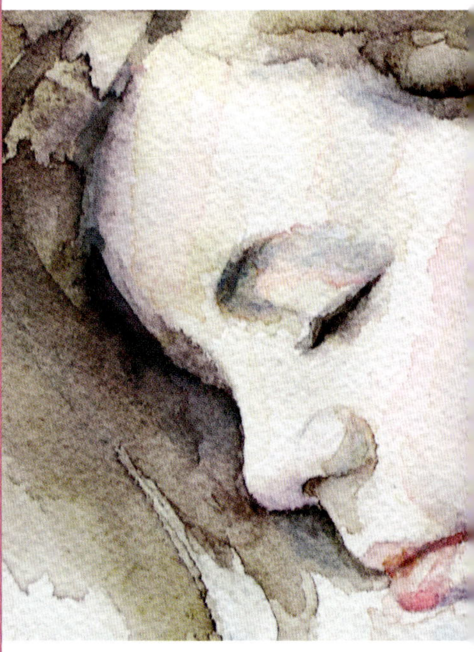

Softening edges (see pp.94–95)

Watercolour paint flows easily and this unpredictable nature is part of its appeal. Learning to control this characteristic is fundamental to working with watercolour, from laying an even wash to incorporating runbacks into your work. Allowing the paint to merge wet-in-wet produces subtle blends and effects. In contrast, you can also work wet-on-dry, to add crisp detail and controlled edges.

A wash is a great starting point for understanding watercolour; practise laying different types of washes, from graduated to the more advanced separating washes. When working from light to dark, you need to consider how to convey highlights, using techniques that either retain lights, from using masking fluid to wax resist, or remove colour through lifting out with a brush, or the more advanced effects of using bleach and salt.

To imbue your painting with light, exploit the transparency of the paint to lay colour in layers, using glazing to build depth or adjust the colour or tone of a wash.

A versatile approach

The range of techniques and approaches available in watercolour make it an ideal medium for many styles of painting. Loose and abstract marks can be complemented with splattered effects or added gouache highlights. Pen and wash is ideal for working in a sketchbook but also adapts to a more illustrative style. Combining watercolour with mixed media opens up myriad options, with applications for illustration and design using detailed drawings and pattern making.

3 Advanced techniques

■ See pp.128–67

In the final section, find out about the principles of perspective and focal points, and how to combine special effects or mixed media – from gouache to charcoal – to develop your style further.

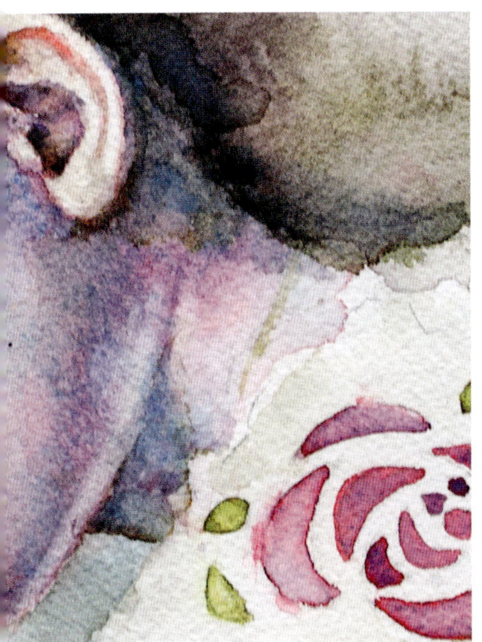

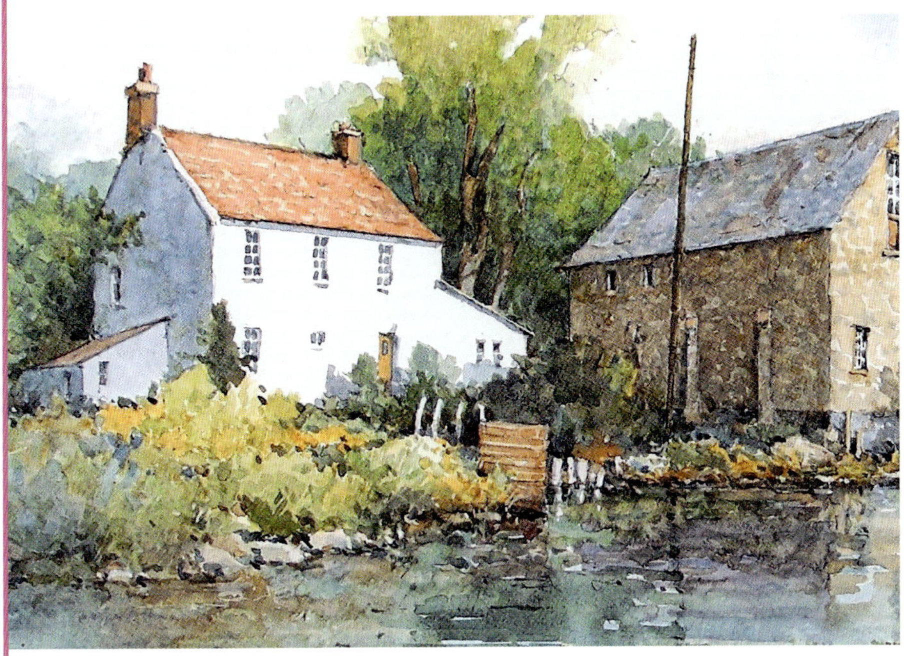

Linear perspective (see pp.134–37)

Wet-on-dry

CONTROLLING BRUSHSTROKES AND EDGES

When wet paint is applied onto dry paper, or onto areas of dry paint, the pigment will spread less than if you apply paint on a wet surface. This gives you more control over your brushstrokes and produces crisp edges, allowing you to achieve precise shapes, definition, and detail.

◾ Controlling the marks

To maintain crisp edges when working on dry paper, always let the first wash dry and don't overwork your washes. For varied effects, use different brushes, from Chinese to mop and rigger, and learn how to control them to build up a vocabulary of marks.

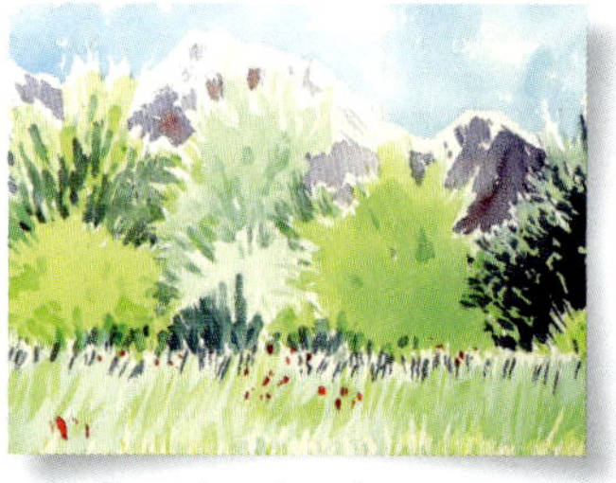

Correct: wet on dry paper   Incorrect: overworked washes

Wet on dry paper

For crisp details on dry paper, the paint shouldn't flow beyond the dry edges of the shape. If you keep adding and pushing more paint beyond the intended area it will mix and you risk diffusing the edges.

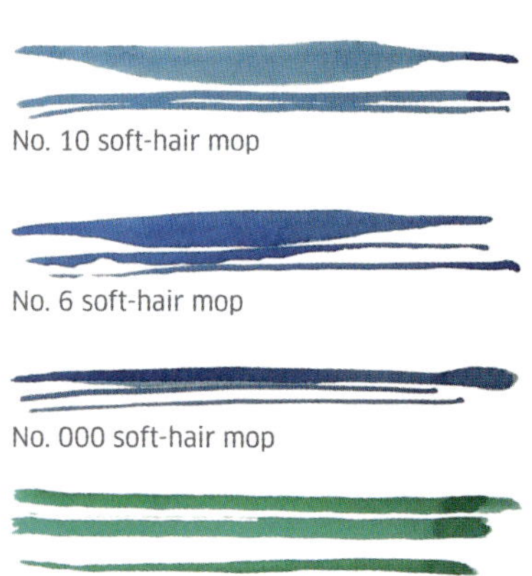

No. 10 soft-hair mop

No. 6 soft-hair mop

No. 000 soft-hair mop

Chinese long brush

Brush marks

Hold the brush close to the ferrule, and use the tip for controlled, detailed marks. Holding the brush higher up will produce looser, featherlike strokes. Use the side of the brush for thicker lines and marks.

PUTTING IT INTO PRACTICE

In this detailed scene, the wet-on-dry technique is used to create leaf shapes in several colours, which vary in tone and intensity. Layers of colour built up over dry underwashes create the reflective water.

You will need

Pure yellow · Green gold · Permanent rose · Caput mortuum violet · Manganese blue · Indanthrene blue · Indigo · Neutral tint · Phthalo green (blue shade)

- ▪ Selection of Chinese brushes
- ▪ No. 10 and no. 000 soft-hair mop brushes
- ▪ 33 x 48cm (13 x 19in) hot-pressed watercolour paper 535gsm (250lb)

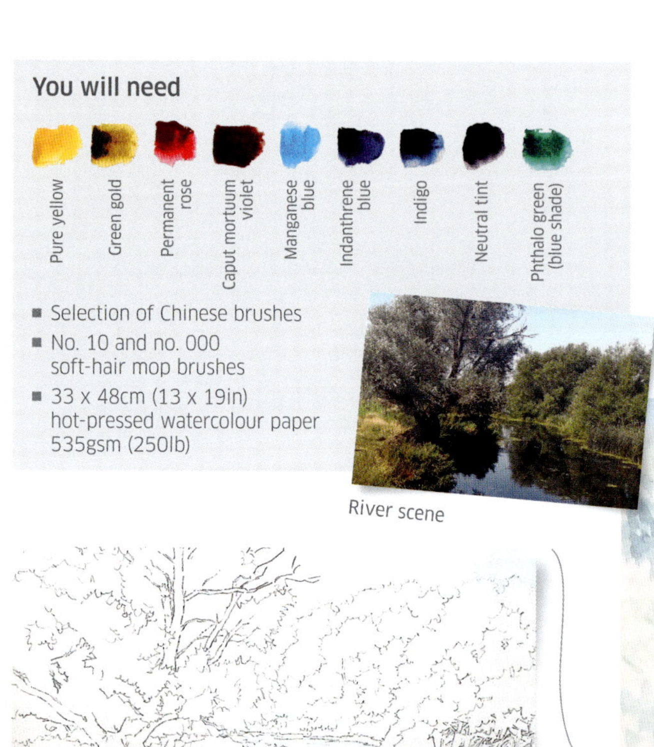

River scene

1 Apply wash for sky and water

On dry paper, paint washes of manganese blue with a no. 10 mop. Pull the brush across to create lines, leaving highlights of dry, white paper.

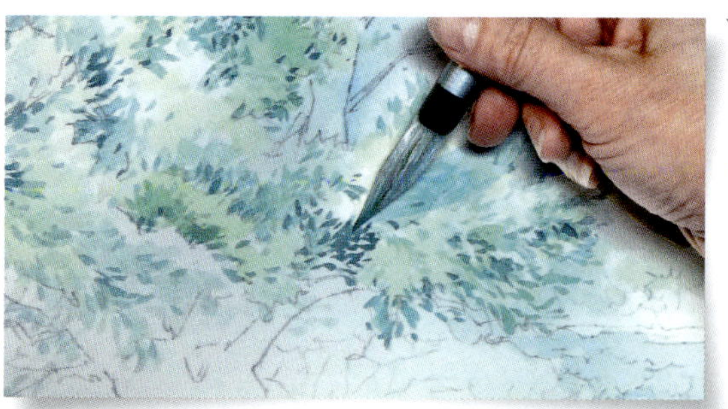

2 Foliage shapes

Apply lightest green for foliage and grasses. With a light touch, slightly fan a Chinese brush to hint at different shapes. When dry, return to fill in gaps.

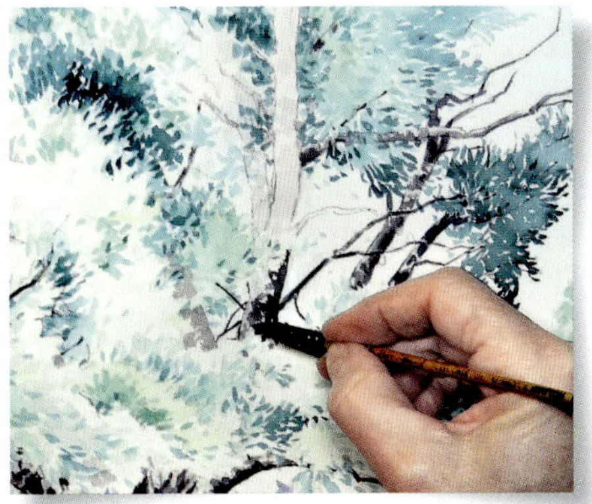

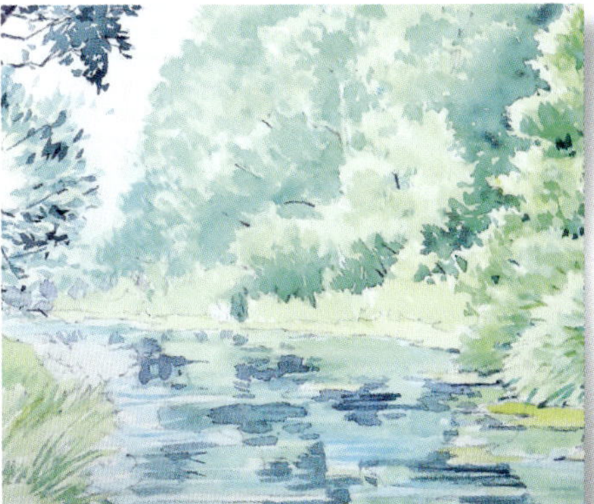

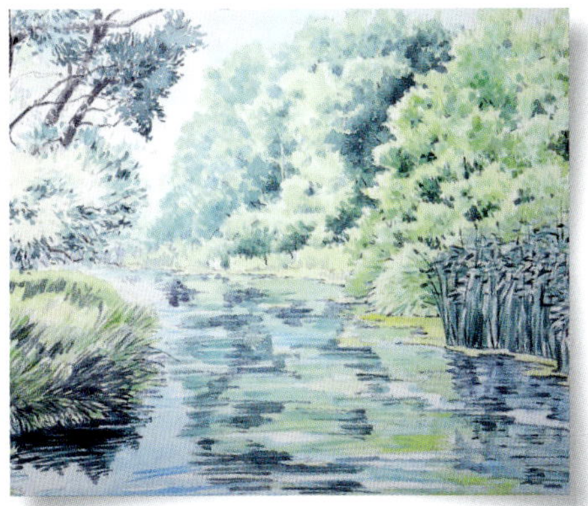

3 Refine the trees

Use different brushes in as many ways as possible to build up layers of colour and tone. Remember to let each wash dry, since earlier laid washes are easily disturbed.

4 Add mid tones

Build up the scene by adding mid tones for the distant trees, river bank, and water, drying in between strokes. Don't be tempted to go back and fiddle; always let the wash dry.

5 Dark tones and details

Add darkest tones and shadows, keeping a balance of light and shade. Use the brush tip to shape leaves and the flat side of a small Chinese brush to pull lines for reflections.

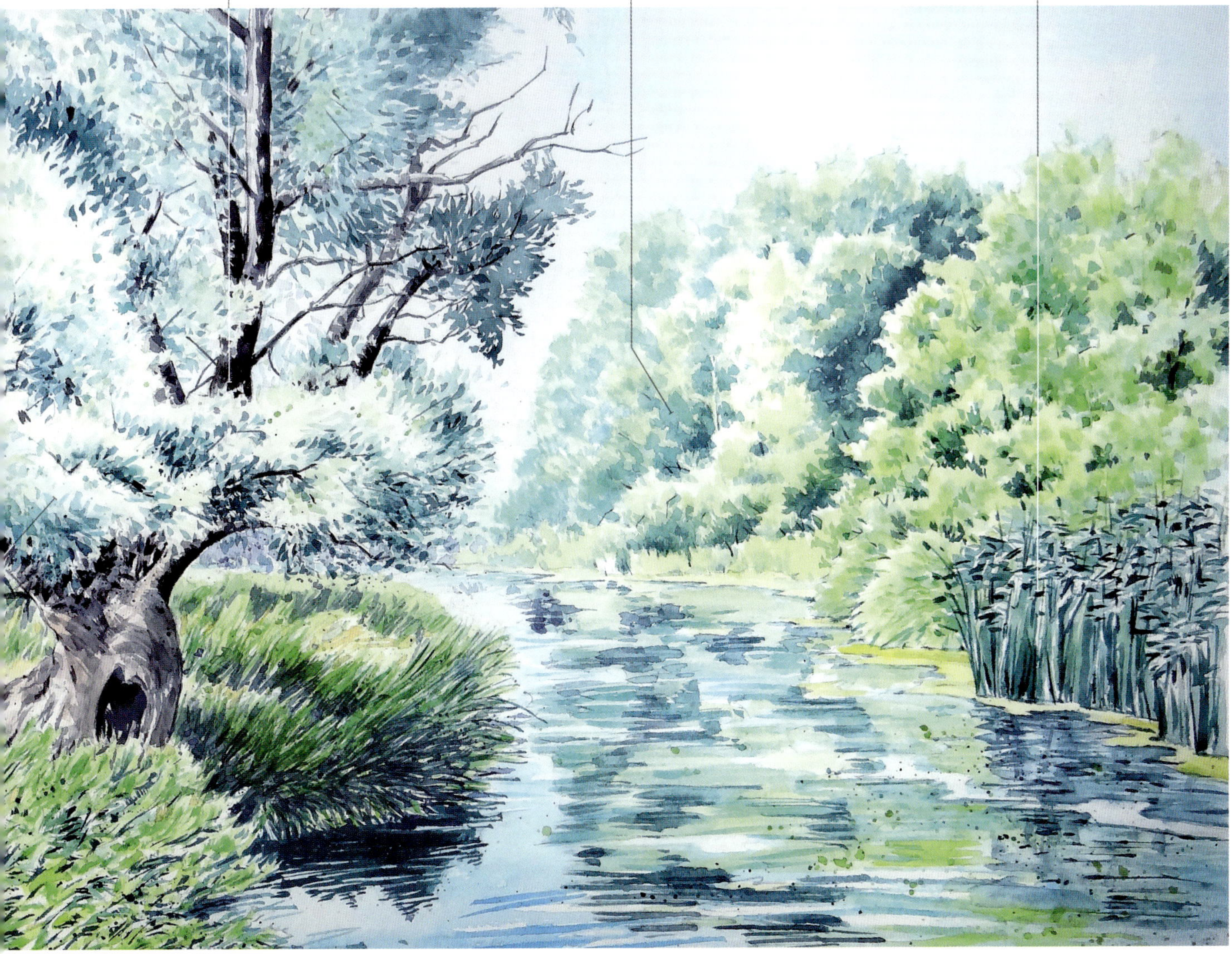

Wet-in-wet

NATURAL BLENDING EFFECTS

By applying paint to wet paper, or into a wet wash, watercolour pigments will merge and blur together naturally, in a way that no other paint medium can achieve. You can use wet-in-wet to blend washes, mix a third colour, or achieve subtle tones in one colour. It is ideal for subjects where subtle changes are required, such as skies or reflections.

■ Encouraging blends

The trick with wet-in-wet is to allow natural transitions and blends to happen – try not to interfere in the blending process with a brush, as the colours will continue to merge as the paint dries. You can impose some control by adjusting the dampness of the paper and choosing which paints to apply together.

Wet paper
The damper the paper the more the wash will spread, leaving tonal variations.

Natural blends
Apply loose drizzles of different colours to wet paper and allow them to blur and blend together.

Adjacent colour blends
Paint an even wash of two separate colours side by side on wet paper and leave them to touch and spread together where they meet.

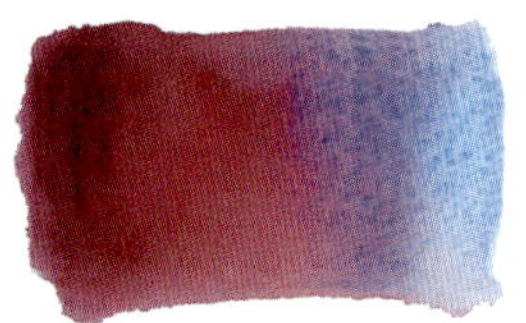

Dominant blends
With a stronger (more pigmented) wash of alizarin crimson added to a weaker one of ultramarine, the crimson dominates as it blends.

PUTTING IT INTO PRACTICE

Wet-in-wet blends are used here to create soft undulations in the water as well as gentle variations in colour on the birds. The fluid nature of the technique mirrors the sense of calm and tranquillity.

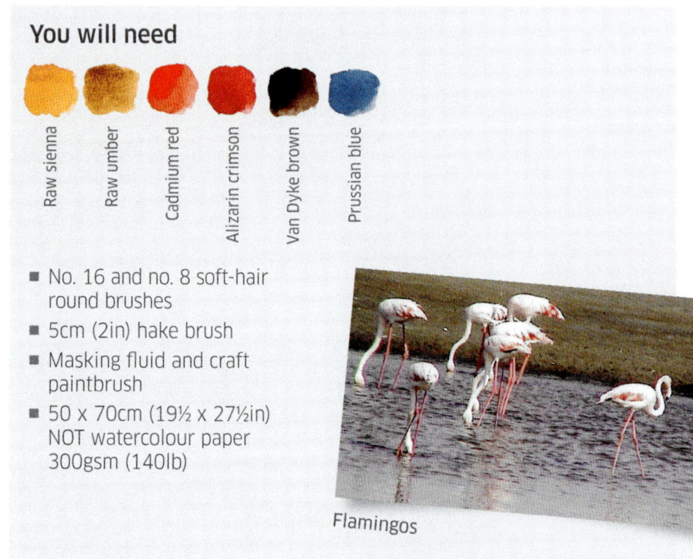

- No. 16 and no. 8 soft-hair round brushes
- 5cm (2in) hake brush
- Masking fluid and craft paintbrush
- 50 x 70cm (19½ x 27½in) NOT watercolour paper 300gsm (140lb)

Flamingos

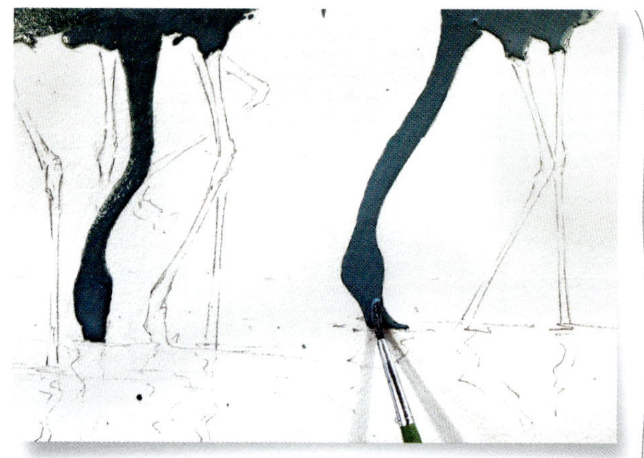

1 Reserve white areas
Using a craft brush, apply masking fluid (see pp.100–101) to the bodies of the flamingos to retain their silhouettes when the initial paint washes are applied. For the water, use swift horizontal strokes to create crisp ripples around their feet, and the end of the brush to splatter spontaneous splashes.

Ripples created with masking fluid

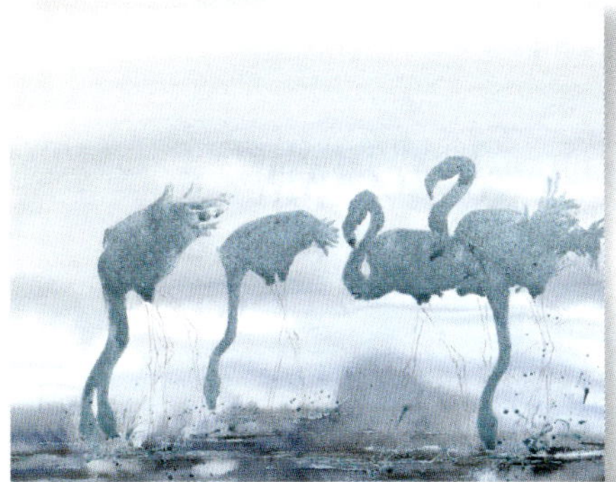

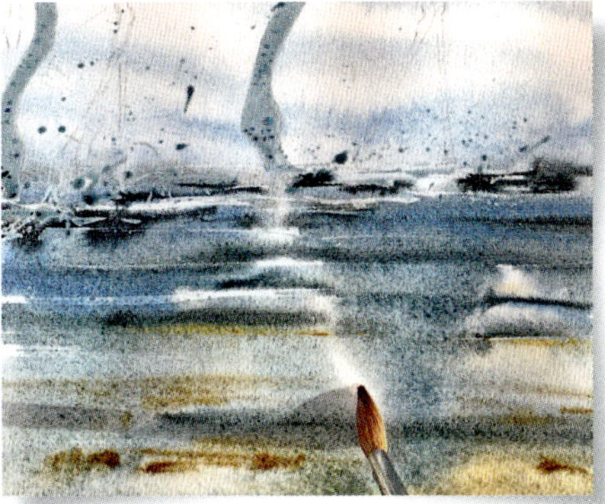

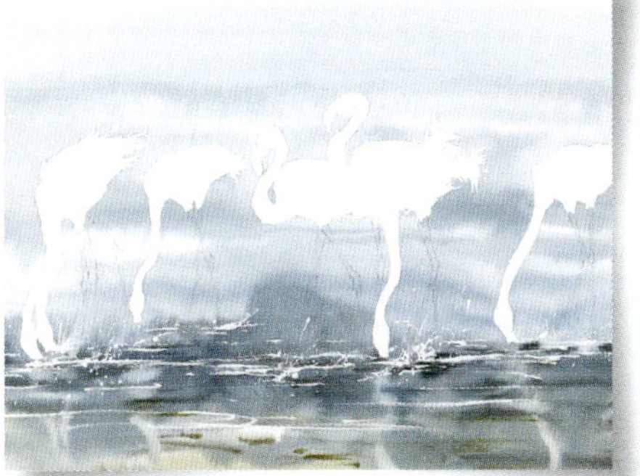

2 Background variegated wash

Use a hake brush to thoroughly wet the paper with washes of Prussian blue and Van Dyke brown, leaving odd chinks in denser tones around the flamingos' feet.

3 Lifting out

Tilt and tip the board to encourage the direction of blend. As the wash dries, lift out the reflected shape of the flamingos' necks with an almost dry brush.

4 Remove masking fluid

Leave the painting to dry slightly propped up so that gravity will encourage the colour to flow downwards and dry paler at the top. Once fully dry, rub off the masking fluid.

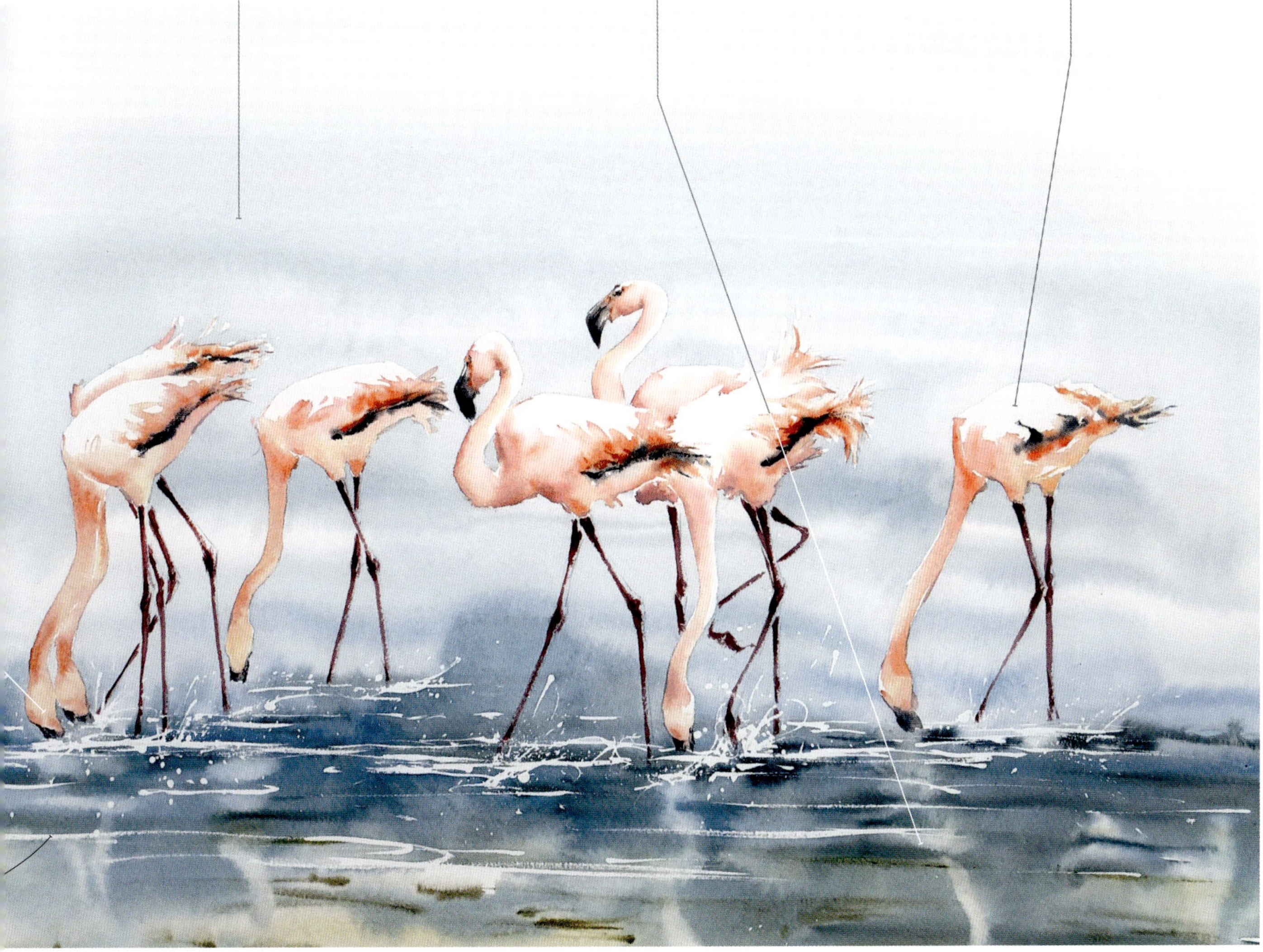

5 Apply water

Wetting each flamingo in turn with clean water, use a varied mix of raw sienna, cadmium red, and alizarin crimson to paint in their form. Dab bolder strengths of the mix into the shadowed areas. While still wet, apply a thicker and more intense mix of cadmium for deeper reds, and a mix of cadmium red and Prussian blue for the black on the wings and beaks. The softened blends will reflect the natural transitions of tones in the birds' feathers.

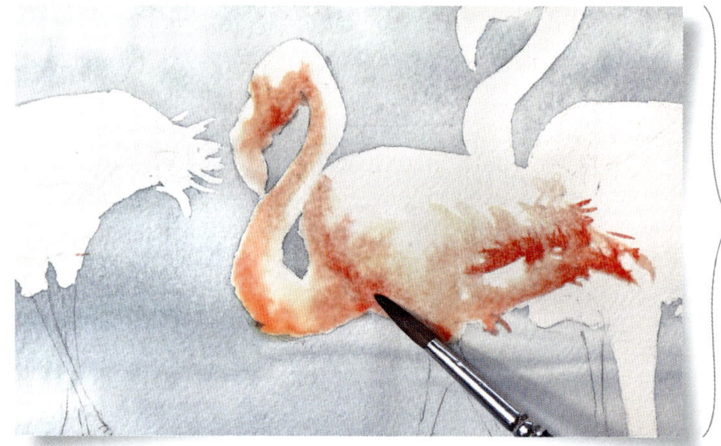

6 Add reflections

There are both shadows and reflections on the water. A reflection naturally extends towards the viewer, whereas the length and direction of the cast shadow is dependent on the angle of the sun. Wet the foreground water slightly, then paint in the reflections loosely with a gentler tone of the flamingo pink. Allow them to fade with soft edges. In contrast to the sharp-edged form of the flamingos, their soft-edged reflections emphasize the effect of the water.

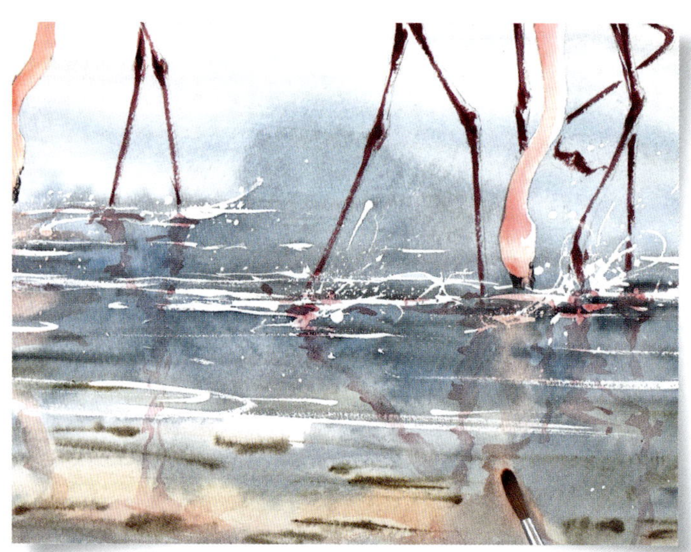

7 Blend shadows

Paint the shadows under the flamingos in touches of Prussian blue, with deeper sharp shadows cast across the water to anchor the flamingos on the lakeshore. Introducing the same Prussian blue from the background into the shadows on the flamingos and foreground water will help to bring the whole painting together. The colours will harmonize, lending a feeling of tranquillity to the scene.

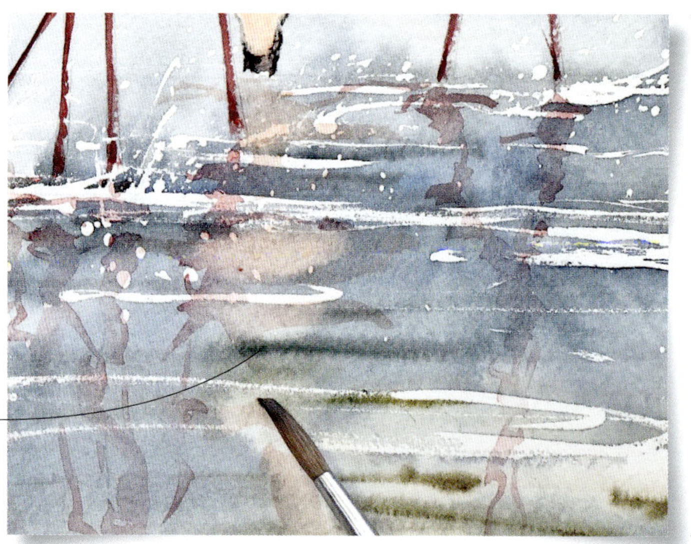

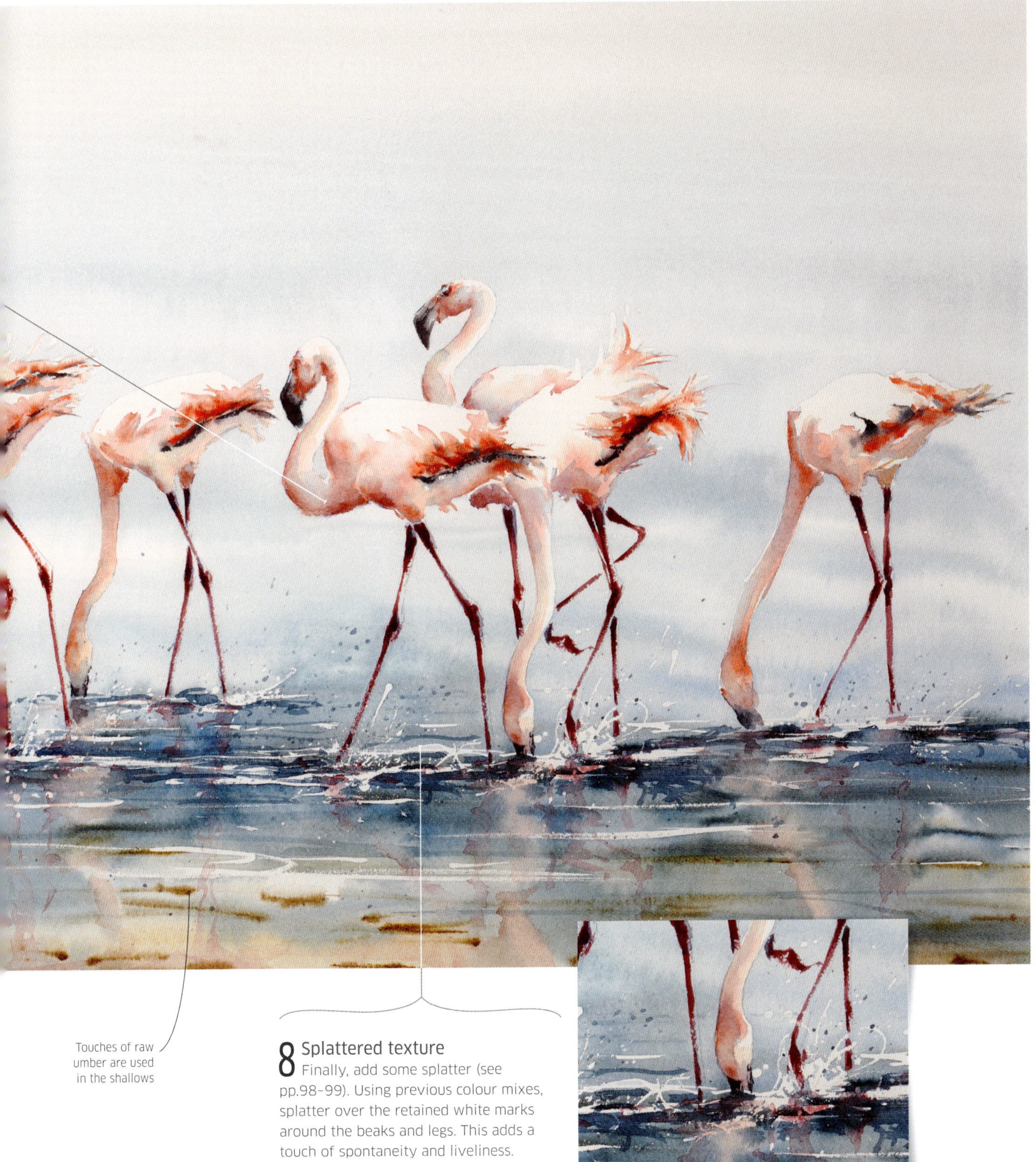

Touches of raw umber are used in the shallows

8 Splattered texture

Finally, add some splatter (see pp.98–99). Using previous colour mixes, splatter over the retained white marks around the beaks and legs. This adds a touch of spontaneity and liveliness.

Dry brush

PAINTING BROKEN MARKS

Dry brush refers to a technique where marks are made with a sparsely loaded brush, resulting in broken edges and textured effects. Simply by varying the angle and direction of the brush you can represent complex subjects such as foliage, the texture of rock or bark, and broken light. Work on rough paper for optimal effect.

Angling the brush

Start with the right ratio of pigment to water in your palette; not too wet that it drips and not so dry that it leaves streaks. Load the brush fully and then use the direction of your brush marks to describe the object you are representing, changing the angle of the brush to control the size and shape of the marks. Choose different brushes, from round to flat, for variety.

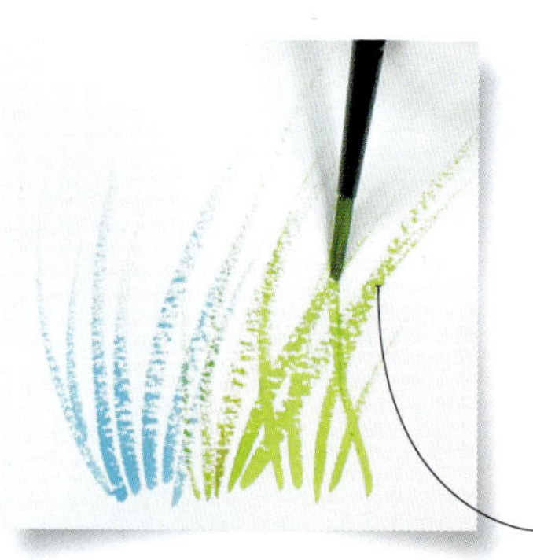

Pulling up
Quickly pull the tip of your brush upward to represent thin subjects like grass, leaving broken marks at the top of the stroke. Either replenish your brush or continue for drier texture. Vary the density of the line with different pressure.

Thin, dry strokes

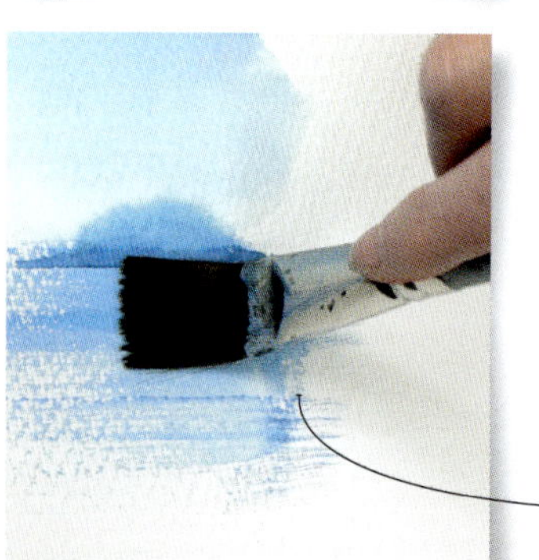

Splaying bristles
A flat brush is ideal for linear subjects. Press near the head of the brush to splay and flatten the bristles, then quickly drag in the direction of your subject; for example, vertically for grass or horizontally for light sparkles on water.

Broken linear marks

PUTTING IT INTO PRACTICE

A soft, wet-in-wet underpainting provides a base for working dry brush to convey the complex autumnal foliage of the tree and hedgerow, using light, directional brush marks at a shallow angle.

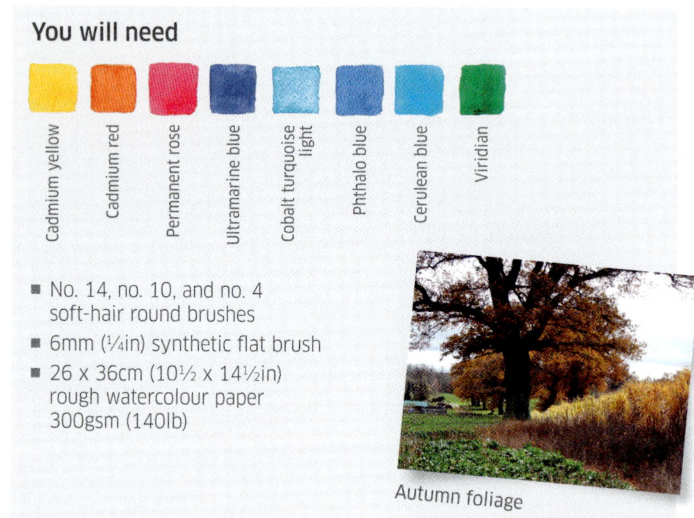

- No. 14, no. 10, and no. 4 soft-hair round brushes
- 6mm (¼in) synthetic flat brush
- 26 x 36cm (10½ x 14½in) rough watercolour paper 300gsm (140lb)

Autumn foliage

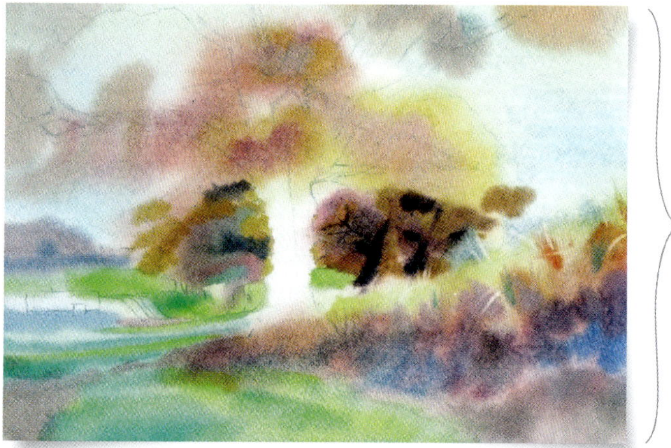

1 Underpainting
After lightly drawing the scene, wet the entire surface of your paper so that you can work all of the underpainting entirely wet-in-wet. Apply washes of orange, green, and violet for the main areas, allowing the pigment to flow freely.

"**The key** to dry brush is **the angle of the brush;** the flatter the better."

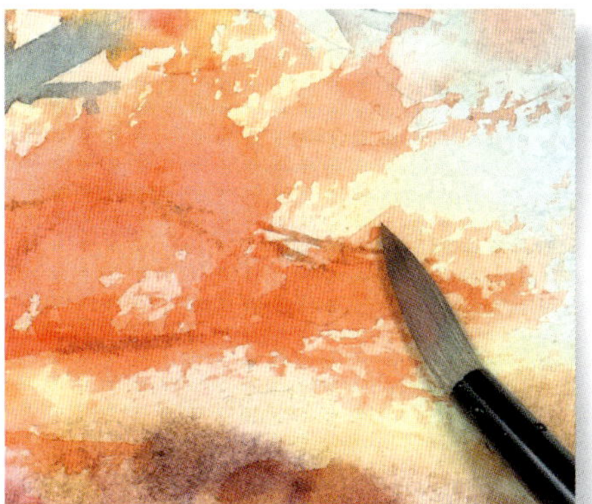

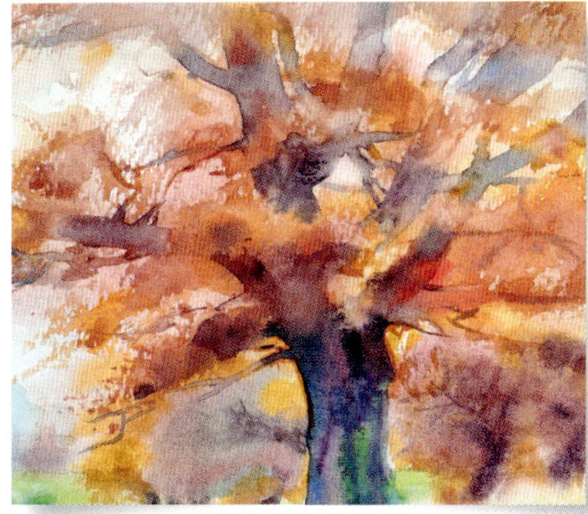

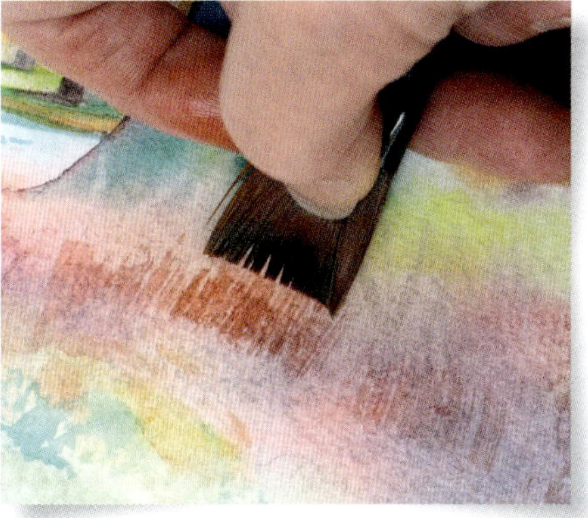

2 Broken edges for foliage
Working wet-on-dry, use an upright brush to apply a flat wash for masses of foliage. Break up the edges with dry brush marks from a flattened brush, without overworking.

3 Preserving edges
To paint the branches in between the foliage, apply a clear wash along the length of a branch and then add pigment between the foliage. This will preserve dry brush edges.

4 Directional strokes
For the long grass in the foreground, separate the bristles of a flat brush with your thumb, and make quick, light, directional dry marks over the soft underpainting.

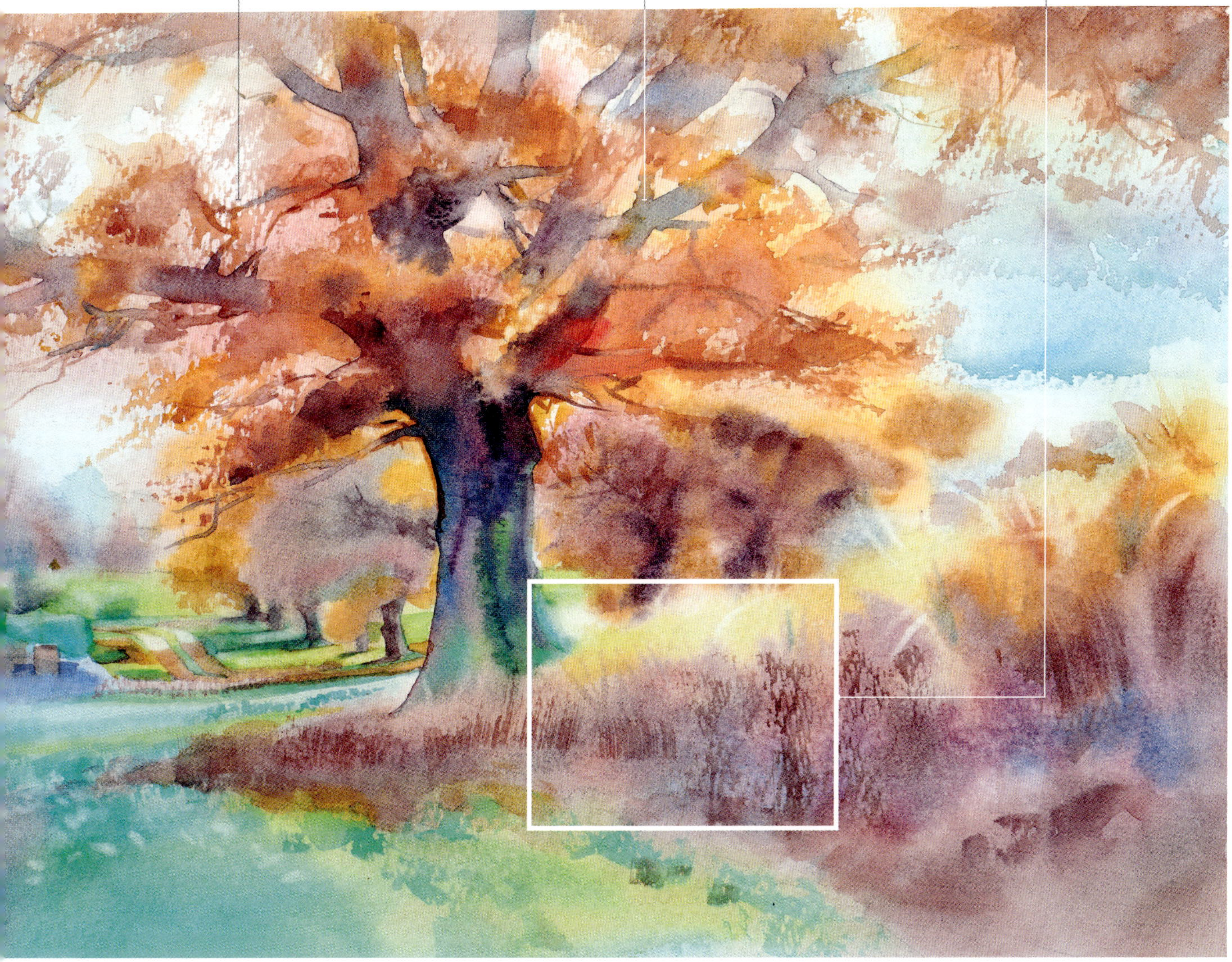

Layering paint

BUILDING WASHES

Watercolours are painted from light to dark and require the whites to be reserved from the outset. Painting transparent washes of individual colours allows you to build them up to create mixes on the paper instead of in a palette. This layering technique produces vibrant watercolours that are unified and harmonious.

■ Working from light to dark

Layering is one of the most important techniques in watercolour. In general, weaker washes and lighter hues are applied first, with successive stronger layers laid after each one has dried; test the strength of your washes on scrap paper before applying. Each transparent layer will influence the colour of the wash laid beneath or on top of it.

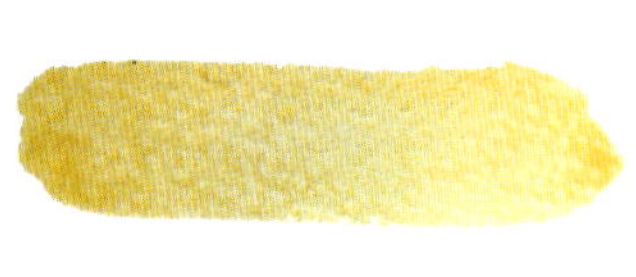

First layer
The initial wash (here, yellow ochre) is applied over a large area to unite the light tones. Where needed, leave the paper unpainted to reserve white.

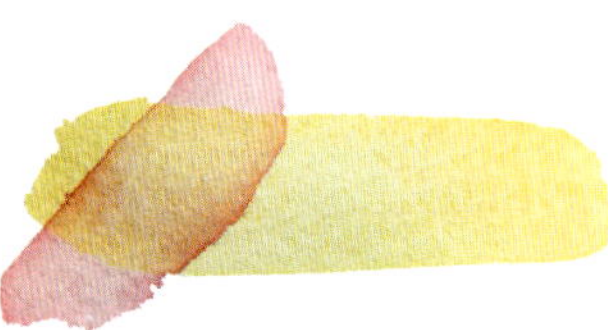

Second layer
Once the first layer is dry, apply a darker colour on top. Here, crimson looks warm over the yellow but appears as a cool pink over the reserved white paper.

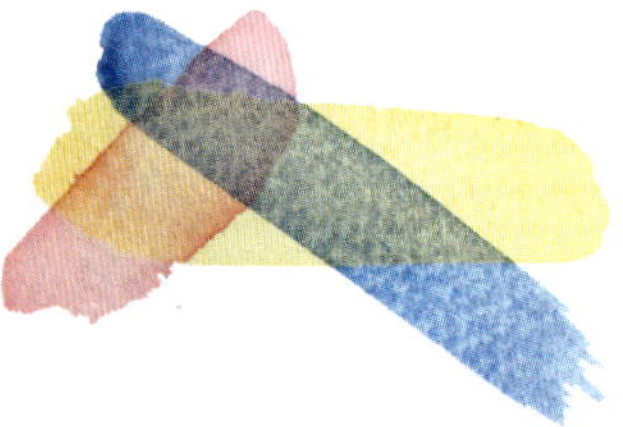

Third layer
Apply the darkest or strongest colour last, after the second layer has completely dried. The darker layer will modify the colours beneath, as cerulean blue does here.

PUTTING IT INTO PRACTICE

The first layer is important in quickly uniting all the light tones. There is no need to preserve edges as the painting will derive its forms from additional colours and tonal values that are overlaid.

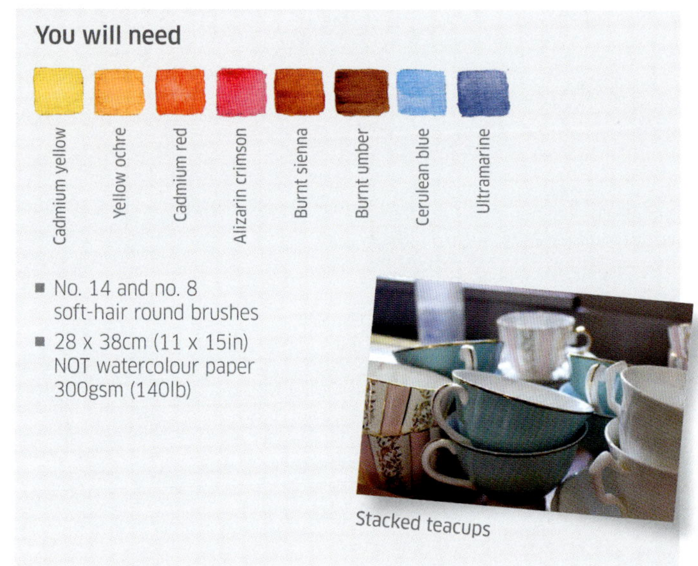

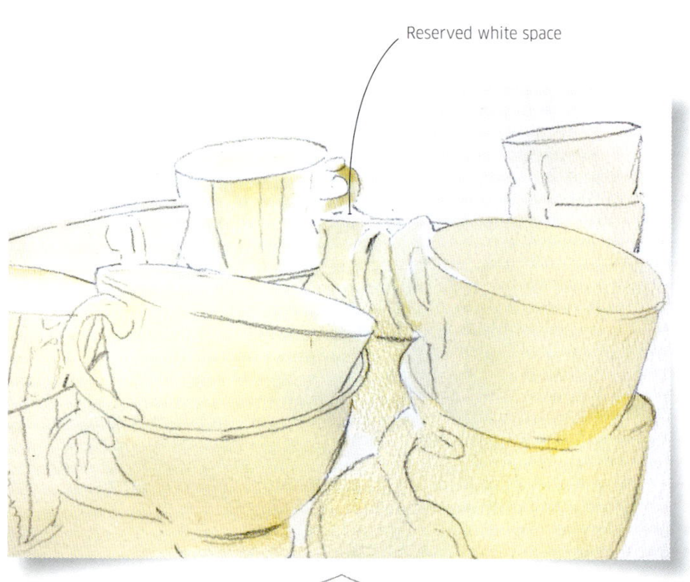

1 Apply a unifying wash
First make a pencil drawing of the cups, taking care to describe the shapes accurately. Once you are satisfied that they are correct, paint them with a wash of yellow ochre to unify them, reserving small white areas of unpainted paper as highlights.

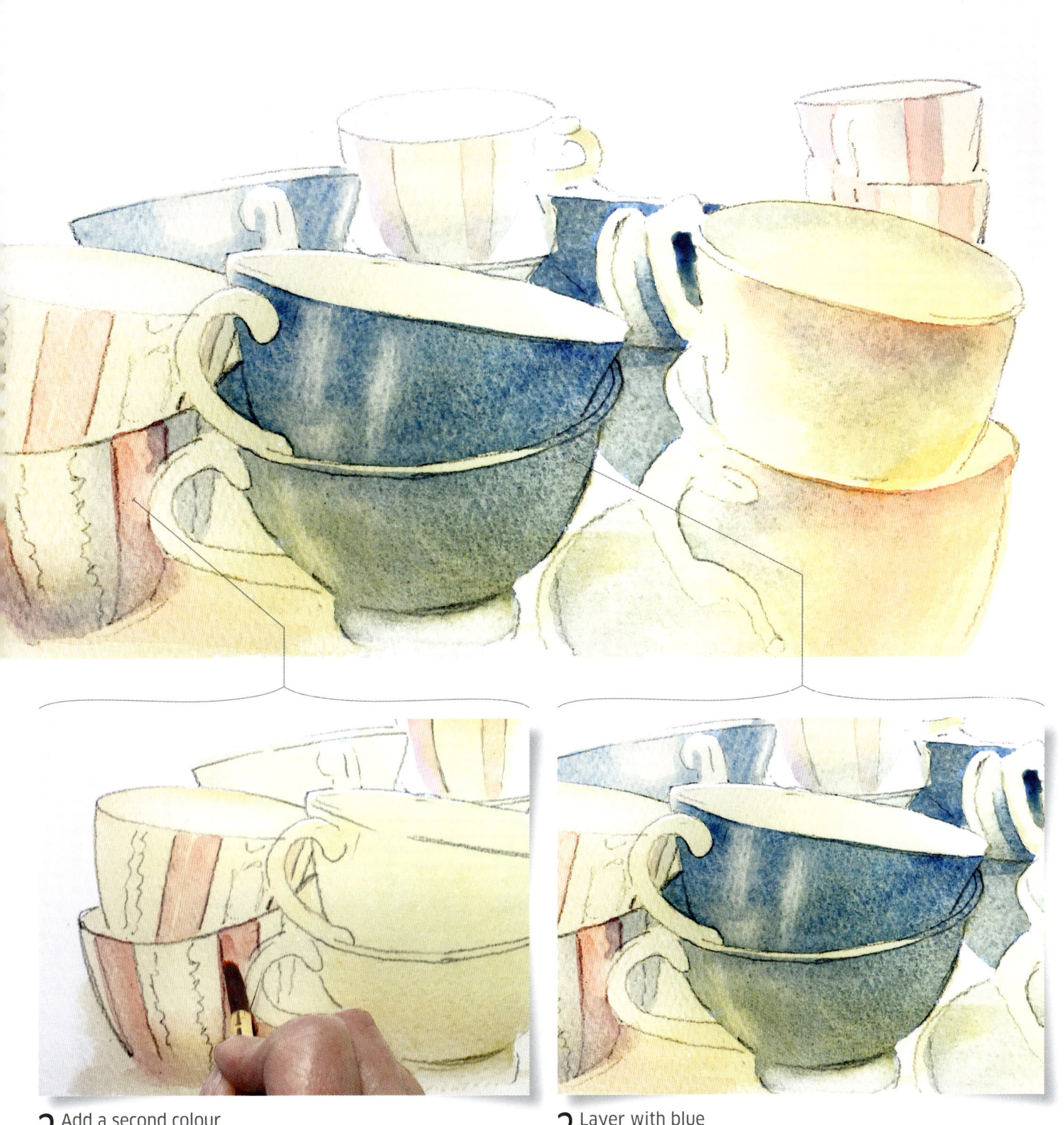

2 Add a second colour

Painting the lightest colours first, lay down a wash of alizarin crimson. This will give warmth to the shadow areas and appear cool pink on the reserved white paper. Paint the pink stripes on the cups, using stronger colour on those in the foreground.

3 Layer with blue

When the paper has dried, mix a wash of cerulean blue and layer it over the top of the yellow and pink mix, allowing the underlayer to show through here and there. This creates a turquoise colour over the yellow ochre and neutralizes the warmer crimson areas.

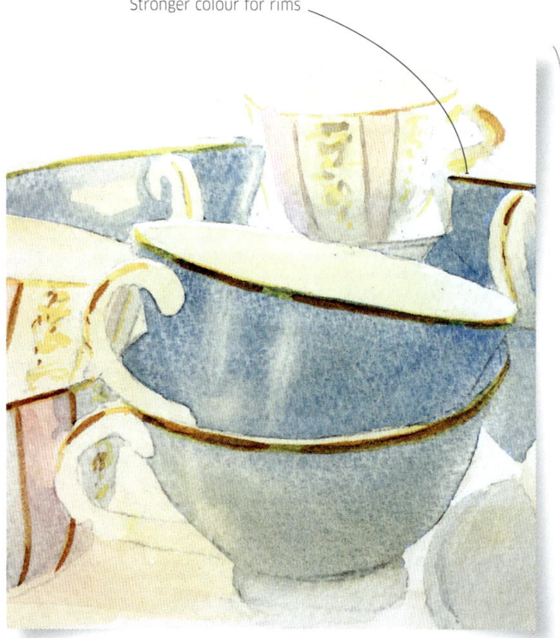

4 Use stronger colour for details

Once the paint is completely dry, erase the pencil drawing. Using stronger mixes to cover the washes, put in cadmium red, cadmium yellow, and burnt sienna for the gold rims and details.

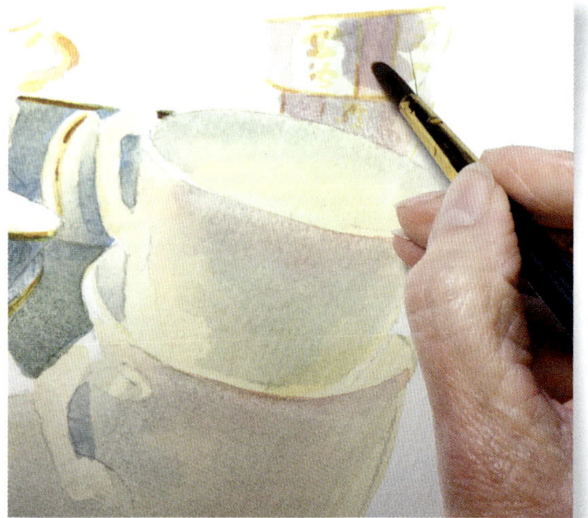

5 Add complementary colours

Layering a complementary hue keeps the colours lively. Mix a lilac from crimson and cerulean and use it in shadows to complement the ochre wash. Cover the turquoise mixes with cadmium red.

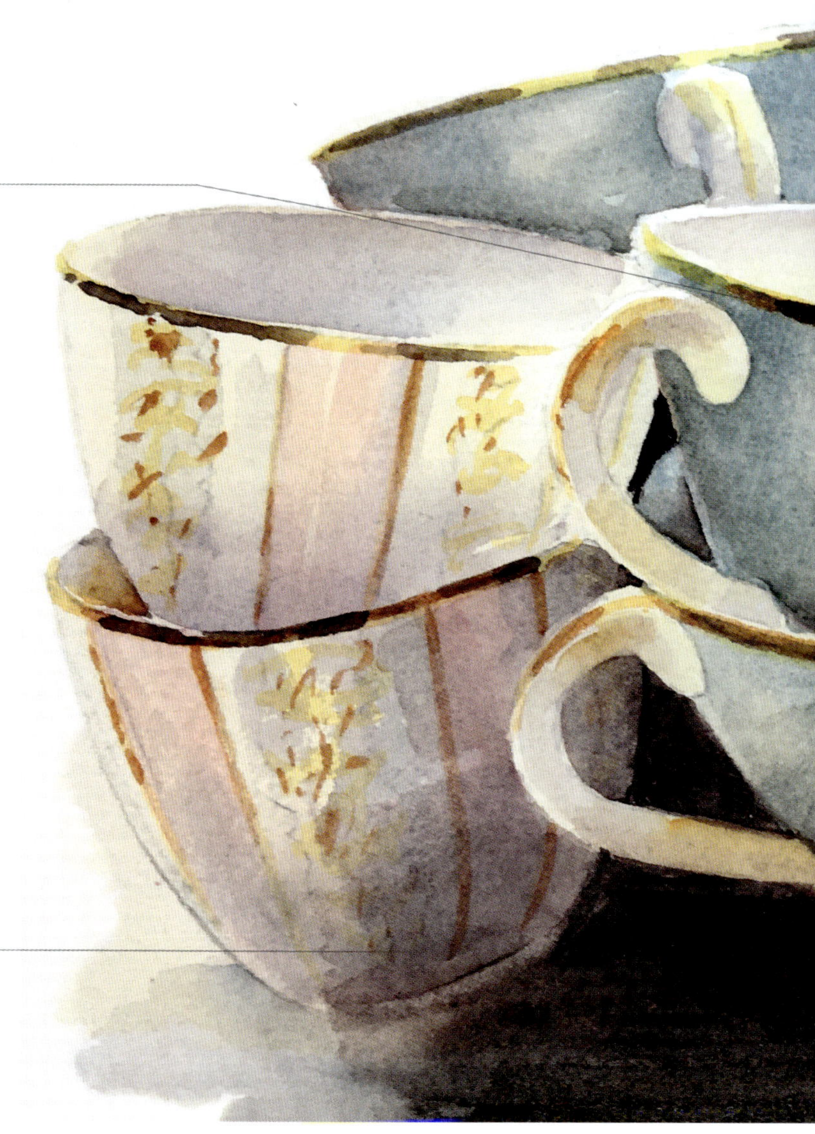

"Even in subtle layers, **complementary colours** give **extra liveliness** to a painting."

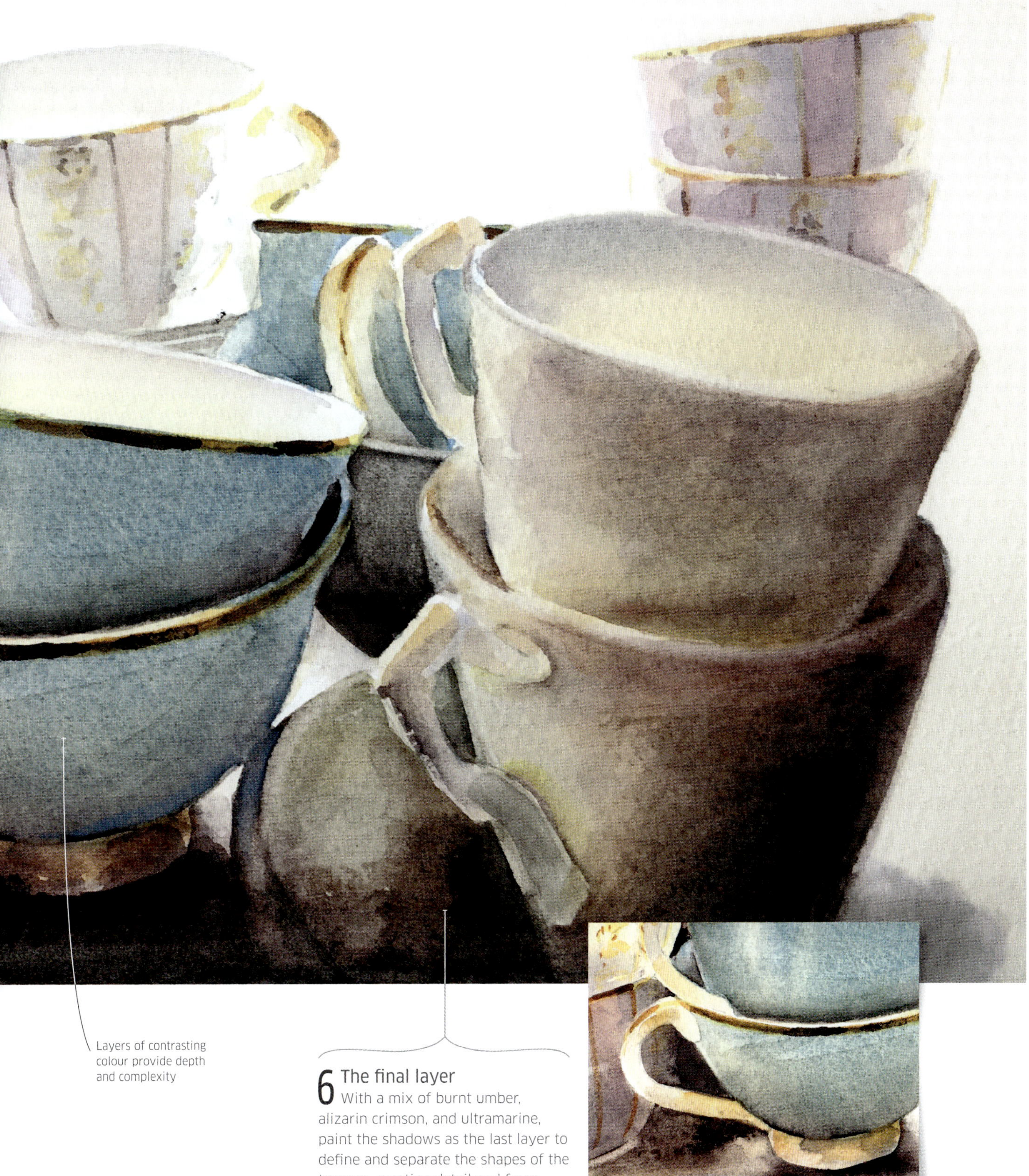

Layers of contrasting colour provide depth and complexity

6 The final layer
With a mix of burnt umber, alizarin crimson, and ultramarine, paint the shadows as the last layer to define and separate the shapes of the teacups, creating detail and focus.

Alla prima

COMPLETING A PAINTING IN ONE SESSION

Sometimes you will want to capture an impression of a scene in one session, known as *alla prima*. It is a great discipline, encouraging you to be organized, to find the essence of your subject through simplification, and to mix and use colours economically. Aim to capture just enough light and colour information about the subject quickly, using as few brushstrokes as possible.

PUTTING IT INTO PRACTICE

A strong first wash sets the tone to capture the warmth and light of this subject. A limited palette of dominant reds with cool blues creates simple contrasts, so that just a few shapes and tones are needed.

You will need

- Cadmium yellow deep
- Cadmium red
- Alizarin crimson
- Burnt umber
- Cobalt blue
- French ultramarine
- Viridian

- No. 14 and no. 8 soft-hair round brushes
- 15 x 25cm (6 x 10in) NOT watercolour paper 300gsm (140lb)

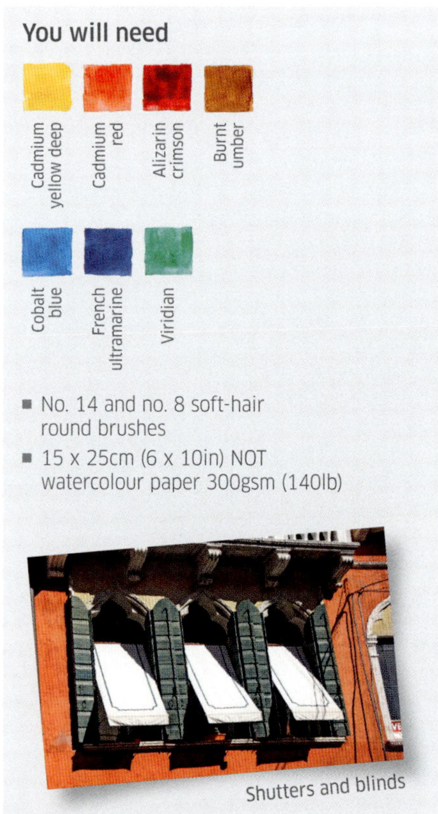
Shutters and blinds

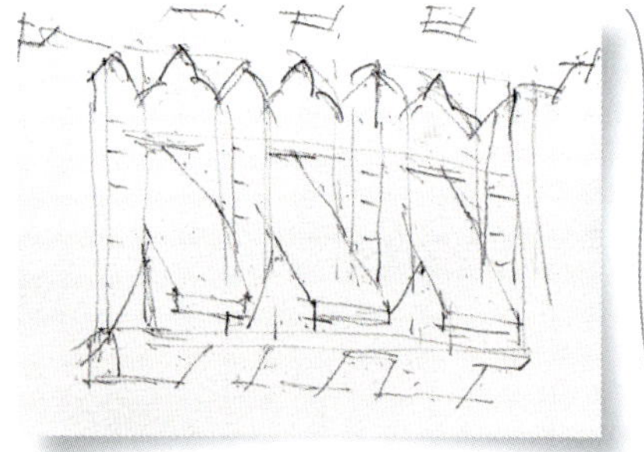

1 Base sketch
Simplify the composition in a quick sketch, noting the main areas of shadow and outlining the whites that you want to retain, here the white blinds. The defined shapes of the cast shadows create the darkest tones: sketch these in so that they can be filled with a dark wash later to give instant depth.

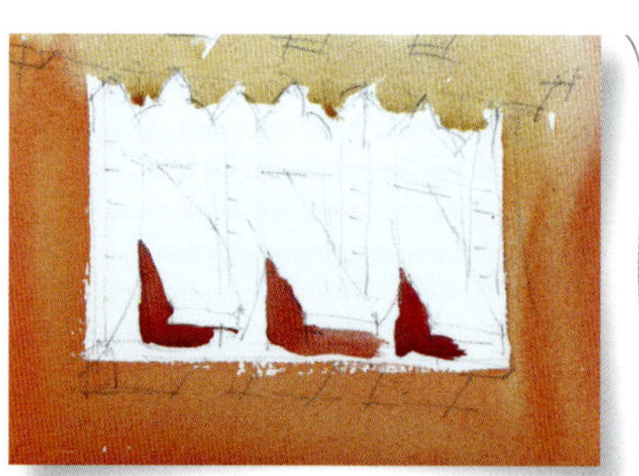

2 First flat wash
Start with a vibrant first wash, mixing alizarin and cadmium yellow deep to establish the tone for the painting. Apply as a strong, flat wash around the window shapes, using burnt umber as an underlay for areas of darker shadow.

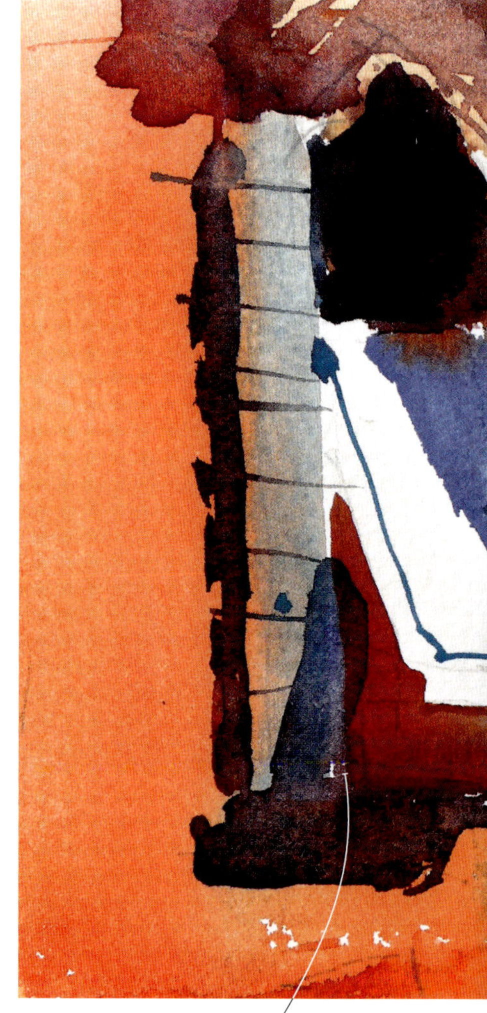
Complementary contrasts add an instant sense of depth

Planning ahead

Lightweight unstretched paper is ideal to use as it dries quickly. Plan your progress beforehand and follow a checklist (right) before putting paint to paper. You will need to wait for washes to dry so keep them to a minimum, breaking the timing down as follows: 5 minutes to apply the first wash, wait 10 minutes; 15 minutes for second and final washes; dry for 5 minutes then add fine details. Don't be tempted to overwork.

Checklist for working *alla prima*

- **Simplify the composition:** Speed up your observational skills and look for shapes rather than objects. Edit peripheral details.
- **Choose a limited palette:** Include a dominant colour for the majority of the composition, with mid and dark tones sharing values; subdue other colours.
- **Plan whites:** Retain the white of the paper for lights and highlights.
- **Limit darks:** Keep dark areas to a minimum, they will have more impact and you only need to strengthen existing washes.
- **Plan blends:** Consider which washes can merge wet-in-wet and which ones need to be kept separate.

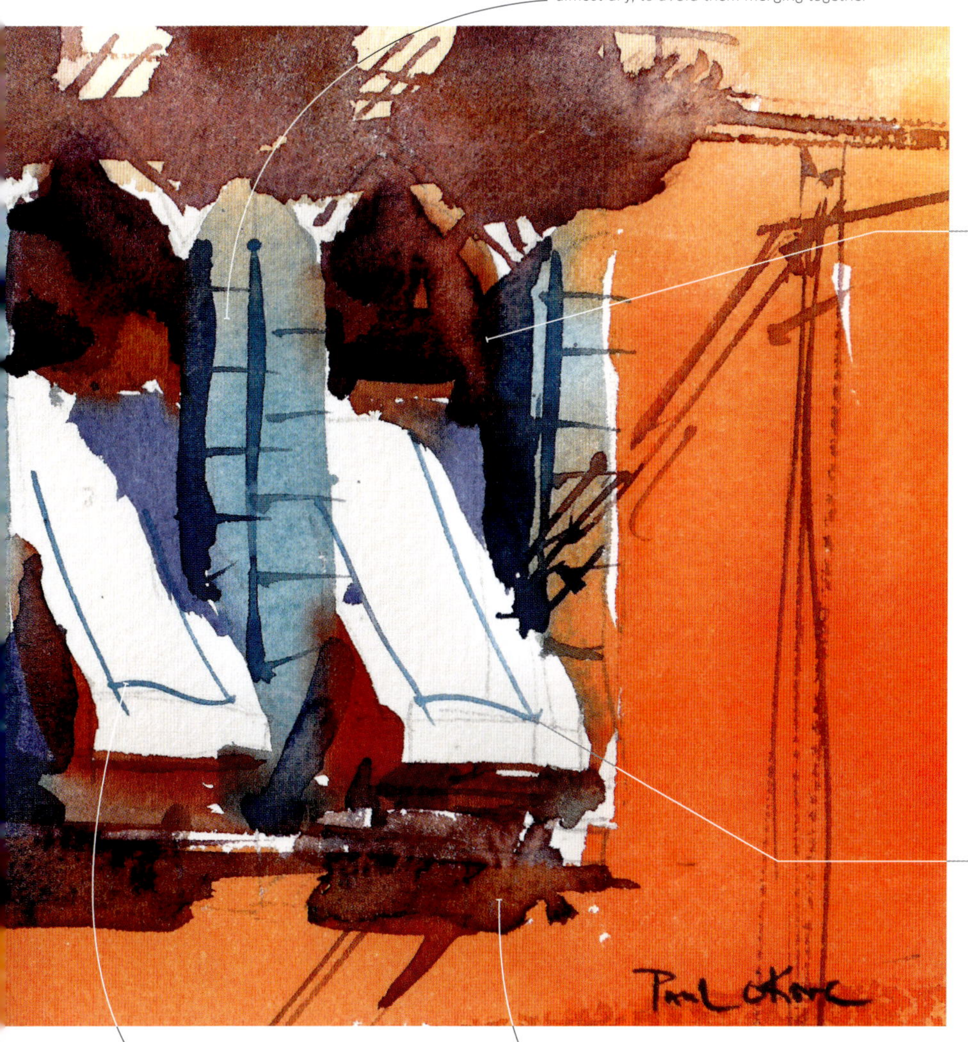

Wait to add the pale viridian wash for the shutters until the warm, second washes are almost dry, to avoid them merging together

Use rich colours for simple, calligraphic marks

Some wet-in-wet merging adds to the sketchy theme

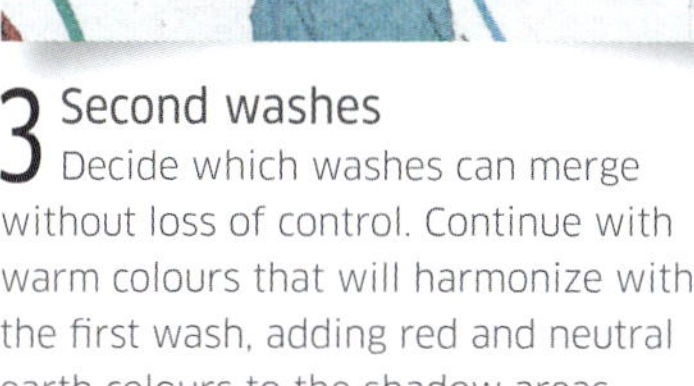

3 Second washes

Decide which washes can merge without loss of control. Continue with warm colours that will harmonize with the first wash, adding red and neutral earth colours to the shadow areas.

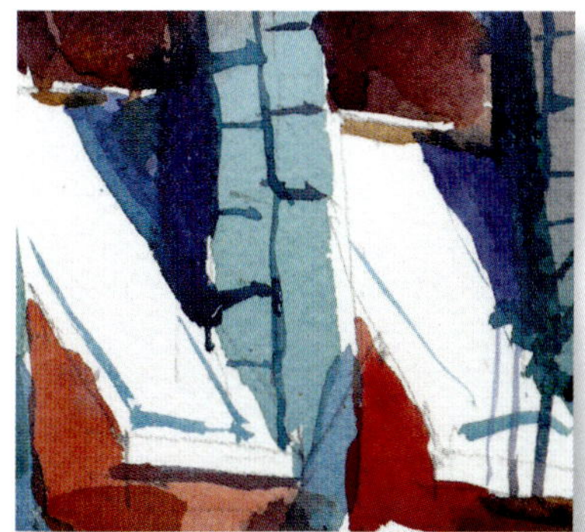

4 Calligraphic marks

When the second washes are dry, add minimal marks to convey details. Focus on the white blinds, using thin, calligraphic lines for the shutters, with just a few shadows on the perimeter.

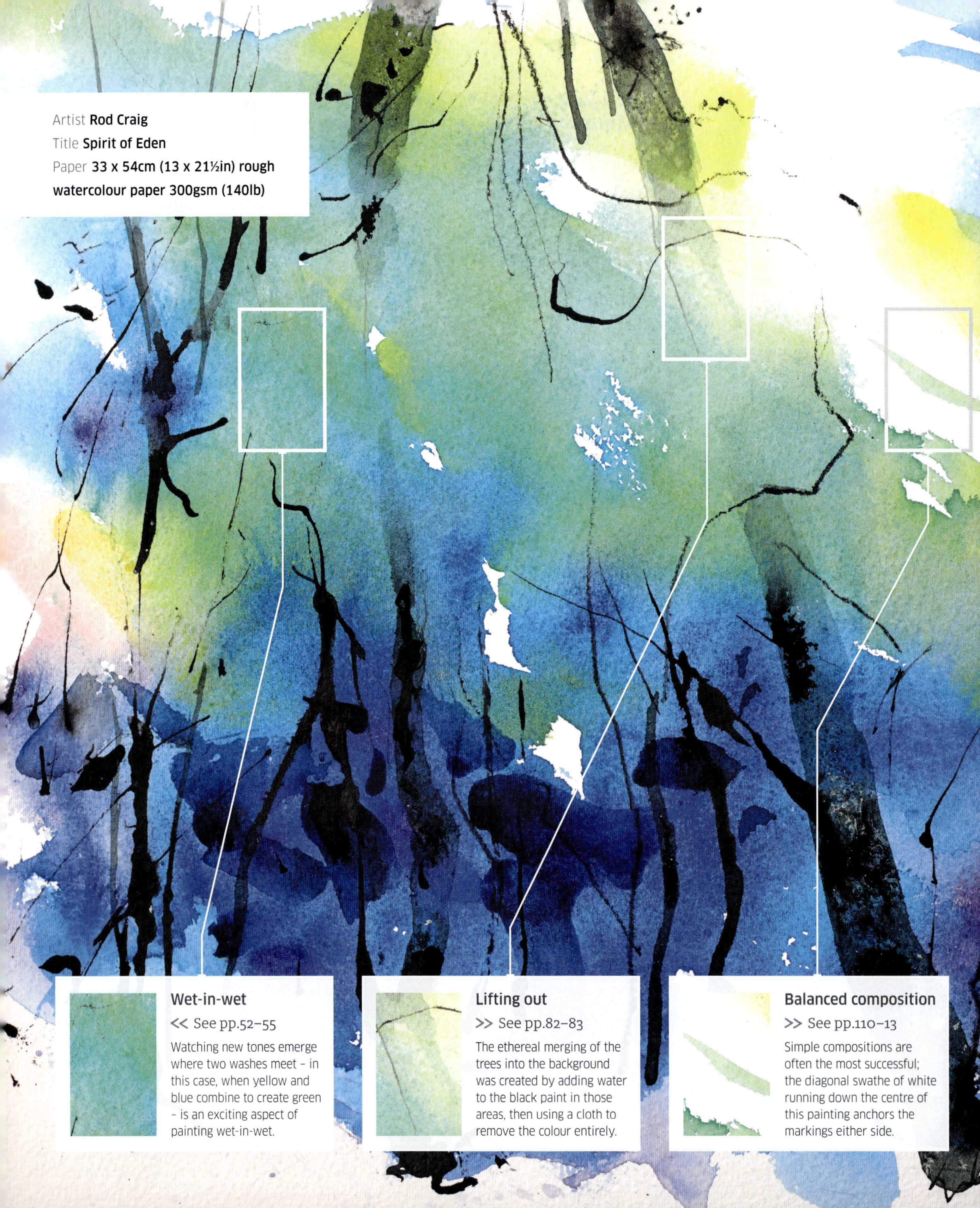

Wet-in-wet

<< See pp.52–55

Watching new tones emerge where two washes meet – in this case, when yellow and blue combine to create green – is an exciting aspect of painting wet-in-wet.

Lifting out

>> See pp.82–83

The ethereal merging of the trees into the background was created by adding water to the black paint in those areas, then using a cloth to remove the colour entirely.

Balanced composition

>> See pp.110–13

Simple compositions are often the most successful; the diagonal swathe of white running down the centre of this painting anchors the markings either side.

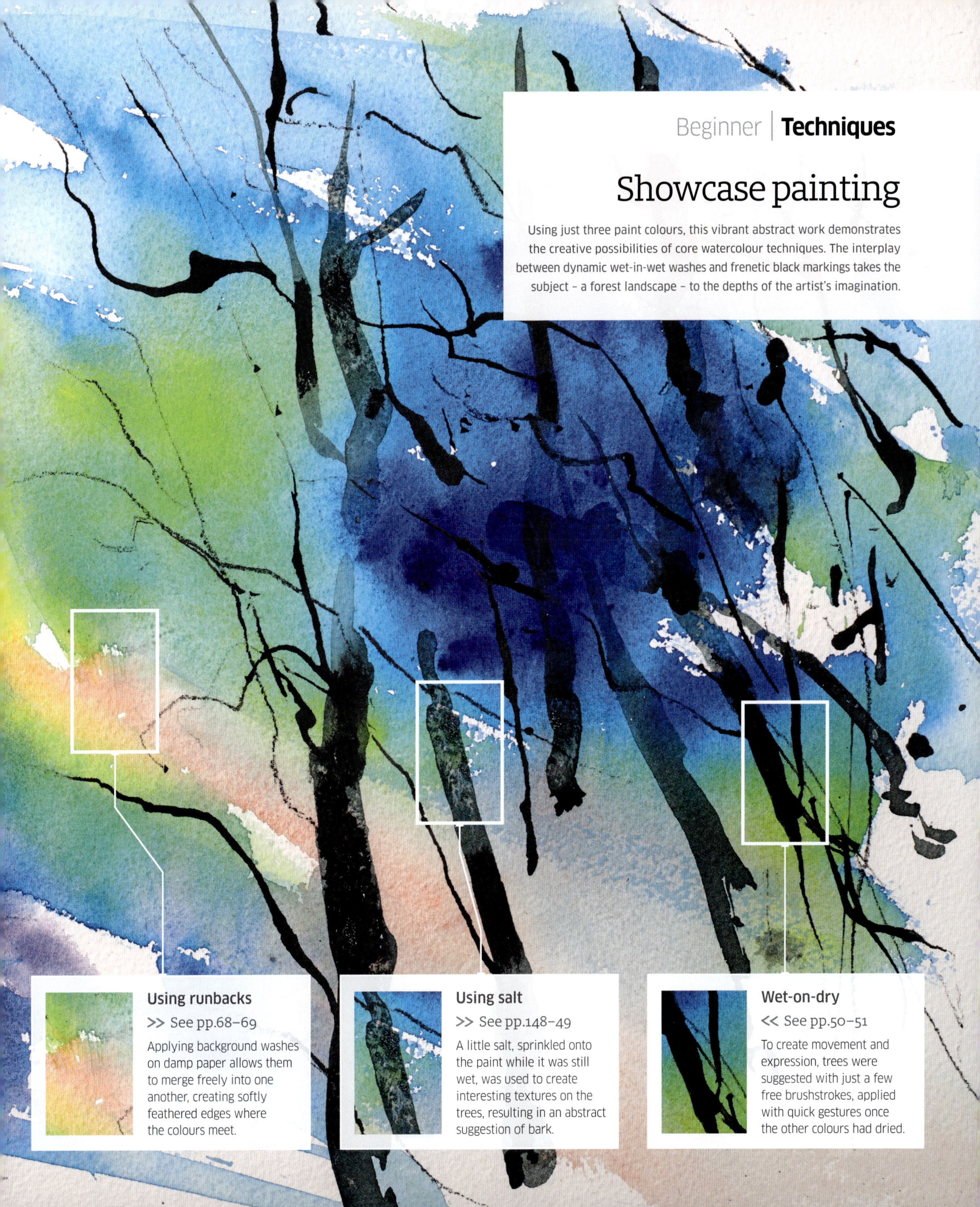

Showcase painting

Using just three paint colours, this vibrant abstract work demonstrates the creative possibilities of core watercolour techniques. The interplay between dynamic wet-in-wet washes and frenetic black markings takes the subject – a forest landscape – to the depths of the artist's imagination.

Using runbacks

>> See pp.68–69

Applying background washes on damp paper allows them to merge freely into one another, creating softly feathered edges where the colours meet.

Using salt

>> See pp.148–49

A little salt, sprinkled onto the paint while it was still wet, was used to create interesting textures on the trees, resulting in an abstract suggestion of bark.

Wet-on-dry

<< See pp.50–51

To create movement and expression, trees were suggested with just a few free brushstrokes, applied with quick gestures once the other colours had dried.

Tone

DESCRIBING FORM AND MOOD

Tone refers to the range of values from black to white – darks, mid tones, and highlights. All colours have a tonal range, but when you look at your work it's easy to become so engaged by the hues, or colours, that you forget about the tonal values. Half-closing your eyes will help you to judge the lights and darks in your composition.

■ Choosing the mood

A knowledge of how to use tone is essential in order to paint convincing subjects, since we understand three-dimensional forms on two-dimensional paper by the light and shade on them, and the shadows they cast. It is also a way to establish an overall mood to a painting, using strong tones for drama or more subtle, close tones to convey a sense of calm and intimacy.

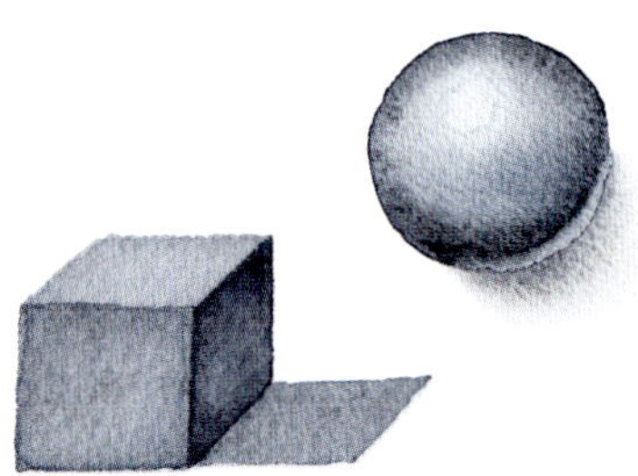

Dramatic tones

The stronger the light source, whether it is artificial or from the sun, the more dramatic the tones on surfaces appear. Dark cast shadows appear on the opposite side to the light source.

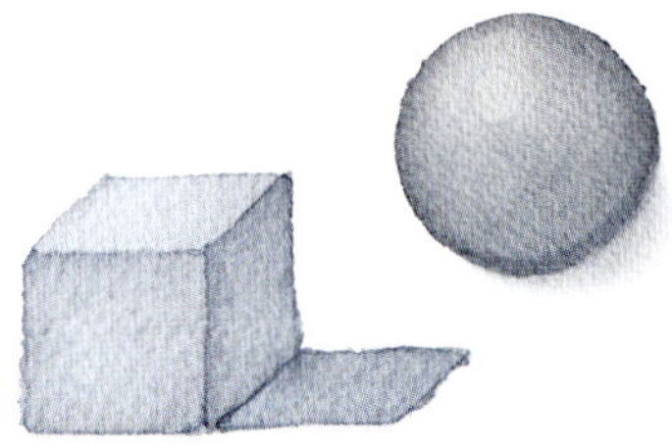

Close tones

When the light is more evenly distributed, such as on a cloudy day or from a shaded lamp, tones become softer and more diffuse. A calmer, more gentle mood is established.

PUTTING IT INTO PRACTICE

Here the use of tone describes the softly rounded shapes of the kitten's body. The colours have been mixed on the paper rather than in the palette, but you can choose whichever method you prefer.

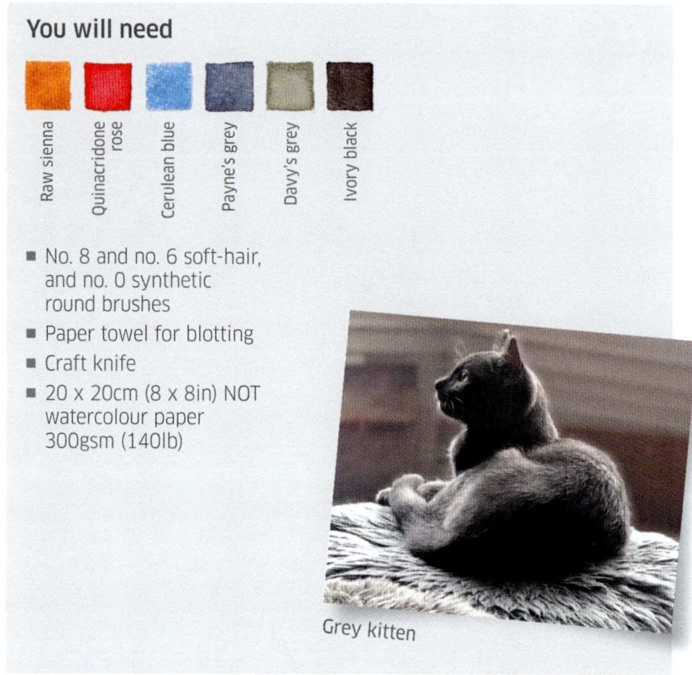

- No. 8 and no. 6 soft-hair, and no. 0 synthetic round brushes
- Paper towel for blotting
- Craft knife
- 20 x 20cm (8 x 8in) NOT watercolour paper 300gsm (140lb)

Grey kitten

1 Lay the first washes

Make a pencil drawing of the kitten, then, with the no. 8 brush, lay a wash of rose and Payne's grey on the darker areas. With clear water, bleed out the transition to the light areas (see pp.94–97). Apply a mid-tone wash of cerulean blue, Payne's grey, and rose to bridge the darks to lights on the kitten's back.

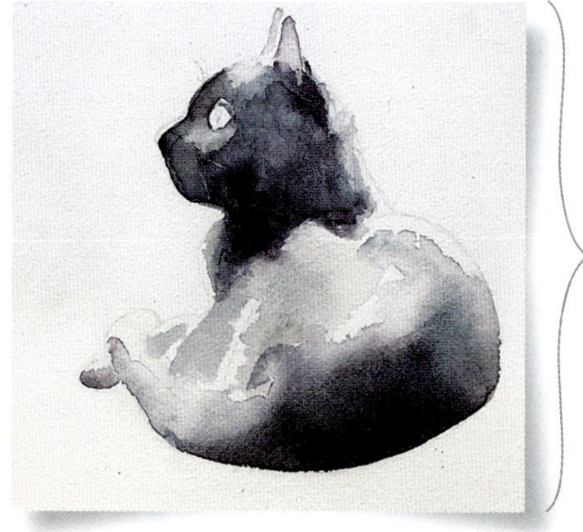

"Cast shadows anchor a subject to a surface."

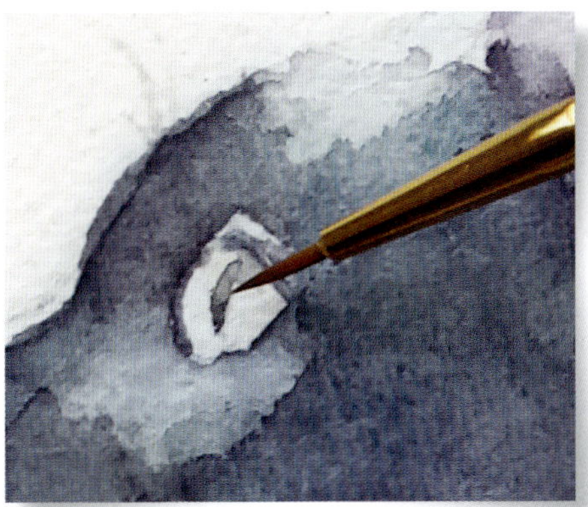 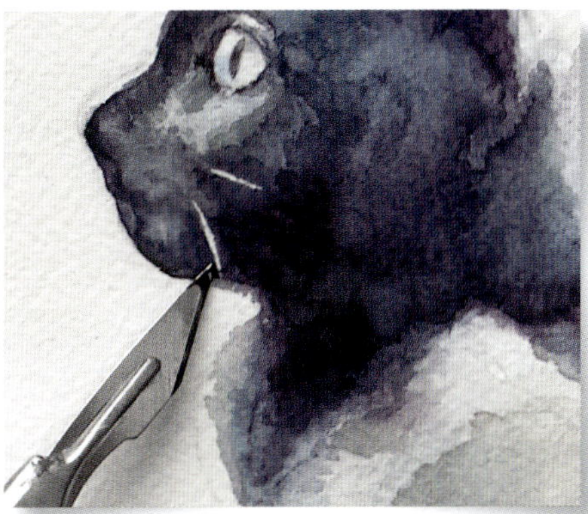 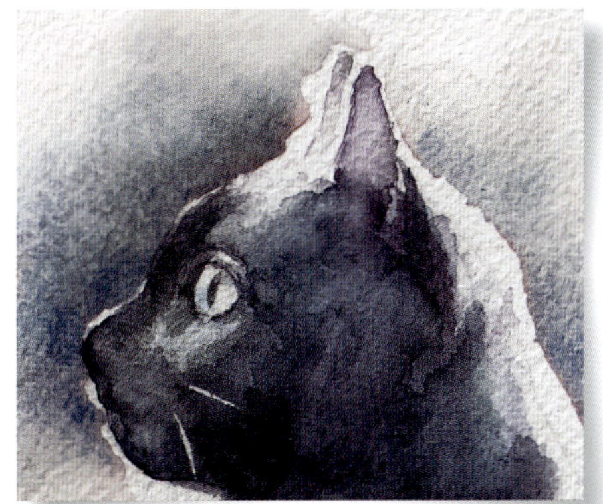

2 Paint in the eye
With the no. 0 brush and black, paint the pupil of the eye. Once it is dry, use very dilute raw sienna for the iris and drop in a little cerulean to create a slight shadow.

3 Add facial details
Use mixes of Payne's grey, black, and rose to refine the dark tones on the face with the no. 6 brush. With a craft knife, gently scratch out the eye highlight and the whiskers.

4 Paint the background
With washes of Davy's grey, rose, and cerulean, work all around the outline of the kitten, leaving the white highlight. Bleed out the edges of the background with clean water.

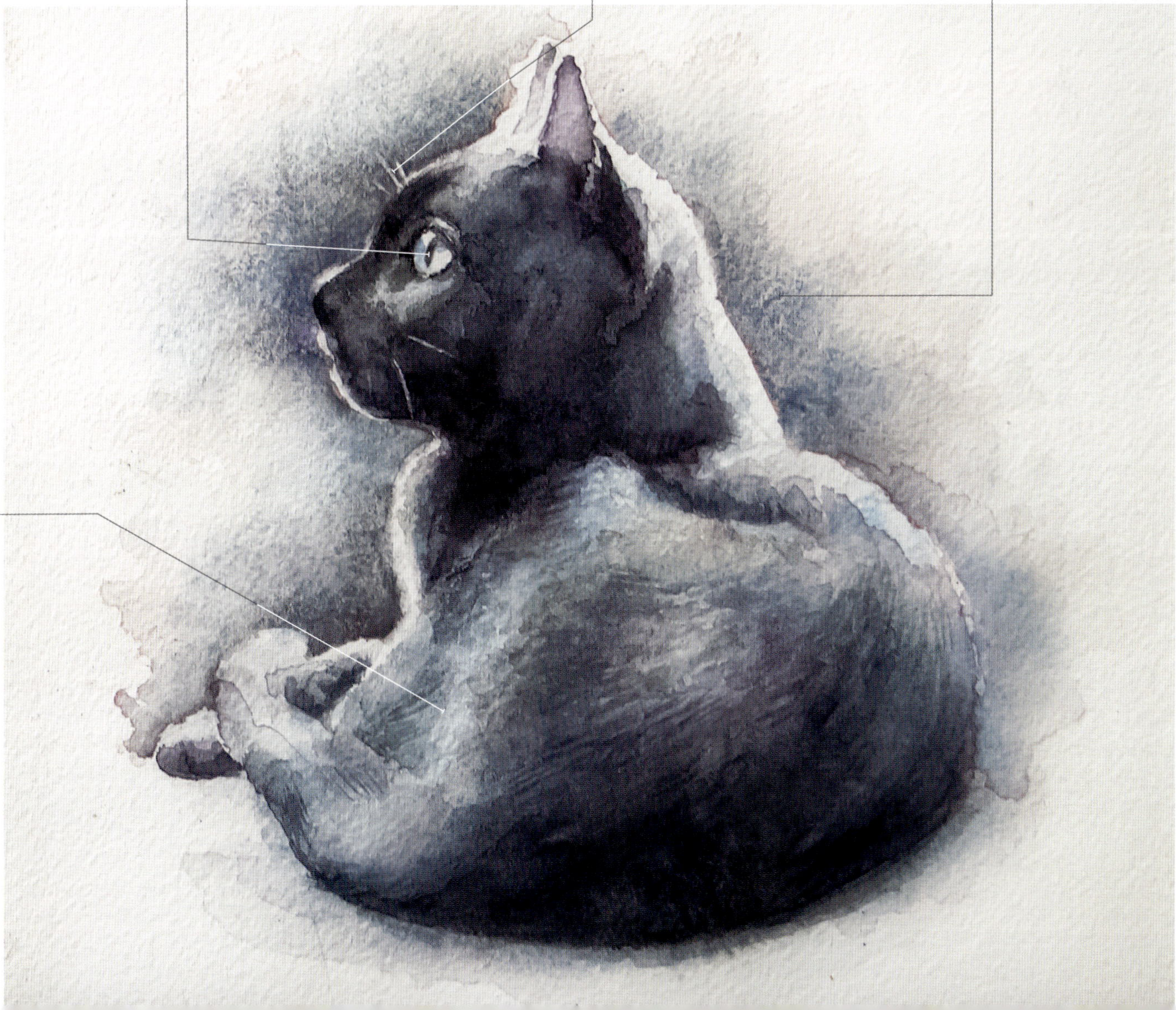

Using runbacks

INCORPORATING ACCIDENTAL EFFECTS

Runs and drips on wet paper create textured edges as they dry, known as runbacks. As a beginner, you may have produced runbacks by accident, but with a little understanding of how they occur, you can use them to your advantage with stunning results.

PUTTING IT INTO PRACTICE

Drips and runbacks are used in this painting to represent the effect of foam breaking on the crest of a wave without painting every droplet of water. The effect is achieved by controlling the dampness of the paper surface.

You will need

- Lemon yellow
- Dioxazine violet
- Ultramarine blue
- Phthalo blue
- Cerulean blue

- No. 20 and no. 10 soft-hair round brushes
- 25mm (1in) flat brush
- Fine mist spray
- 29 x 42cm (11½ x 16½in) rough watercolour paper 300gsm (140lb)

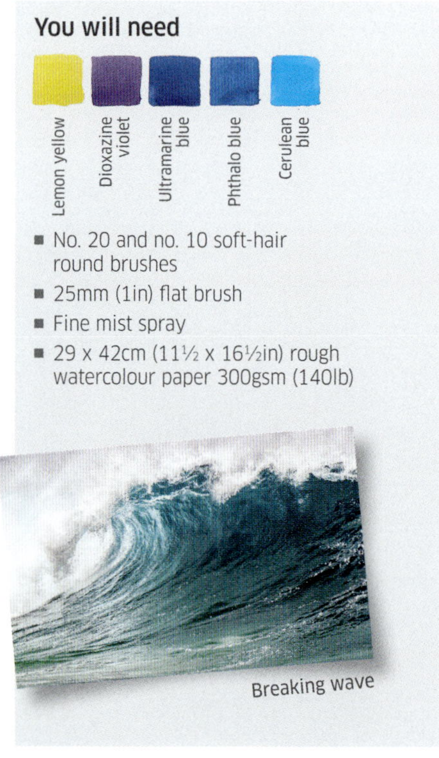
Breaking wave

1 Define edge of wave
Using a no. 20 round brush, apply a clear, solid wash with broad brushstrokes from the top. Break up this wash where you want to represent the curve of the wave head, and leave dry any highlights that you want to appear white on the finished painting.

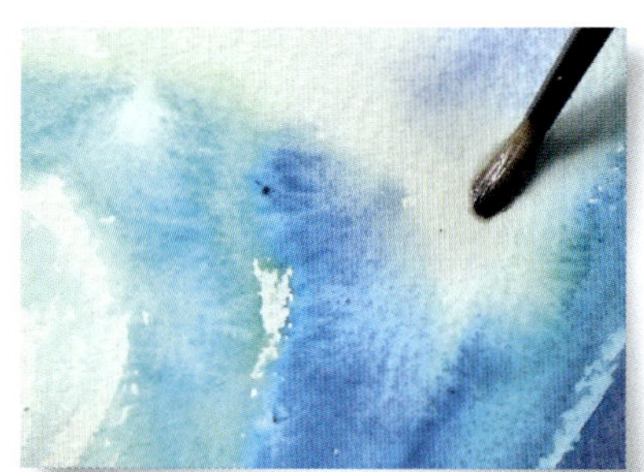

2 Add water to crest
Apply colour to the body of the wave in bold strokes. As soon as the sky area dries to damp and has lost its sheen, apply small amounts of clear water to areas on the crest of the wave where they meet the damp pigment.

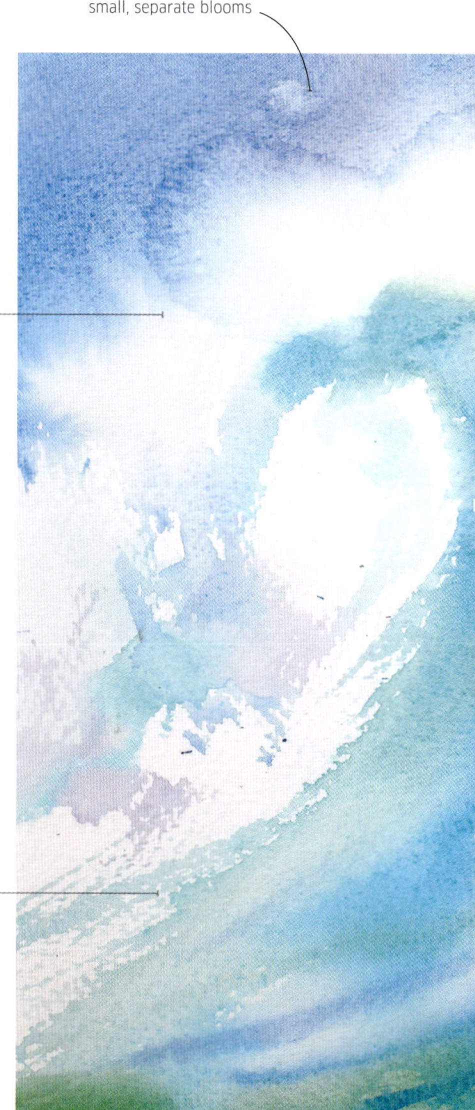
A drop of water creates small, separate blooms

Assisting runbacks

Runbacks need a damp surface. To encourage their formation you must ensure that the paper surface maintains the same level of wetness throughout the painting. As the painting dries to damp, continue to add water to the same wetness, using a brush or fine mist spray to apply the water. Judge when to add your wet wash to the damp paper so that it spreads to leave a bloom or feathery edge as it dries.

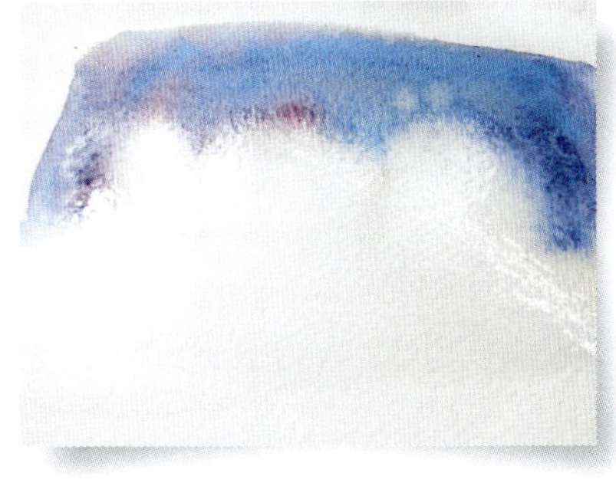

Judging surface water
The shine on wet paper indicates it is damper than the pigment area, so the water will mix with the drier paint edges. Check this surface reflection constantly.

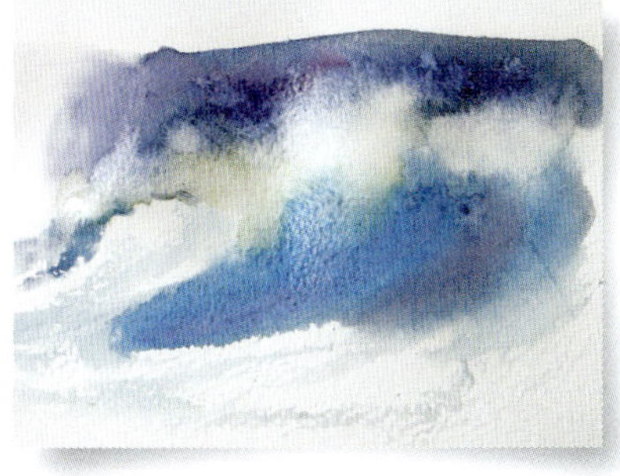

Timing paint application
Let an area dry to damp before adding water next to it; done too soon, you will simply have a smooth wet-in-wet blend. Allow the runback time to develop.

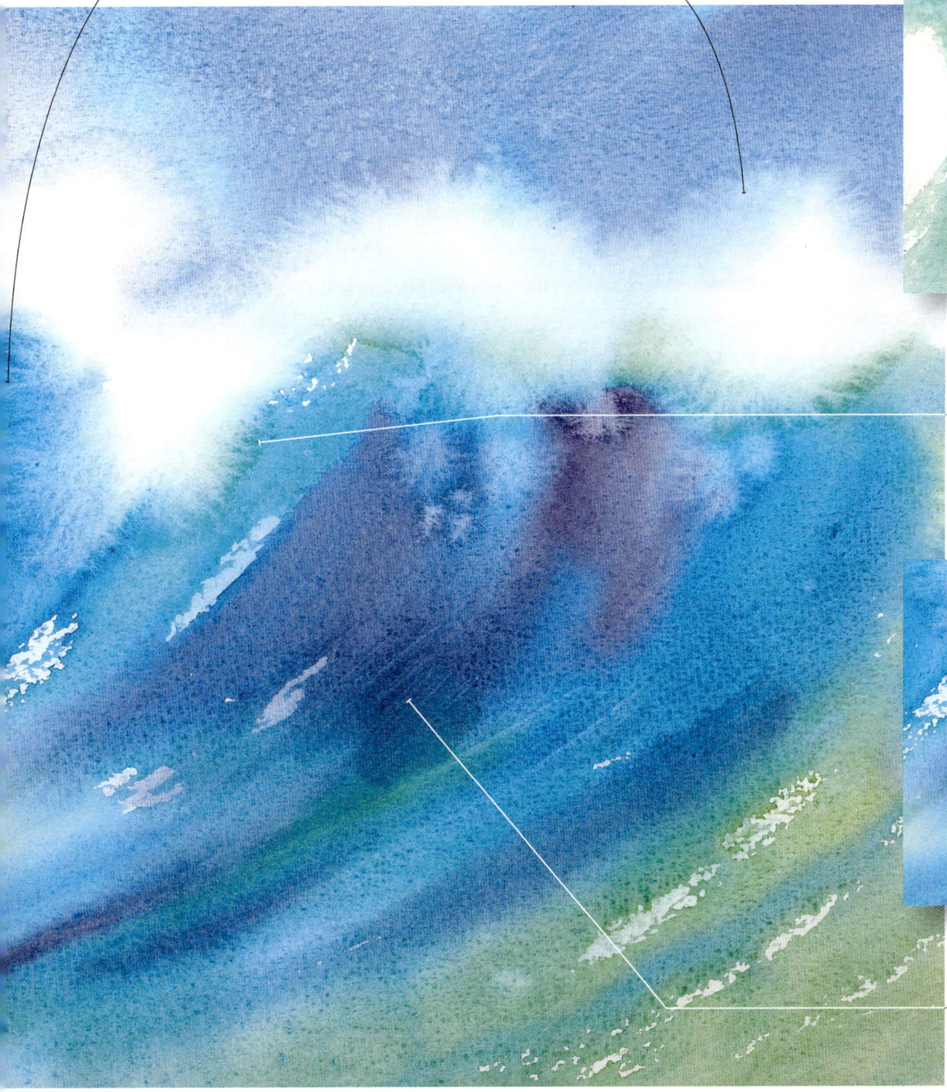

Space the runbacks so that they don't merge together

Soft edges appear where the water spreads into the drier sky

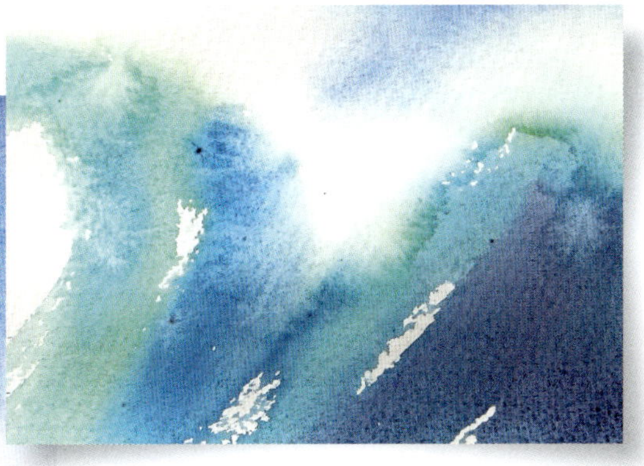

3 Tilt the paper
To encourage the runbacks, tilt the paper in the direction of the flow of the wave. Soft edges will emerge where the run meets with a slightly drier area. Harder edges form where the damp bleed meets the dry wash beneath.

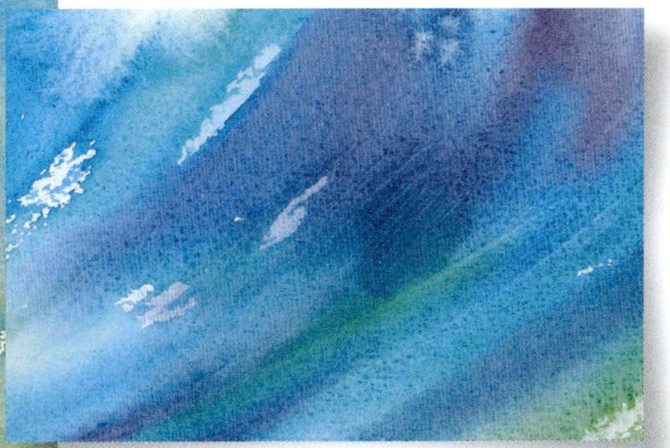

4 Final solid marks
Add a little more definition to the body of the wave. Re-wet it with an even mist of water and apply a few streaks with a small brush, keeping the detail understated in this area.

Flat wash

APPLYING SMOOTH COLOUR

A fundamental technique to master in watercolour is applying smooth layers of colour that dry to an even tone. Flat washes can represent large areas such as sky or water, and define architecture and features in a landscape. A smooth, flat layer is also a good base for adding details in darker mixes, or building layers to vary the tone.

■ Laying a flat wash

Use a soft-hair brush or a large synthetic-fibre brush that will hold the most paint. Before you start, make sure that you mix sufficient colours – there is nothing worse than running out of a particular mixture before the wash is complete. Try not to stop in the middle of laying a wash, as any variation in application could lead to patches or stripes showing as the wash dries. When the wash is complete, leave the paper to dry.

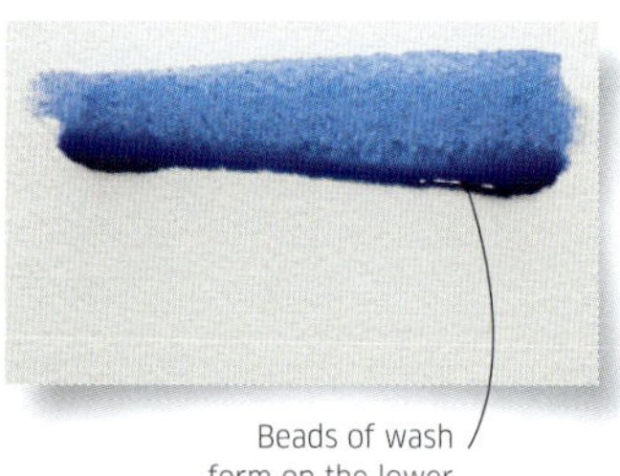

First stroke

Hold the paper at a shallow angle (around 30º), so that the paint retains a wet lower edge. Load the brush fully and start at the top, painting across the paper in one continuous stroke.

Beads of wash form on the lower edge of each stroke

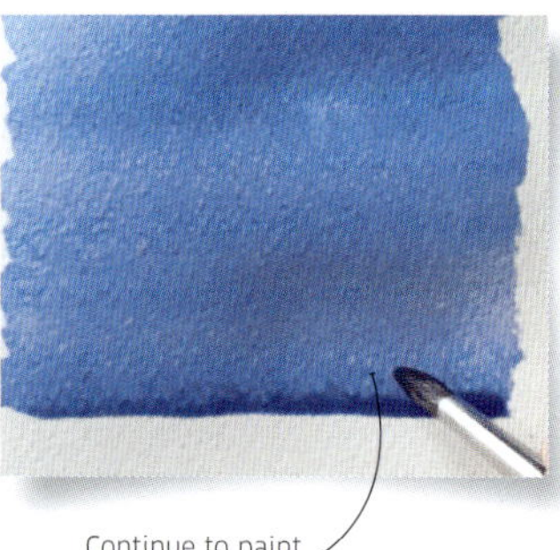

Blending brushstrokes

Re-load the brush, pick up the wet edge, and blend it smoothly into the next stroke. Continue, keeping the brush well loaded so that you can cover an area quickly and evenly. Absorb any excess at the bottom with a dry brush or paper towel.

Continue to paint across the paper in the same direction

PUTTING IT INTO PRACTICE

In this view of Istanbul, flat washes were applied to give solidity to the building, contrasting with the lighter sky. Visual interest is created by varying the tone of the flat washes from light to dark.

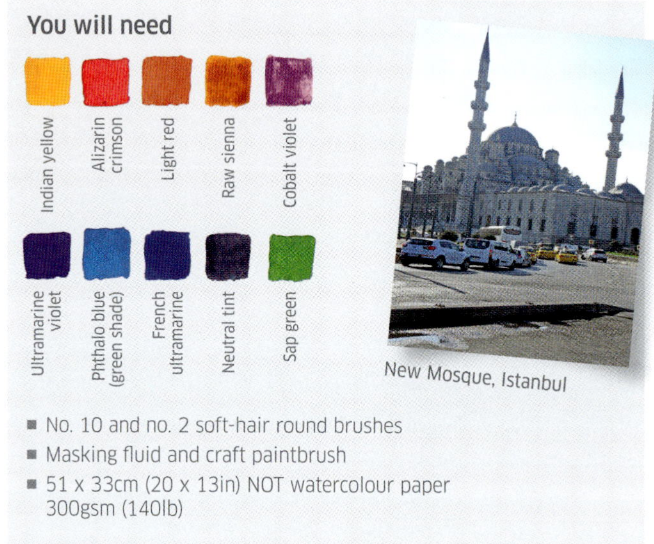

- No. 10 and no. 2 soft-hair round brushes
- Masking fluid and craft paintbrush
- 51 x 33cm (20 x 13in) NOT watercolour paper 300gsm (140lb)

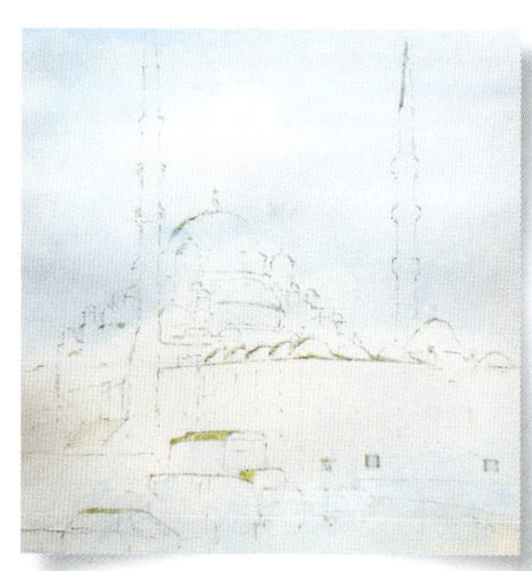

1 First layer

Lightly sketch the outlines of the main composition and mask any areas that are to remain unpainted with masking fluid, and leave to dry. Apply a sky wash in loose patches from top to bottom, and on the road, leaving white for the clouds, buildings, and vehicles.

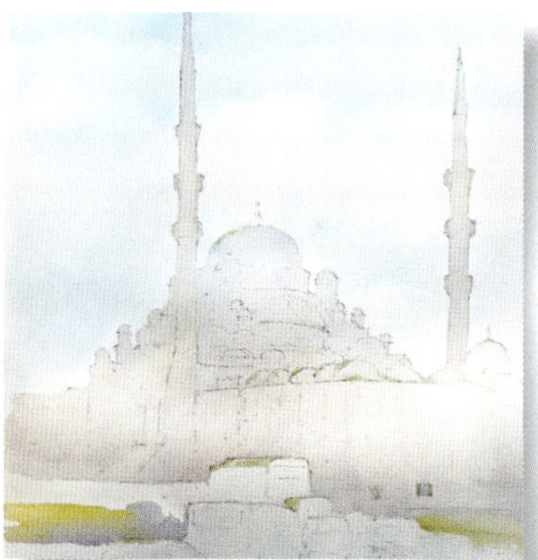

2 Add mid-ground colour

When the sky wash is dry, lay a flat wash of solid colour to the building. Start at the top of the minarets and lay the wash within the outline in one smooth area. Apply the first layers of wash for the vehicles and road.

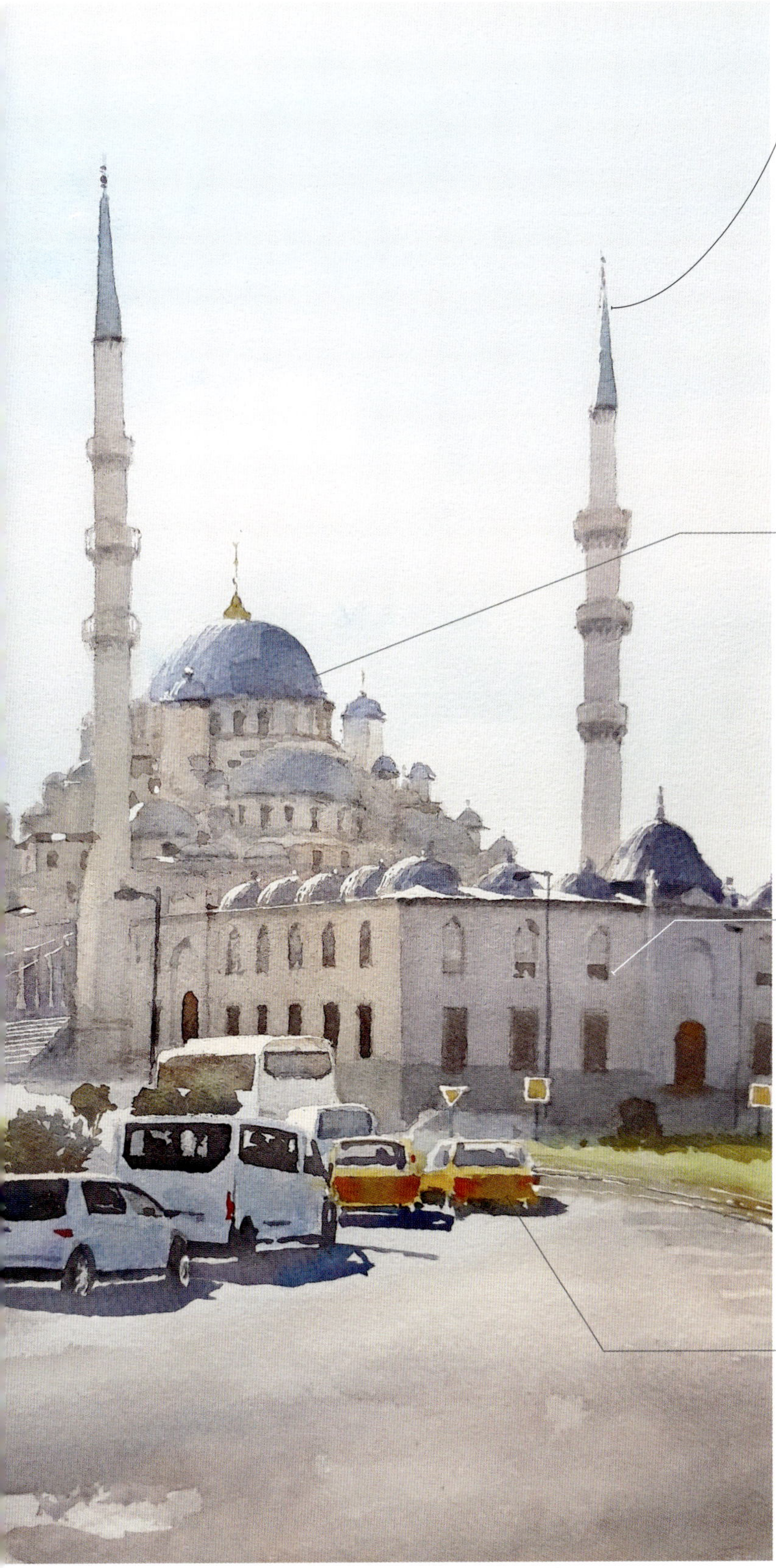

"Watercolour **lightens as it dries**, so apply a **darker wash** than you think."

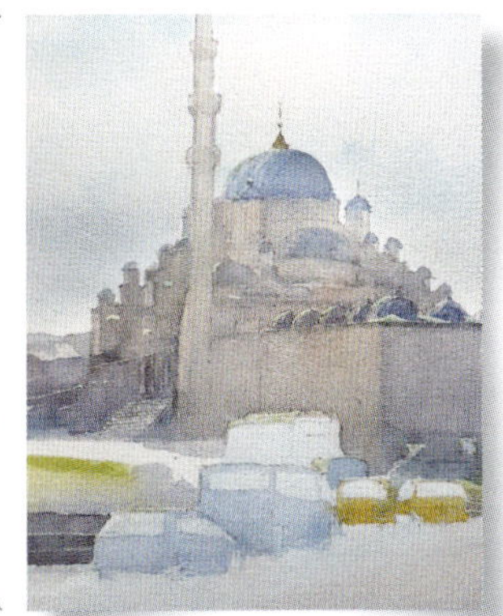

3 Define features

Lay a third wash over the building to define the larger features and separate each façade. Use darker values to accentuate the domes and roofline. The contrast of colour with the bright taxis adds foreground interest.

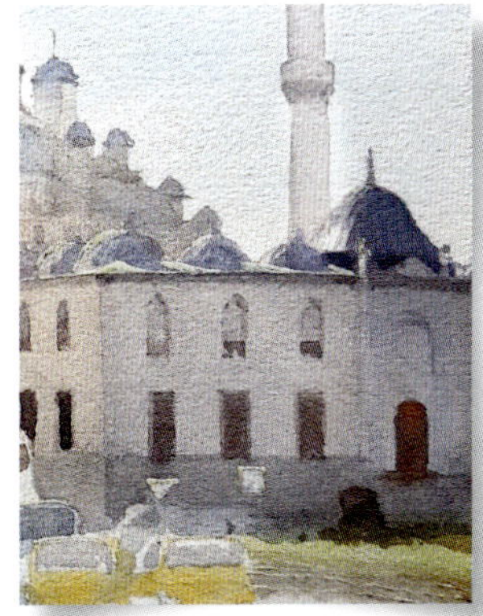

4 Dark details

Working over the flat wash, use a darker neutral mix to add details to the buildings. The windows and doors create a sense of scale with the darker details of bushes and cars, drawing the eye into the composition.

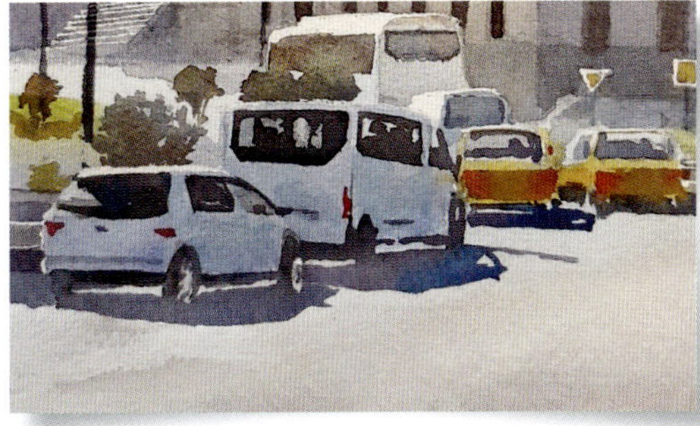

5 Refine foreground features

In the final stage, add the darkest shadows and features. The strong shadows of the vehicles have several colours of the same tonal value (see pp.66–67) to suggest reflected light and avoid them looking flat.

Graduated wash

DILUTING COLOURS IN WASHES

Watercolour pigment can be manipulated with just water and gravity to run freely over the paper, creating beautiful effects that are unique to the medium. A graduated wash fades as the pigment becomes progressively diluted, making this an especially effective technique for painting skies and indicating distance.

Two ways to lay a graduated wash

The most common way to lay a graduated wash is to brush clean water into the paint as you work down the paper, but stripes or bleeding may occur if the paper dries unevenly. Wetting the paint on the paper with a spray bottle instead avoids this.

Using the brush

Working from top to bottom and painting from left to right (if you are right-handed), lay a stroke of paint with a wet brush on dry paper. With each successive stroke, dilute the same mix with one dip of the brush into clean water.

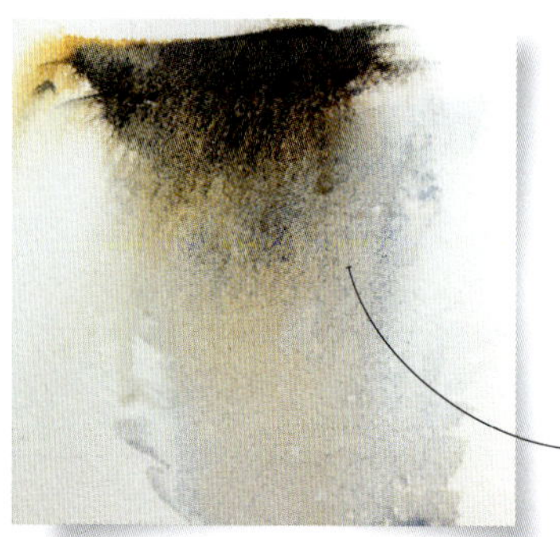

Spraying

Using a spray bottle to wet the paint instead gives a smooth and even result. Using two colours in the mix sometimes results in them separating into a lovely haze.

Separating paint

PUTTING IT INTO PRACTICE

A graduated wash is ideal for a day when mist reduces a complicated landscape to just a few tonal passages. Use a large brush and tilt the paper at an angle of about 45 degrees.

You will need

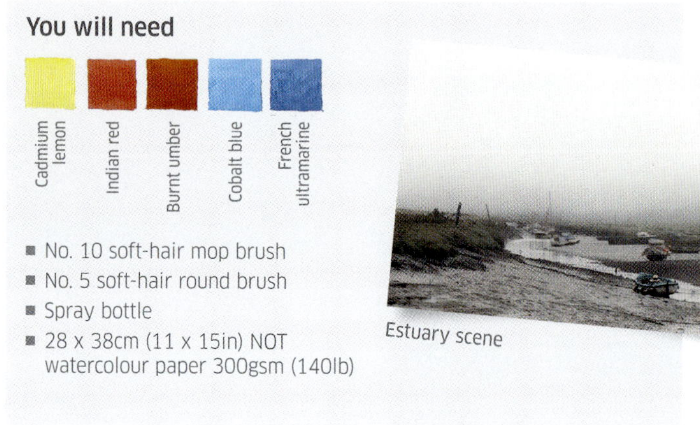

- No. 10 soft-hair mop brush
- No. 5 soft-hair round brush
- Spray bottle
- 28 x 38cm (11 x 15in) NOT watercolour paper 300gsm (140lb)

Estuary scene

1 First loose washes

With a mix of French ultramarine and burnt umber, start from the top of the page and work downwards, to create a graduated wash by dipping the mop brush in clean water before each horizontal stroke. Allow to dry.

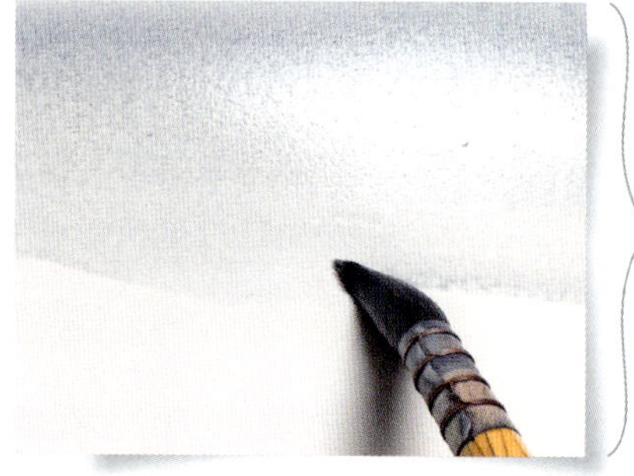

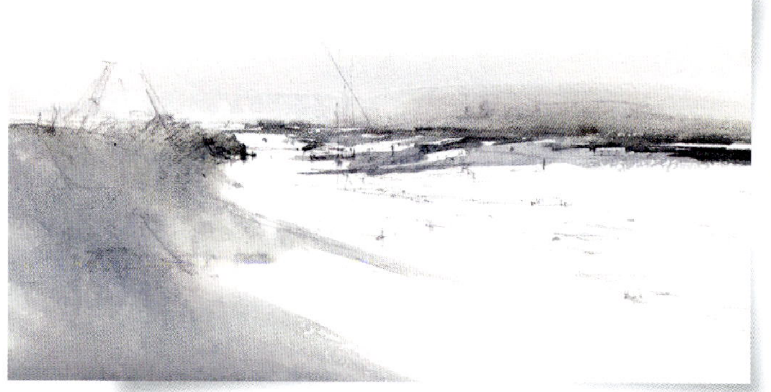

2 Add the boats and banks

Starting at the horizon, with the same mix but adding a touch of cadmium lemon, paint in the distant and foreground banks and highlight the boat shapes. Use less lemon as you work down towards the mud banks.

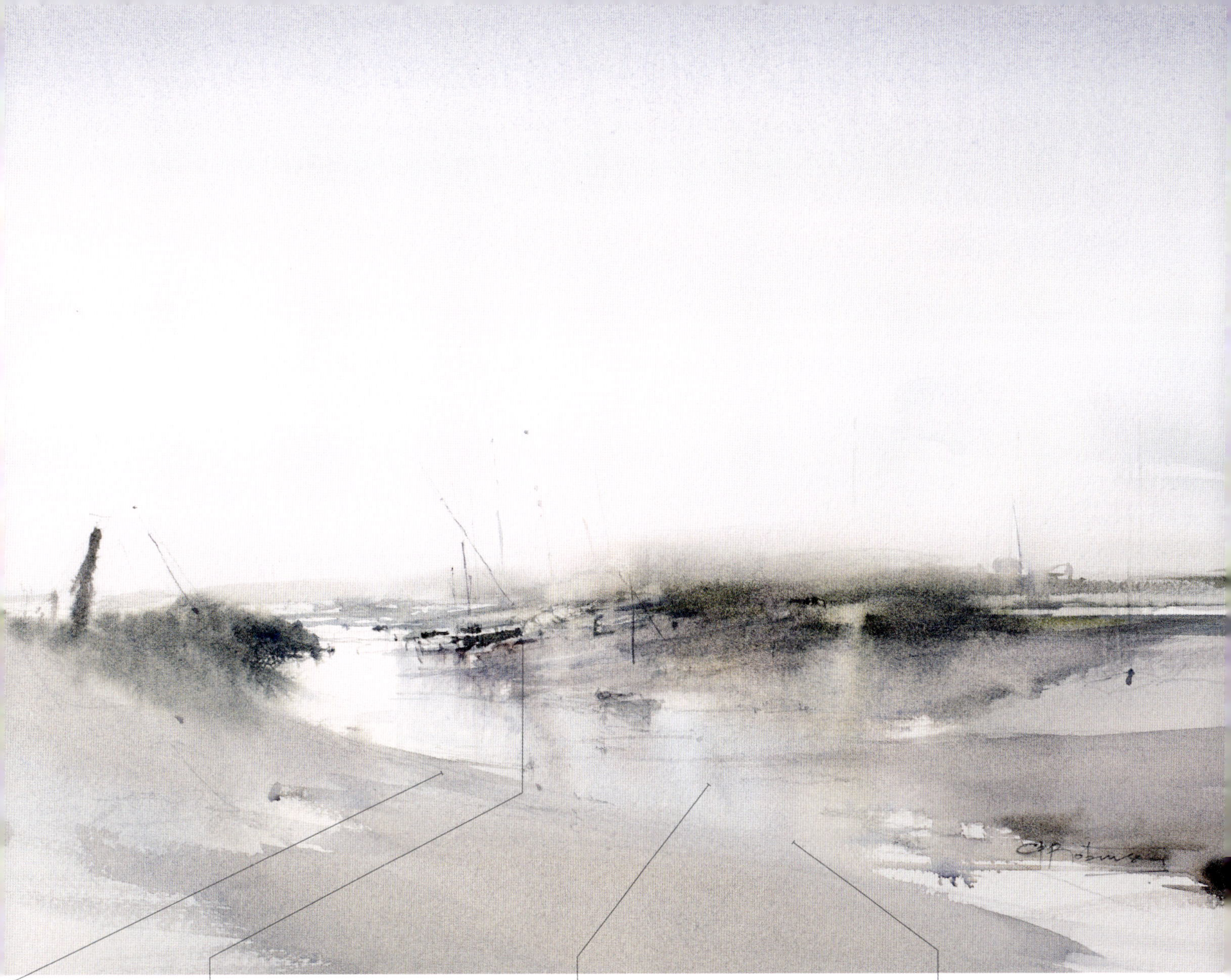

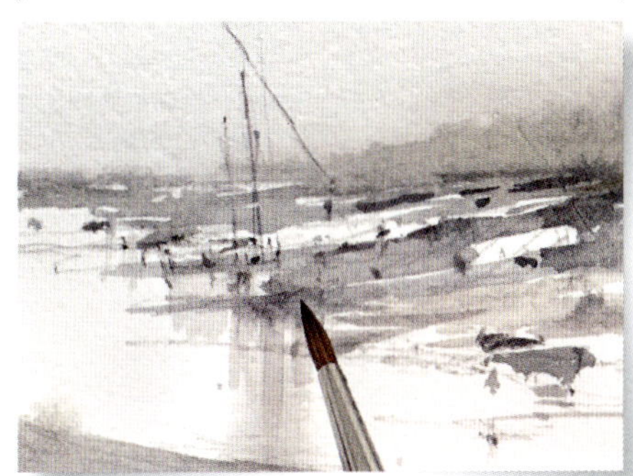

3 Describe details
Once dry, use the round brush and a stronger mix of French ultramarine and burnt umber to add details such as the boats, masts, and posts and the shadows on the banks.

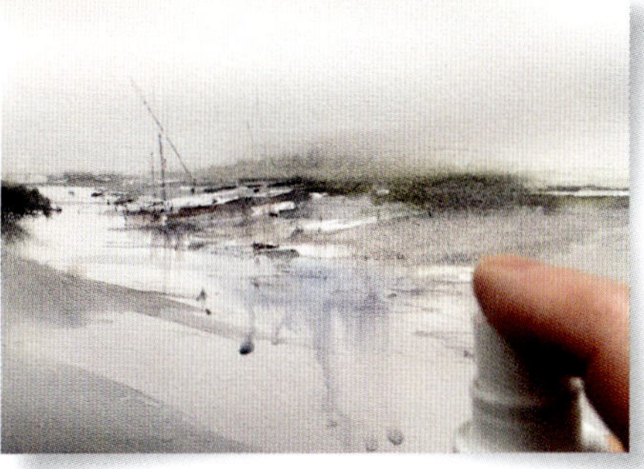

4 Graduated wash for wet mud
To create the feeling of wet mud, add a graduated wash of cobalt blue using the spray bottle and allow the mud to merge with the water. Guide the paint down with the mop.

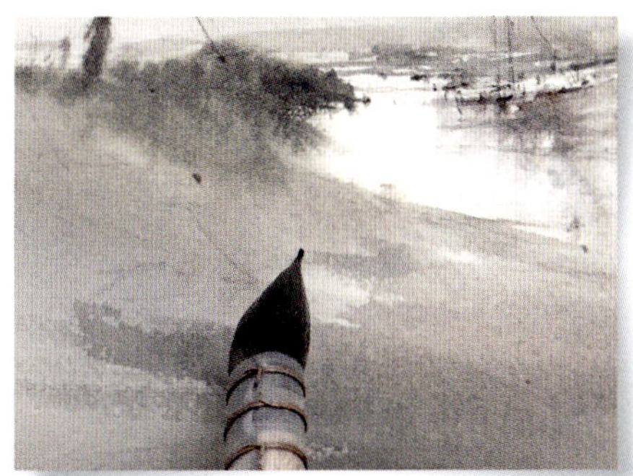

5 Strengthen the foreground
When the painting is dry, add a foreground wash using the mop with a mix of French ultramarine, burnt umber, and a touch of Indian red.

Variegated wash

MINGLING COLOURS IN A WASH

You can create fantastic backgrounds and stormy skies with initial washes that transition from one colour to another. It takes some practice and confidence to conquer, so enjoy some experimentation until you're happy with the results for backgrounds before moving on to other details. Wetting the paper in places can add to the way in which the colours spread and also avoid any obvious stripes.

■ Marbled and smooth effects

For a random marbled effect, background washes are applied to wet paper and then further paint is washed on, catching the moments when the paper is damp in some places and dry in others. Mixing while the paints are both wet allows softer blending which is key for natural-looking and picturesque effects.

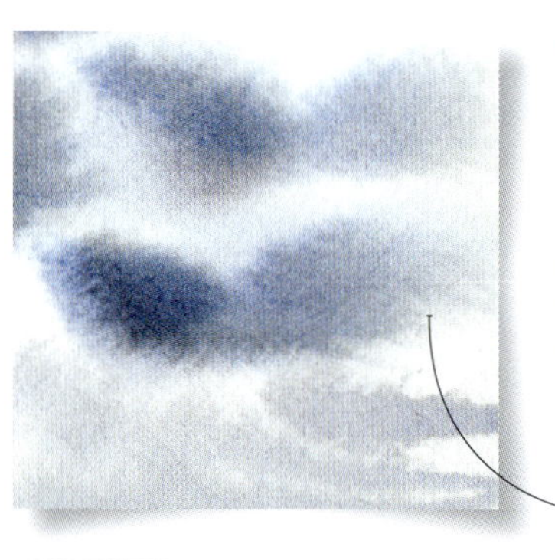

Random colour transitions

Applying small areas of wet paint to wet paper creates random transitions of colour. You can tilt the paper to influence the direction of paint flow. Using a stronger wash enables you to add intensity.

Visible colour edge

Smooth colour transitions

For a gradual transition of colour, tilt your board at an angle of at least 45 degrees. Lay your first wash from the top, with plenty of dilute paint on your brush. Apply a wash of another colour, allowing the diffuse edges to blend together.

Gradual colour variation

PUTTING IT INTO PRACTICE

There is no need for a pencil sketch here. After the background wash, build up the clouds with stronger mixes, using different brushes on damp and dry areas of the paper to create an impressionistic effect.

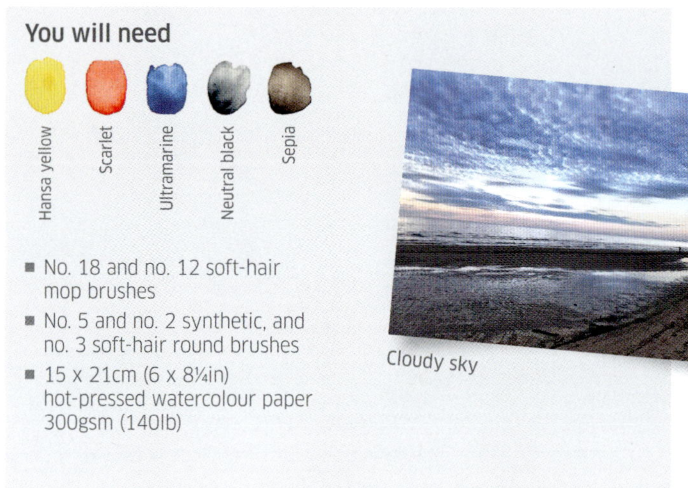

You will need
- No. 18 and no. 12 soft-hair mop brushes
- No. 5 and no. 2 synthetic, and no. 3 soft-hair round brushes
- 15 x 21cm (6 x 8¼in) hot-pressed watercolour paper 300gsm (140lb)

Cloudy sky

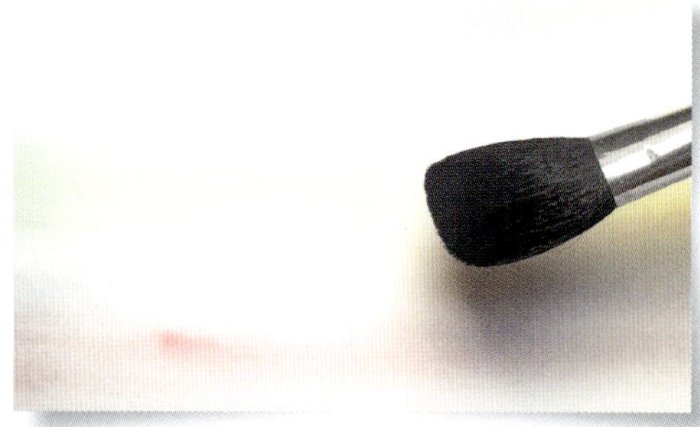

1 Background wash
Wet the paper all over. Lay washes of blue and black in the upper third, then yellow with a band of scarlet below. Use more blue and black at the base.

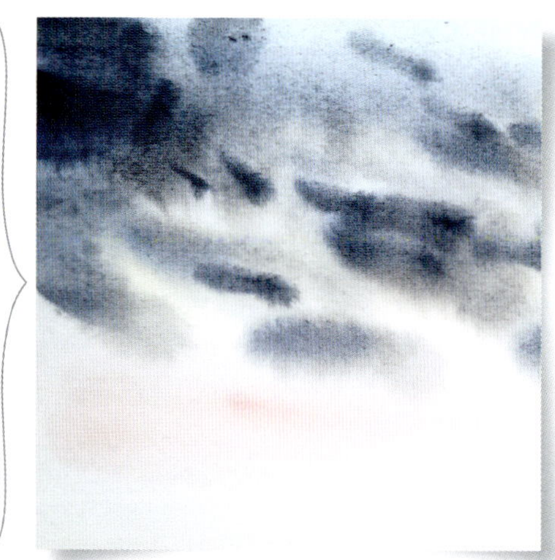

2 Paint the clouds
While the paper is still wet, mix blue, sepia, and black. Use strokes of colour for clouds, tilting the paper to create movement. When the paper dries a little, use a finer brush for a variety of small clouds.

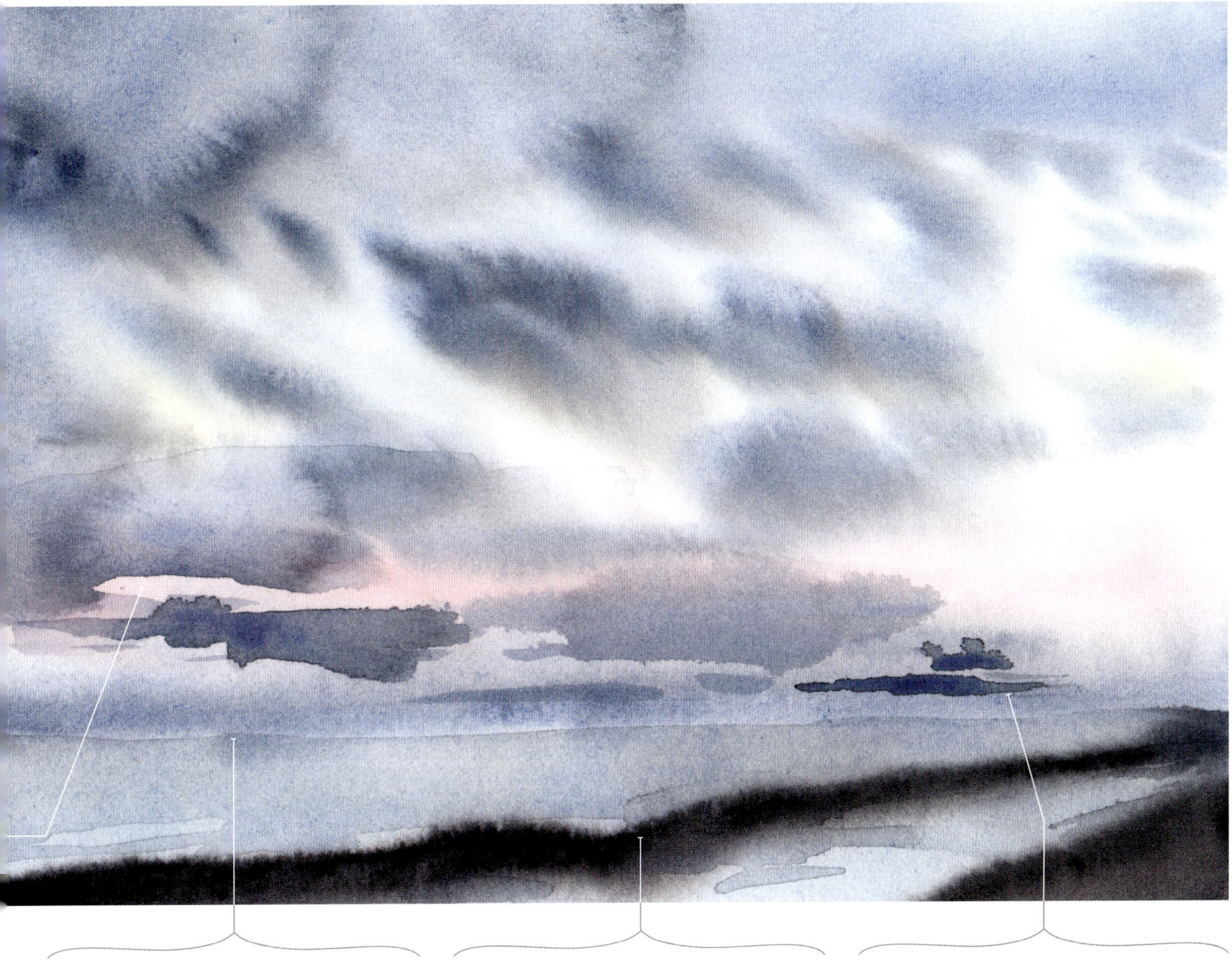

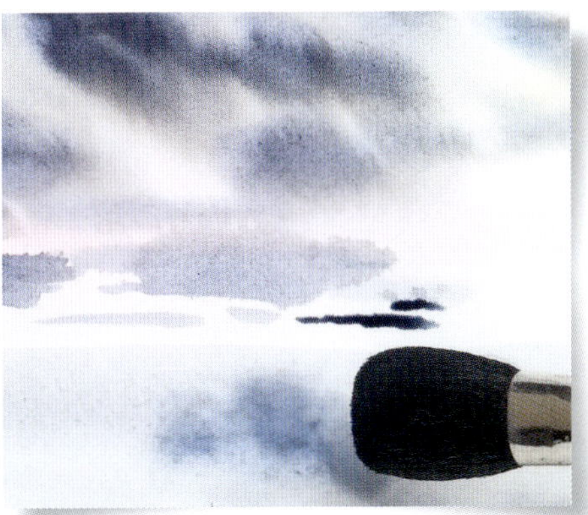

3 Detail around the horizon
When the paper dries, paint the remaining clouds above the horizon. Then paint the sea and horizon in a watery wash, adding a little blue and black in places for some depth.

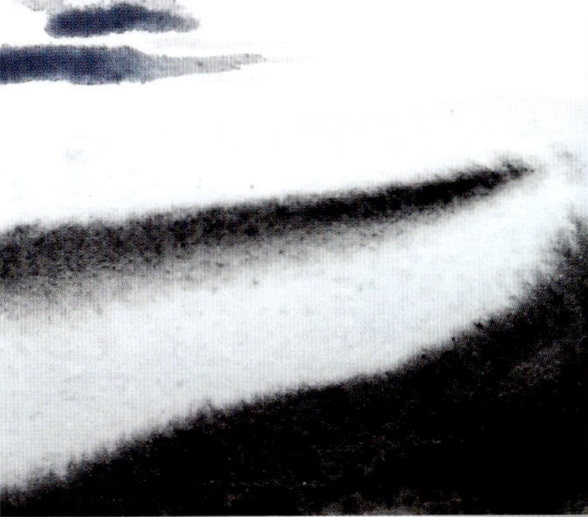

4 Foreground setting
When the paper is just damp, paint the beach with an expressive stroke of sepia with a little black and blue. When it is dry, add small strips of sand and some details.

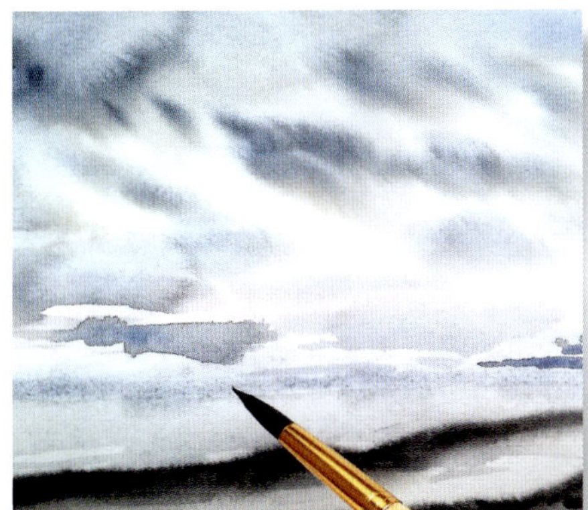

5 Add depth
Apply water to the horizon area then use a little blue mixed with sepia to create a stronger impression of depth and firm up the horizon.

Line and wash

COMBINING WATERCOLOUR WITH PERMANENT INK

Working in pen and ink opens another means of expression for the watercolourist, with the opportunity to use spontaneous drawing marks in waterproof ink that become an integral part of your painting. Employ the descriptive range of lines either as a foundation for your washes, or as a final signature to enhance your subject matter with an illustrative style.

Using sketch lines

The portability of watercolour makes it an ideal sketching medium, and combining it with ink as a drawing tool will encourage you to approach your work with confidence, as you learn to accept the permanency of marking pen on paper. Start with a small, smooth-paper sketchbook to make a feature of ink sketches.

Finalizing with lines

For a more illustrative approach, line is very effective over a dried wash to add the finishing touch to a painting. Simple outlines and defined edges will visually enhance shapes but it is also an opportunity to draw freely, using fluid, freehand marks that add an additional element to your painting.

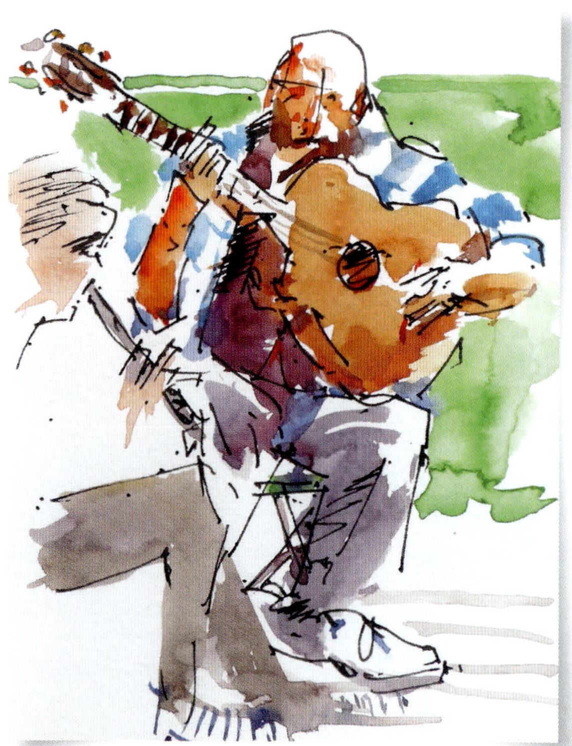

Loose marks and impressions
Different pens and nibs give lines of varying thickness; check the ink flows smoothly so that you can work spontaneously and freely. If your ink line looks too dominant, use richer paint and allow the lines to be part of the finished piece for a bold yet effortless effect.

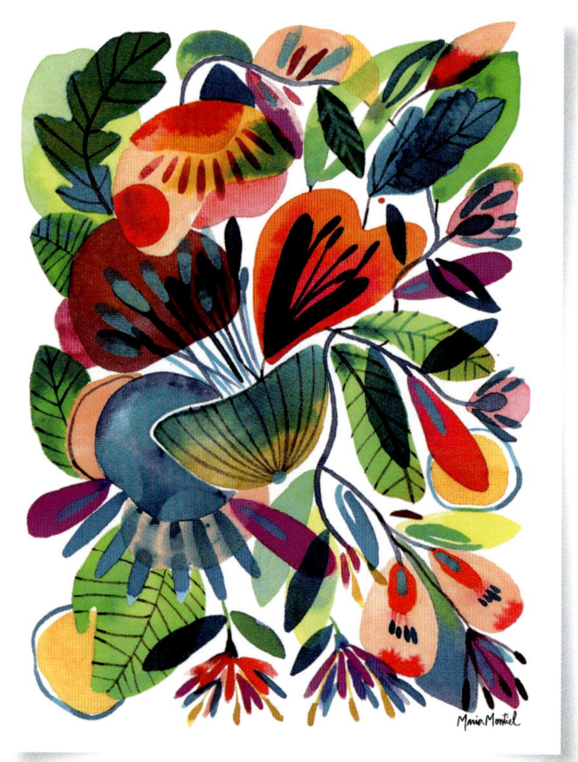

Outlines and details
The use of abstract washes and shapes mixed with organic, sketchy lines adds definition to your artwork and provides vibrant points of interest throughout. Choose bold, contrasting colours from the rest of the painting to define outlines and details for a sense of playful impact.

SKETCHING WITH INK

Here, a quick sketch in waterproof ink uses line to capture the figure and the detail of the fishing rod. Strong and simple washes are used to complement the pared-back nature of the image.

You will need

White gouache
Cadmium yellow
Cadmium red
Burnt sienna
Raw sienna
Cerulean blue
French ultramarine

- No. 14, no. 10, and no. 8 soft-hair round brushes
- 25mm (1in) and 13mm (½in) synthetic flat brushes
- 0.5mm technical pen
- 23 x 30cm (9 x 12in) NOT watercolour paper 300gsm (140lb)

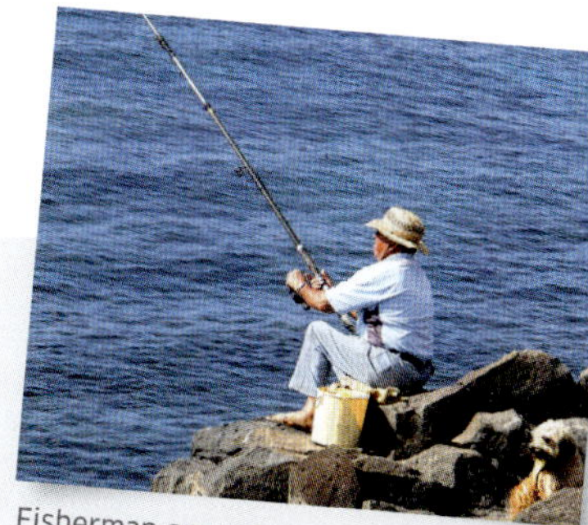
Fisherman on rocks

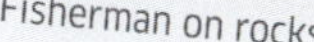

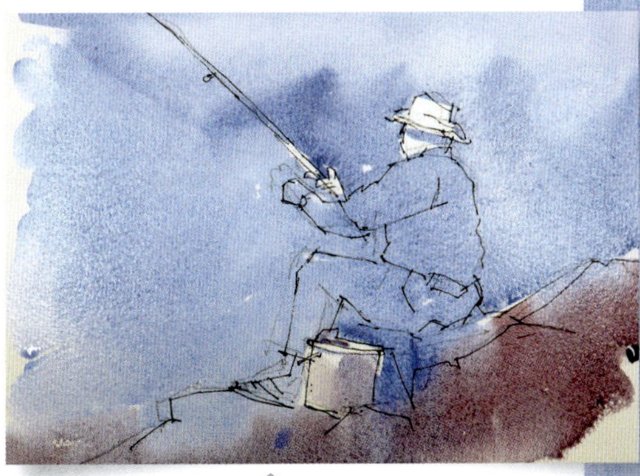

1 Simplify the image
Sketch the image confidently with waterproof ink, simplifying the scene to the main components. Apply a wash of ultramarine over almost the entire image, leaving hints of white for the face and hat.

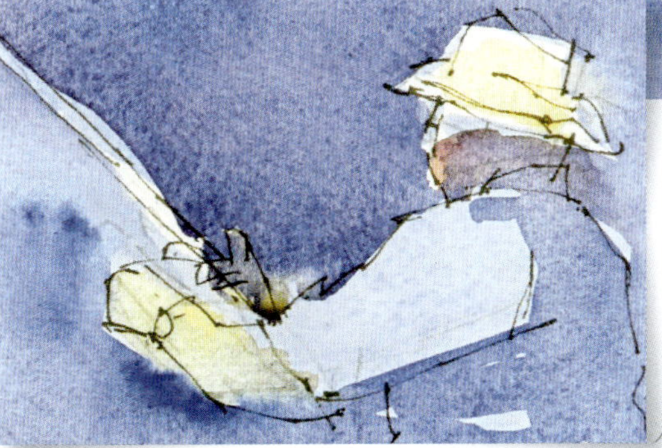

2 Vary base colours
Keep it simple by using tones of blue; add more ultramarine around the figure to make the arm and leg appear lighter. Use the pen outlines to guide the shapes, making sure that they are still visible.

White gouache on the rod leads the eye to the drawn shape

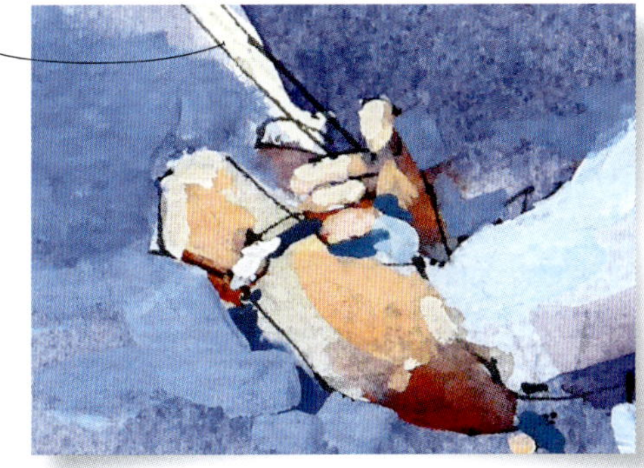

3 Balance colour and line
Reinforce darker tones using as few strokes as possible to retain the sketchy feel without losing the ink lines. Mix gouache in the lighter tones for final highlights.

DESCRIPTIVE OUTLINES

The dark background to the reference image has been reversed to provide a light, neutral foundation for the intense flower colours. Enclosing all the shapes in inked lines gives a sense of containment to the painting, combining precise outlines with loose, fluid strokes.

You will need

Watercolour
- Lemon yellow
- Light brown
- Transparent orange
- Crimson red
- Opera rose
- Perylene violet
- Ultramarine
- Cobalt turquoise light
- Cobalt green
- Viridian

Liquid watercolour
- Pastel green

- No. 2 mop brush
- No. 4, no. 1, and no. 0 soft-hair round brushes
- Watercolour pencil
- Fine permanent marker, ink pen, or calligraphy pen

- 30 x 20cm (12 x 8in) NOT cotton watercolour paper 300gsm (140lb)

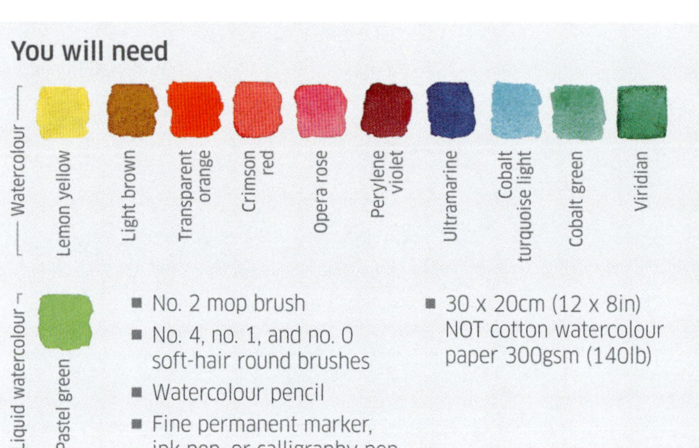

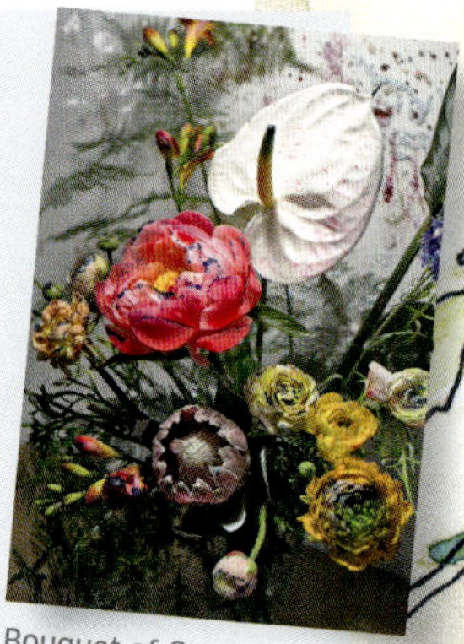

Bouquet of flowers

1 Background wash

Use a watercolour pencil to sketch the main elements and any connections between them. Mix a light, neutral wash for the background and apply it around the main shapes to provide a foundation for the flower and leaf colours. A pale wash will ensure that pen lines stand out.

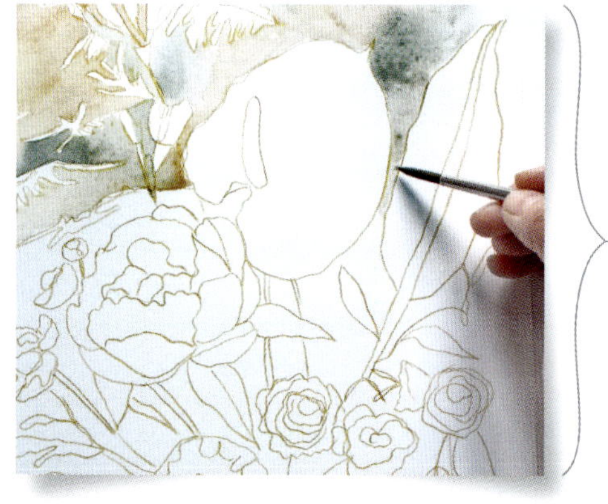

2 Fill shapes

Add light and mid tones to the leaf and flower shapes, keeping within the drawn lines so that the shapes have defined edges that you can follow with a pen later. Let each stage dry before continuing to add darker tones to the bouquet.

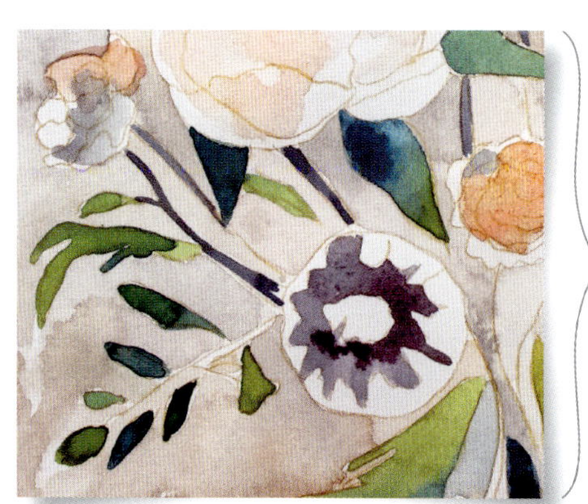

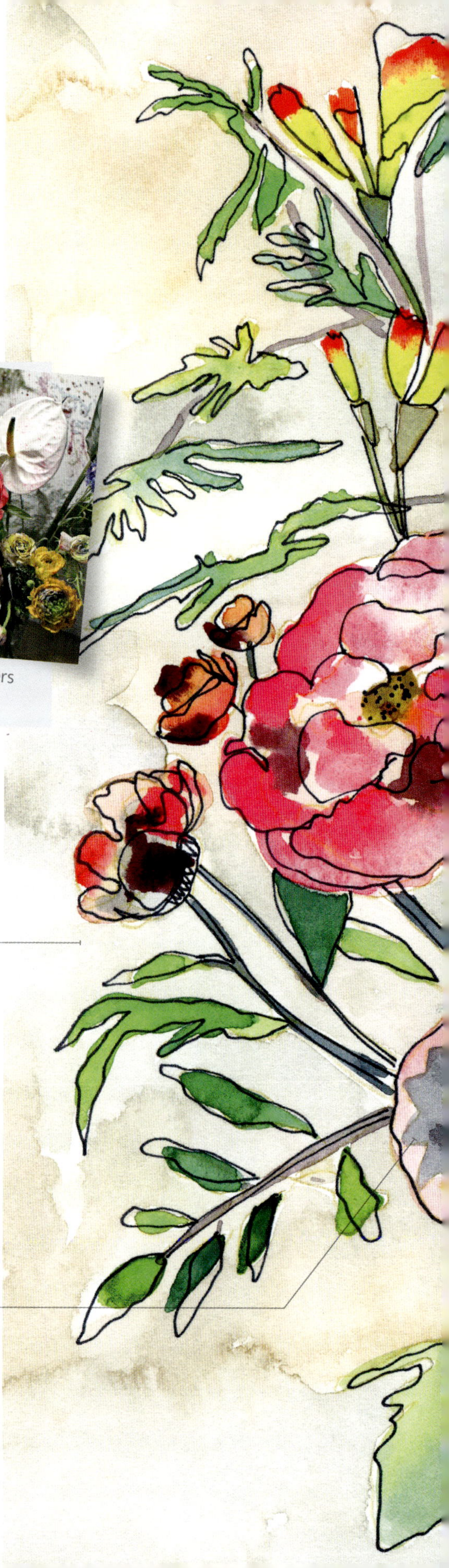

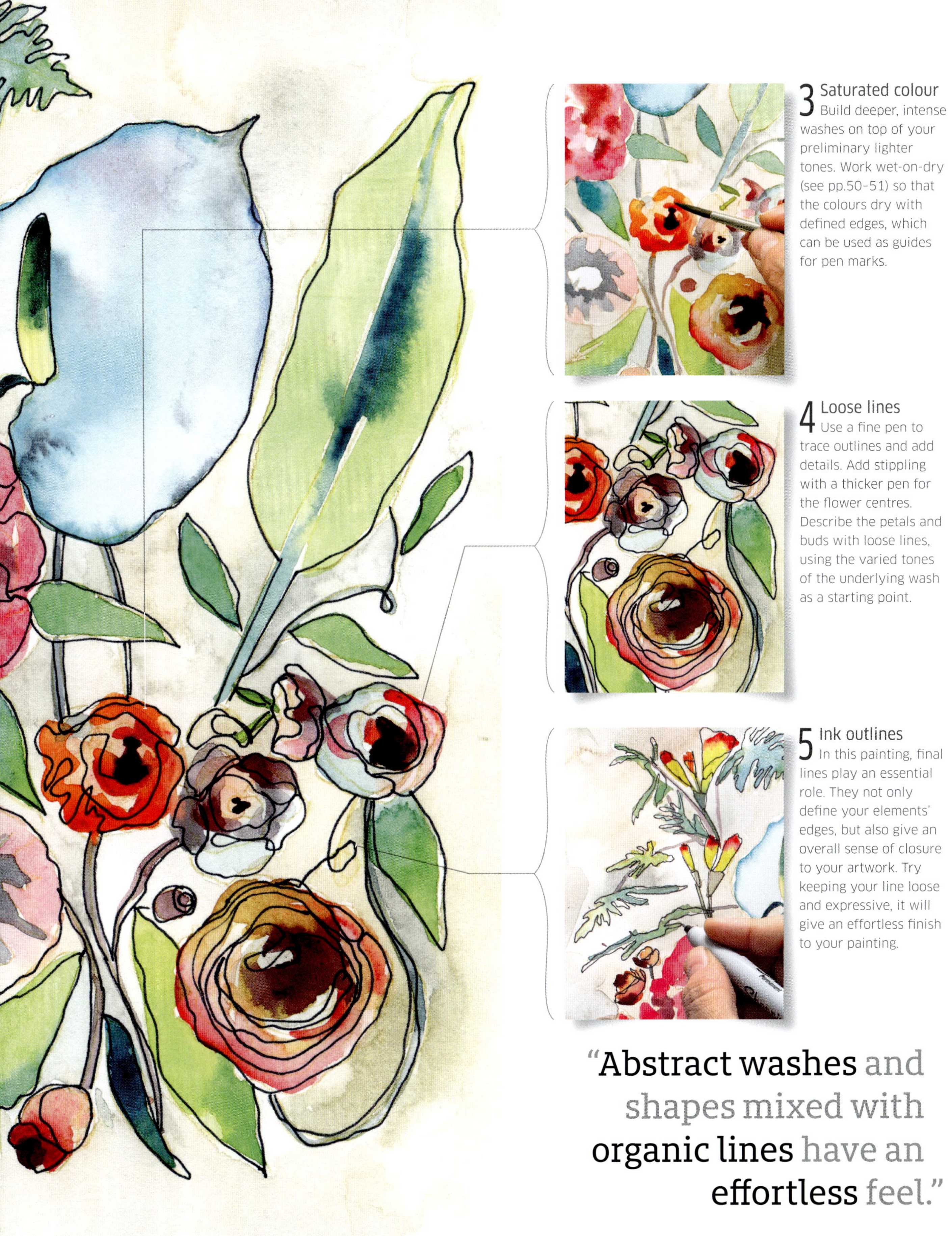

3 Saturated colour

Build deeper, intense washes on top of your preliminary lighter tones. Work wet-on-dry (see pp.50–51) so that the colours dry with defined edges, which can be used as guides for pen marks.

4 Loose lines

Use a fine pen to trace outlines and add details. Add stippling with a thicker pen for the flower centres. Describe the petals and buds with loose lines, using the varied tones of the underlying wash as a starting point.

5 Ink outlines

In this painting, final lines play an essential role. They not only define your elements' edges, but also give an overall sense of closure to your artwork. Try keeping your line loose and expressive, it will give an effortless finish to your painting.

> "Abstract washes and shapes mixed with organic lines have an effortless feel."

Straight edges

PAINTING AN EVEN LINE

Almost all man-made elements in a subject will have some straight lines. Surprisingly, these do not necessarily need to be painted perfectly straight. Variety in the line is always preferable, but there are some subjects, such as telegraph poles, where bends will look incongruous. There are a few ways to help keep lines straight without a ruler, so that they look like a natural part of the painting process.

■ Aids for achieving natural lines

Painting a freehand straight line does not often come easily, but you can employ various tools, either from your painting kit or made from materials close at hand, to help you achieve a natural line. To make the line appear painterly rather than graphic, vary the pressure to adapt the line's width and solidity.

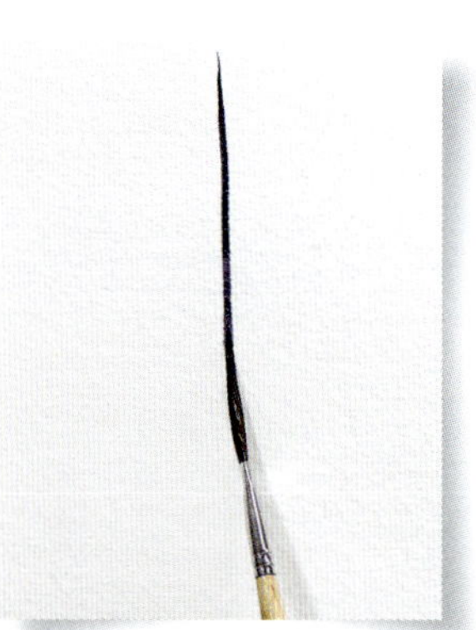
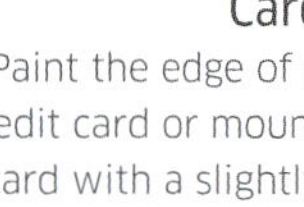

Swordliner
Gently lie the curved "blade" of the brush on the paper, then lightly draw it down.

Card
Paint the edge of a credit card or mount card with a slightly stronger mix and stamp or drag.

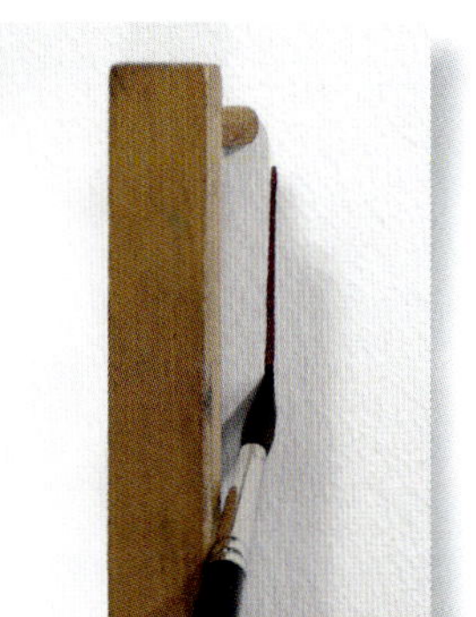
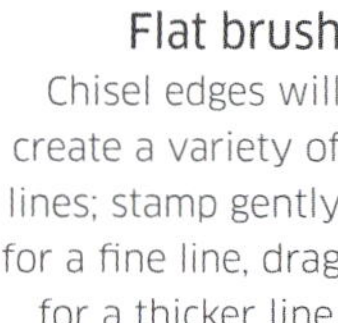

Mahlstick
Use a straight edge or mahlstick as a guide; draw down with the ferrule against the stick.

Flat brush
Chisel edges will create a variety of lines; stamp gently for a fine line, drag for a thicker line.

PUTTING IT INTO PRACTICE

Here, different aids were used to convey the variety of lines, from the corrugated iron to the telegraph poles that are so integral to the composition.

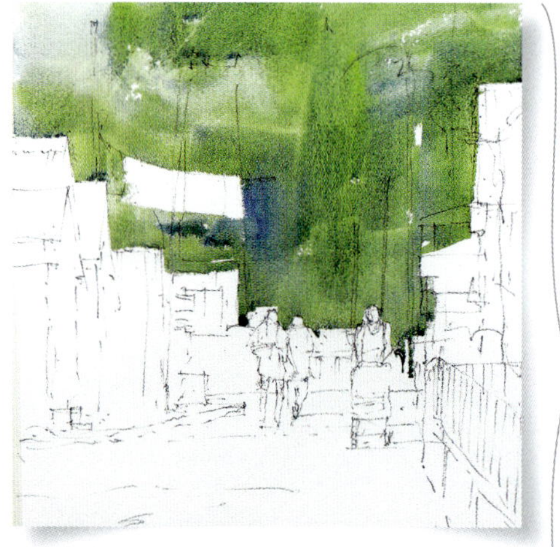

1 Background wash
Paint the background vegetation using the flat brush and a French ultramarine and cadmium yellow mix. Vary the mix as you paint. Use the edge of the brush to create the squared edges of negative roof shapes.

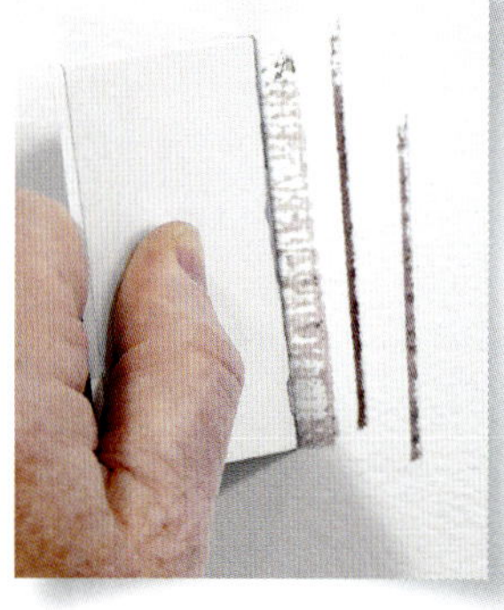
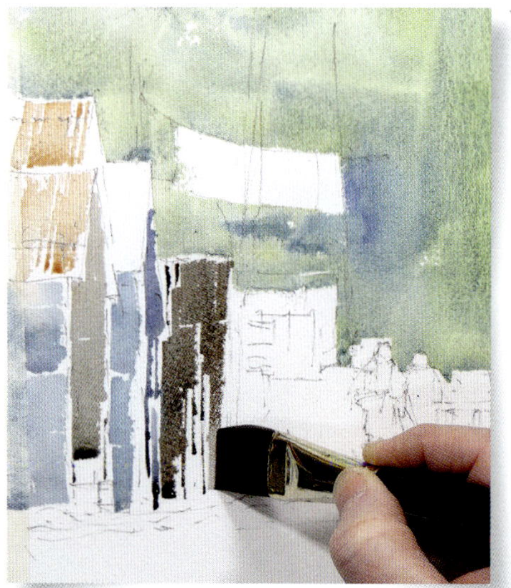
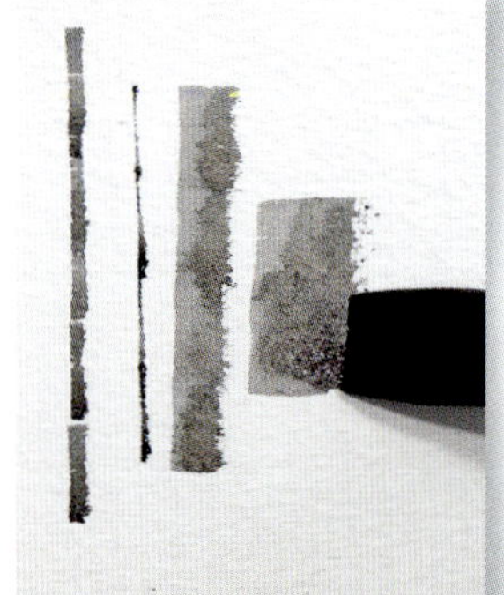

2 Brush lines
Continue with the flat brush to fill in the buildings, using the edge for corrugations and planks. Vary the line width and colour, using a variety of blues, browns, and greys.

You will need

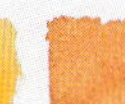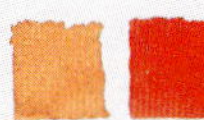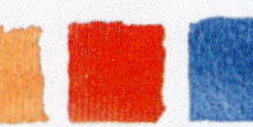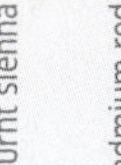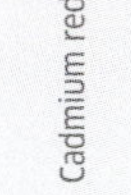

Cadmium yellow

Burnt sienna

Cadmium red

French ultramarine

- 25mm (1in) soft-hair flat brush
- No. 10 soft-hair round brush
- 6mm (¼in) swordliner brush
- Ruling pen

- Mount card or mahlstick, and credit card
- 25 x 35cm (10 x 14in) NOT watercolour paper 300gsm (140lb)

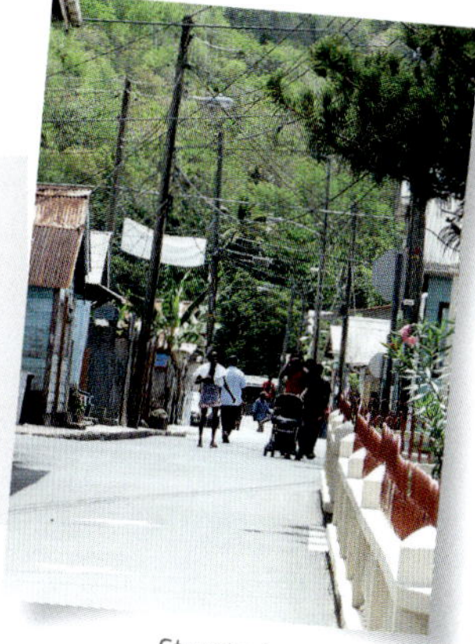
Street view, St Lucia

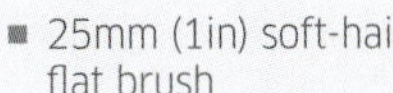

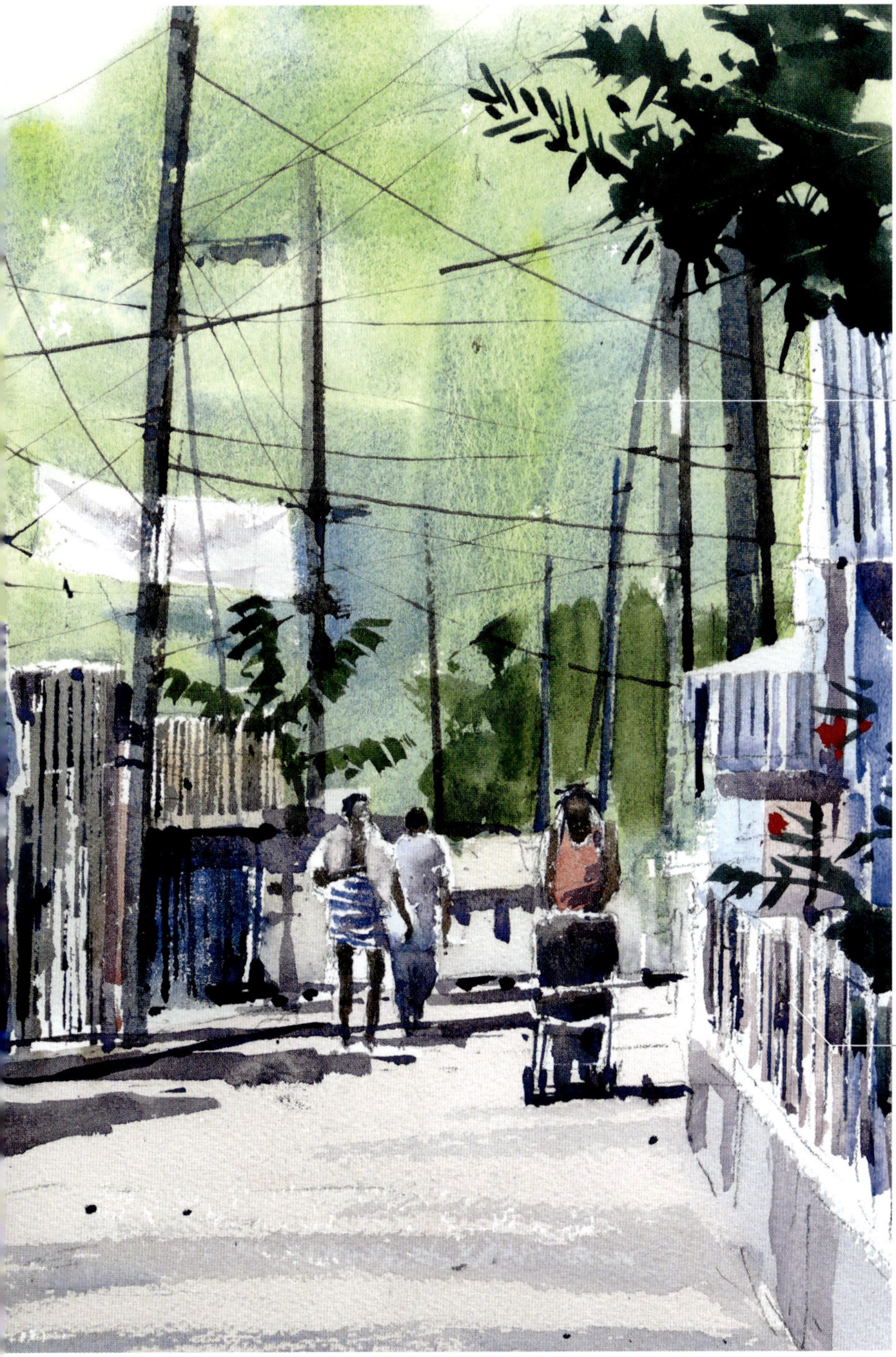

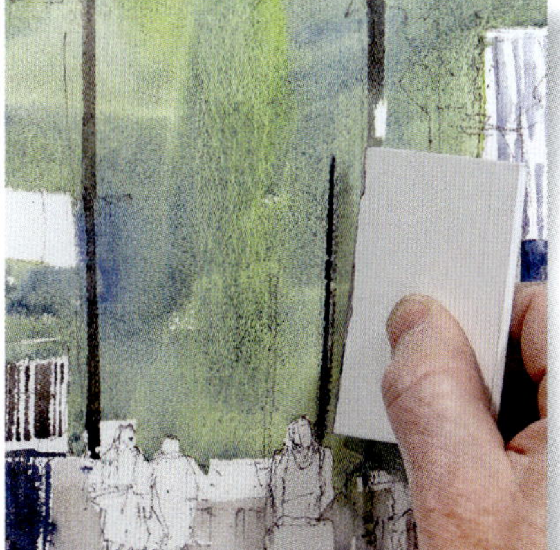

3 Assisted lines
Use the mahlstick or the edge of a mount card to create the poles, using a variety of darker mixes. Cut the card to different lengths and drag it sideways to broaden the line for the wider poles.

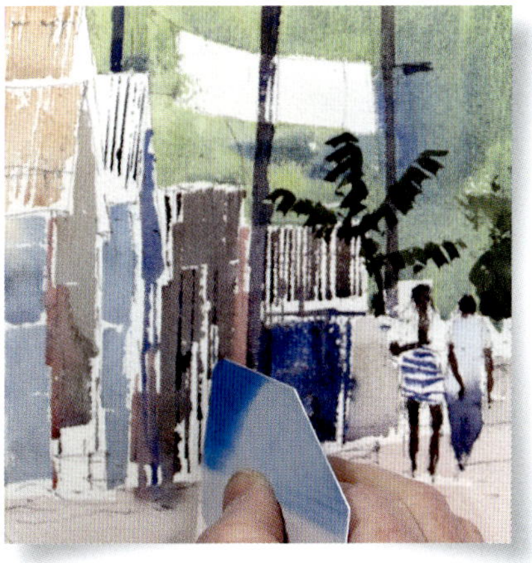

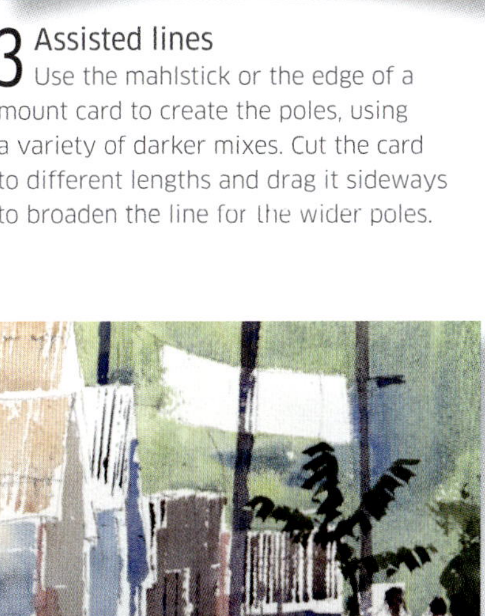

4 Fine lines
With a strong shadow mix, apply finer lines with a credit card for the corrugated sheets and straight cables. Use a ruling pen (see pp.20–21) for the slightly curved lines.

Lifting out

REMOVING PIGMENT

You can control the level of definition in a painting by taking pigment away, rather than adding more and more. Lifting out lets you decide on the amount of looseness you want in a more considered way, giving you control to define edges and shapes; it is ideal for portraying patterns of light.

■ Ways to lift out pigment

There are several options available for removing a coloured wash and manipulating it to leave shapes or edges in the paint. A sponge will leave a textured effect (see pp.84–85), or try a cotton bud for small details, or a paper towel to absorb larger areas. Apply a brush to absorb pigment; it is easy to control and can be used to soften wet edges, or leave a more defined dried edge. Use a medium such as gum arabic to assist lifting out; it binds pigment so that you can lift off all the colour.

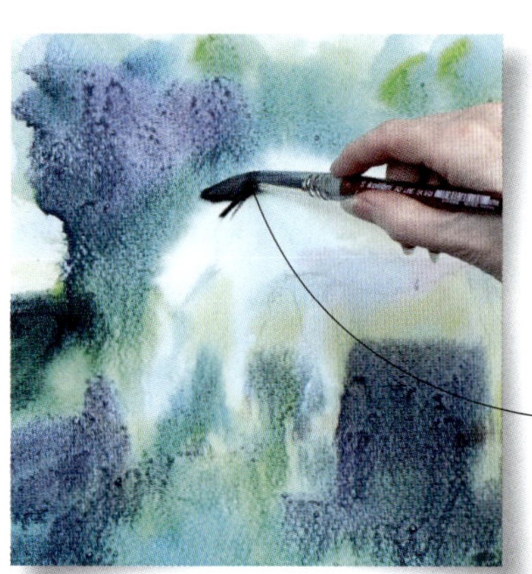

Using a brush
To lift off an area of wash, use a clean, dry brush, pressing quite hard with every brushstroke to avoid replacing the pigment.

Stroke a dry brush to absorb the wash and soften edges. White paper is revealed where pigment is removed

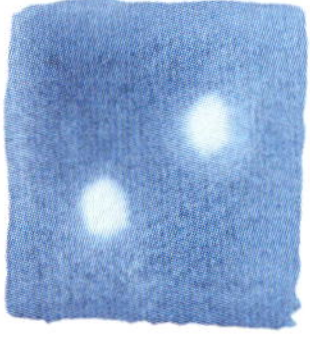

Soft edges

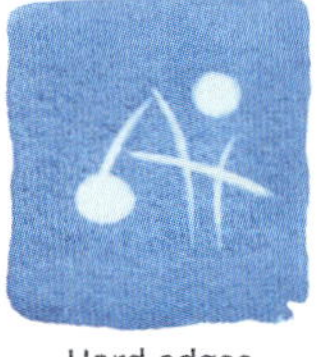

Hard edges

Soft and hard edges
For soft edges, use a dry brush to lift off when your wash is still wet, leaving a diffused mark. For a hard edge, apply a clean, damp brush when the wash is drying, or completely dry.

PUTTING IT INTO PRACTICE

Gum arabic has been used in this painting to slowly allow definition to appear out of a mist, by lifting out the highlights that create a dappled pattern of light on the horse's body.

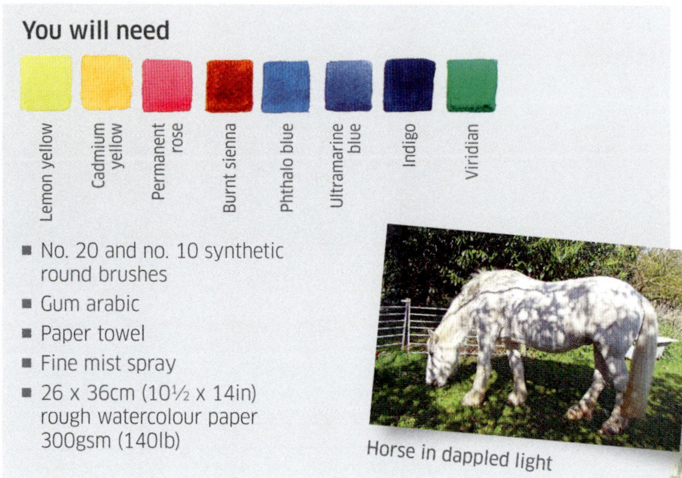

- No. 20 and no. 10 synthetic round brushes
- Gum arabic
- Paper towel
- Fine mist spray
- 26 x 36cm (10½ x 14in) rough watercolour paper 300gsm (140lb)

Horse in dappled light

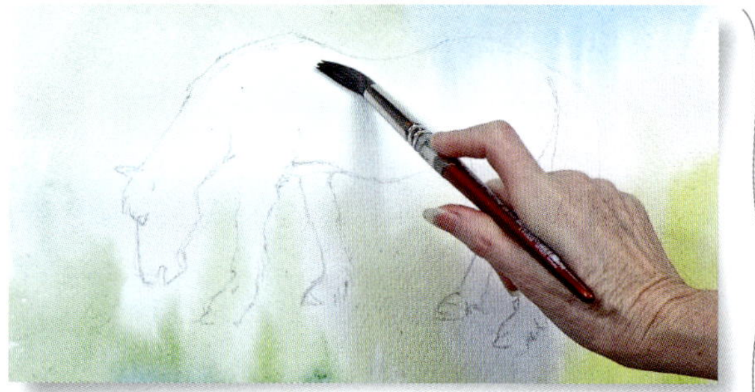

1 Underpainting
Lay the background colour around the horse's body, using colours that will form highlights when lifted out later. Mop up any runs with a clean, dry brush.

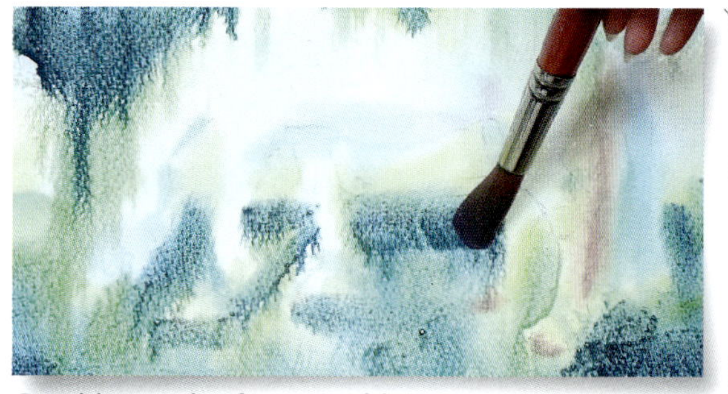

2 Add a wash of gum arabic
When dry, apply a 50:50 mix of gum arabic and water over the entire painting. Add pigment to the background wet-in-wet to soften shadow edges.

3 Apply light markings

Start applying the rough areas of dappled light and shade on the horse's body with a smaller, drier brush. Detail is not necessary at this stage, let the wash flow and run naturally to define the form. Lift off soft edges.

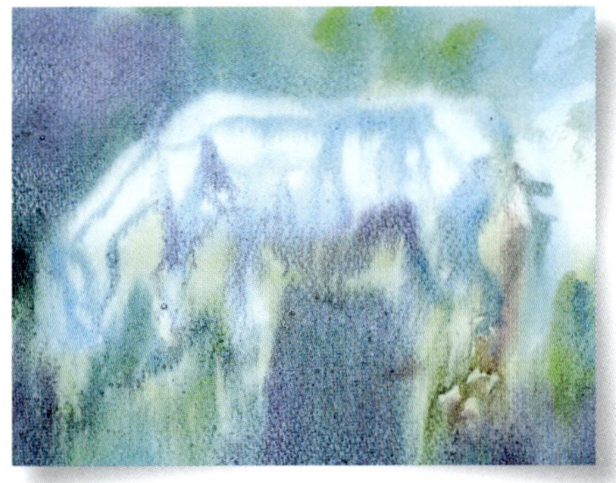

4 Lift off edges

Continue to add pigment to the wet surface so the wash maintains a soft edge. When dry, lift out hard edges of the pools of light, so that the lines of pigment that are left read correctly as shadows, not random marks.

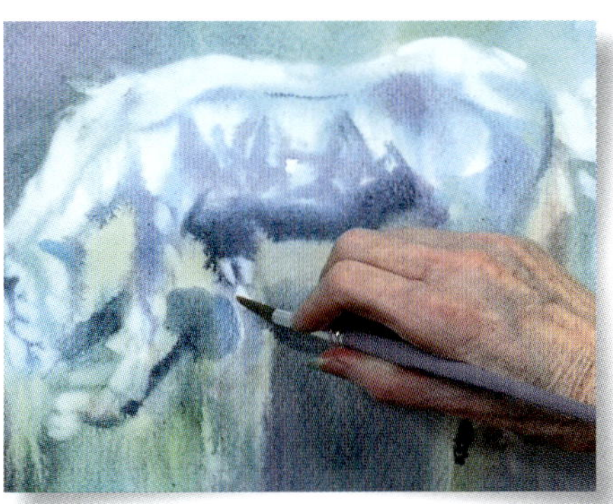

5 Mottled texture

Create texture by pressing a paper towel onto damp paper, either by spraying a dried area, or before a wash has completely dried. Try spraying then tipping your painting and allowing the droplets to run in rivulets.

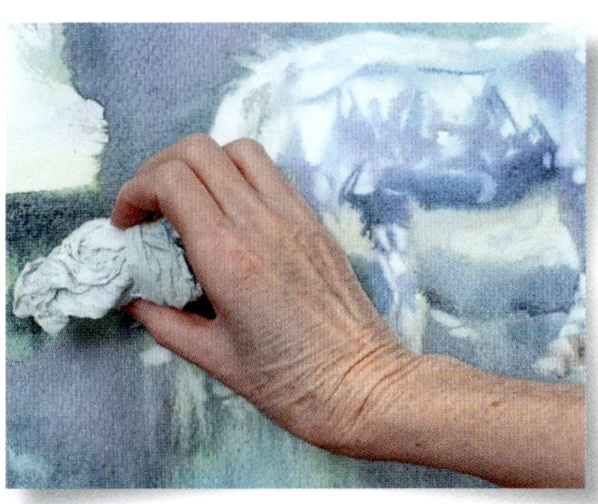

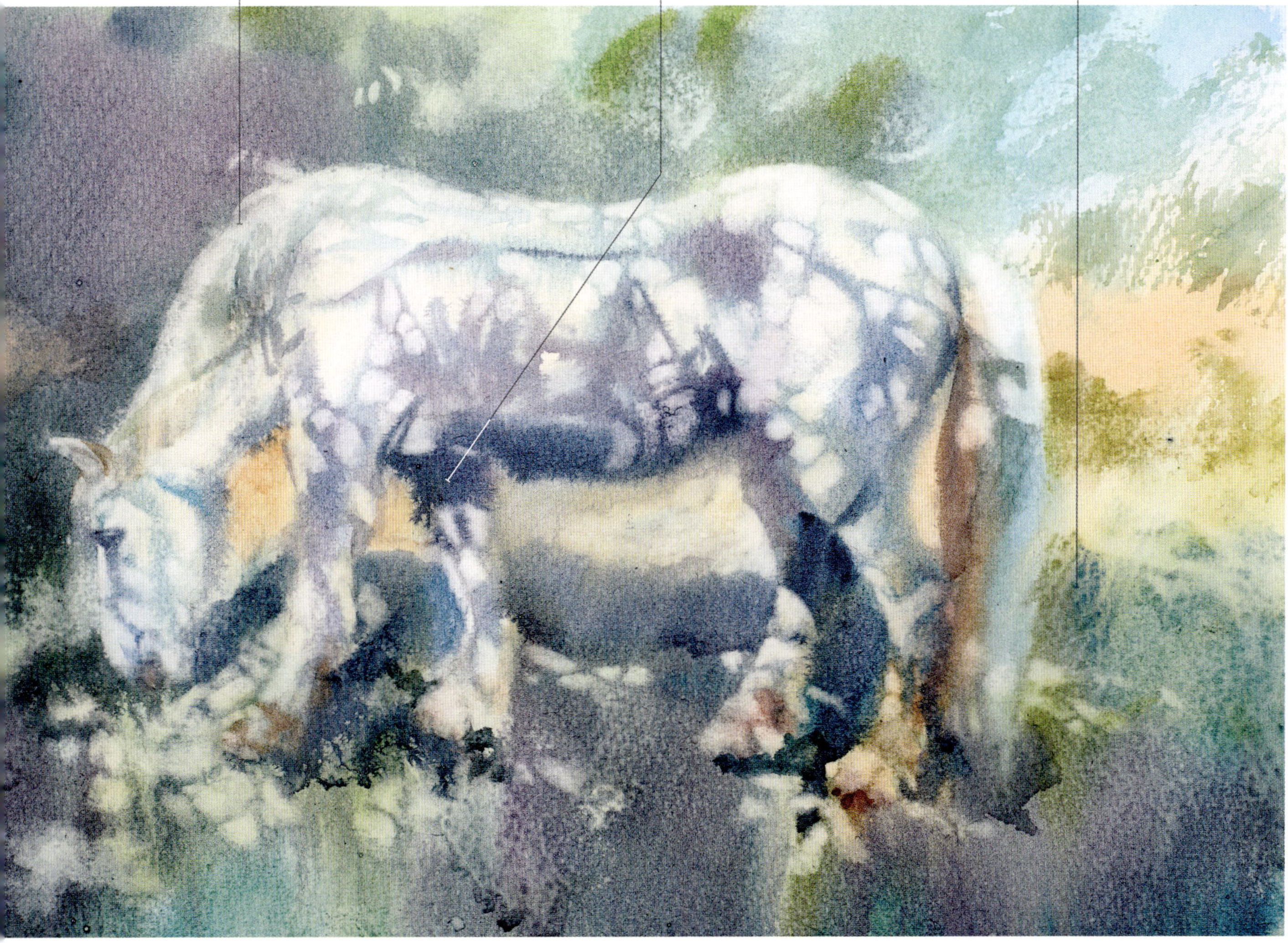

Using a sponge

CREATING TEXTURES IN PAINT

Sponging is an easy-to-control technique that adds texture and vibrancy to your painting. The natural dimples in a sponge are ideally suited to creating loose effects in watercolour, either by making marks or lifting out colour. Use sponging for many subjects from foliage, dappled light, sea spray, clouds, and smoke, to fur or fabric.

■ Making textured marks

For best results use a natural sponge. Prepare it by submerging in clean water and squeezing out the excess with a paper towel. Dip into your prepared wash and test before applying. Lightly dab or drag the sponge to add textured marks, or lift out for softened edges.

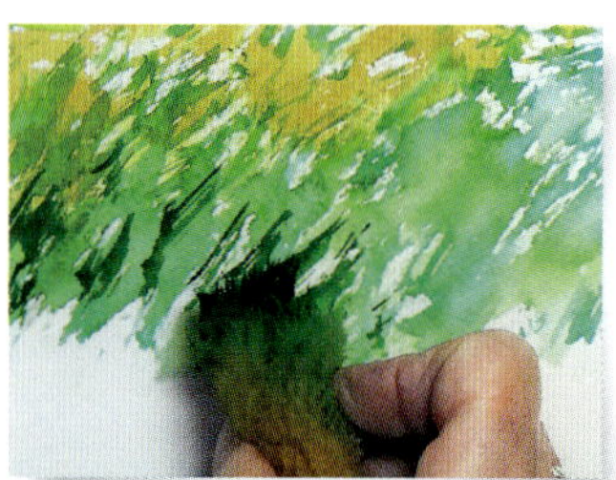

Dragging

Working dark over light, drag the sponge in short strokes, taking care not to overwork an area and muddy the washes. This method will cover large areas quickly and is suited to grasses, trees, and branches.

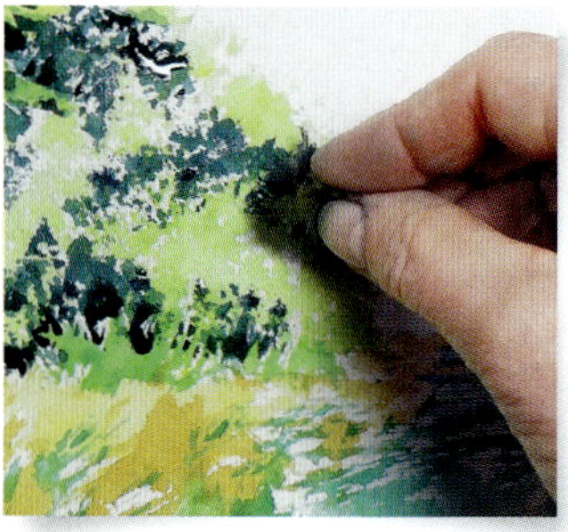

Stippling

Build texture or add natural highlights by lightly dabbing the sponge. Test the amount of paint and water; too much water will cause the texture to be lost.

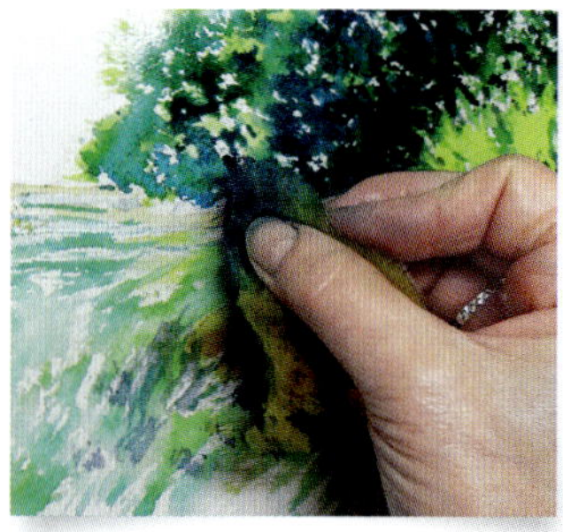

Alter wetness

The wash doesn't always have to be dry. Alter the wetness of your paint to achieve different effects, using wet-in-wet where you want the colours to blend.

PUTTING IT INTO PRACTICE

Working from light to dark, the textured background of flowers and grasses was created by stippling and dragging layers of colour. A trail of smoke was added by sponging out colour when the painting was dry.

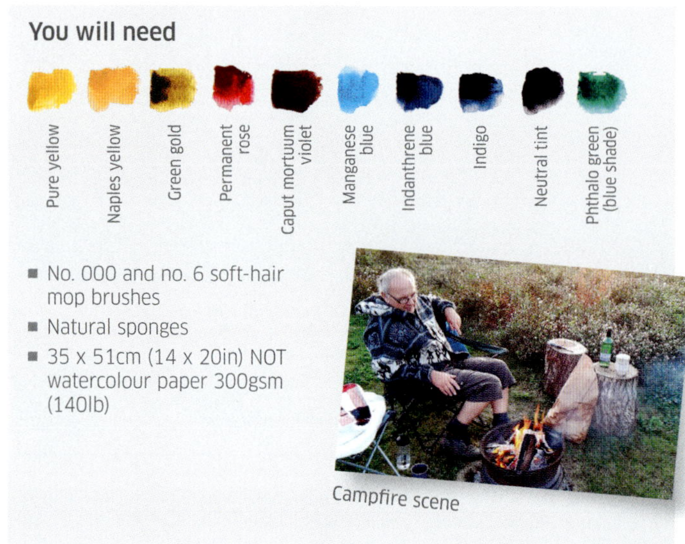

You will need

- No. 000 and no. 6 soft-hair mop brushes
- Natural sponges
- 35 x 51cm (14 x 20in) NOT watercolour paper 300gsm (140lb)

Campfire scene

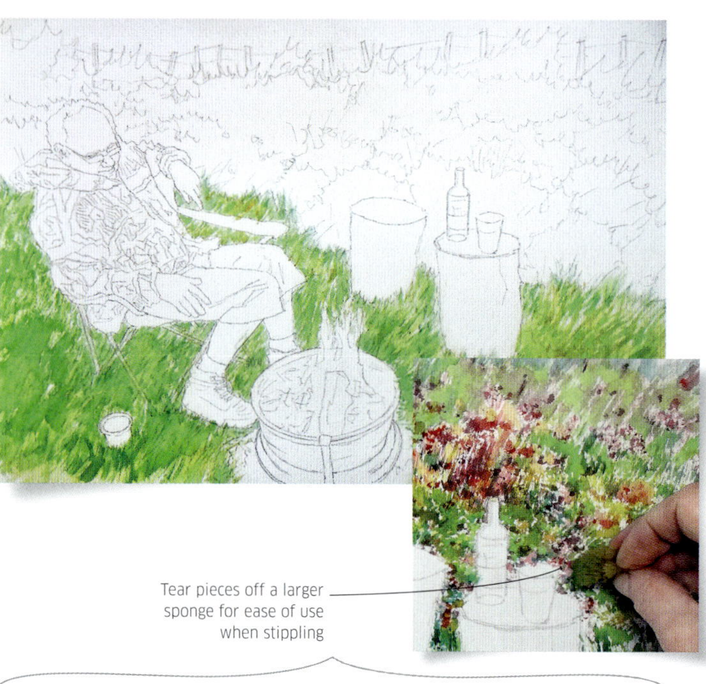

Tear pieces off a larger sponge for ease of use when stippling

1 Light first layers

Add the foreground grasses by dragging the sponge in short strokes, building layers of colour. Stipple colour for the background flowers and seedheads, building oranges, pinks, and copper browns.

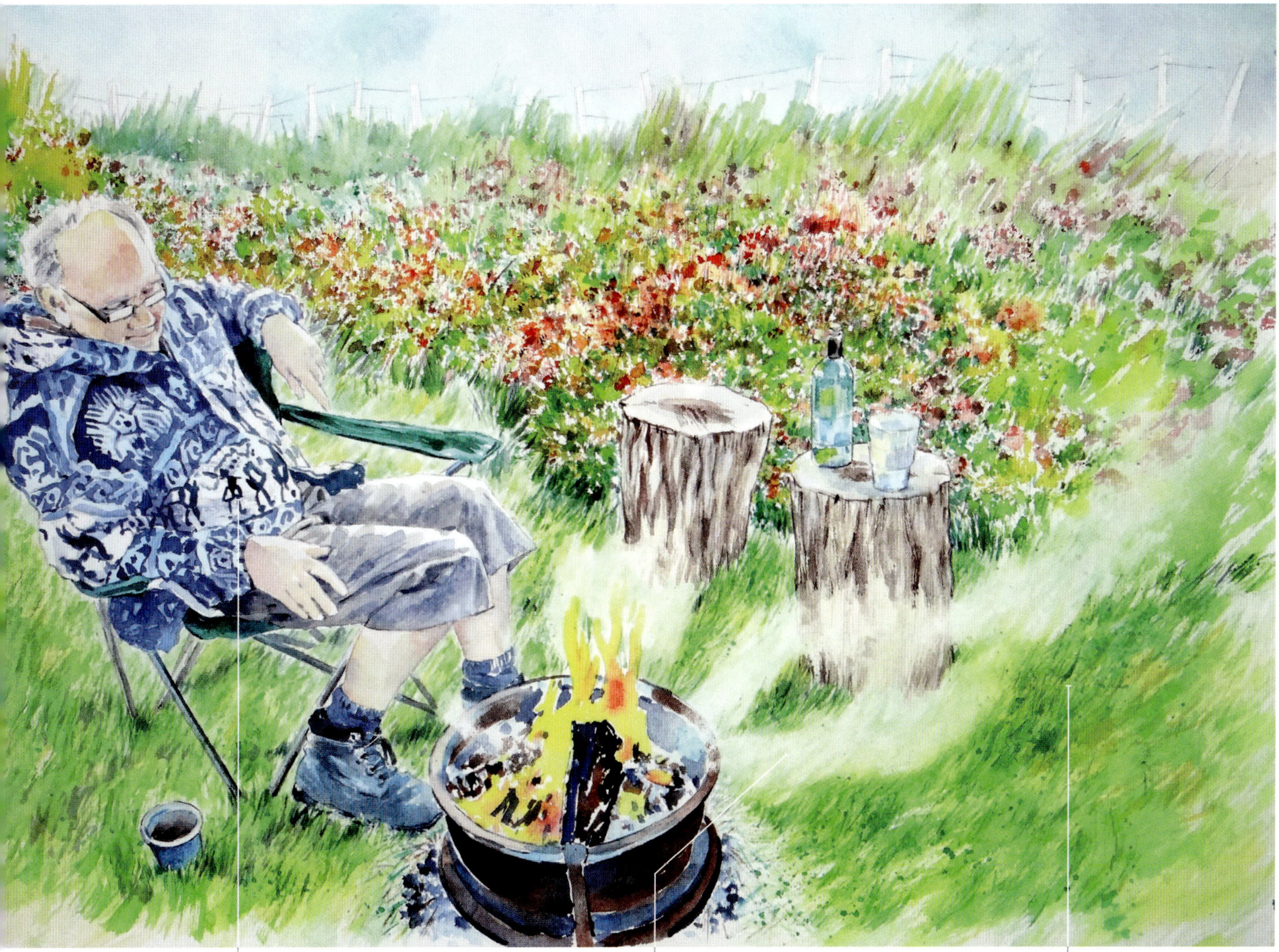

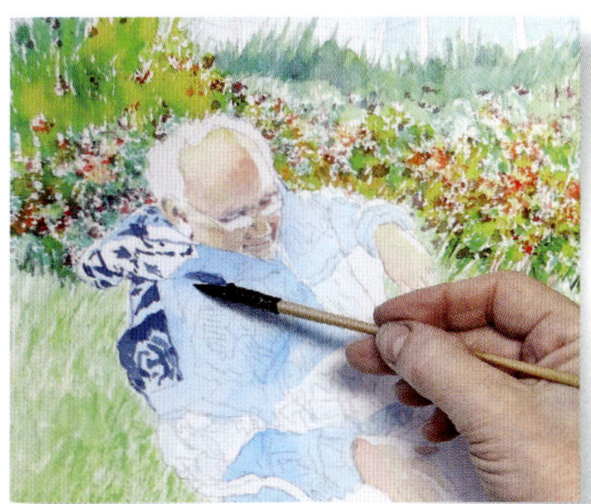

2 Begin painting the figure
Use different-sized brushes to paint the more detailed figure and the fire in the foreground, using wet-in-wet and wet-on-dry techniques to build up the layers.

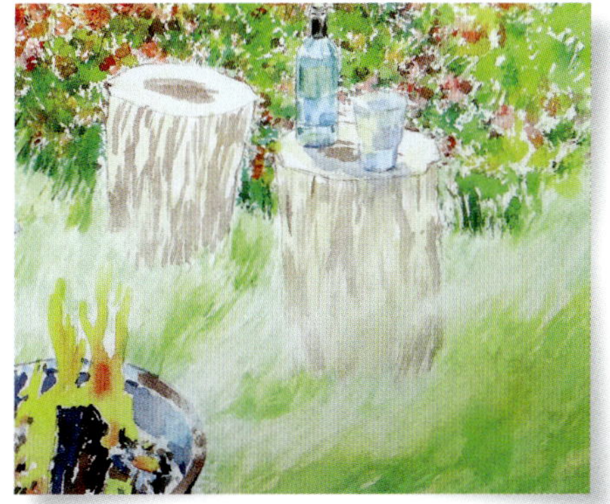

3 Lift off dry colour
Leave the painting to dry completely, then use a clean, damp sponge to gently rub the path of the smoke trail to diffuse and lift the colour away. Be careful not to rub a hole!

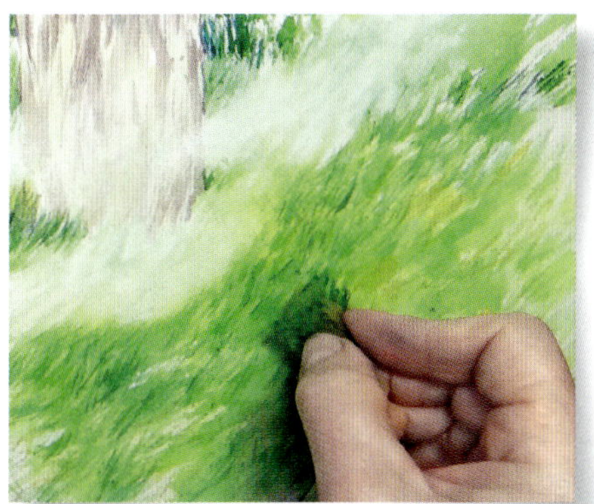

4 Build texture
Drag and stipple with the sponge to build up the darker tones and shadows in the foliage and grass, creating more layers of texture and interest. Add any final details.

Correcting mistakes

REMOVING UNWANTED MARKS

Unwanted spills, bleeds, and runs can be hard to control and will dry to leave a stain. But making mistakes in watercolour needn't be the end of the world; by being prepared and ready to act quickly, you can rescue your work and repaint the area when dry. There are also methods for revising or removing more permanent marks, allowing you to correct your painting at a later stage.

◼ Removing spills

To avoid a spill or run bleeding or drying over other washes, act quickly to blot and remove the wet paint. Do not scrub to avoid scuffing the paper surface.

You will need
- Paper towel
- Clean, damp brush

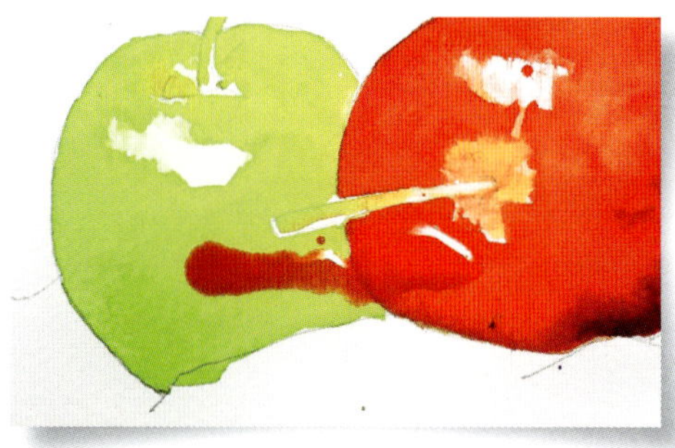

Paint run
Excess red wash has run across the dried light-green wash. You must respond instantly to prevent the run from drying with a hard edge. Always have paper towels to hand so that you can act swiftly.

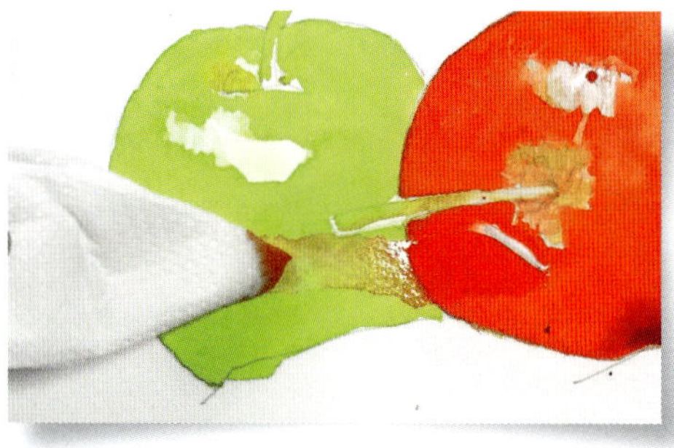

Blot excess
Lightly dab on the spill with a small piece of paper towel to gently soak up the excess. Let the paper dry and continue painting. If a mark remains, re-wet the area and remove it with either a damp brush or paper towel.

◼ Removing bleeds

Watercolour can be difficult to control and often colours will run into one another just where you don't want them. One solution is to remove the paint with a brush.

You will need
- Clean, damp brush

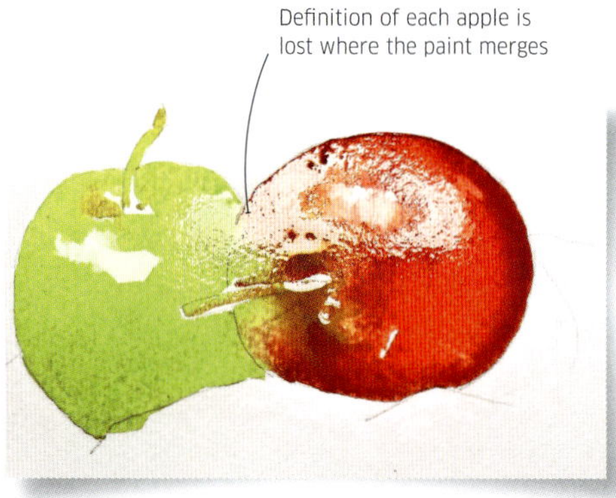

Merging colours
If you apply areas of wet watercolours too closely together, it is likely they'll bleed into one another, creating unwanted blends and colour mixes. Here, the red and green washes have merged to create a brown.

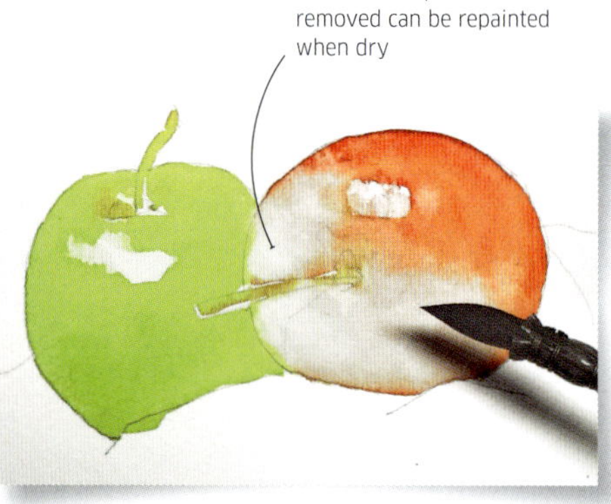

Brush away bleed
Soften the area of the bleed by brushing it with a clean, damp brush to remove the excess paint. Leave to dry, then repaint, letting each area dry completely so that the colours don't bleed together again.

■ Removing dry paint

Watercolour is water-soluble, which means most unwanted marks can be re-wetted and lifted off the painting. You can also scrape off marks on thick paper.

You will need
- Natural or synthetic stiff-bristle brush
- Paper towel
- Sponge or Magic Watercolour Eraser
- Craft blade

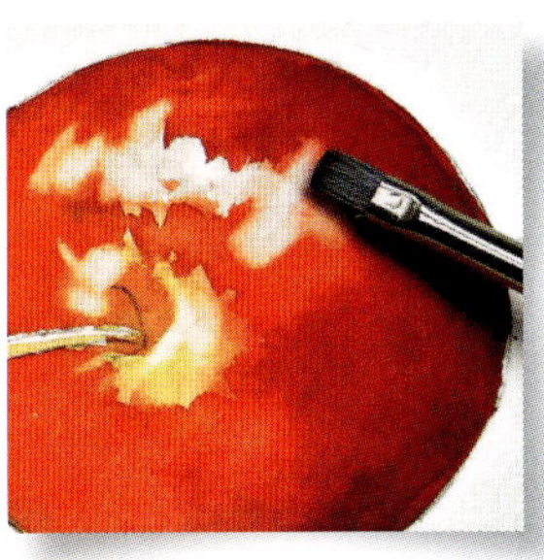

Damp brush
Gently scrub the area with a damp bristle brush. Blot with a paper towel, rinse the brush, and repeat.

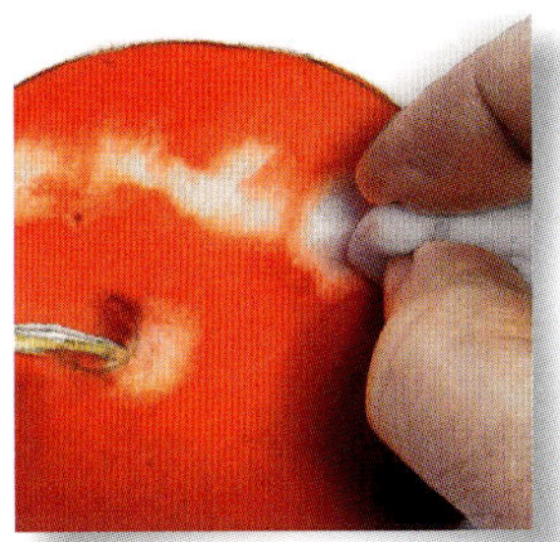

Sponge eraser
Lift or erase dry paint with a sponge or white "magic" eraser. Tear off a piece, wet, rinse, then "rub" off an error.

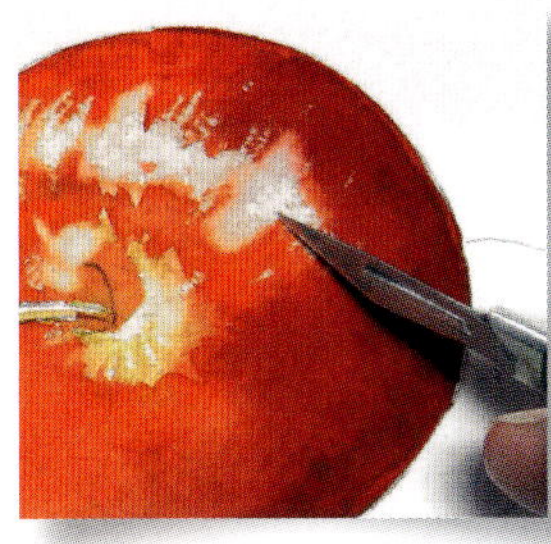

Craft blade
To remove a light stain left after blotting, let it dry then scrape away layers of paint with the edge of a blade.

■ Preventing runbacks

A runback is an area that has dried with a feathery edge where washes have mingled. Working quickly will reduce the likelihood of runbacks happening.

You will need
- Paper towel
- Clean, damp soft brush

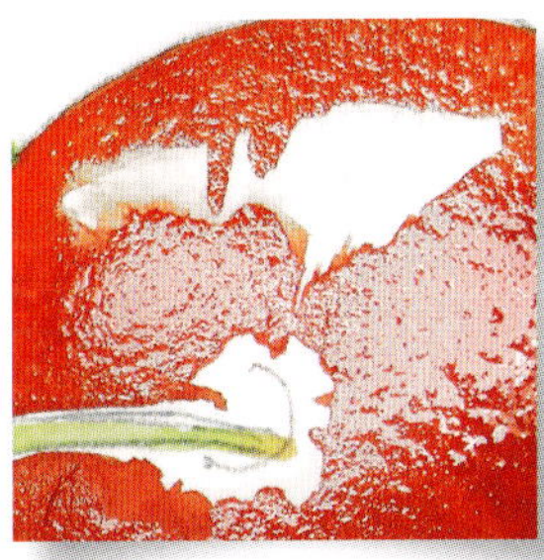

Causes of runbacks
Excess paint will seep back towards an area of drier paint, causing the washes to feather together.

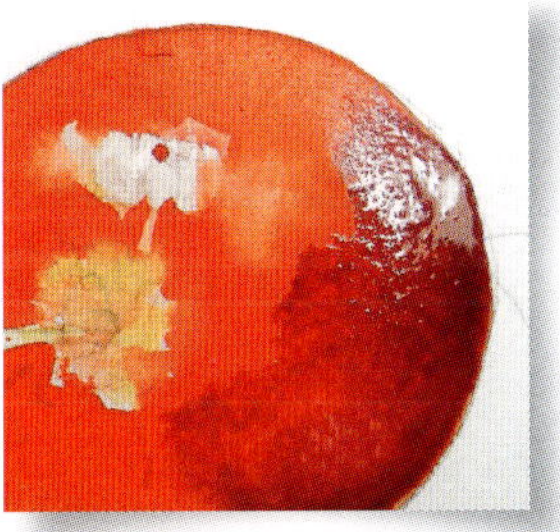

Runback marks
Unintentional water marks known as runbacks, blooms, or cauliflowers, are left as the area dries.

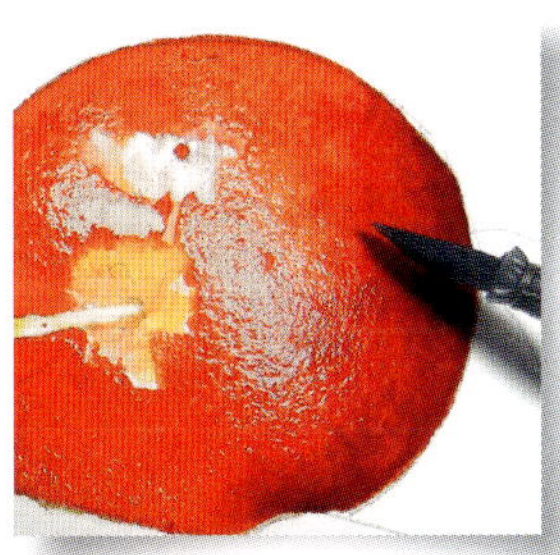

Taking action
As soon as a runback appears, dab it with a soft brush or paper towel to lift off the excess paint.

■ Solutions for permanent mistakes

Some pigments stain and won't allow you to lift out using the quick fixes above. Repainting is one option, either dark over light or using white gouache, or wash away to start again.

You will need
- White gouache
- Soft brush
- Tap or shower

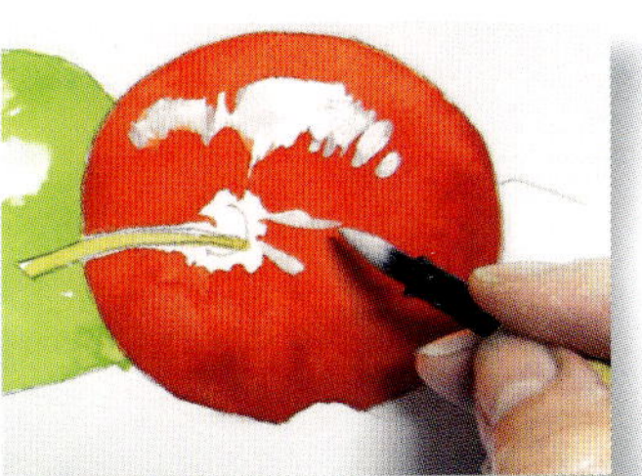

Restoring highlights
Opaque white gouache can be applied over a dried wash to bring back lost highlights.

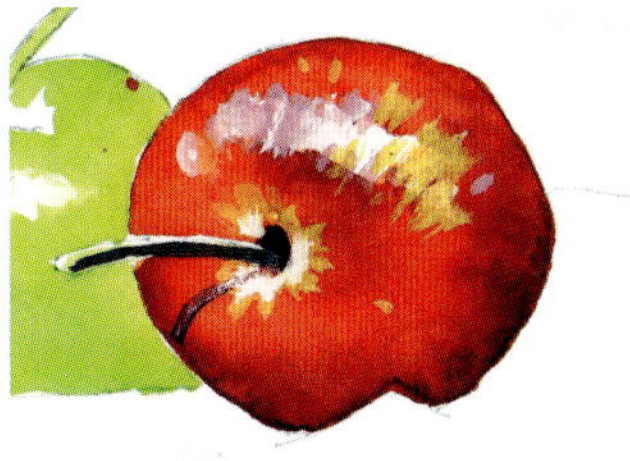

Colour mixing
Mixing white gouache with transparent watercolour on the paper will cover mistakes.

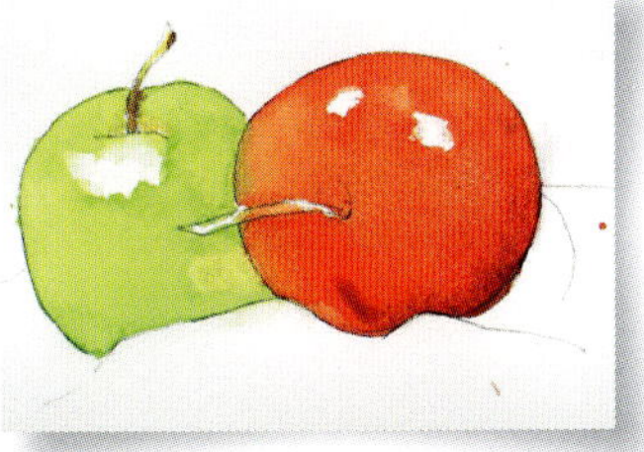

Overworked piece
If painted on thick, heavy paper, an overworked piece can be washed away and repainted.

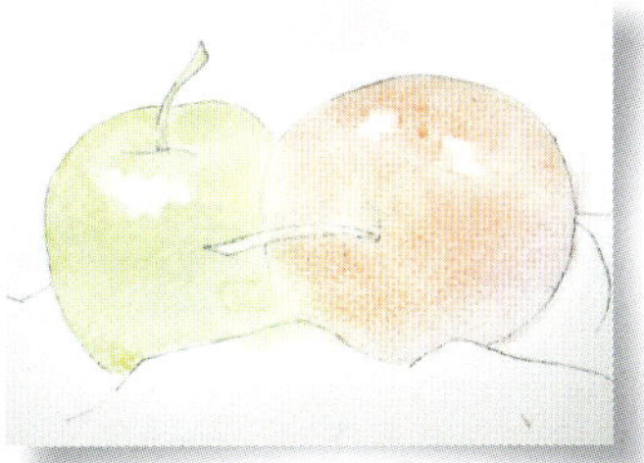

Washing off
Gently wash the colour away with a brush under running water to leave a "ghost".

Artist **Julia Trickey**
Title **Fading Hydrangea Study**
Paper **28 x 45cm (11 x 17½in) hot-pressed watercolour paper 640gsm (300lb)**

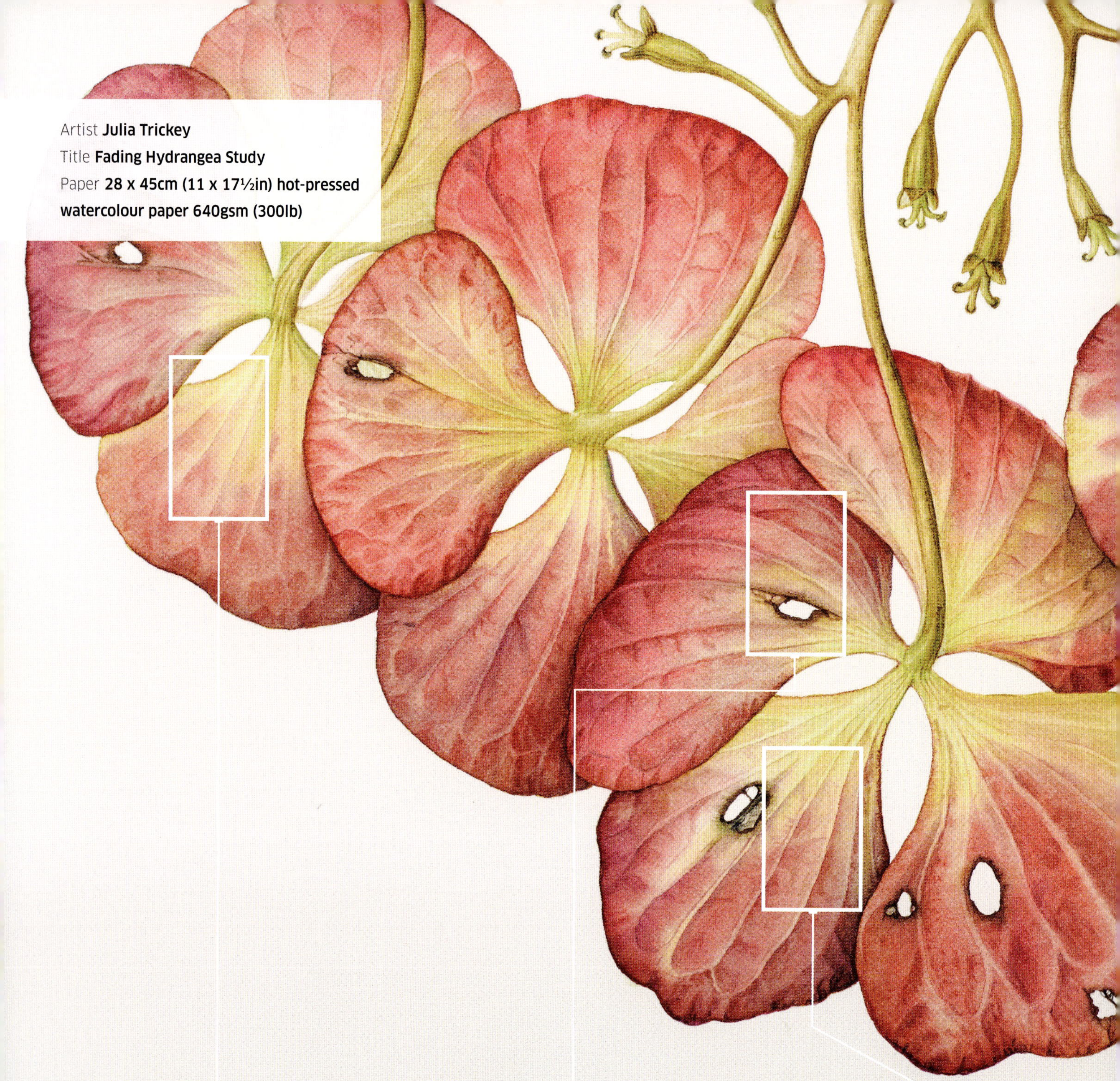

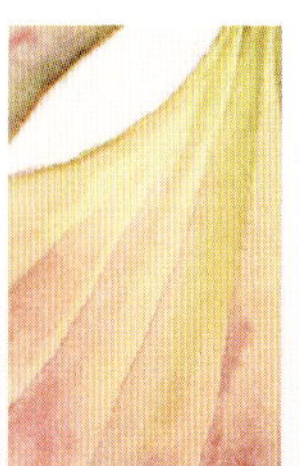

Wet-on-dry

<< See pp.50–51

Pale green was painted over the whole of each petal, then left to dry completely, creating a background on to which subsequent colours were built.

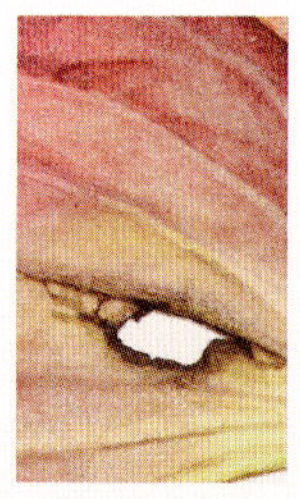

Using masking fluid

>> See pp.100–101

Masking fluid was used for small flower stems and petal blemishes in order to lay down initial washes without having to work around these areas of precise detail.

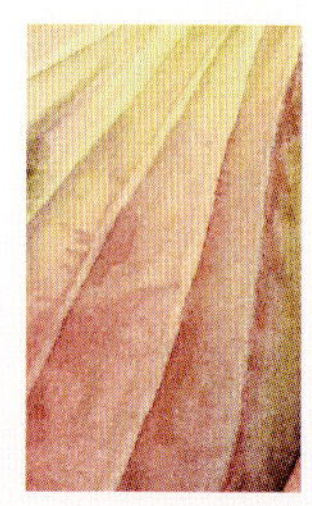

Lifting out

<< See pp.82–83

To create the veins on the petals, a slightly damp brush was gently agitated along the path of each vein, then blotted using paper towel or a cloth.

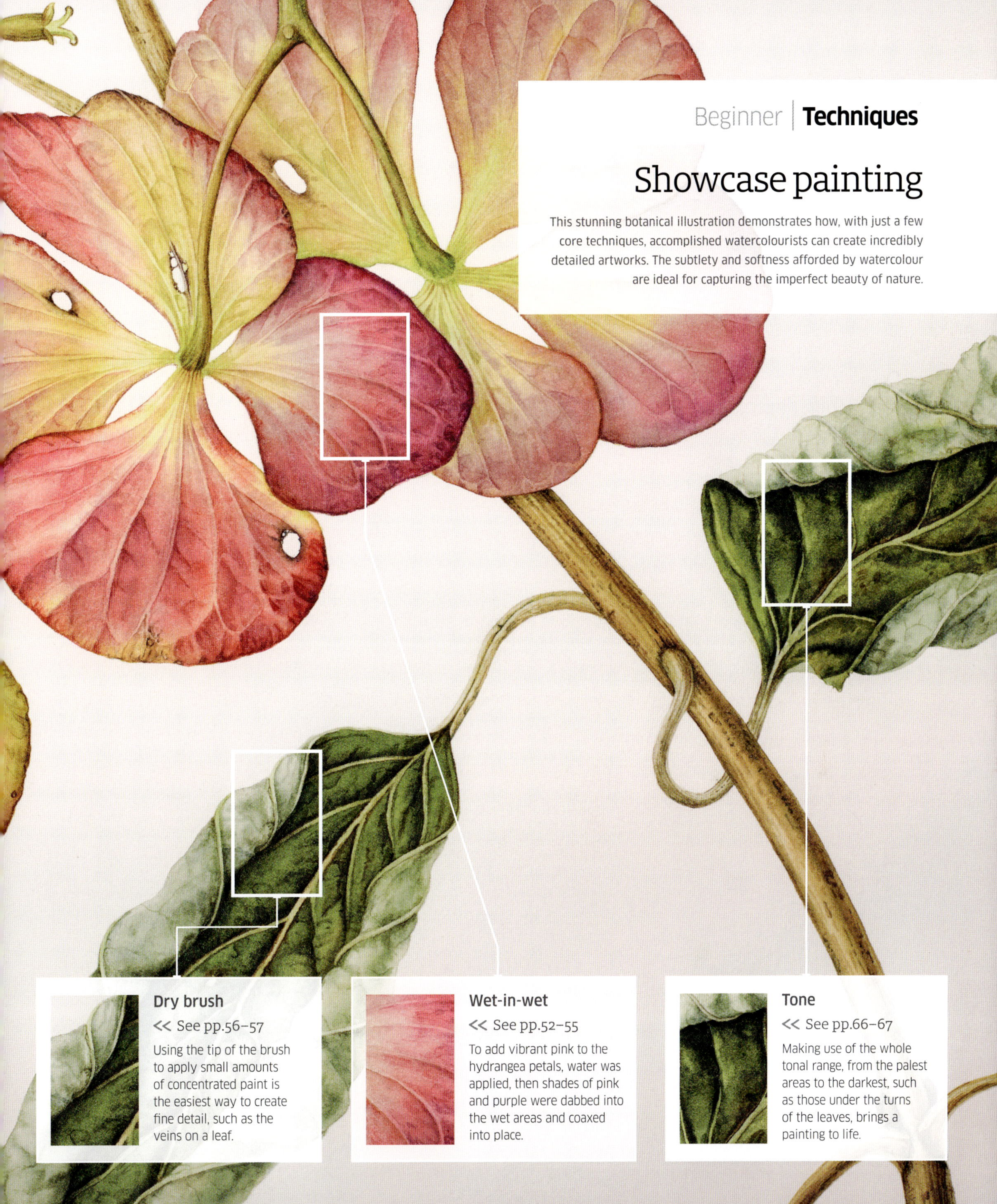

Showcase painting

This stunning botanical illustration demonstrates how, with just a few core techniques, accomplished watercolourists can create incredibly detailed artworks. The subtlety and softness afforded by watercolour are ideal for capturing the imperfect beauty of nature.

Dry brush
<< See pp.56–57

Using the tip of the brush to apply small amounts of concentrated paint is the easiest way to create fine detail, such as the veins on a leaf.

Wet-in-wet
<< See pp.52–55

To add vibrant pink to the hydrangea petals, water was applied, then shades of pink and purple were dabbed into the wet areas and coaxed into place.

Tone
<< See pp.66–67

Making use of the whole tonal range, from the palest areas to the darkest, such as those under the turns of the leaves, brings a painting to life.

Granulated wash

EFFECTS WITH GRAINY PIGMENT

When the pigments in your paint separate and clump together to create a speckled effect, this is called granulation. Choosing granulating colours for part or all of a painting can bring delicate textures, variety to washes, and overall interest.

■ Experimenting with granulation

There are many ways to encourage granulation. Use a rough paper that will hold the pigments in the surface, working flat on wet paper where you want the granulation to occur. Use granulation medium for a more intense effect or mimic it with salt crystals (see pp.148–49). Mix pigments in a separated wash (see pp.92–93) to extend the effects.

PUTTING IT INTO PRACTICE

With a palette that comprises nearly all granulation pigments, mixes of greys and strong darks are used to convey the dramas in this stormy view of Venice. Granulation medium is used for added texture in wet washes.

You will need

- White gouache
- Cinabrese
- Raw sienna
- Burnt sienna
- Burnt umber
- Caput mortuum violet
- Cerulean blue
- French ultramarine
- Viridian

- No. 10, no. 3, and no. 2 soft-hair round brushes
- Granulation medium
- 50 x 61cm (19½ x 24in) NOT watercolour paper 425gsm (200lb)

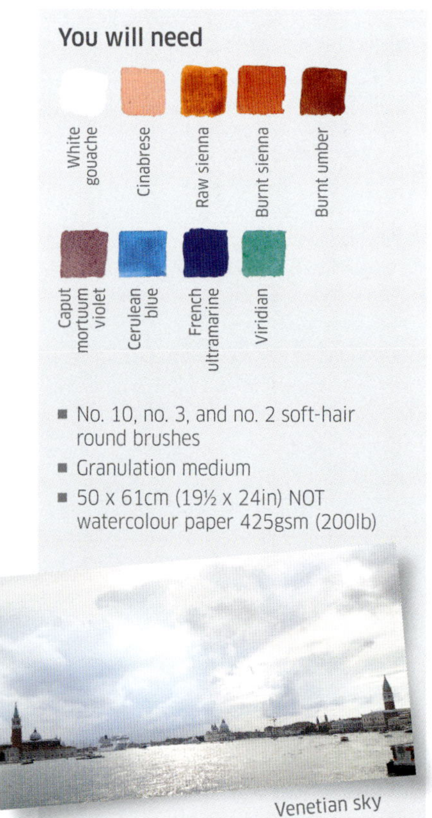

Venetian sky

1 Foundation wash
Apply a pale wash of cerulean blue and raw sienna to tint the paper and provide a transparent foundation with subtle texture. Cover the whole paper.

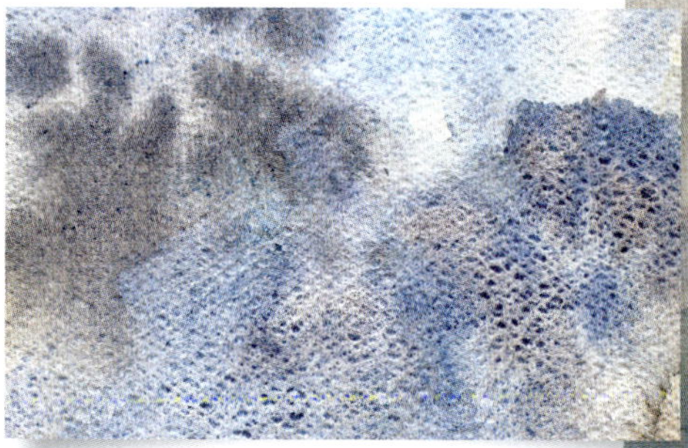

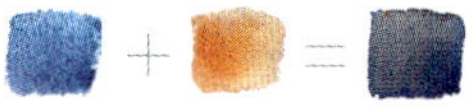

Cerulean blue + Burnt sienna = Granulated sky mix

2 Granulated sky
Apply blue and brown granulating pigments to the wet paper, mixing some washes with granulation medium instead of water, and allowing them to blend.

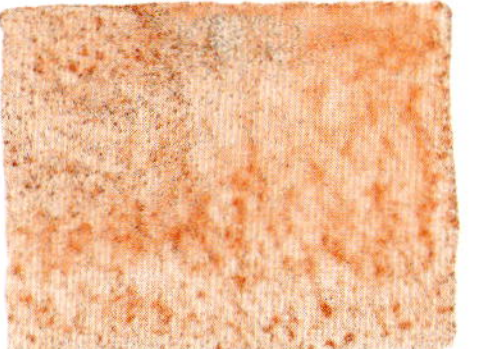

Light red

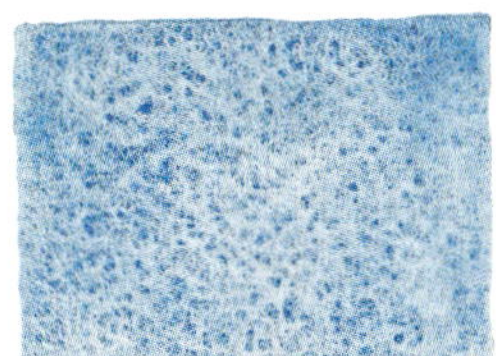

Cerulean blue

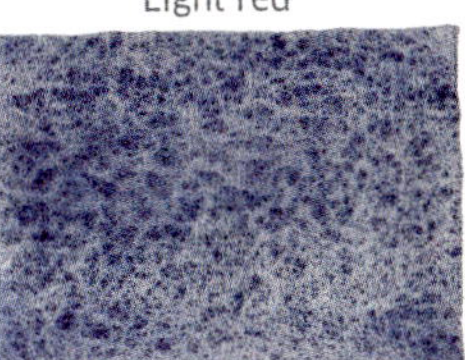

French ultramarine

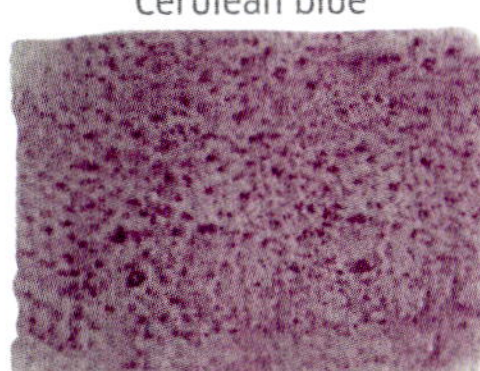

Violet with granulation medium

Natural and enhanced granulation

Wet paper helps naturally granulating pigments to separate and settle, leaving a grainy effect when dry. Add granulation medium for similar effects in smooth washes, or to enhance naturally granulating pigments.

Suitable granulating pigments

Not all colours granulate but the following pigments all produce natural granulation effects, either used alone or mixed together.

- Burnt sienna
- Burnt umber
- Cadmium red
- Cerulean blue
- Cinabrese
- Cobalt blue
- Cobalt violet
- French ultramarine
- Light red
- Pozzuoli earth
- Raw umber
- Rose madder genuine
- Terre verte
- Ultramarine violet
- Viridian

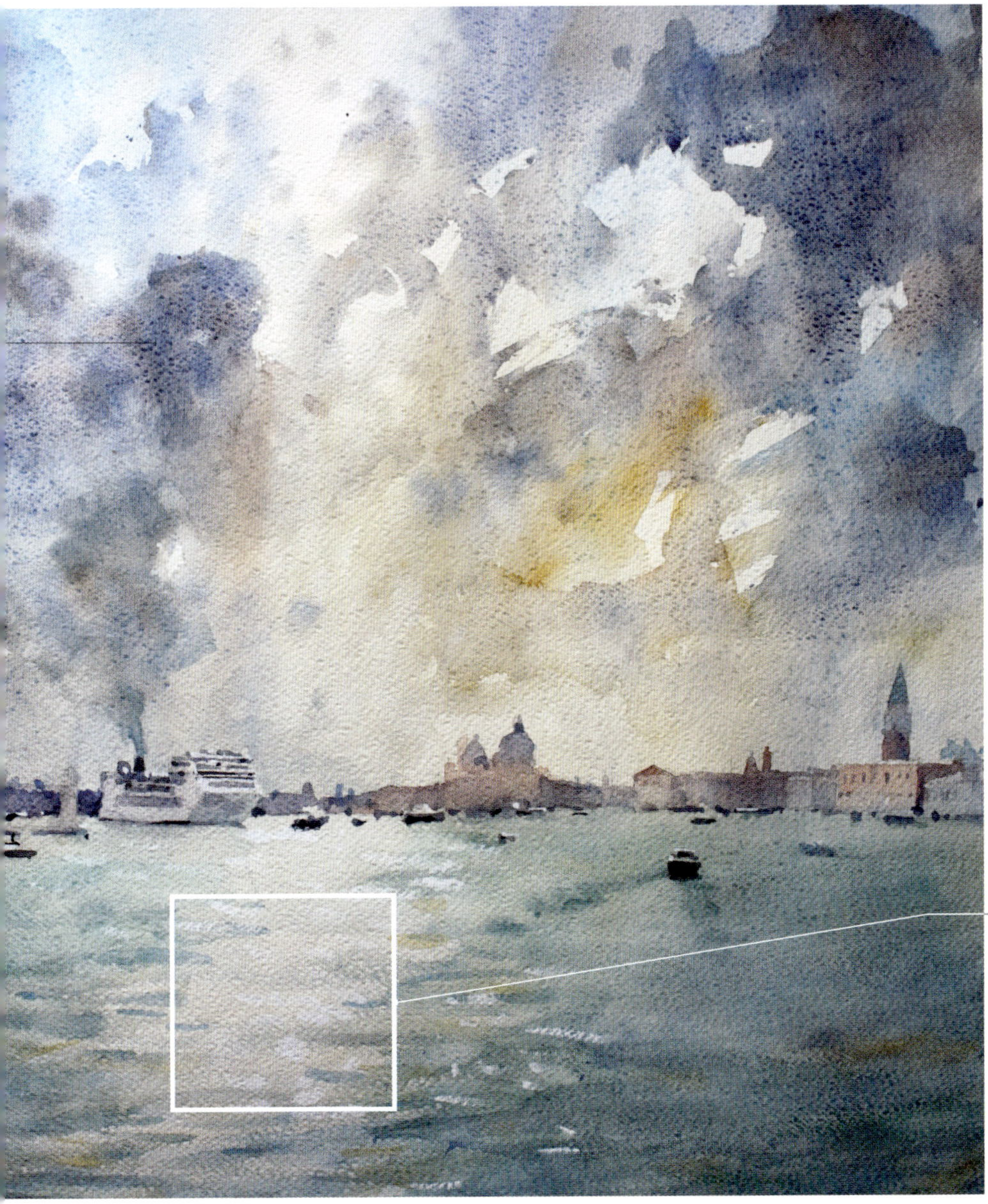

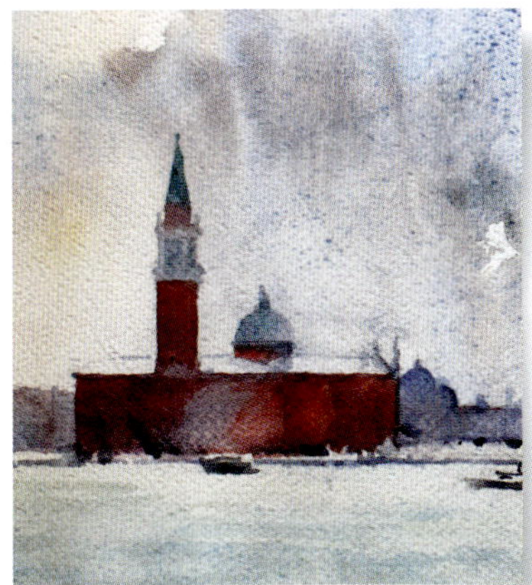

3 Architectural details

The buildings add a sense of scale and solid drama to contrast with the transient sky. Use dark mixes and granulated textures to make the façades stand out.

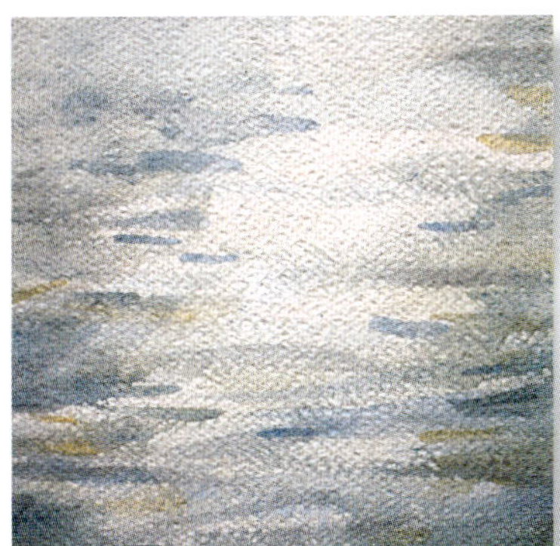

4 Final highlights

When the previous layers are dry, add finer details, such as the boats and stanchions, with a no. 2 brush and dark tints. Apply touches of thick white gouache at the end to give glittering highlights.

Separated wash

ENCOURAGING REACTIONS BETWEEN PIGMENTS

Properties of certain pigments react when mixed with others to create an effect known as a separated wash. The reactions vary, from a granulated texture to patterns caused by restricted bleeds. You can use these natural reactions to your advantage; they can be employed over large areas to create mottled effects for skies and water, or to suggest more detailed patterns such as animal markings or fabric designs.

■ Special effects

Knowing how certain colours behave (see Granulating, Repelling, and Separating Pigments pp.246–247) can enhance your painting, creating natural effects that you may otherwise struggle to achieve. Some pigments react by blocking and pushing other colours away; others leave grains of intense pigment that add random texture.

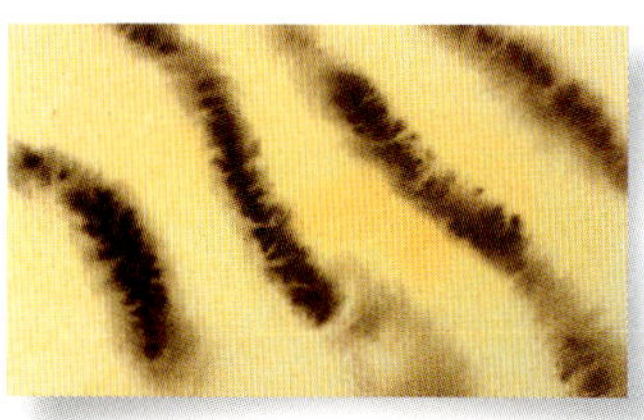

Restricting spread
This mix of opaque Naples yellow and cadmium orange has completely restricted the spread of the Van Dyke brown. The stripes are perfect for animal markings.

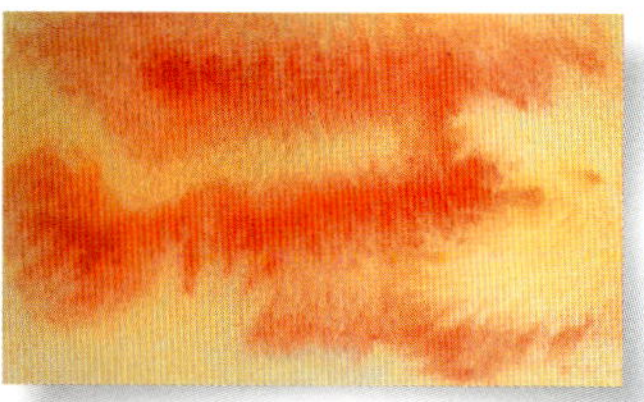

Feathered bleeds
On a wet Indian yellow wash the cadmium red struggles to fully merge. Indian yellow likes to run away and bleed. The resulting effect is useful for flowers and sunsets.

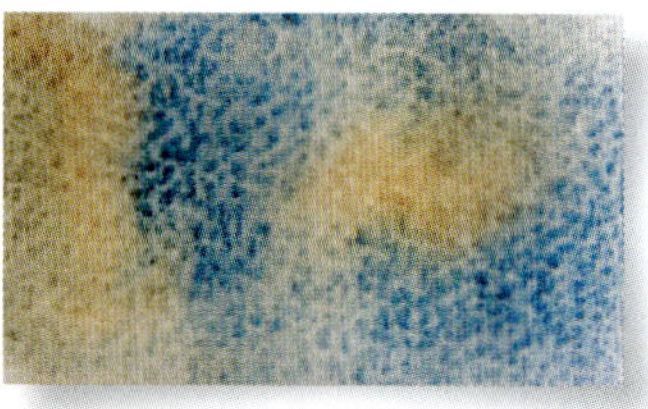

Rough texture
Cerulean and raw umber are both very granulating and don't like to spread evenly. When mixed they naturally separate, resulting in a textural effect that is useful for painting rock.

PUTTING IT INTO PRACTICE

Here, the granulating effects of the burnt sienna and French ultramarine produce an interesting sky with depth. The blocking properties of Naples yellow allow the wing markings to blend naturally.

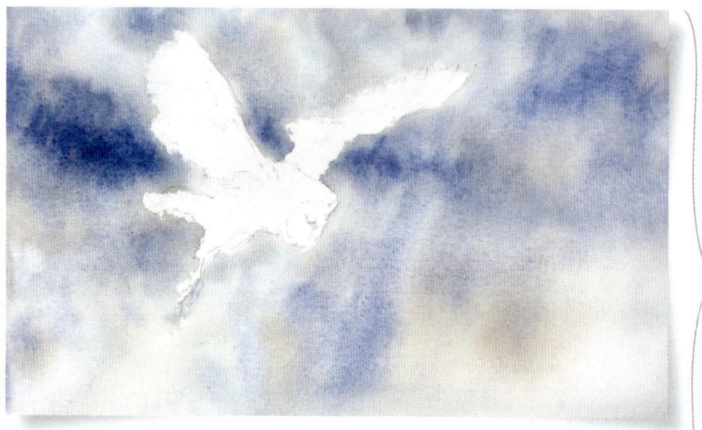

1 Granulated wash
Lay loose mixes of ultramarine and burnt sienna diagonally across the wetted paper to create a wet-in-wet background. Tilt the board at differing angles, so the colours merge naturally.

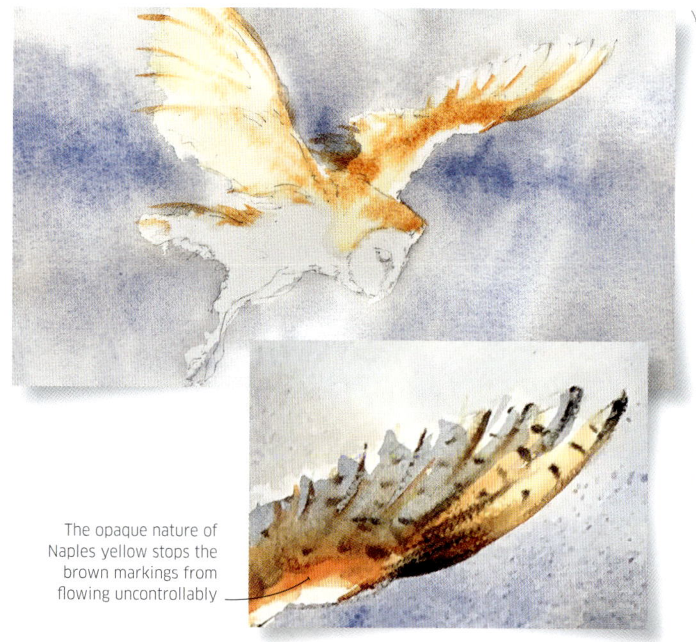

The opaque nature of Naples yellow stops the brown markings from flowing uncontrollably

2 Wet-in-wet glazes
When the background is dry, paint the owl with a wet-in-wet glaze of Naples yellow and raw sienna, taking the yellow out to the wing tips. Add the wing bars with a swift stroke in Van Dyke brown.

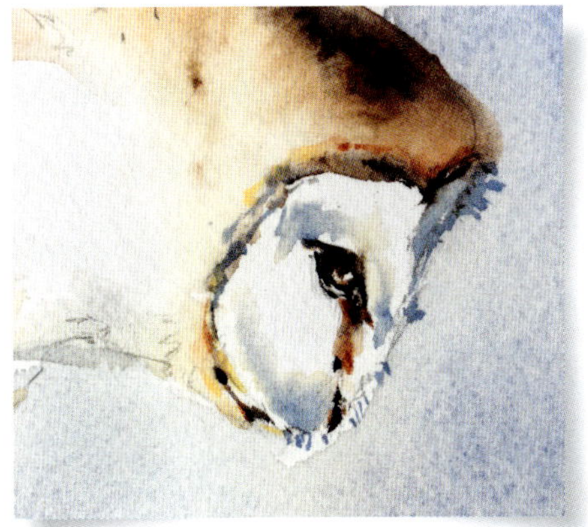

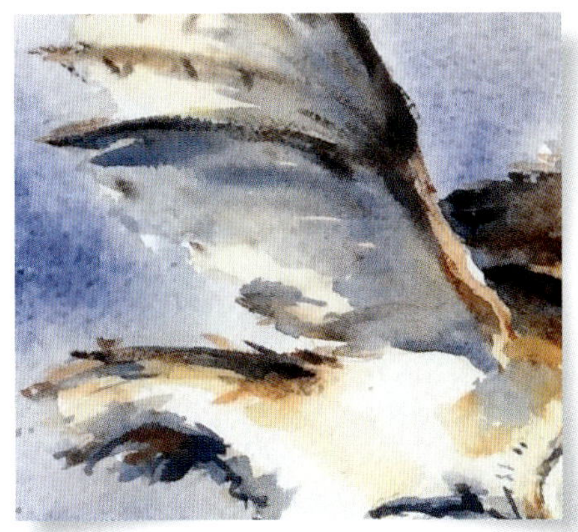

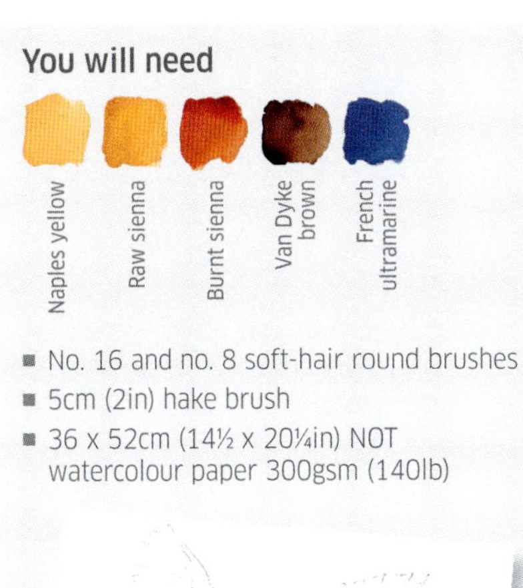

You will need

- Naples yellow
- Raw sienna
- Burnt sienna
- Van Dyke brown
- French ultramarine

- No. 16 and no. 8 soft-hair round brushes
- 5cm (2in) hake brush
- 36 x 52cm (14½ x 20¼in) NOT watercolour paper 300gsm (140lb)

Owl in flight

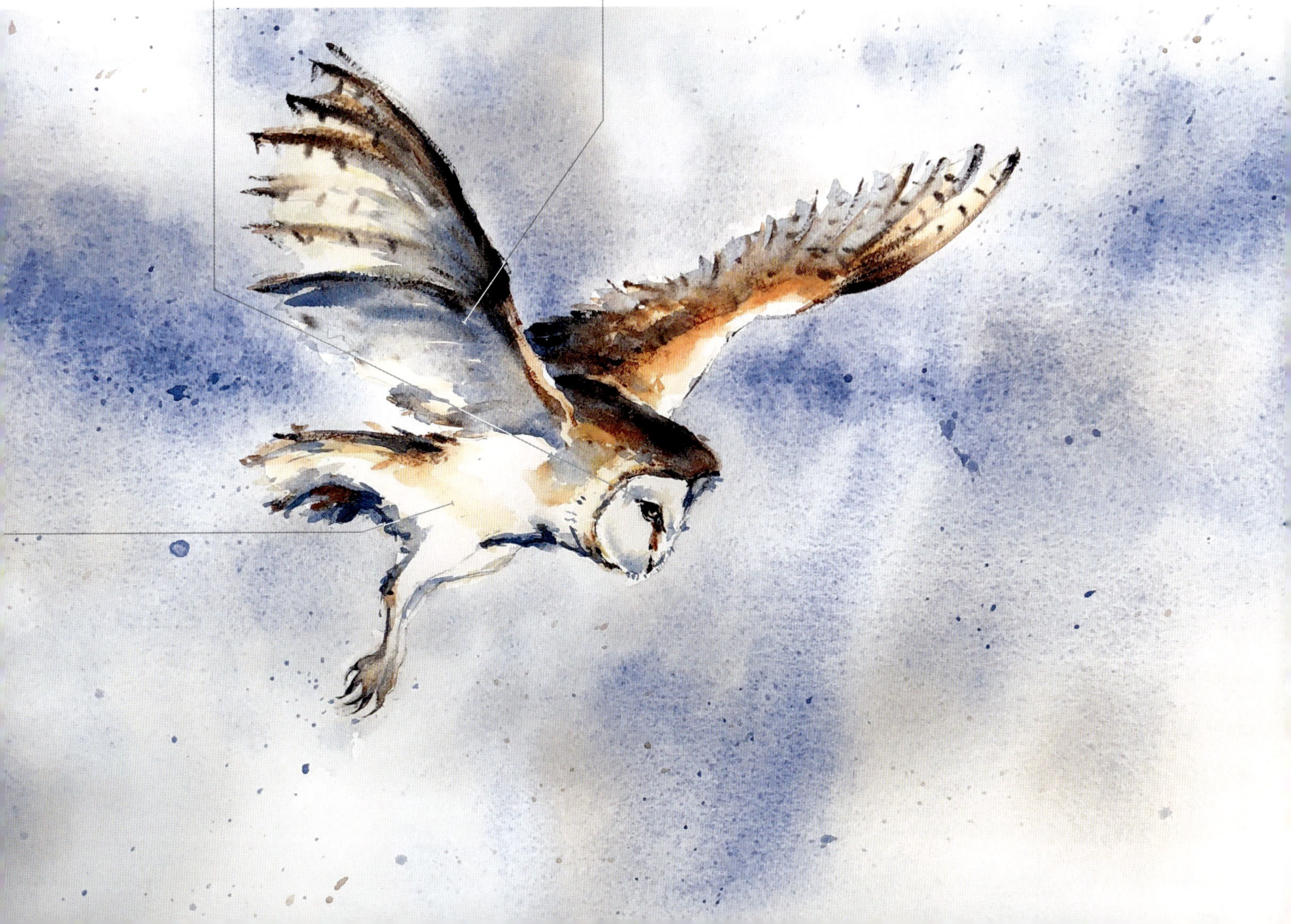

3 Face detail

Paint the eye, leaving a chink of paper unpainted for the highlight. Use the granulating properties of French ultramarine and burnt sienna with dry brushwork to add the feathered edge to the face.

4 Final shadows

Paint the shadow under the wings in a clear wash of ultramarine. Add Van Dyke brown to the blue wash to strengthen the shadow under the body and tail. Add splatter to the background for a sense of immediacy.

Softening edges

MAKING DECISIONS ABOUT EDGES

Any mark that is made by a brush has an edge, and it is the artist's choice what sort of edge that will be. Soft edges can be employed to suggest surfaces, indicate depth, and evoke atmosphere. Combining them with hard edges can help create focal areas and give a three-dimensional feel. Many subjects, including portraits (see right) and landscapes (see pp.96–97) benefit from the use of soft edges.

■ Manipulating the paint

The easiest way to soften edges in a watercolour is to brush clean water on the outer edge of the paint while it is still wet. This gives a fading-out effect, for example, where a shadow meets a highlight. Alternatively, you can blend the paint before it dries, moving it gently with a brush, or lay wet areas of paint adjacent to each other so that the edges merge.

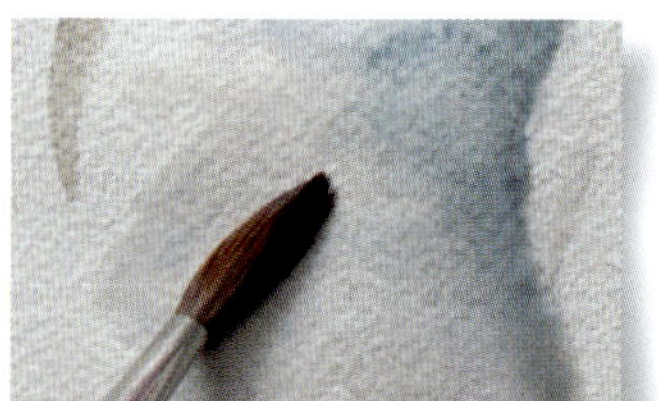

Wetting the edge
To achieve a gently fading soft edge, dip the brush in clean water and brush it over the edge before the paint has dried.

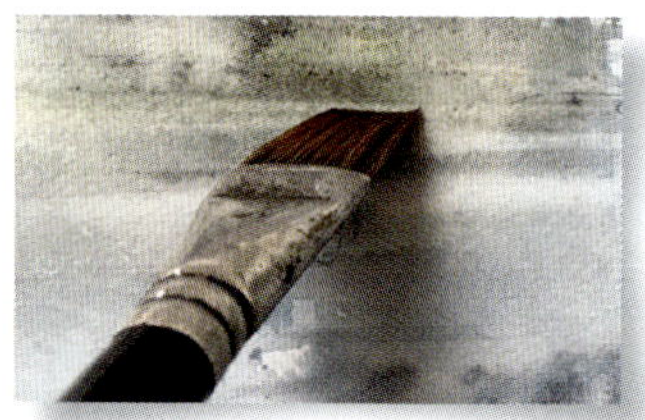

Blending when damp
With the first wash still damp, add a stronger mix so that the paint blends into the wash without losing its intensity.

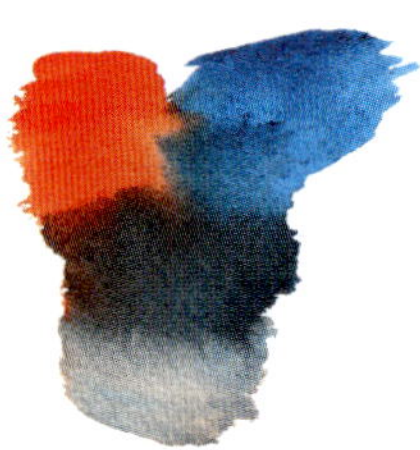

Wet-in-wet edges
Tilt the paper enough to allow the paint to run downwards. As it collects at the bottom of the paper, use a damp brush to soak up the paint so it avoids runbacks.

TEXTURE AND ATMOSPHERE

For this portrait of a sleeping child, the soft edges that are used not only convey the texture of hair, silk, and youthful skin, but they also suggest repose in peaceful surroundings.

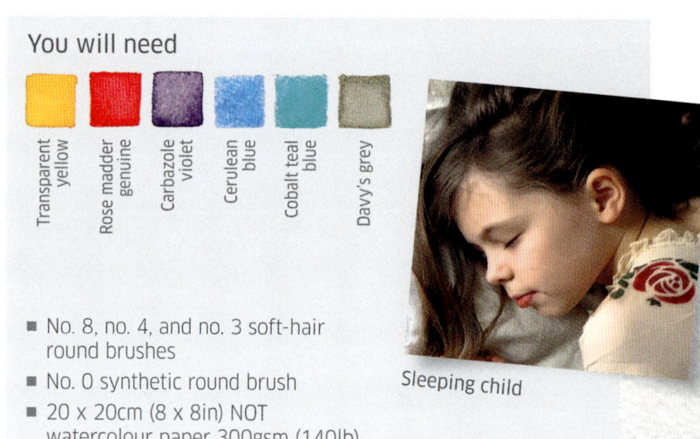

- No. 8, no. 4, and no. 3 soft-hair round brushes
- No. 0 synthetic round brush
- 20 x 20cm (8 x 8in) NOT watercolour paper 300gsm (140lb)

Sleeping child

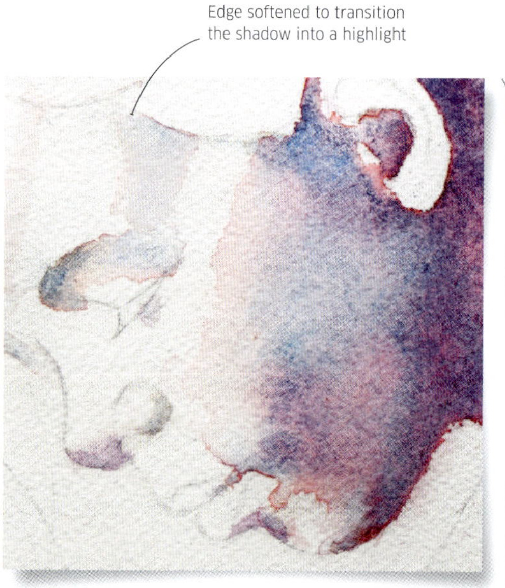

Edge softened to transition the shadow into a highlight

1 Soften tonal transitions
With the no. 8 brush, make mixes of rose, cerulean, and teal and lay in the shadow areas of the face. Apply clean water to the edge of your mix to soften the transition into the highlights.

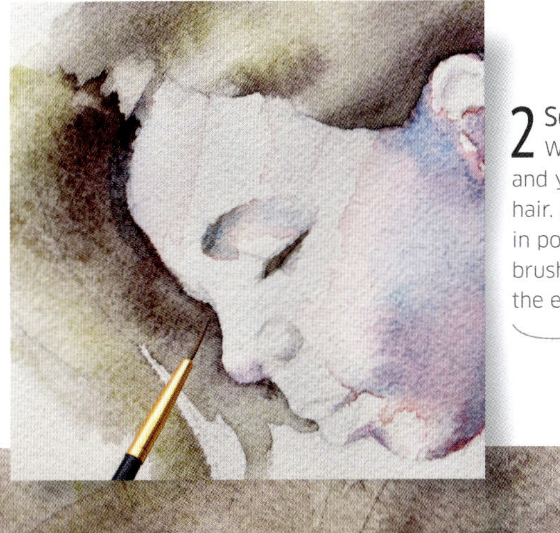

2 Soft edges for hair
With the same brush, mix violet and yellow for the eyelashes and hair. Apply it freely and confidently in pools on the paper. Use the no. 0 brush for the small areas such as the eyelashes. Paint the rose motif.

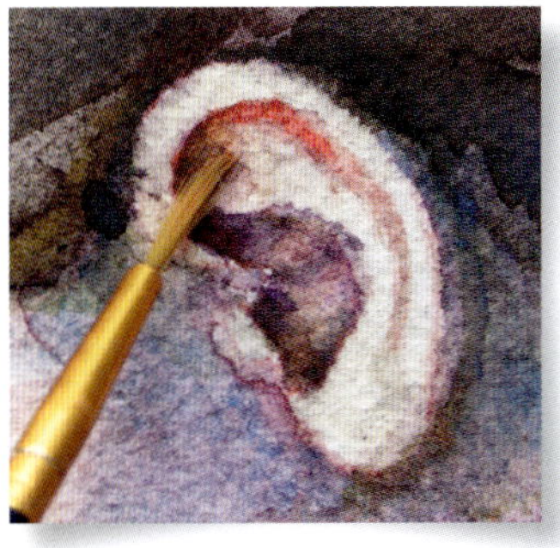

3 Refine the ear
With the no. 0 brush, add small amounts of the violet mixed with rose and cerulean to create more strength in the shadows of the ear.

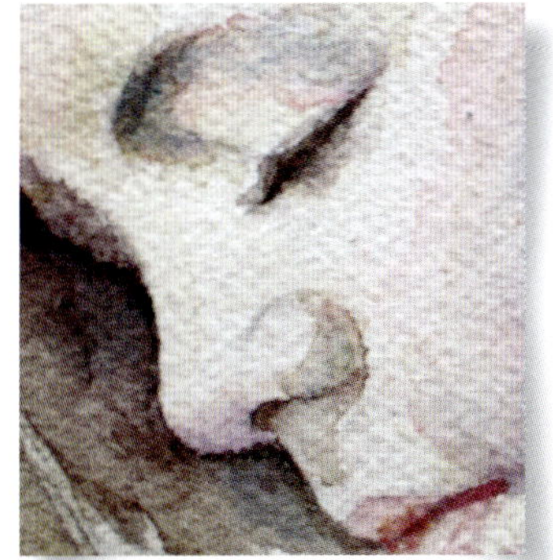

4 Strengthen the features
Use a violet and yellow mix for the shadows of nose and eyes. Mix rose and violet for the lips. Apply grey behind the shoulder.

5 The final touches
Apply a violet and yellow mix to darken sections of the hair. With the no. 0 brush, refine the features. To finish, mix rose and cerulean to emphasize the cheekbone.

ILLUSION AND MYSTERY

Softening edges creates an illusion of a scene rather than describing it, adding to the mystery of a painting. The most common occurrence in nature where edges are softened is reflections in water. Not surprisingly, watercolour is the best paint medium for capturing this quality. Keep your paper tilted at 45 degrees to allow the paint to flow.

You will need

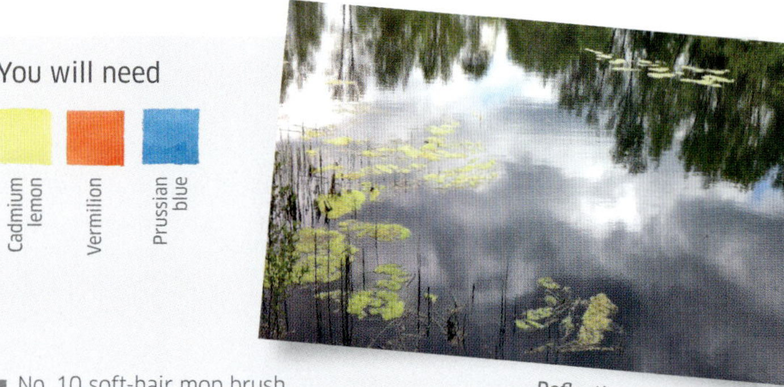

Cadmium lemon

Vermilion

Prussian blue

- No. 10 soft-hair mop brush
- No. 5 soft-hair round brush
- No. 10 synthetic flat brush
- Masking fluid and an old brush
- 28 x 38cm (11 x 15in) NOT watercolour paper 300gsm (140lb)

Reflections in water

1 Mask out white areas

Roughly draw the outline of the floating weeds then, with an old brush, use masking fluid to highlight these areas. Remember to make the weeds larger towards the foreground to add a sense of perspective (see pp.26–27).

2 Soften sky reflections

After wetting the paper, wash in mixes of Prussian blue and vermilion with the mop brush, leaving patches of white and blue to reflect the sky above. This wet-in-wet wash technique softens the sky and gives the painting a sense of drama.

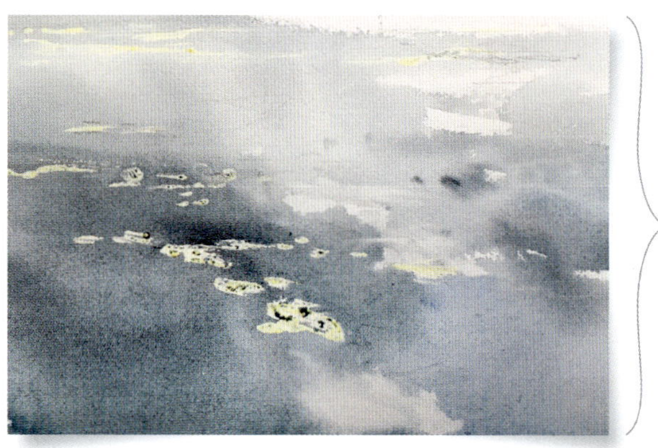

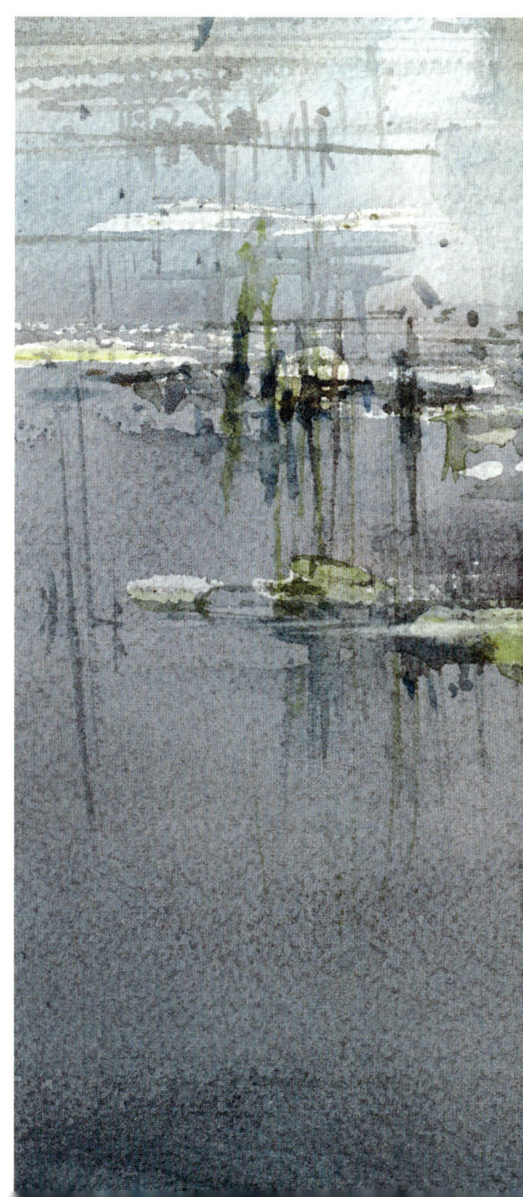

"Softened edges are perfect for **evoking reflections** in water, contrasted with **crisp details.**"

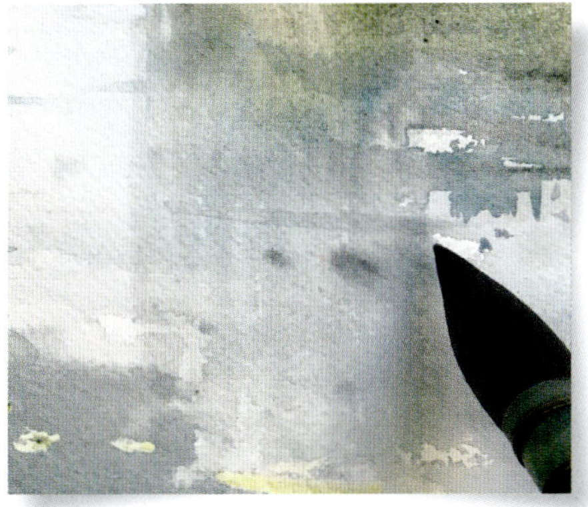

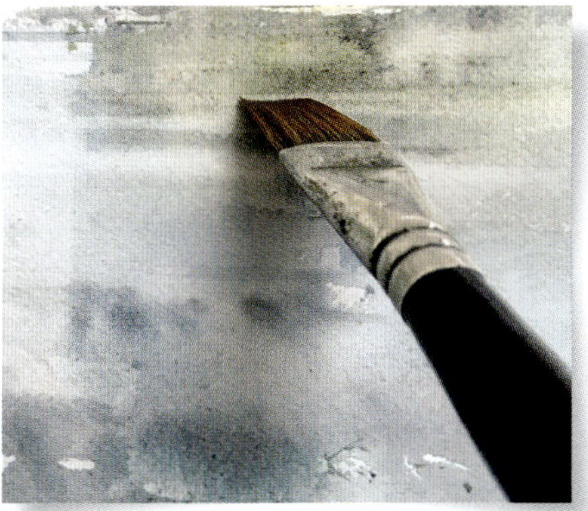

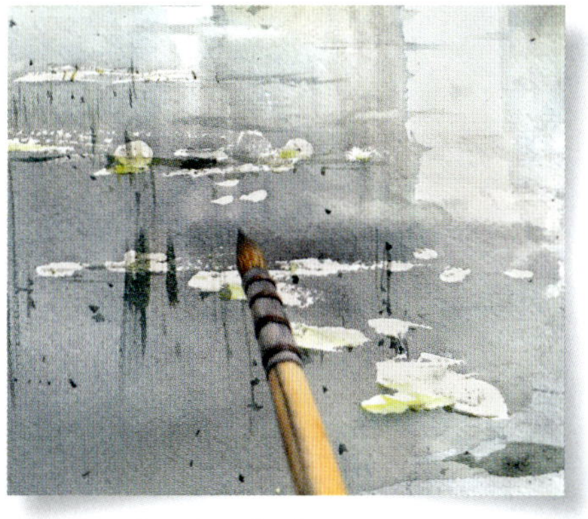

3 Allow the paint to run
To add distant trees and other reflections, wet the paper, holding it almost vertical, and mix in the same colours to run downwards. Touch up with a little of the lemon on the tree.

4 Soften the edges of ripples
While the paper is still a little wet, using a damp brush, slide across the reflections from left to right and over the untouched paper to give a soft edge to distant ripples.

5 Add crisp details for contrast
Remove the masking fluid when the paper is dry. Add the reeds and weed reflections with the no. 5 brush. Keep them crisp so they contrast with the softened background.

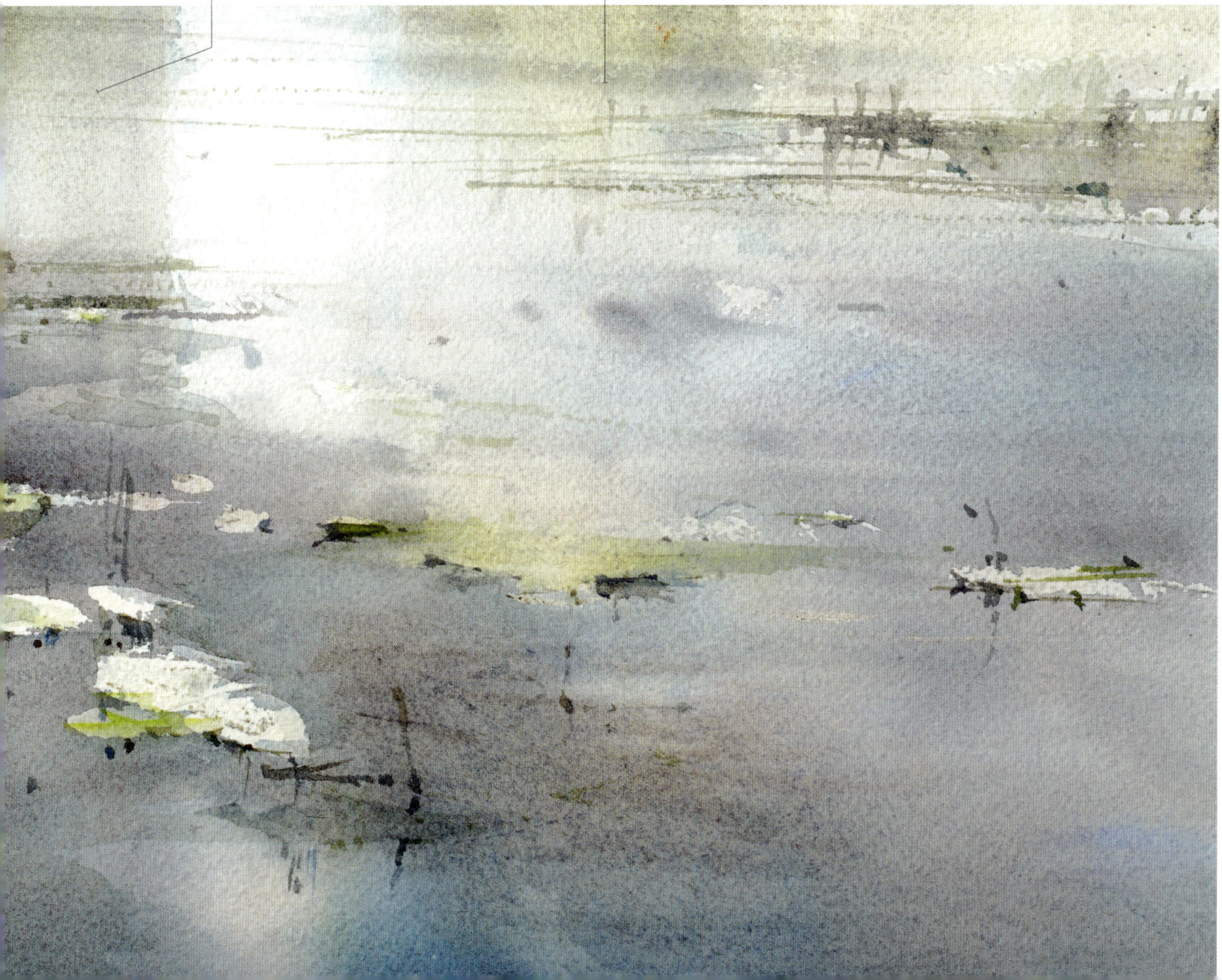

Splattering and spattering

USING SPOTS AND SPRAYS OF PAINT

Splattering and spattering techniques create interesting background textures, and can also represent gravel, sand, stonework, falling snow, and splashes of water or rain.

Splatter and spatter techniques

Loading a round brush and tapping the handle creates splatters, or large spots of paint. A toothbrush will create spatter, or small speckles. Spraying onto wet or dry paper produces different effects.

PUTTING IT INTO PRACTICE

In this painting of Chinese lanterns, the background is tied in with the main subject by using sprays of paint in similar colours. They are more defined where the paper is dry and softer where it is still wet.

You will need

- Transparent pyrrol orange
- Aureolin
- Raw sienna
- Moonglow
- Burnt umber

- No. 8 soft-hair liner brush
- No. 1 soft-hair rigger brush
- Old toothbrush
- Paper towel or tissue
- 38 x 28cm (15 x 11in) rough watercolour paper 300gsm (140lb)

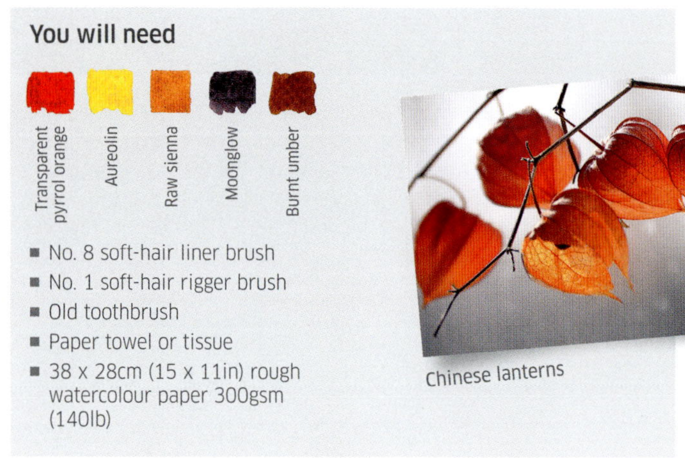
Chinese lanterns

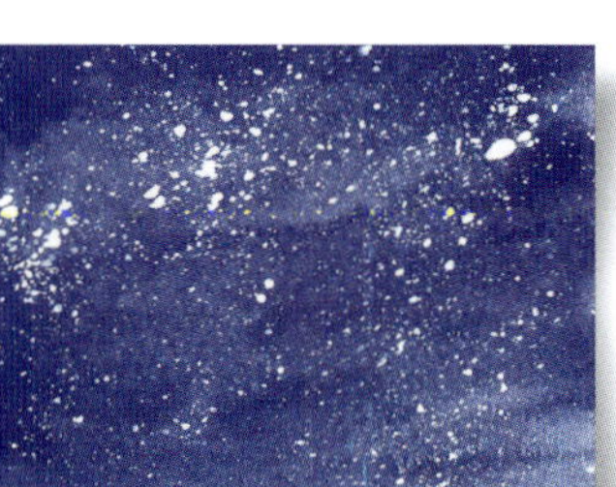

Spattering on dry paper
Pull the bristles of a toothbrush backwards with your thumb to create a fine mist of paint.

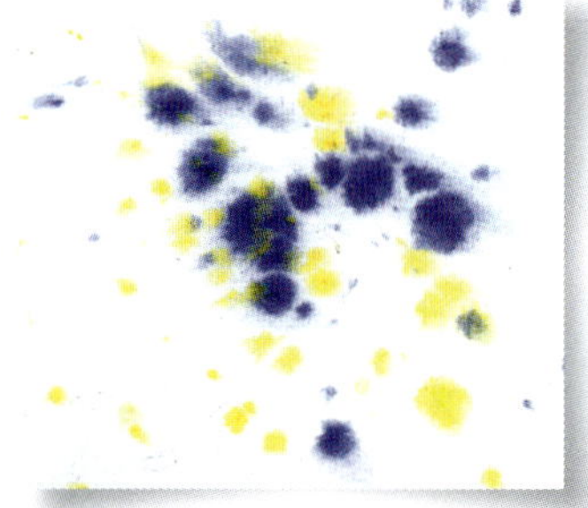

Splattering on wet paper
Splatter or spatter on wet paper for a softer effect, using either a toothbrush or a paintbrush.

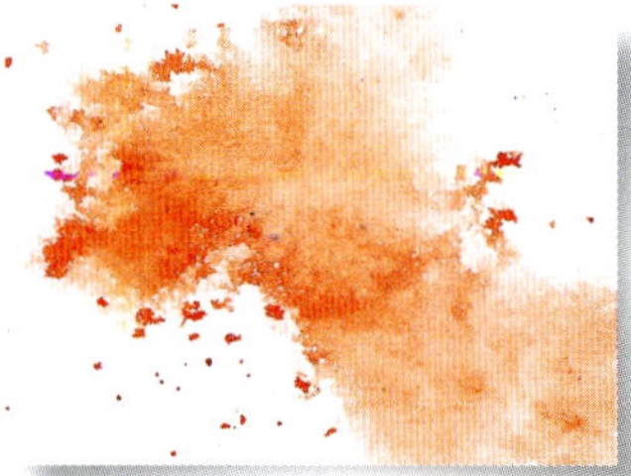

Spatter with white gouache
Using a toothbrush, spatter white gouache onto a background wash to represent falling snow.

Splatter and spritz
Spritz areas of splattering with water from a spray bottle to give random diffuse effects.

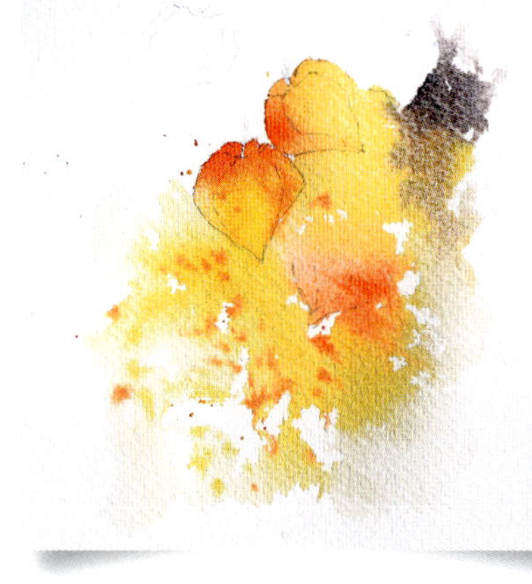

1 First washes
Sketch the main lanterns. Mix four separate washes of orange, aureolin, moonglow, and sienna. Paint the central lanterns with dilute orange, varying with aureolin. Paint sienna in the background and allow the orange to run in. Add moonglow to the background top right, leaving the edges quite rough and ragged.

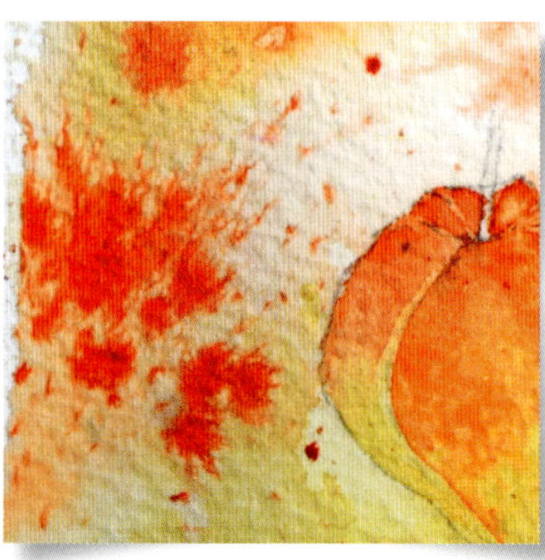

2 Add texture
Flick paint from your round brush into the wet background, or use a toothbrush if you prefer finer paint spots. Have some kitchen towel or tissue ready to blot if necessary. Keep adding more lanterns and background, progressing round the painting.

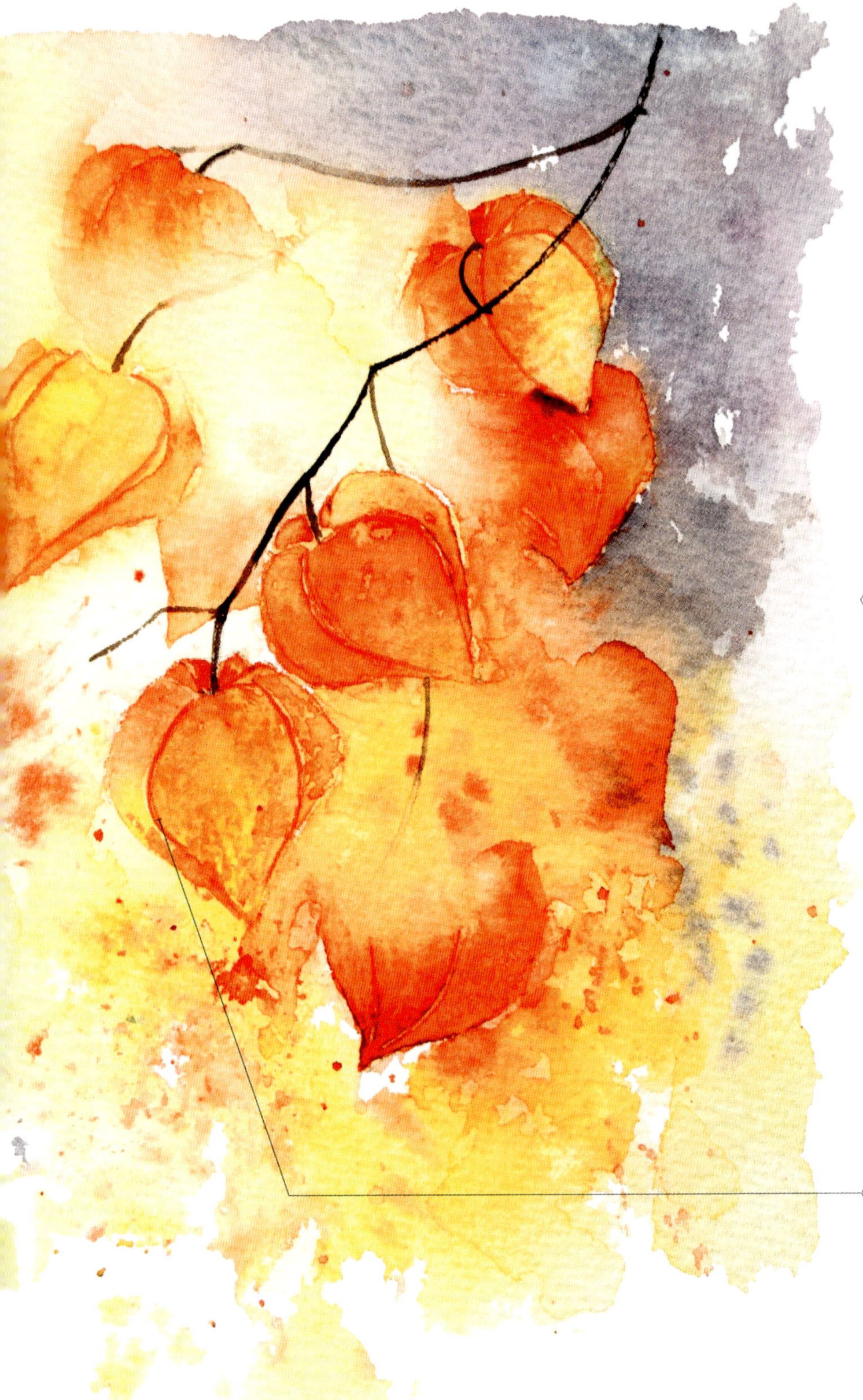

"Use splatters and spatters to suggest background textures."

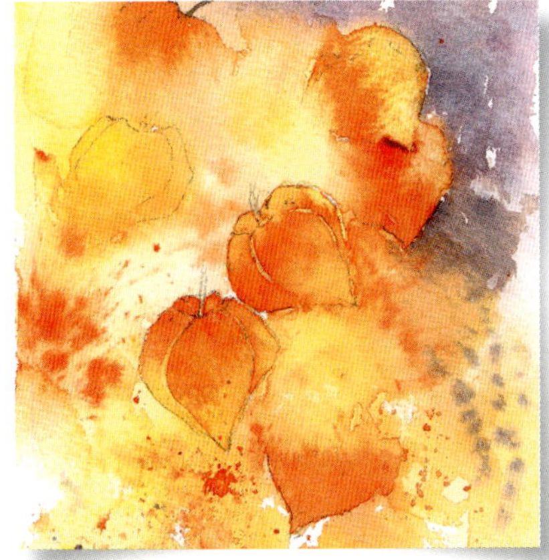

3 Build up layers

Continue to build up the layers, ensuring that you maintain a balance of light and darker tones, and a mix of diffuse and defined edges. Allow the paper to dry before adding the final details.

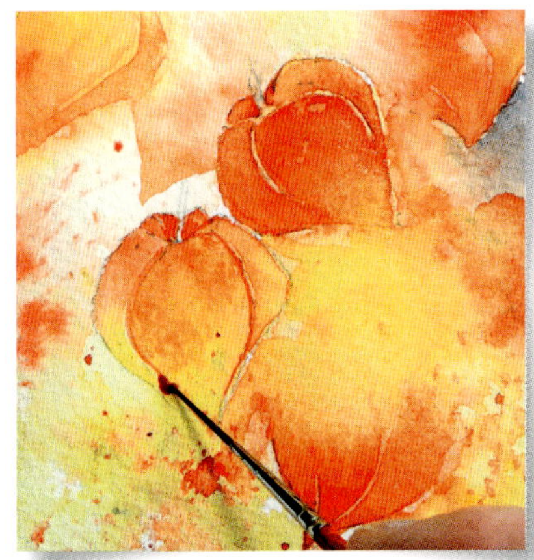

4 Finalize details

Using the rigger and a stronger mixture of orange, paint some ribs on the lanterns. Spatter a bit more orange on dry paint for fine textures. Mix a small amount of umber with moonglow and paint some fine stems.

Using masking fluid

PRESERVING WHITE AND LIGHT AREAS

Also known as liquid frisket, masking fluid is a water-based medium used to repel paint and preserve white or light areas on the paper. This technique is useful for creating small or complex details that would be too difficult to paint around. Masking off can produce unusual effects that would be impossible to do by hand with just a brush.

■ Working with masking fluid

You can paint freely with masking fluid, using it at the start to reserve the white paper beneath or to create highlights; or at later stages to preserve lighter colours when darker washes are laid on top. Always apply and remove the fluid when the paper is completely dry, to avoid damaging the surface.

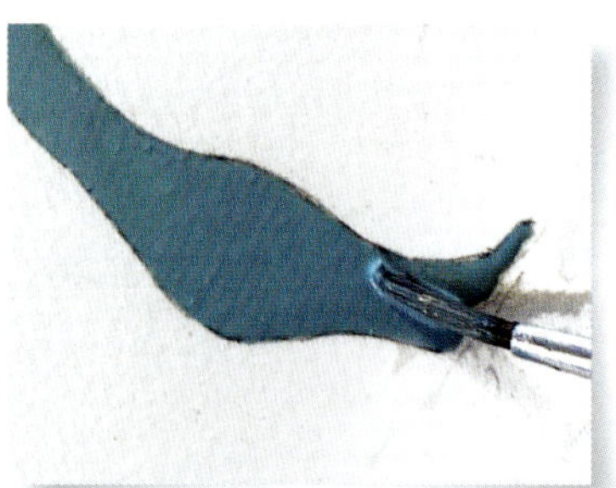

Using a brush
A brush gives you control when applying the fluid but as masking fluid can damage brushes, protect them by soaking first in a mix of one teaspoon liquid soap in a glass of water. Wash the brush immediately after use.

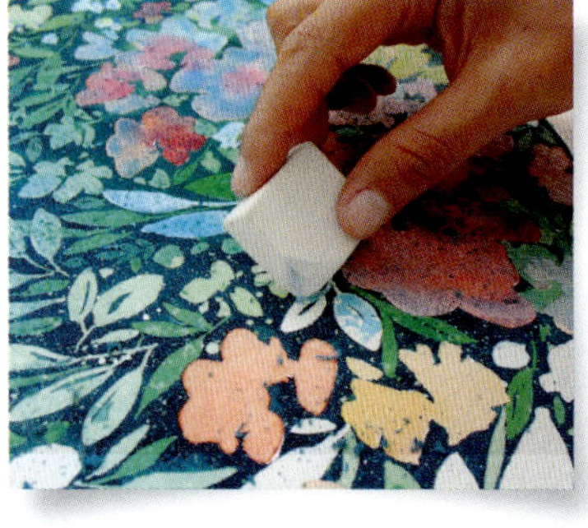

Removing masking fluid
When the paint is dry, blot any excess pigment on the masked areas to avoid transferring it to the white areas. Remove masking by rubbing with fingertips or an eraser for small areas, or with a stiff piece of cloth for large areas.

PUTTING IT INTO PRACTICE

Here, masking fluid is used to create complex layers and lots of texture. The masking fluid was painted on not only to preserve the white but also to maintain the colours of several layered washes.

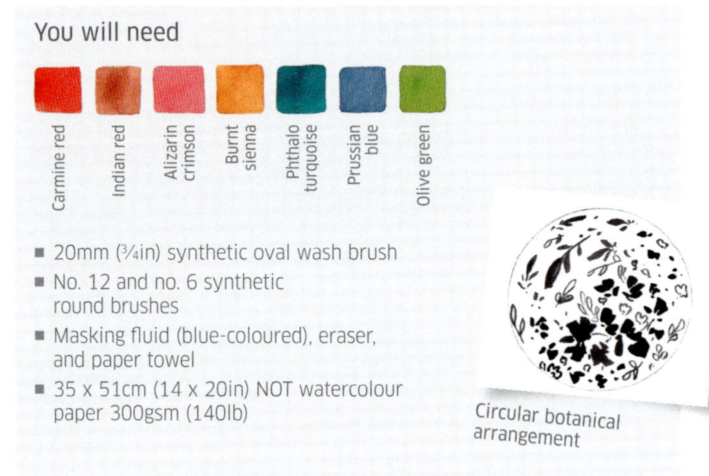

- 20mm (¾in) synthetic oval wash brush
- No. 12 and no. 6 synthetic round brushes
- Masking fluid (blue-coloured), eraser, and paper towel
- 35 x 51cm (14 x 20in) NOT watercolour paper 300gsm (140lb)

Circular botanical arrangement

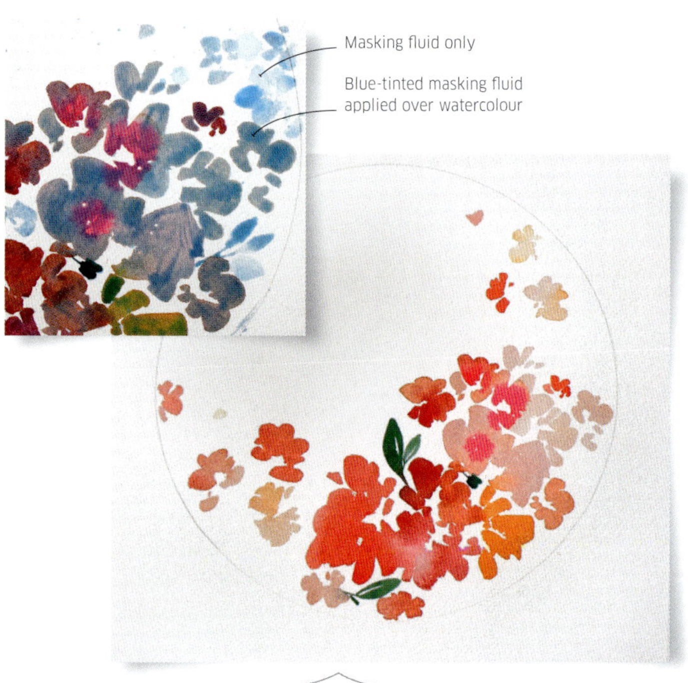

1 Paint masked shapes
Draw a circle in pencil and paint the shapes of loose flowers and leaves inside, varying wash strength from concentrated to transparent. When the layer is dry, paint over the shapes with masking fluid. Then, paint more flowers, shapes, and spatters using only masking fluid; these will be white in the finished painting.

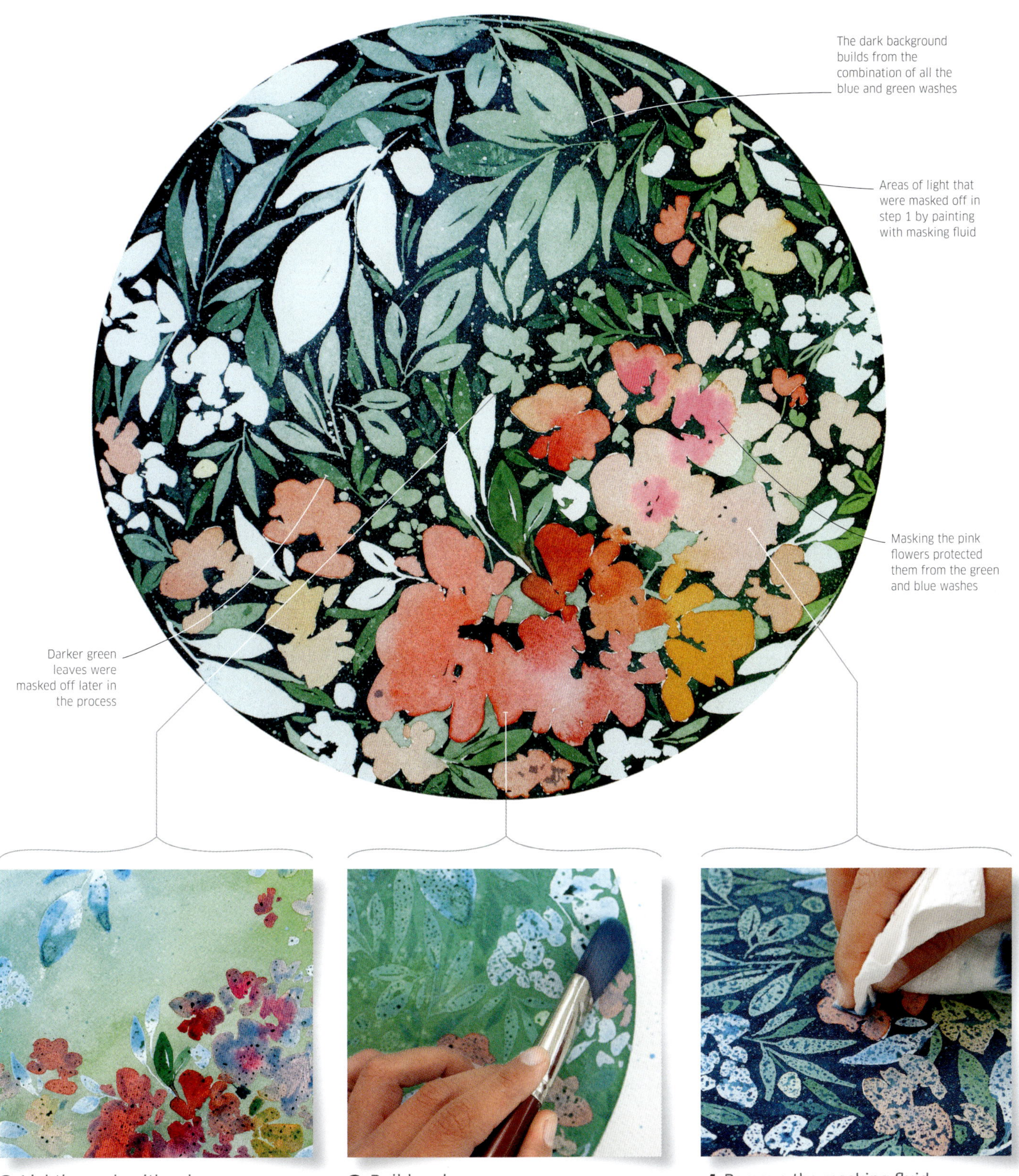

2 Lightly wash with colour
Once the fluid is dry, paint a light wash of blues and greens. When that layer is dry, paint another layer of masking fluid shapes.

3 Build up layers
Repeat step 2 for more layers of colour and masking fluid to preserve the lighter colours. The washes can be more saturated each time.

4 Remove the masking fluid
When the paper is totally dry, blot off the masked areas then peel off the masking fluid; it is easiest to start with a corner.

Using wax resist

ALTERNATIVE HIGHLIGHTS

Wax crayons, candles, and oil pastels can all add elements of colour and texture to your painting. Their water-resistant properties are useful for creating highlights over which you can paint uninterrupted washes.

■ Exploring wax effects

Watercolour and wax don't mix, so watercolour will only settle into the paper around your waxed marks. Unlike removable masking fluid, these marks are permanent and will become part of the painting. Experiment with different wax materials, from clear candle wax to crayons that give coloured and textured marks.

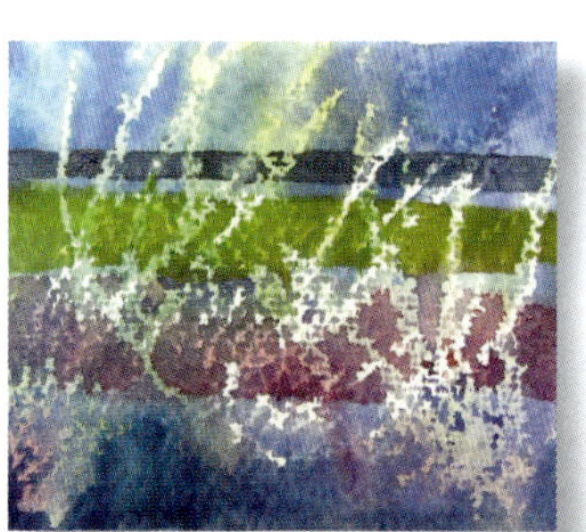

Applying candle wax
Candle wax is clear and preserves the layers beneath. Apply it before your first wash to retain any whites. When dry, add more candle marks to preserve the colour of your first wash under any subsequent washes applied freely on top.

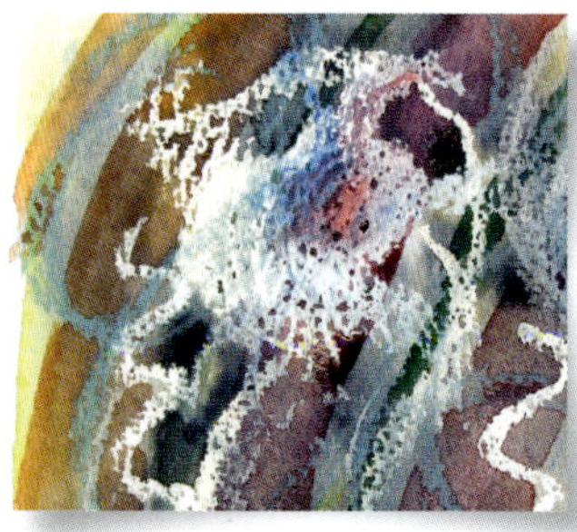

Applying oil pastel
Use coloured oil pastels or wax crayons to build textured and descriptive marks that will be visible through a transparent wash applied over the top.

Relief rubbing
Place lightweight paper over a textured surface, such as a plank of wood, and rub with the flat side of a candle. The texture will be visible through your wash.

PUTTING IT INTO PRACTICE

To create an effect of animation, a loose drawing with wax crayons and oil pastels captures the vibrant pose. Melted wax combined with disjointed small washes completes the vitality of the image.

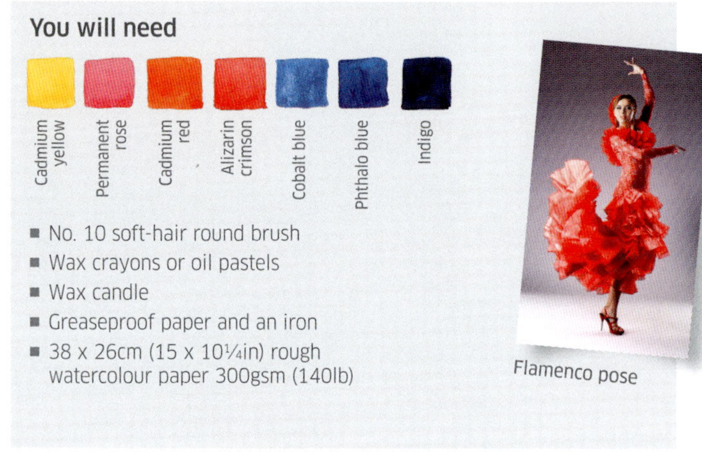

- No. 10 soft-hair round brush
- Wax crayons or oil pastels
- Wax candle
- Greaseproof paper and an iron
- 38 x 26cm (15 x 10¼in) rough watercolour paper 300gsm (140lb)

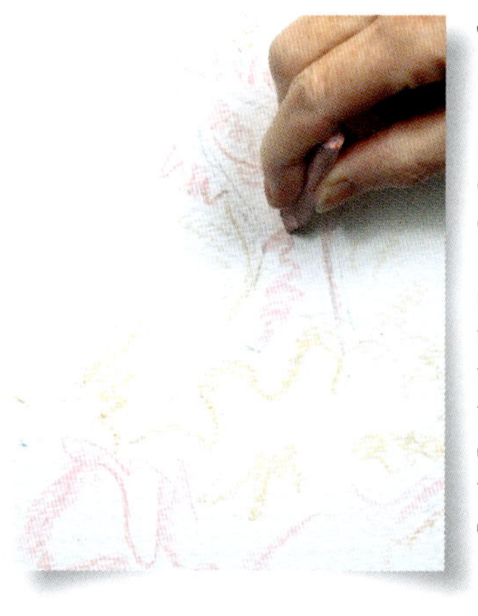

1 Wax marks
Draw over a light supporting pencil sketch with oil pastels and crayons. Make loose, expressive marks with both the sharp tip and the flat edge of the pastel or crayon to vary the thickness of your coloured strokes.

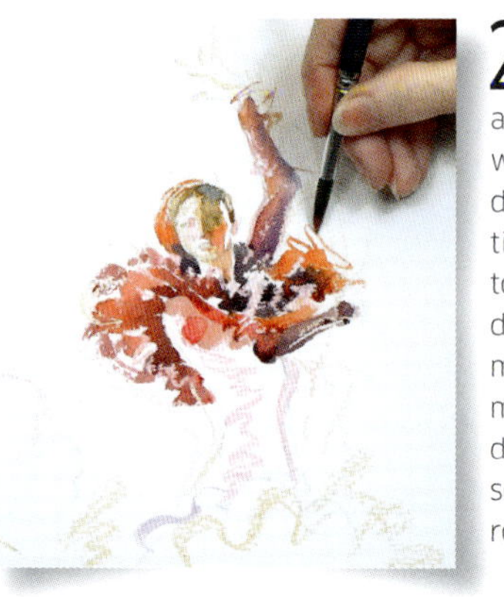

2 Fill colour
Apply small areas of disjointed washes wet-on-dry, using the tip of your brush to add more description and movement. Keep marks loosely described, with some gaps to retain vitality.

"Drawing with wax under a wash gives you freedom to be expressive and creative."

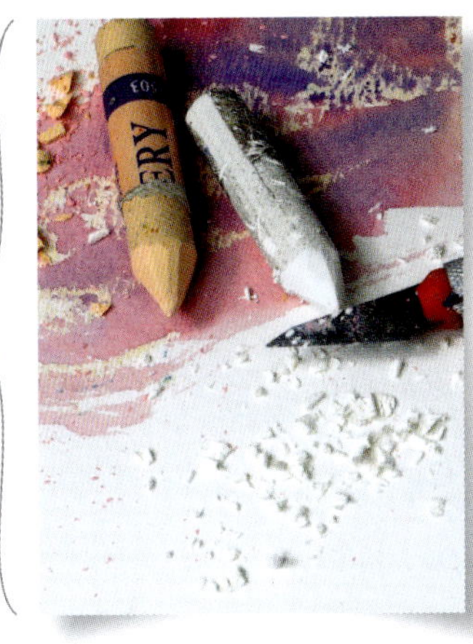

3 Wax shavings
When shaving oil pastels or wax crayons, keep the shavings to one side because they can be used to add texture and colour. Scatter these wax or oil shavings around the edge of the figure.

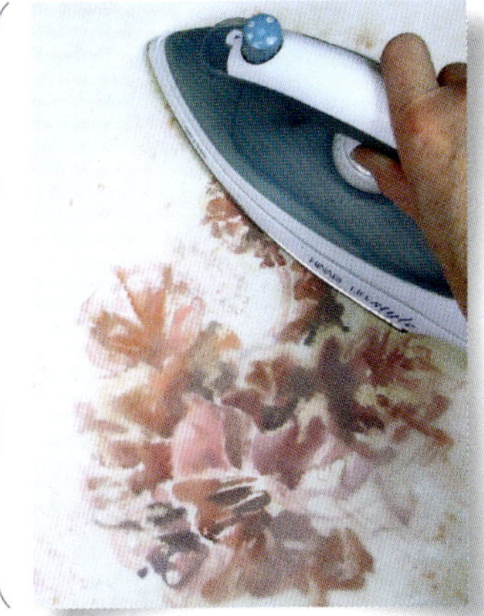

4 Melt wax
Place a sheet of greaseproof paper over the top of the painting. Apply a warm iron over the greaseproof paper until the shavings melt beneath and spread a little, depending on how thickly you cluster the shavings.

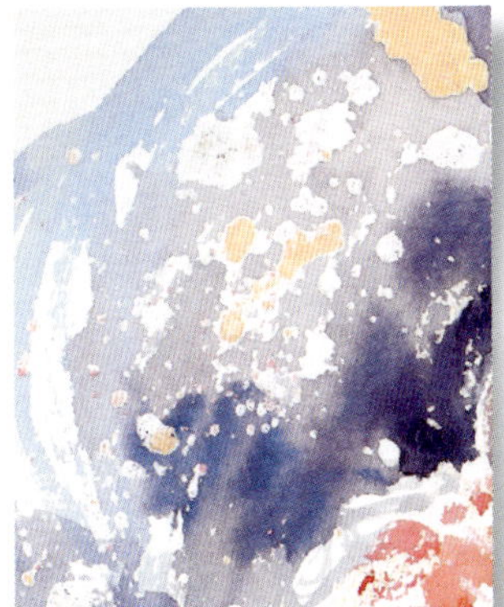

5 Overpaint wax
Peel back the greaseproof paper and remove; your splattered wax will now be firmly fixed. Apply a final darker background wash to expose any white or coloured wax you have melted. Paint loosely to keep the sense of animation.

Highlights

CREATING DRAMATIC LIGHT EFFECTS

When painting with watercolour, natural and dramatic light effects are usually best achieved by leaving areas of white paper untouched rather than adding white pigment. Working this way, light will reflect off the surface of the paper with greater luminosity. However, you can also use other techniques to create added light, texture, and movement.

Using white effectively

Painting around white space is the classic way of reserving the lightest areas you want in your painting, but you can also add highlights to areas where you have laid colour in order to bring more life and interesting texture to your work. Additional flicks of white can suggest the sparkle of light and reflections.

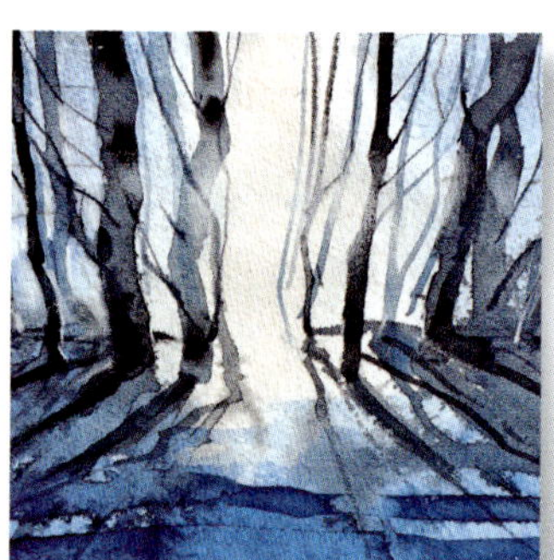

Reserving white paper
Leaving some areas of paper unpainted is a classic technique. It works best where edges are fractured or faded to give a natural effect rather than a harsh even line. Here the background trees appear bleached by strong light.

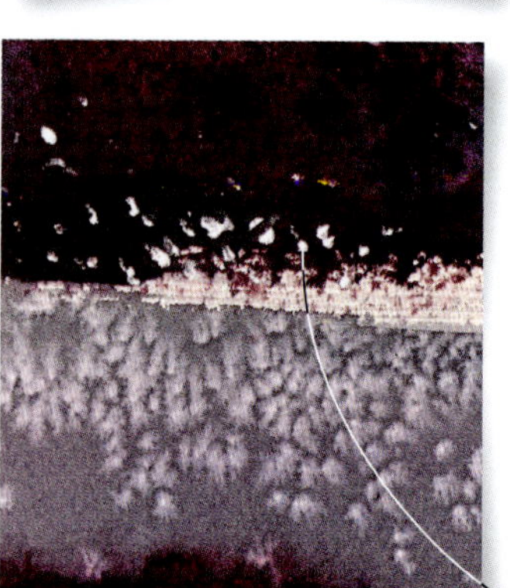

Watercolour pencil markings

Textural highlights
Scattering salt into wet paint gives small, diffuse highlights that are ideal for suggesting the play of light on the surface of water. A white watercolour pencil dipped in white watercolour ground provides a brighter, defined highlight.

PUTTING IT INTO PRACTICE

This painting has strong contrasts of tone between the dark land and the sea and sky, which are illuminated by the use of reserved white paper, added salt, and some touches of white ground.

You will need

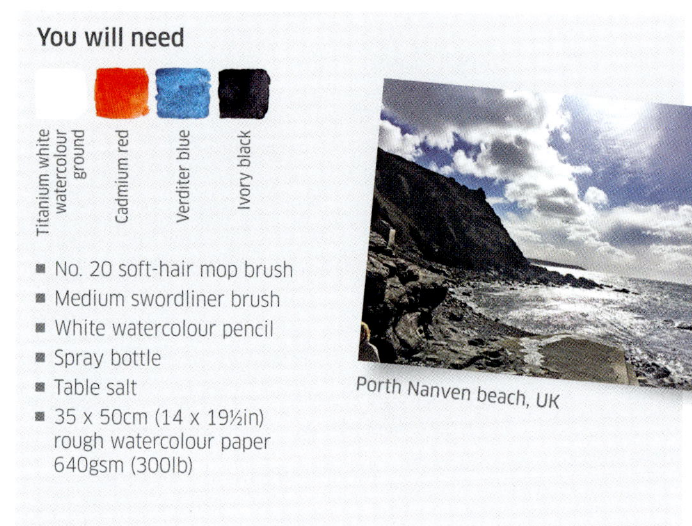

Porth Nanven beach, UK

- No. 20 soft-hair mop brush
- Medium swordliner brush
- White watercolour pencil
- Spray bottle
- Table salt
- 35 x 50cm (14 x 19½in) rough watercolour paper 640gsm (300lb)

1 Apply the first colour
Spray the paper all over with water, just enough to dampen it. Apply the blue loosely with a broad brush, leaving a larger area of white than you need, as the paint will spread.

2 Add dark and light
While the paint is wet, add some black. Dab with a damp paper towel to create softer effects, then make some quick strokes with fresh paper towel for bursts of light. Allow to dry.

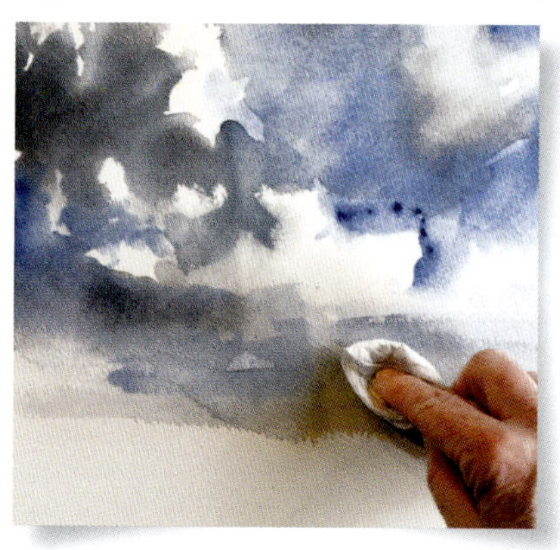

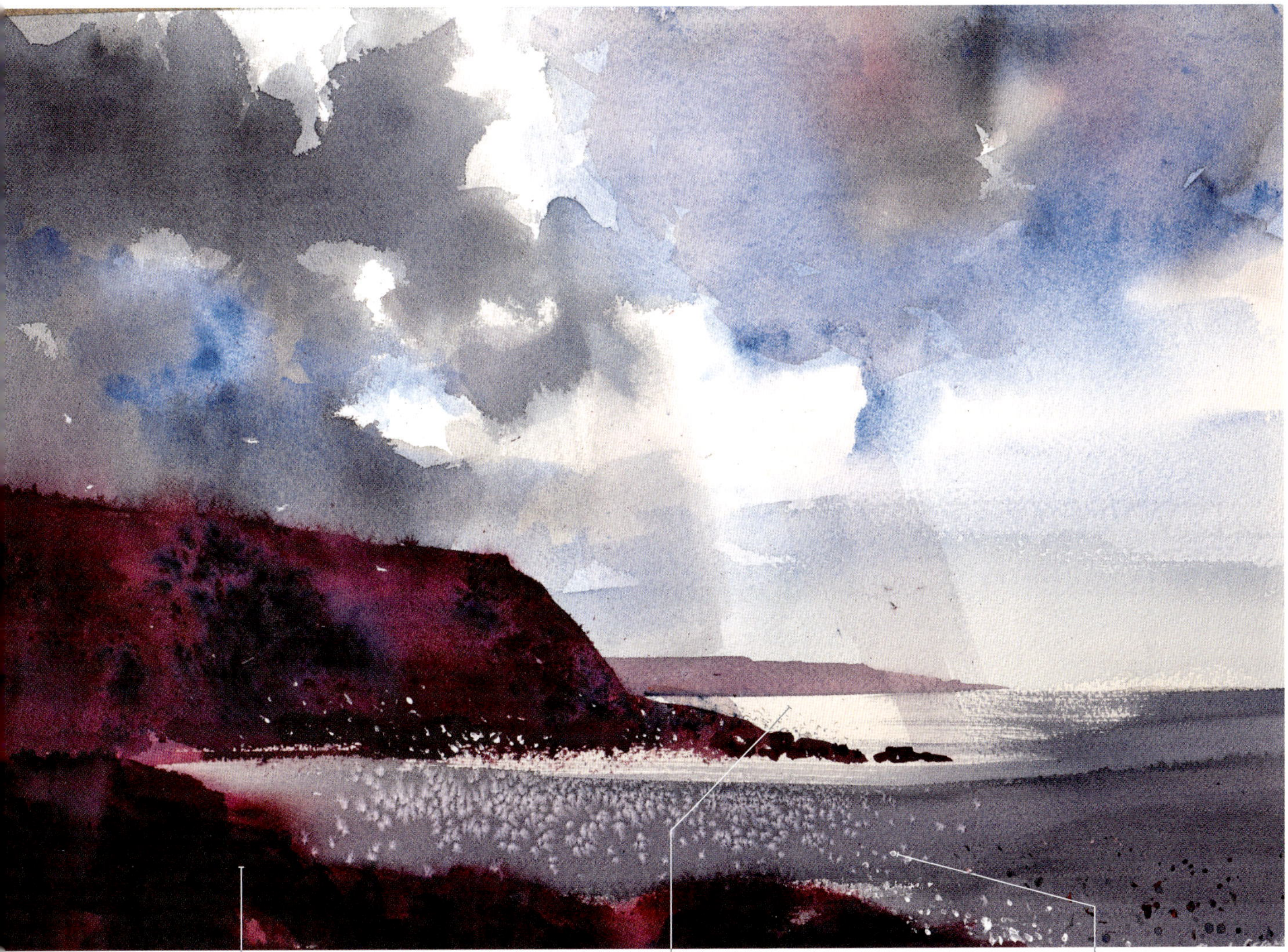

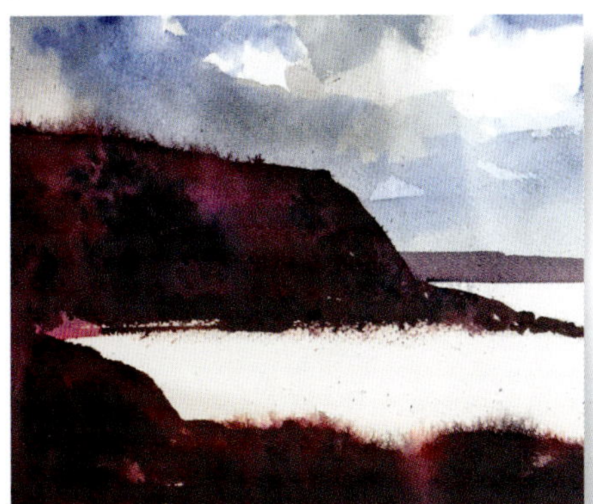

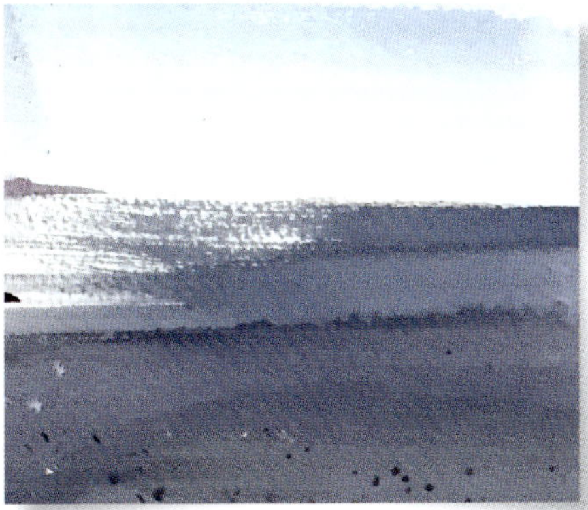

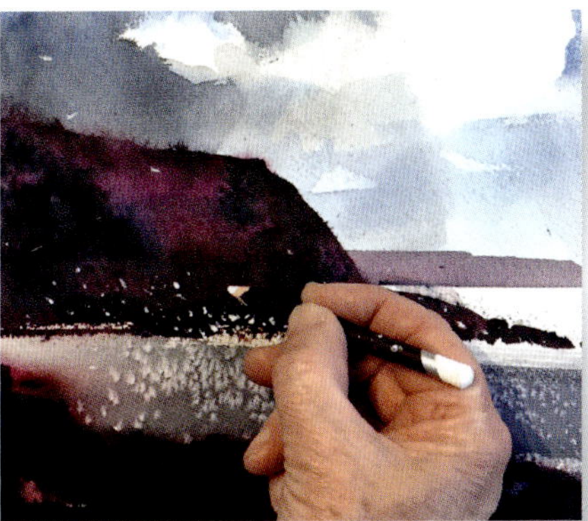

3 Add the land shapes
Paint a strong mix of blue and red on the cliffs. Dilute the mix and paint the far coast. As the dark areas begin to dry, spray lightly with water to add texture and soften edges.

4 Light on the water
Paint a wash of mixed blue and black, lifting off the brush to leave white paper where the light hits. Sprinkles of salt added to the wet paint will add a textured light effect.

5 Add highlight details
Once the paint has dried, dip a watercolour pencil into undiluted titanium white ground to add a suggestion of spray and birds in flight. These touches will add depth and movement.

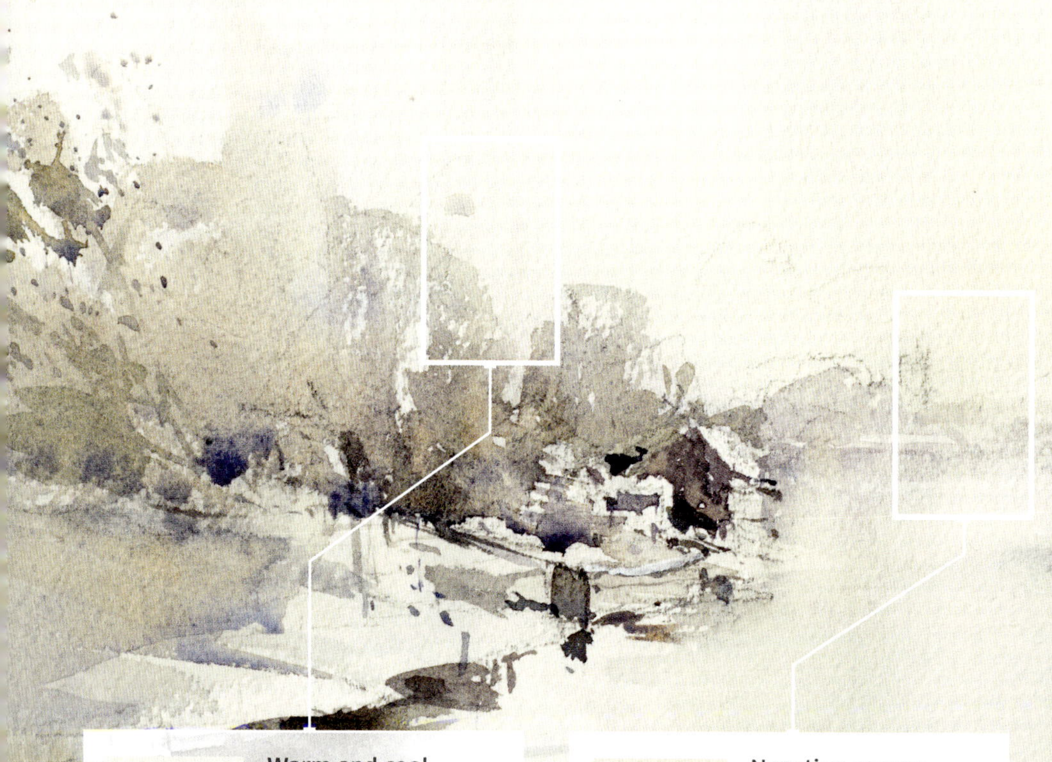

Artist **Chris Robinson**
Title **By the Thames at Old Isleworth**
Paper **38 x 56cm (15 x 22in) NOT**
watercolour paper 300gsm (140lb)

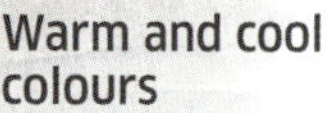

Warm and cool colours

>> See pp.120–21

Cool blues and brown greys are the predominant colours, offset only slightly by the warm red tiled roof and yellow morning light.

Negative spaces

>> See pp.114–15

The gap between the banks of the river is an area of visual interest and the focal point of the painting, allowing the viewer's gaze to drift into the distance.

Graduated wash

<< See pp.72–73

The reflections in the water are painted in a wash that starts at the hard edge of the quay; a spray bottle can be used to help the paint run down the paper.

Showcase painting

This moody, watery landscape combines a structured composition with loose, expressive techniques, capturing the dramatic interaction of nature and a semi-urban setting. Watercolour is the ideal medium to depict weightless clouds and glassy reflections in the river.

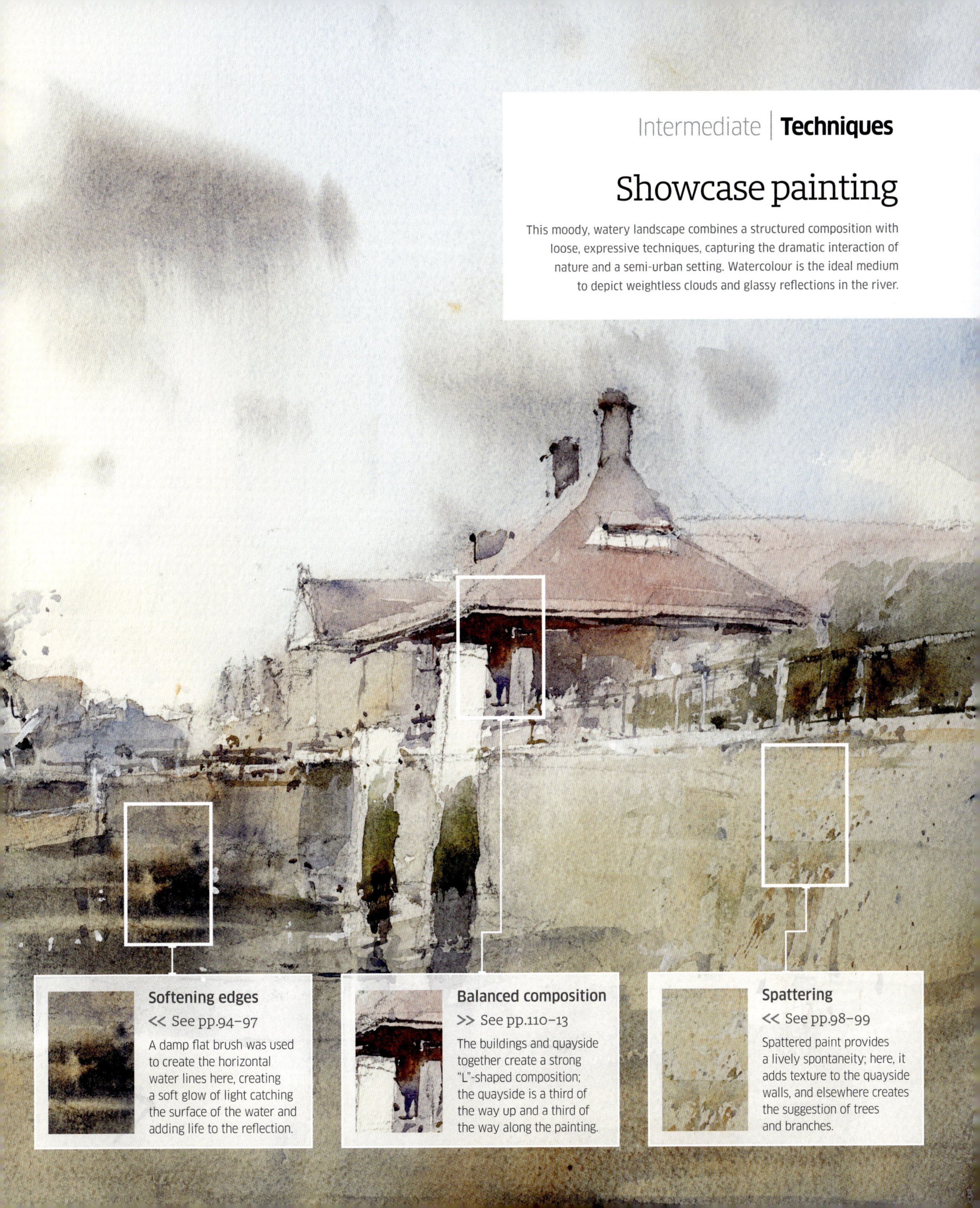

Softening edges

<< See pp.94–97

A damp flat brush was used to create the horizontal water lines here, creating a soft glow of light catching the surface of the water and adding life to the reflection.

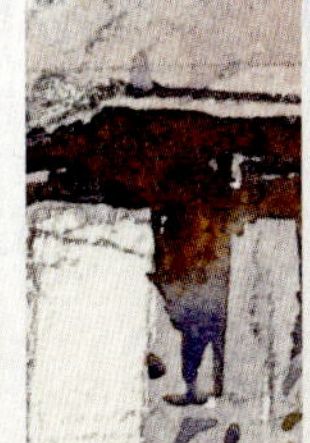

Balanced composition

>> See pp.110–13

The buildings and quayside together create a strong "L"-shaped composition; the quayside is a third of the way up and a third of the way along the painting.

Spattering

<< See pp.98–99

Spattered paint provides a lively spontaneity; here, it adds texture to the quayside walls, and elsewhere creates the suggestion of trees and branches.

Repetition

COMPOSING WITH SHAPE AND COLOUR

Repetition simply means to feature an element, shape, or colour more than once. This simple yet powerful technique allows you to create visually interesting paintings, whether they're landscape, still life, or abstract. Repeatedly painting motifs also helps to improve your brushwork.

Adding subtle variations

Repeating a shape, for example fence poles in a landscape or a snowflake in a snow-themed pattern, is a good way to create harmony in a painting. Working with a limited palette also maintains cohesion. However, repeating exactly the same shape can look boring, so incorporate variations in size, colour, orientation, and position. Making such small tweaks will bring a sense of visual rhythm to your piece.

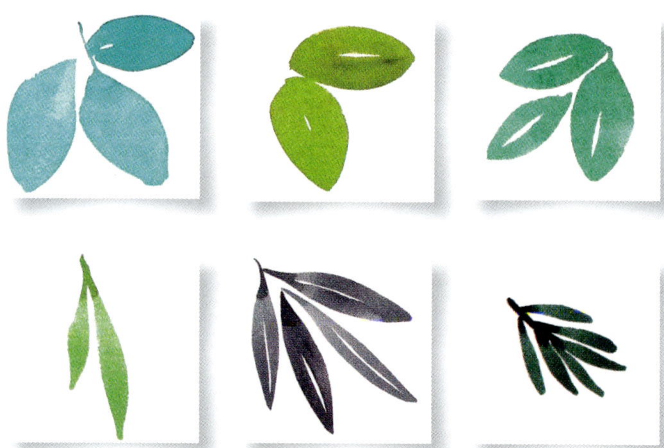

Vary shape, size, and colour
Paint just two or three different but connected shapes from the same theme, changing the size, shape, and orientation when repeating them around the page, and using a limited palette to create a cohesive whole. If you need more shades, mix the colours or adjust their strength.

PUTTING IT INTO PRACTICE

For this repetition exercise, three main leaf shapes were painted in a limited palette of three colours. The leaves vary in size and position around the page but the overall effect is one of unity and cohesion.

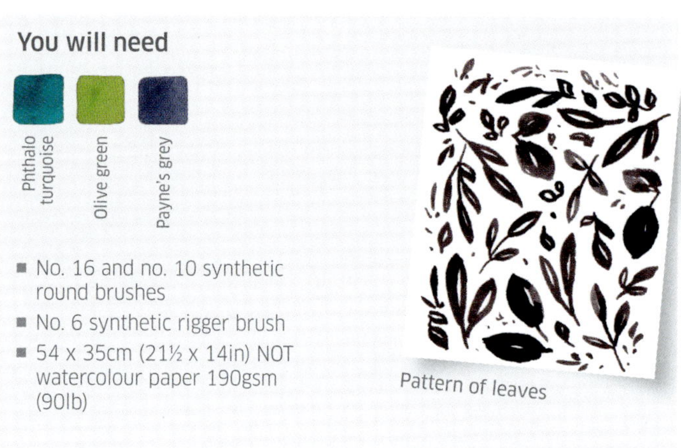

- No. 16 and no. 10 synthetic round brushes
- No. 6 synthetic rigger brush
- 54 x 35cm (21½ x 14in) NOT watercolour paper 190gsm (90lb)

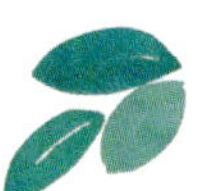
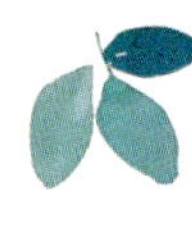
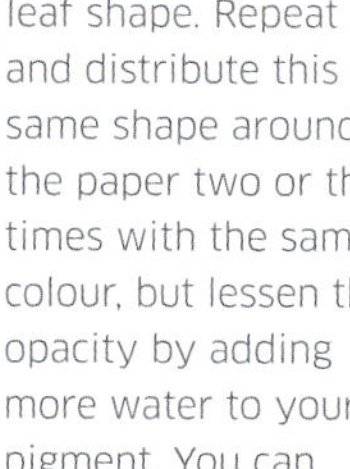

1 First shape
Paint your first leaf shape. Repeat and distribute this same shape around the paper two or three times with the same colour, but lessen the opacity by adding more water to your pigment. You can also vary the size of your leaves.

Painted dots or lines can resemble leaves or flowers in the empty spaces between the leaves

> "Varying the **shape, position, or colour** of a motif can bring a sense of **movement** and **rhythm**."

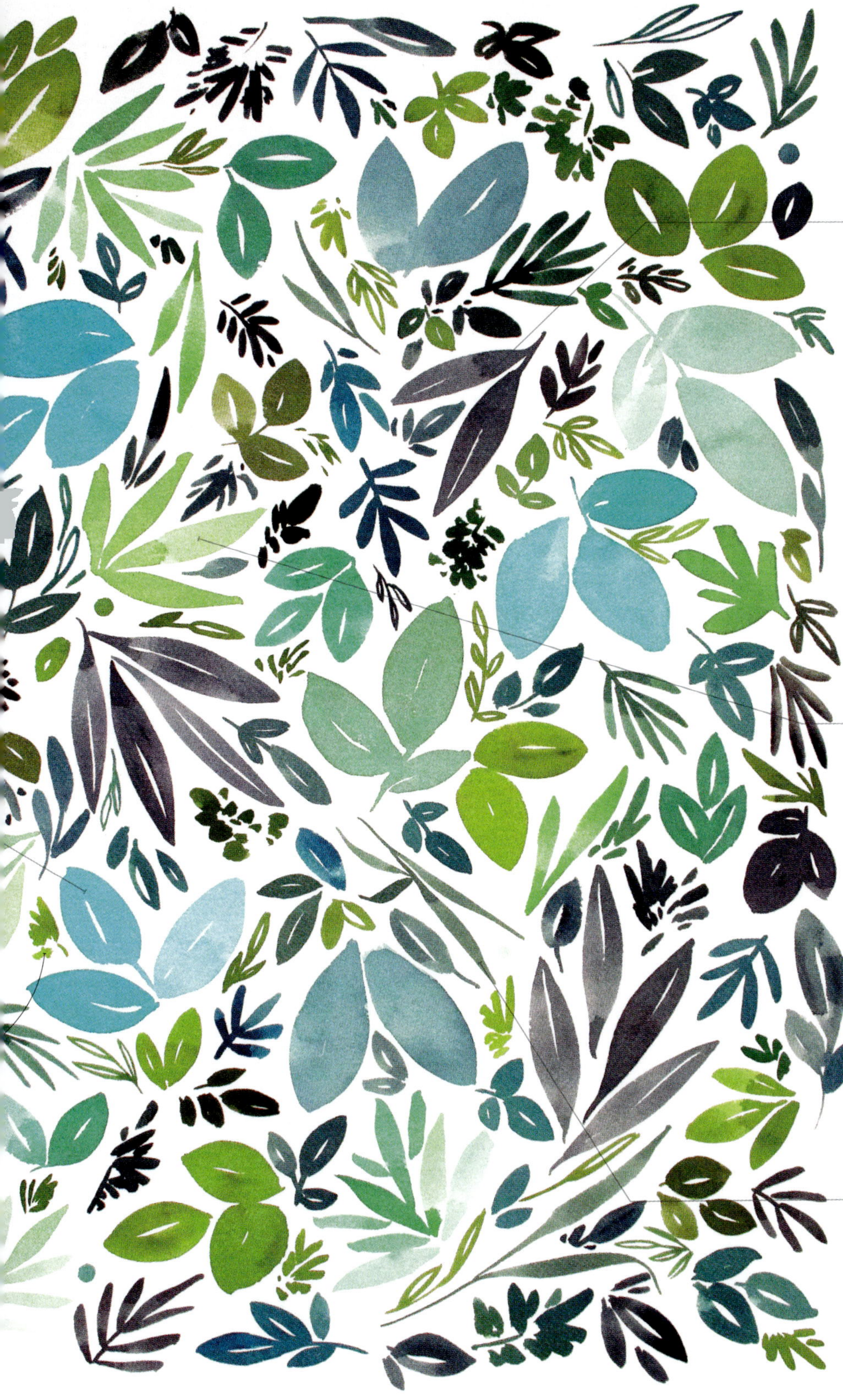

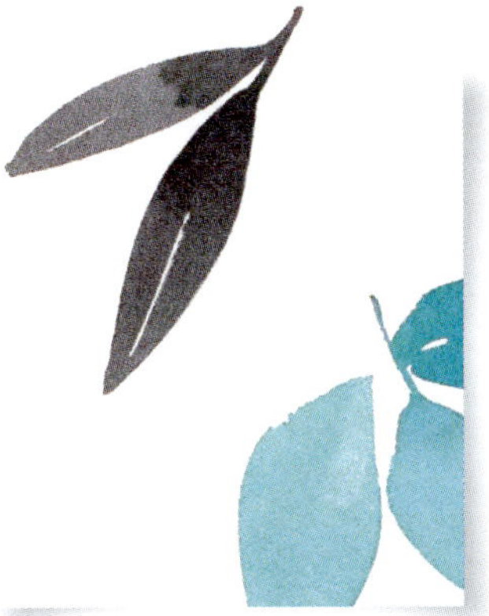

2 Second shape and colour

Repeat step 1 but with a second leaf shape and a second colour. Do change the orientation of the leaves each time.

3 Third shape and colour

Repeat for a third leaf shape and a third colour. To vary the scale, be sure to paint a big leaf here and there.

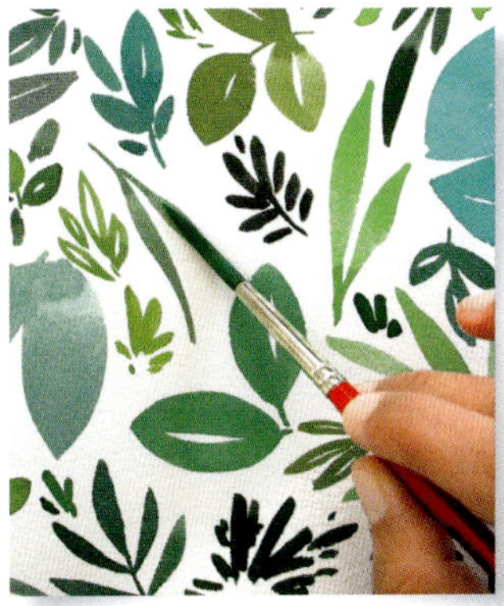

4 Fill the gaps

Continue filling your paper. Mix new shades as you go within the same palette; if more contrast is needed, add a drop of black.

Balanced composition

CREATING STRUCTURE AND SHAPE

Whether you are painting a landscape, figures (see p.112–13), or other subject, a good structural composition will engage the viewer. The "rule of thirds" (see right) is one classic technique. Another is to use alphabet letters, such as L, V, Z, C, T, and S, as compositional shapes. You do not need to paint objects to lead the eye – colours, tones, and individual shapes provide just as much interest.

USING V AND Z SHAPES

Your painting must have a background, a middle distance, and a foreground to succeed. To balance the composition, this painting relies on the strategy of using "V" and "Z" shapes.

You will need

- No. 15 and no. 10 soft-hair mop brushes
- No. 10 stiff-bristle round brush
- No. 5 soft-hair round brush
- 56 x 38cm (22 x 15in) NOT watercolour paper 300gsm (140lb)

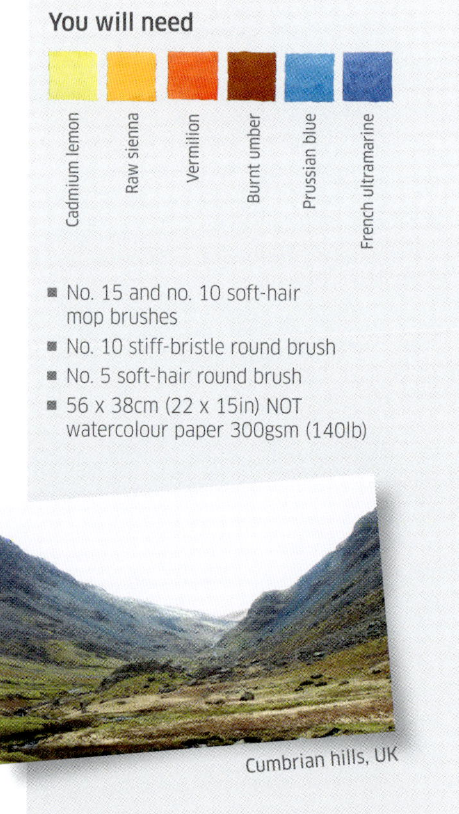

Cumbrian hills, UK

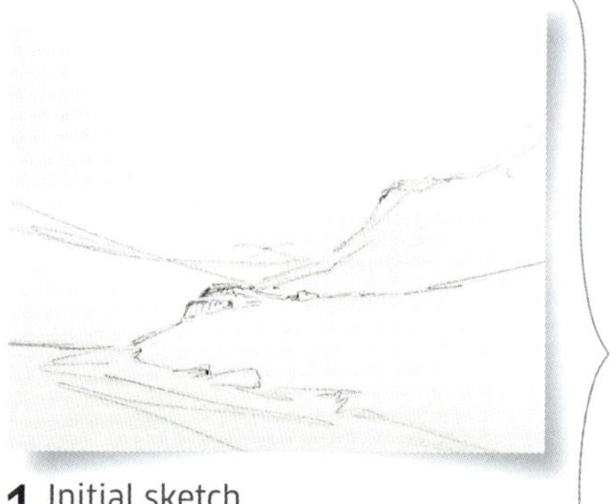

1 Initial sketch
For a valley amid steep mountains, a "V" structure is ideal. Also, a strong "Z" composition connects the foreground stream, the middle-distance rocks, and the background mountain.

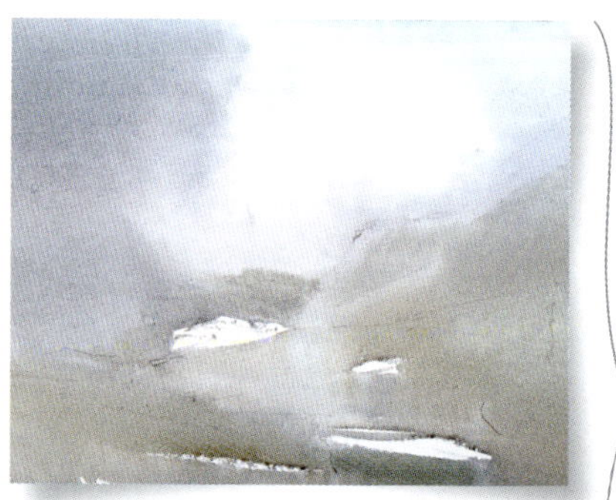

2 Background wash
Dampen the paper with the no. 15 mop brush, leaving areas untouched. Mix Prussian blue, vermilion, and a little raw sienna to paint the sky and carry the wash over the ground. Add a touch of lemon for the valley in the wet wash.

Selecting your scene

Even a scenic landscape can struggle to interest the viewer without a good composition, whereas an apparently mundane view can make an exciting painting if the composition is strong. The rule of thirds involves dividing a picture into thirds and placing a focal point where the thirds intersect. Finding other shapes to lead the eye will help you to arrive at a scene that will engage the viewer's eye.

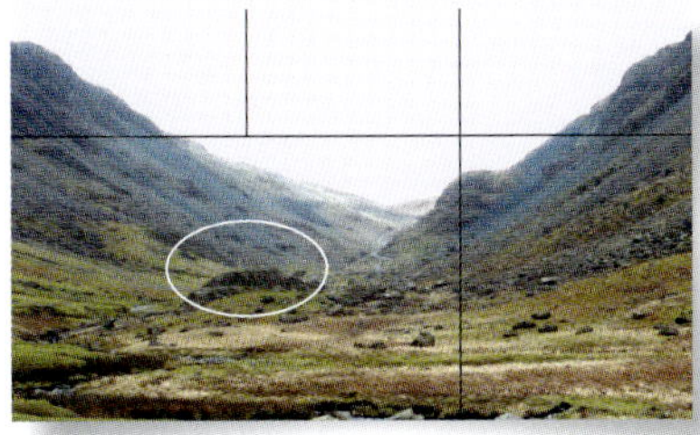

The rule of thirds
Make sure the scene has a focal point for the eye to travel to, placing it at the intersection of thirds rather than in the centre.

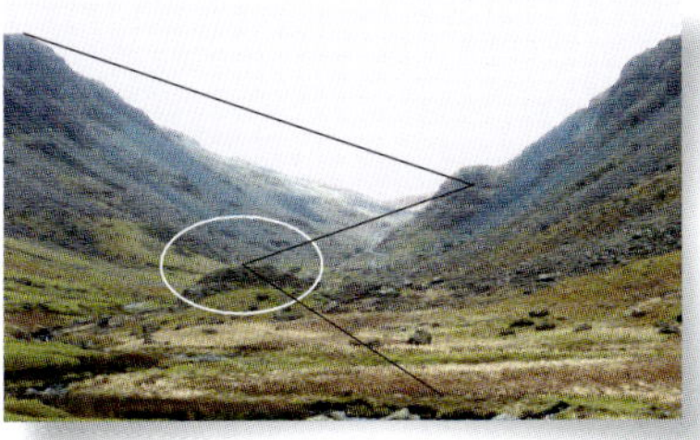

Connecting the shapes
Find a connection between the main shapes. The simplest way here is to use the stream, the distant road, and the mountains for a hidden "Z" shape.

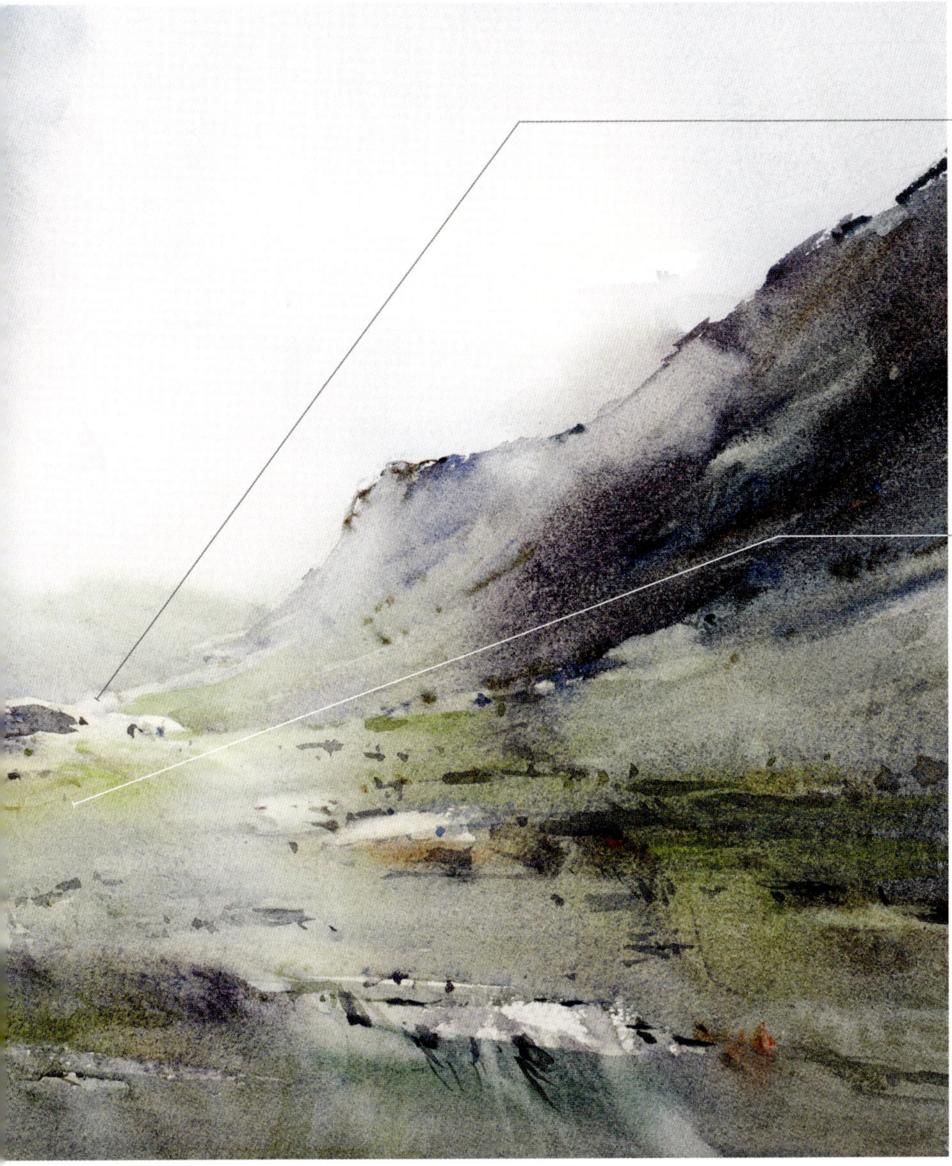

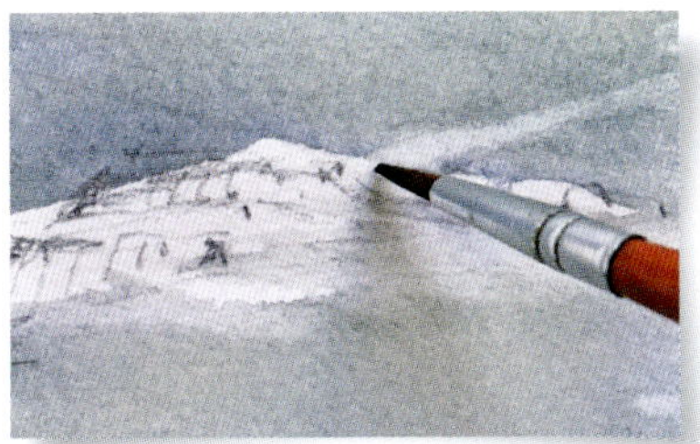

3 Define the shapes
While the paint is still wet, lift out the road and stream with a dry brush to connect the white areas and form a "Z" composition.

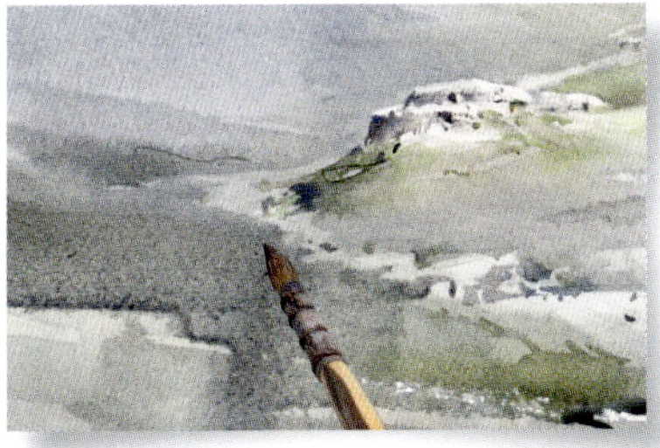

4 Strengthen shapes and tones
Paint the rocks wet-on-dry. Give the middle and foreground a wet-in-wet wash of ultramarine, lemon, and umber.

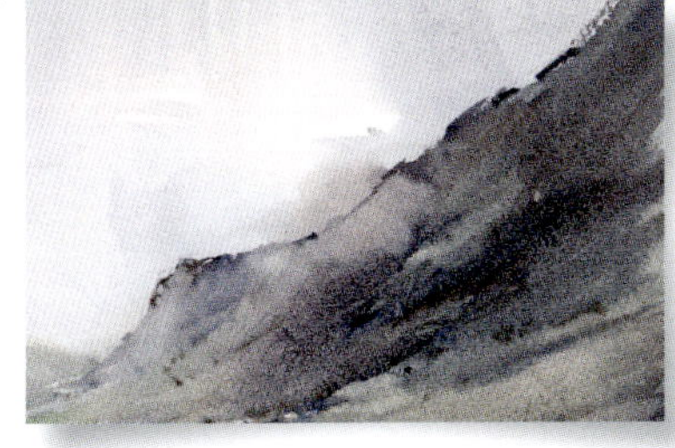

5 Balance the colour
Add cloud shadows, wet-in-wet, with umber, ultramarine, and lemon to the upper part of the mountain on the right to balance the composition.

USING AN S-SHAPED COMPOSITION

The compositional technique of following an "S" shape has been used in this painting to add intrigue and keep the viewer looking at the piece for longer. This is a more interesting and dynamic way to arrange multiple figures than placing them all standing together. Here the figures, faces, and limbs create the shape.

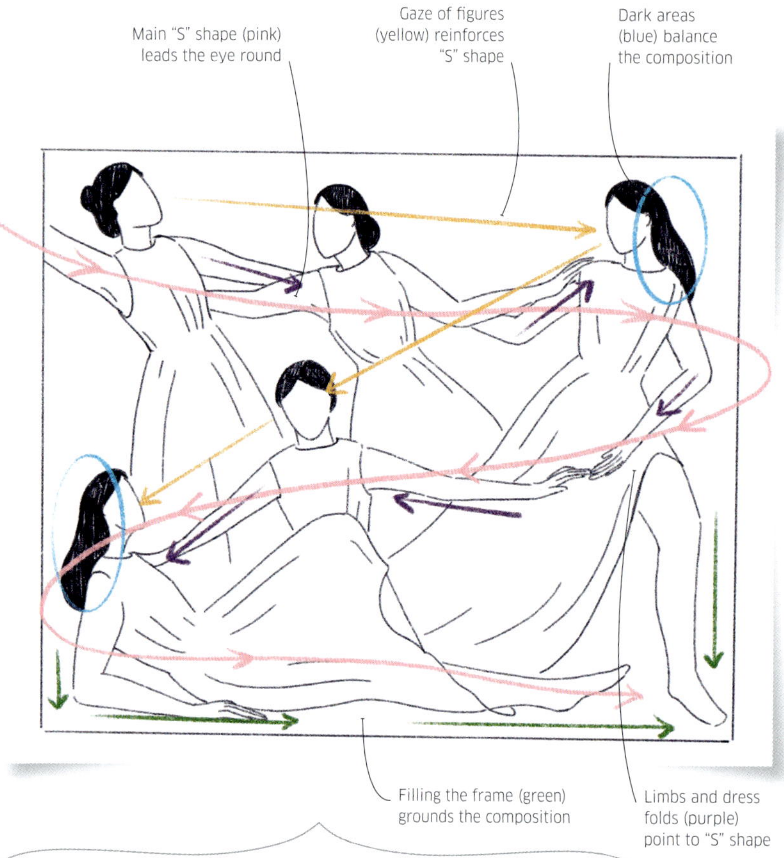

1 Planning out the composition

Achieving the correct angles is crucial to the success of this flowing composition, so begin by making a drawing. Start with the "S" shape shown here, which will become the line around which you place your elements. Use the limbs of the figures to follow the sketched line as closely as possible, while still being believable in their angle. Vary the heights of the figures so you can follow the shape. Next, map out the areas of darker tone.

"A dynamic composition can be both simple and powerful if the forms and angles work well."

You will need

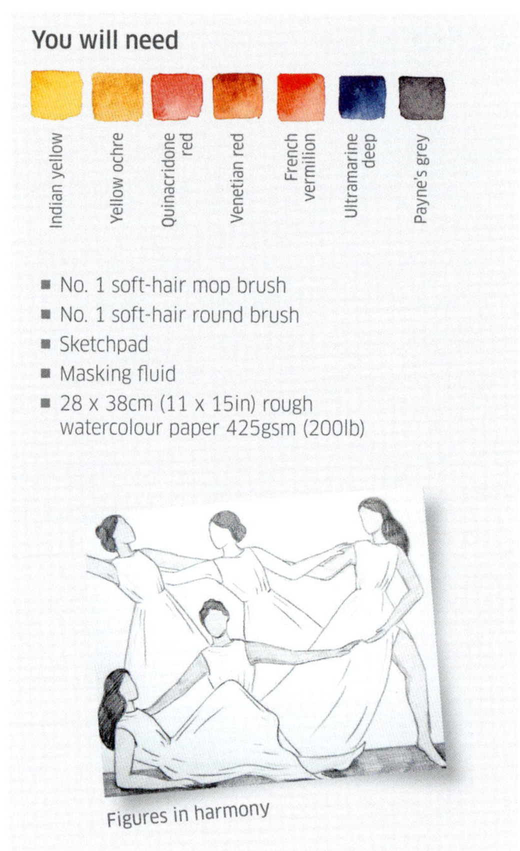

- No. 1 soft-hair mop brush
- No. 1 soft-hair round brush
- Sketchpad
- Masking fluid
- 28 x 38cm (11 x 15in) rough watercolour paper 425gsm (200lb)

Figures in harmony

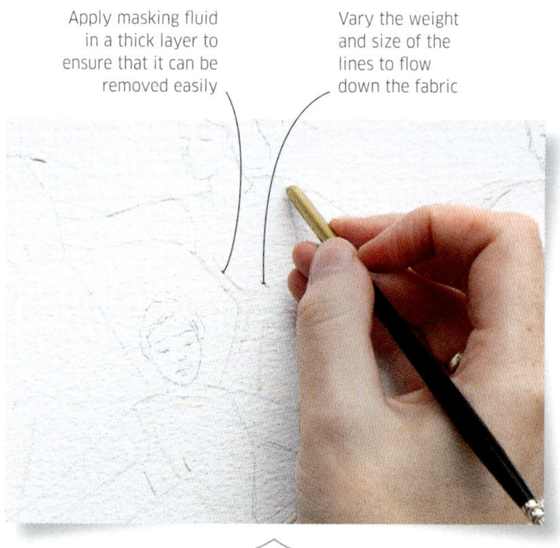

2 Sketch and mask the highlights

Once you are confident about the composition, draw it on your watercolour paper. Using the wooden end of a paintbrush, apply masking fluid to the highlights of folds on the fabric and high points on the lighter figures.

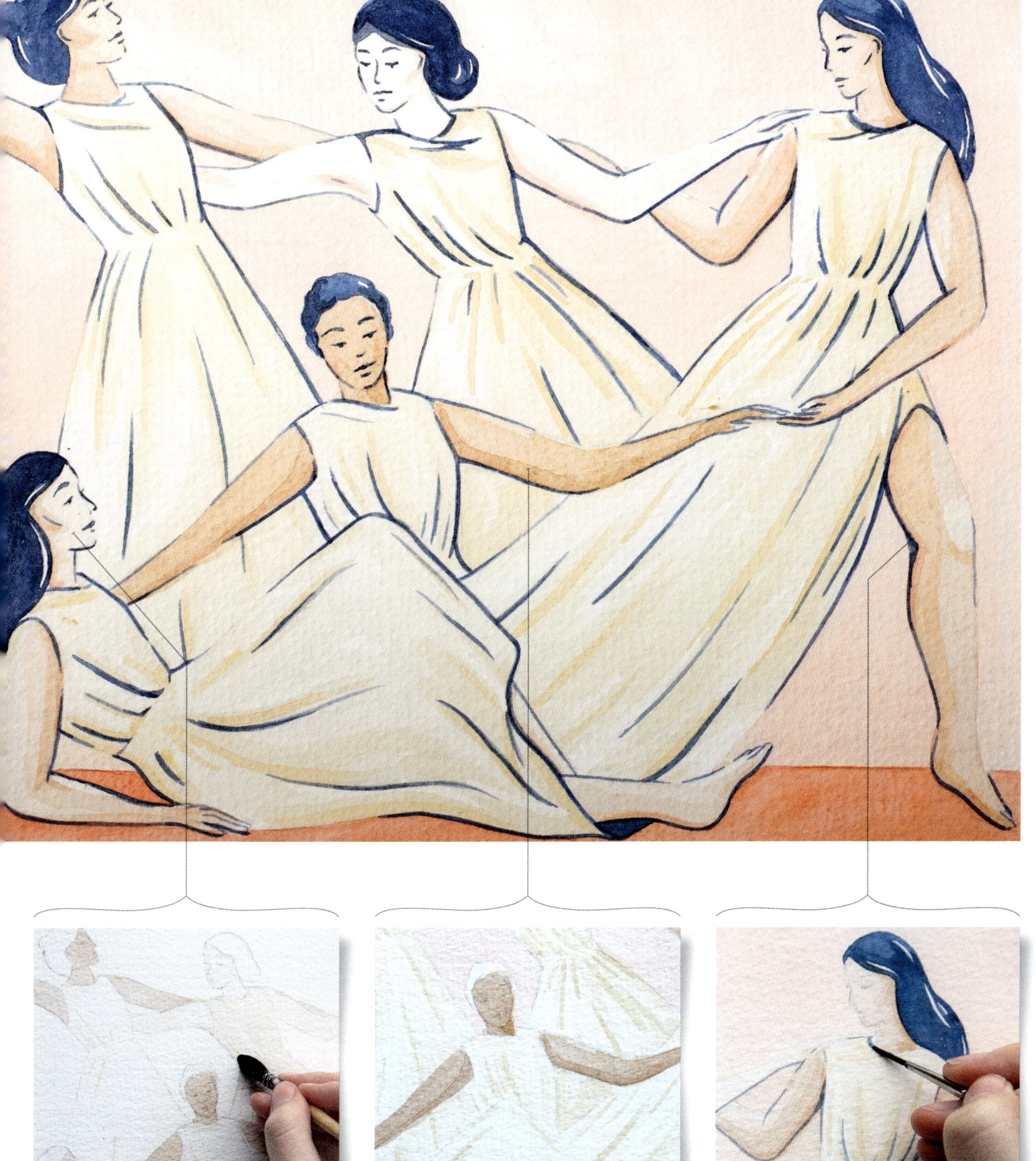

3 The first skin tones
Using the mop brush, mix very dilute skin tones and apply in flat layers. Allow the washes to dry completely before painting adjoining areas.

4 Deeper tones and shadows
Work from the lightest remaining tone, in this case the background, to the darkest. For shadows on the figures, overlay the same light skin tone used in the previous step.

5 Darker details
Make a thicker mix of the darkest tone using blue and grey and apply with the round brush, using as few strokes as possible. Finally, remove the masking fluid.

Negative spaces

DEFINING THE SHAPES IN BETWEEN

The areas that create voids inside a subject, or around the outside of a shape, or "positive" form, are called negative spaces. In a landscape this could be the sky behind a wood, or the gaps between the trees. By following the shape of the negative, sometimes seen as a silhouette, you will define the shape of the positive form.

■ Looking for the negative

Negative spaces can be dark or light. To find a negative, concentrate on observing the space around or in between solid objects. Observe differences in tone to define either a light solid against a dark space, or dark solids in a light space. For some subjects, try viewing your subject as a silhouette to help find the solid form.

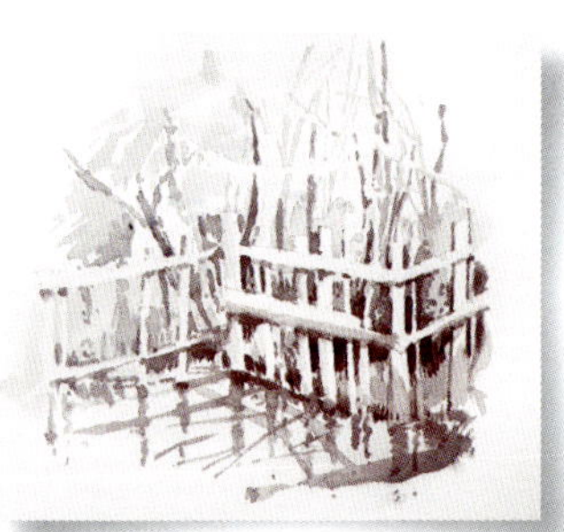

Tonal differences
It can be useful to see the negative spaces in and around an object as an aid to drawing a complicated shape. Here, the dark spaces in between the fence posts recede, which brings the light fence forwards and clarifies the solid structure.

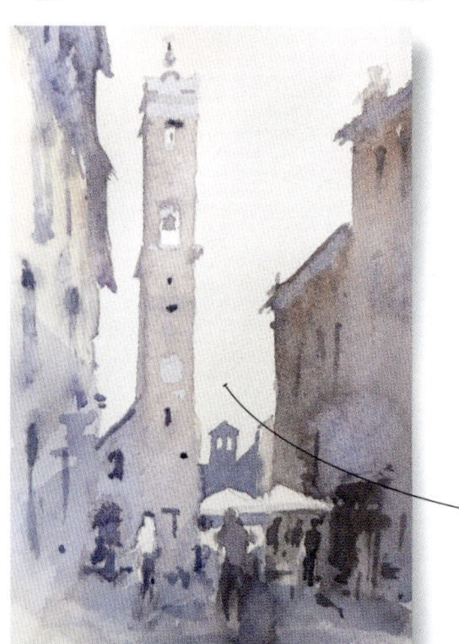

Silhouetted shapes
Look at the shapes around an object or in the voids between shapes. These can be found in skies in landscapes or the backdrops to a still life or figure study, where the empty space creates a silhouette that defines the solid form.

The light sky behind the buildings creates a silhouetted skyline

PUTTING IT INTO PRACTICE

In this painting the negative spaces help to define the character of the classical architecture and its features. The spaces around and between the solid objects are all negatives that bring a sense of depth to the composition.

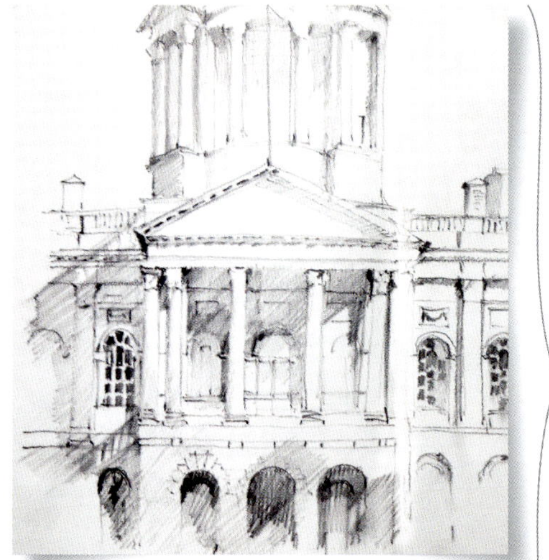

1 Preliminary drawing
The strong shadows in this location sketch help to articulate the architecture and can be used as a guide for defining the negative shapes. Plot outlines of the building to organize the proportions.

2 Paint silhouettes
First, apply the pale colour of the building and foreground, with a few touches of cerulean blue wet-in-wet. Next, paint the sky around the silhouette of the buildings.

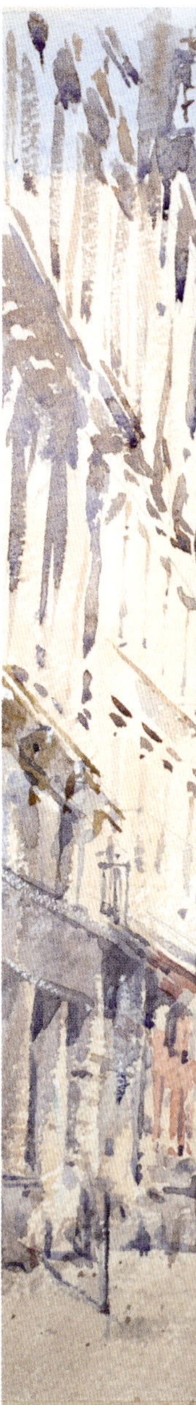

You will need

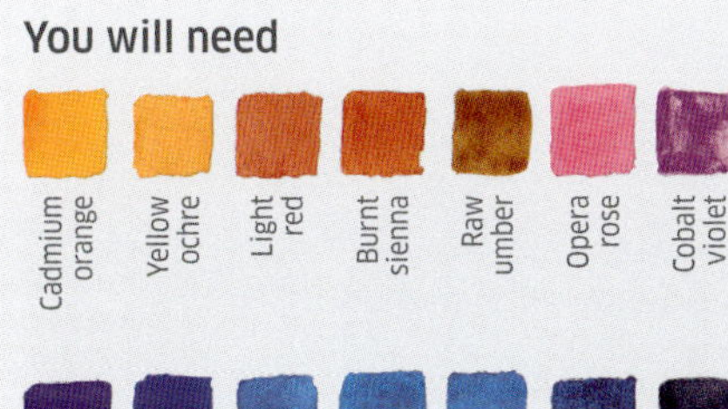

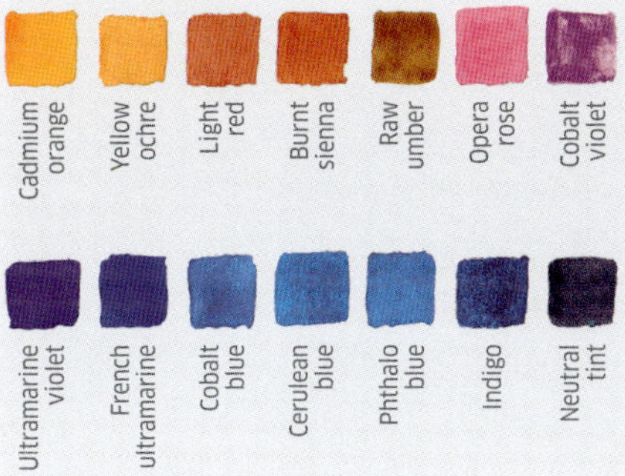

Cadmium orange · Yellow ochre · Light red · Burnt sienna · Raw umber · Opera rose · Cobalt violet

Ultramarine violet · French ultramarine · Cobalt blue · Cerulean blue · Phthalo blue · Indigo · Neutral tint

- No. 10 and no. 3 soft-hair round brushes
- 50 x 56cm (19½ x 22in) NOT watercolour paper 425gsm (200lb)

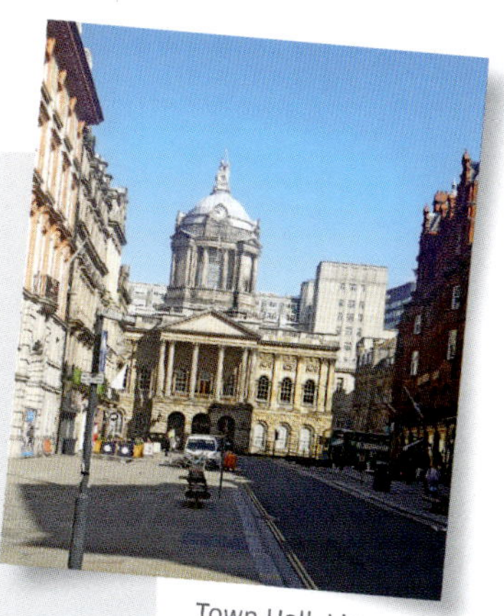

Town Hall, Liverpool

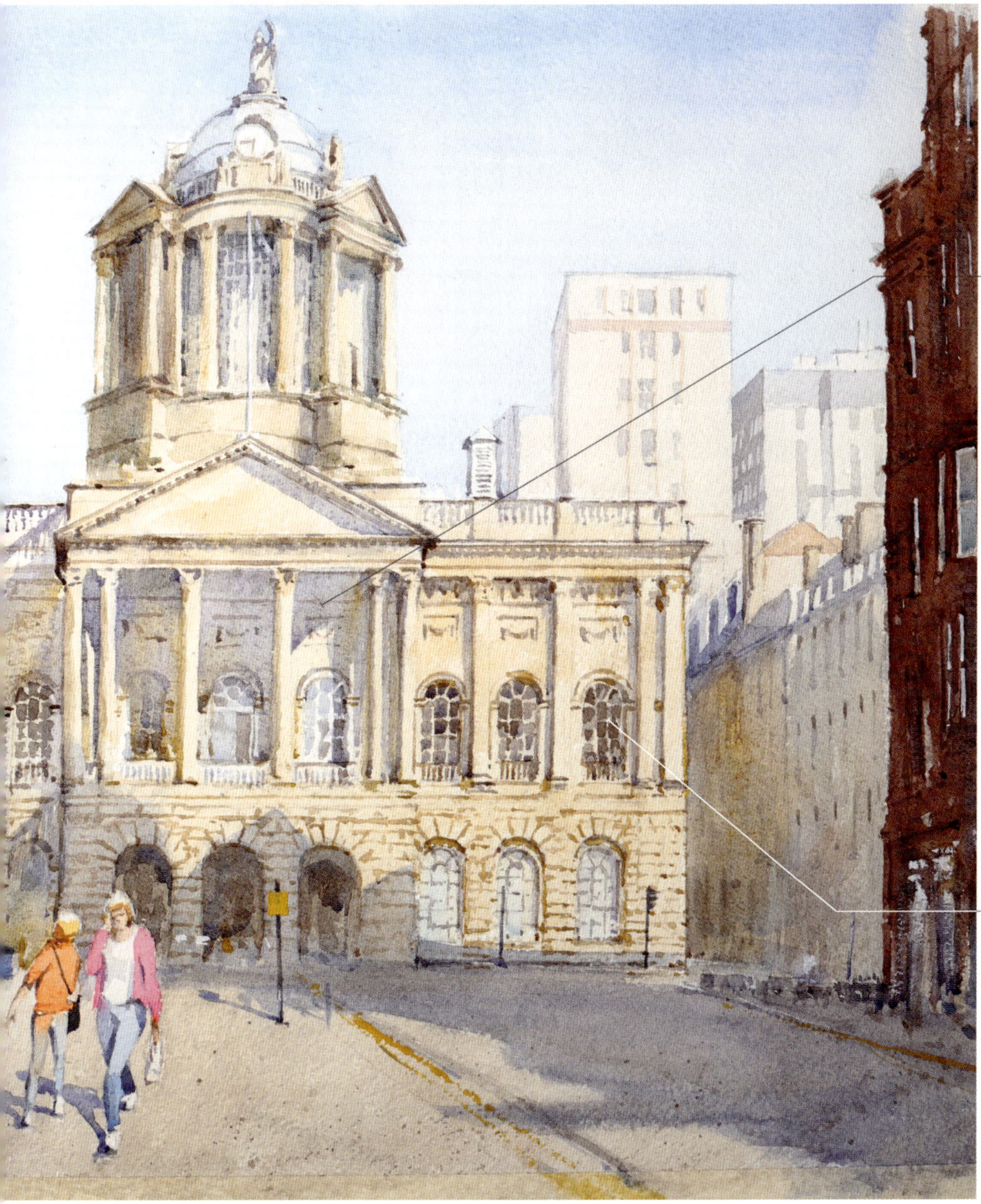

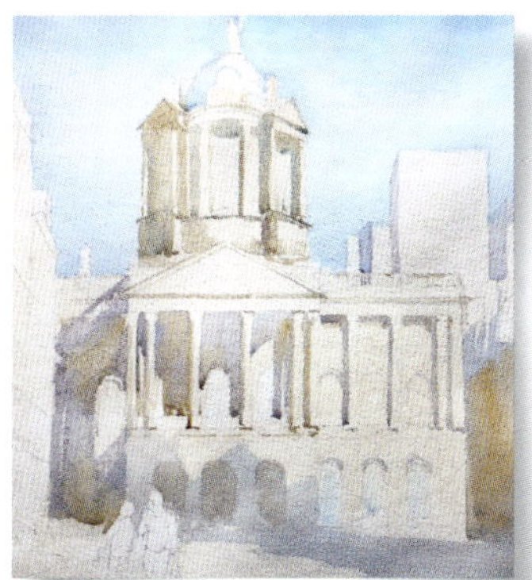

3 Define shadowed spaces

Use a cool blue to add the main shadows between the columns, the spaces between the balustrades, and the ones inside the arches. These negative spaces will clarify the structure of the building.

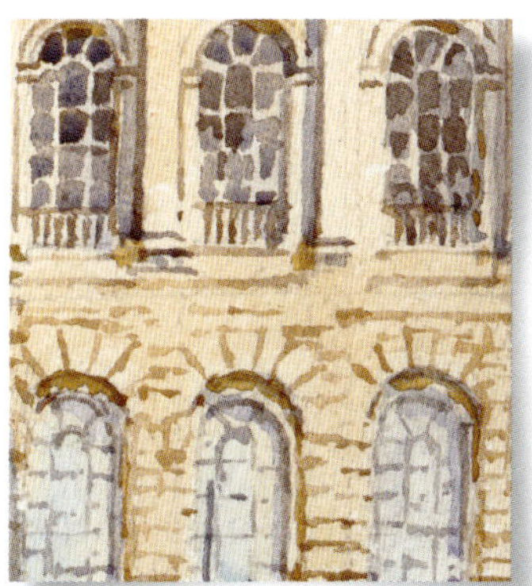

4 Structural details

There can be more than one layer of negative space; the windows between the columns are also negatives. Add the darker details within the architecture with a no. 3 brush to ensure the shapes are not flooded.

Analogous colours

USING COLOURS THAT HARMONIZE

Analogous colours are those that sit next to each other on the colour wheel (see below). When used together they create a calm and harmonious feeling. They can also be used to bring life into a solid colour by varying the colour as you paint.

■ Harmony and interest

While complementary colours placed adjacent to each other appear brighter (see pp.118–19), analogous colours are more subtle and harmonious. They are ideal when you want to add interest to an area of colour without introducing bold, clashing effects.

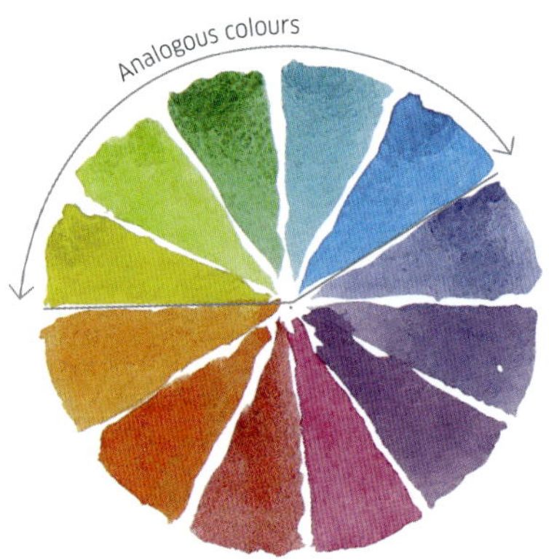

Adjacent colours
The colour wheel is arranged in terms of analogous colours – for example, green is analogous with blue and yellow. Choose a sequence of up to five colours to create a harmonious scheme.

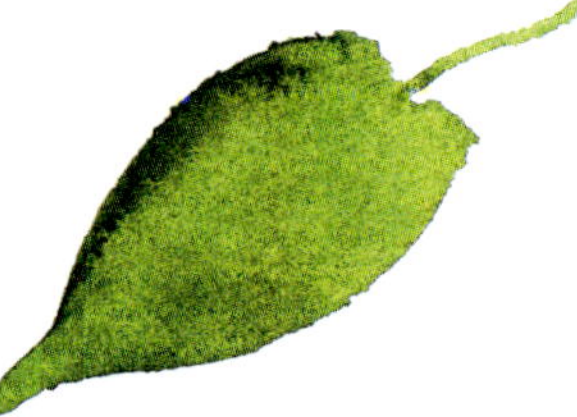

Single colour
If you mix just one green and use it to paint a leaf the effect can be rather flat and dull.

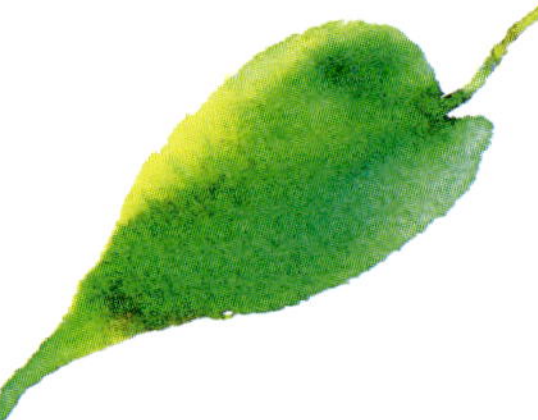

Analogous colours
A leaf painted with some added yellow and blue has more variety and therefore looks more lively.

PUTTING IT INTO PRACTICE

This painting of pansies uses a set of colours analogous with purple, so they range from crimson through purple to blue. The bright yellow centres of the flowers provide small splashes of contrast.

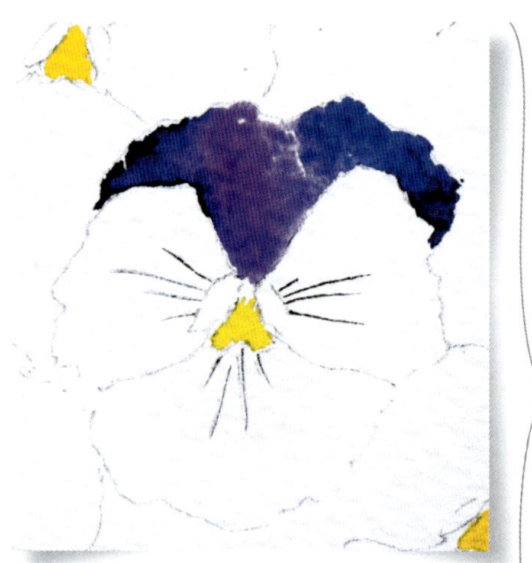

1 Establish a focal point
Draw two or three pansy flowers. Mix several pink, purple, and blue colours. Start with the central flower, painting the centre and two top petals but leaving the others as mainly white paper to act as a focal point.

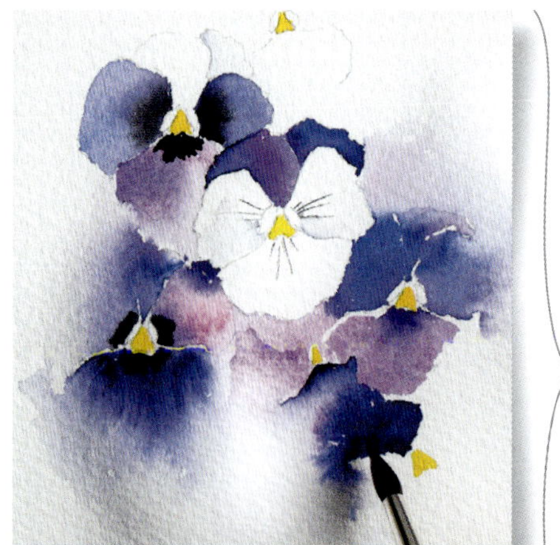

2 Build up the colours
Keep adding more flowers, allowing the colours to overlap and run into each other, but leaving the paper dry for the yellow centres. Paint these in with crisper edges.

You will need

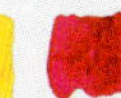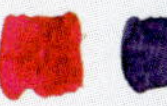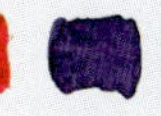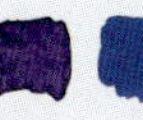

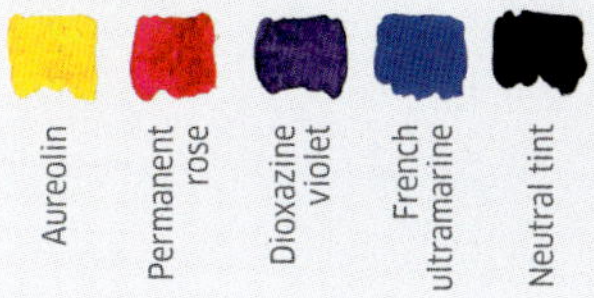

Aureolin

Permanent rose

Dioxazine violet

French ultramarine

Neutral tint

- No. 8 soft-hair reservoir liner brush
- 38 x 28cm (15 x 11in) rough watercolour paper 300gsm (140lb)

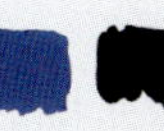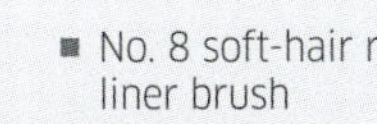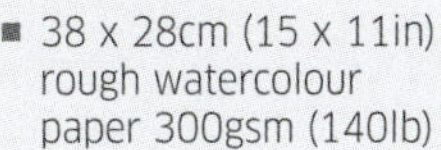

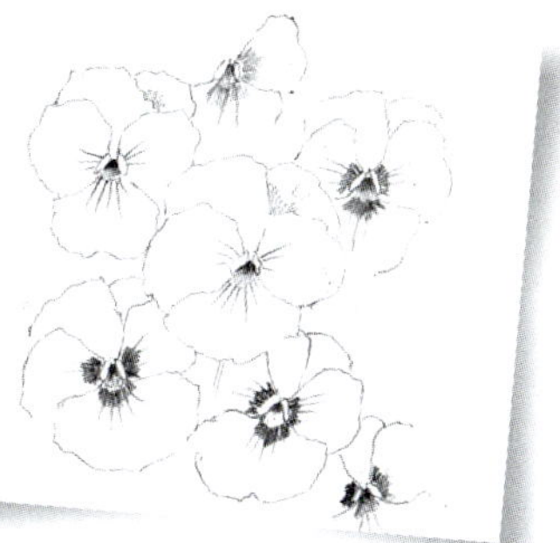

Sketch of pansies

"**Analogous colours** are harmonious and provide subtle effects."

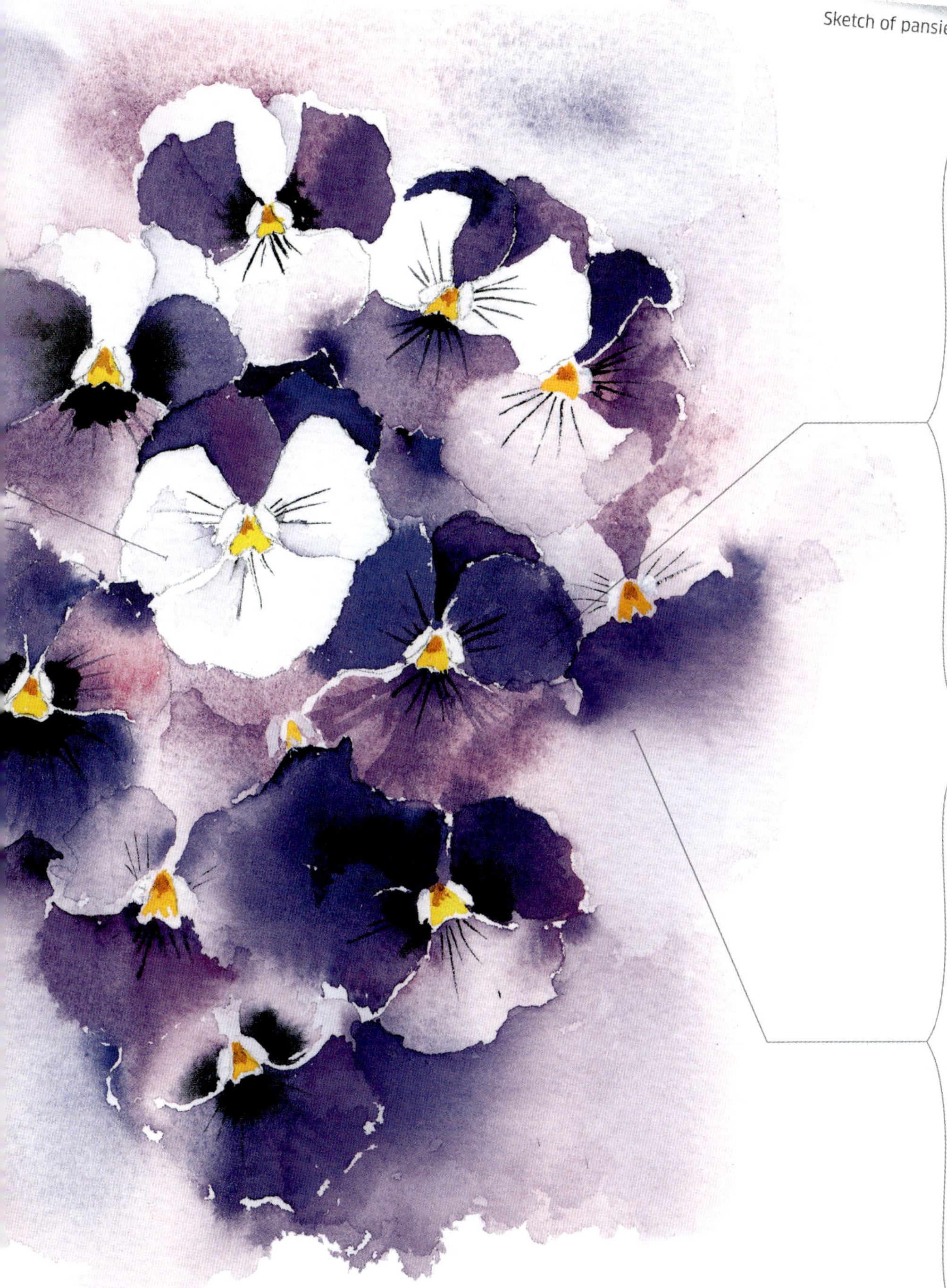

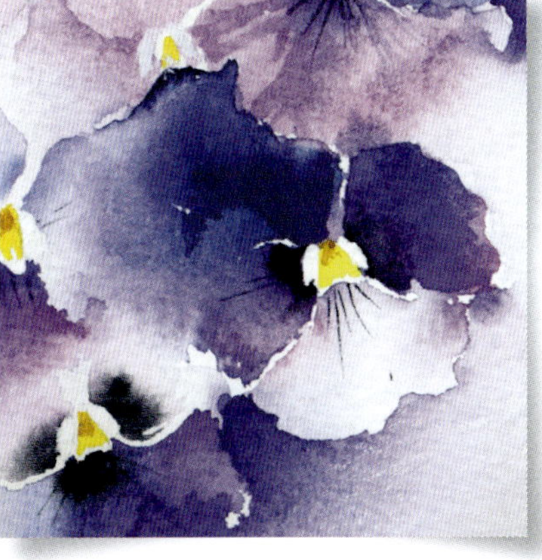

3 Darker centres

Put in the dark markings as the paint dries, painting with a strong mix of neutral tint. Use water to blur the edges of the petals into the background to keep a loose, painterly style.

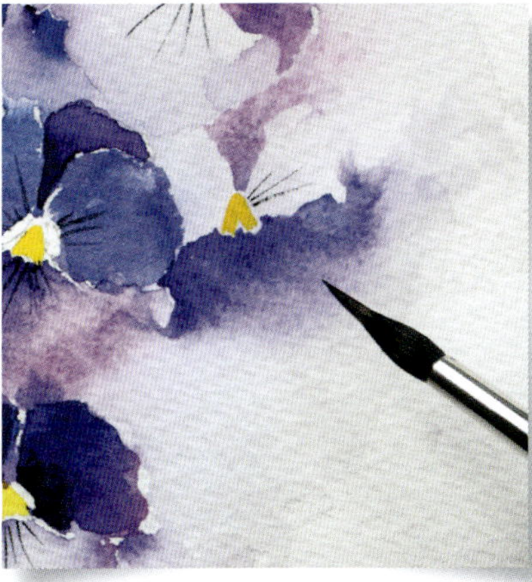

4 Work into the background

Keep adding more flowers, leaving some unfinished. Use the analogous colours in the background, fading out with water to soften edges (see pp.94–97).

Complementary colours

USING CONTRASTING COLOUR FOR VISUAL EFFECT

Complementary colours lie opposite each other on the colour wheel. They are naturally contrasting colours that enhance each other. By choosing a limited palette of complementaries, you can exploit this visual relationship as a key part of your composition, especially in subjects that include light and shade. They can bring balance to a painting, especially when used as transparent washes.

Complementary options

Artists can use complementary colours in various ways to visually change the perception of an image. Placing them side by side enhances their vibrancy. You can exploit this effect either in details, or as the basis of your composition in a palette built on one or two pairs. Mixing complementary colours to create a range of neutrals is an advanced way to unify a painting. Consider colour bias (see p.34), too, to extend your options and keep your painting lively.

PUTTING IT INTO PRACTICE

To recreate the glowing golden light and cool shadows of an Italian evening, a limited palette of yellow and orange was used with complementary purples and blues, mixed to make spectral greys.

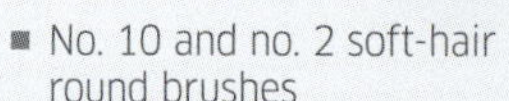

You will need

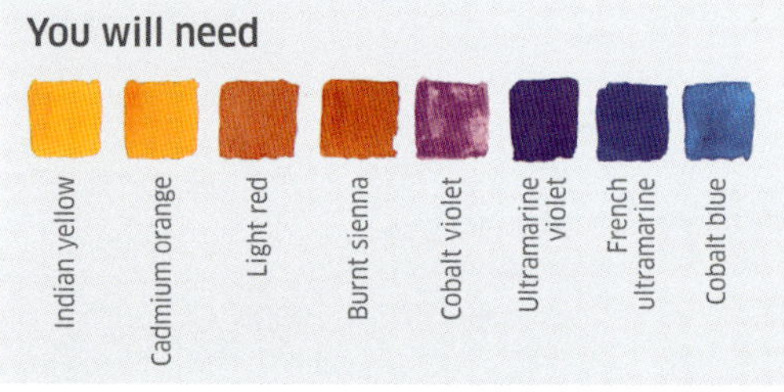

Indian yellow | Cadmium orange | Light red | Burnt sienna | Cobalt violet | Ultramarine violet | French ultramarine | Cobalt blue

- No. 10 and no. 2 soft-hair round brushes
- 48 x 51cm (19 x 20in) NOT watercolour paper 300gsm (140lb)

Matera, Italy

> "**Create a range** of neutrals from **complementary pairs** to unify your painting."

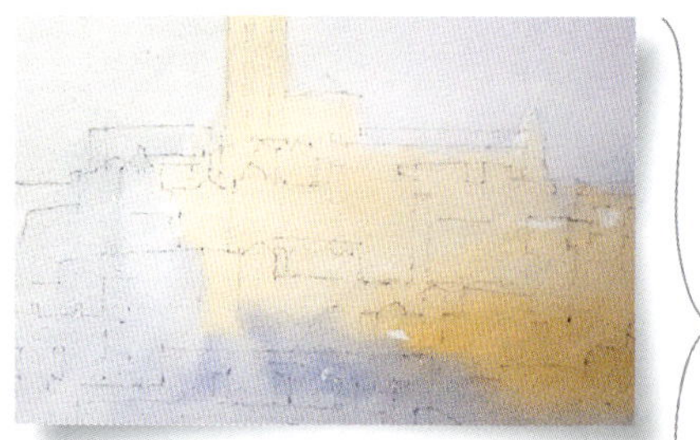

1 Complementary washes
Paint a blue sky wash next to orange, to make the orange stronger and create the impression of light and warmth.

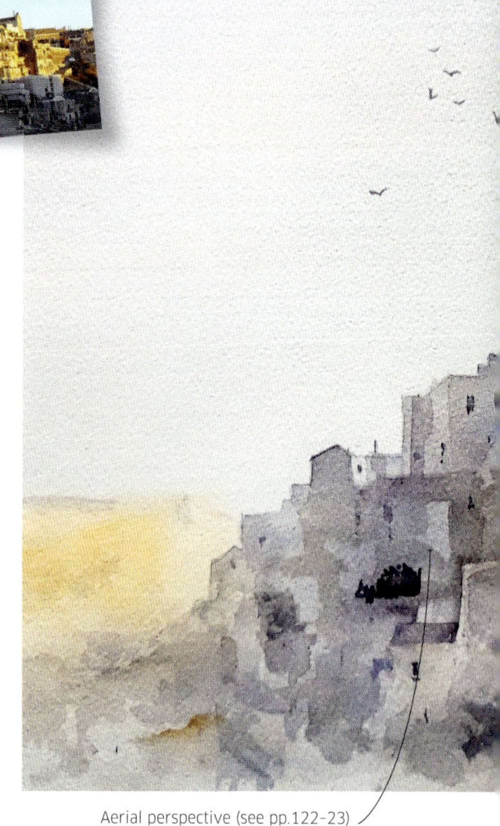

Aerial perspective (see pp.122–23) is enhanced by using cooler colours in the background shadows

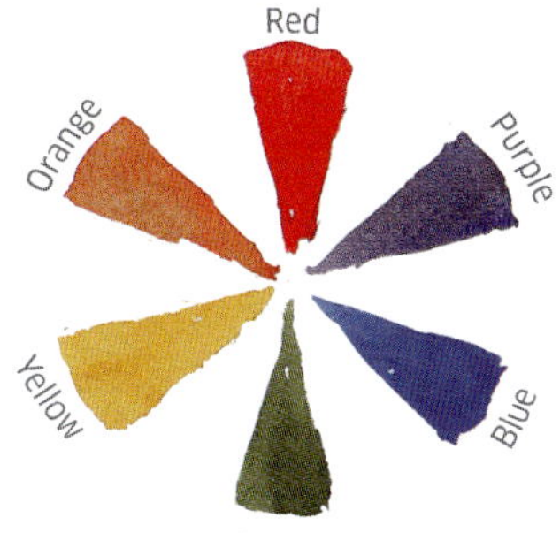
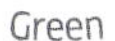

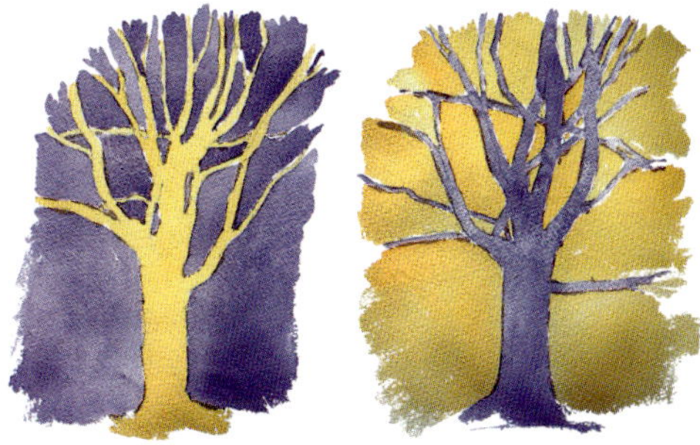

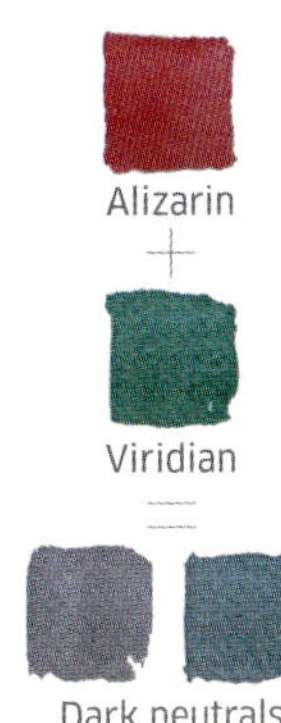
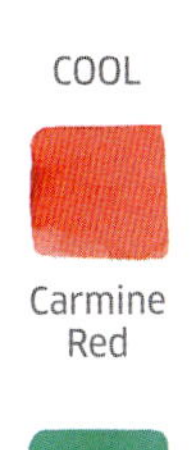
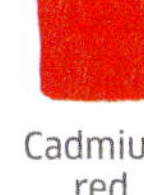
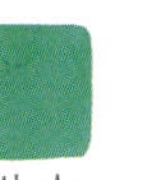

Complementary pairs

The colours that lie opposite each other on the colour wheel (see p.32) are complementary: red with green, orange with blue, and yellow with purple. Consider using pairs to give your painting visual excitement.

Visual effect

Using complementary colours together, either juxtaposed or in an optical mix, will enhance their effect, throwing the colours forward. Using complementary pairs in your composition, adding one colour against the other, will draw attention. Take care to balance their use as the visual effect can be jarring.

Mixing neutrals

Create warm, cool, and coloured greys by mixing complementaries in different ratios, ensuring the neutrals vary in temperature and give a strong enough dark.

Colour bias pairs

Paint pigments often have an undertone with a warm or cool bias. To ensure a broad range of mixes, include both warm and cool complementary pairs in your palette.

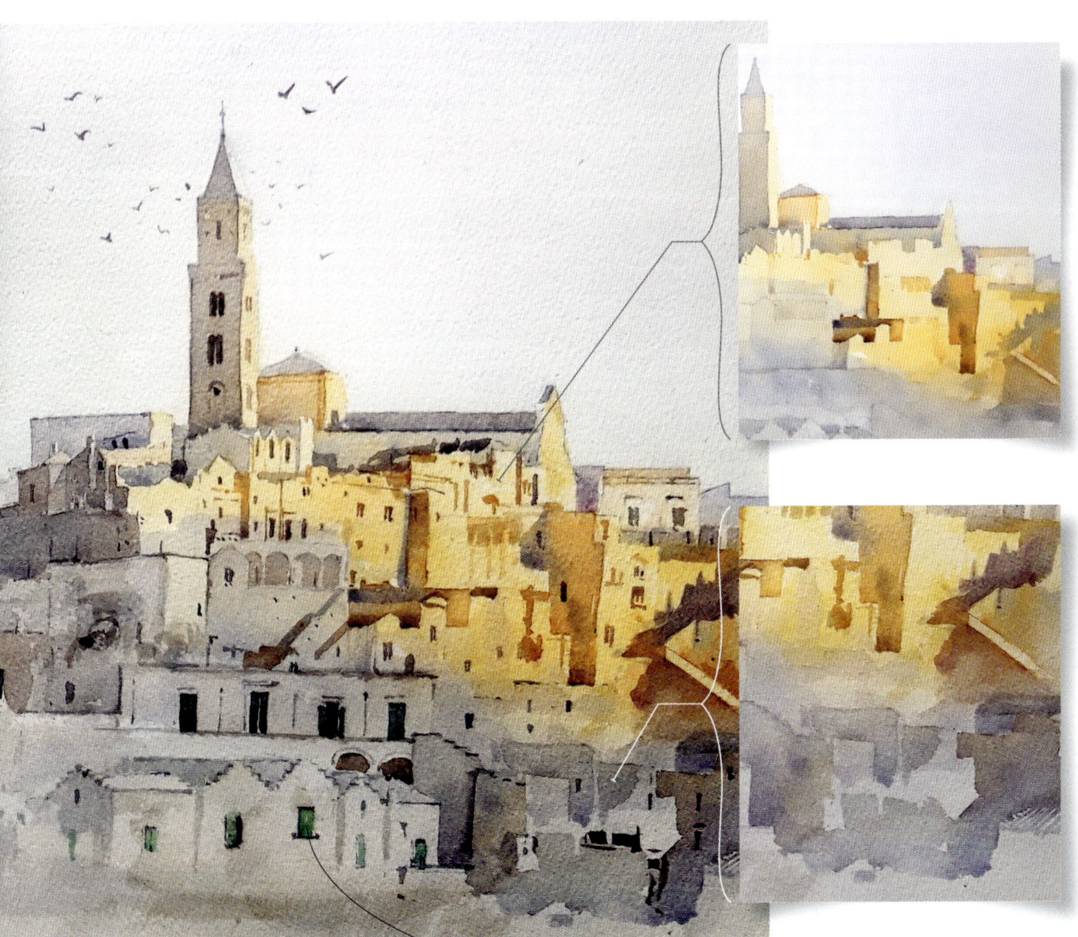
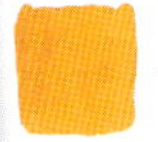
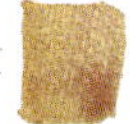
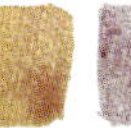
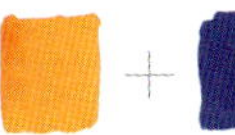
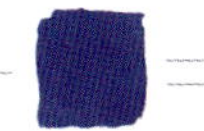
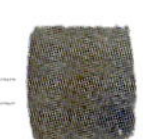
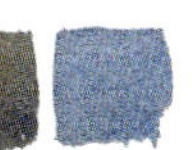

2 Warm shadows

When the first layer is dry, block in the architecture with pale tones of mixed greys using complementary colours. Yellow and violet give neutrals with a warm colour temperature (see p.34) that reflect sunlit shadows.

3 Cooler tones

For the areas furthest away from the light or in deep shadow, use a mix with a cooler feel, creating blue-toned neutrals from orange and blue.

A bright green was used for the window shutters as a contrast to the complementary palette

Warm and cool colours

USING COLOUR FOR HARMONY OR CONTRAST

The colours in your paint palette can be divided in many ways, and colour temperature is one that you can use to influence a composition. Warm and cool colours have properties that work individually, or influence each other when combined, and how you use them can create harmony or discord. Understanding these properties, and how to balance or combine them, will help you to create compositions that are visually stimulating and engaging.

PUTTING IT INTO PRACTICE

These examples are a valuable exercise to help you understand the visual effects of colour, using fluid watercolour mixes to explain how our perception of the same image changes according to colour temperature.

Contrasts add energy

Analogous colours
(see pp.116–17) work together

Cobalt violet

Ultramarine

Aqua green

Turquoise blue (liquid watercolour)

Cobalt turquoise light

Cobalt green

Pastel green (liquid watercolour)

Lemon yellow

Gold ochre (liquid watercolour)

Transparent orange

Crimson red

Opera rose

Perylene violet

Cool colour scheme

A composition using only cool colours is gentle on the eye and will convey a sense of tranquility, serenity, and coldness. Although these colours work well together, the image is flat and subdued, and lacks focus. A painting using only cool colours will struggle to hold your attention.

Warm colour scheme

Choose a predominantly warm palette to stimulate sensations of warmth, tension, and energy. These colours can be intense and overly saturated, creating vibrations at a visual level, which may suit particular subjects but these same effects may create disharmony in a colour scheme.

Perceiving temperature

We associate certain colours with perceived temperature and it is relatively simple to use these qualities to influence the feel of a painting. The predominant colours in your palette will give your work either a warm or cool atmosphere, for example using blues for a snowy scene.

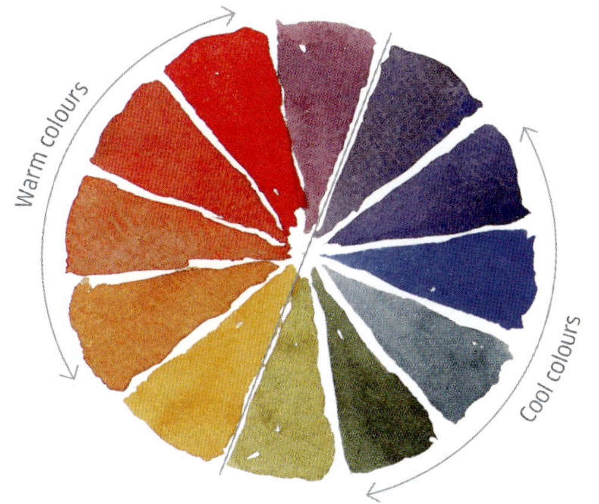

Warm and cool colour wheel

We associate warmth with the yellow-orange-red half of the colour wheel, and the green-blue-purple half is seen to be cool. Bear in mind that paint colours also have a temperature bias (see p.34), with cool reds and warm blues, to extend your mixes.

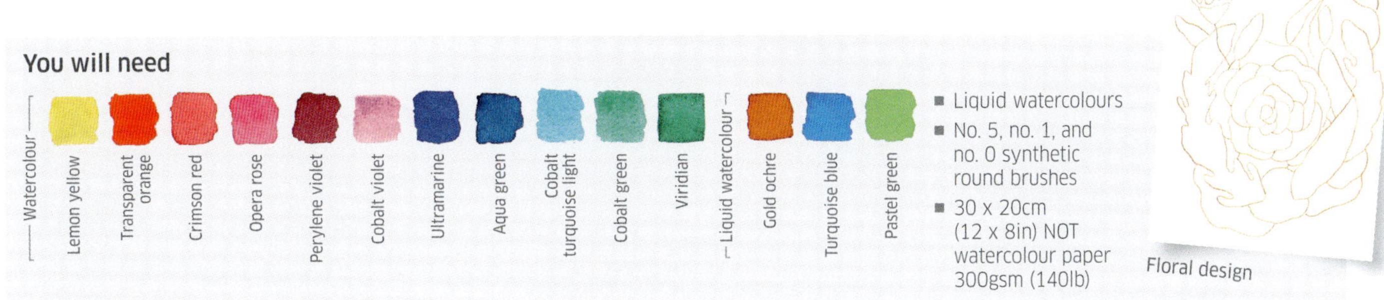

You will need

Watercolour: Lemon yellow, Transparent orange, Crimson red, Opera rose, Perylene violet, Cobalt violet, Ultramarine, Aqua green, Cobalt turquoise light, Cobalt green, Viridian — Liquid watercolour: Gold ochre, Turquoise blue, Pastel green

- Liquid watercolours
- No. 5, no. 1, and no. 0 synthetic round brushes
- 30 x 20cm (12 x 8in) NOT watercolour paper 300gsm (140lb)

Floral design

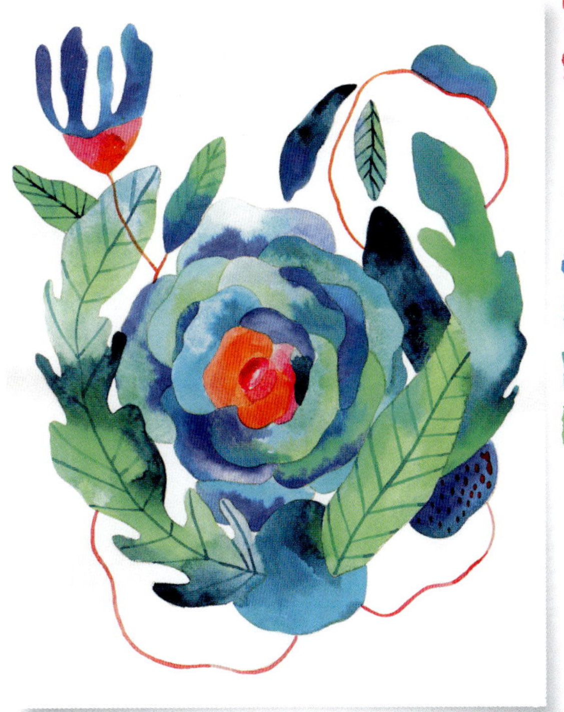

Contrasting colour scheme

To highlight one or more elements in a composition, exploit the visual effect that cool colours recede and warm colours advance. Using a warm or complementary colour against a cool colour scheme, immediately creates a focal point, adding depth to the flower.

Transparent orange · Opera rose · Ultramarine · Aqua green · Turquoise blue (liquid watercolour) · Cobalt turquoise light · Cobalt green · Pastel green (liquid watercolour)

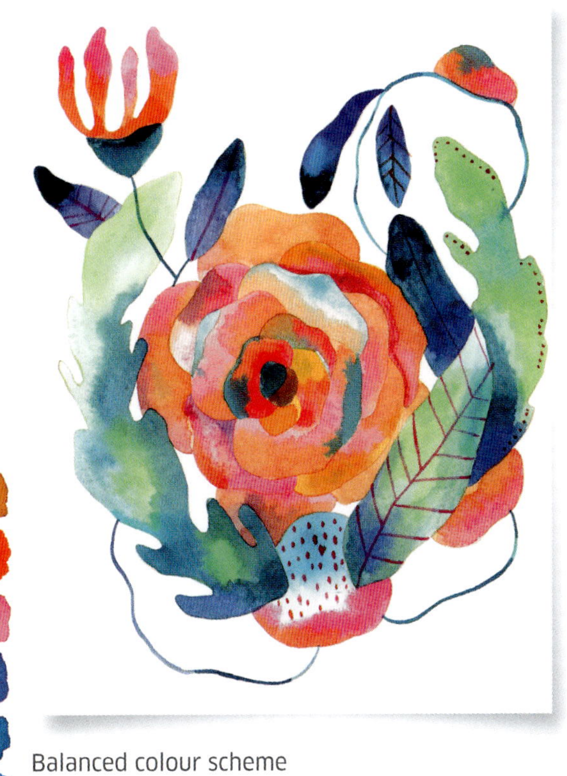

Balanced colour scheme

Using tones from both the warm and cool sides of the colour wheel will create a balanced composition in which each element will stand out and complement each other. Choose three or four colours from each side to achieve harmony, using them equally across the image.

Gold ochre (liquid watercolour) · Transparent orange · Opera rose · Ultramarine · Aqua green · Turquoise blue (liquid watercolour) · Cobalt turquoise light · Viridian

Aerial perspective

THE ILLUSION OF DISTANCE

To create depth on the flat paper surface, artists can simulate the natural effects of the atmosphere – known as aerial perspective – on objects as they recede into the distance. For realistic landscapes, observe how objects lose colour, tone, definition, and detail in the distance.

Contrasts of colour and tone

Divide the landscape into back, mid, and foreground. As objects recede in the background note that their colour leans towards cooler blue or grey, with mid tones in the middle ground, and warm, strong tones in the foreground. When painting, you may need to exaggerate this natural effect with glazes or deeper mixes.

PUTTING IT INTO PRACTICE

Here, the atmospheric effect of the distant mountain has been exaggerated by adjusting the warmth and coolness of the landscape colours, changing what you see to reflect the mood.

You will need

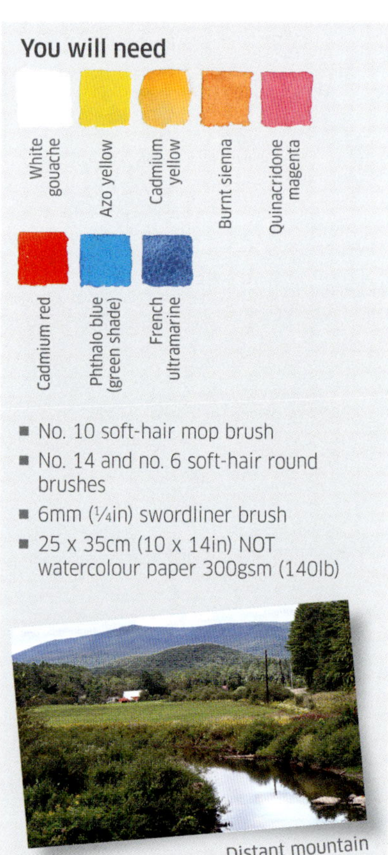

- No. 10 soft-hair mop brush
- No. 14 and no. 6 soft-hair round brushes
- 6mm (¼in) swordliner brush
- 25 x 35cm (10 x 14in) NOT watercolour paper 300gsm (140lb)

Distant mountain

1 Cool and warm washes
Paint a background wash from top to bottom, starting with a cool blue mix of phthalo blue with a touch of quinacridone magenta at the top, and a warm ochre colour mixed from quinacridone magenta and yellow at the bottom.

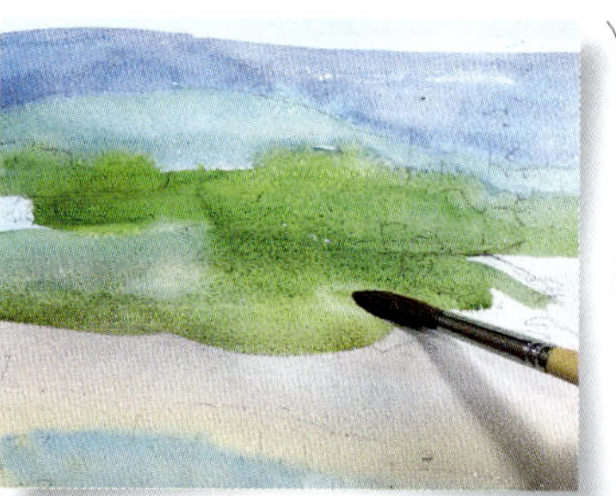

2 Enhance distant contrasts
Exaggerate and push the mountain further back using richer, cool tones from French ultramarine with a little quinacridone magenta and yellow. Add more yellow to the distant trees to bring them forward.

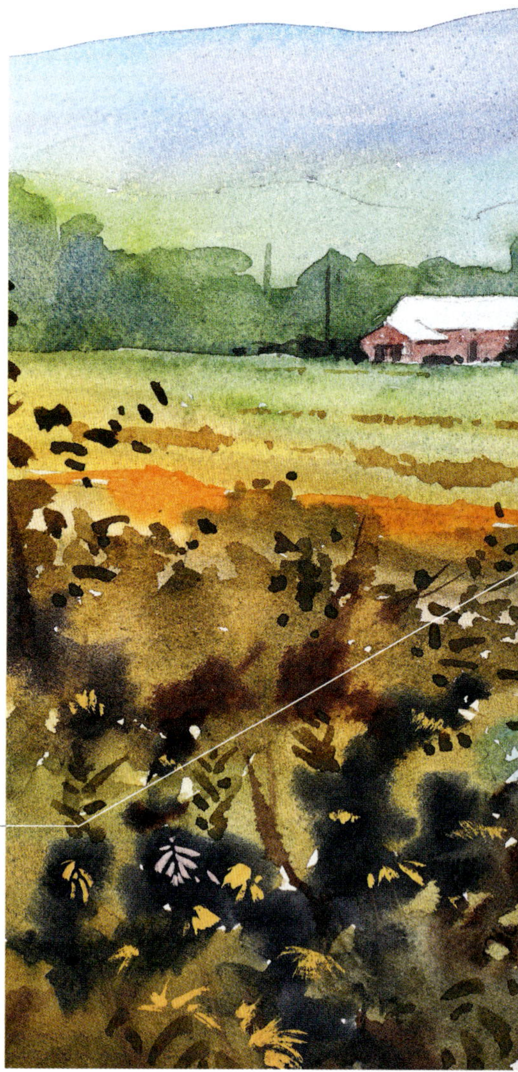

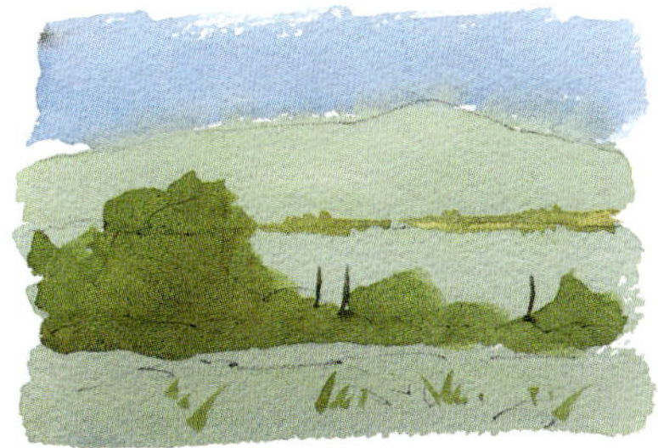

Minimal contrast

If the background, middle, and foreground are painted in the same tonal value, the landscape appears flat, with no illusion of depth.

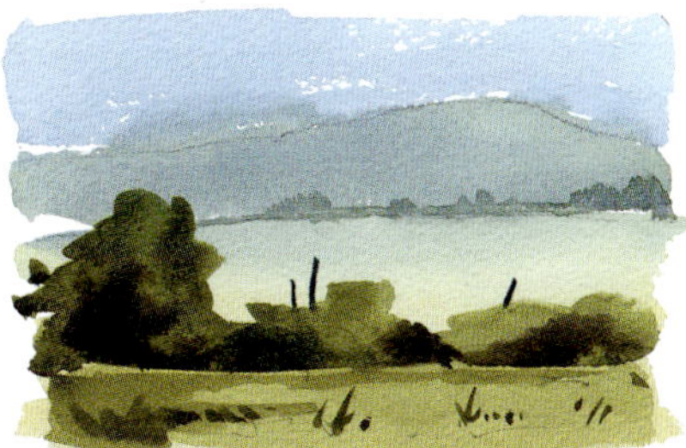

Strong contrast

A more natural approach uses warm colours and stronger tones in the foreground with cooler, weaker tones in the background.

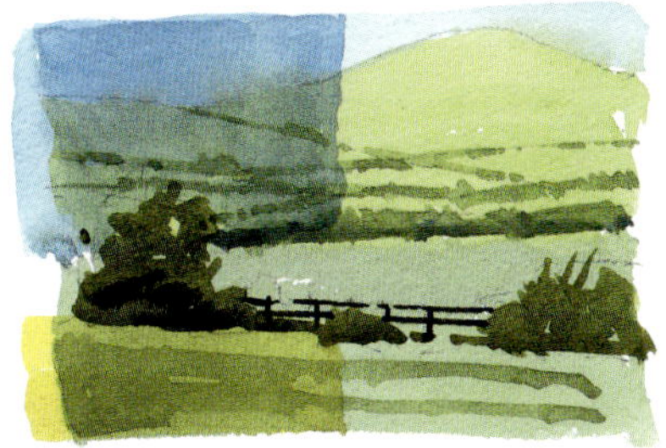

Emphasizing the contrast

If your painting still lacks depth, enhance the contrasts with glazes: a cool blue over the background and warm yellow coming forward.

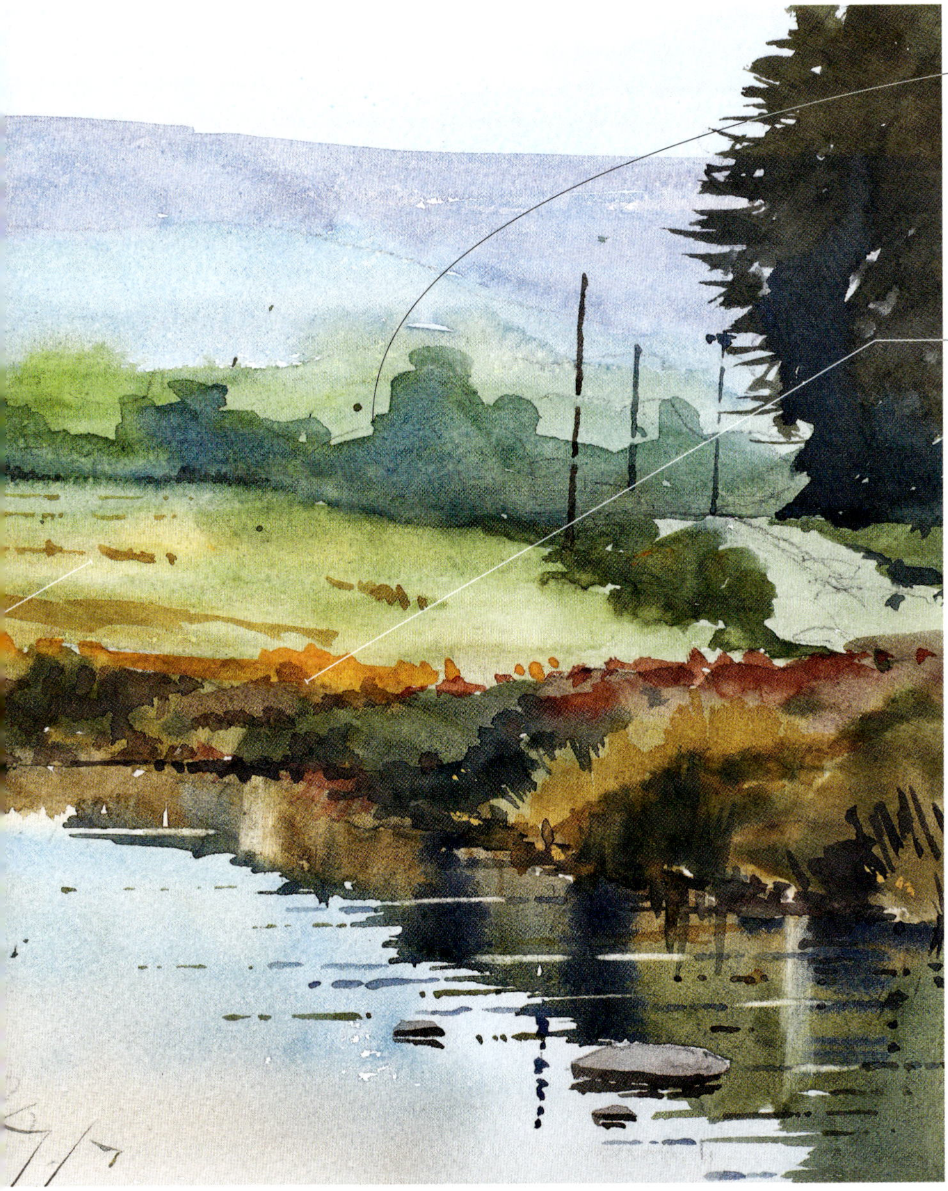

Tonal variation increases towards the foreground

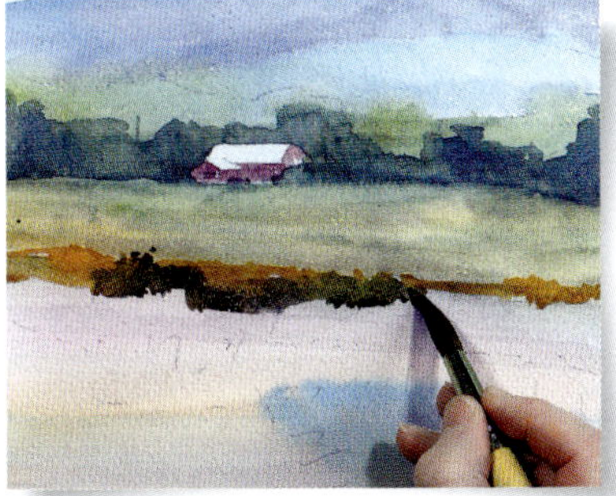

3 Warm mixes

Add warmer Indian yellow to mixes with plenty of pigment to make a warmer, strong green that brings the middle ground forward. A touch of red for the barn will enhance the effect.

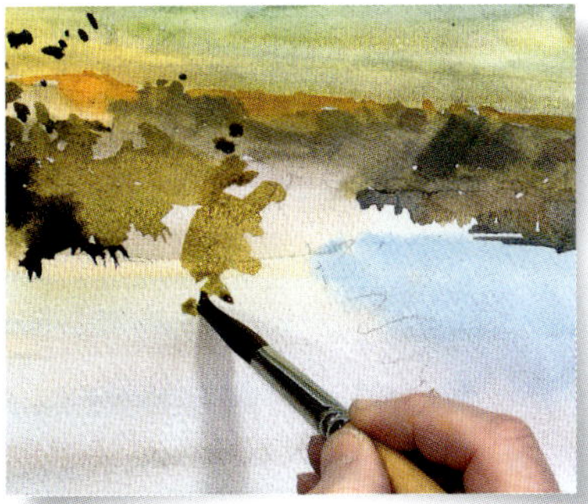

4 Foreground detail

For the foreground, use a variety of colour and tone and add almost all the detail, which brings this area forward; resist putting detail in the background. Mix a little white gouache with red and yellow to add a few light highlights.

Glazing

APPLYING TRANSPARENT LAYERS

This useful technique simply involves laying one thin wash, or glaze, of colour over another dry layer of paint, either to build colours from light to dark, or to interact with the underlying colour to create a colour mix or alter colour temperature. Use transparent glazes to adjust large areas of tone across a landscape, or over small pockets of local colour.

■ Altering layers

Before applying a glaze, consider its effect on the dried wash underneath, and how that will modify the feel of your painting. A glaze can be used to enhance aerial perspective; a cool glaze helps a background recede, whereas a warm glaze makes it advance. Use glazes to modify shadows or add colour to a monochrome sketch.

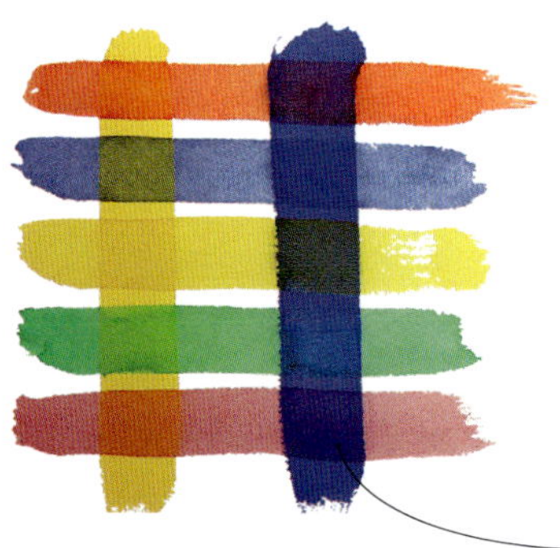

Modifying colour

Change the underlying colour with a transparent glaze in a different hue to create optical mixes, such as purple where red and blue meet, or orange where yellow and red cross. You can also use warm or cool glazes to alter colour temperature.

Blue is warmed by red glaze

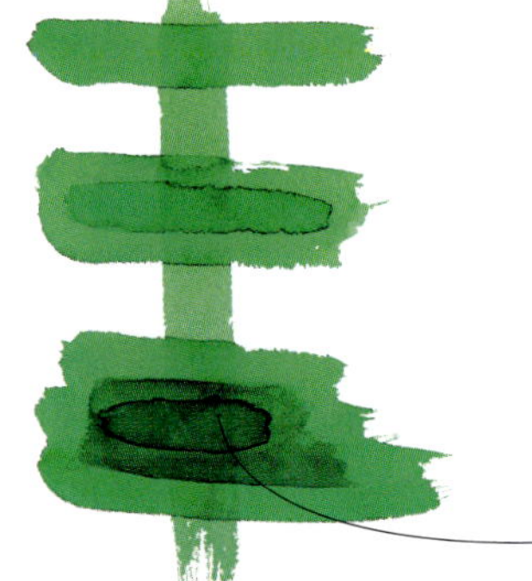

Modifying tone

Build tones from light to dark by layering thin glazes on top of each other. The subtle effect can be used over a large area, such as a sea or sky, and will give a light, transparent feel with modulations of tone.

Glaze layers build darker tone

PUTTING IT INTO PRACTICE

The calm, peaceful mood of this scene is conveyed in a few stages, taking note of the three main areas of light, mid, and dark tone. Glazing is used to add depth to the water and to warm the foreground.

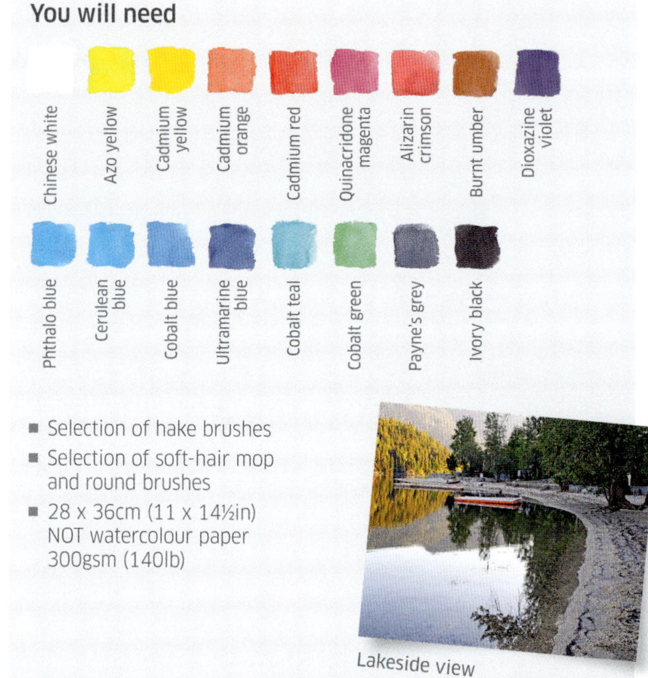

You will need

Chinese white · Azo yellow · Cadmium yellow · Cadmium orange · Cadmium red · Quinacridone magenta · Alizarin crimson · Burnt umber · Dioxazine violet

Phthalo blue · Cerulean blue · Cobalt blue · Ultramarine blue · Cobalt teal · Cobalt green · Payne's grey · Ivory black

- Selection of hake brushes
- Selection of soft-hair mop and round brushes
- 28 x 36cm (11 x 14½in) NOT watercolour paper 300gsm (140lb)

Lakeside view

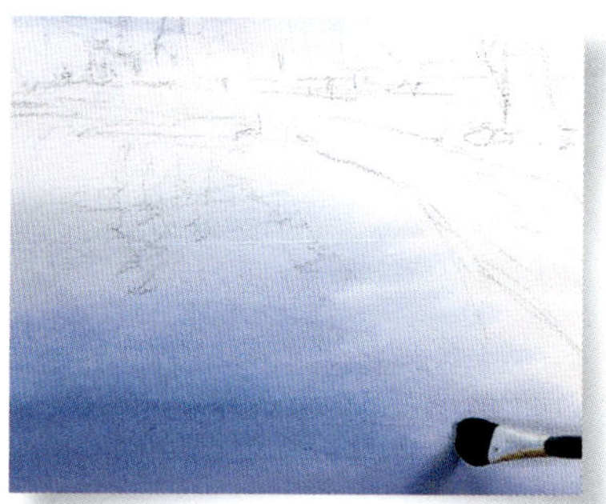

1 Establish lightest tone
Simplify the scene into areas of light, mid, and dark tone. Lay a single wash for the lightest areas of the distant mountains, becoming slightly darker towards the foreground water.

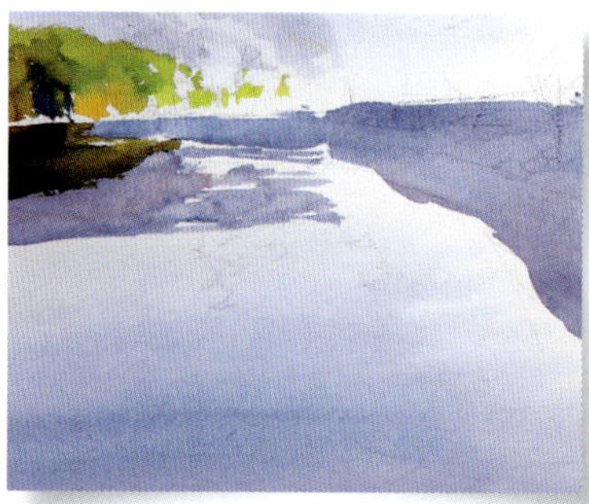

2 Medium tones
The lit green mountain and the shoreline are part of the medium value, so work on these at the same time to make sure that the tonal relationship with the water and distant mountains is correct.

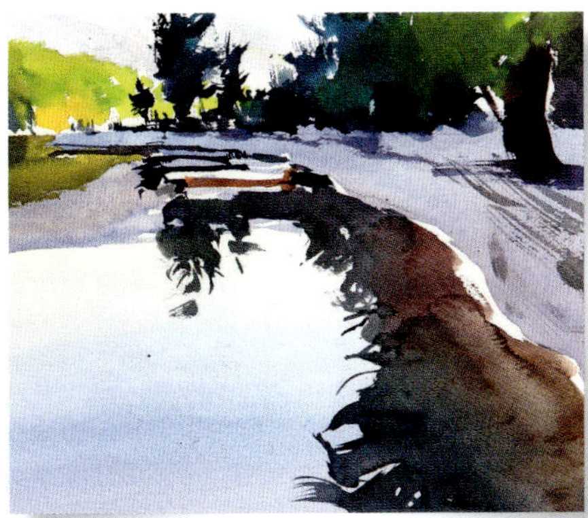

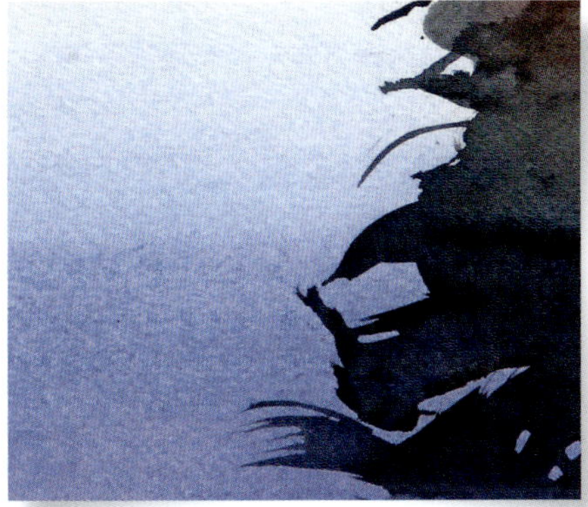

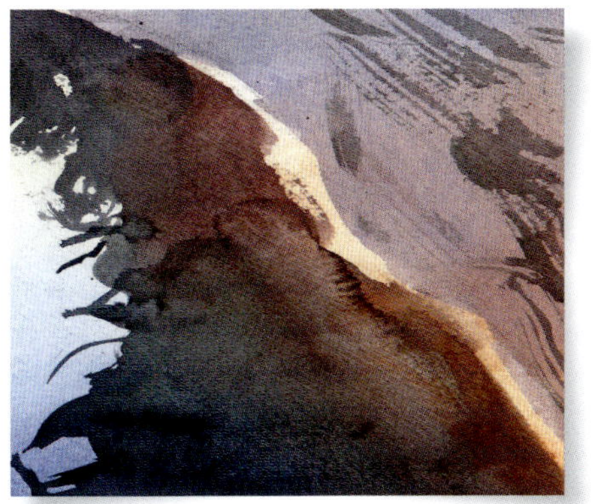

3 Assess the tones
After blocking in the dark trees and the water reflections, assess your painting. Here, the foreground shoreline needs to be warmer and the near water needs to be darker.

4 Darker glaze
Glazing is the simplest way to modify these areas. Apply a deeper blue glaze to darken the foreground water, taking the glaze over the shadow areas to unite each element.

5 Warm glaze
To help the foreground advance, apply a warm orange glaze over the base blue and add a light magenta glaze over the trees to warm the middle ground against the cool sky.

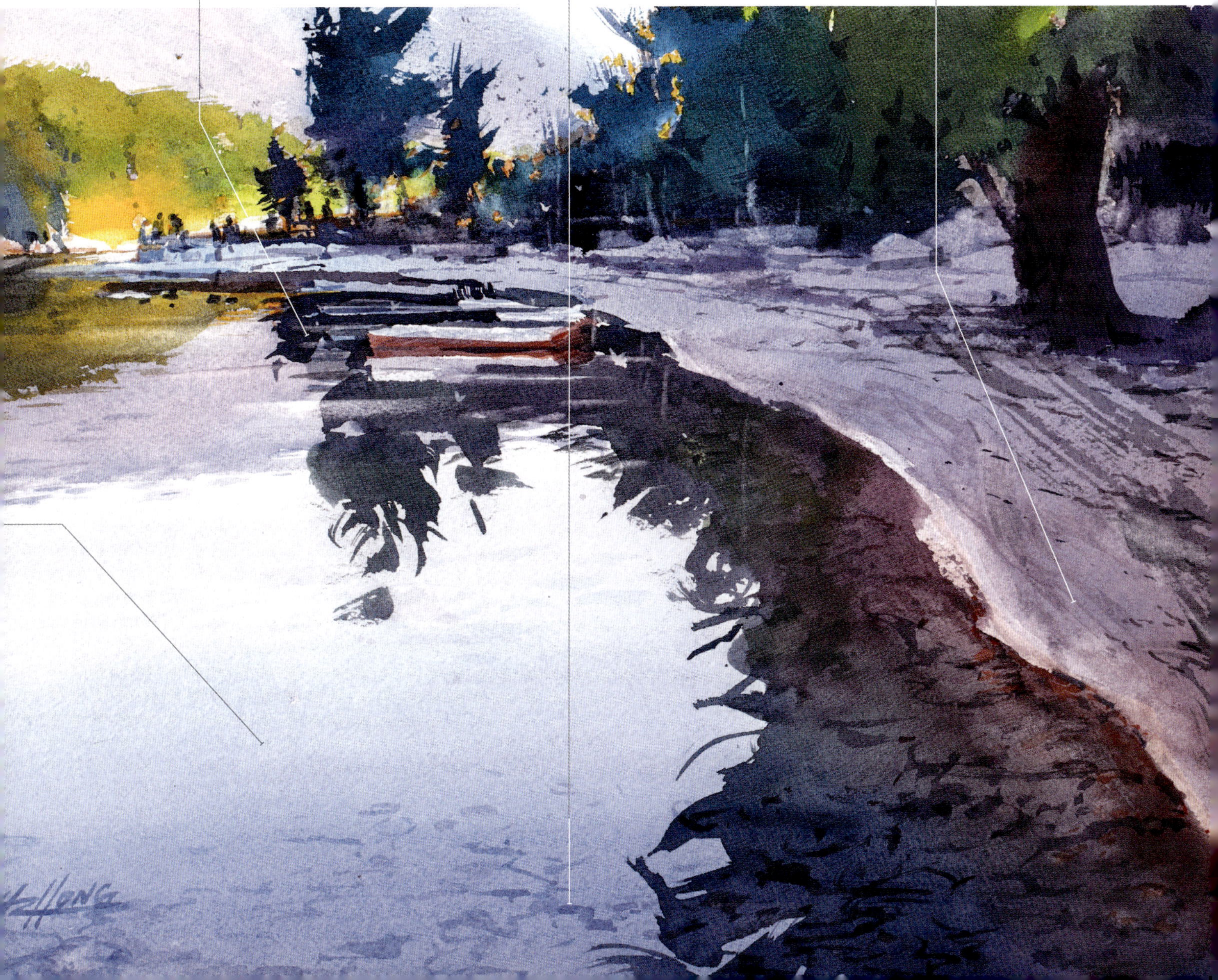

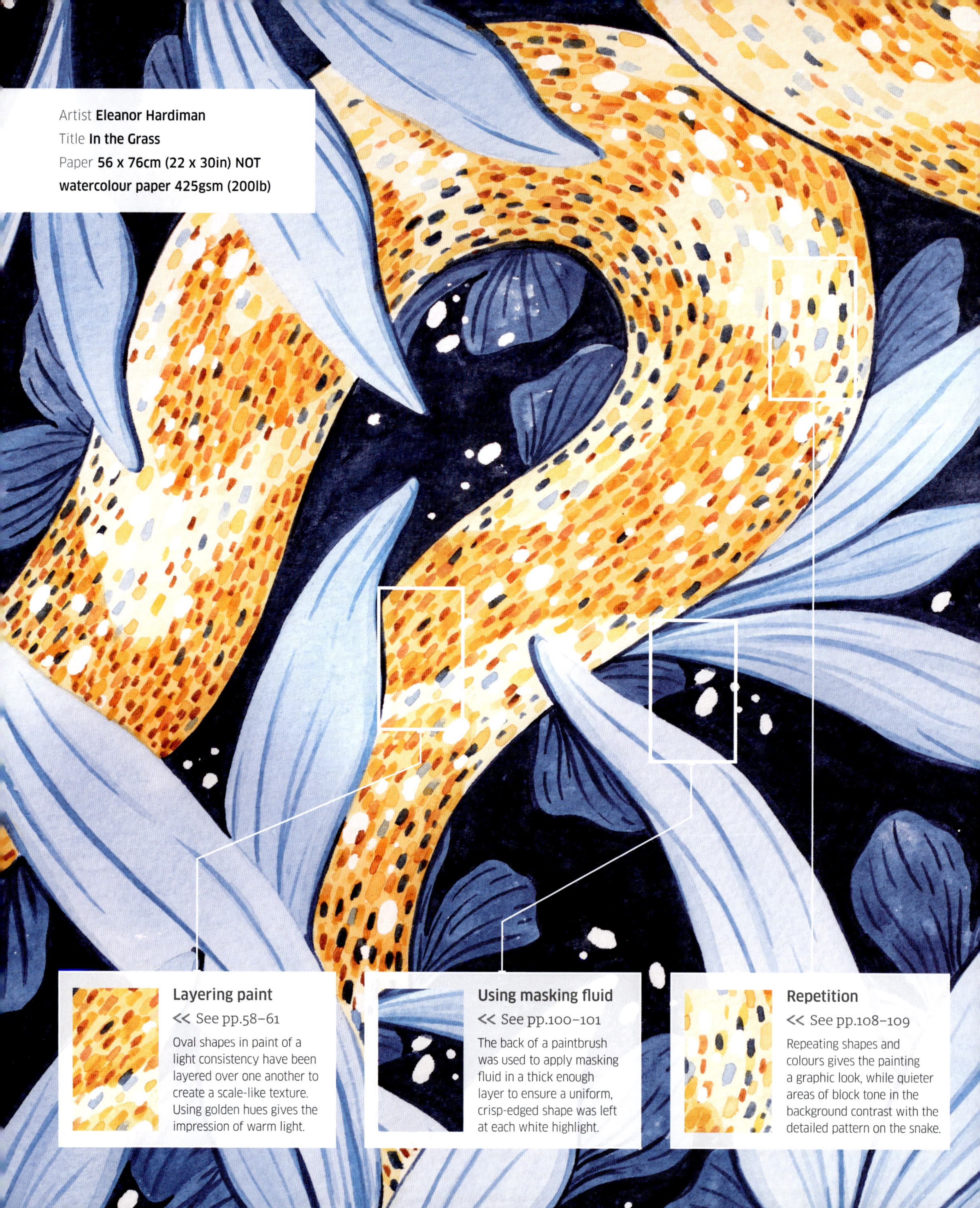

Layering paint
<< See pp.58–61

Oval shapes in paint of a light consistency have been layered over one another to create a scale-like texture. Using golden hues gives the impression of warm light.

Using masking fluid
<< See pp.100–101

The back of a paintbrush was used to apply masking fluid in a thick enough layer to ensure a uniform, crisp-edged shape was left at each white highlight.

Repetition
<< See pp.108–109

Repeating shapes and colours gives the painting a graphic look, while quieter areas of block tone in the background contrast with the detailed pattern on the snake.

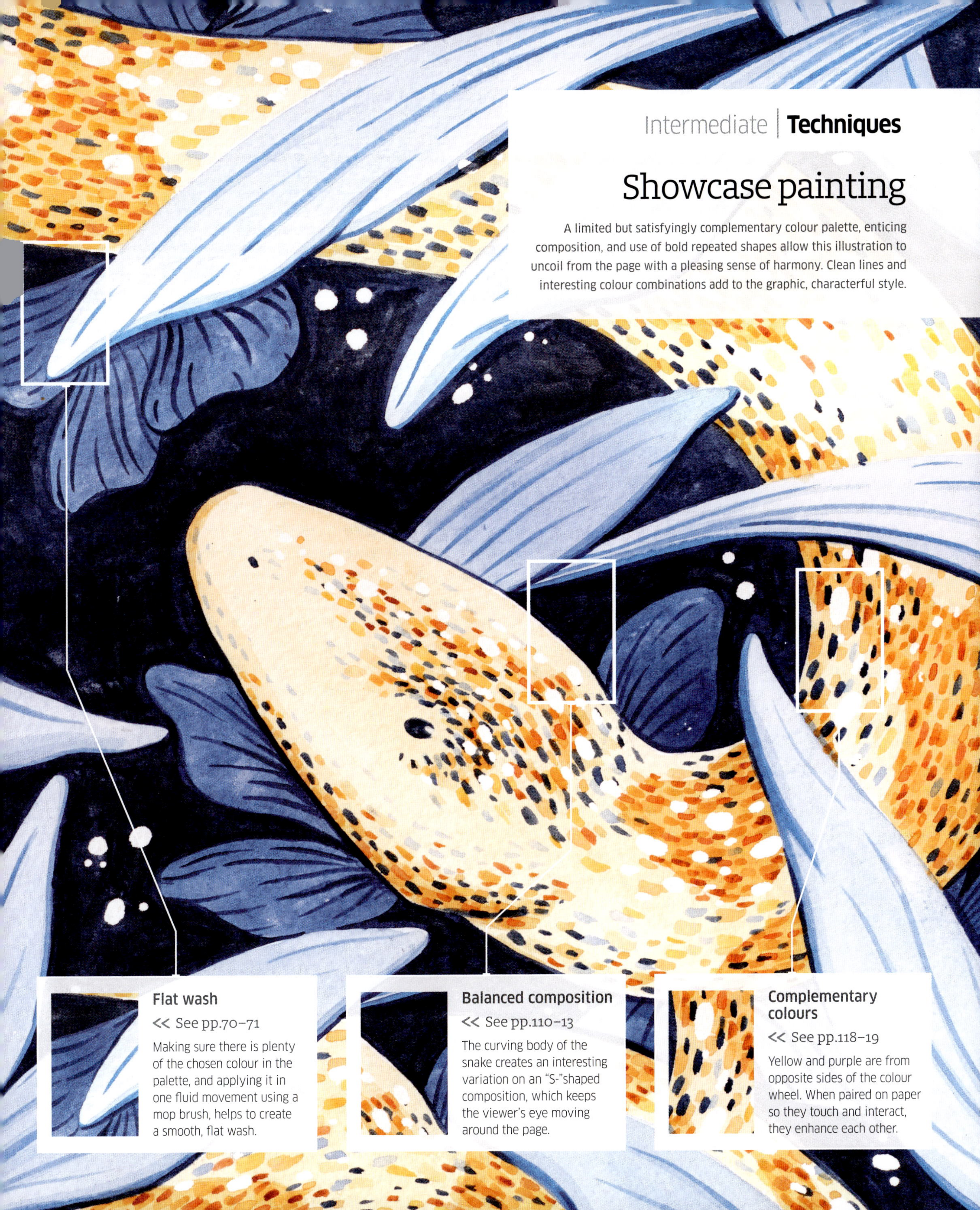

Showcase painting

A limited but satisfyingly complementary colour palette, enticing composition, and use of bold repeated shapes allow this illustration to uncoil from the page with a pleasing sense of harmony. Clean lines and interesting colour combinations add to the graphic, characterful style.

Flat wash

<< See pp.70–71

Making sure there is plenty of the chosen colour in the palette, and applying it in one fluid movement using a mop brush, helps to create a smooth, flat wash.

Balanced composition

<< See pp.110–13

The curving body of the snake creates an interesting variation on an "S-"shaped composition, which keeps the viewer's eye moving around the page.

Complementary colours

<< See pp.118–19

Yellow and purple are from opposite sides of the colour wheel. When paired on paper so they touch and interact, they enhance each other.

Working in monochrome

FOCUSSING ON TONAL VALUES

The structure of a painting is based on tone, or value, not colour. It is important to understand the difference between the two. Colour refers only to the hue, but tone is the lightness or darkness of that hue (see also pp.32–33). By painting in one colour and concentrating on tone, you will be able to produce simple interpretations of even the most difficult subjects.

PUTTING IT INTO PRACTICE

If working in monochrome, a colourful subject forces you to think tonally. Here, the scene is reduced to three base values: lights are left as white paper, mid tones are reduced to one wash and darks are built up on top.

You will need

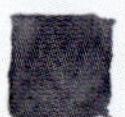

Neutral tint

- No. 14 and no. 6 soft-hair round brushes
- 25 x 35cm (10 x 14in) NOT watercolour paper 300gsm (140lb)

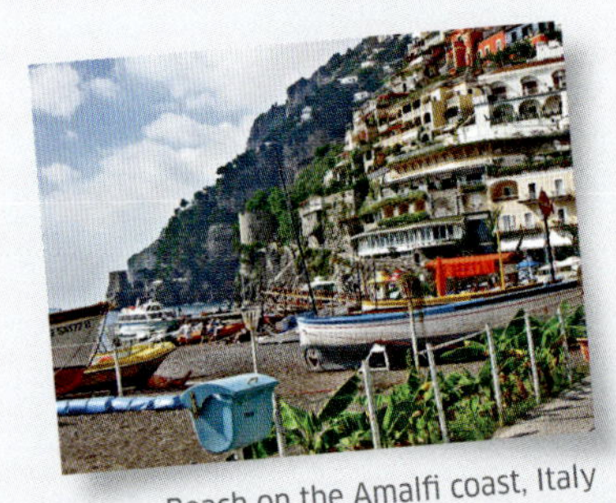

Beach on the Amalfi coast, Italy

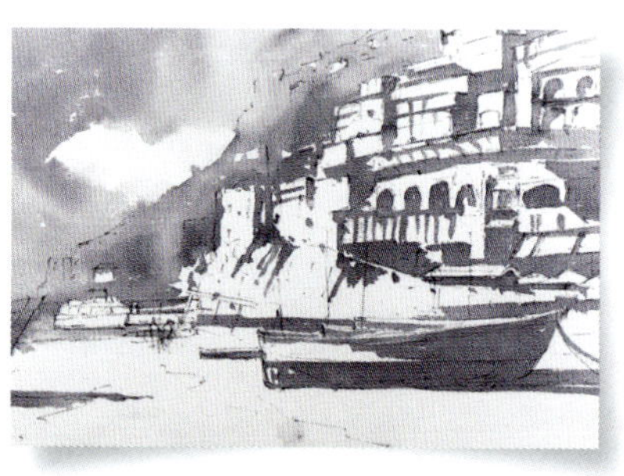

1 Mid-tone base
Merge light tones together and render the whole subject with a light, mid-tone wash, except for the lightest lights left as white paper. Forget colour – look for light and dark only, to define the structure.

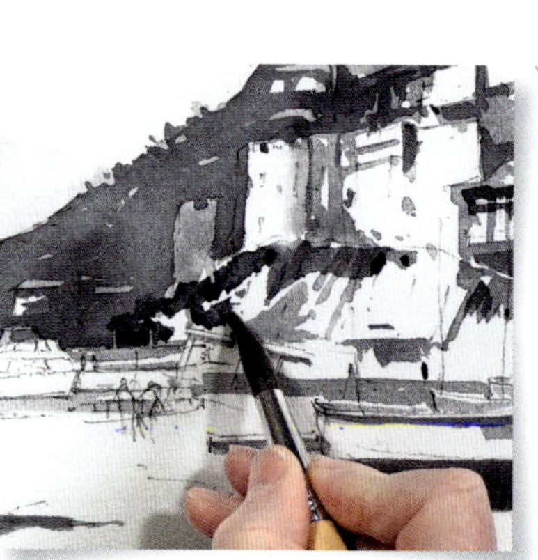

2 Selective second wash
With a second, darker mid-tone wash, cover everything except for the lightest lights and the mid tones from the first wash. Converting colour to monochrome makes you see the importance of strong tonal shapes rather than detail.

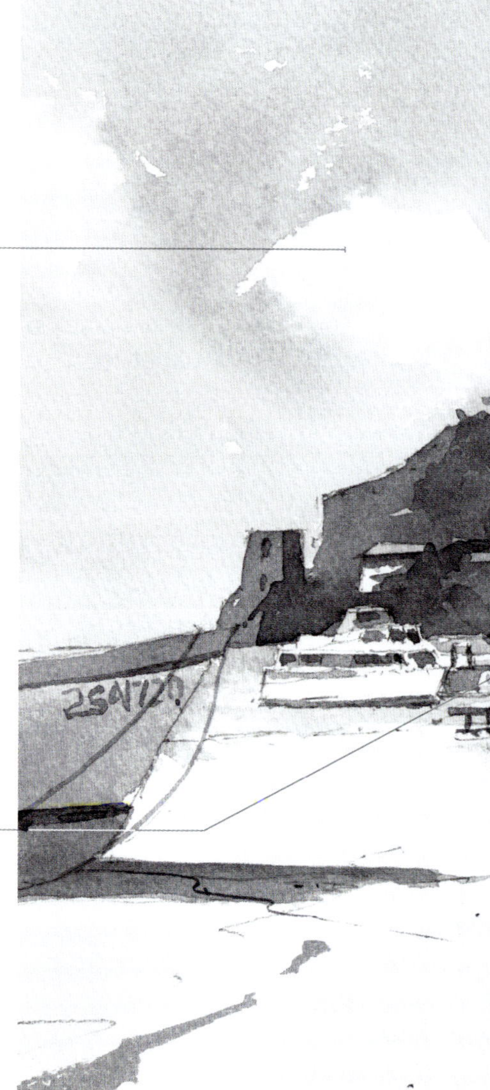

Converting colour to tone

To assess tones, convert colour into value, or greyscale; light, mid, and dark. Paint your subject in one colour, using a paint that is naturally dark, such as neutral tint, black, sepia, or indigo. Start with a mid-tone wash, leaving the white of the paper for the lights. Don't differentiate between the lightest tones, even if they are different colours; allow them to merge together. Mix a darker wash for the stronger colours and details.

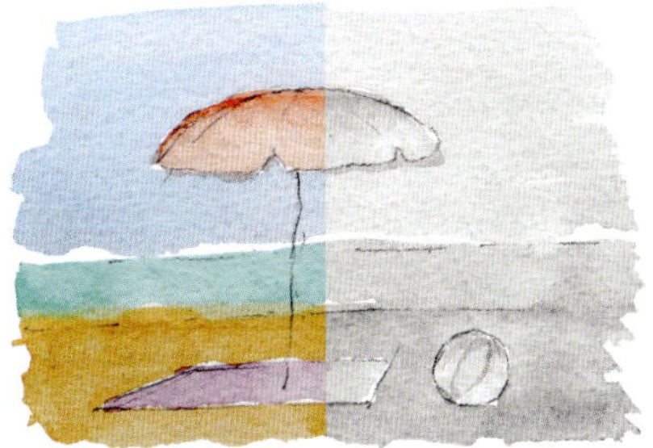

Little tonal contrast

If you think only in colour you could end up with a flat and uninteresting image. Convert the subject to greyscale (right), and everything merges into one.

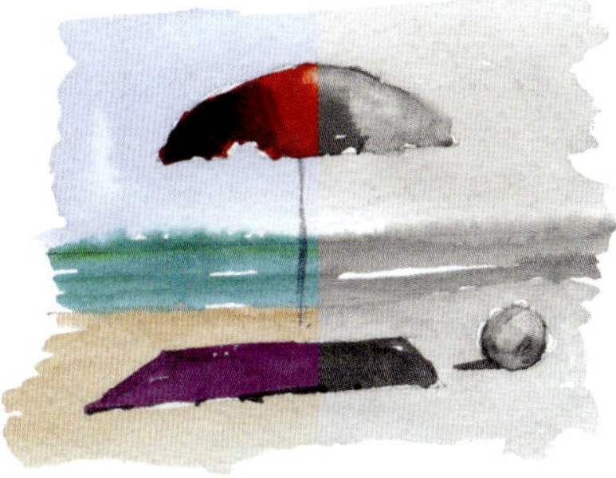

Stronger tonal contrast

By also thinking of the tone of colours, you will produce something where the structure can still be clearly seen when converted to greyscale (right).

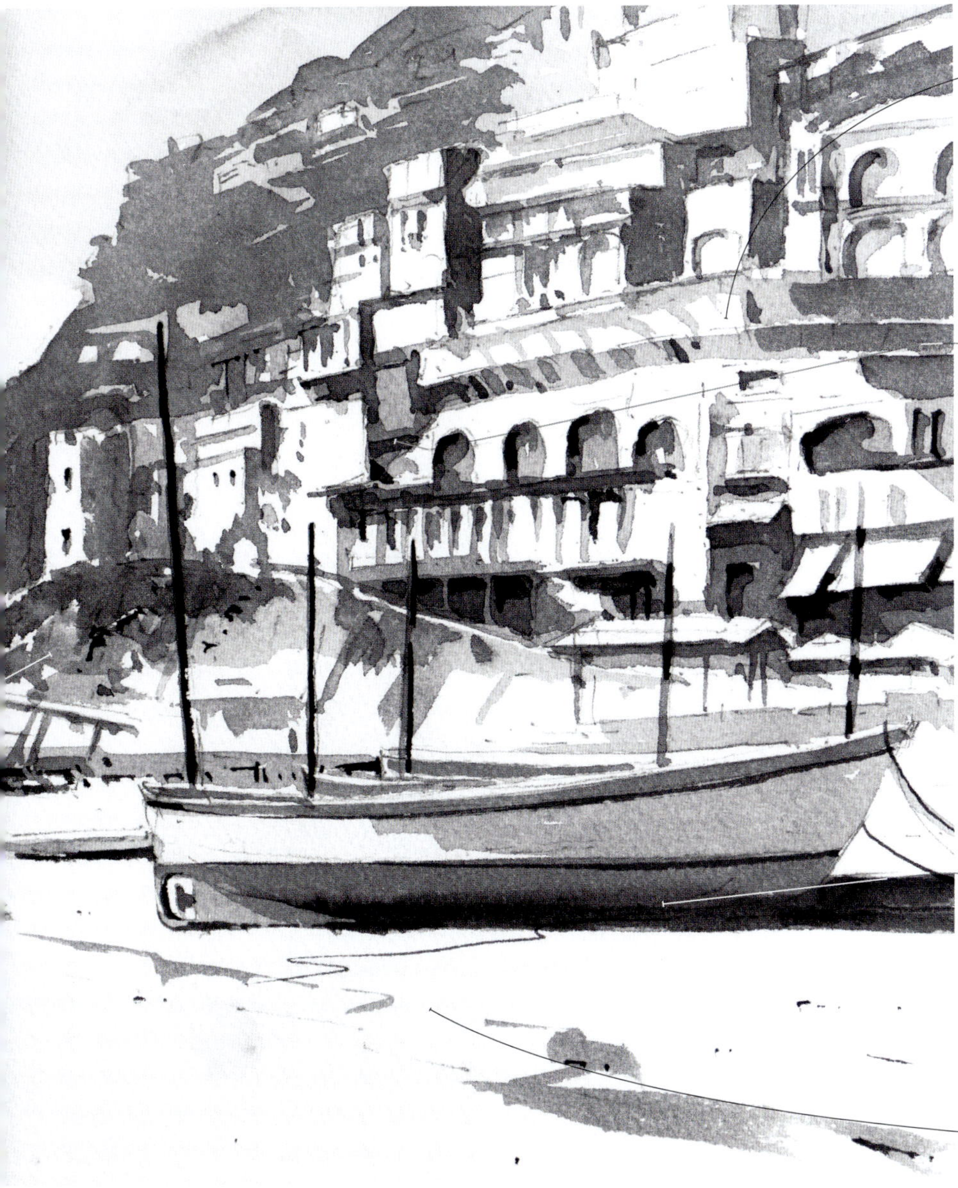

Don't differentiate between the lightest tones of different colours; allow all of them to merge together

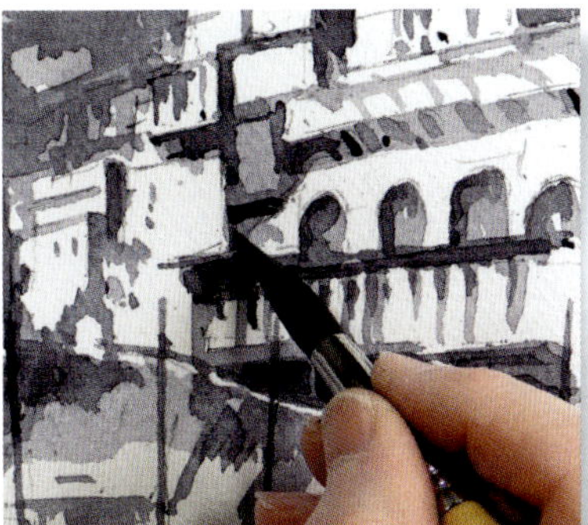

3 Reinforce darker areas
With the third wash, cover only those darker-toned areas. You will find areas where you are itching to use colour, but resist and enjoy the process.

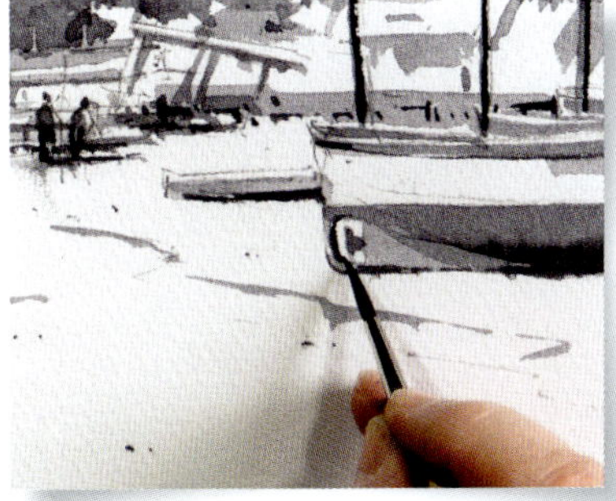

4 Intense darks
Use almost neat paint to create the darkest darks for the final details that help to pull the painting together.

Monochrome emphasizes the need to reserve the light areas from the earlier stages

Simplifying figures

USING SIMPLE SHAPES

Tackling the drawing of figures can seem intimidating, but in fact they can be broken down into simple shapes to create convincing human beings in a contemporary graphic style. By using flowing lines a stylized figure can be drawn that still remains believable.

◾ Drawing the essentials

This technique can be used when drawing from life, from a reference, or even from the imagination. It uses lines running through the centre of the body to make the figure flow convincingly. The figure is drawn in sections, starting with the torso. Reducing the complex human form to simple graphic shapes makes figures easier to draw in any position. Once the shapes are determined the form is drawn over with darker lines.

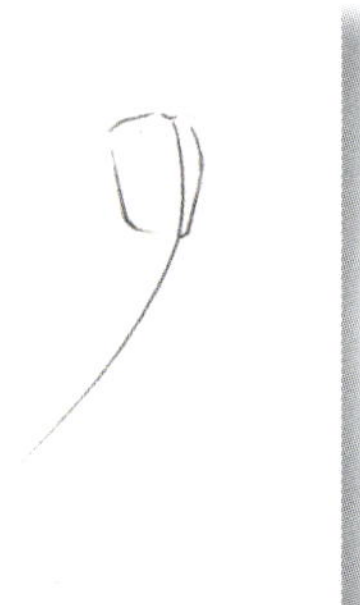

The initial lines
Sketch a line, imagining it going through the centre of the body from the neck to the hips. Draw the torso as a simple oblong shape.

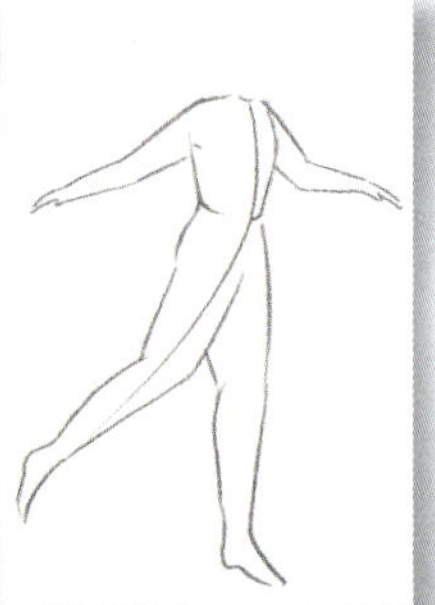

Adding the limbs
Next add curved hips and render the legs and arms as simple shapes, splitting the legs into two parts, above and below the knee.

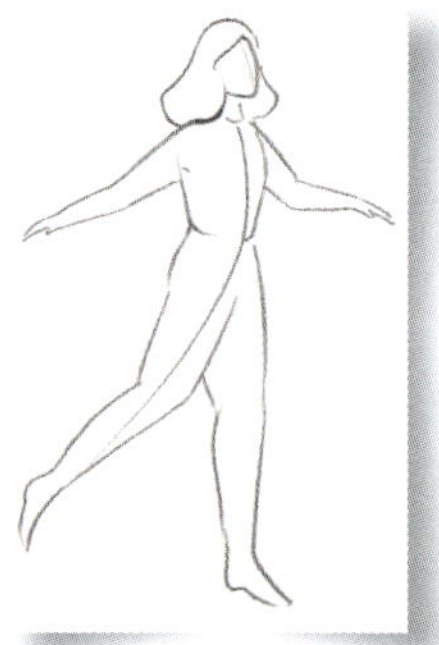

The head and neck
Add the neck and an egg shape for the head. Draw a central line between the eyes and down the nose. Base the features on this central point.

PUTTING IT INTO PRACTICE

This stylized watercolour is painted from the palest tone to the darkest detail colour, using light and medium washes that are layered to create blocks of shadows and a graphic style.

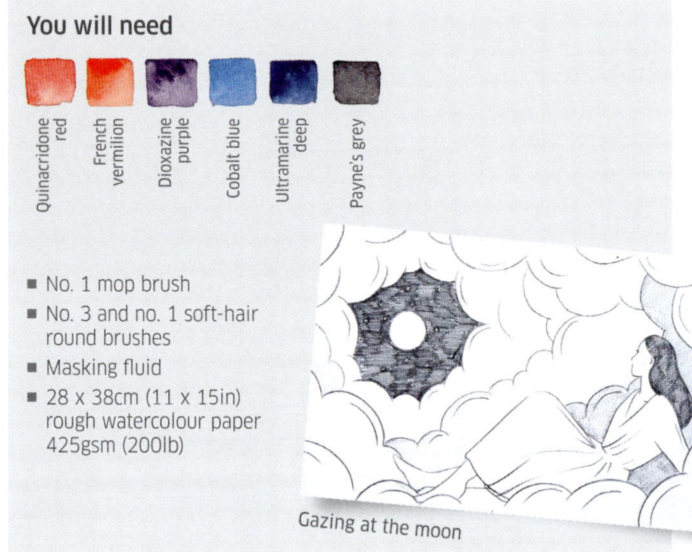

- No. 1 mop brush
- No. 3 and no. 1 soft-hair round brushes
- Masking fluid
- 28 x 38cm (11 x 15in) rough watercolour paper 425gsm (200lb)

Gazing at the moon

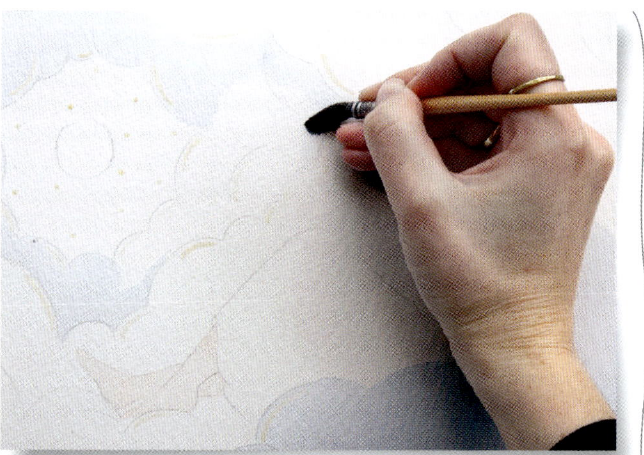

1 Sketching and masking
Using the reference sketch, lightly draw the composition. With the end of a paintbrush, apply masking fluid in the areas that are to remain white. When it is dry, mix plenty of very dilute colour and paint in the lightest tone using a mop brush. Try to paint these areas in one go to keep the colour as flat as possible. Mix the reds together for the skin tones.

2 Building up tones

Once the first layer is dry, paint shadows on it in the same colour. The moon is the light source, so follow the direction of the light. You should now have two tones.

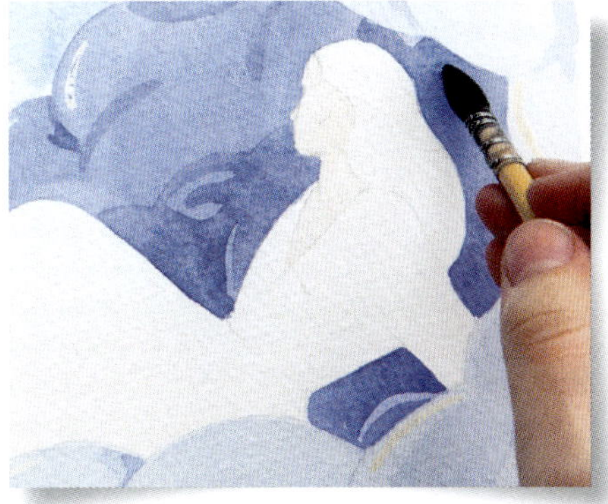

3 Painting the negative shape

Mix a darker blue wash and paint round the figure in a flat layer. Repeat the areas of the first wash with the darker wash and paint flowing cloud shapes.

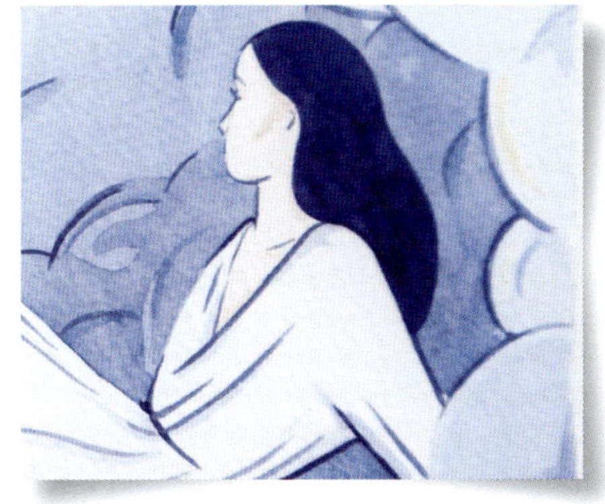

4 Add detail with the darkest tone

Mix the darkest tone and, using a round brush and small strokes, paint details such as the face, hair, sky, and edges of some of the clouds. Finally, remove the masking fluid.

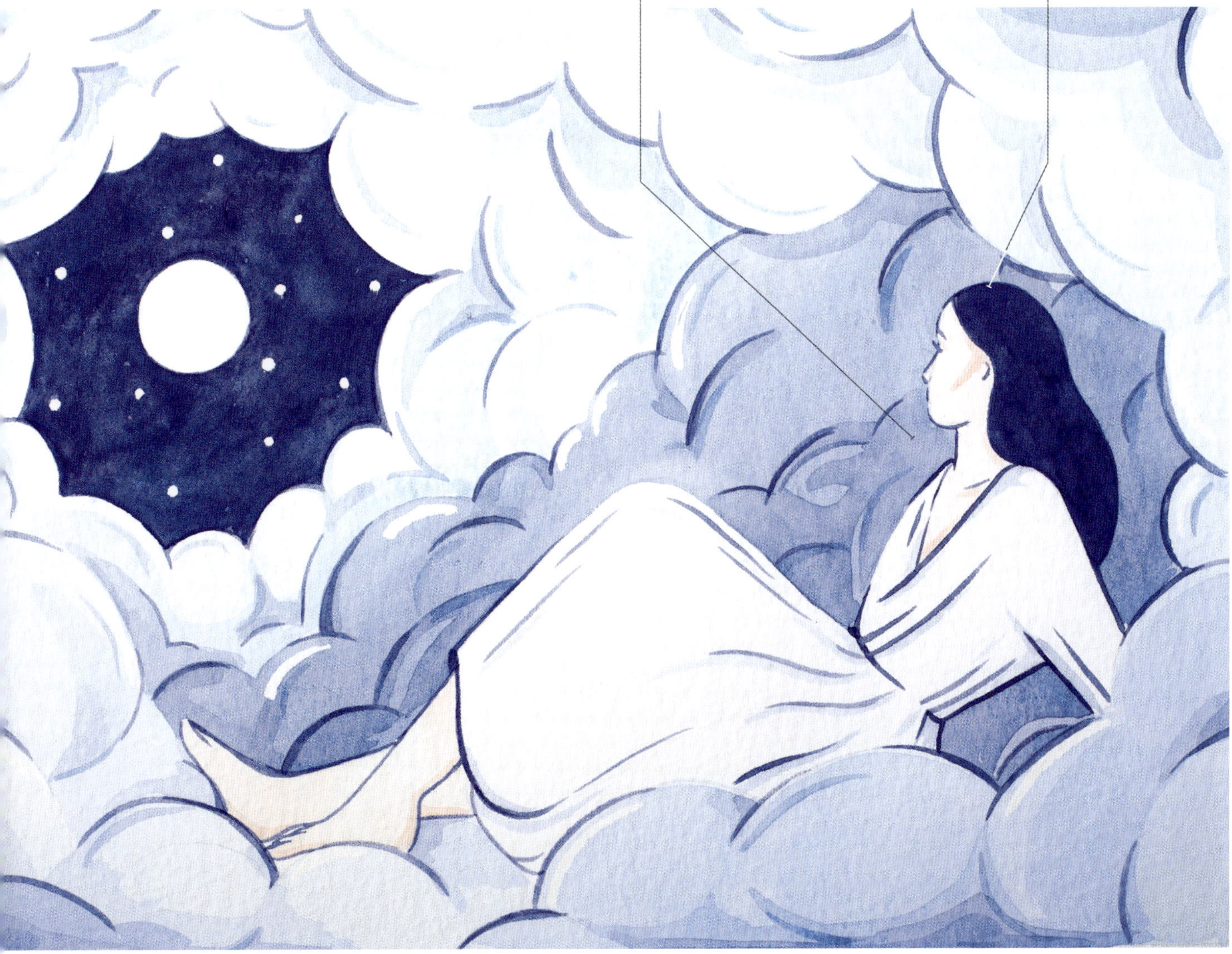

Simplifying a scene

ELIMINATING DETAILS

Townscapes can tempt the watercolour artist to overcomplicate a scene and lose the freshness of the medium. Instead, look for a few main shapes and lines that direct the eye. Use tonal contrasts that emphasize the shapes and make them three-dimensional without the need to add explanatory detail.

◼ Using washes for effect

Limiting the number of washes you apply can simplify shapes by creating impressions rather than more realistic representations. Blending colours helps to link shapes and also allows you to create the illusion of depth by using colour temperature.

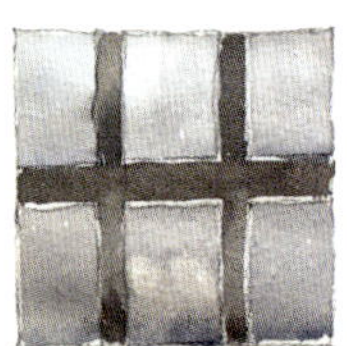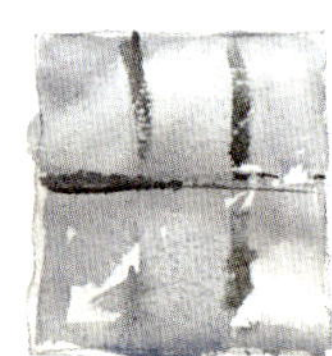

Using fewer washes
On the left, the window has been given seven washes, each pane carefully painted. On the right it is loosely painted with just two washes, the glazing bars painted over the first one.

Blending colours
Keep a limited palette and control the tone by strengthening the colours towards the foreground. Blending colours from cool to warm creates depth without requiring detail. Ideally use one wash, painting from background to foreground.

Background (light wash) cool colours

Middle distance (medium wash) mid-temperature colours

Foreground (heavy wash) warm colours

PUTTING IT INTO PRACTICE

This is a subject that has strong tonal shapes, few colours, and a sense of depth, with shadows masking a host of complicated details. Avoid using small brushes as they create a temptation to fiddle.

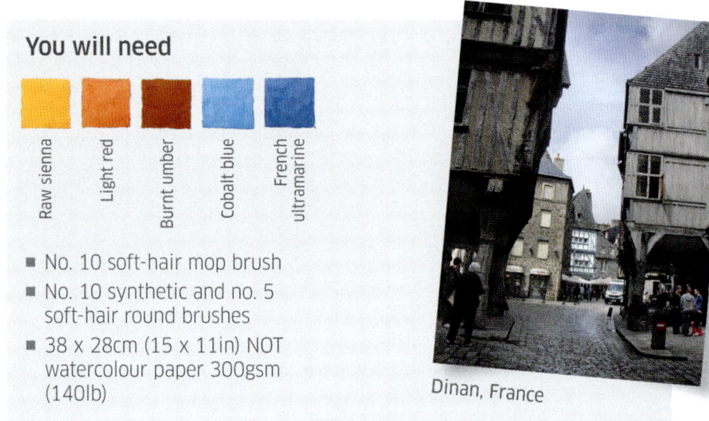

- No. 10 soft-hair mop brush
- No. 10 synthetic and no. 5 soft-hair round brushes
- 38 x 28cm (15 x 11in) NOT watercolour paper 300gsm (140lb)

Dinan, France

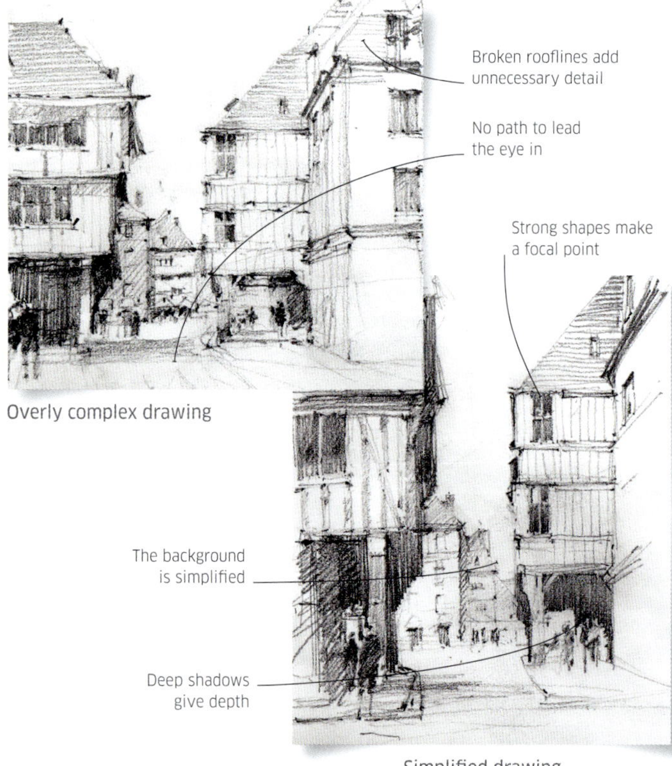

Overly complex drawing

Simplified drawing

1 Identifying key shapes and tones

It helps to draw the scene from different angles first. In the top drawing there are too many fussy details and no deep shadows to give distance. The view above is simpler, with depth and strong shadows, and captures the essence of the timber-framed houses.

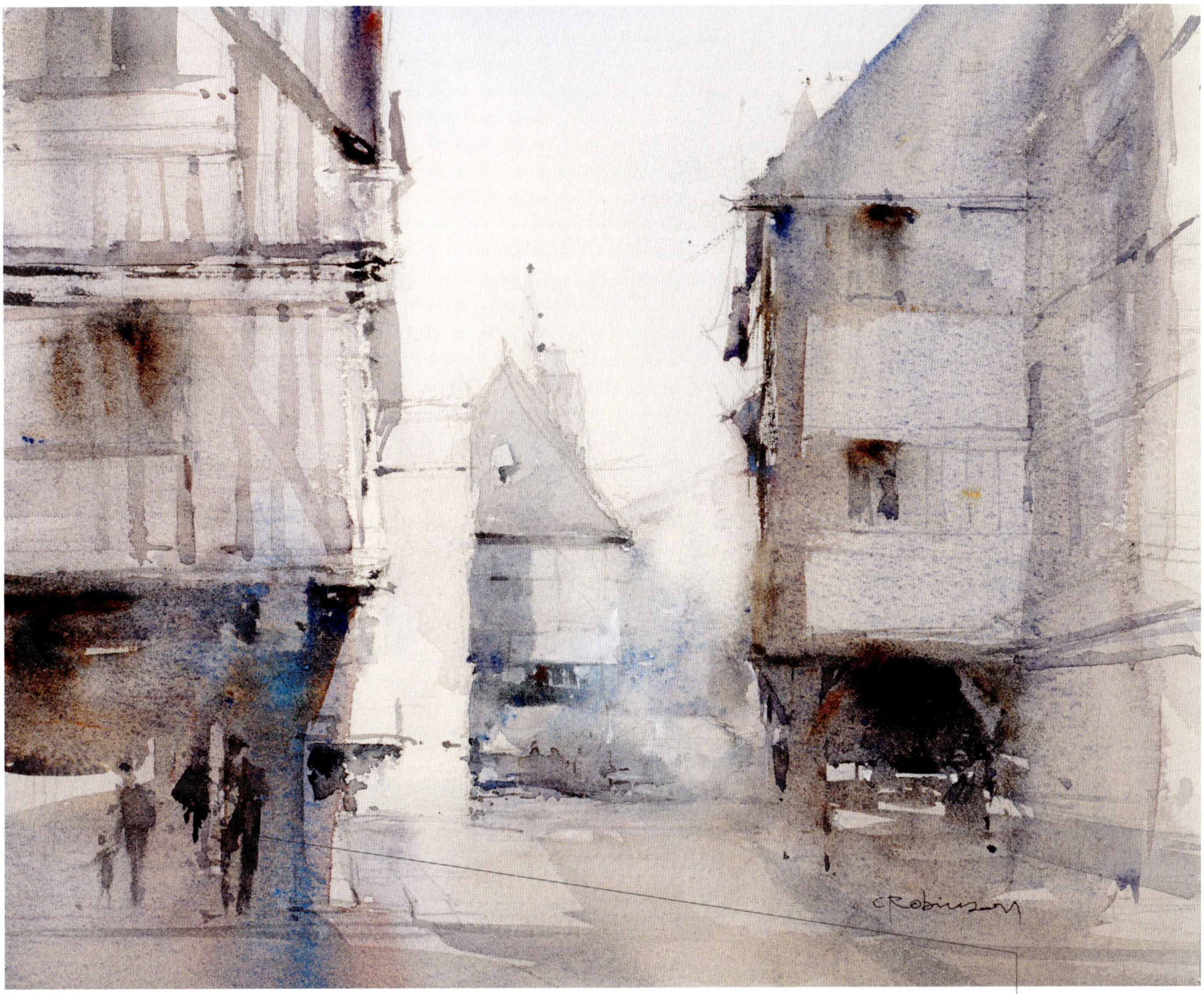

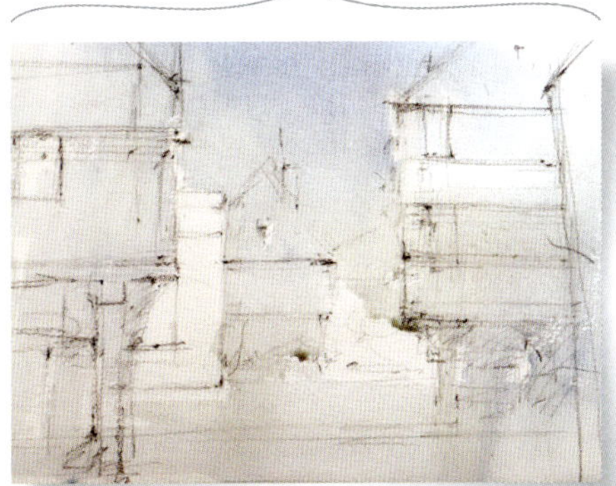

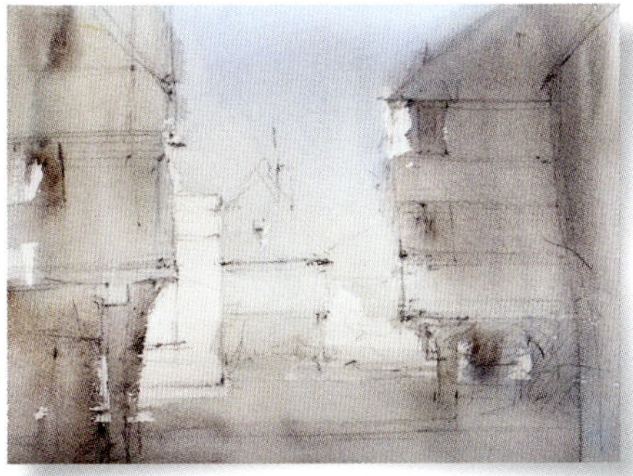

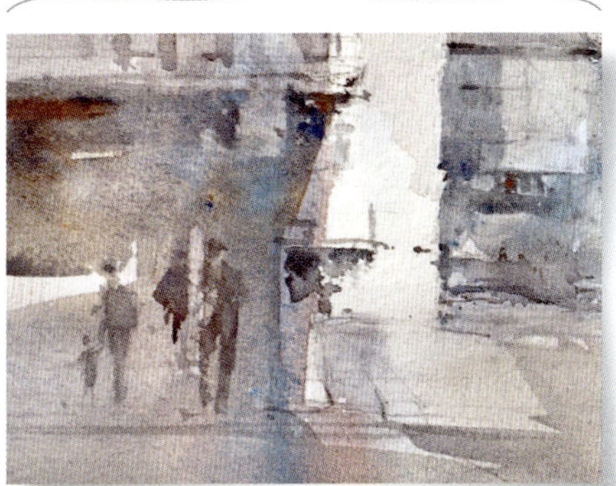

2 Putting in the palest tones
Draw a rough outline of the positions of the buildings and add a general wash of cobalt blue. Add light red and raw sienna over the lower part of the paper.

3 Emphasizing the main shapes
As the paint starts to dry, tilt the paper to 45 degrees and, with the mop brush, add a second wash of burnt umber and French ultramarine over the two main buildings.

4 Picking out details
With the synthetic brush, paint over the pencil marks. Strengthen deep shadows with a stiffer mix of the same colours. Add figures and the timber frames with the no. 5 brush.

Linear perspective

DEPICTING DISTANCE AND THREE-DIMENSIONAL SPACE

A sense of perspective is one of the tools that an artist can use to give a drawing or painting depth and substance. These examples explain linear perspective, a concept most often found in landscapes where it is used to show how objects diminish in size into the distance. These principles can also be applied to other subject matter, from still lifes to life studies.

■ One-point perspective

The simplest form is one-point perspective. Here all lines of perspective vanish to one focal point positioned on the horizon line. Parallel lines above the horizon will slope down to meet it, and those below will slope up, getting closer together towards the vanishing point.

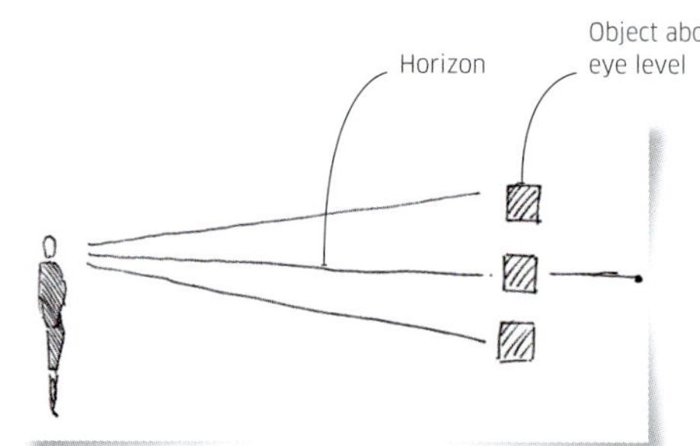

Viewpoint
The horizon is the viewer's eye level. Place objects above the horizon to imply looking up, or below the horizon to imply looking down.

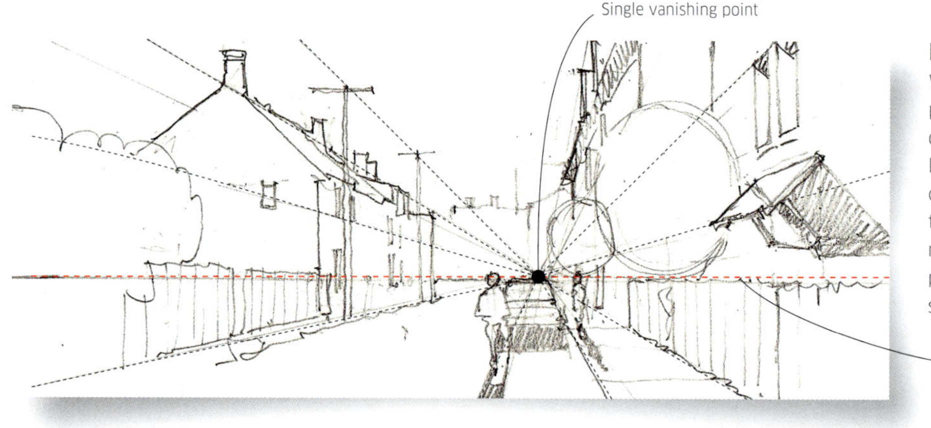

Elements of perspective
When planning a painting with one-point perspective, note how objects seen face on remain flat, but the parallel lines of buildings and the road follow the slant of linear perspective, getting closer as they approach the horizon until they meet at a single vanishing point. Objects placed following these lines become smaller towards the vanishing point.

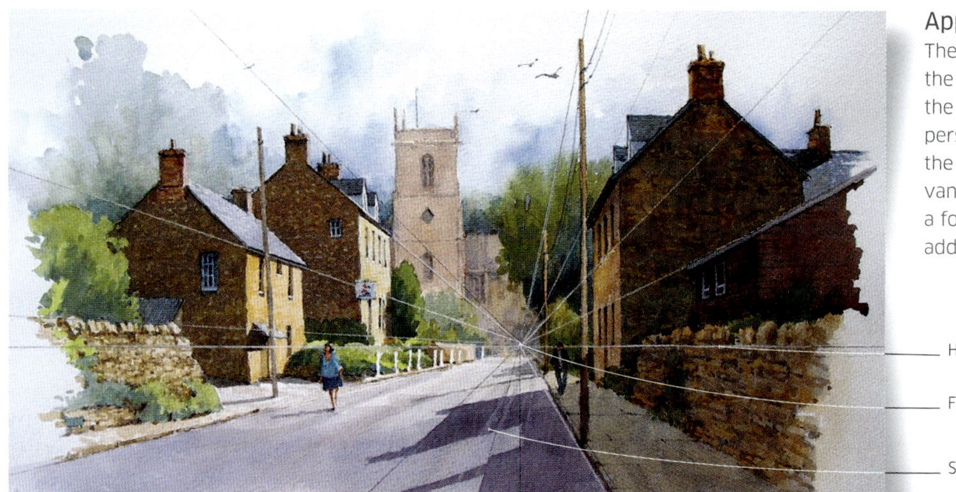

Applying perspective
The horizon represents the eye level of the artist or viewer and helps to position the different elements that convey perspective. The parallel lines, such as the sides of the road, converge at the vanishing point on the horizon. Placing a focal point here, such as the church, adds to a sense of depth.

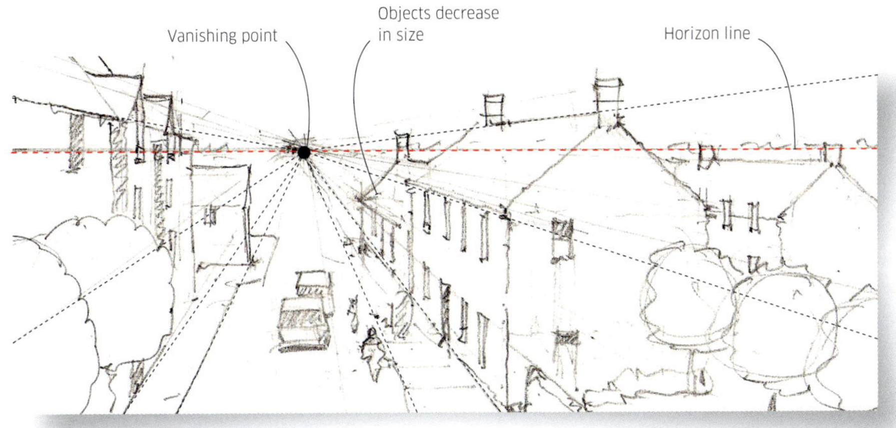

Elevated viewpoint

This scene is viewed from a high viewpoint with most objects placed below the horizon. An off-centre vanishing point is reflected in different perspective lines, with shorter lines on the left. The high viewpoint means most lines slope up, with only the rooflines above the horizon sloping down.

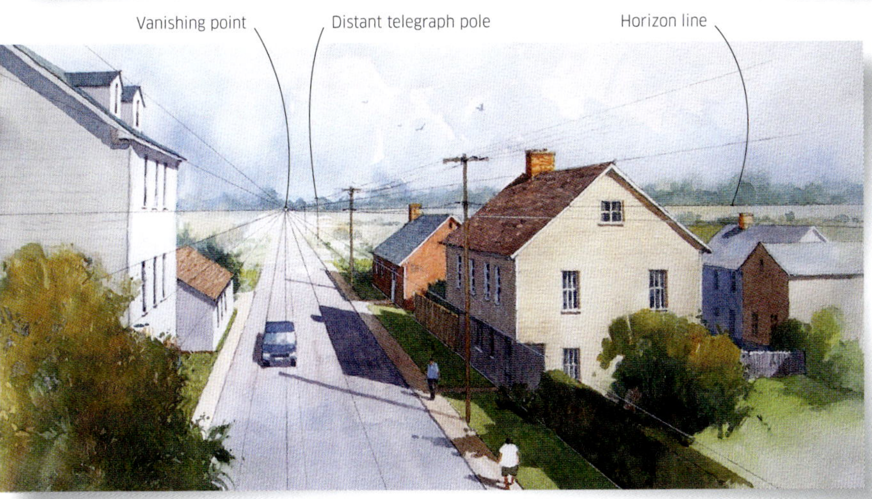

High horizon

In the finished painting, the high horizon is placed about one-third down from the top of the painting, following the composition principle known as the "rule of thirds" (see p.27). The extended foreground uses perspective to draw the viewer's eye into the distance. The telegraph poles enhance the sense of depth as they decrease in size, following the sloping parallel lines to accurately portray distance.

■ Two-point perspective

A less confined composition often includes objects seen from an angle to all surfaces, where both sides are distorted by perspective. The surfaces (usually perpendicular to each other) will diverge to two different vanishing points.

Two vanishing points

When painting objects with surfaces perpendicular to each other, ensure the lines of perspective vanish to two distant points, both on the same horizon line.

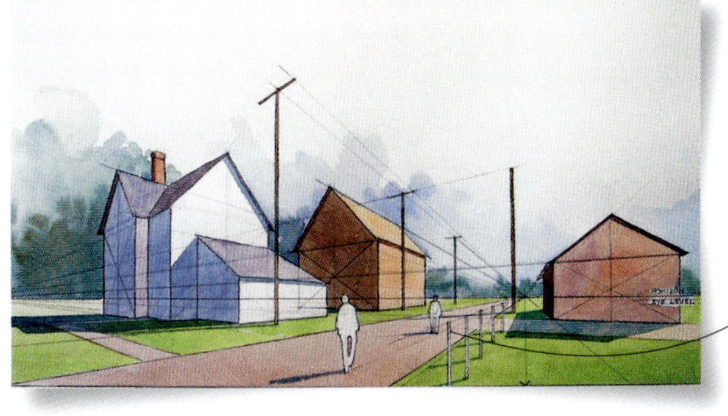

Relative size

Vertical lines defining the height of objects, such as the telegraph poles and fence posts, should reflect their relative size correctly as they diminish. Including figures with their eye level on the horizon, will help to judge scale correctly.

Smaller, distant figure is placed on the same eye level on the horizon line

PUTTING IT INTO PRACTICE

As this group of buildings are viewed from an angle, two-point perspective is used to render them accurately in the setting. The receding river, river bank, and fence posts all converge in the distance towards a vanishing point just behind the tree, leading your eye through the scene. The sides of the buildings in shadow follow perspective lines to a second vanishing point on the left.

You will need

Yellow ochre · Burnt sienna · Burnt umber · Ultramarine blue · Sap green

- No. 18, no. 12, and no. 8 soft-hair round brushes
- No. 4 and no. 2 stiff-bristle fan brushes
- 32 x 55cm (12½ x 21¾in) hot-pressed watercolour paper 300gsm (140lb)

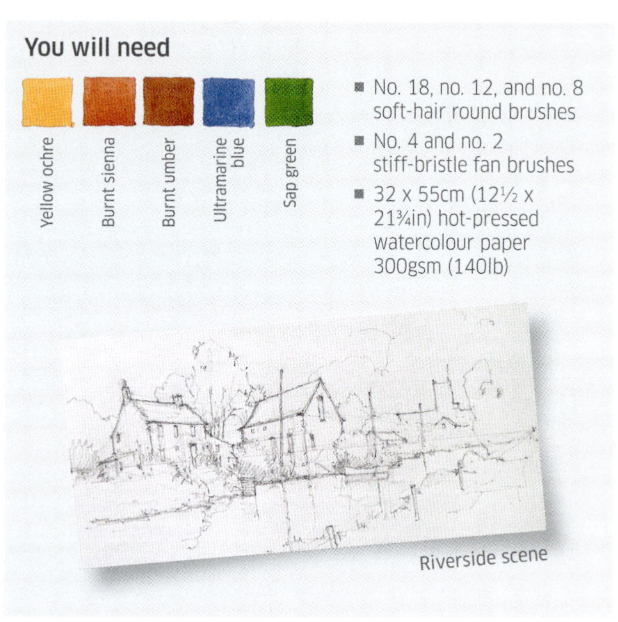
Riverside scene

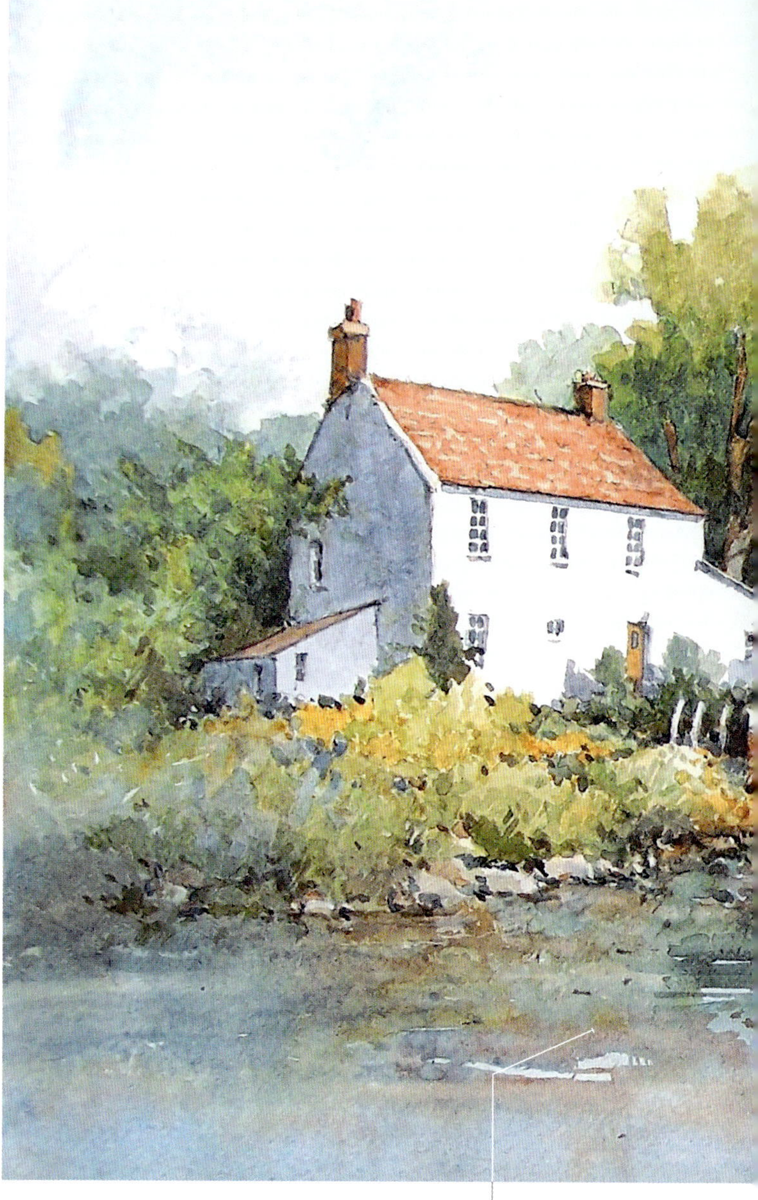

"**Linear perspective** aids a composition by **drawing the eye** towards a **focal point.**"

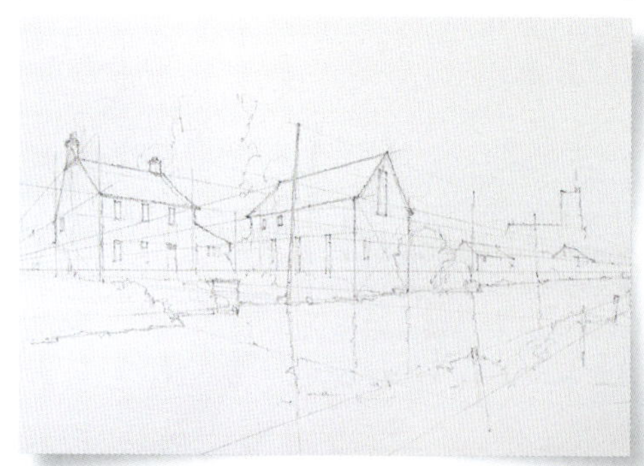

1 Sketch perspective lines
Draw perspective lines over a light pencil sketch. Follow the lines from two focal points, adding in the roof, window, and wall surface lines along with vertical lines, such as poles and posts.

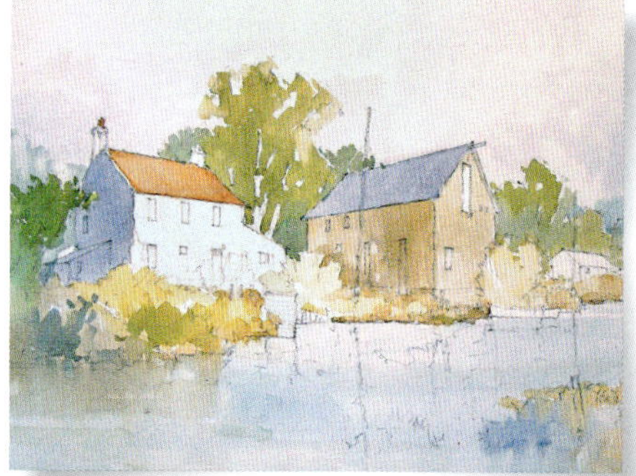

2 Establish base washes
When the underdrawing is complete, erase the perspective lines. Apply basic washes to the sky and water first then add initial colours to the main surfaces, using a warm palette.

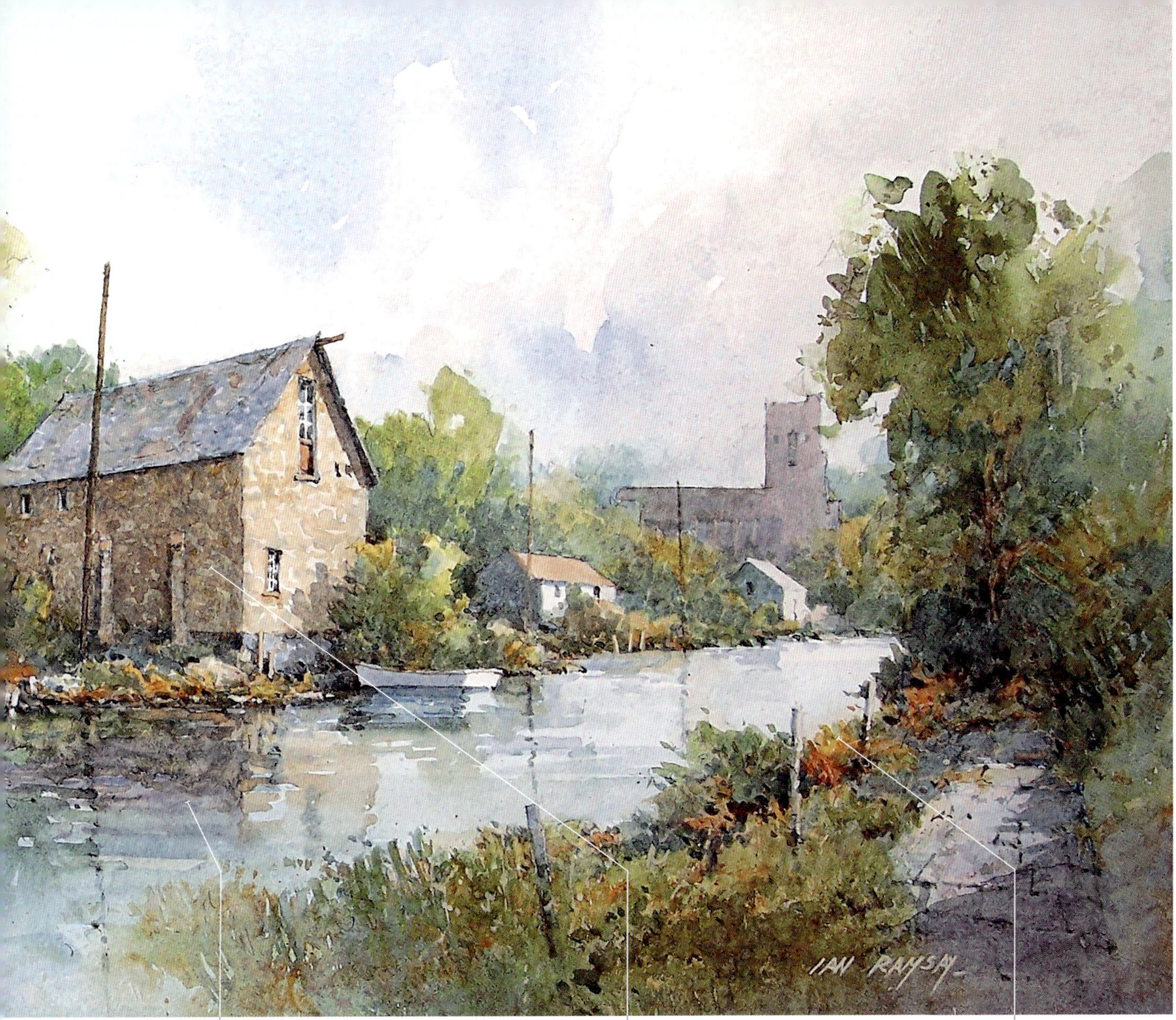

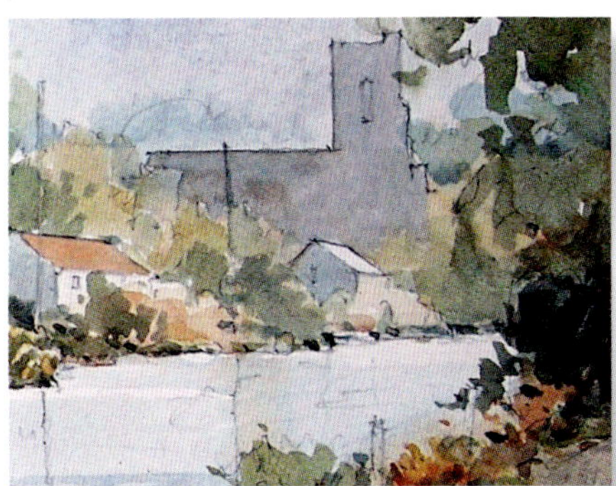

3 Suggest movement

Work on the river, using a fan brush to add surface movement to the water. Washes on the distant buildings give them depth and emphasize the flat face of the church.

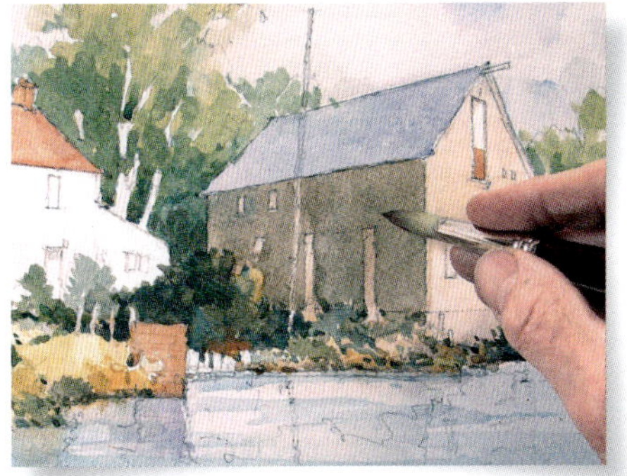

4 Layer tones

Add stronger tones to all surfaces with a round brush. Using darker tones on the shadowed sides of the buildings will enhance the perspective and three-dimensional effect.

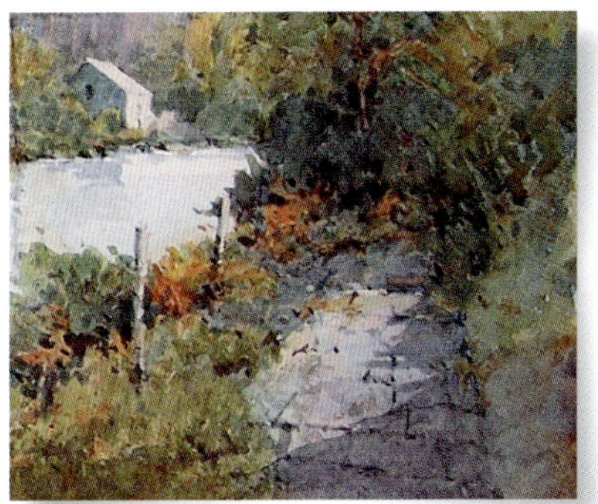

5 Foreground detail

Build the foreground details where the converging lines of the path and diminishing fence posts lead to the vanishing point hidden behind the trees.

Shadows and sunlight

CREATING A SENSE OF LIGHT

Sunshine in a painting is only obvious when there are shadows. Avoid subjects that are either totally in shade or with the sun behind you. Instead, look for a balance of light and cast shadow that translates into highlights and soft tones on paper.

◼ Suggesting realistic shadows

Shadows are not random shapes and colours. For a convincing cast shadow, note how its length and direction is determined by the position of the sun. Realistic shadows needn't always be based on local colour; unify multiple shadows with a single wash.

Shadow direction

Shadows have a vanishing point on the horizon and in the sun. To calculate shadow length, draw a line from the sun across the top of the object until it intersects the shadow.

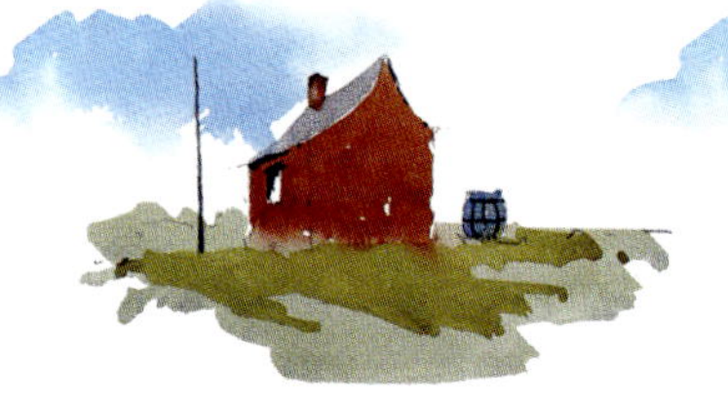
Without shadow wash

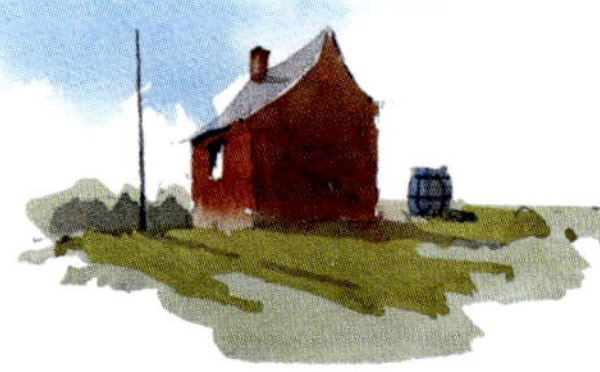
Shadows added in grey wash

Shadow wash

The transparency of watercolour means you can create the look of shadows with a single, grey shadow wash. This darkens the underlying wash and avoids the need to mix dark versions of each colour.

PUTTING IT INTO PRACTICE

Here, sunlight from the right creates rims of light on the backlit figures, with subdued and softened edges in the muted background, unified with a shadow wash. Cast shadows bring sunshine to the foreground.

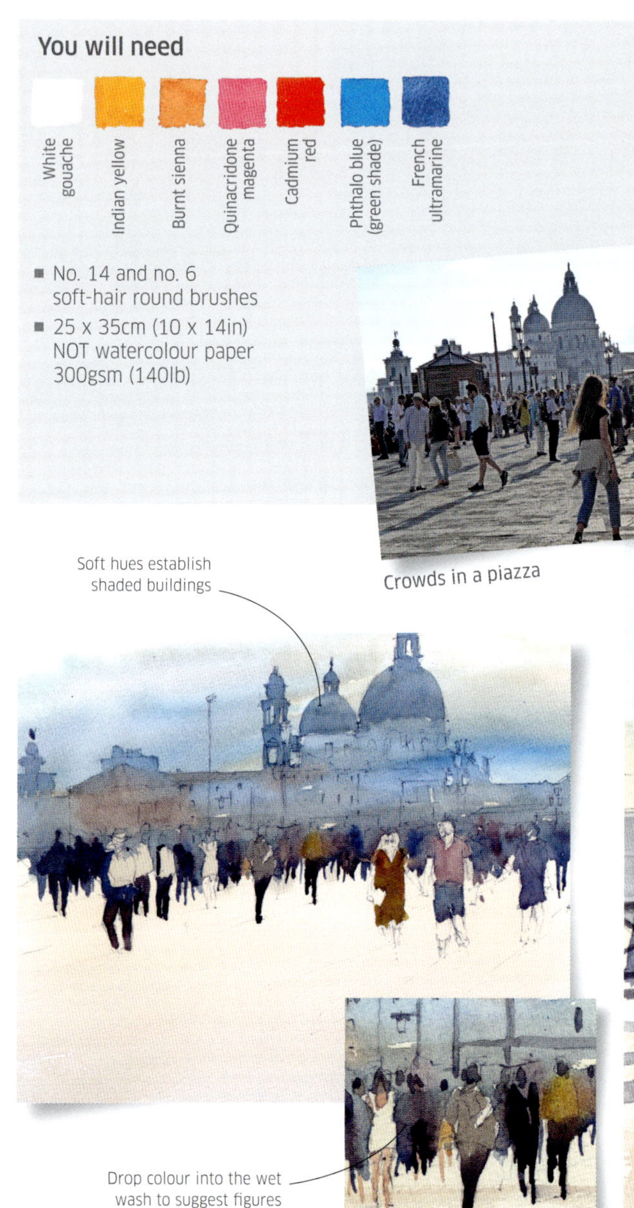

- No. 14 and no. 6 soft-hair round brushes
- 25 x 35cm (10 x 14in) NOT watercolour paper 300gsm (140lb)

Crowds in a piazza

Soft hues establish shaded buildings

Drop colour into the wet wash to suggest figures merging in the crowd

1 Subdued tones
Cover the paper with a warm wash and paint the main shapes. Backlighting has the effect of blending everything in subdued colour, so paint the background in a grey wash of French ultramarine and burnt sienna.

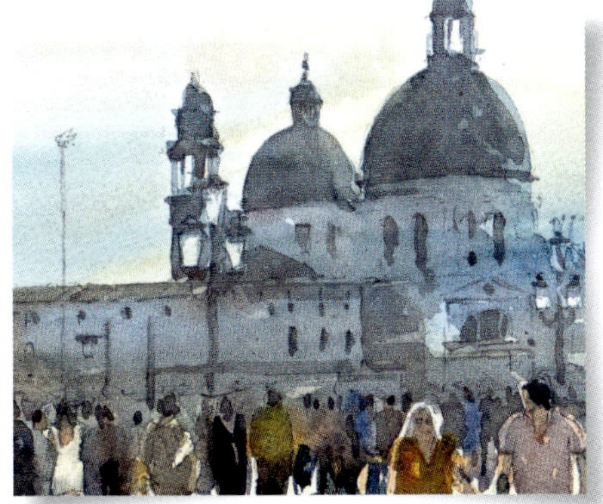

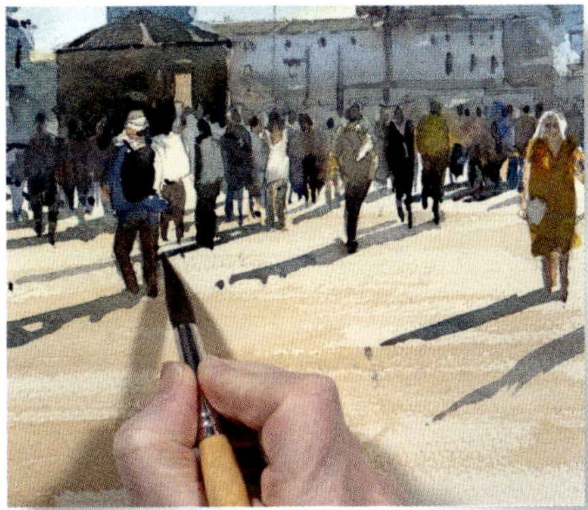

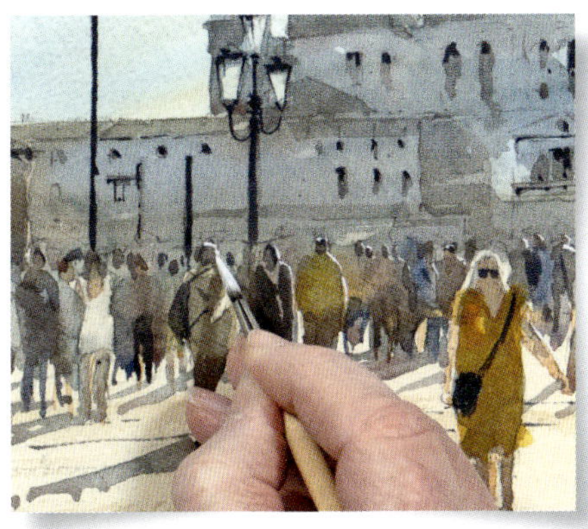

2 Add shadow wash

Add a shadow wash of ultramarine and cadmium red over the buildings and figures. Keep the wash as transparent as possible so that underlying colours are visible.

3 Cast shadows

Use the shadow wash for cast shadows, checking their length and direction, but don't worry too much about precise shapes. Keep edges soft; don't let them dry as you paint.

4 Final contrasts

With the no. 6 brush, add the deep darks with a strong shadow mix, using white gouache to add some highlights to the right edges of the figures, where the sun hits.

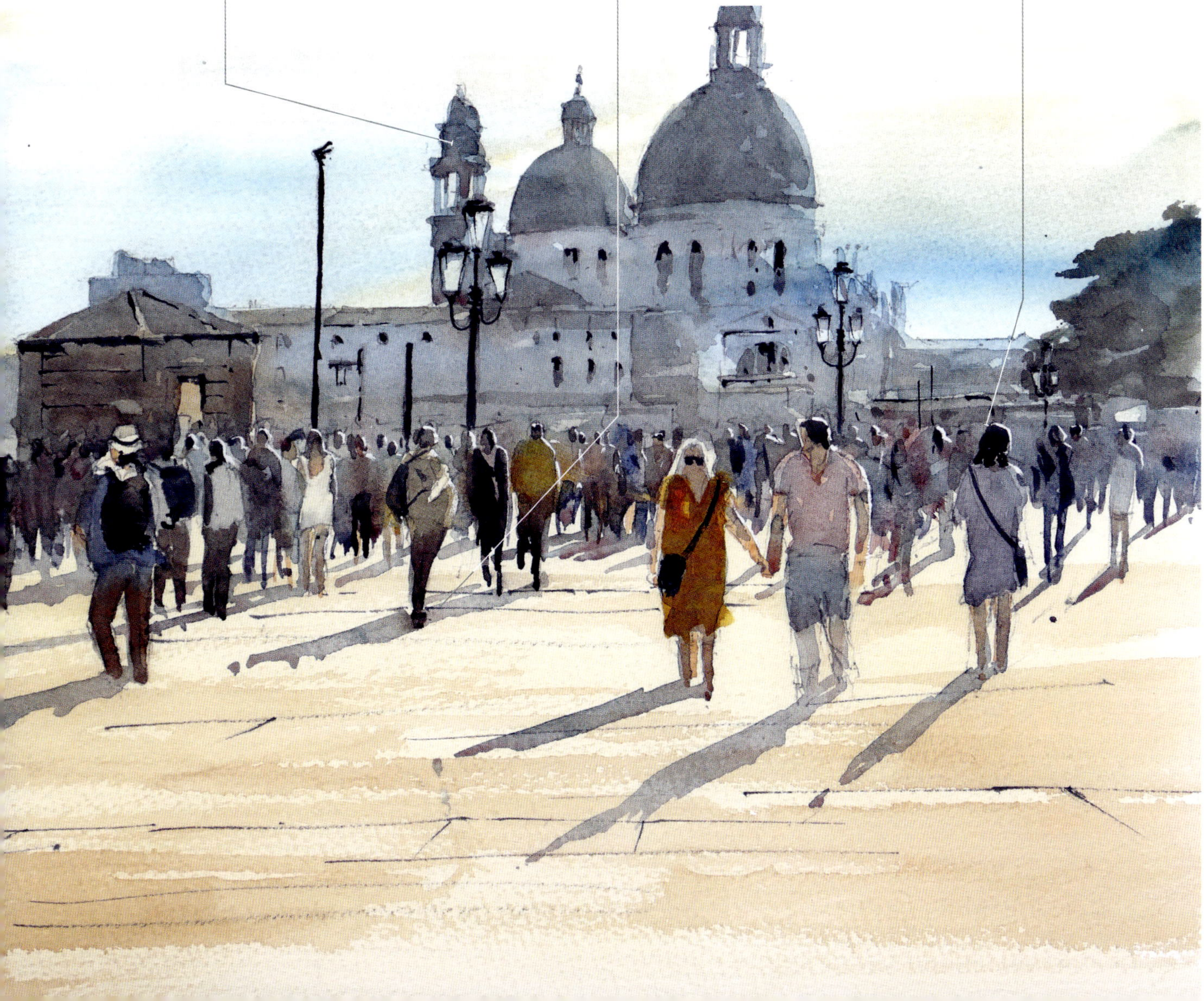

Focal points

DIRECTING THE VIEWER'S EYE

The focal point is the centre of interest in a painting. Your chosen focal point should not be too difficult to paint, and its position should clearly tell the story of the scene. Once you have chosen your focal point, don't be tempted to change paths or the painting will become muddled.

PUTTING IT INTO PRACTICE

Here the cows are the focal points. Using recognizable shapes and adding warm colour attracts the viewer's eye. Adding details of the bridge, softening the trees, and showing ripples in the river puts the cows into context.

You will need

Cadmium lemon | Raw sienna | Light red | Burnt umber | Prussian blue | French ultramarine

- No. 10 soft-hair mop brush
- No. 10 and no. 5 soft-hair round brushes
- No. 10 synthetic flat brush
- 28 x 38cm (11 x 15in) NOT watercolour paper 640gsm (300lb)

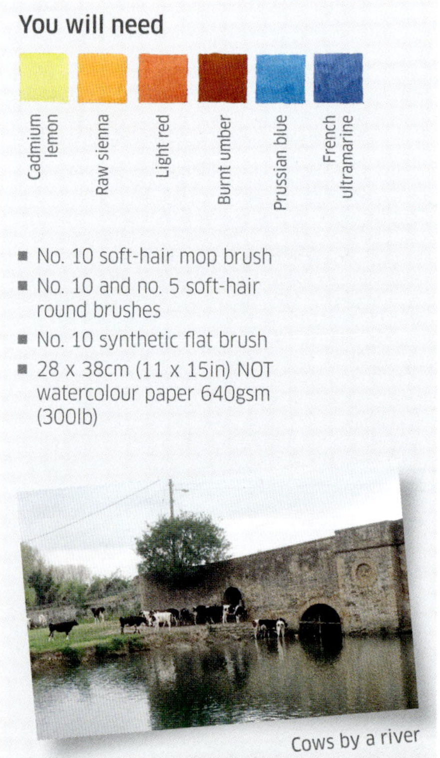
Cows by a river

▪ Emphasizing key areas

We usually focus on recognizable objects or shapes, but sometimes it is the gaps between them that draw our attention. Try to connect your focal point to other shapes, then look for complementary colours so your focal point contrasts with the other colours in the painting. Contrasts of light and dark can also create a focal point.

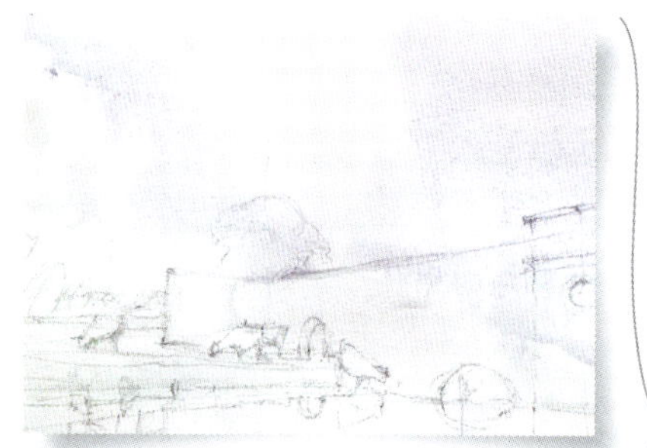

1 Planning and painting
First sketch the positions of the key shapes, such as the bridge, the cows, the tree, and the reflections. Then tilt the paper to 60 degrees. Mix French ultramarine and burnt umber. Wet the paper and paint in the clouds with the mop brush, adding some French ultramarine to the sky.

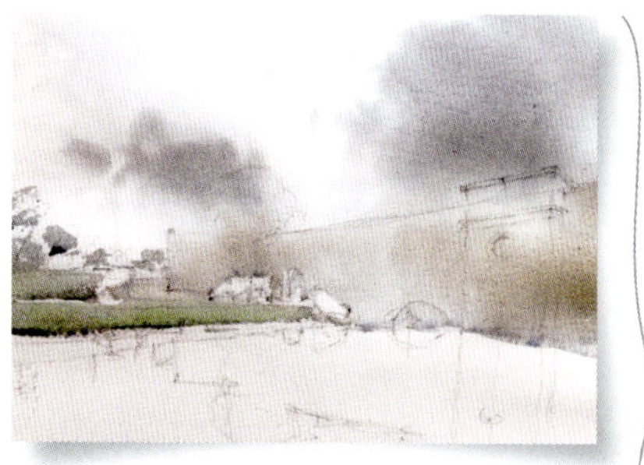

2 Establish depth with colour
While the paint is still wet, run the wash over the bridge but add raw sienna to give it a warm colour, working around the cows so they remain white. Add Prussian blue and cadmium lemon to the fields, leaving the river untouched.

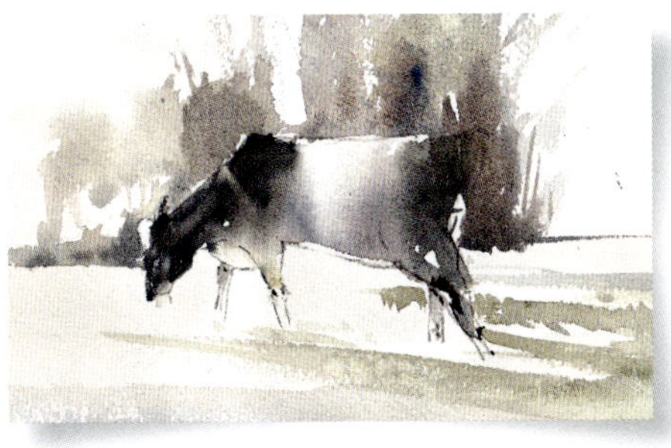

Tonal contrast
Recognizable shapes catch the eye. The contrast of the dark cow's head against a light background achieves this here.

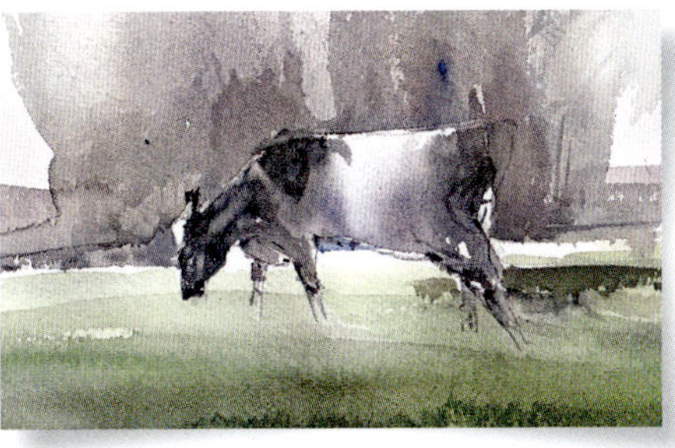

Detail
Add some surrounding detail so the focal point sits convincingly in context and looks natural rather than over-emphasized.

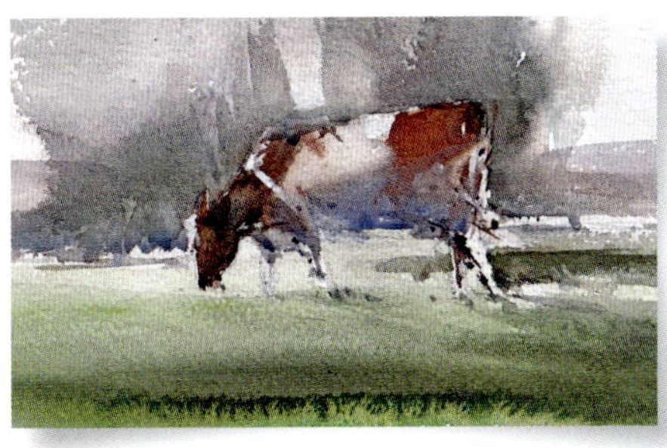

Colour
Use complementary colours. Here the red-brown of the cow is highlighted against the grey-greens of the trees and grass.

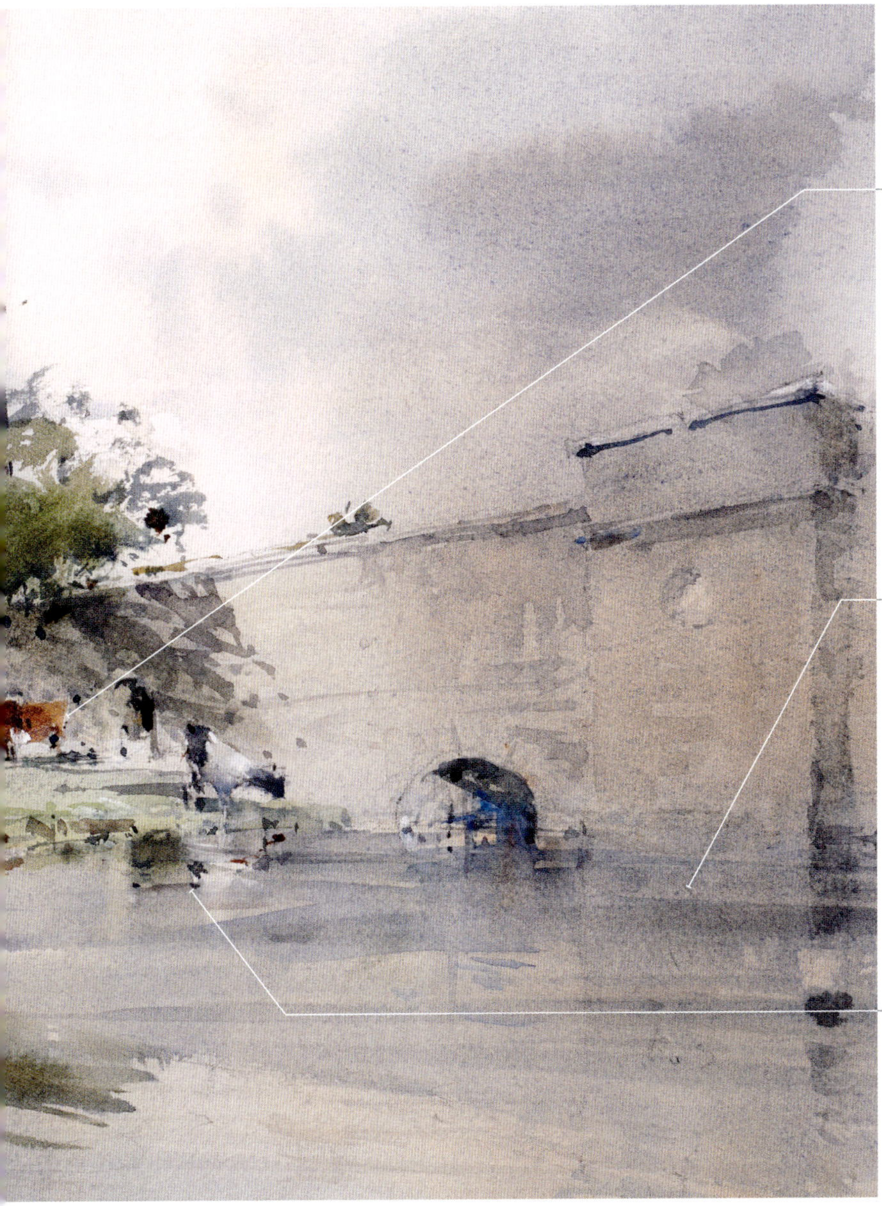

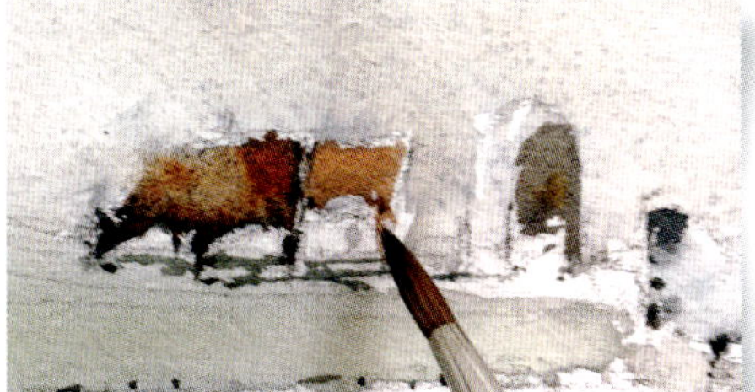

3 Paint in the details
Using Prussian blue, lemon, and light red, dry-brush the tree. Then paint the cows, using burnt sienna and ultramarine.

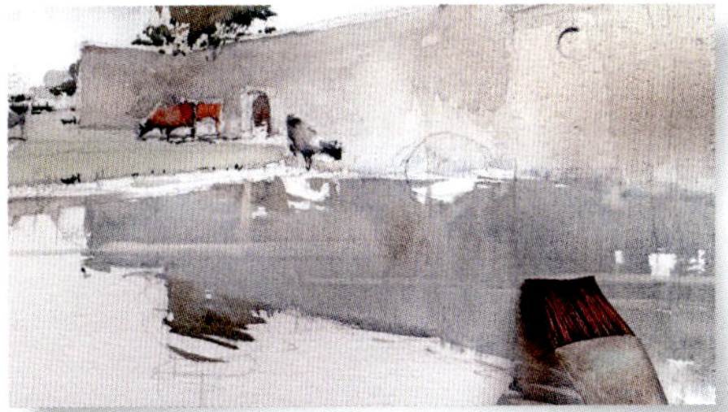

4 The foreground river
Mix ultramarine, umber, and a little raw sienna. Wet the paper and paint the reflections, starting from the bank. Add green for the tree.

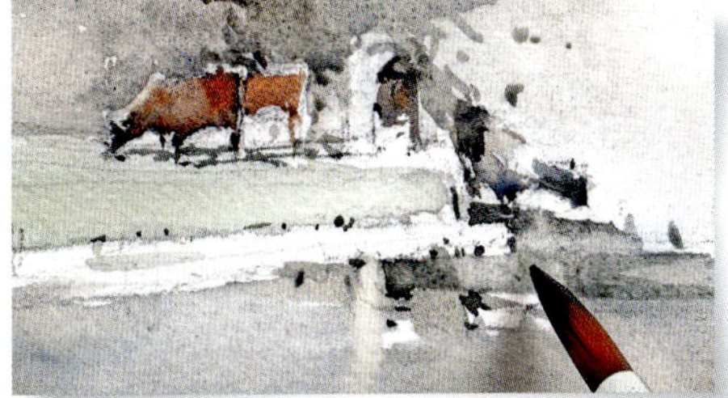

5 Enhance the focal points
With the same mix, add shadows under the tree and bridge. Add more reflections and detail to the cows so they come into sharp focus.

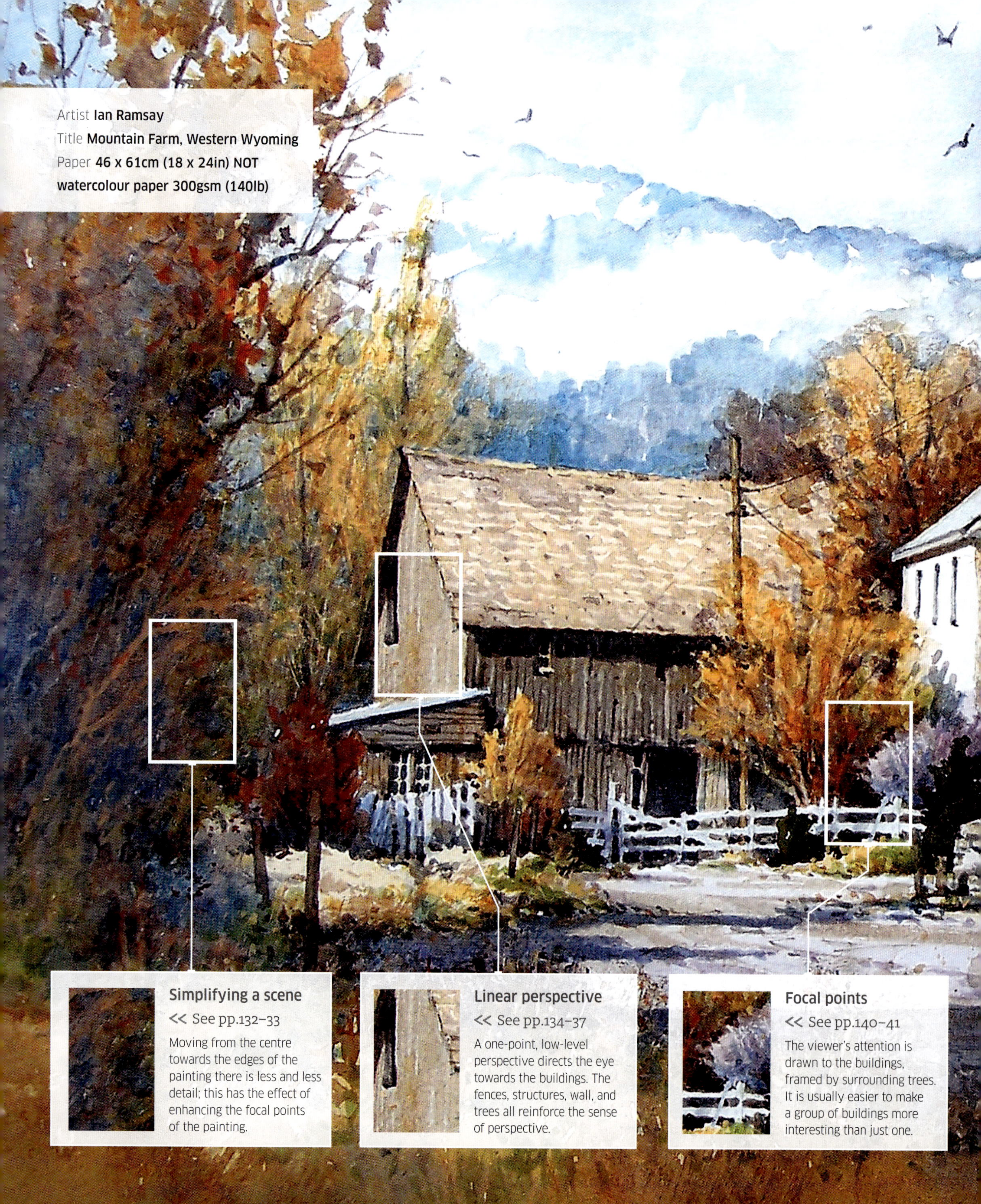

Simplifying a scene
<< See pp.132–33

Moving from the centre towards the edges of the painting there is less and less detail; this has the effect of enhancing the focal points of the painting.

Linear perspective
<< See pp.134–37

A one-point, low-level perspective directs the eye towards the buildings. The fences, structures, wall, and trees all reinforce the sense of perspective.

Focal points
<< See pp.140–41

The viewer's attention is drawn to the buildings, framed by surrounding trees. It is usually easier to make a group of buildings more interesting than just one.

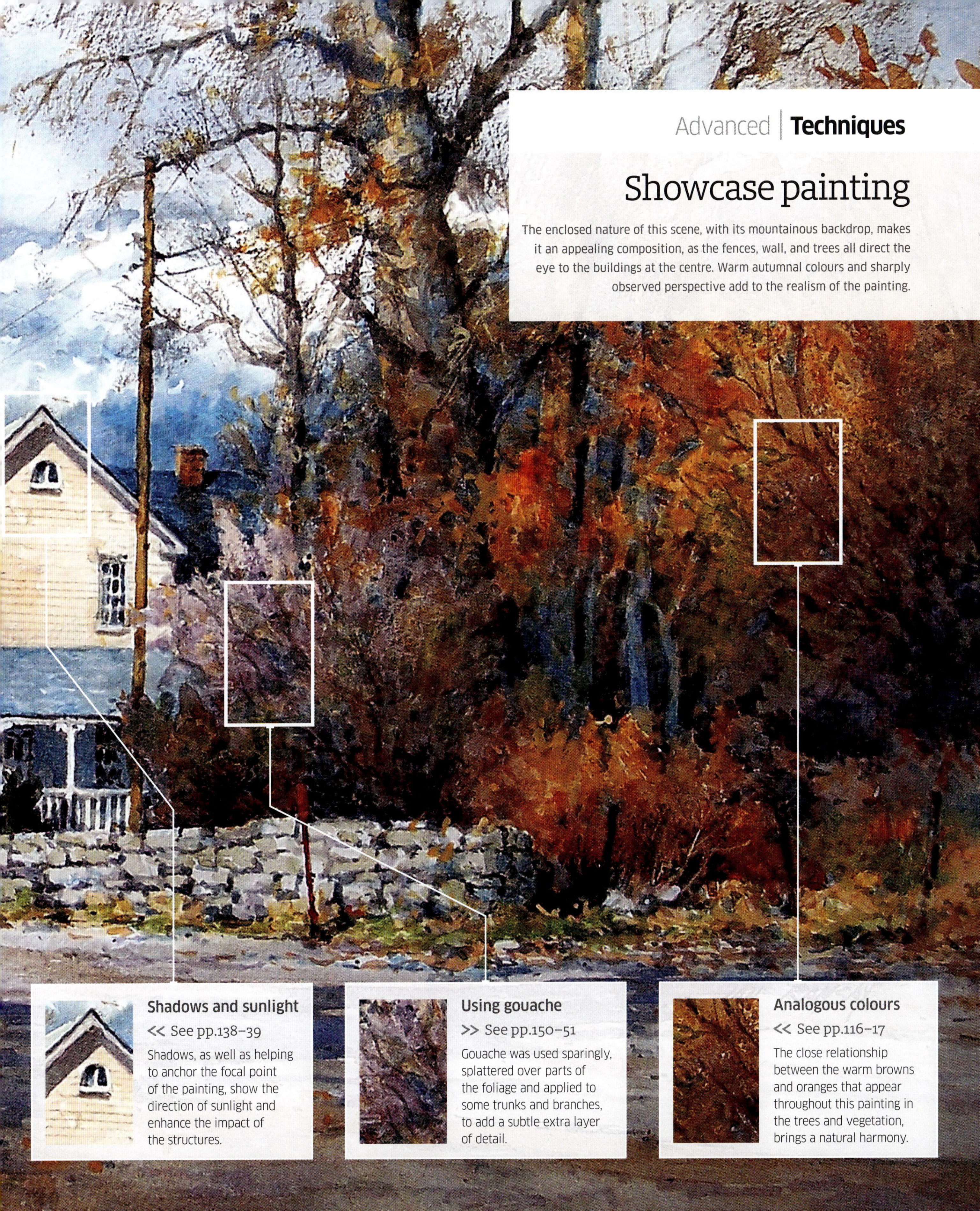

Showcase painting

The enclosed nature of this scene, with its mountainous backdrop, makes it an appealing composition, as the fences, wall, and trees all direct the eye to the buildings at the centre. Warm autumnal colours and sharply observed perspective add to the realism of the painting.

Shadows and sunlight

≪ See pp.138–39

Shadows, as well as helping to anchor the focal point of the painting, show the direction of sunlight and enhance the impact of the structures.

Using gouache

≫ See pp.150–51

Gouache was used sparingly, splattered over parts of the foliage and applied to some trunks and branches, to add a subtle extra layer of detail.

Analogous colours

≪ See pp.116–17

The close relationship between the warm browns and oranges that appear throughout this painting in the trees and vegetation, brings a natural harmony.

Scraping back

SCRATCHING AT THE PAPER'S SURFACE

Scraping back is a useful technique to remove layers of colour, create light shapes, and add texture to a painting when a brush can't do the job. The best scraping tools – from old credit cards and penknives to palette knives and plastic spoons – have relatively flat edges. Judicious scraping is always called for; don't get carried away.

■ Judging when to scrape

When the wash is still damp, you can scrape out details with your chosen tool. Paint removed from the paper's fibres reveals the lighter area beneath. Paper types that absorb more paint make it harder to lift out colours, and some colours, such as phthalo blue, are more staining.

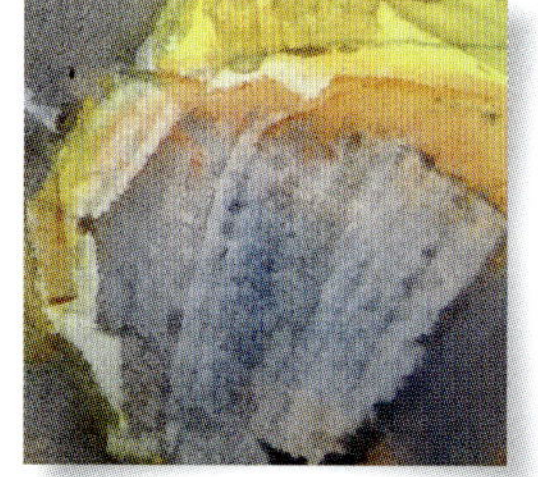

Scraped paint

Staining pigment

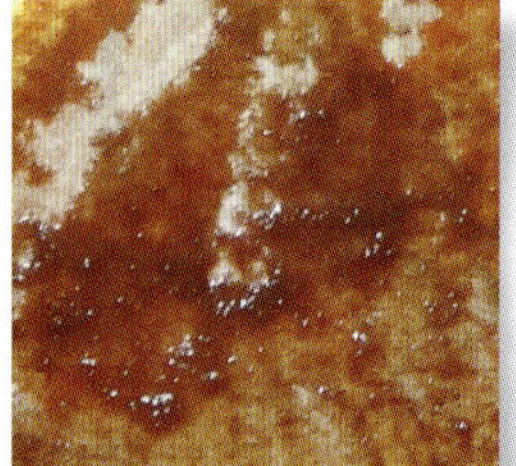

Too wet

Too dry

Wet or dry?

Move damp colour with your chosen tool, scraping and rotating the tool at the same time. If you try to move the paint when it is too wet, pigment will creep back into the shape instead being lifted out; if the paper is too dry, you won't be able to scrape the paint away.

PUTTING IT INTO PRACTICE

Scraping back creates points of interest through varied marks and is an effective way to suggest texture, as shown in this painting of a stone Buddha monument in Sri Lanka.

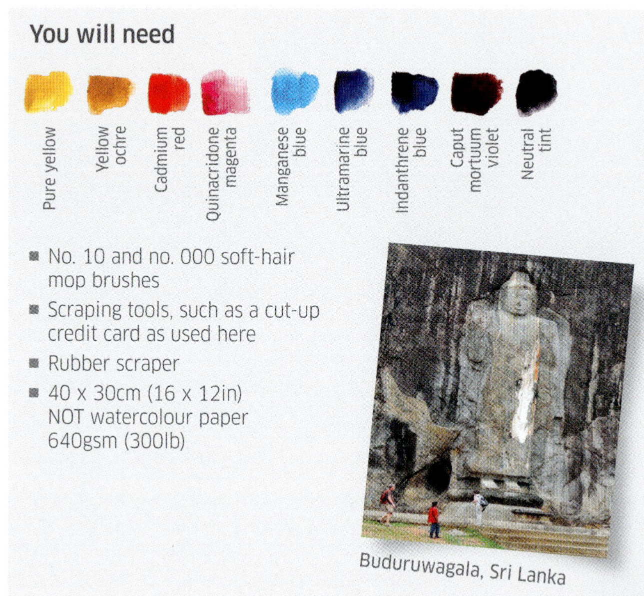

- No. 10 and no. 000 soft-hair mop brushes
- Scraping tools, such as a cut-up credit card as used here
- Rubber scraper
- 40 x 30cm (16 x 12in) NOT watercolour paper 640gsm (300lb)

Buduruwagala, Sri Lanka

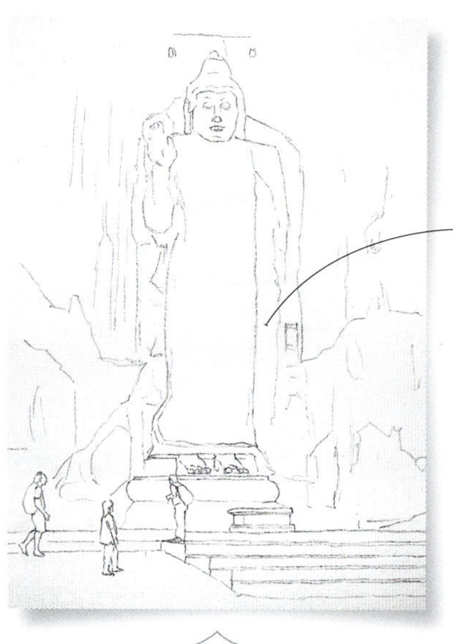

1 Prepare the paper

Draw out your composition on heavy watercolour paper, then dampen evenly with a large mop brush, keeping the figures and rest of the foreground dry.

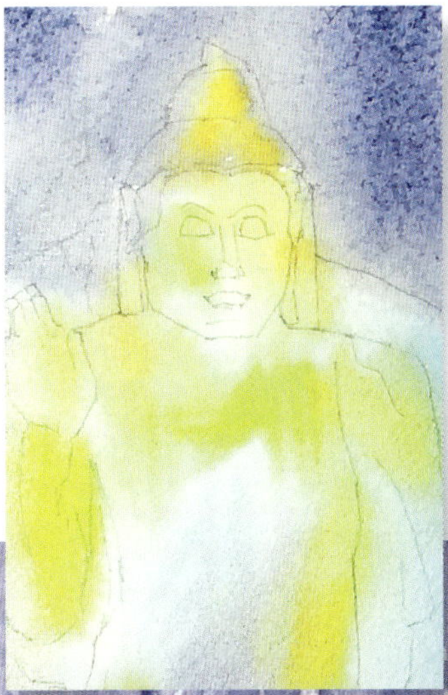

2 **The first wash of colour**
Lay in a variegated wash of yellows, oranges, and purples mixed from indanthrene and quinacridone magenta, letting the colours mix gently on the paper. Leave the wash for a minute before scraping – the paper must have just the right amount of wetness.

> "You can scrape out **subtle details, lines, and irregular shapes** with your tool of choice."

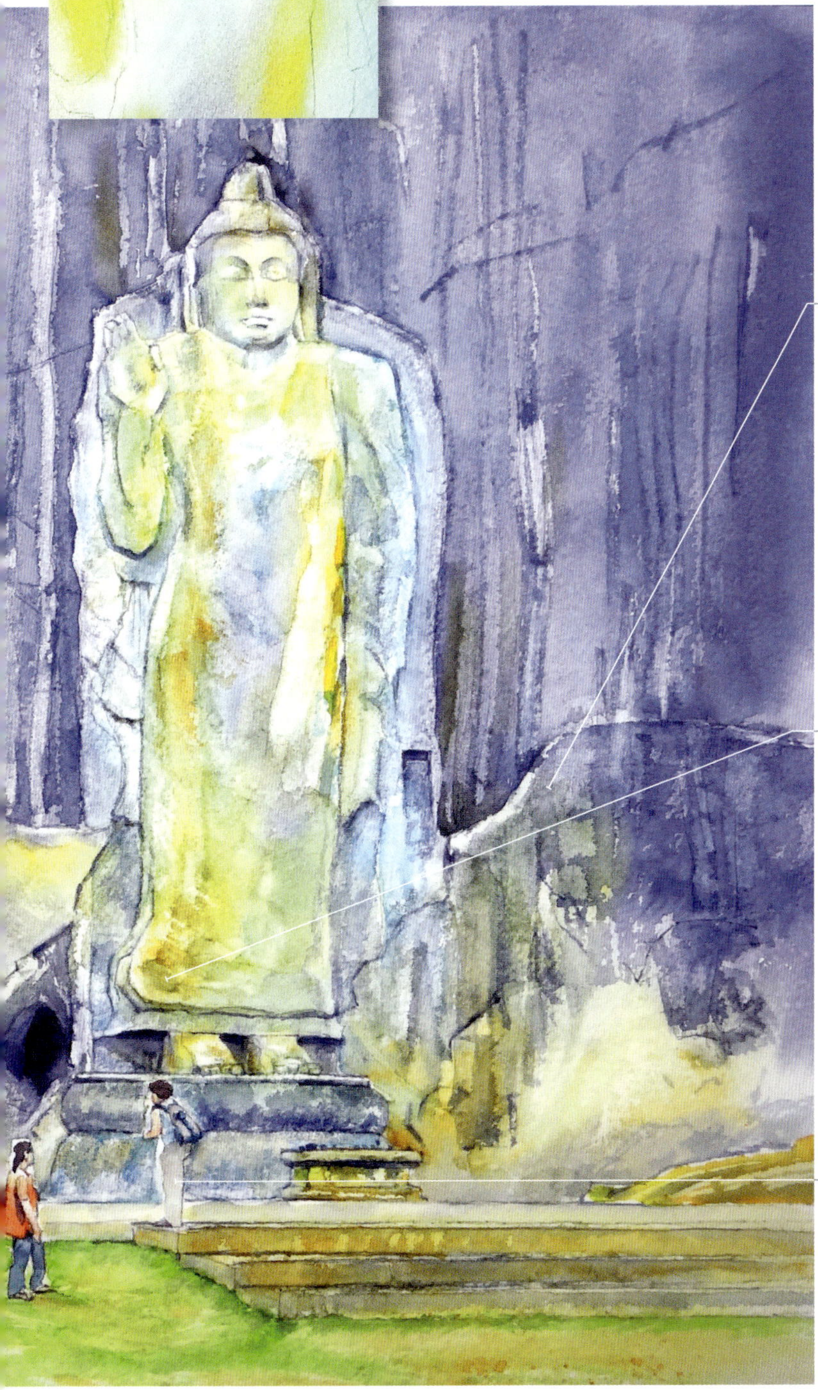

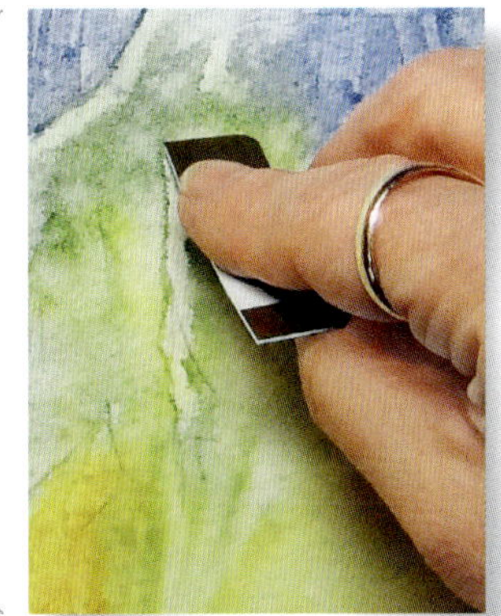

3 **Scrape shapes**
Press hard into the wash with the edge of your tool and pull or drag the paint away – you want to scrape and rotate the tool at the same time. If the paper feels too wet, the paint will fill back in, so leave it a few minutes to dry before you start.

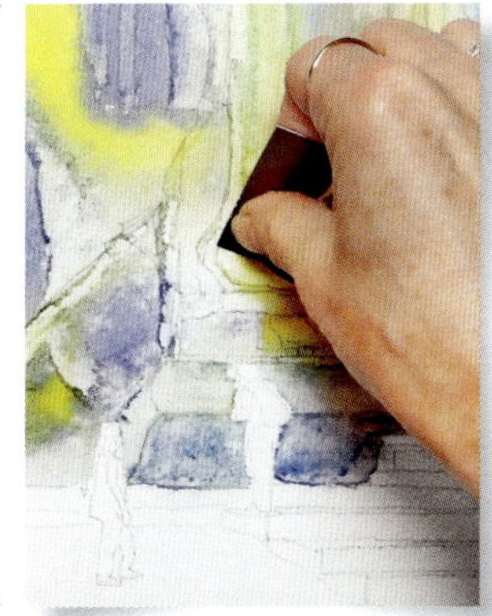

4 **Scrape details**
When the first shapes are dry, repeat the process in smaller areas using finer tools. Let the paint soak in a little before lifting out the colour, and wipe the tool clean between scrapes to prevent colour transfer.

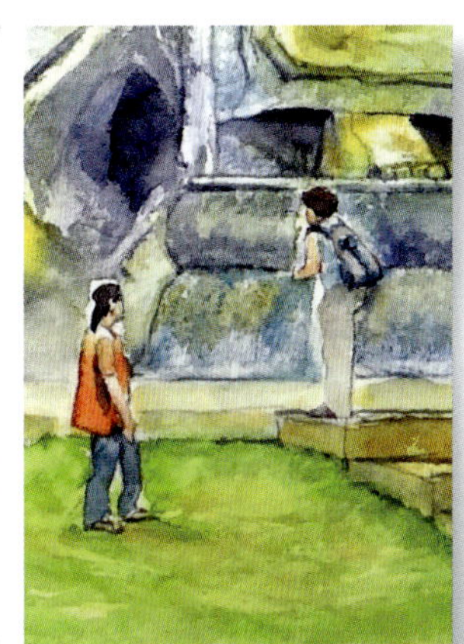

5 **Finishing touches**
Stand back to assess the overall effect and, if required, finish any last details with a small brush, adding more local colour in the desired areas, without overworking them.

Using cling film

CREATING RIPPLED AND WRINKLED TEXTURES

By applying cling film to a wet wash and creasing it on the wet paint you can create interesting textures. This is great for adding character to stones, patterns in foliage, and ripples in water. The paint becomes lighter in areas where the plastic touches the paper and the wrinkles create sharp outlined shapes.

PUTTING IT INTO PRACTICE

For this painting of a turtle in the sea, cling film is used to create lines and shapes to suggest waves and ripples in the water. It is an easy way to achieve random, unforced changes of tone and line.

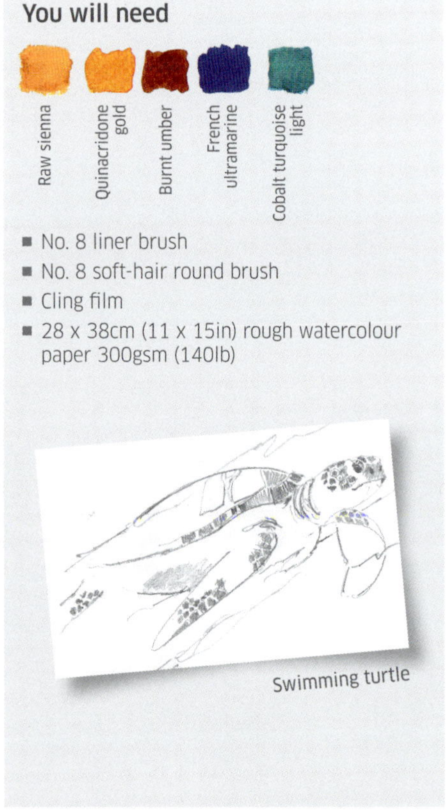

You will need

- Raw sienna
- Quinacridone gold
- Burnt umber
- French ultramarine
- Cobalt turquoise light

- No. 8 liner brush
- No. 8 soft-hair round brush
- Cling film
- 28 x 38cm (11 x 15in) rough watercolour paper 300gsm (140lb)

Swimming turtle

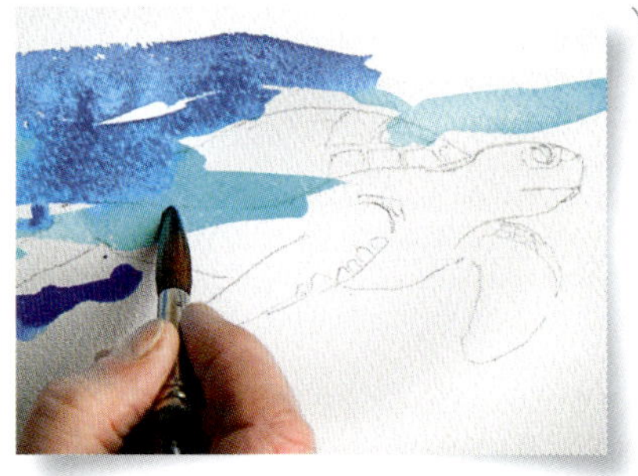

1 Initial drawing and first wash
Sketch in the turtle. Mix up washes of two or three different blues. These need to be strong in colour but liquid. Paint the area around the turtle in diagonal strokes, using your different blues. Allow the colours to run together and invade the outline of the turtle.

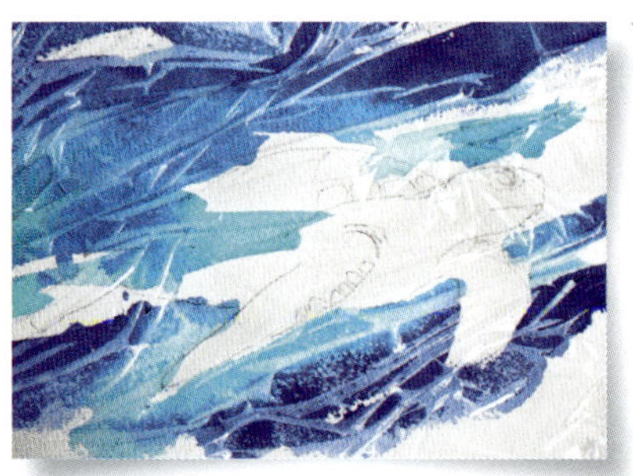

2 Apply cling film
Before the blue has had time to dry, place the cling film on the whole painting. Use your fingers to create wrinkles and folds in a broadly diagonal direction to make rippling shapes. Leave to dry, overnight if possible.

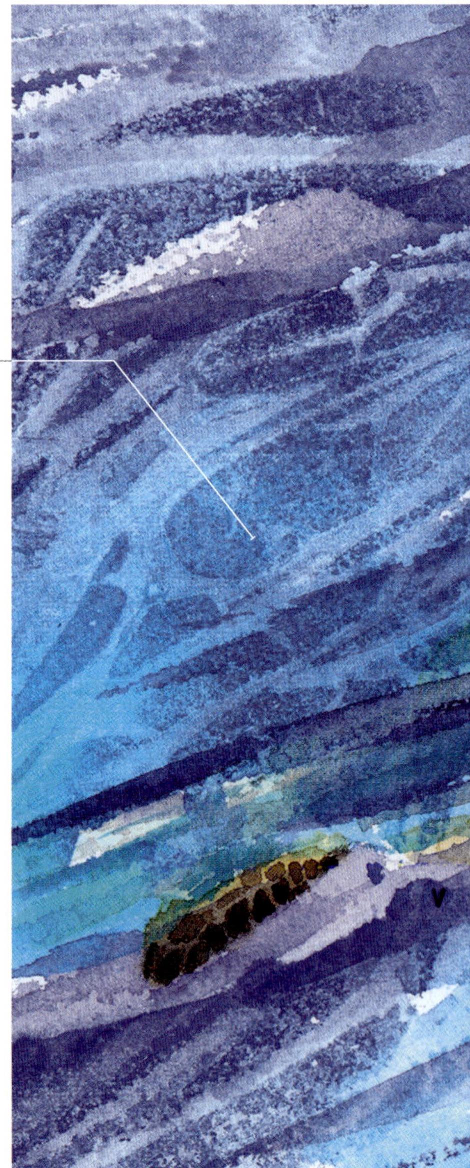

Imprinting wet paint

Using cling film to make shapes in a wash helps to suggest forms and textures that are hard to achieve with a paintbrush – for example, rocks, heavily textured vegetation, or the movement of water. The cling film must be applied while the wash is still wet and allowed to stay in place until it is completely dry; if you remove it too soon you run the risk of your textures fading or even disappearing altogether.

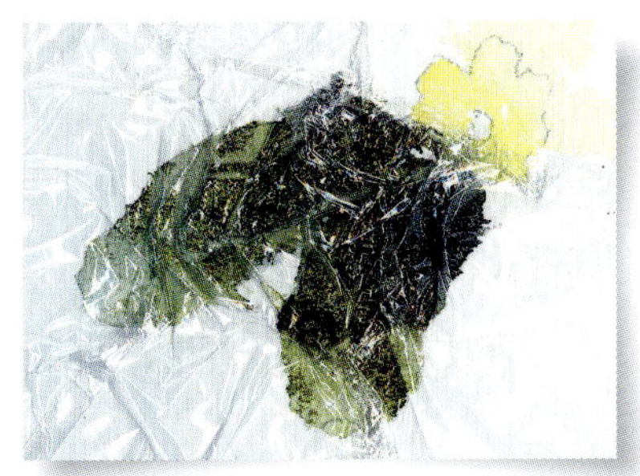

Applying cling film
For a texture such as the crinkled leaves of primroses, cling film is ideal. Lay it flat on the paper then crease it with your fingers to make appropriate shapes.

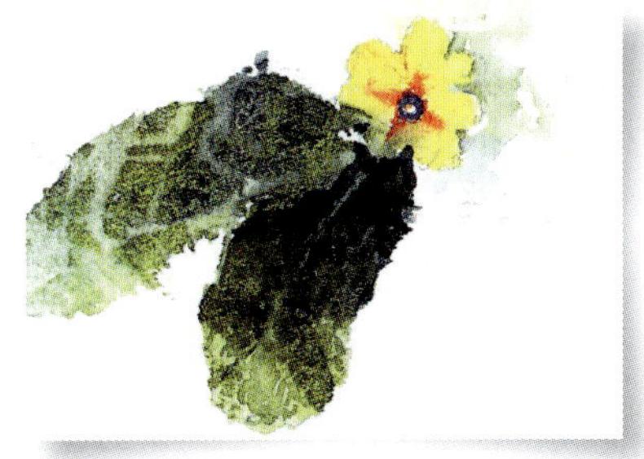

Texture and pattern
Carefully remove the cling film when the paint is absolutely dry. The flat paint wash will be transformed with interesting textures and patterning.

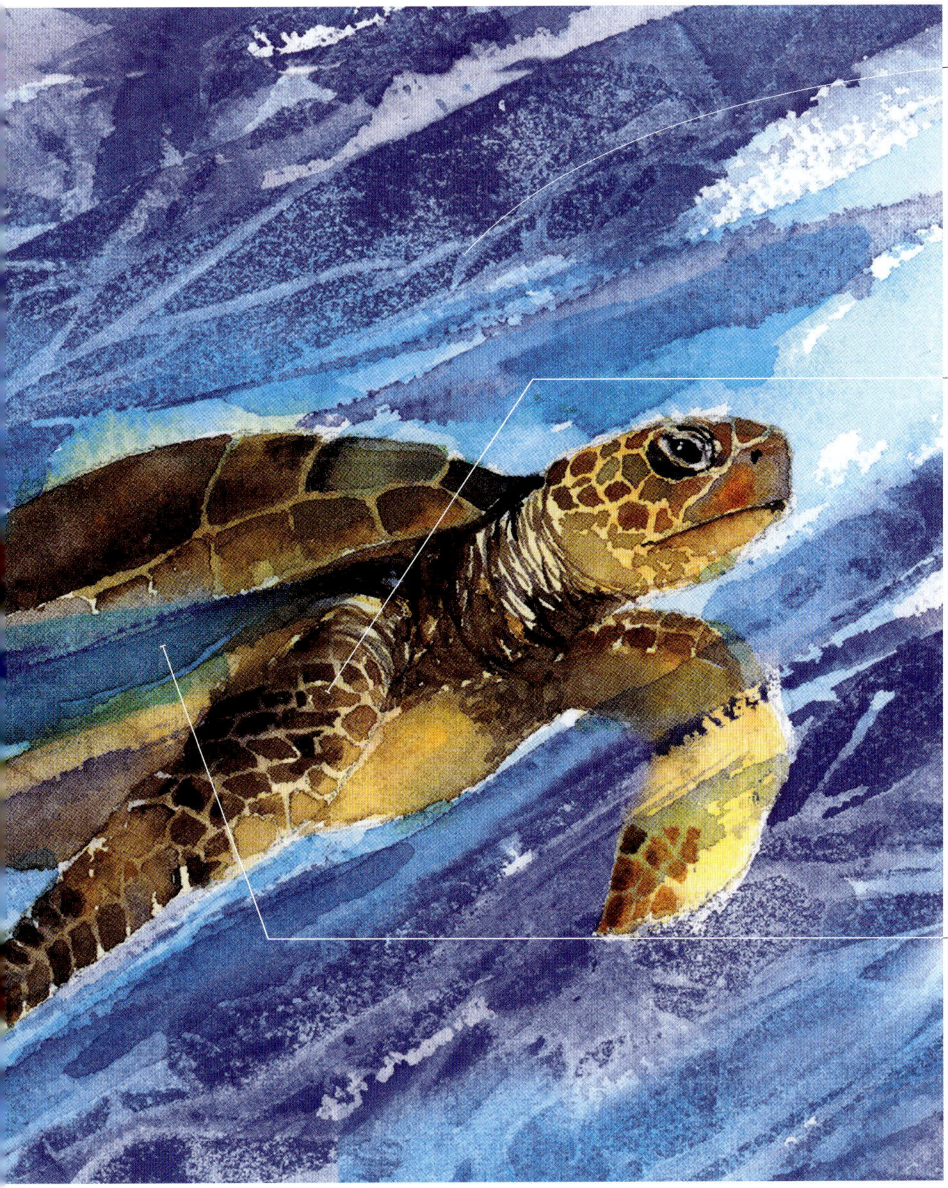

Random textured marks made by the cling film

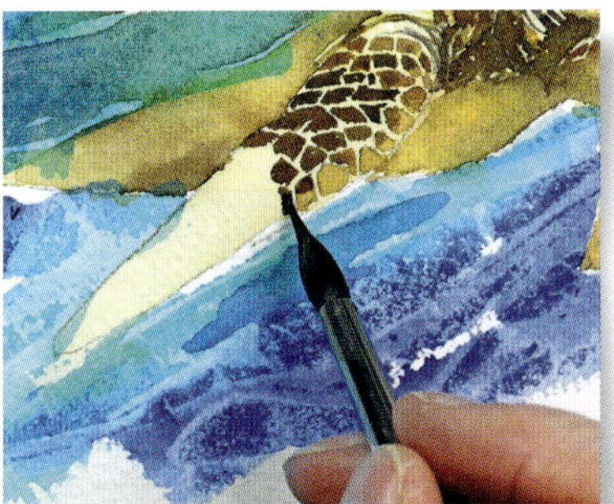

3 Paint the turtle
Remove the cling film. Mix washes of umber, sienna, and gold. Start with a thin wash of sienna over all the turtle. Let that dry, then add the pattern of his scaly skin and shell with darker colours.

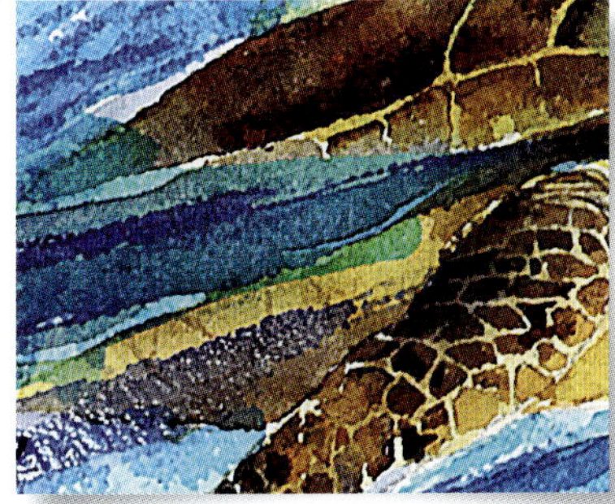

4 Finishing touches
When the paint is dry, add further diagonal strokes of a thinner mixture of blue to make darker waves of water. These can go over the turtle a little and can also be used to fill in white areas.

Using salt and bleach

EXPERIMENTAL EFFECTS

The creative use of salt and bleach will add a different dimension to your work. Consider how best to employ their abilities to lift out areas of colour, whether for texture or to play with hues and add back whites. These special effects suit many subjects, from flowers to fabric patterns.

■ Adding light and texture

Bleach offers some interesting effects for creating white and lights. It is best applied to strong pigments, such as liquid watercolours, and bear in mind that the effects are permanent and you won't be able to paint on top. Rinse your brushes well after use. Table salt also lifts out colour but leaves grainy, textural marks.

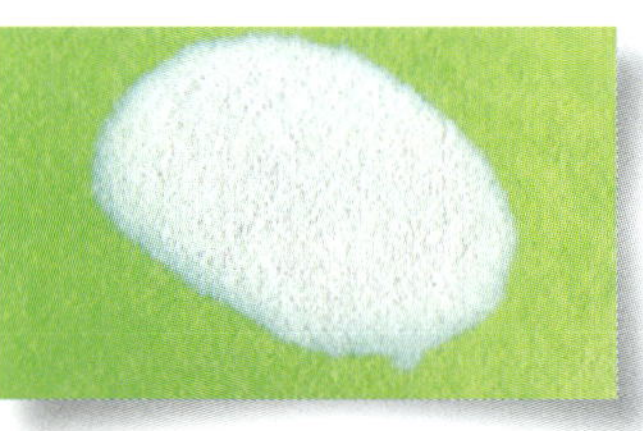

Bleach on dry wash
Apply bleach to a dry wash and let it dry to achieve a complete white with a hard edge. If you want to lighten tones, interrupt the process by lifting off the bleach with a paper towel.

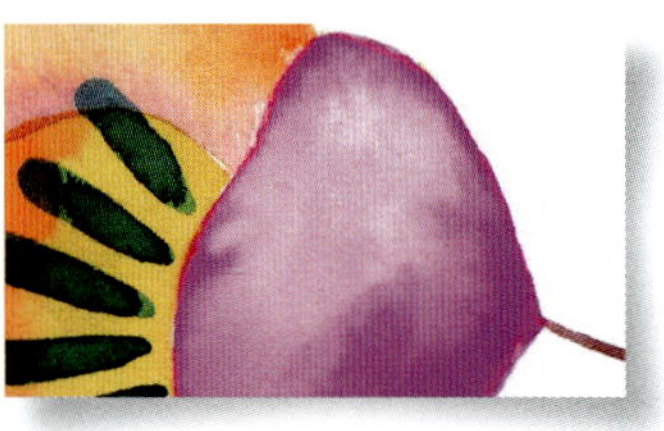

Bleach on wet wash
While the surface is still wet, apply bleach to create random lights as it spreads and blends. You can also lift it out before it turns completely white.

Table salt
Sprinkle over fine grains of salt while the watercolours are still wet. Let it dry completely before removing with a paper towel to reveal mottled marks. Rock salt can also be used.

PUTTING IT INTO PRACTICE

Salt has been used here to give a special effect of textured elements to the abstract florals. Bleach is used to lighten the petals and add pale spots on the leaves, enhancing the variety of shapes and colours.

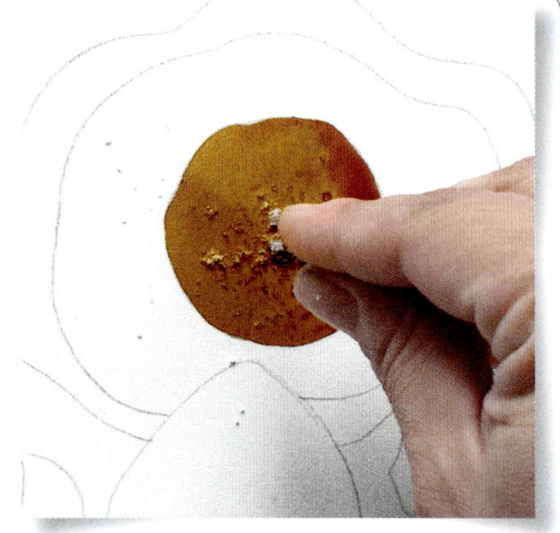

1 Apply salt grains
Draw the outlines of the main elements with watercolour pencil. Fill some flower centres with colour and add salt. Before continuing to paint, wait until these areas are completely dry and remove the salt.

2 Mix tones
Rather than using flat washes for the leaves and petals, experiment by mixing two or three tones on one element, or using cool and warm colours together (see p.120).

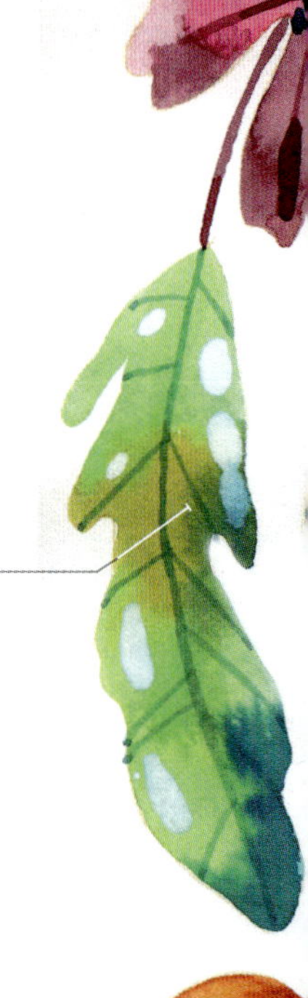

You will need

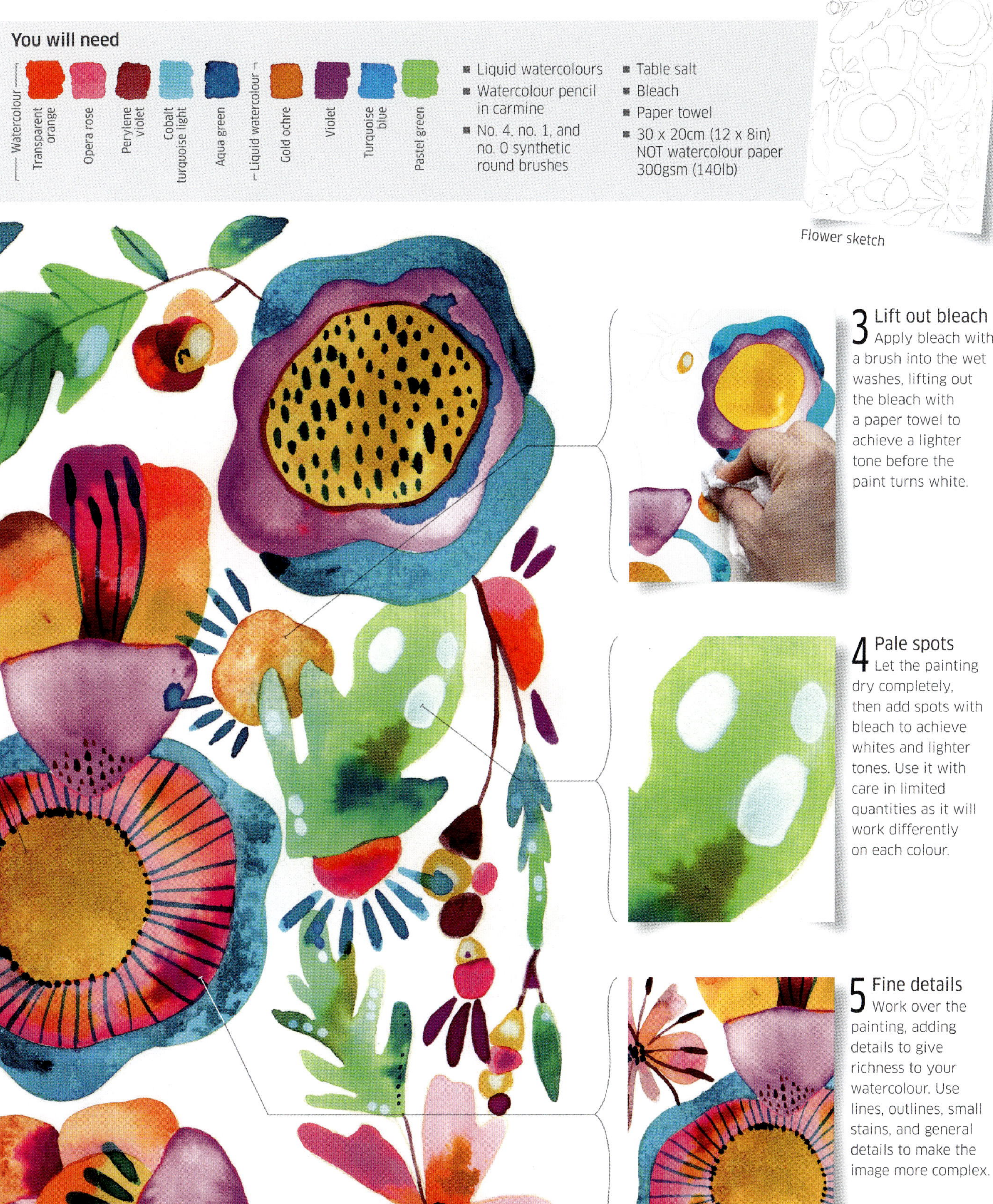

Watercolour
- Transparent orange
- Opera rose
- Perylene violet
- Cobalt turquoise light
- Aqua green

Liquid watercolour
- Gold ochre
- Violet
- Turquoise blue
- Pastel green

- Liquid watercolours
- Watercolour pencil in carmine
- No. 4, no. 1, and no. 0 synthetic round brushes

- Table salt
- Bleach
- Paper towel
- 30 x 20cm (12 x 8in) NOT watercolour paper 300gsm (140lb)

Flower sketch

3 Lift out bleach

Apply bleach with a brush into the wet washes, lifting out the bleach with a paper towel to achieve a lighter tone before the paint turns white.

4 Pale spots

Let the painting dry completely, then add spots with bleach to achieve whites and lighter tones. Use it with care in limited quantities as it will work differently on each colour.

5 Fine details

Work over the painting, adding details to give richness to your watercolour. Use lines, outlines, small stains, and general details to make the image more complex.

Using gouache

ADDING OPACITY TO COLOURS AND HIGHLIGHTS

Including gouache paints in your palette will extend your range of techniques. Opaque effects add contrast to transparent washes, with the opportunity to add light over dark in any colour. Any subject with white or light components is suitable, from snowy scenes to falling water or breaking waves.

■ Enhancing light-coloured shapes

Remembering to leave clean, white shapes in the paper for highlights and lights, can be slow and clumsy, interrupting the flow of a wash and perhaps losing edges. Instead, use gouache to paint light-coloured areas on top of a watercolour wash, giving you more control of your marks and to add defined lights.

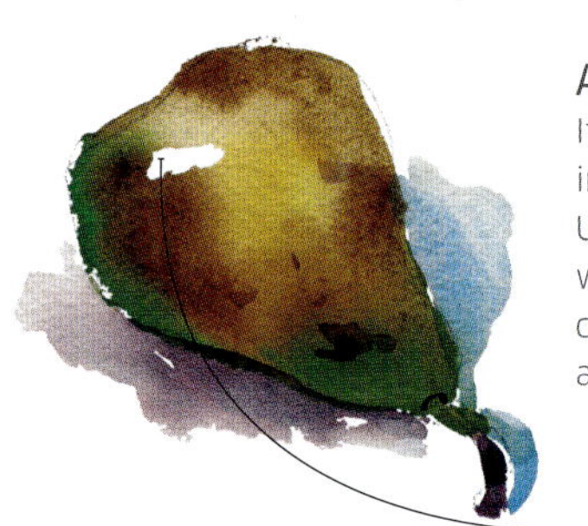

Adding highlights

It can be difficult to leave shapes in white paper for small highlights. Use gouache, either as a pure white or mixed with a wash to create an opaque light that gives added dimension to the shape.

Using white gouache can be easier than painting around small spaces

Uneven edges in watercolour

Defined edges in gouache

Defining edges

Painting around intricate light shapes in watercolour makes it difficult to create crisp edges. Apply gouache over a wash to paint in detailed shapes and retain a defined edge.

PUTTING IT INTO PRACTICE

The tracks across the snowy field are represented here in a few blue washes. Rather than trying to paint around the highlighted snow furrows, opaque shapes are added on top of the watercolour wash.

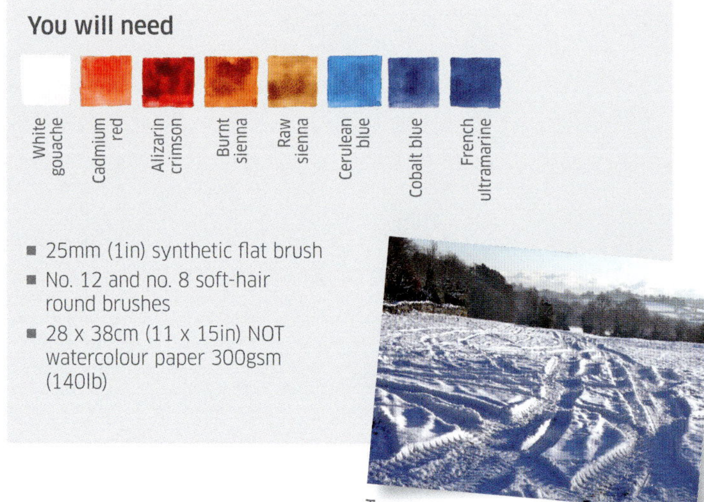

- 25mm (1in) synthetic flat brush
- No. 12 and no. 8 soft-hair round brushes
- 28 x 38cm (11 x 15in) NOT watercolour paper 300gsm (140lb)

Tyre tracks in snow

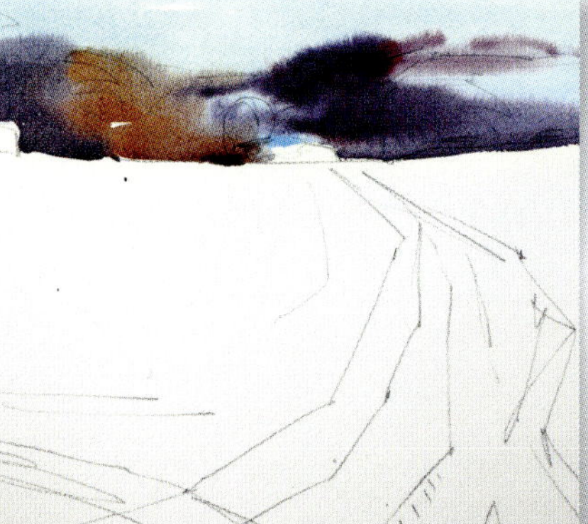

1 Base washes
Establish the main composition with a light pencil sketch. Start with a sky wash of cerulean blue and while still wet, paint simple shapes for the background trees with bold, transparent mixes of French ultramarine and alizarin crimson, adding burnt sienna to the left.

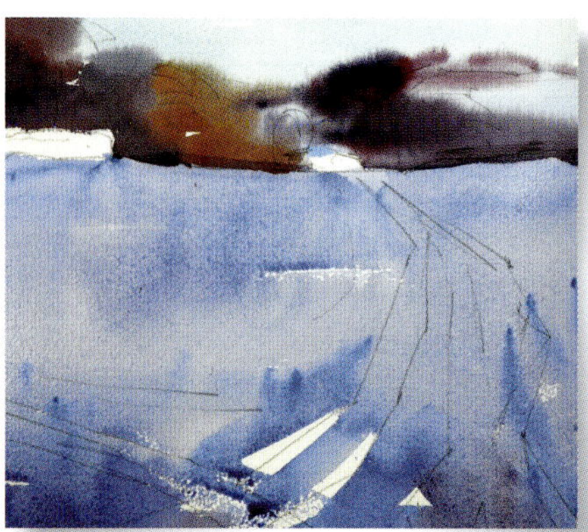

2 Foreground snow
It is important to apply all the snow as one continuous wash, only leaving a few highlights and breaks to show the white paper, to enable a comparison with the gouache at a later stage. Allow sky and background to merge wet-in-wet.

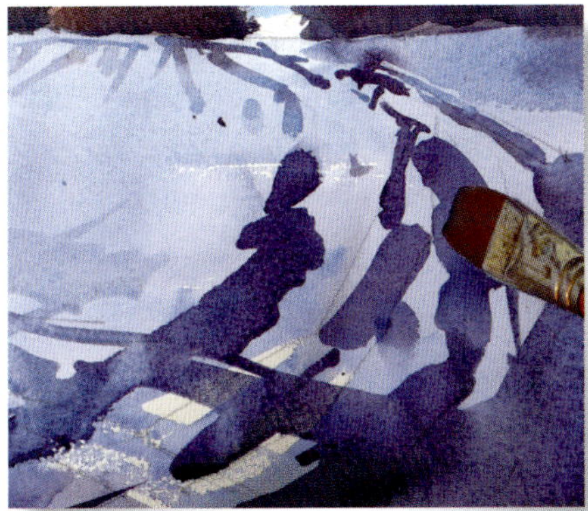

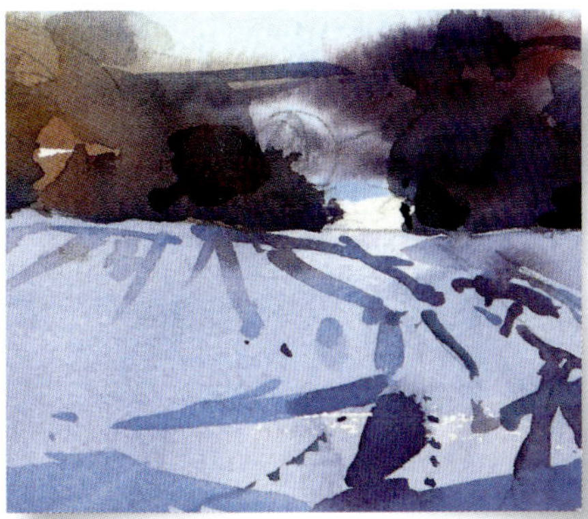

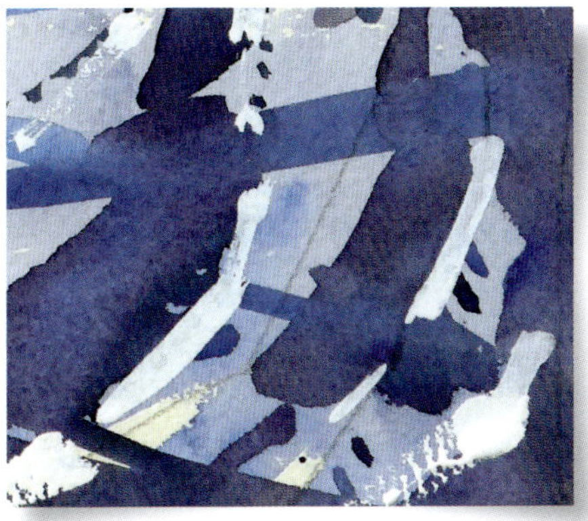

3 Blue shadows

Mix a range of blues for the dark shadows. Apply simple strokes in different brush sizes, using cobalt for the mid ground and transition to a warmer tone darkened with red.

4 Warm contrasts

Darken blue washes with red, burnt sienna, and some alizarin crimson, letting the warmer tones blend in the trees. Add dashes of the shadow colours for the tyre treads.

5 Opaque texture

Use dry brush marks in pure gouache with a little water added to highlight the edges of the furrows against the blue shadows. Contrasts with the white paper add textural interest.

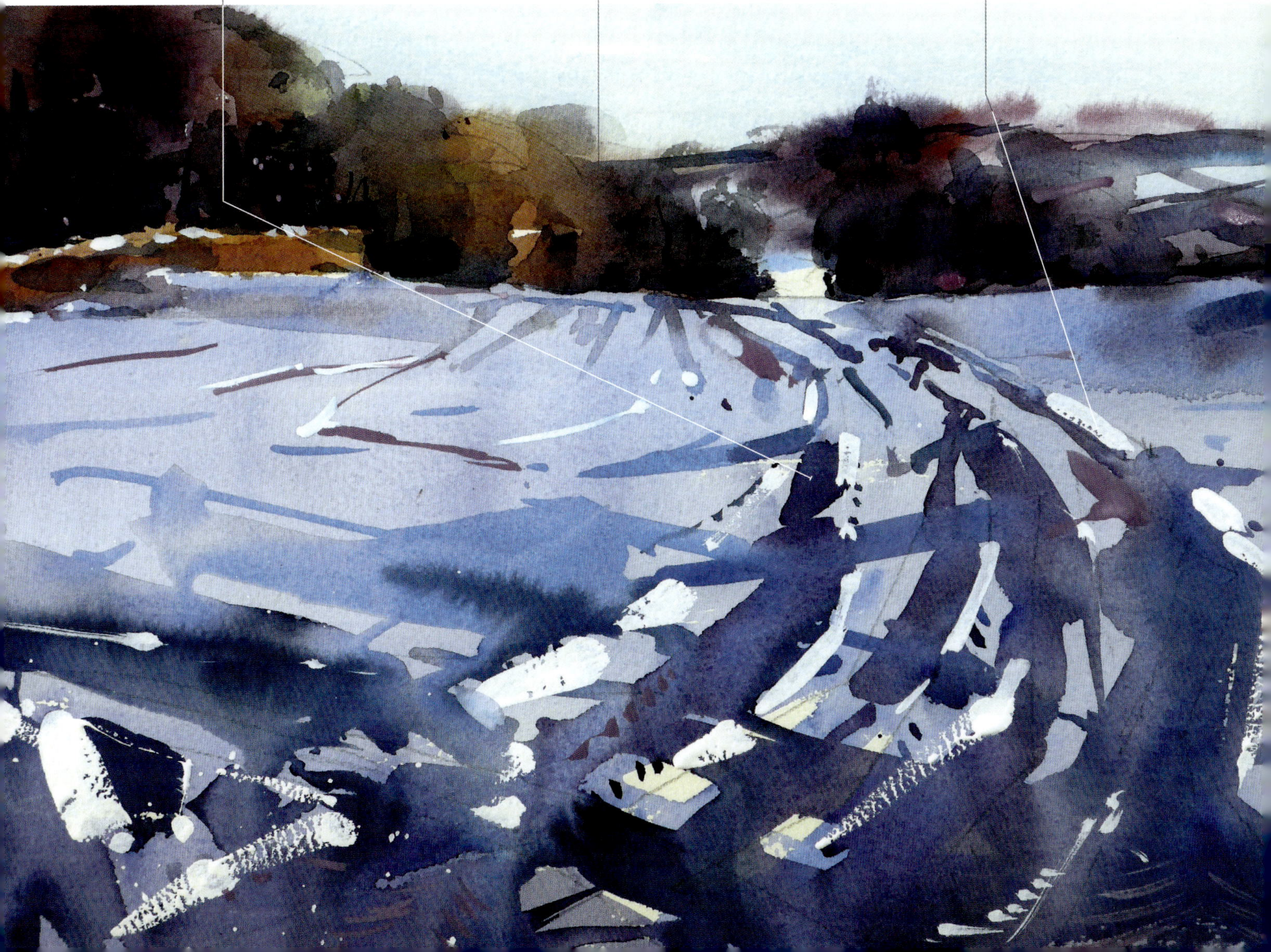

Using charcoal

CONTRASTING TONAL QUALITIES WITH COLOUR

Combining an expressive drawing tool such as charcoal with watercolour adds different qualities to your paintings. Its fluid nature lends itself to fast sketches, and its tonal qualities are ideal for adding shadows and textures. Filling a charcoal outline with watercolour suggests a graphic, illustrative style, adding colour effects that aren't possible in charcoal alone.

■ Tonal effects

Charcoal lends itself to tonal studies, from rich blacks to light smudges. Use it to establish shadows, outlines, and tones: either dry, or wet the marks to smooth and intensify them. Blend with water to create a light wash, or lay colour on top.

■ Textural effects

Broken charcoal marks will add texture to a painting and this effect can be enhanced by working on paper with a rough surface. Apply a wash over the top so that both the grain of the paper and the charcoal marks become integrated with the painting.

Combining media
Vine charcoal smudged into the paper results in a granulated effect when light washes are applied on top. White gouache adds accents of light.

Creating tone
Charcoal is easy to apply and marks vary in intensity according to how hard you press. Use the different tones for shadows and form.

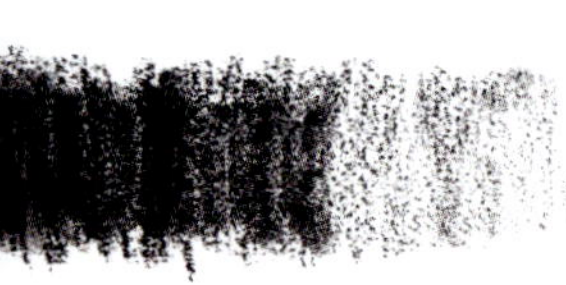

Wet charcoal
Apply a little water to the charcoal mark to smooth and intensify the effect, creating a velvety black with a unique, matt texture.

Add colour
Lay a relatively dry wash over charcoal to create layers of tone and texture. Use more water to blend the tones, if preferred.

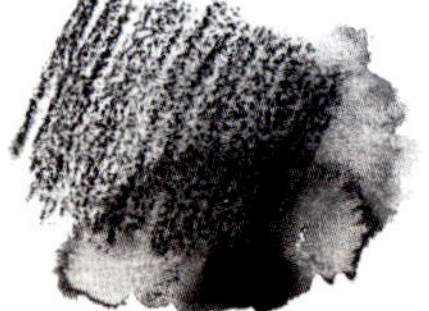

Charcoal wash
For more varied marks, add water to dissolve the charcoal and move the wash with a brush or let it bleed and spread naturally.

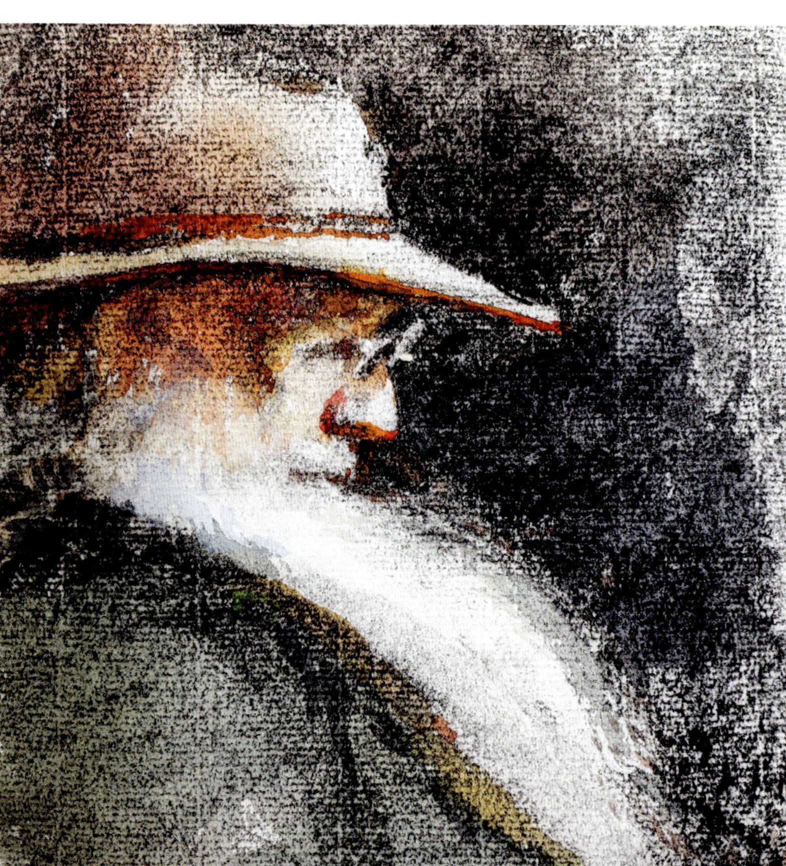

PUTTING IT INTO PRACTICE

This still life uses the contrasting textures of the charcoal outline and the watercolour wash to imbue the simple subject matter with colour and immediacy. Intense mixes of the liquid watercolours are used for dark tones, blending the contrasting colours for mid tones and highlights.

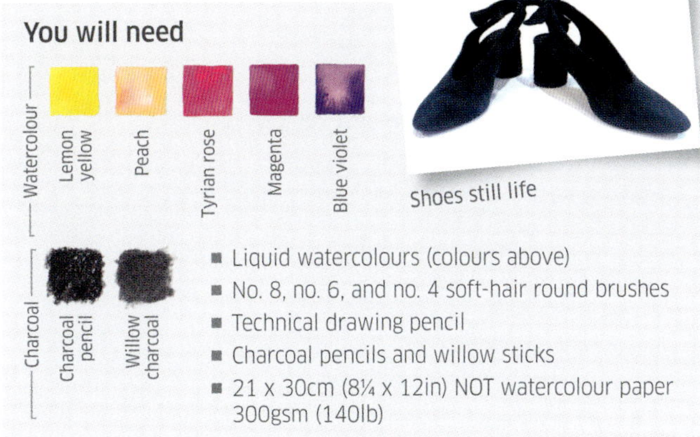

- Liquid watercolours (colours above)
- No. 8, no. 6, and no. 4 soft-hair round brushes
- Technical drawing pencil
- Charcoal pencils and willow sticks
- 21 x 30cm (8¼ x 12in) NOT watercolour paper 300gsm (140lb)

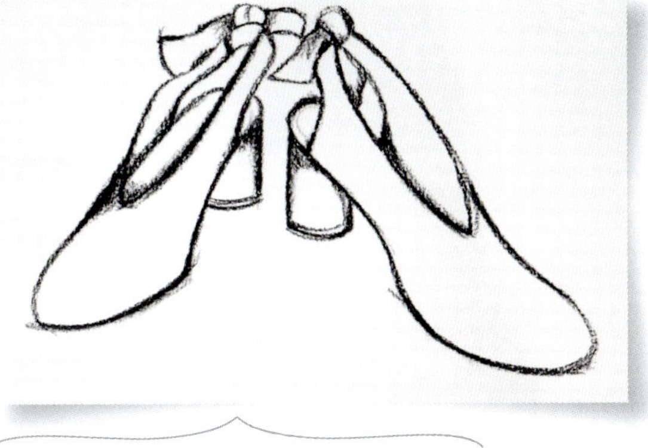

1 Charcoal outlines
Draw light, simple outlines with a technical pencil. Using different thicknesses of charcoal, draw over the underdrawing in a more sketchy style, avoiding smudges. Hold the charcoal with a loose grip and don't apply too much pressure.

Different tones are achieved with dry and wet charcoal

Charcoal wash for inner shadows

When applying the colour you don't need to fill the shape perfectly

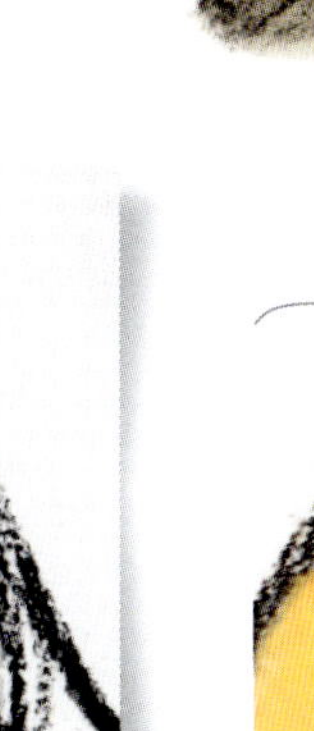

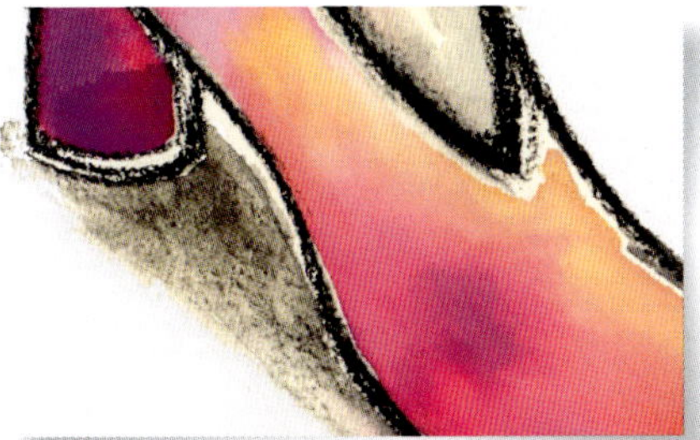

2 Smooth charcoal
Moisten and smooth the outlines with a small amount of water on your brush, moving the charcoal wash to areas of darker tone.

3 Fill with liquid colour
Add liquid colour in a mix of tones inside the lines, with undiluted wash for darker tones over the charcoal marks.

4 Blend shadows
Add shadows beneath the shoes with smudged charcoal. Use a little water to create a lighter tone wash around the outside of the shape.

Using inks

WORKING WITH INTENSE COLOUR

Inks are super-concentrated and more vibrant than standard watercolour paints. There are a few types, but all can be used neat for bold colour, or diluted with water for less impact. The brilliant colours offered by inks make them popular with illustrators.

◼ Types of inks

Liquid watercolours (also called watercolour inks), water-soluble drawing inks, and Indian inks are great when you're looking for vibrant and colourful results. Those made from dyes rather than pigments are usually not lightfast, and therefore better suited to illustration for print rather than paintings for display.

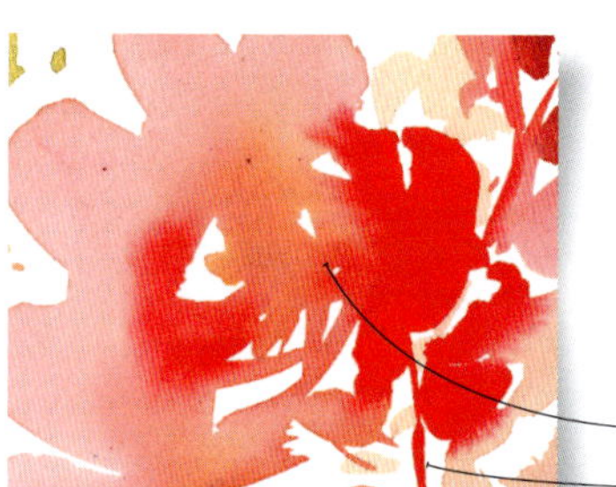

Liquid watercolours

These are very concentrated watercolours. Just a drop will give intense colour, and they blend beautifully wet-in-wet. You can also use them neat to pick out details.

— Blending colour

— Intense detail

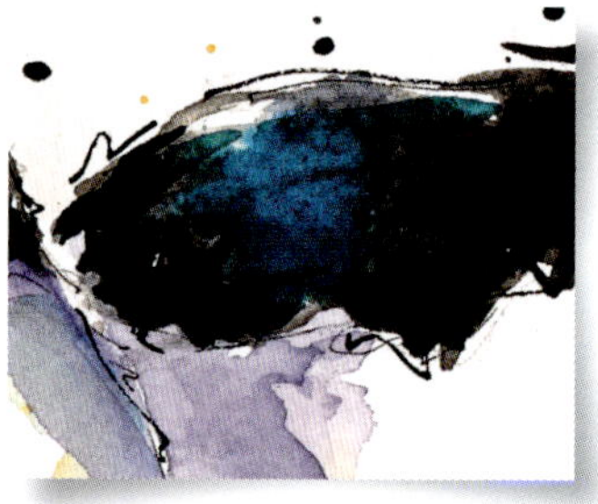

Water-soluble inks

Some drawing inks are water-based. They blend well with watercolour washes without losing intensity and impact. They are usually made with dyes, and are not lightfast.

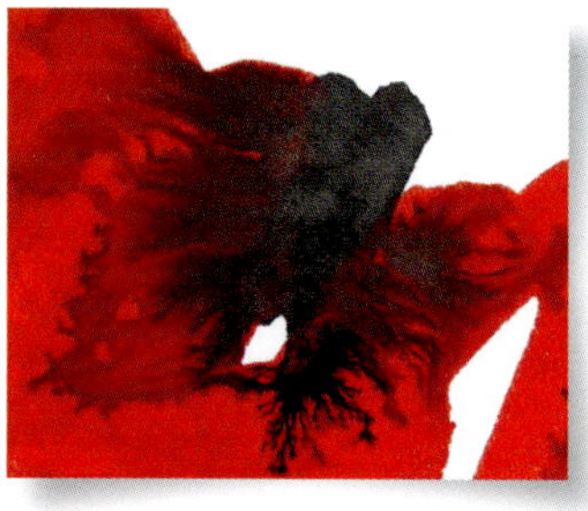

Indian inks

Made with lamp black pigment and binder, Indian inks are waterproof when dry, making them great for the "line" in "line and wash" paintings. They mix with wet watercolour, but can repel the paint to create interesting effects.

PUTTING IT INTO PRACTICE

This floral abstract is created by introducing liquid watercolours in strategic places in every layer of the painting, from base washes to accents of saturated colour that highlight the simplified botanical shapes.

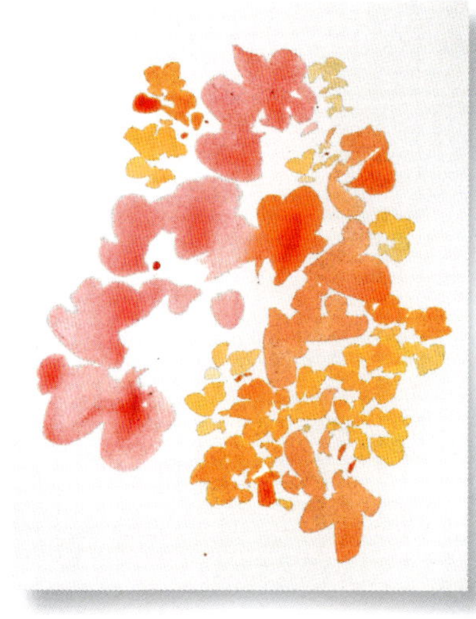

1 A watery mix
Dilute your colours to create a watery mix in your palette. Paint the first shapes of flowers loosely, alternating between your coloured water and the watercolour inks. Make sure this layer is very wet – you should be able to see mini-pools of colourful water.

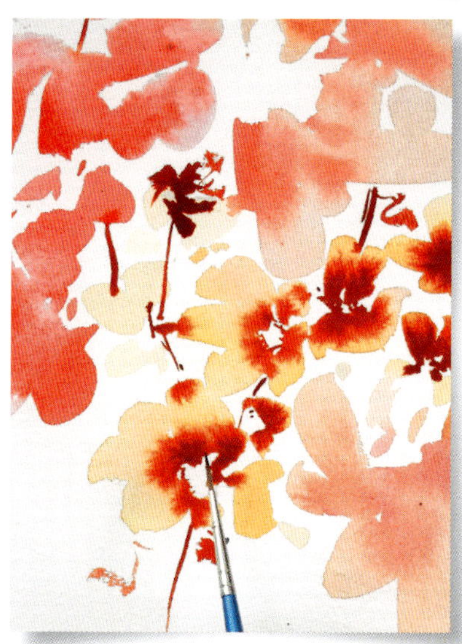

2 Drops of colour
To gain immediate vibrancy, use a brush or dropper to add the contrasting liquid watercolour to the bright flower centres. Ensure that the first layer is damp enough for the colours to blend naturally. Add fine stems with the darker colour.

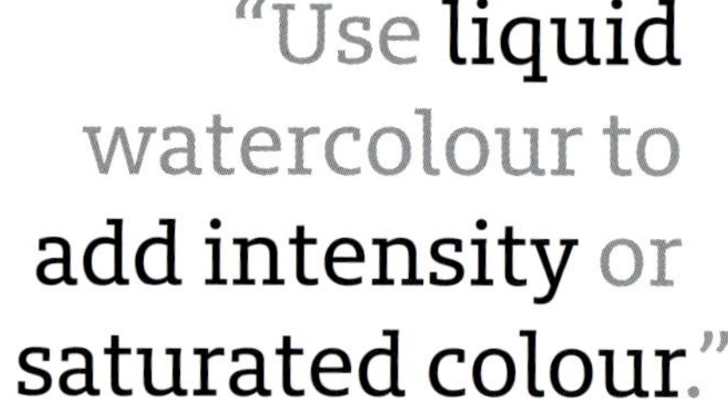

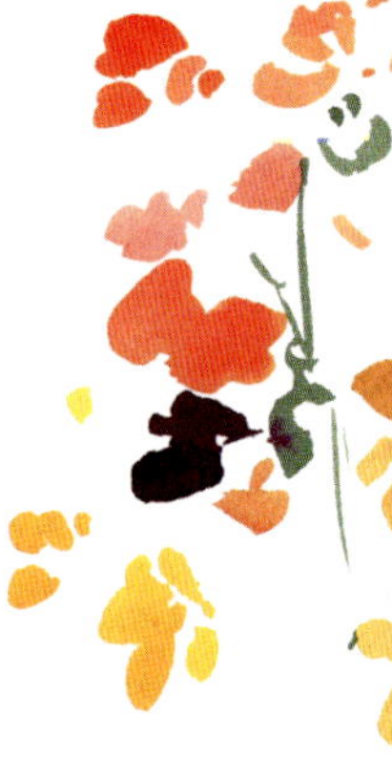

"Use **liquid watercolour** to **add intensity** or **saturated colour.**"

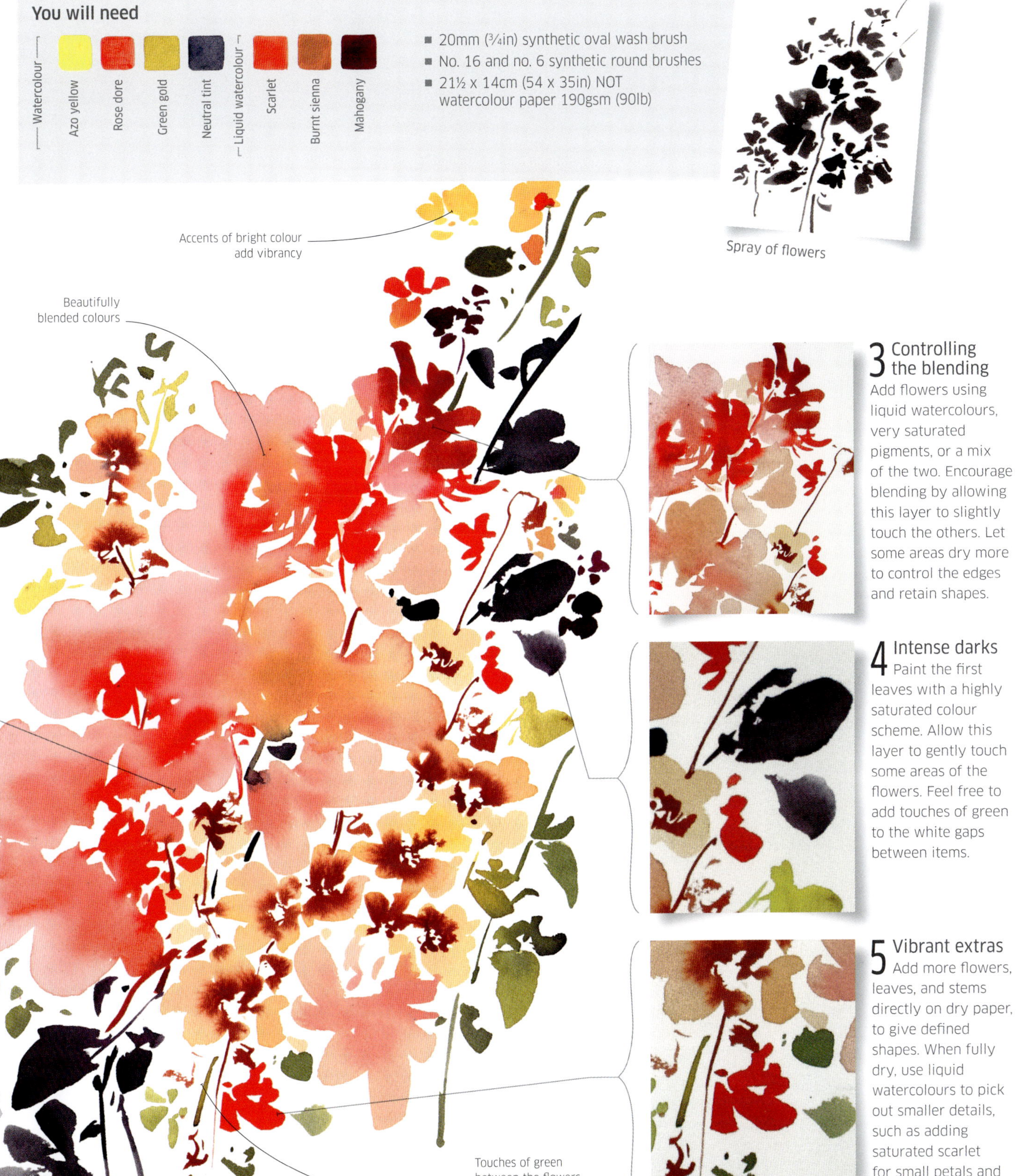

You will need

Watercolour
- Azo yellow
- Rose dore
- Green gold
- Neutral tint

Liquid watercolour
- Scarlet
- Burnt sienna
- Mahogany

- 20mm (¾in) synthetic oval wash brush
- No. 16 and no. 6 synthetic round brushes
- 21½ x 14cm (54 x 35in) NOT watercolour paper 190gsm (90lb)

Spray of flowers

Accents of bright colour add vibrancy

Beautifully blended colours

Touches of green between the flowers gives cohesion and direction to the work

3 Controlling the blending

Add flowers using liquid watercolours, very saturated pigments, or a mix of the two. Encourage blending by allowing this layer to slightly touch the others. Let some areas dry more to control the edges and retain shapes.

4 Intense darks

Paint the first leaves with a highly saturated colour scheme. Allow this layer to gently touch some areas of the flowers. Feel free to add touches of green to the white gaps between items.

5 Vibrant extras

Add more flowers, leaves, and stems directly on dry paper, to give defined shapes. When fully dry, use liquid watercolours to pick out smaller details, such as adding saturated scarlet for small petals and flower centres.

Watercolour pencils and pens

USING PIGMENTED DRAWING TOOLS

With a high concentration of water-soluble pigment, watercolour pencils and pens are a versatile and quick way to draw and paint. They give you much more control over finer details and marks than a brush and wash, and create a smooth surface with subtle variations. Use alone or combine with traditional washes for detailed studies.

Surface marks

The effects from water-soluble drawing tools depend on whether you work on wet or dry paper. Laying tone on dry paper and wetting with a brush creates an even wash, whereas drawing on damp paper translates your drawn marks into intense pigment in one stroke.

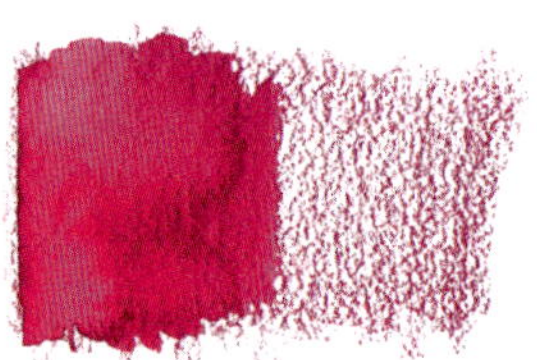

Adding water to pencil

Lay your pencil marks on dry paper, drawing or shading where required. Load a clean brush with water and work over the pencil mark to dissolve the pigment and create a wash.

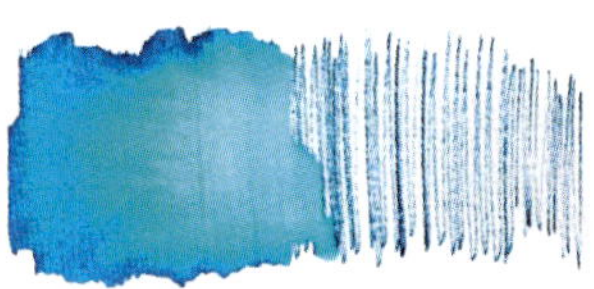

Adding water to pen

Treat water-soluble pen marks in the same way as pencil, using a clean brush to apply water. Move the brush to blend and spread the wash.

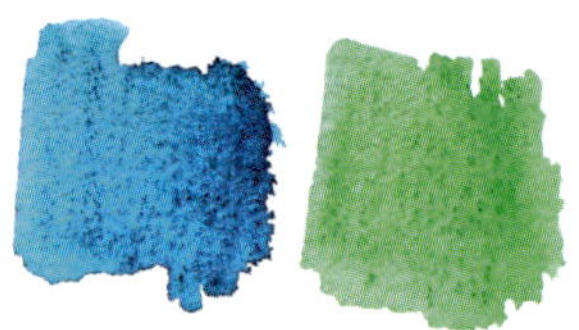

Drawing on wet paper

Damp your paper with clean water applied with a brush or spray. Draw with a watercolour pencil to create rich and intense marks where the pigment blends into the paper.

PUTTING IT INTO PRACTICE

This colourful rendering of a beetle combines liquid washes, watercolour pencils, and markers to create a varied and detailed surface. Controlled application maintains the precision of the initial drawing.

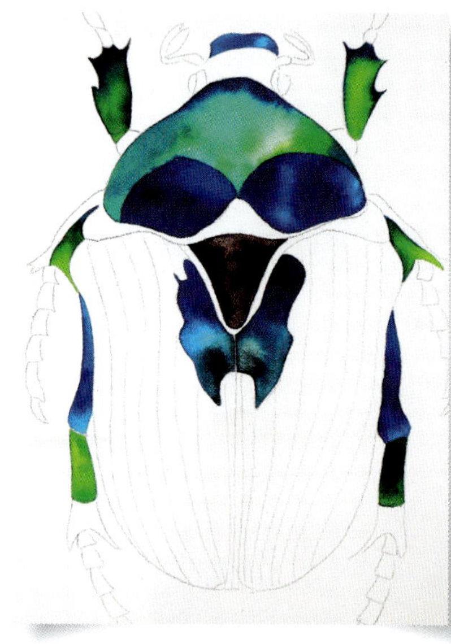

1 Fill outline with liquid colour
Draw precise outlines that will be used as guides for washes or pencil shading. Using a no. 10 brush, fill the largest sections of the beetle's shell with bold washes. Use plenty of water for a more transparent effect.

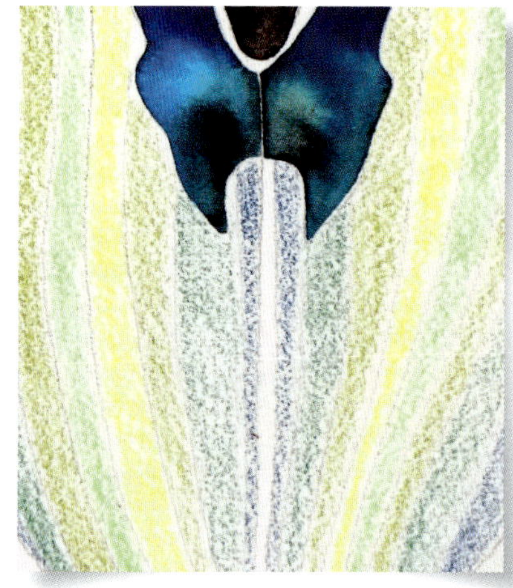

2 Pencil shading
When the liquid watercolour washes are completely dry, use watercolour pencils to continue to fill in the smaller parts of the design, laying different colours and staying within the outlines.

"Create different **shades** or tints by varying the pressure of your pencil marks."

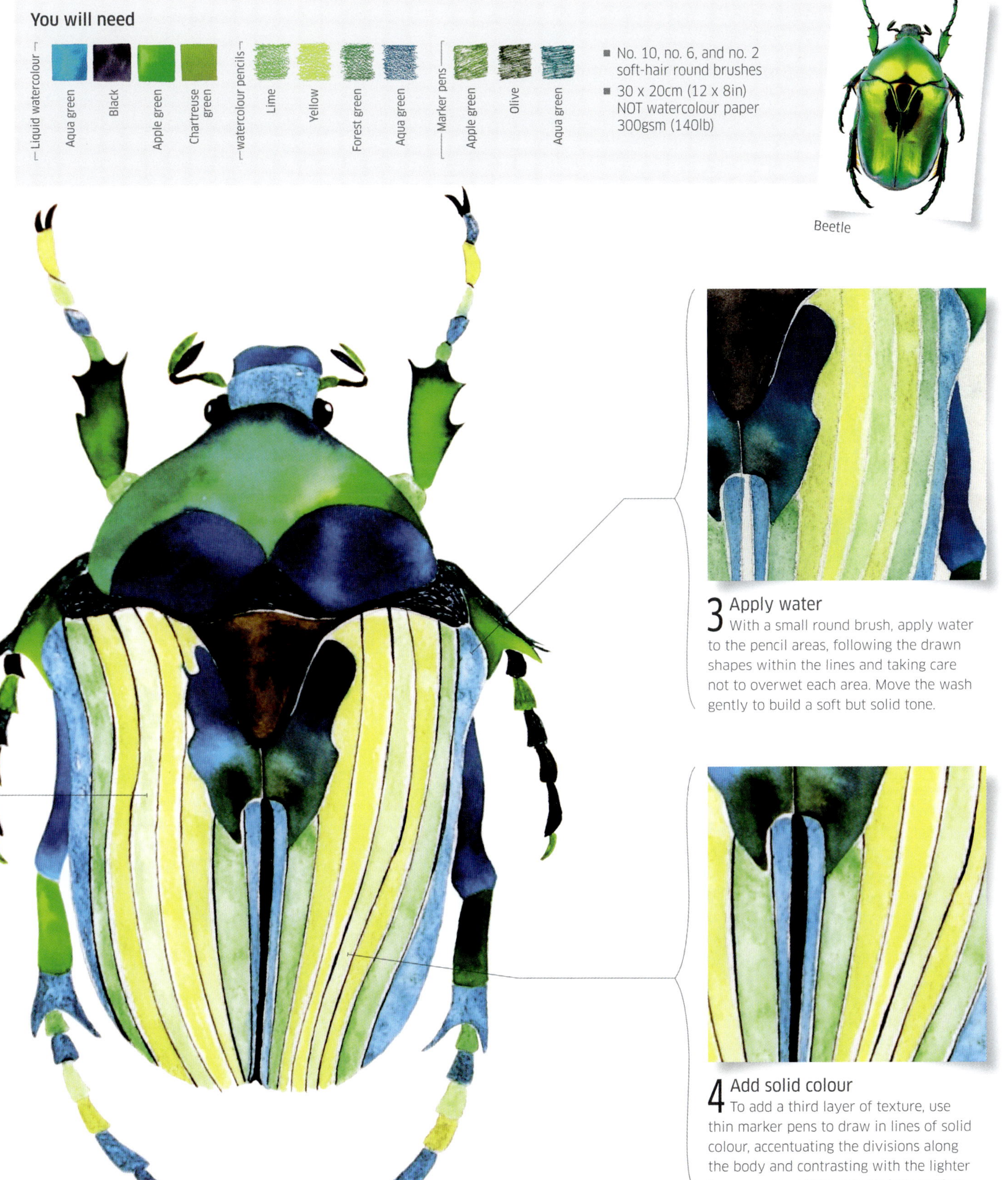

You will need

- No. 10, no. 6, and no. 2 soft-hair round brushes
- 30 x 20cm (12 x 8in) NOT watercolour paper 300gsm (140lb)

Beetle

3 Apply water
With a small round brush, apply water to the pencil areas, following the drawn shapes within the lines and taking care not to overwet each area. Move the wash gently to build a soft but solid tone.

4 Add solid colour
To add a third layer of texture, use thin marker pens to draw in lines of solid colour, accentuating the divisions along the body and contrasting with the lighter transparency of the watercolour washes.

Effects with gouache

ADDING OPAQUE COLOUR AND SURFACE TEXTURE

Combining gouache with watercolour can be very liberating, allowing you to paint light passages over your darks and adding another surface layer of opacity. Pure gouache contains much more pigment than pure watercolour – used on its own it has a powerful impact, but by mixing it in watercolour washes you can merge seamlessly between the two media.

PUTTING IT INTO PRACTICE

This painting combines both media, with watercolour providing a light, translucent setting of sea and sky, against which the strong opaque mixes solidify the boat with texture and bold colour.

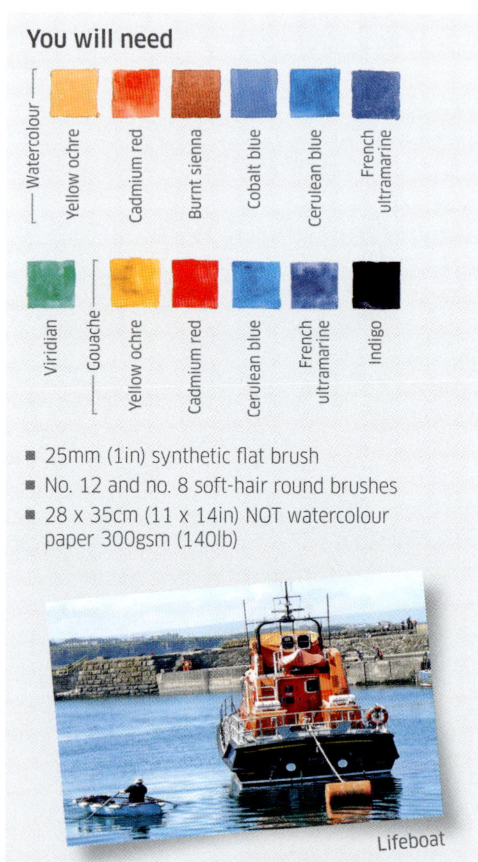

You will need

- 25mm (1in) synthetic flat brush
- No. 12 and no. 8 soft-hair round brushes
- 28 x 35cm (11 x 14in) NOT watercolour paper 300gsm (140lb)

Lifeboat

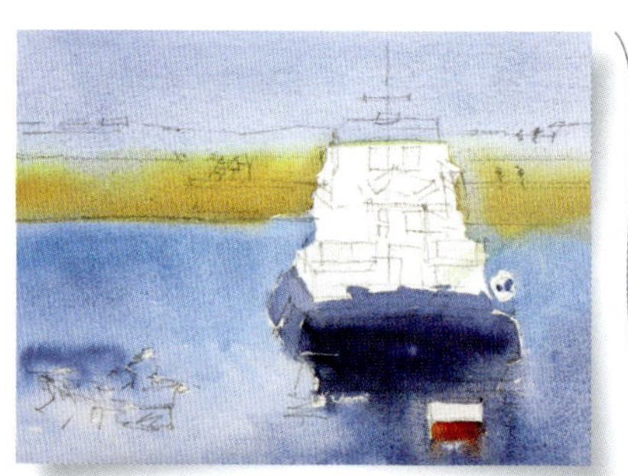

1 Bold washes
Loosely sketch the scene. Next, fill the paper with a continuous wash of cerulean sky merging with an ochre harbour wall. Apply a cobalt and French ultramarine blend in the foreground. Paint around the top of the boat where you will apply an orange wash later.

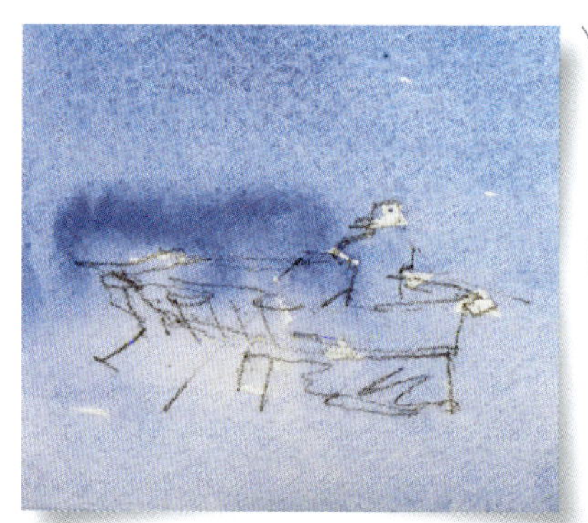

2 Ignore highlights
When using gouache, you don't need to plan ahead for highlights; lay a flat wash in one go across all the elements. The small boat and figure here will be worked on later.

■ Benefits of opaque paint

Employ gouache to bring body and texture to your paintings. Its opacity and high pigment content adds strength to lighter colours, creating better coverage with a chalkiness that can be used in contrast to transparent washes. Working light over dark means you don't have to plan for highlights, adding lights and whites with control at the end. Gouache is naturally thick and works well as an impasto texture, too.

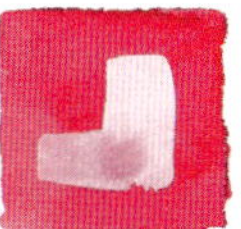

Chinese white

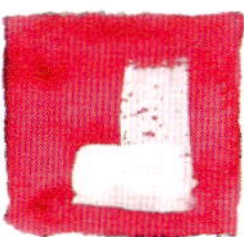

White gouache

Adding body
Chinese white leaves a semi-opaque, mixed tone compared to the matt effect of gouache.

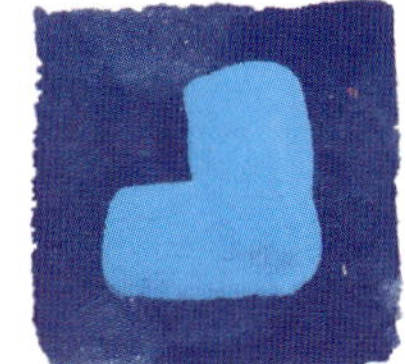

Adding colour
The rich pigment in pure gouache leaves fresh, bold marks that retain their shape.

Adding texture
Use undiluted gouache to create texture through impasto effects or with dry-brush techniques.

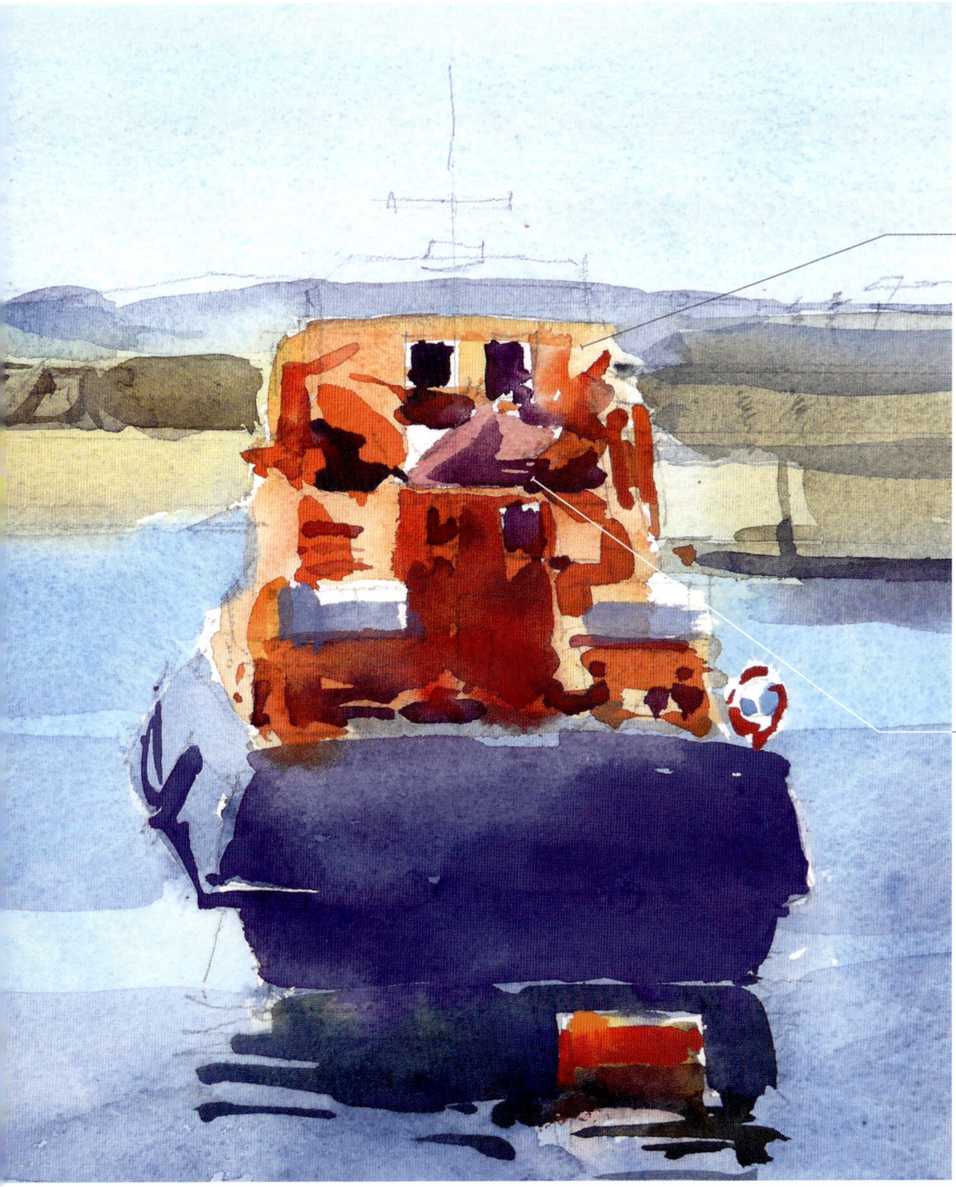

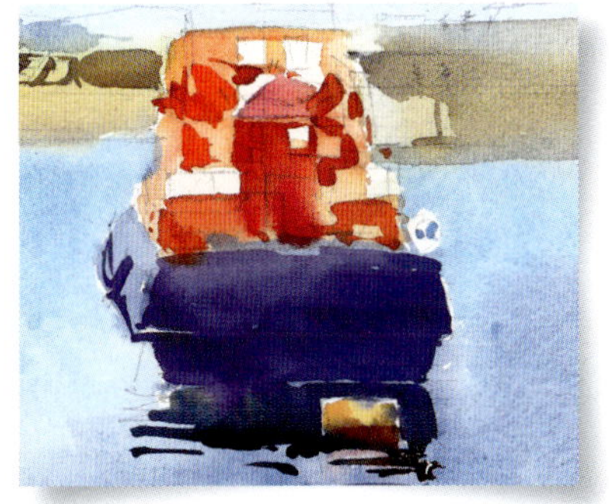

3 Contrasting washes
Paint the deck with mixes of red and orange, laying in the main shapes and avoiding detail. Orange instantly appears bolder against the blue.

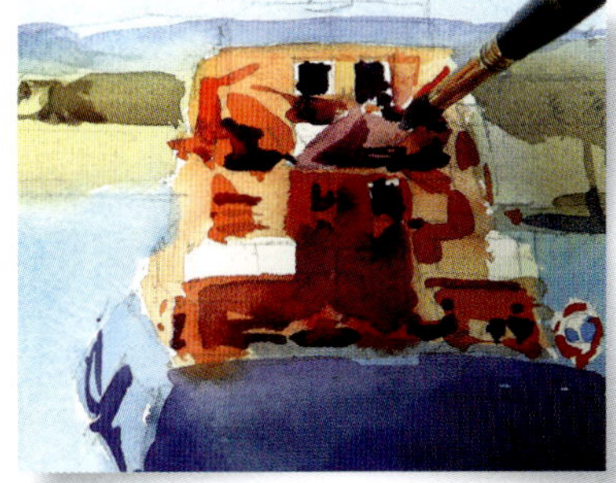

4 Watercolour darks
Use a dark orange for the shadowed shapes, letting it blend slightly. Apply the darkest darks with a mix of indigo and ultramarine on the boats and water.

5 Assess your painting
After building watercolour darks, stop to assess if you can continue to inject colour without muddying the mixes. At this point, introduce gouache to strengthen your colours.

6 Mix lights and brights

Enhance the bright colours using pure red and orange gouache to bring light back to the boat's upper levels. The opaque orange mix stands out clearly over the darker undertones. Applied thickly, it adds surface texture, too.

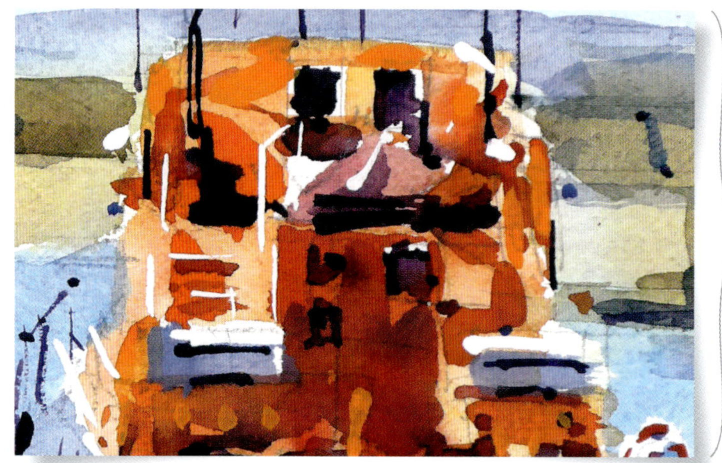

7 Highlight shadows

Use a pale blue gouache mix to bring light and life back to the ripples of water behind both boats, adding strokes over the dark shadow wash beneath. Use pale opaque blue as a grey for the off-white shadow areas on the main boat.

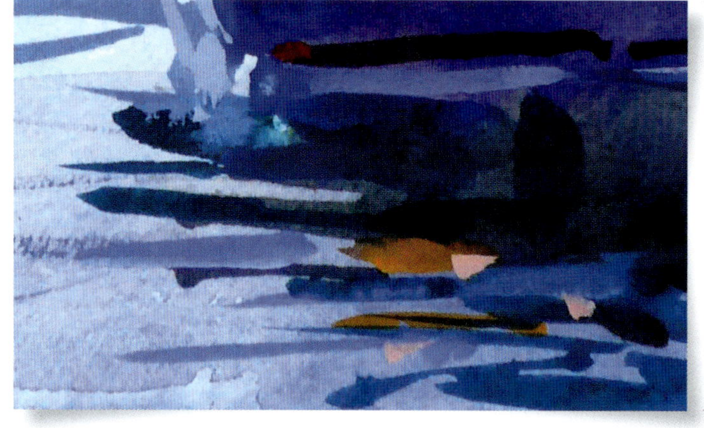

8 Detailed highlights

Use dabs of pure white gouache for the bright highlights on the boat and fisherman, and the lightest reflections in the water. Mix a range of blue tones in gouache to add light over dark.

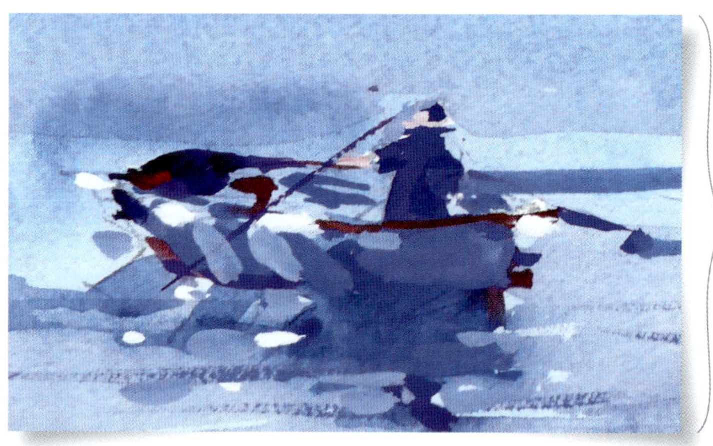

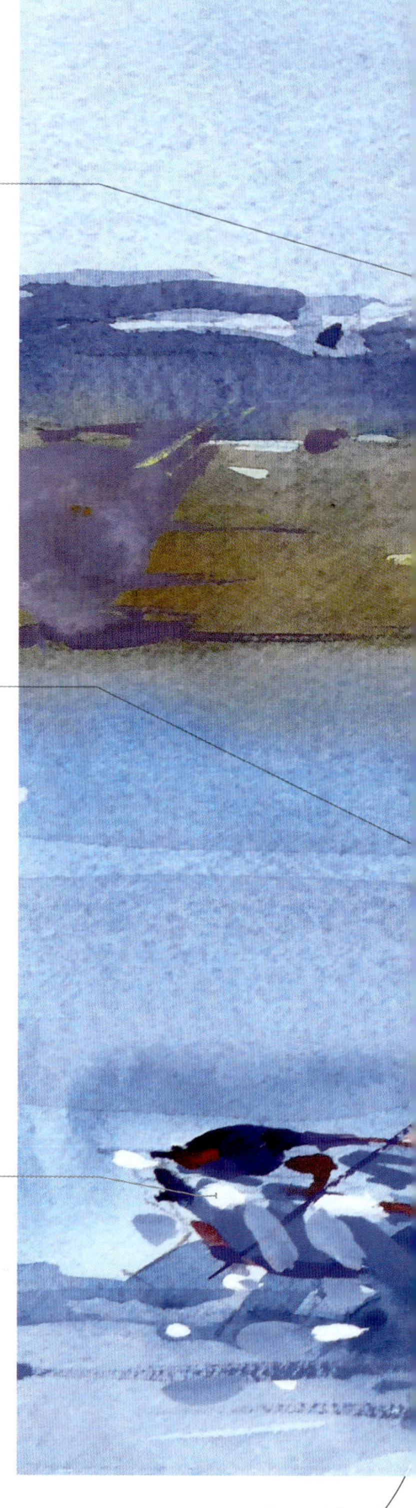

Pure cadmium red watercolour

"**The opaque qualities** of gouache will enhance your watercolours with added **body and light**."

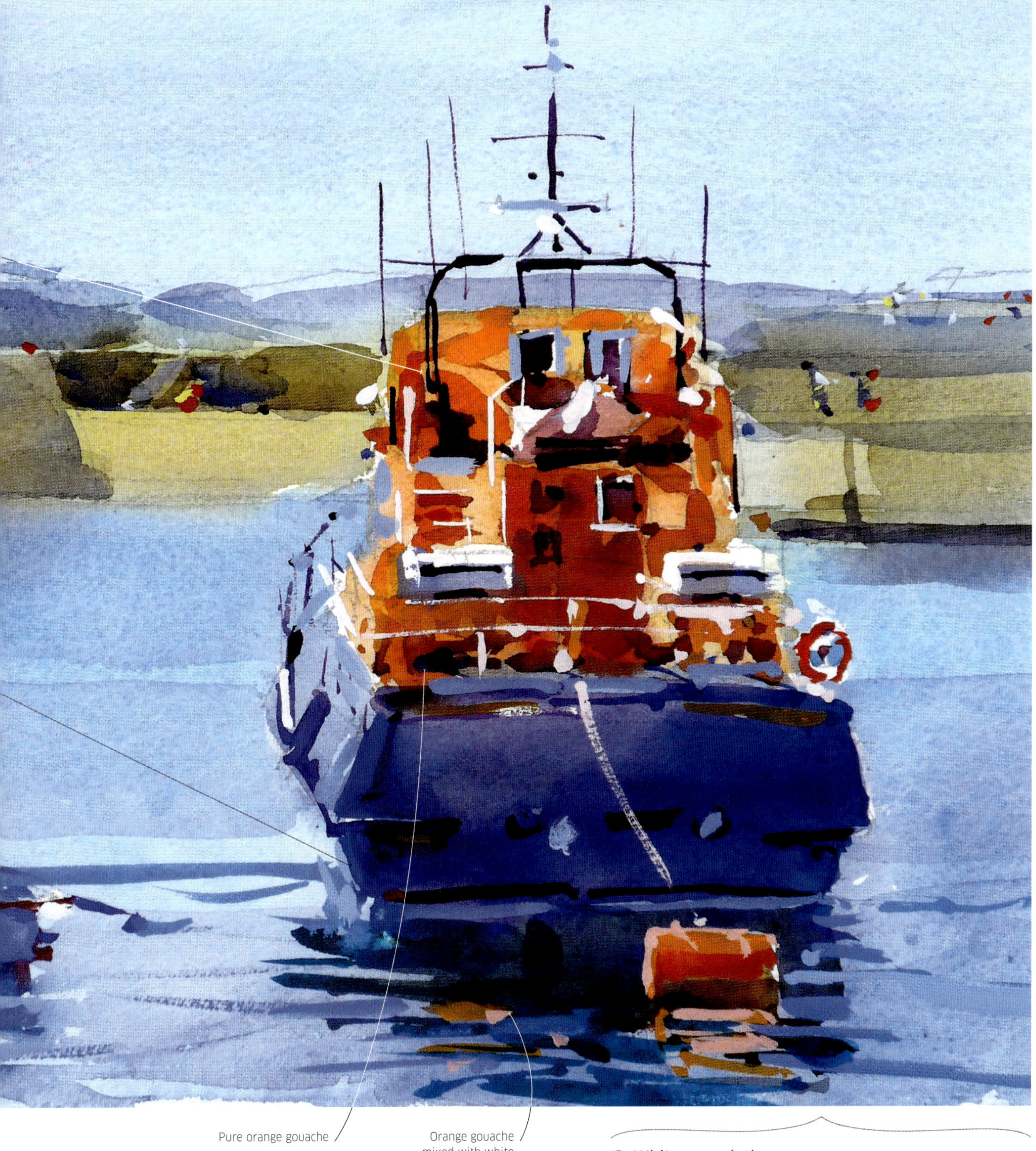

Pure orange gouache

Orange gouache
mixed with white

9 White over dark

Use pure white gouache to draw in the fine lines of the boat rails and steps, over the dark underlayers. A broken stroke is all that is needed to suggest the tethering rope to the buoy.

Towards abstraction

PAINTING INTUITIVELY

In the absence of clearly identifiable objects, abstract painting relies on interesting shapes and successful colour combinations to please the viewer's eye, giving the artist endless opportunity for expression. The "controlled accidents" you can achieve in watercolour add real excitement and freedom to a painting.

■ Abstract principles

Making the first marks is an exciting experience in an abstract painting, since they will often determine the direction of the piece. In the absence of a scene or subject that the viewer can relate to, concentrate on interesting shapes, edges, colours, and textures. Rough papers are great for this type of work. Use a lot of water, strong colours, and large brushes.

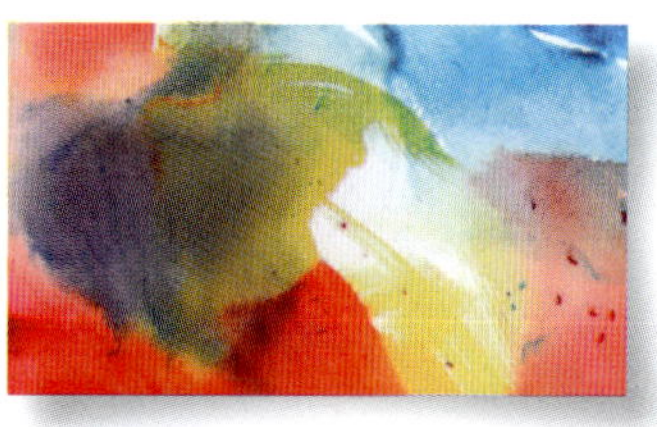

Colour palette
In an abstract, colours do not have to resemble real life. Choose any colours that work well together (see pp.116–21), and experiment with hues you don't see in nature.

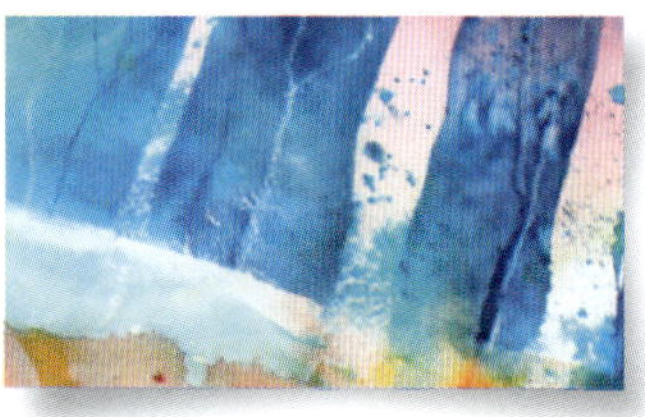

Shapes and composition
Assemble shapes in a form that makes a strong composition. Some shapes may hint at recognizable objects while others may come from your imagination.

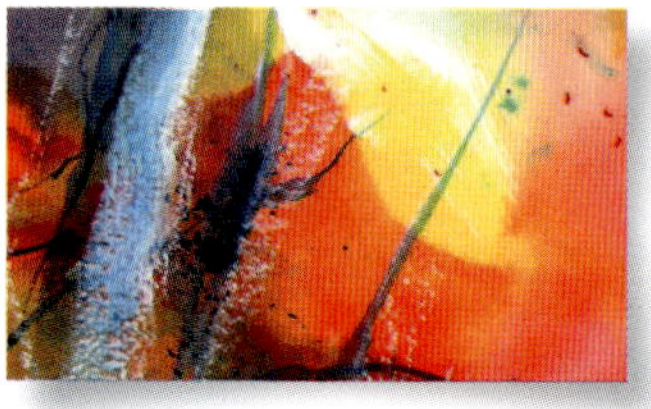

Hard and soft edges
Incorporating a range of hard and soft edges adds visual stimulation. In the absence of representational forms for the viewer to identify, they can be of any shape.

PUTTING IT INTO PRACTICE

Watercolour is a wonderful medium for achieving abstract and semi-abstract images, since the colours blend to create tones and shapes you might not have visualized. This painting, done from the imagination, has bright, warm colours that suggest a heightened version of autumn. The background shapes can be read as trees, though there is no attempt at realism.

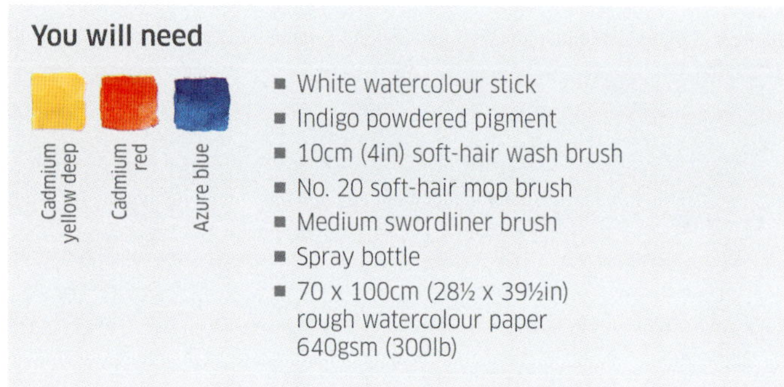

You will need

Cadmium yellow deep • Cadmium red • Azure blue

- White watercolour stick
- Indigo powdered pigment
- 10cm (4in) soft-hair wash brush
- No. 20 soft-hair mop brush
- Medium swordliner brush
- Spray bottle
- 70 x 100cm (28½ x 39½in) rough watercolour paper 640gsm (300lb)

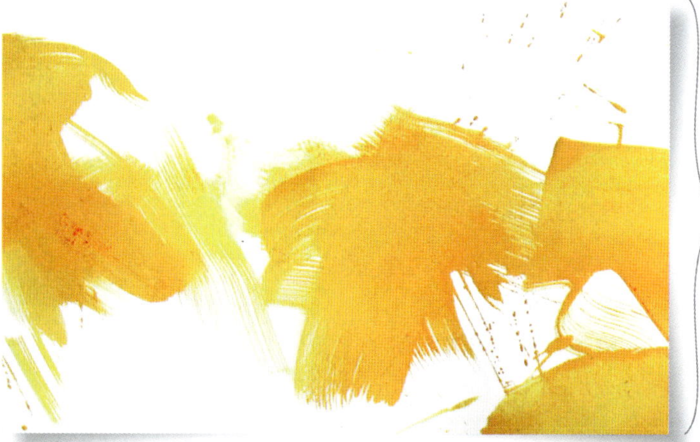

1 The first marks
Having decided on a colour palette, work from light to dark. A deep yellow is a good base for subsequent colours to blend with. Just make some vigorous marks with a large brush.

> "**Encourage** the paint to move and blend by angling the board."

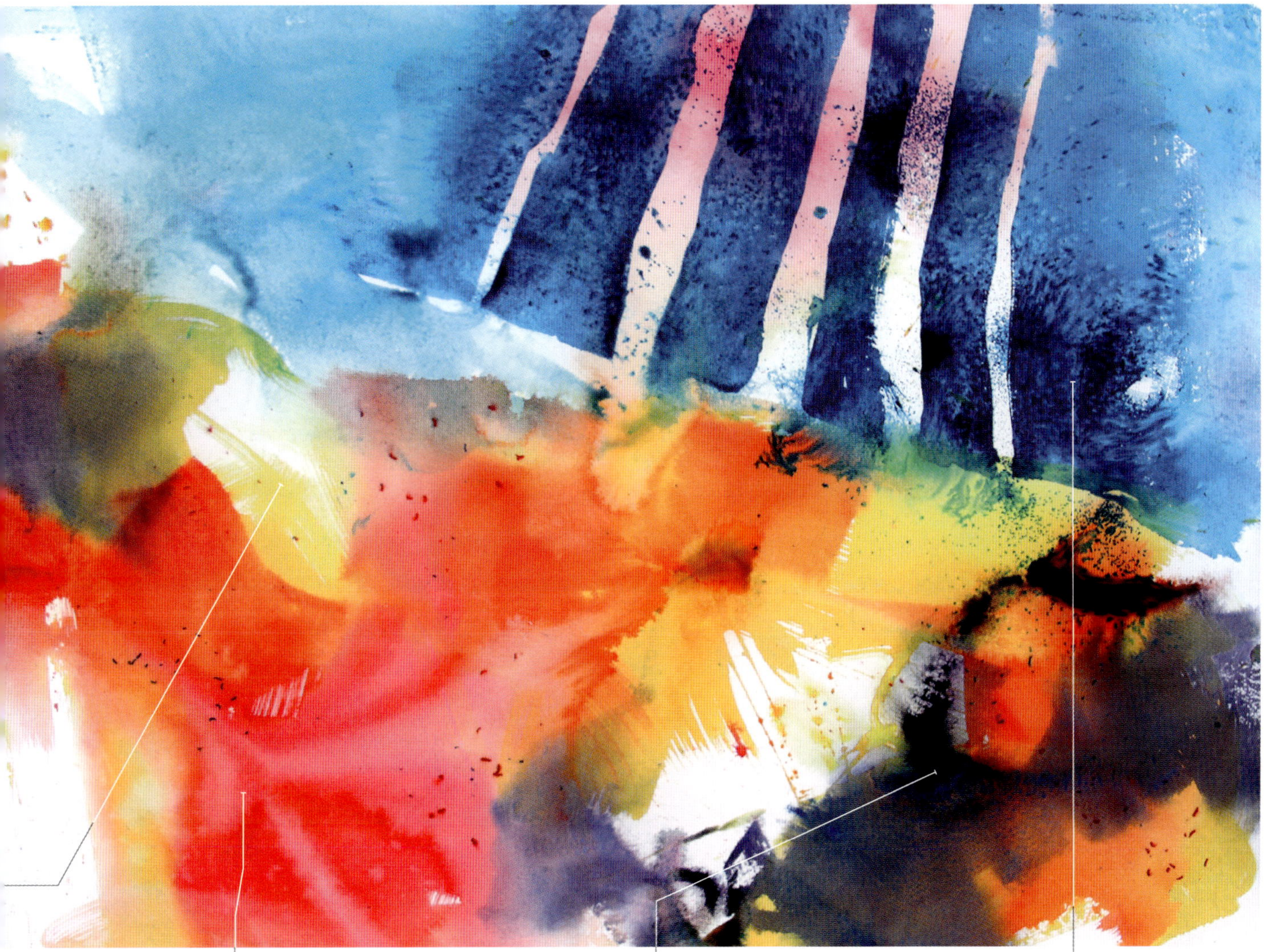

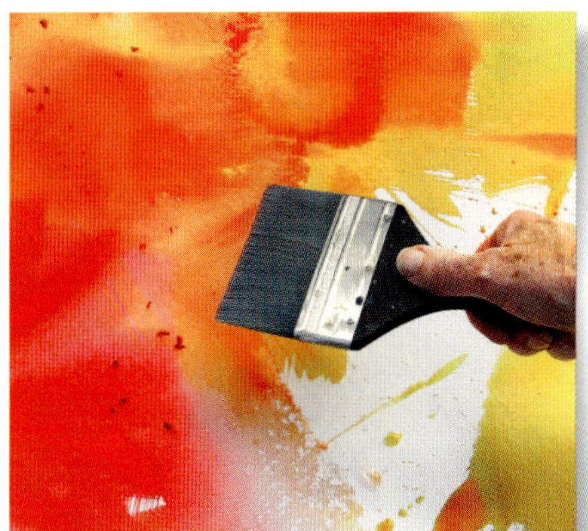

2 Introduce a second colour

While the paint is still wet, mix plenty of strong red and work it quickly onto the paper. Begin to establish a horizon line.

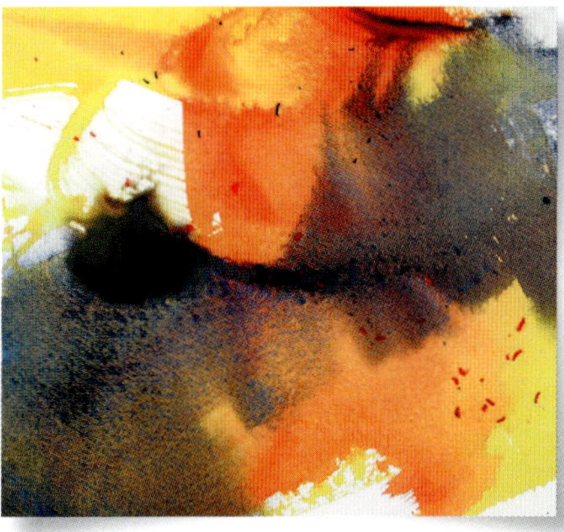

3 Add deeper tones

Work in deep blue which will mix to create warm browns and purples and produce blue where the paper was still white.

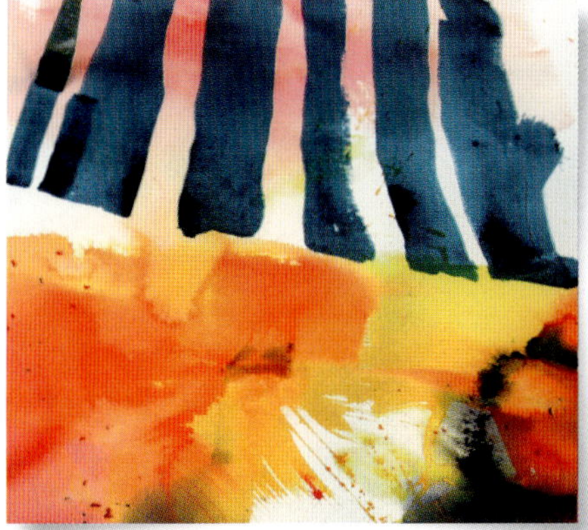

4 Develop a composition

Let the paint dry then, using the same blue, outline a suggestion of trees. Add water to the outer edges to blend them in.

5 Add white highlights

Loosely add white highlights and a suggestion of branches with a watercolour stick. This gives the painting a real lift, but keep the marks moderate so that the eye is not too distracted. This technique works best on more textured papers.

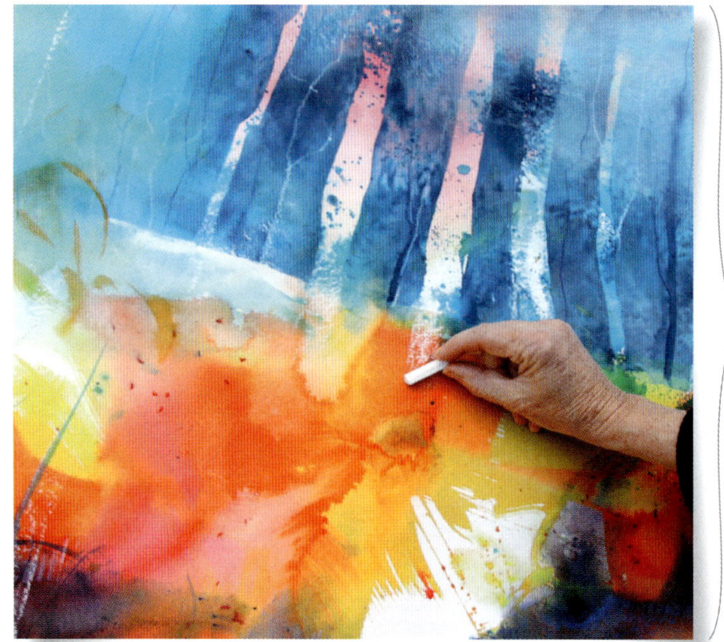

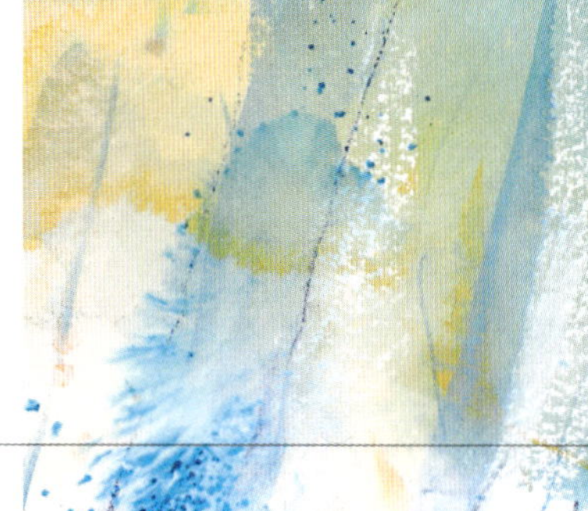

6 The final brushstrokes

Add some fine blue brushstrokes to the foreground and woodland areas to create an increased sense of movement and landscape. The more you add, the less abstract the painting will become; it is your choice how far to take this.

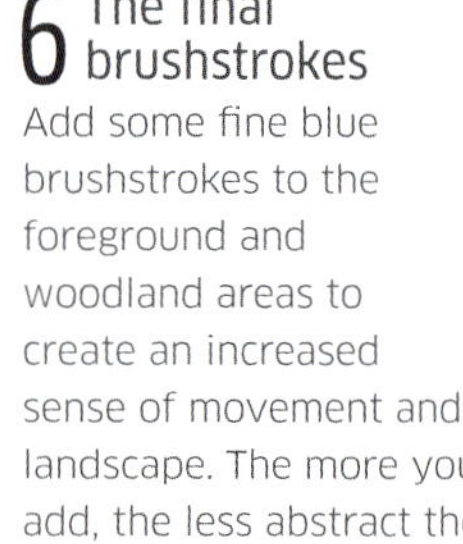

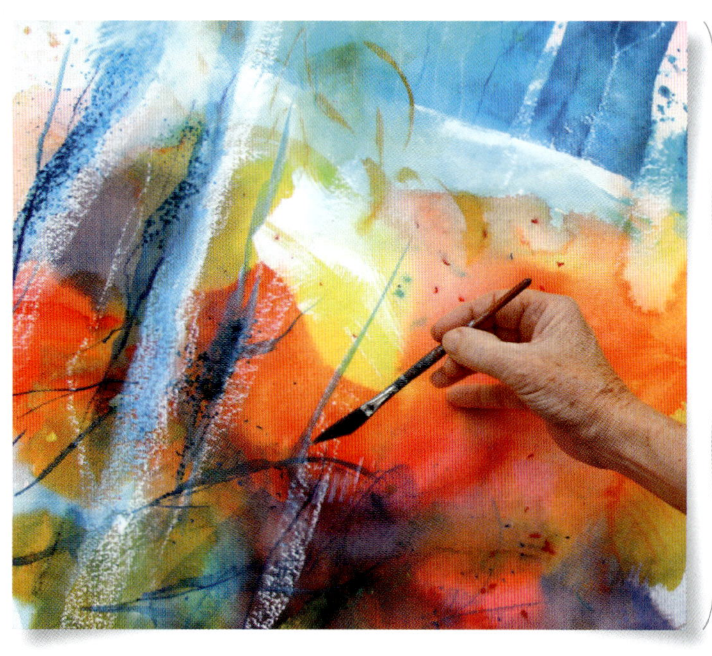

Marks from a white watercolour stick suggest rough, natural textures

"**Abstract paintings** give you total freedom of **shape, texture, and colour** as long as you arrive **at a pleasing result.**"

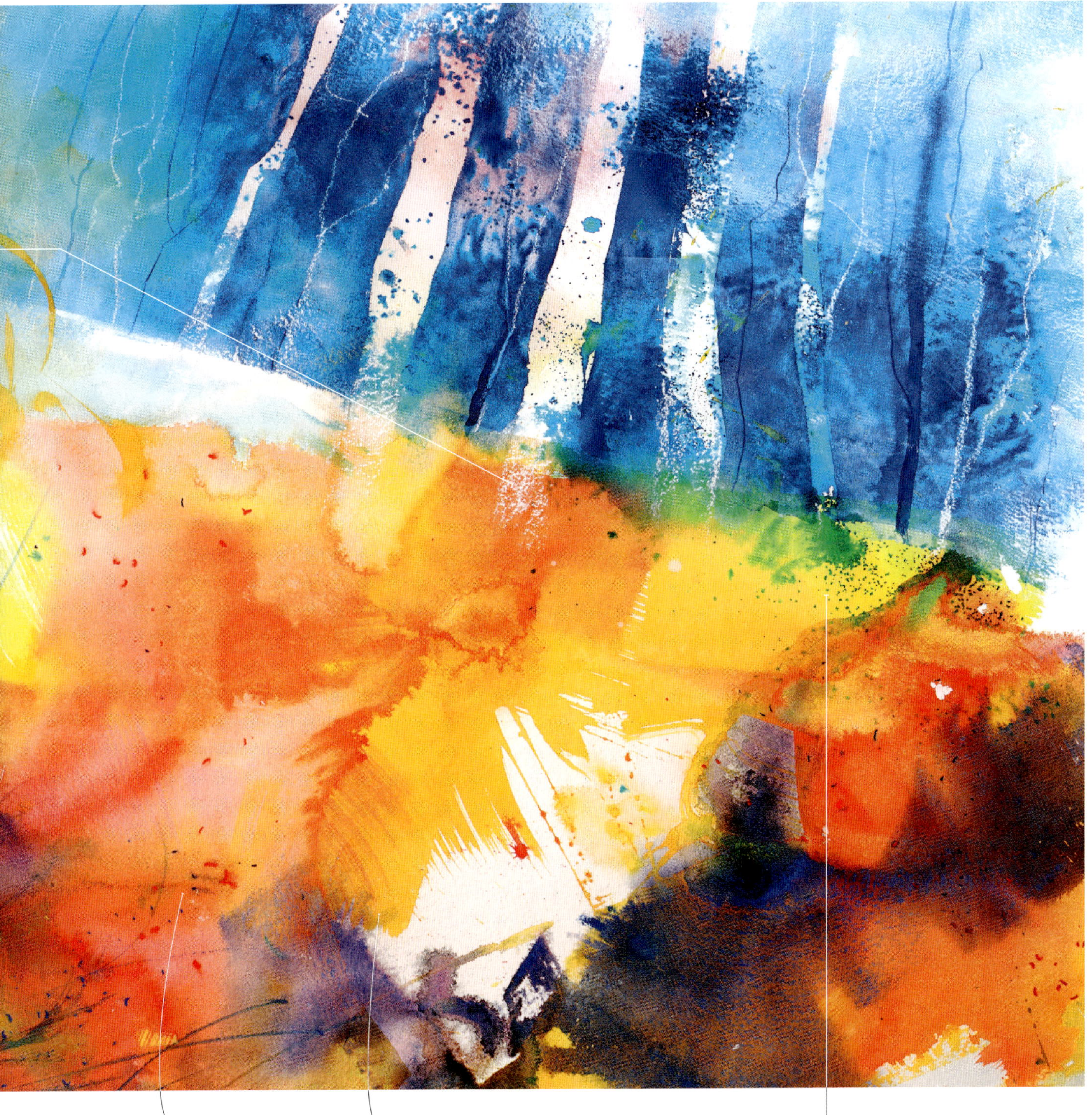

Soft edges create depths that invite the viewer to explore them

Hard edges give definition, offering contrast for the eye

7 Use dry pigment for texture

Before the painting has dried, sprinkle powdered pigment randomly over the blue area and spray with water. This creates beautiful textures and makes the trees less defined.

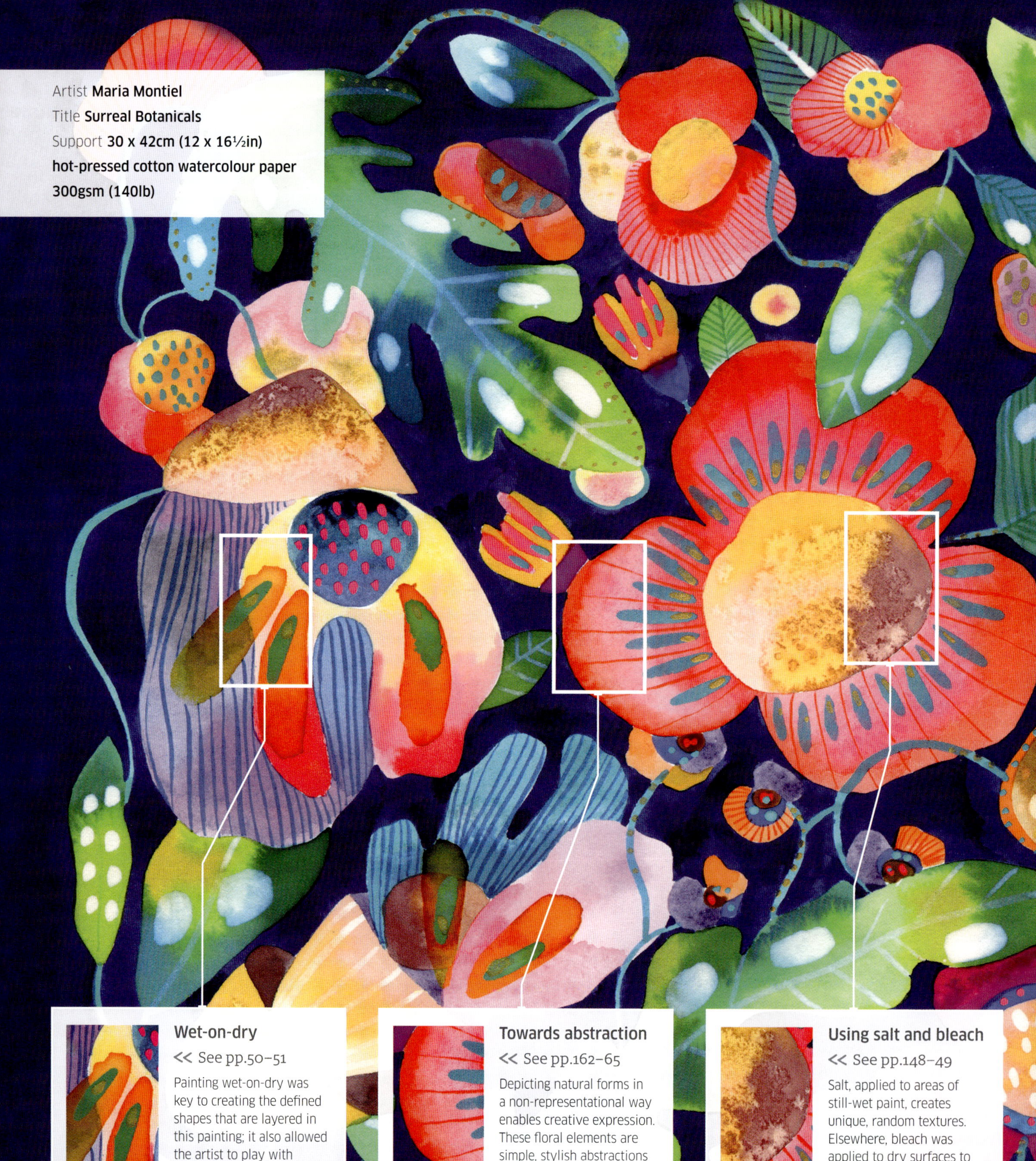

Artist **Maria Montiel**
Title **Surreal Botanicals**
Support **30 x 42cm (12 x 16½in)**
hot-pressed cotton watercolour paper
300gsm (140lb)

Wet-on-dry

≪ See pp.50–51

Painting wet-on-dry was key to creating the defined shapes that are layered in this painting; it also allowed the artist to play with transparencies.

Towards abstraction

≪ See pp.162–65

Depicting natural forms in a non-representational way enables creative expression. These floral elements are simple, stylish abstractions of real flowers.

Using salt and bleach

≪ See pp.148–49

Salt, applied to areas of still-wet paint, creates unique, random textures. Elsewhere, bleach was applied to dry surfaces to create glowing lighter tones.

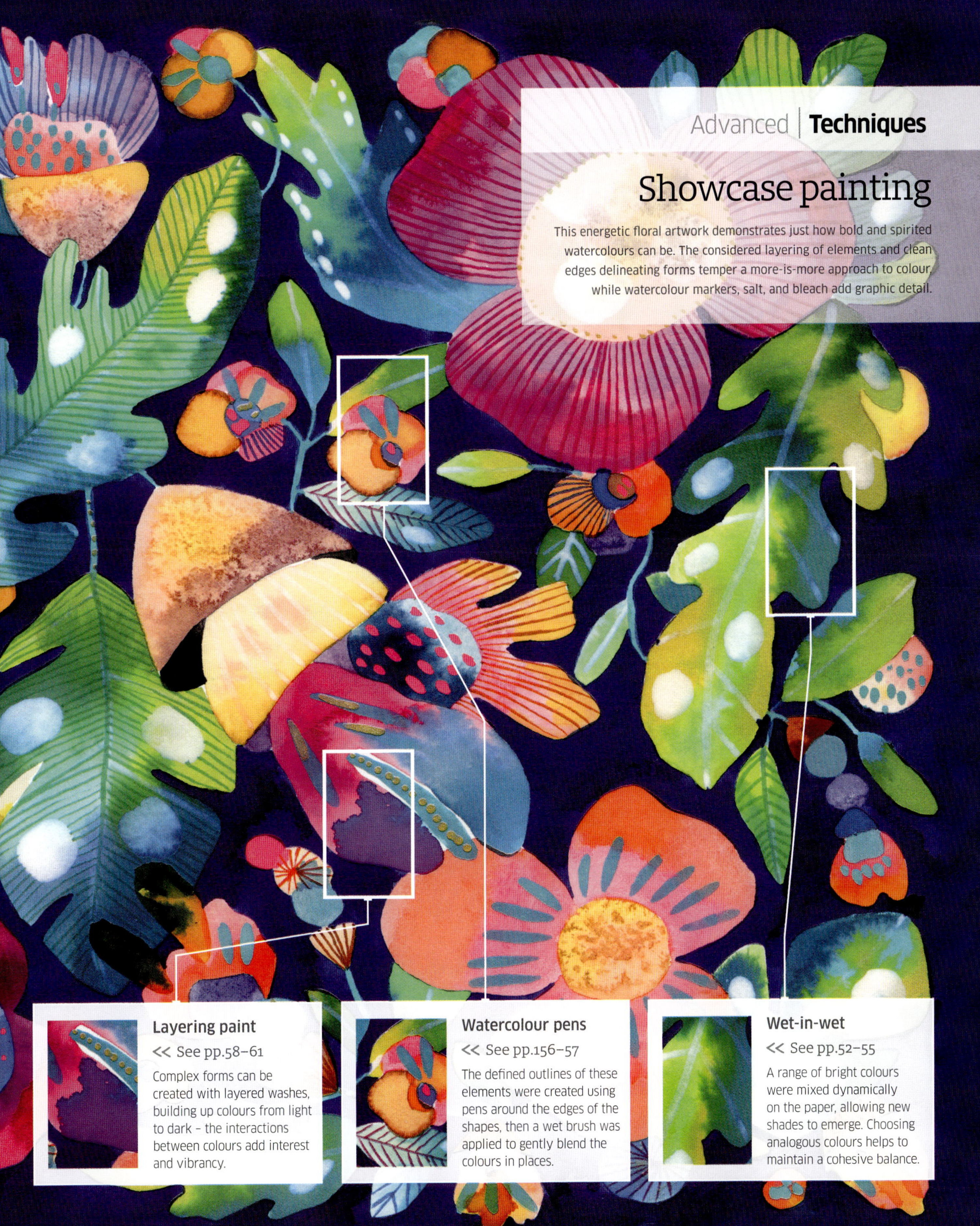

Showcase painting

This energetic floral artwork demonstrates just how bold and spirited watercolours can be. The considered layering of elements and clean edges delineating forms temper a more-is-more approach to colour, while watercolour markers, salt, and bleach add graphic detail.

Layering paint

≪ See pp.58–61

Complex forms can be created with layered washes, building up colours from light to dark – the interactions between colours add interest and vibrancy.

Watercolour pens

≪ See pp.156–57

The defined outlines of these elements were created using pens around the edges of the shapes, then a wet brush was applied to gently blend the colours in places.

Wet-in-wet

≪ See pp.52–55

A range of bright colours were mixed dynamically on the paper, allowing new shades to emerge. Choosing analogous colours helps to maintain a cohesive balance.

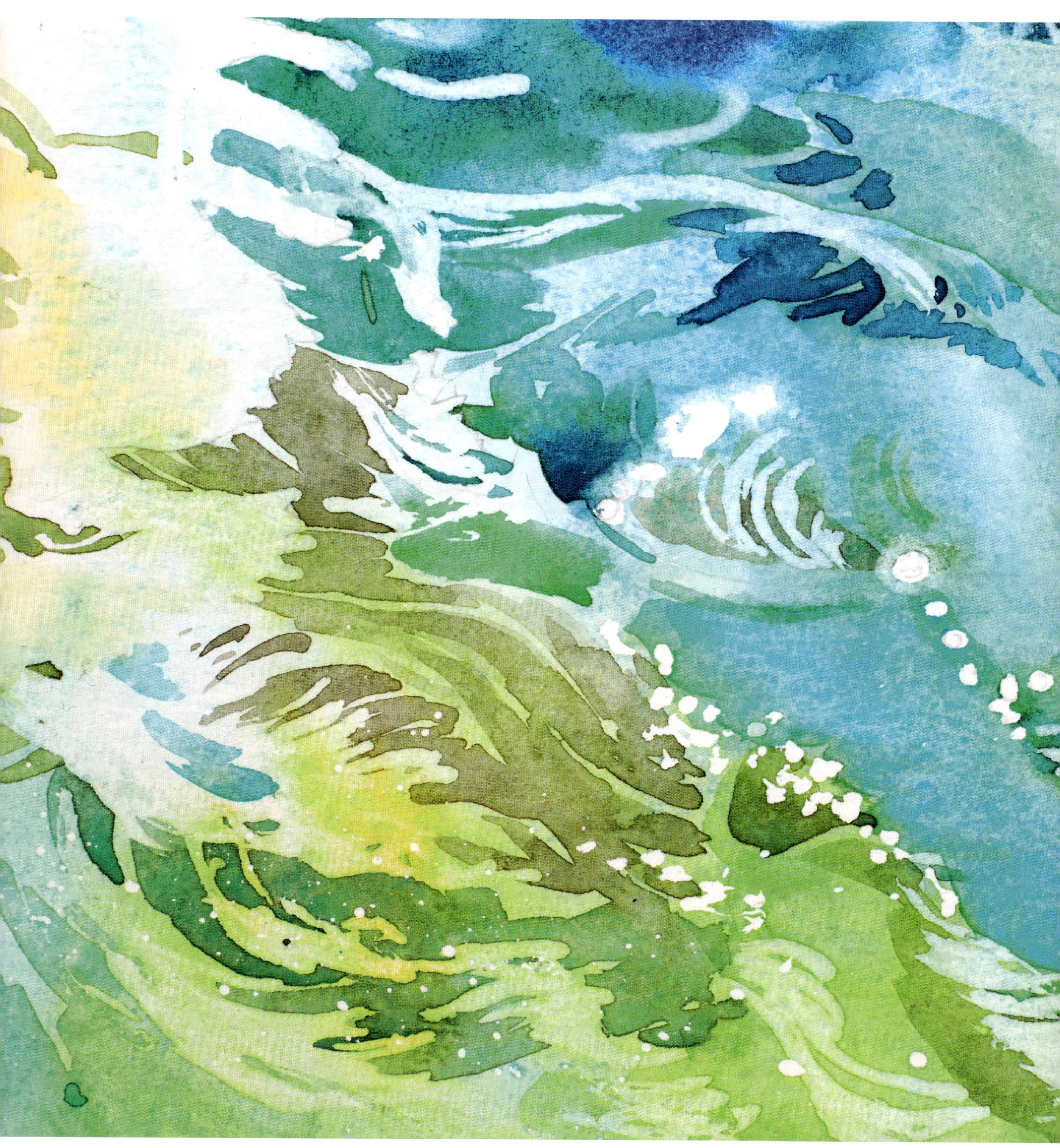

Subjects

Choosing a **subject**

Traditionally used for landscape paintings, watercolour is now employed by artists to convey anything from portraits to fashion illustrations. Each subject presents its own challenges, whether portraying reflections in water, shadows in snow, or capturing a fleeting impression of an animal. Mastering these challenges will help to convey the essence of your subject.

On the following pages, subjects have been divided into three groups, with approaches for landscapes and townscapes discussed in detail, followed by a guide to still life and flower subjects, thinking about pattern and texture. In the final section, the challenges of figures and portraits are addressed, along with the skills needed to paint animals. Showcase paintings by different artists illustrate the range of styles that can be used.

Landscapes and townscapes

■ See pp.172–203

This section gives you examples of different approaches to the perennially favourite subject of the landscape, breaking it down into not only classic views but also how to convey snow, water, skies, and urban settings in varied styles.

Harbour scene (see pp.188–89)

Patterns, still lifes, and flowers

■ See pp.204–17

The second section focusses on those subjects that require close-up attention, from flower studies and patterns, to still lifes and textures. Find inspiration for illustrative designs and impressionistic interpretations.

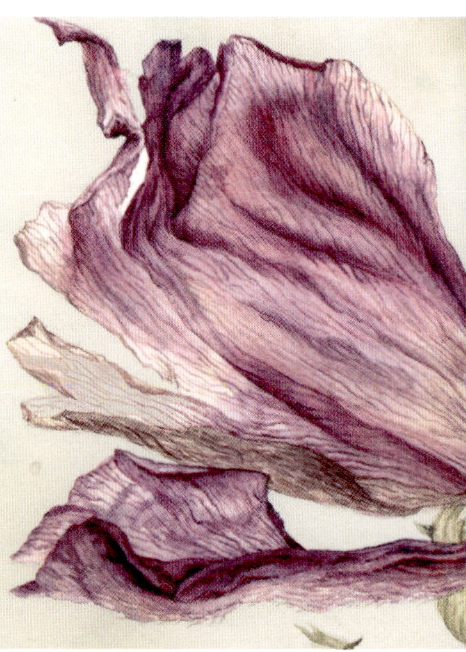

Botanical painting (see pp.212–15)

Watercolour adapts to any subject. When planning your painting, take into consideration the myriad ways to approach a subject, illustrated in this chapter with examples from different artists who demonstrate how they plan and execute a painting, with insights into their methods, from how to handle the composition of a busy street scene to painting a crashing wave.

Some work in a representational way, capturing scenes such as sunlit water by exploiting the luminosity of watercolour. Others work in a more abstract style, breaking subjects down by colour or tone, rendering trees as abstract shapes, or reducing a moving animal to soft, minimal brushstrokes.

For a more graphic approach, take inspiration from artists who use intensely saturated liquid watercolours to create patterns or illustrations, particularly suited to flower studies.

Extending your options

Certain subjects lend themselves to particular techniques or media to convey key elements, such as texture, details, and movement. Consider how your painting could be enhanced by introducing other media; use gouache, for example, to add contrasting opaque effects.

Extending your repertoire of skills to include techniques that help with details or texture, such as using bleach or salt, will enable you to plan and work at greater speed and with greater confidence. Continue to experiment, drawing inspiration from the artists and subjects shown here, and translating it into your own individual style.

Portraits, figures, and animals

■ See pp.218–45

The final section explains how best to approach figures, whether as a portrait or incorporating figures in a setting or as an illustration. Find out how to paint animals, capturing the essence of a wild animal or the character of a family pet.

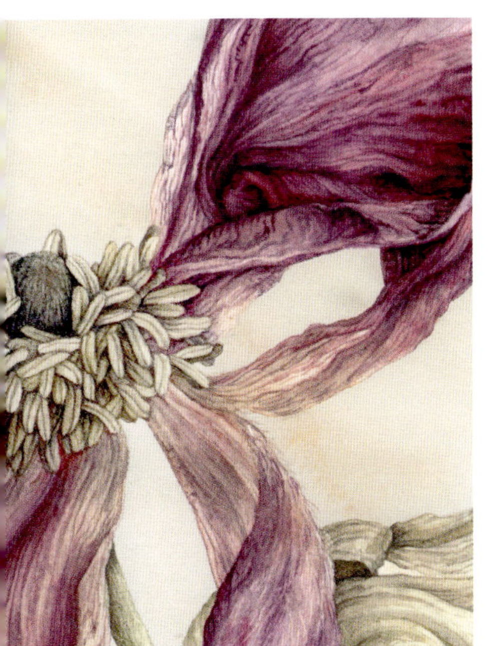

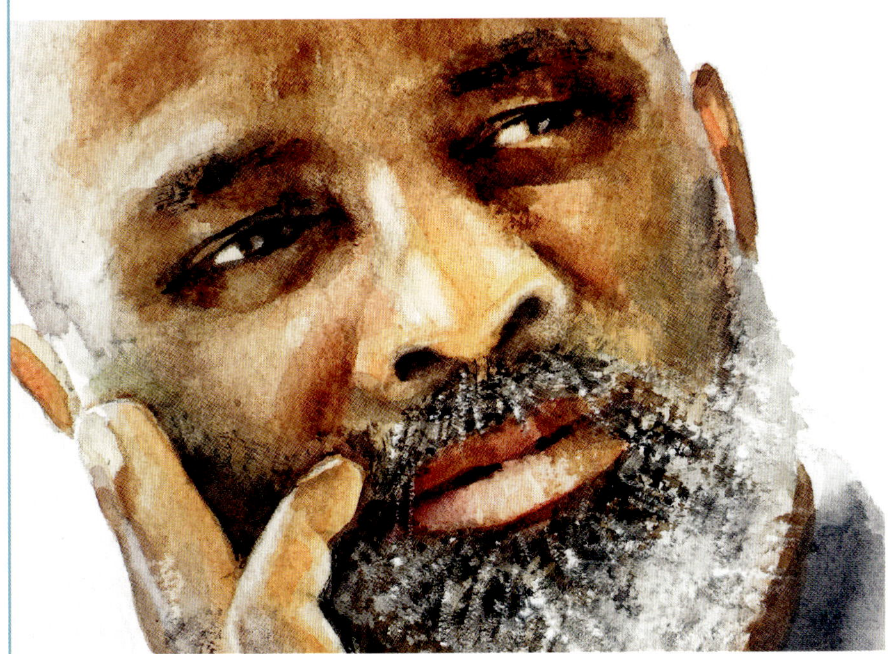

Skin tones (see pp.220–23)

Woodlands

SHAPING MASSES OF TREES AND FOLIAGE

Trees are an almost universal component of a landscape. To create a feeling of depth, trees must be painted in different ways to capture both the essential simplicity of a distant mass of woodland, along with the infinite variety of colour, tone, and shape seen in the foreground. To maintain a sense of a group of trees, ensure that each element blends naturally with the next.

PUTTING IT INTO PRACTICE

A feeling of dense woodland is captured here through the effects of aerial perspective; soft washes map out the distant trees, with warmer mixes and varied strokes used to define the trees that advance in the foreground.

You will need

- Cadmium yellow
- Burnt sienna
- Cadmium red
- Phthalo blue (green shade)
- French ultramarine

- No. 14 and no. 6 soft-hair round brushes
- 6mm (¼in) swordliner brush
- 25 x 35cm (10 x 14in) NOT watercolour paper 300gsm (140lb)

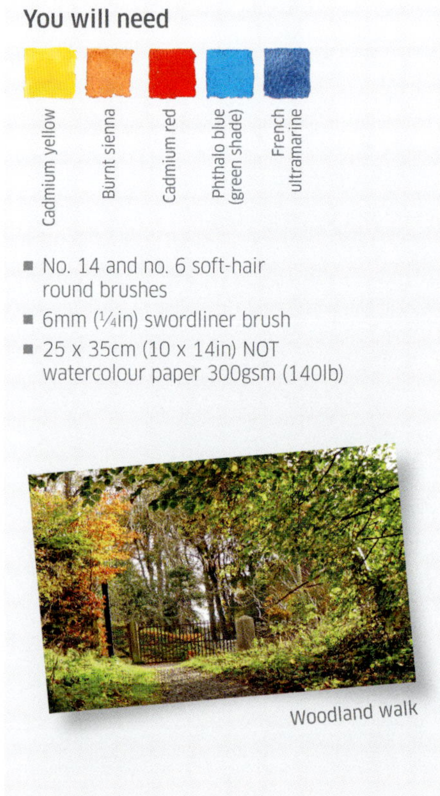

Woodland walk

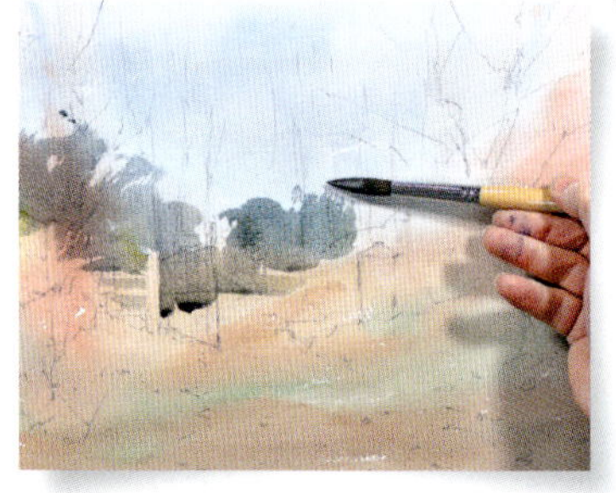

1 Distant mass
Apply a simple first wash of blue sky followed by warm mixes for the local colour in the foreground. Add a flat wash of French ultramarine and burnt sienna to give the impression of the distant trees, using the side of the brush to suggest the broken edge of the leaf canopies. Leave to dry.

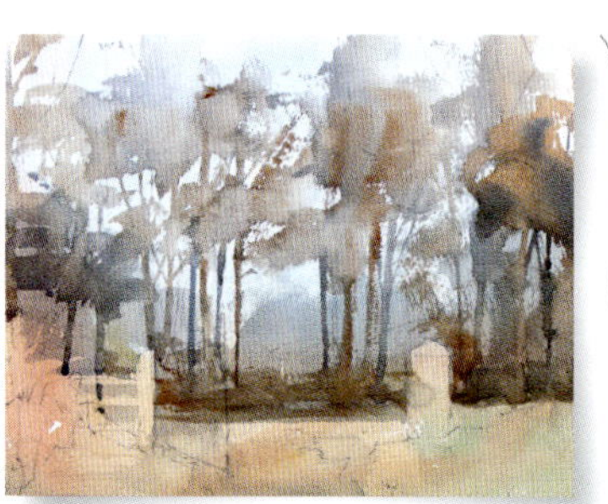

2 Tree groups
Use the point of a no. 14 brush to paint the middle distance trees. Add detail to the branches and trunks using varied mixes of the same wash to connect them. Aim for a group, not separate trees, and allow to dry.

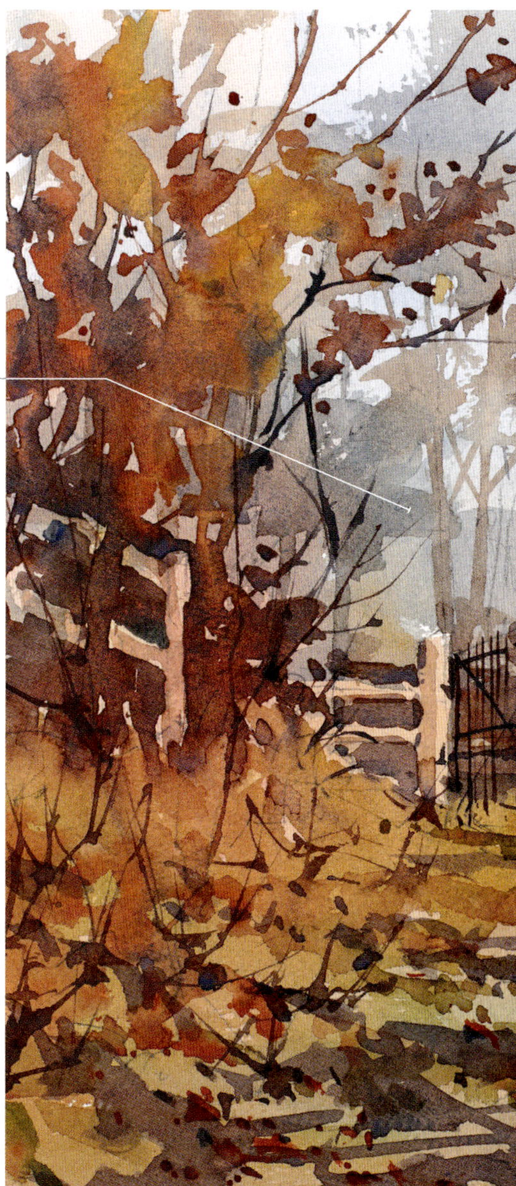

Three-dimensional shapes

Foreground detail gives depth to any painting and is especially important in landscapes, helping to differentiate the woods from the trees. While distant tree trunks can be rendered with tonal lines, those in the foreground should be more complex, with the suggestion of solidity and a rounded form. Simplify the shape into light and dark tones, adding texture for bark with dry brushstrokes.

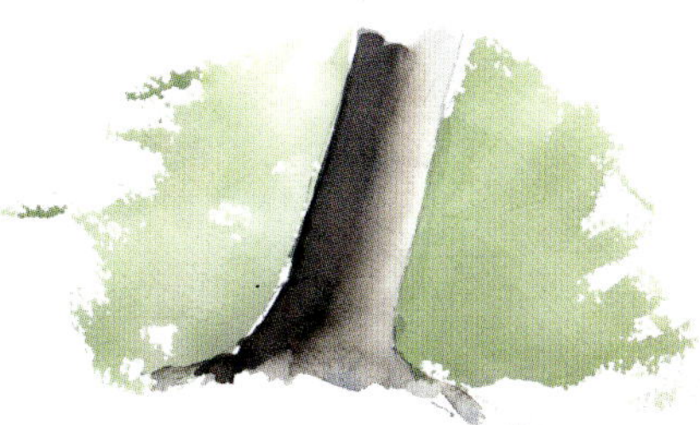

Light and shade
The main trunk of a tree is essentially a cylinder. Use a soft blend between the light and dark side of the trunk to give a three-dimensional effect.

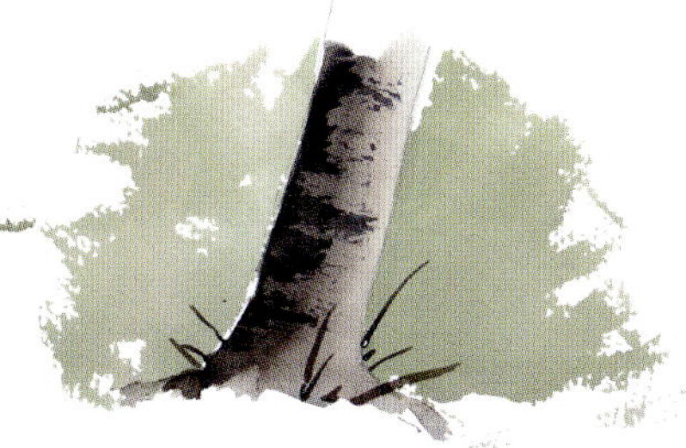

Bark texture
When the wash is dry, apply linear marks using dry brush (see pp.56–57) and a rigger or swordliner, to create a convincing suggestion of bark texture.

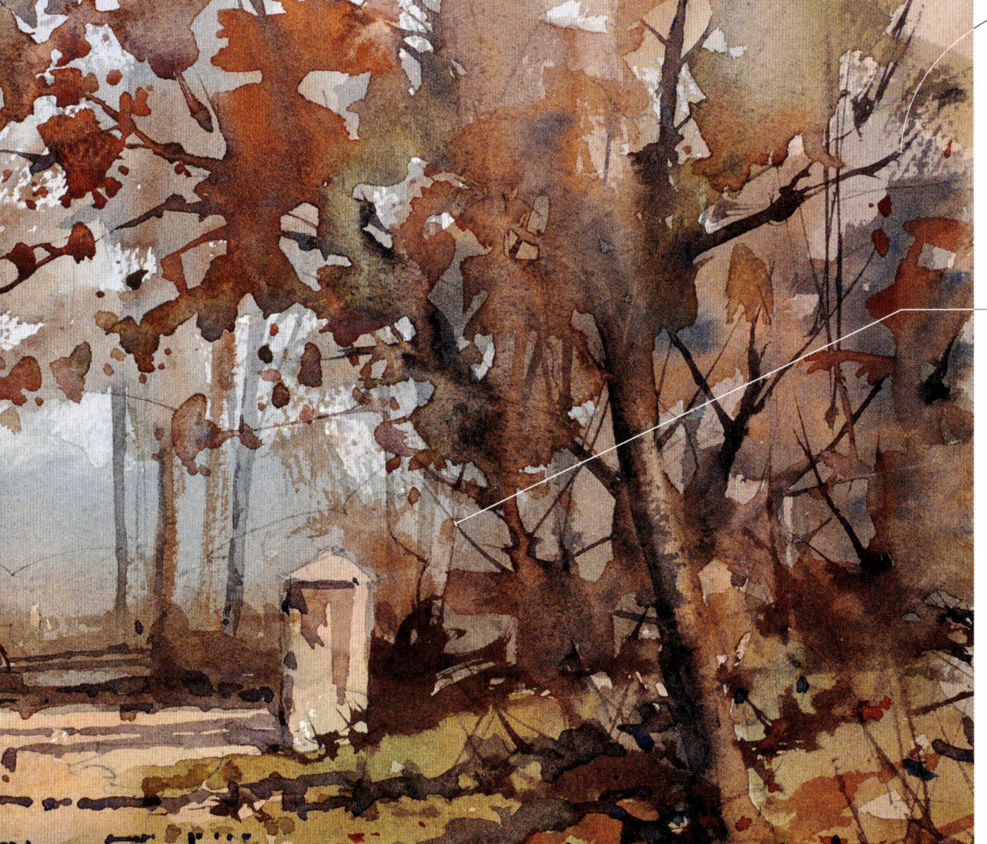

Connect the shapes of the masses of leaves together with softly blending twigs

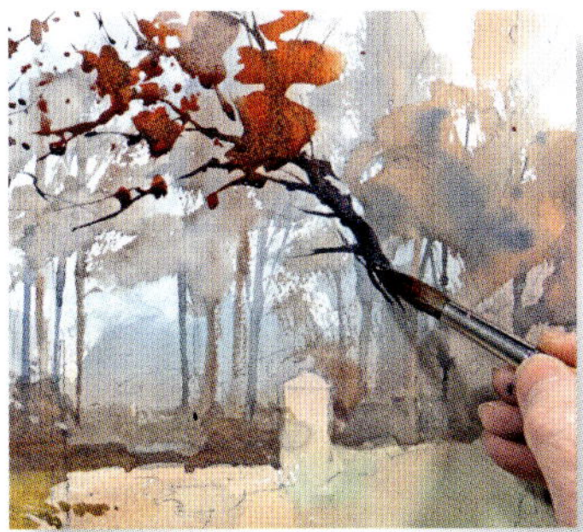

3 Foliage shapes
In the foreground, use stronger mixes and varied shapes to suggest the leaf cover and twigs, working wet-in-wet; complete sections of a tree before moving on. Blend the base of the trees with the ground.

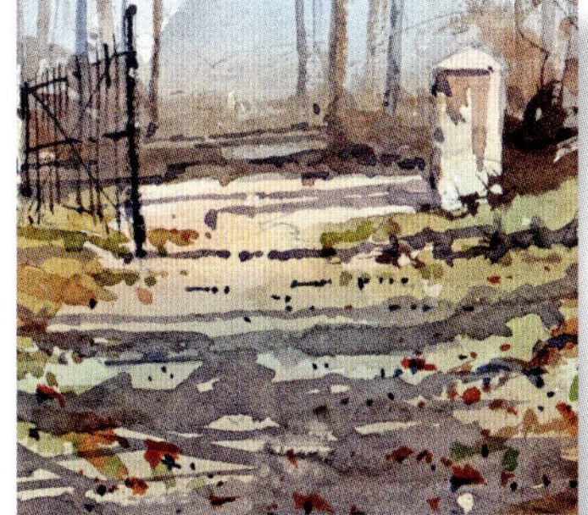

4 Foreground detail
Use a strong mix of burnt sienna and French ultramarine for the dark shadows that connect the trees. Hint at leaves on the forest floor with dots and dashes of splatter.

Tree blossom

CREATING THE EFFECT OF MASS PETALS

It is impossible to paint individual cherry blossom flowers with a brush. Instead, you can use a sponge on top of a wash in order to create the texture and varied shades of the blossom. Some white gouache mixed with the pink in one layer gives better coverage and a more realistic expression of blossom petals on a tree.

■ Key techniques

When painting blossom or any other flowers *en masse*, it is important to avoid heavy, solid blocks of colour and concentrate on suggesting a surface of varied depth and colour in a lively manner. To prevent background colours affecting the flowers, lay a light wash of your flower mix first.

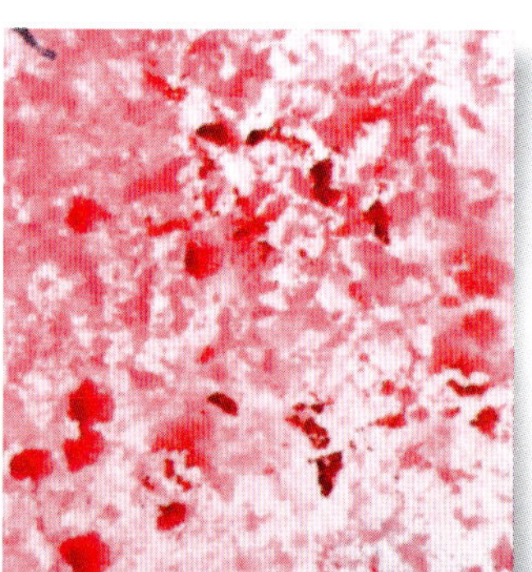

Stippling and splattering
Suggest blossom through a mixture of sponging and splattering or spattering the paint expressively, without having to paint every flower. Layering analogous colours (see pp.116–17) creates extra depth and dimension.

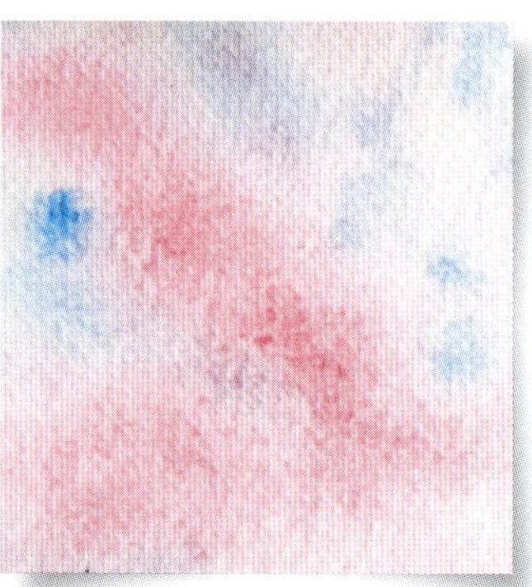

Background colour
To prevent the sky colour affecting the colour of the blossom, paint a "blush" of pink in the underpainting where you will place the blossom. This will keep the blossom colour bright and vibrant.

PUTTING IT INTO PRACTICE

Painting the blossom first may seem counter-intuitive, but this way the branches can be threaded in and out to look natural. Using a rigger for the finer branches helps to show their gradually diminishing size.

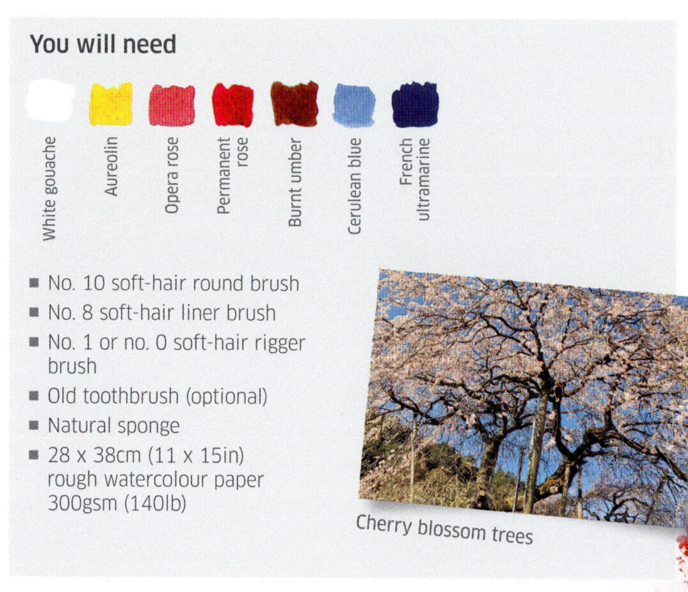

- No. 10 soft-hair round brush
- No. 8 soft-hair liner brush
- No. 1 or no. 0 soft-hair rigger brush
- Old toothbrush (optional)
- Natural sponge
- 28 x 38cm (11 x 15in) rough watercolour paper 300gsm (140lb)

Cherry blossom trees

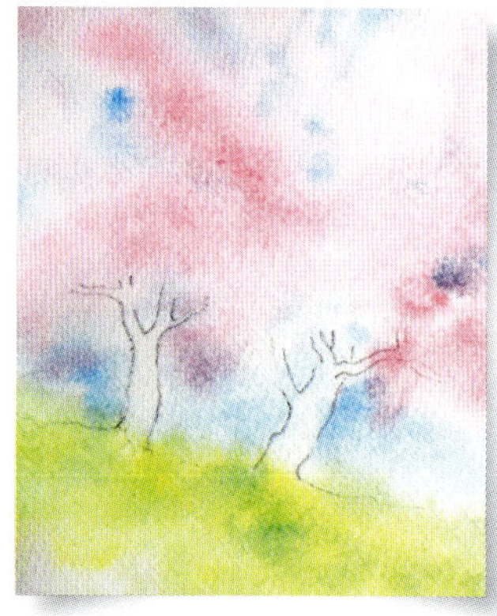

1 First washes
Mix three washes of rose, cerulean, and aureolin. Wet the paper with your round brush and quickly lay the pink areas of blossom. Add cerulean to the sky then aureolin for the grass.

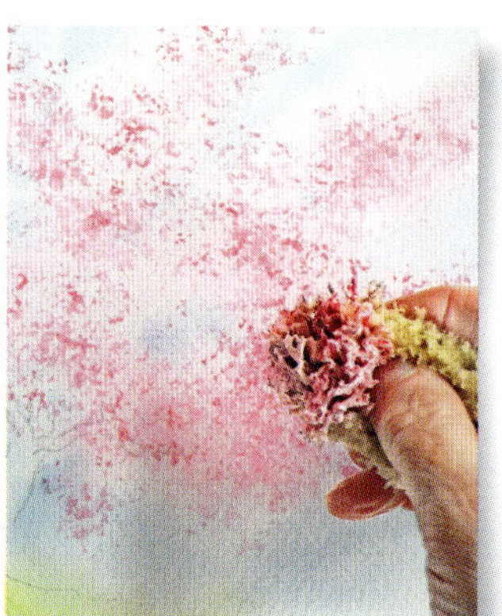

2 Add texture
When all is dry, mix a strong rose wash and one of rose with white gouache. Dip a just-damp sponge in the rose and lightly dab over the tree. Repeat with the gouache mix.

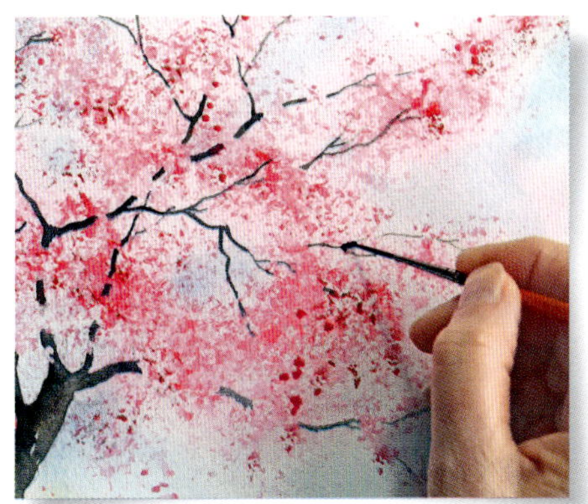

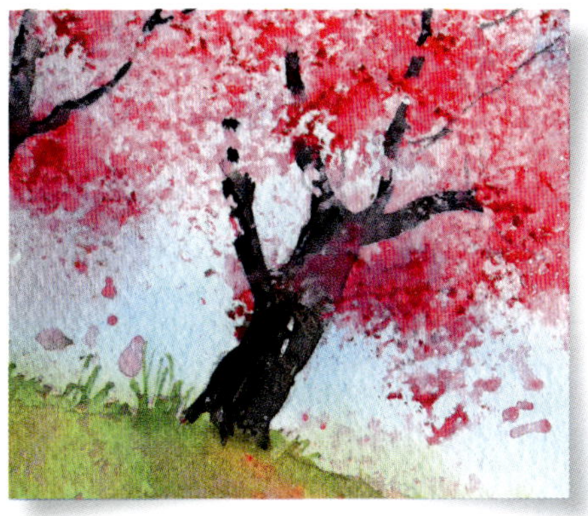

3 Add dark trunk and branches
Paint an ultramarine and umber mix on the trunk. Using a clean damp brush, fade the branches and trunk into the blossom and grass. Switch to the rigger for the finer twigs.

4 Finishing touches
With the sponge and pink mix, add more blossom but this time let it go over the trunk and branches a little. Repaint the grassy area with aureolin mixed with a little cerulean.

> "For blossom, use texture and variation of colour for a lively effect."

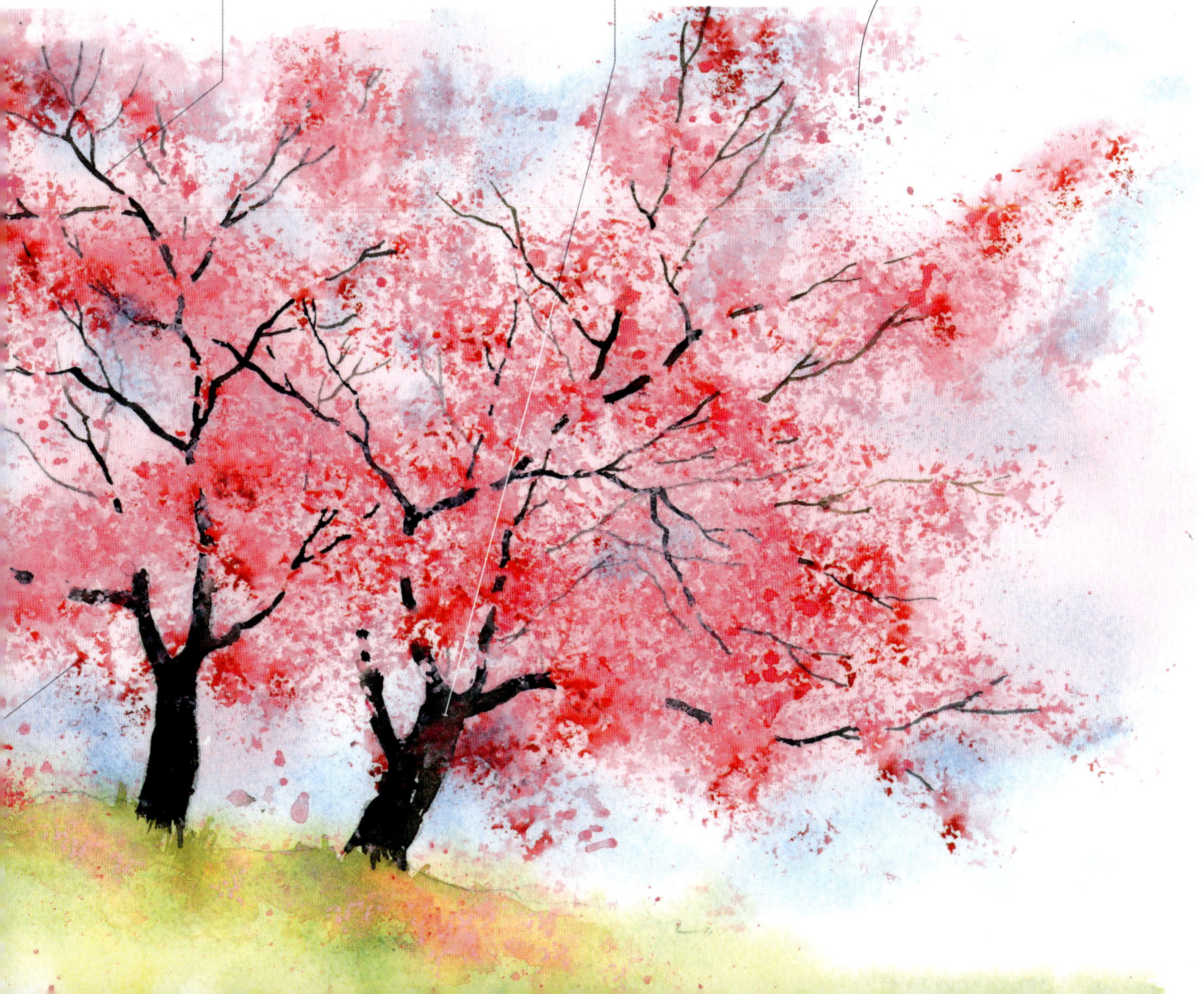

Splatter or spatter some pink with a brush or toothbrush at the branch tips and on the ground

Open landscapes

EVOKING A SENSE OF SPACE

Aerial perspective techniques (see pp.122–23), using paler tones and colours in the distance, are well-suited to an open landscape. Conveying depth and drama, and creating the illusion of walking through the landscape, will draw your viewer in. Avoid unnecessary details, which will lose the spontaneity of the work, and keep the foreground loose to help to maintain a painterly rather than linear feel.

PUTTING IT INTO PRACTICE

Broad brushstrokes with minimal fuss are needed for this type of landscape. Use wet-in-wet washes and suggest atmospheric haze to convey the sense of the landscape receding from the viewer.

You will need

- No. 15 and no. 10 soft-hair mop brushes
- No. 5 soft-hair round brush
- Small penknife
- 38 x 56cm (15 x 22in) NOT watercolour paper 300gsm (140lb)

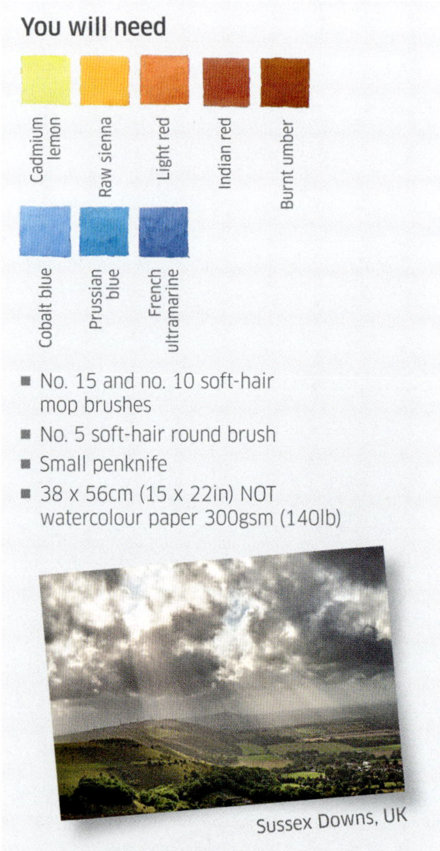

Sussex Downs, UK

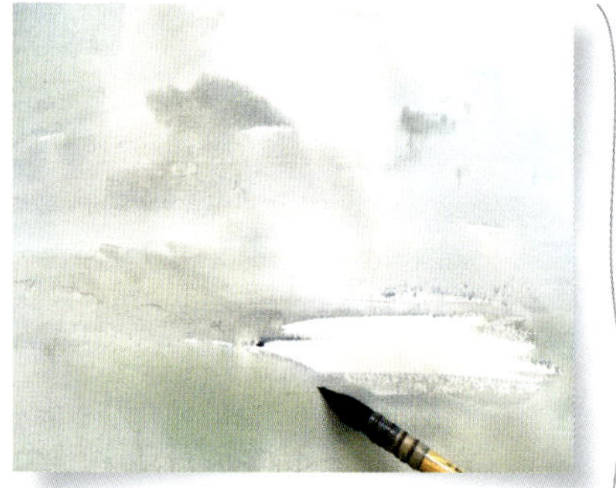

1 The first washes
Dampen the paper and paint the sky using ultramarine and umber. Leave white paper for clouds, fields, and blue sky. As the paint dries, add darker cloud colour and cobalt blue in the sky, and green for hills and foreground.

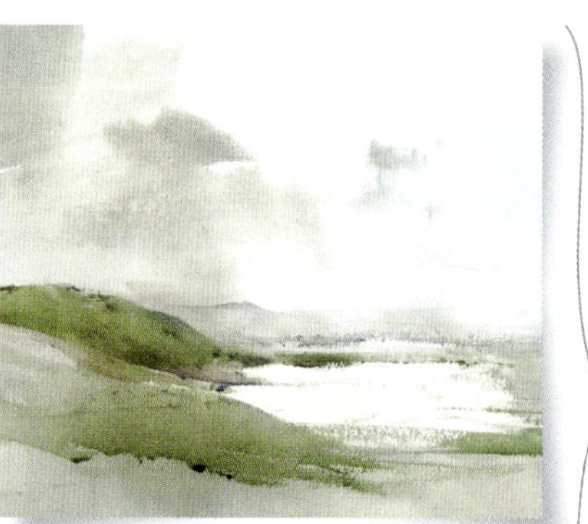

2 Paint the distant view
With the no. 10 mop, paint the distant hill and trees with cobalt blue and Indian red. Use the same technique for the middle-distance hills and trees with a mix of Prussian blue, lemon, and red.

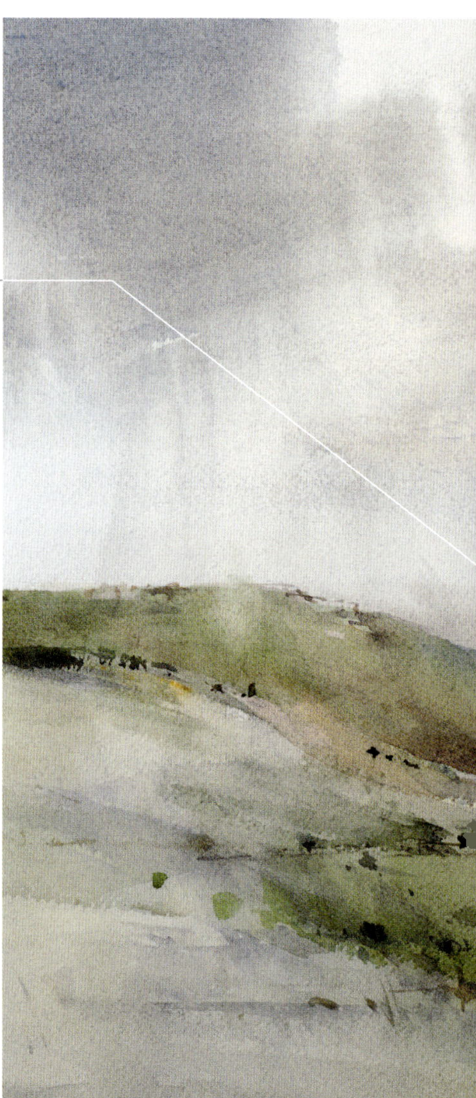

Impressionistic techniques

To make the background recede, use loose, impressionistic techniques. Hills and trees can be kept loose with a single wash of colour, usually blue, to give the effect of atmospheric haze. Pick up the "bead" of paint that collects at the base of a wash (see p.70) to paint loose, continuous washes down the paper, avoiding details in the distance. Add texture and details in the foreground to bring it closer to the viewer.

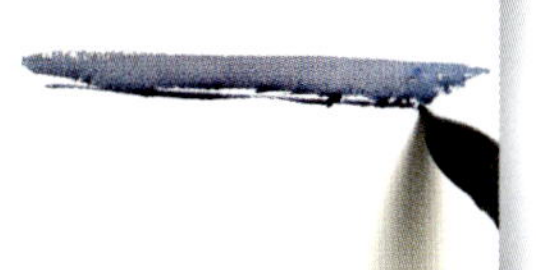

Using a bead of paint
Add to your first wash with the same paint to create a bead at its base. Use this to continue down with horizontal strokes.

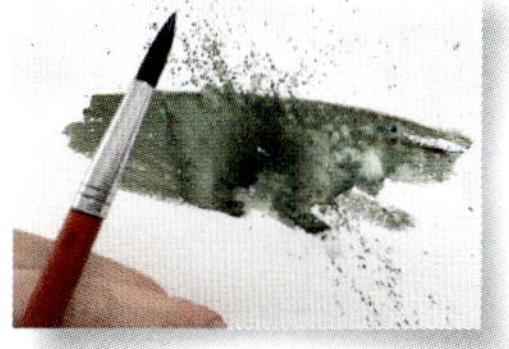

Splattering
Wet paint thrown from the brush into existing wet washes creates the impression of foreground vegetation and stones.

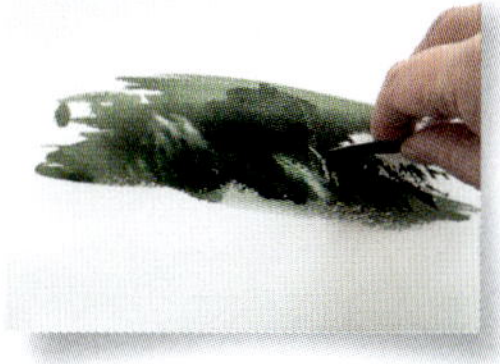

Lifting out
Lifting the existing wet washes with a penknife or a dry brush also produces the effect of foreground elements.

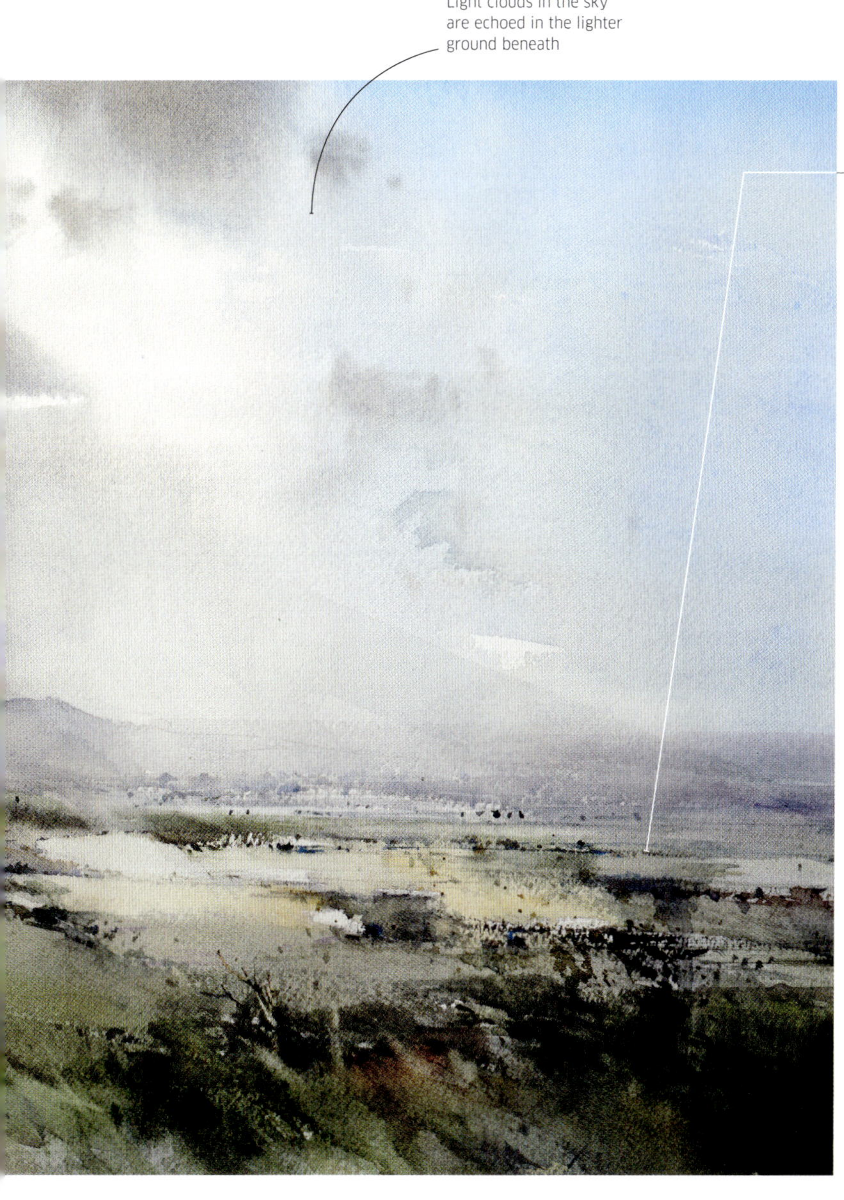

Light clouds in the sky are echoed in the lighter ground beneath

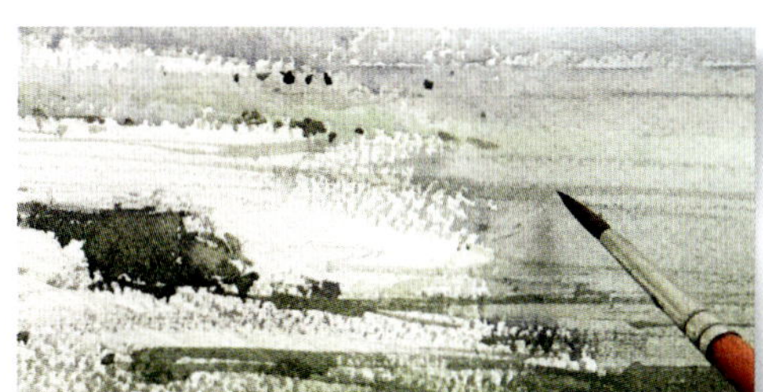

3 Build up the foreground
With the no. 5 brush, emphasize the perspective by making the trees larger towards the foreground. Add a light wash of raw sienna over the fields.

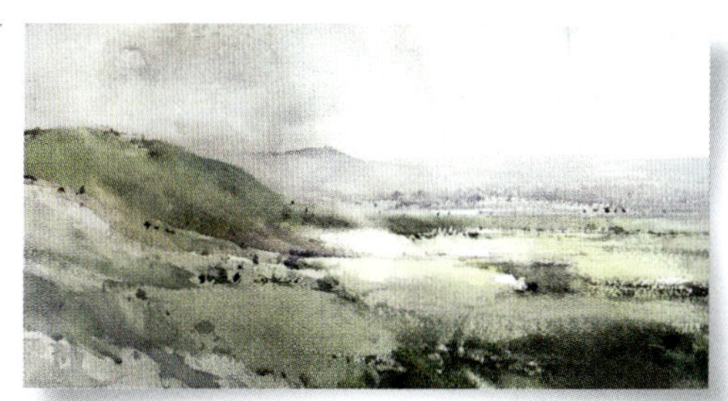

4 Add warmth and detail
Use ultramarine and red for cloud shadow over the foreground. Scratch a tree out of the wet paint with the knife. Lift out other areas with a dry brush.

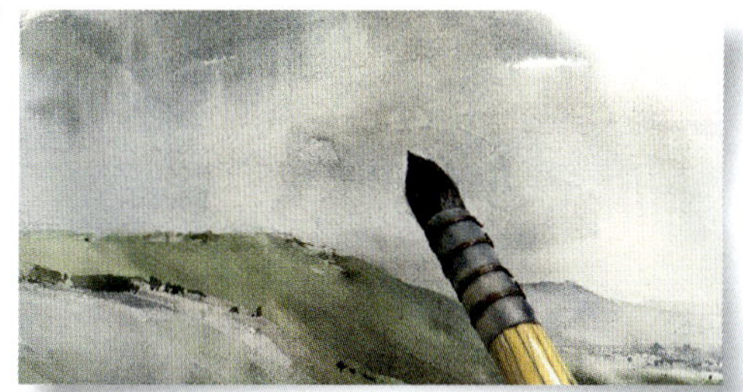

5 Strengthen the sky
Wet the sky and lay a wash of ultramarine and umber over the dark clouds to strengthen the top. Keep the clouds towards the horizon much lighter.

Abstracting a landscape

SIMPLIFYING AND INTERPRETING

The key to abstraction is to simplify the composition and eliminate detail while retaining elements of the landscape – sky, a hillside, or a suggestion of foliage can be enough to establish a sense of place. Use bold, energetic marks and strong colours that can suggest a rugged scene or gentler washes for more of a serene feel.

■ Using identifiable shapes

While a representational painting describes a scene or subject, a semi-abstract relies on the power of suggestion. In a landscape subject, large shapes imply landmasses or dense vegetation, while smaller blotches of colour and vertical strokes of paint can be read as individual trees.

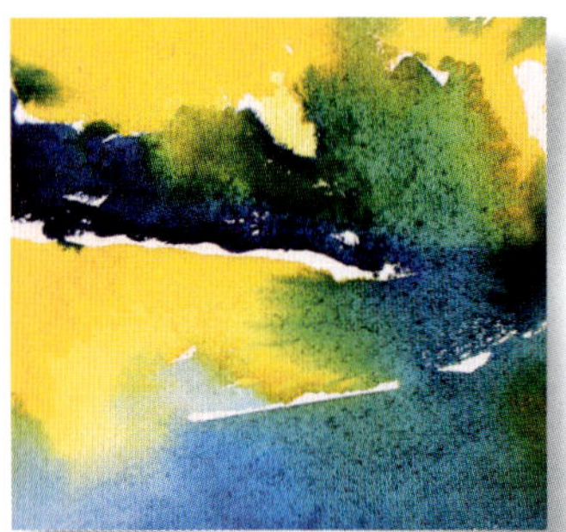

Washes and large shapes
Broad washes of colour are familiar in landscape scenes, but in a semi-abstract painting they do not necessarily aim to describe a recognizable place; colours are chosen to work as part of the composition rather than to be realistic.

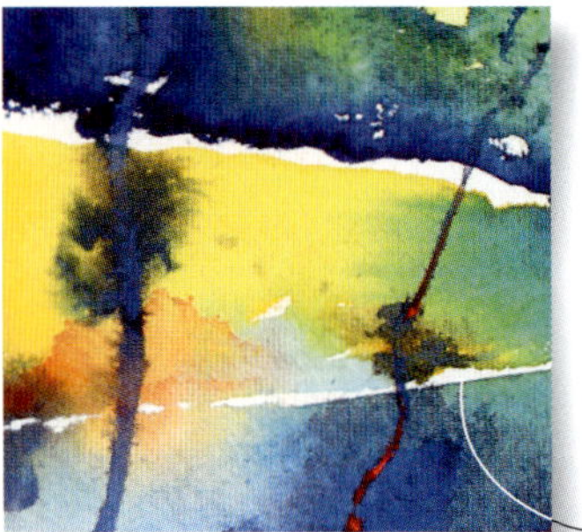

Lines and breaks
Vertical and horizontal linear shapes and crisp-edged colours provide some structure and lead the viewer's eye round the painting. Reserved white paper suggests a circular passage which is broken by the implied tree trunks.

Reserved white paper

PUTTING IT INTO PRACTICE

Part of the process of abstraction can be to opt for less obvious colours. The deep yellow and blue hint at a tropical scene, but using yellow for sky and blue for land gives the painting a more surreal quality.

You will need

Cadmium yellow deep

Cadmium red

Phthalo blue

- No. 20 soft-hair mop brush
- Medium swordliner brush
- Spray bottle
- 30 x 42cm (12 x 16½in) rough watercolour paper 640gsm (300lb)

1 Make the first marks
Having decided on your main colour, make your first marks. You may have a composition in mind – maybe something as simple as a horizon line. This is purely a starting point.

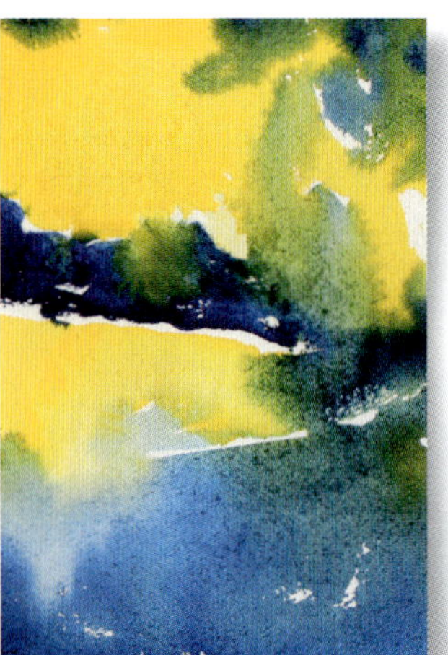

2 Merge washes
Quickly block in the second colour, allowing the two washes to merge and random shapes to form. This stage will determine the direction and personality of the painting. Allow to dry.

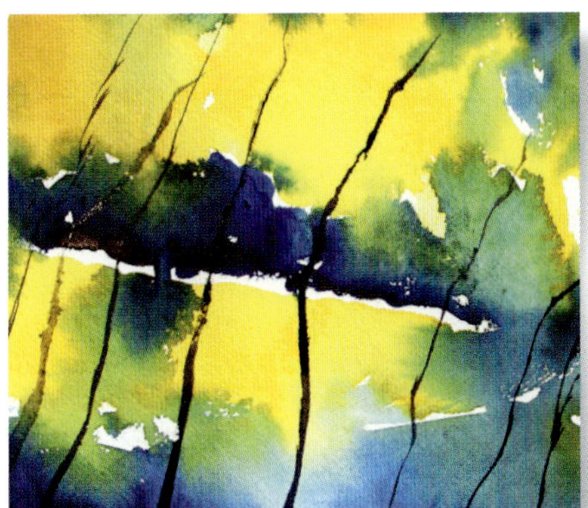

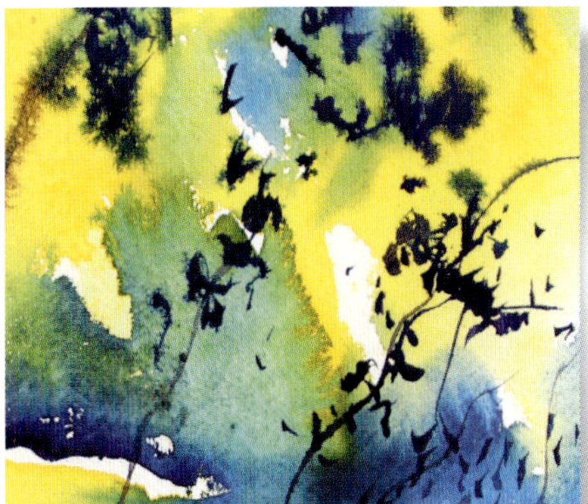

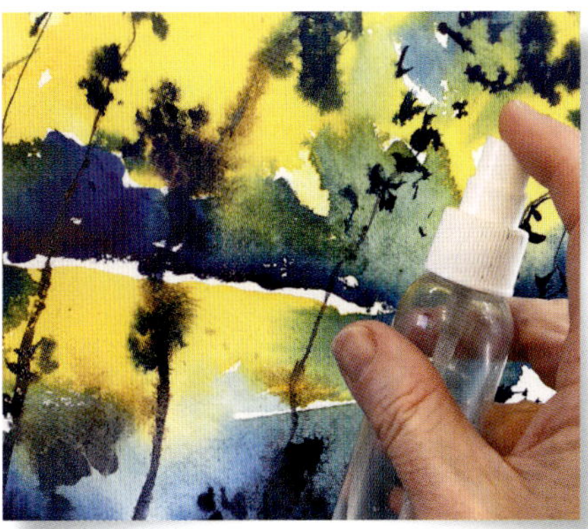

3 Add perspective

You now need to achieve a sense of perspective. Drawing tree-like shapes with a strong mix will contrast with the softer wash and give the illusion of foreground.

4 Paint the foliage

Quickly add loose blobs of the same strong colour rather than trying to engage with the detail of branches or leaf shapes; a swordliner brush is perfect for this.

5 Achieve random effects

While they are still wet, spray the foliage areas with water to soften the edges and give random effects as the colours bleed. Add a few red highlights to contrast with the blue.

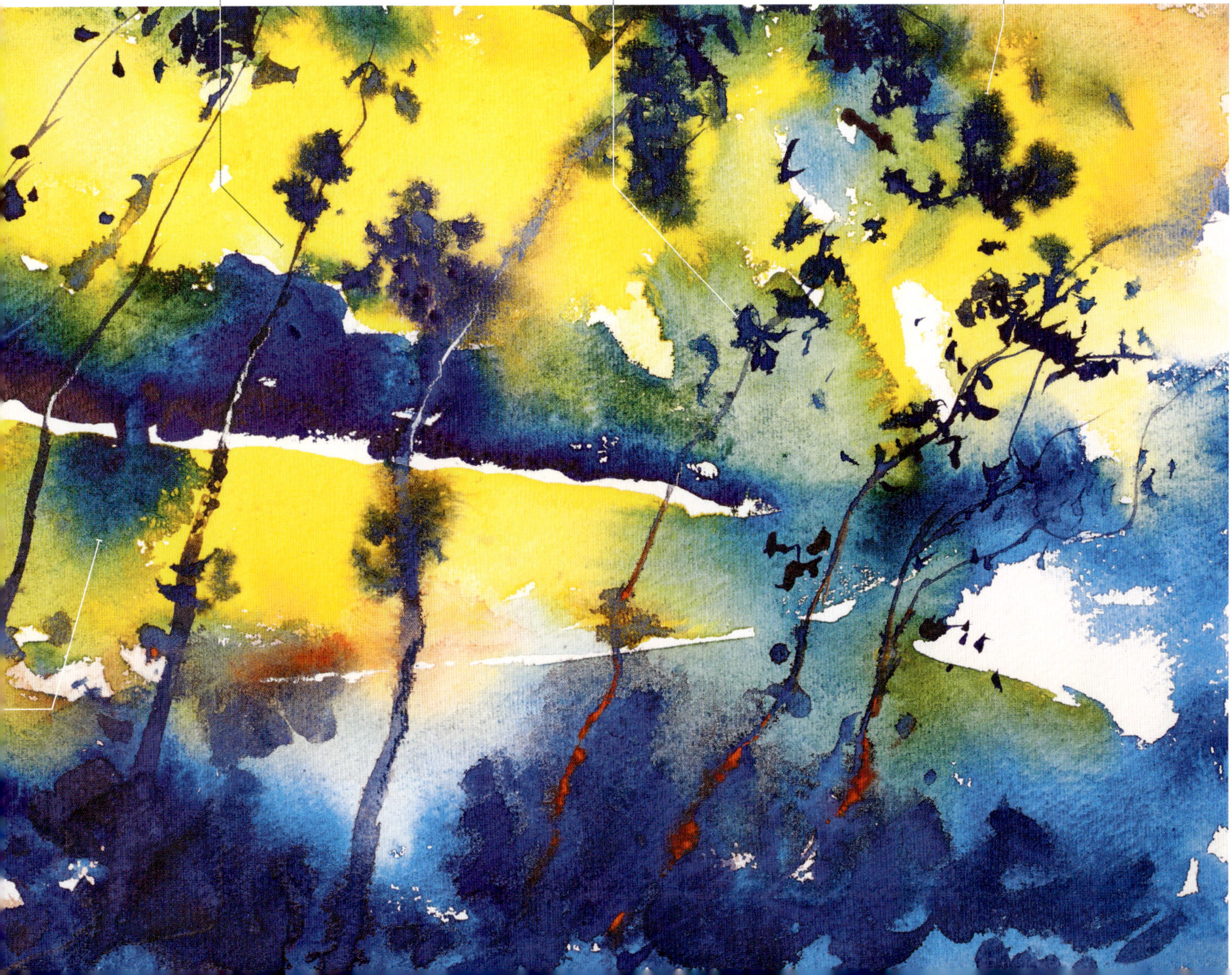

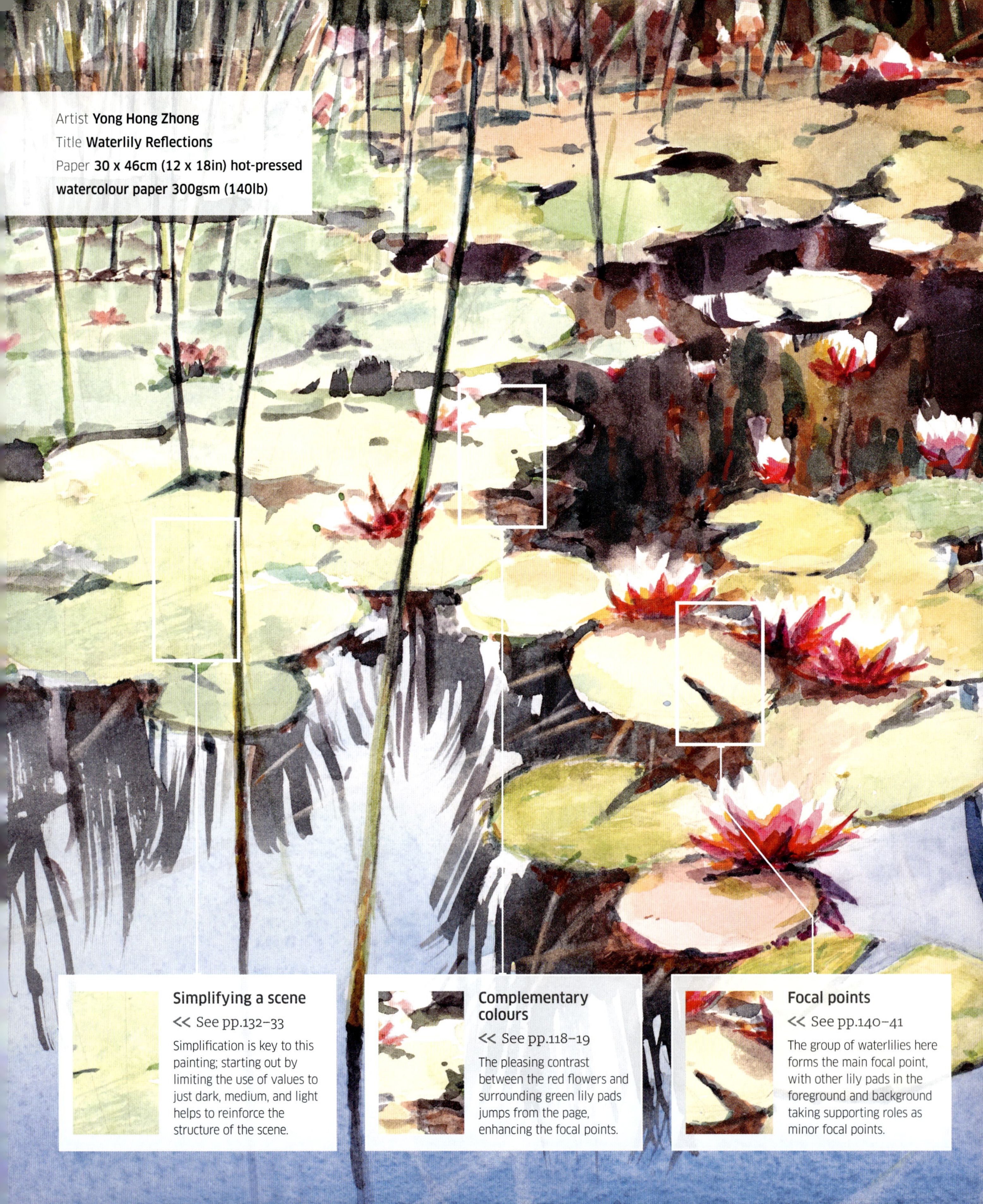

Simplifying a scene

≪ See pp.132–33

Simplification is key to this painting; starting out by limiting the use of values to just dark, medium, and light helps to reinforce the structure of the scene.

Complementary colours

≪ See pp.118–19

The pleasing contrast between the red flowers and surrounding green lily pads jumps from the page, enhancing the focal points.

Focal points

≪ See pp.140–41

The group of waterlilies here forms the main focal point, with other lily pads in the foreground and background taking supporting roles as minor focal points.

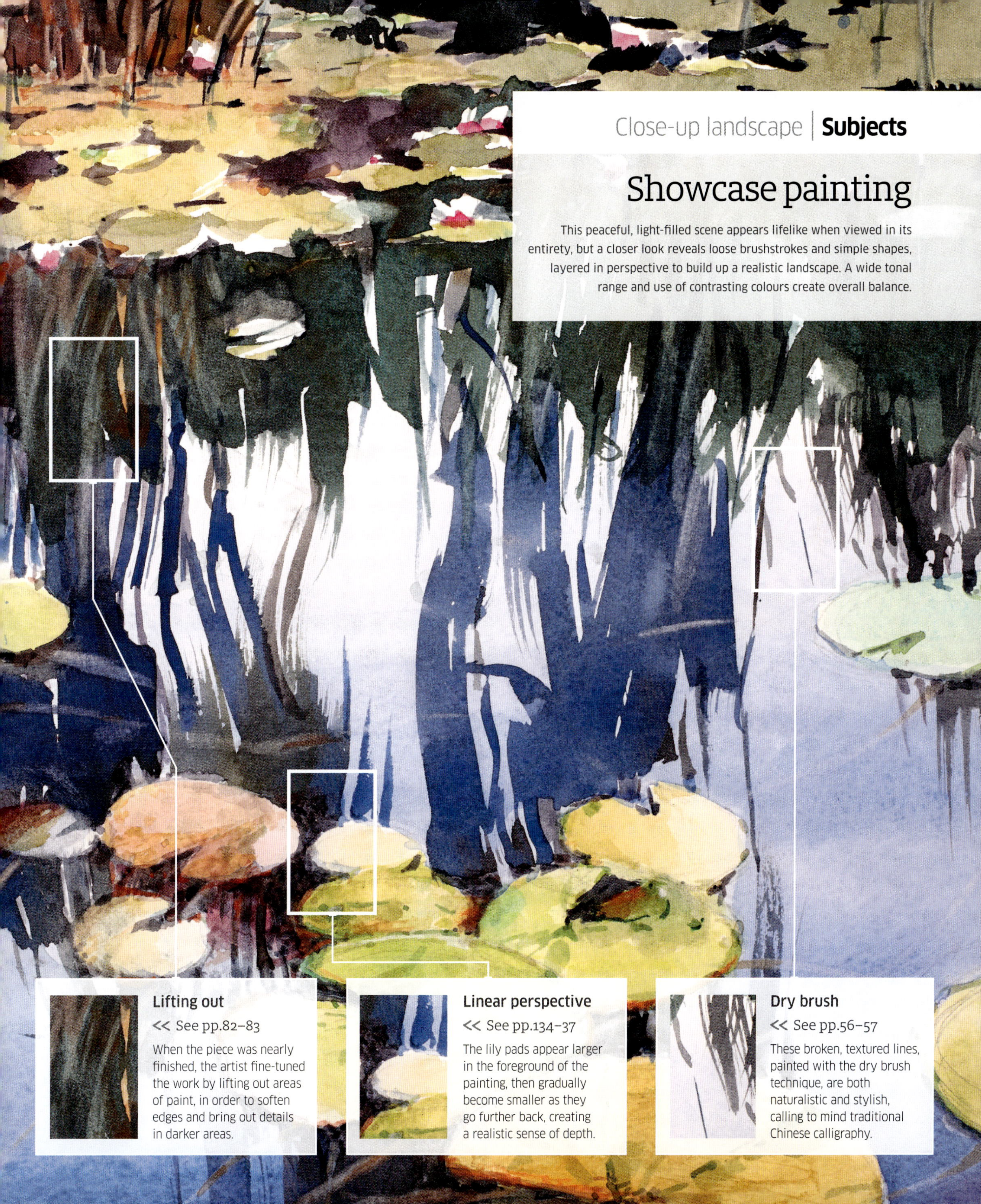

Showcase painting

This peaceful, light-filled scene appears lifelike when viewed in its entirety, but a closer look reveals loose brushstrokes and simple shapes, layered in perspective to build up a realistic landscape. A wide tonal range and use of contrasting colours create overall balance.

Lifting out

<< See pp.82–83

When the piece was nearly finished, the artist fine-tuned the work by lifting out areas of paint, in order to soften edges and bring out details in darker areas.

Linear perspective

<< See pp.134–37

The lily pads appear larger in the foreground of the painting, then gradually become smaller as they go further back, creating a realistic sense of depth.

Dry brush

<< See pp.56–57

These broken, textured lines, painted with the dry brush technique, are both naturalistic and stylish, calling to mind traditional Chinese calligraphy.

Still water

REFLECTIONS, RIPPLES, AND SHADOWS

It is important to consider how water moves and the way reflections appear when tackling still water in a landscape. Exploit the natural transparency of watercolour paint to capture the delicate sense of light on water, where colourful reflections, ripples of light, and shifting shadows are integral to the composition.

▪ Capturing subtle movement

Use a mixture of techniques to convey the sense that water is gently animated: combine larger flat washes; wet-in-wet modulations of colour; and dry brush for texture to provide variety and interest. Use with care so as not to overpower the whole composition.

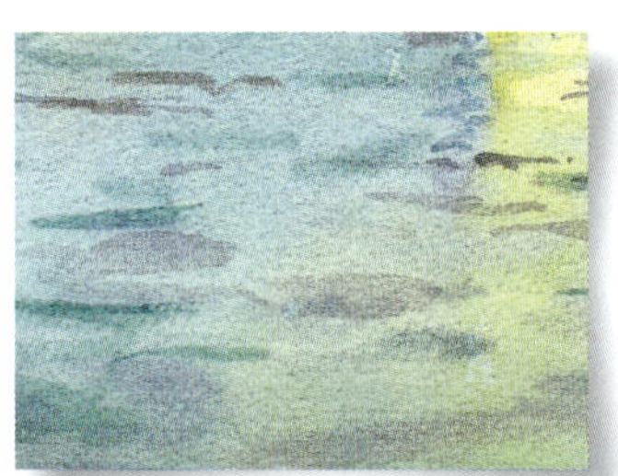

Wet-in-wet reflections
Where reflected colours merge and shift, apply pigments quickly and allow them to blend on the paper. Paint colours either side by side or into each other while they remain wet.

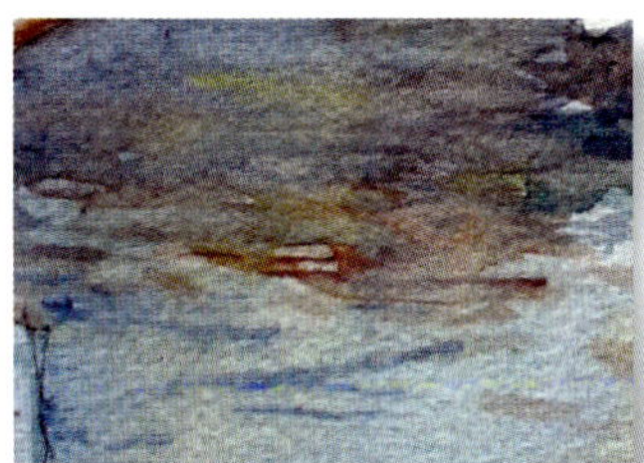

Glazing
Use thin, transparent glazes (see pp.124–25) for shifting colours and tonality or changing the temperature from warm to cool. Avoid opaque colours as they can obscure the layers.

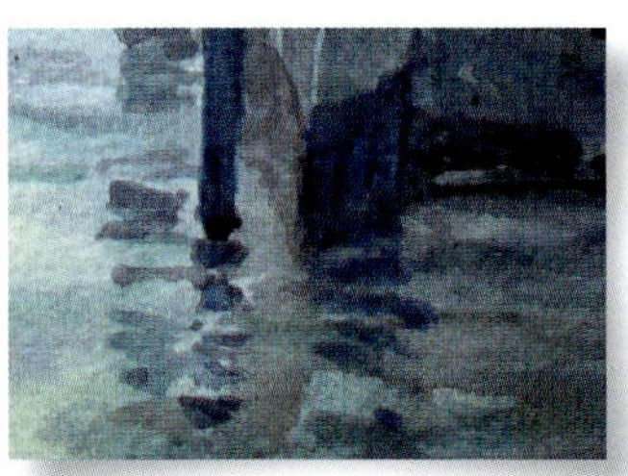

Wet-on-dry shapes
Work wet-on-dry, manipulating the brush to make marks and dashes for ripples and gentle waves. Build dark washes over a flat layer, with a mix of tones to add a sense of movement.

PUTTING IT INTO PRACTICE

The glittering reflections in a gently rippling canal are captured here using soft glazes and wet-in-wet blends that create atmospheric effects to envelop the scene with subtle cool and warm colouring.

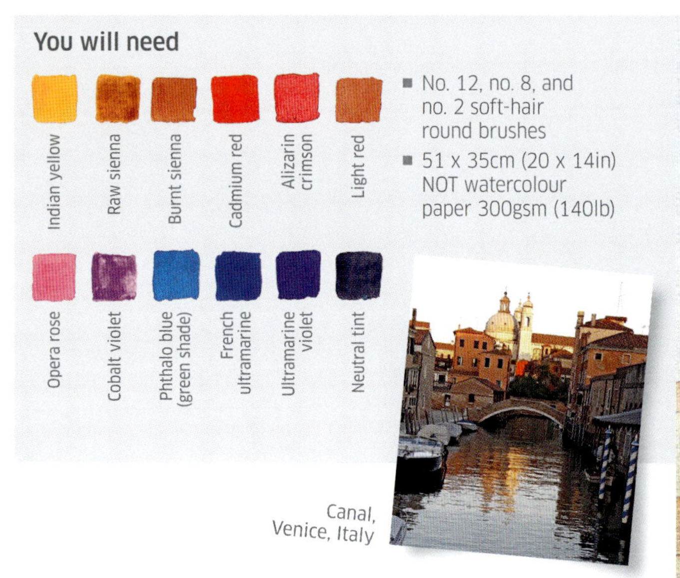

- No. 12, no. 8, and no. 2 soft-hair round brushes
- 51 x 35cm (20 x 14in) NOT watercolour paper 300gsm (140lb)

Canal, Venice, Italy

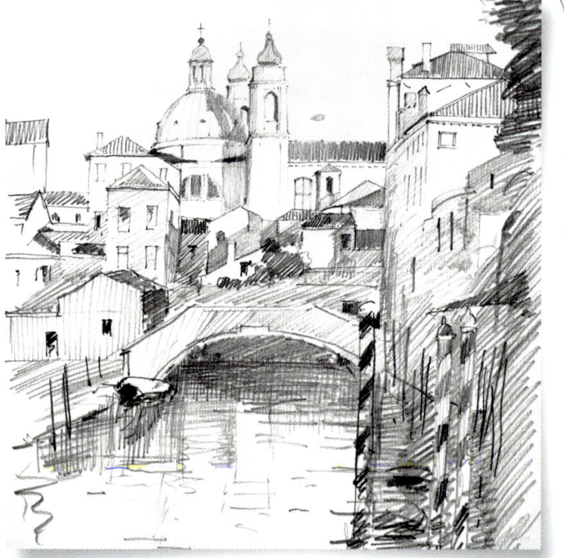

1 Tonal study
A pencil study helps to organize the relationships between the buildings and the water. Note the shadows beneath the bridge and the darker tones along the canal edges, which can be referred to when painting.

Add darker tones beside the reflection to enhance the effect of light

"Use soft, **wet-in-wet edges** to convey the shifting colours of reflections in water."

Apply warm washes to the buildings and their roofs, with bright mixtures where the light hits

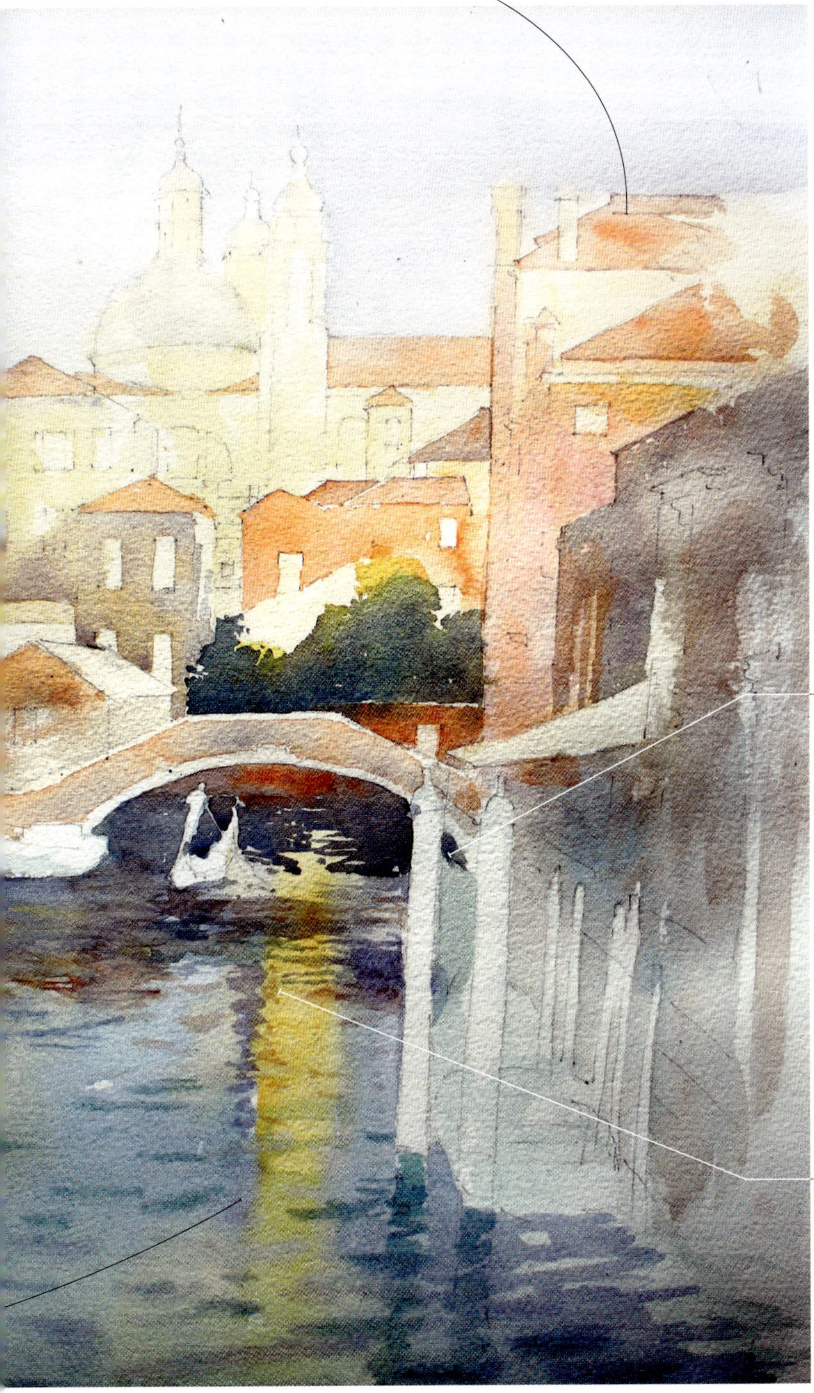

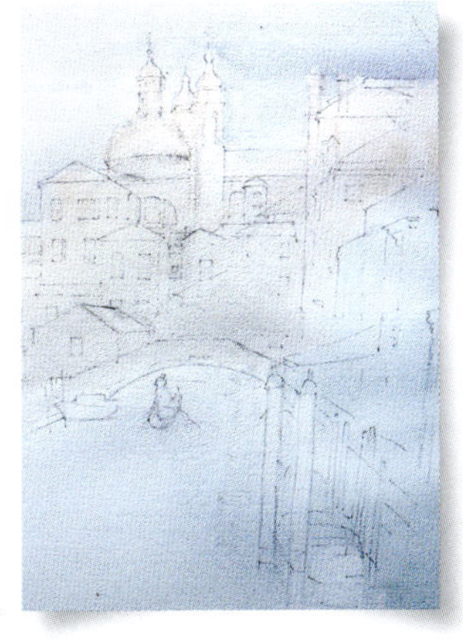

2 Establish light

Add a first wash to establish the general light in the view. The violet-blue colour of the sky is complemented by the light yellow wash falling over the buildings. At this stage, leave the area for the water unpainted.

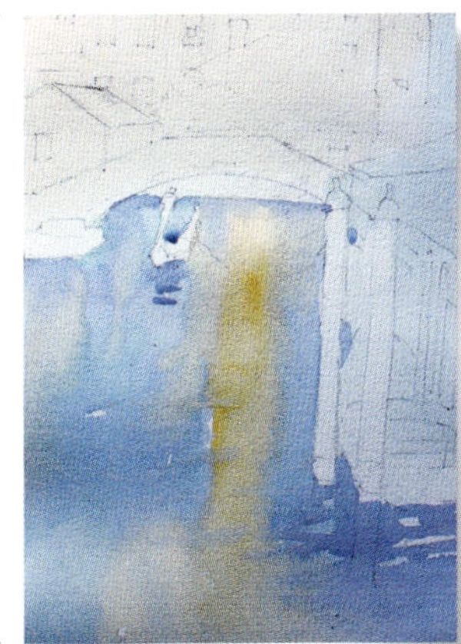

3 First wet-in-wet layer

Quickly add the first base layer of water wet-in-wet within the shape of the canal and around the boats and gondola. Leave clean paper where the sunlit tower is reflected. Add bright yellow into this space and let it spread.

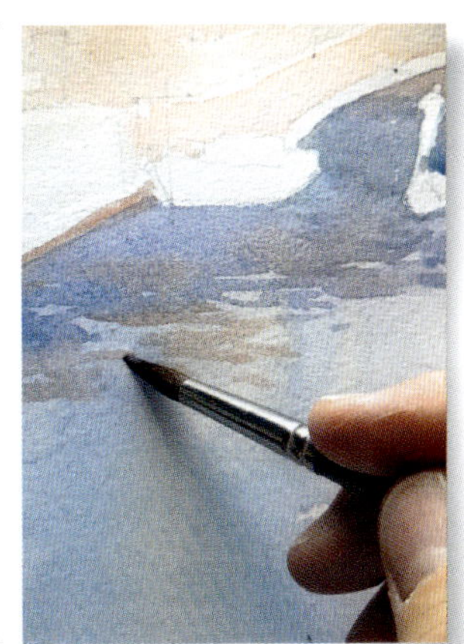

4 Add ripples

Use the tip of a no. 2 brush to add a layer of ripples under the bridge, painting small points and lines of the darker ripples. Apply ripples in the foreground, then damp the paper with clean water and leave so that the ripples soften out.

5 Strengthen shadows

The strong lighting in the scene casts dramatic shadows on the buildings. Use a variety of colours in the basic shadow mixture to keep the painting interesting. Add a second, slightly darker sky layer to allow the light effects to shine out.

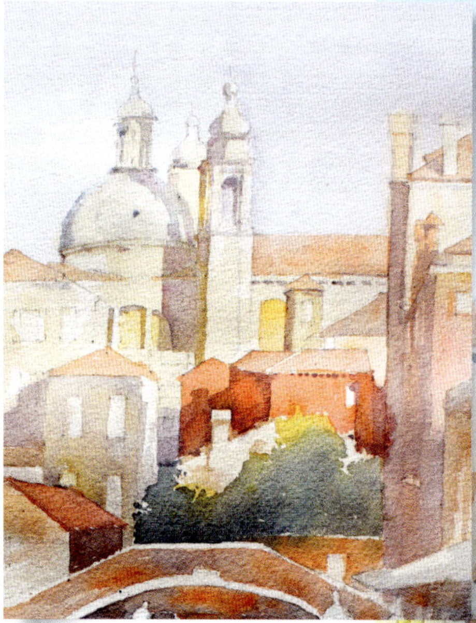

6 Foreground detail

Add the dramatic darks of the boats and striped mooring posts. Here the cool, neutral colouring is a good foil to the rich variety of colour in the background. Keep the boats, pole, and reflections as simple as possible, working wet-on-dry for the dark tones of the reflected solid shapes.

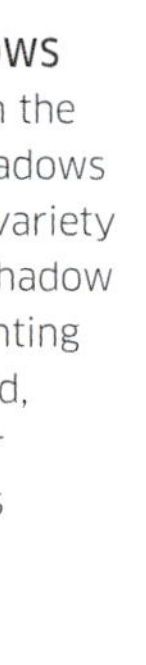

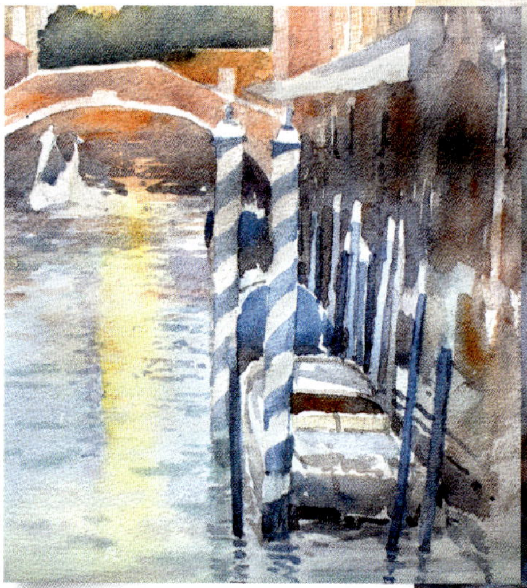

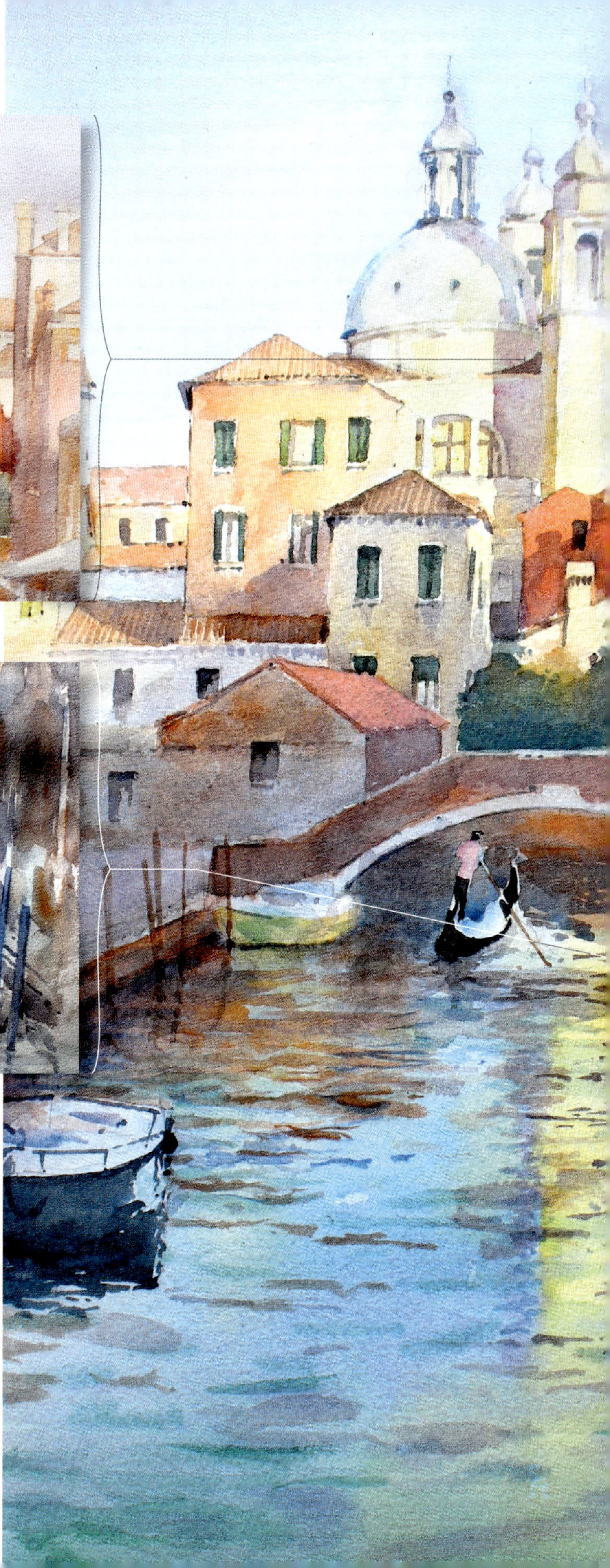

"**The golden hour** in Venice is the **ideal moment to paint** reflections on rippling water."

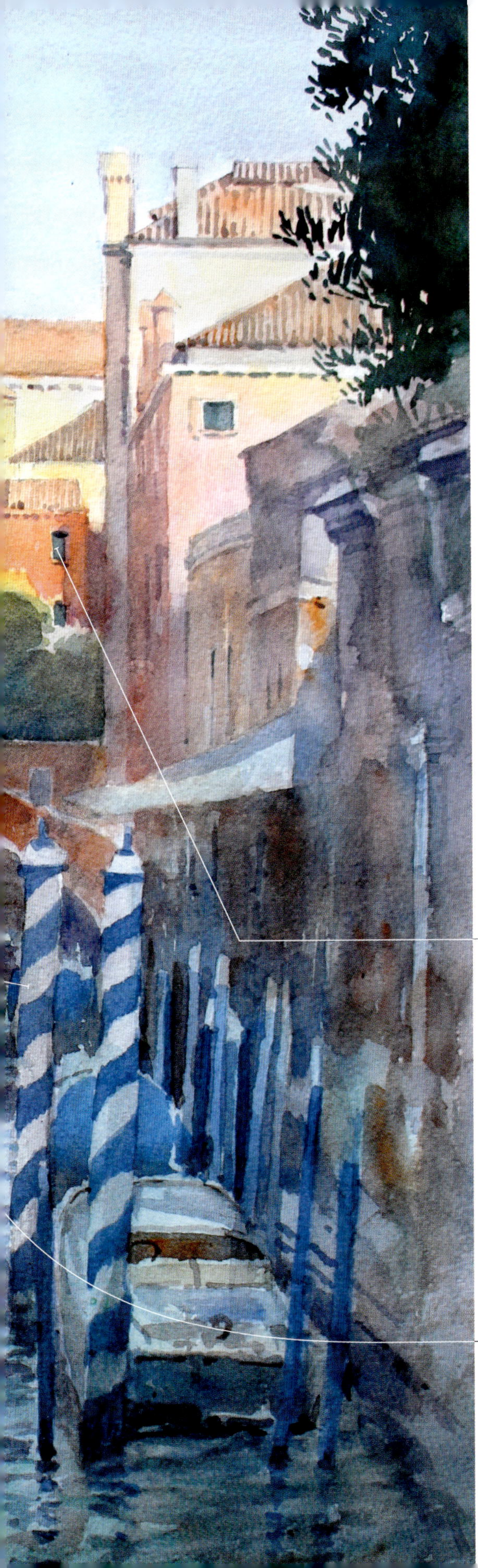

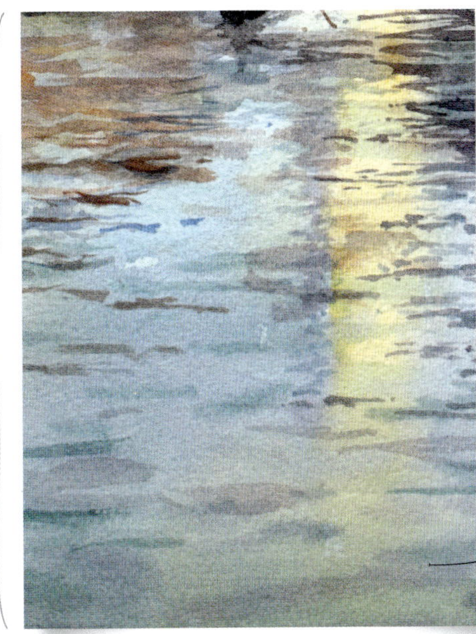

7 Transparent glazes

Apply thin, transparent glazes over the dry layers to shift the tonality and colouring in the painting, using warm glazes to connect the reflections to the buildings. Add successive glazes to give depth. Apply a gentle glaze of viridian to the lower section of the water, adding more ripples while the glaze is still wet.

Viridian glaze brightens the foreground

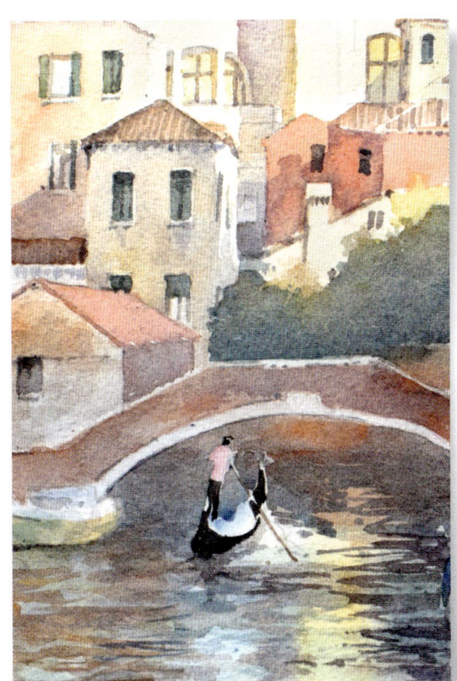

8 Fine details and final glazes

Use different colours for the windows, carefully observing shapes to bring character and scale to the buildings, adding the finer edges to the roof cornices and tiles. Balance the composition with a few additional glazes on the buildings to create a richer sense of space, and finally paint the gondolier to give a sense of movement.

Adjust thin glazes to modulate and unite the composition throughout the painting process

Waves

CAPTURING MOVEMENT AND DRAMA

A crashing wave is so exciting and dynamic to watch, but so difficult to paint as it only lasts for a few seconds. Use field sketches and photographs as a reference to help "freeze" the action and manipulate your composition to focus on the wave, keeping it in context but subduing the rest of the scene.

▪ Making waves

Work from reference photographs to edit the composition, focussing on the wave. Decide in advance which tones to lighten or darken; which edges to soften or harden; which colours to mute or saturate. Leaving whites and planning dark contrasts throws action into the picture plane. Use opaque lights to give body to the spray.

Leave whites
Use initial washes to describe the shape of the wave as a negative space (see pp.114–15), painting around it to leave the white paper. Consider the height of the crashing foam, extending the white into the top of the picture plane.

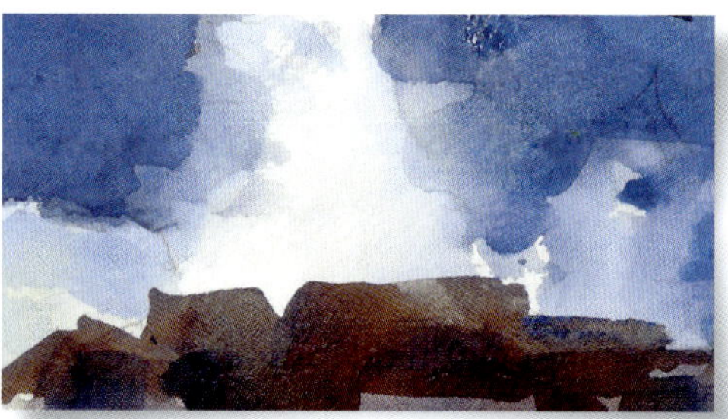

Soften edges
Where washes have dried with a hard edge around the white wave, use a clean brush and water to gently blend and soften the edges (see pp.94–97).

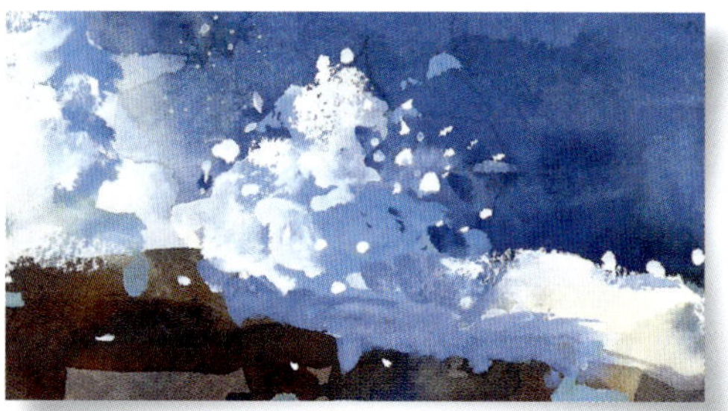

Opaque colour and detail
To contrast against transparent washes, use gouache to add opaque lights (see pp.150–51), splattering white blobs to add movement (see pp.98–99).

PUTTING IT INTO PRACTICE
Here, the wave in the reference photograph has been made taller, to fall into the centre of the picture. Contrasts of tone and colour help to focus the action.

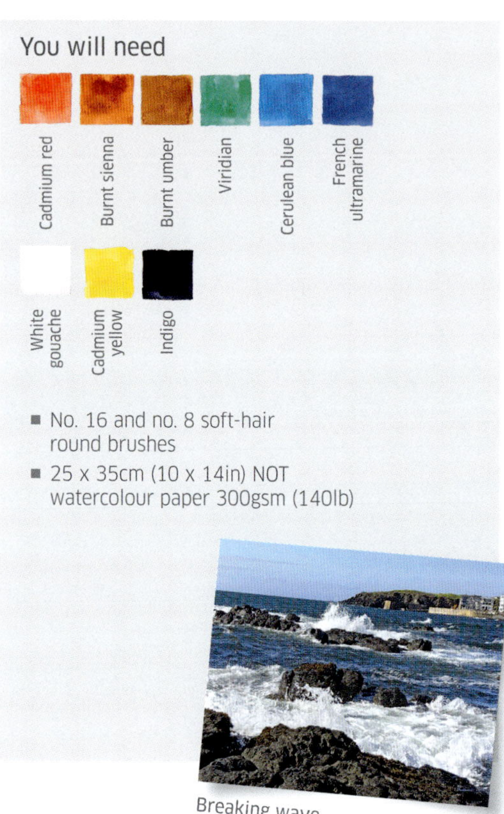

- No. 16 and no. 8 soft-hair round brushes
- 25 x 35cm (10 x 14in) NOT watercolour paper 300gsm (140lb)

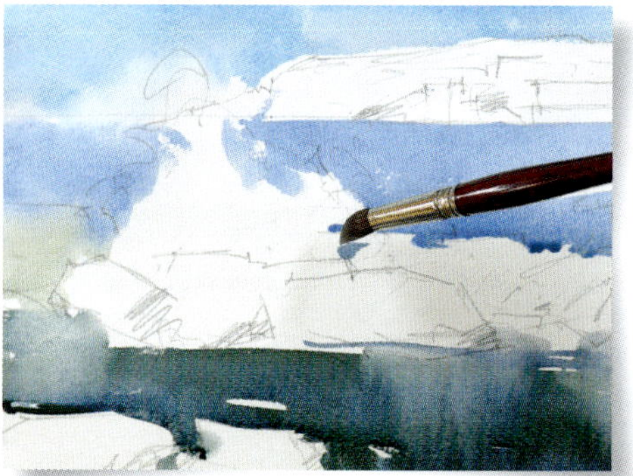
Breaking wave

1 Define main areas
With the composition divided into thirds, establish a cool sky with cerulean and a warm sea with ultramarine, using hard edges to define the horizon. Leave white paper for the rocks and breaking wave.

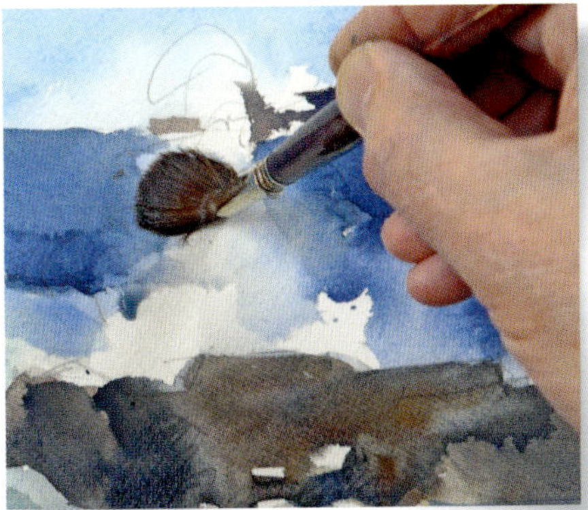

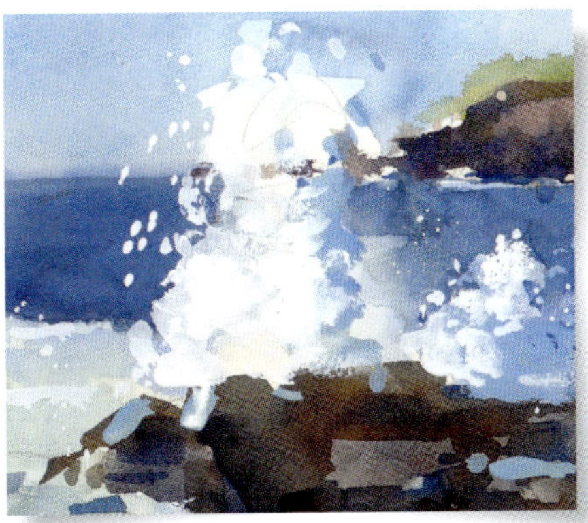

2 Emphasize dark contrasts
A white wave needs a dark backdrop; use a stronger mix for the sea to define the wave's shadow side. The rocks ensure a dark area adjacent to the lightest light of the wave.

3 Blend edges
To merge the white paper into the sea colour, use clean water to soften the hard edge of the adjacent blue, moving the wash to blend light tones where the wave breaks.

4 Opaque effects
When the watercolour is completely dry, splatter white gouache to achieve the dash of wave droplets and mix opaque wave shadows in cobalt to complement transparent washes.

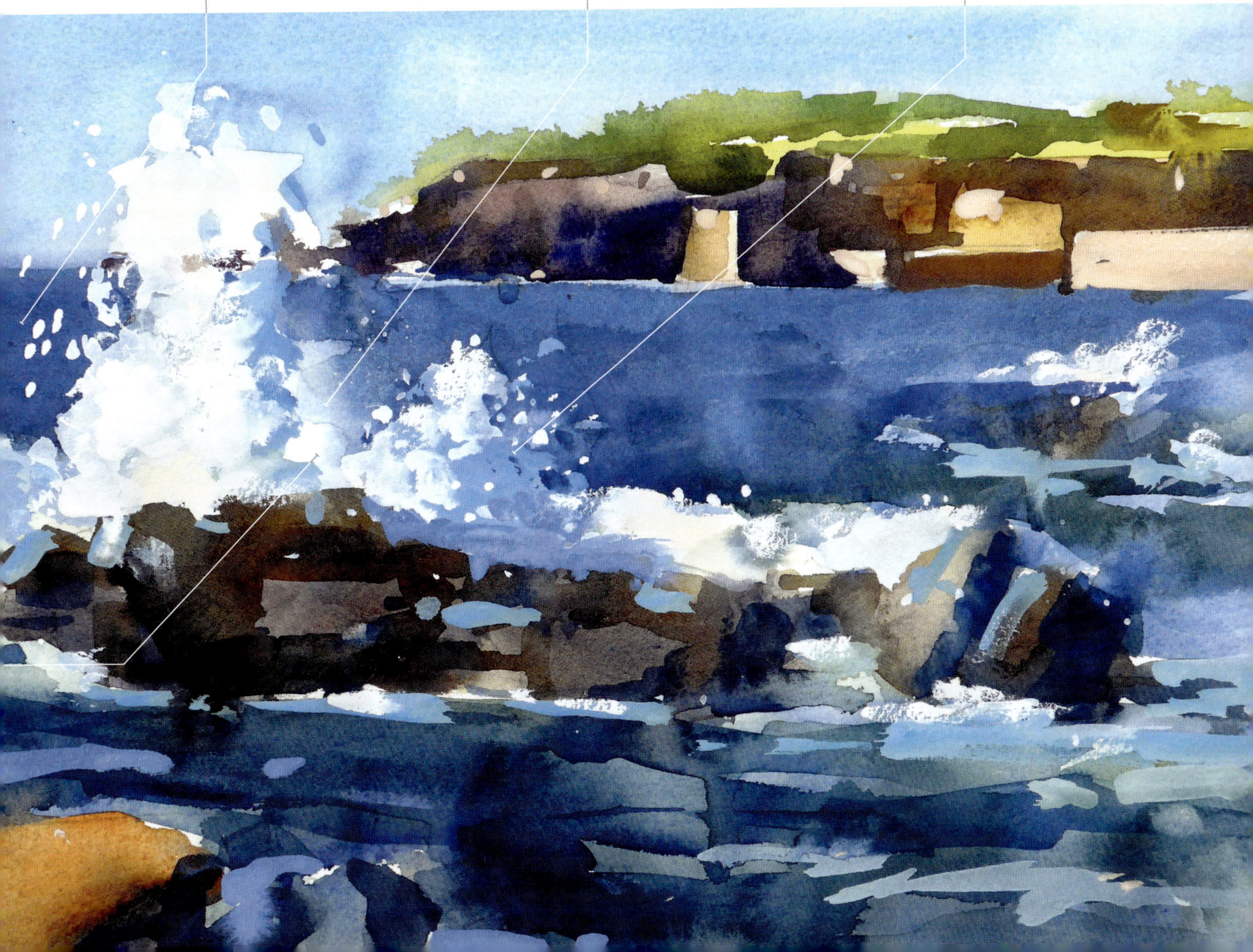

Harbour scene

CAPTURING A NAUTICAL LANDSCAPE

There is so much material to work with in a harbour scene. The colours and shapes of the boats, the rigging, reflective water, the mood created by the weather, and all of the structure that makes up a harbour are of endless fascination for the artist. Employ different techniques to capture the shifting layers of colour in the water against the solid forms of the dock and boats, using dark and light values to create visual contrasts.

PUTTING IT INTO PRACTICE

The boats and harbour setting draw your eye through the scene, following the path of light on the water where the reflections connect to the sea. Be alert to the contrast between light and dark values.

You will need

White gouache

Yellow ochre

Permanent yellow deep

Deep scarlet

Burnt sienna

Burnt umber

Ultramarine blue

Cobalt blue

Phthalo green (blue shade)

Sap green

- Selection of soft-hair flat and round brushes, rigger brush, stiff-bristle fan brush
- 41 x 51cm (16 x 20in) NOT watercolour paper 300gsm (140lb)

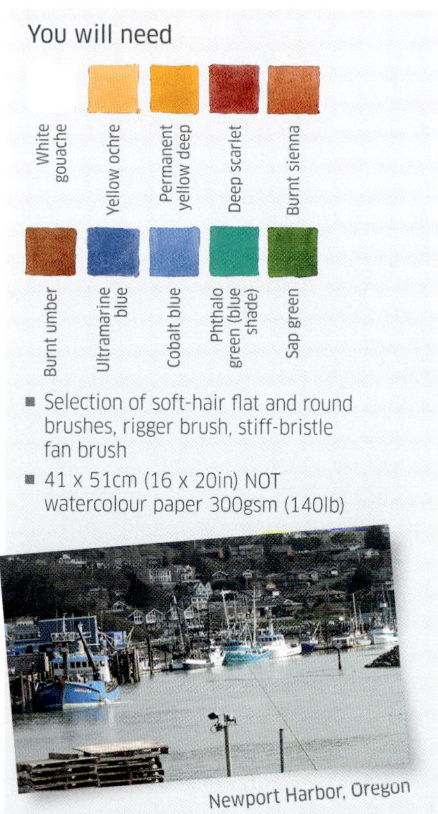
Newport Harbor, Oregon

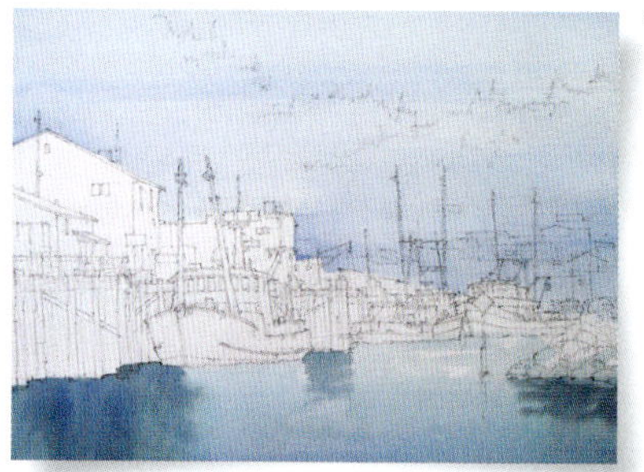

1 Foundation washes

Lightly draw your sketch in pencil, making sure all the elements are resolved before you begin to paint. Smoothly apply a flat wash of ultramarine mixed with a little burnt sienna with a flat brush and overlay it with cobalt blue. Use a slightly richer mix to begin the areas of major reflection.

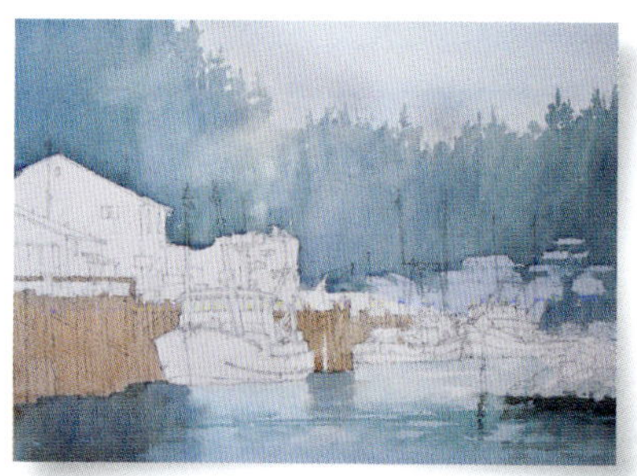

2 Add background

Work rapidly with a large mop brush with a good point to render the background hills. Use plenty of water to apply layers of ultramarine with yellow ochre. Soften the tree shapes as you work, blending with a stiff fan brush.

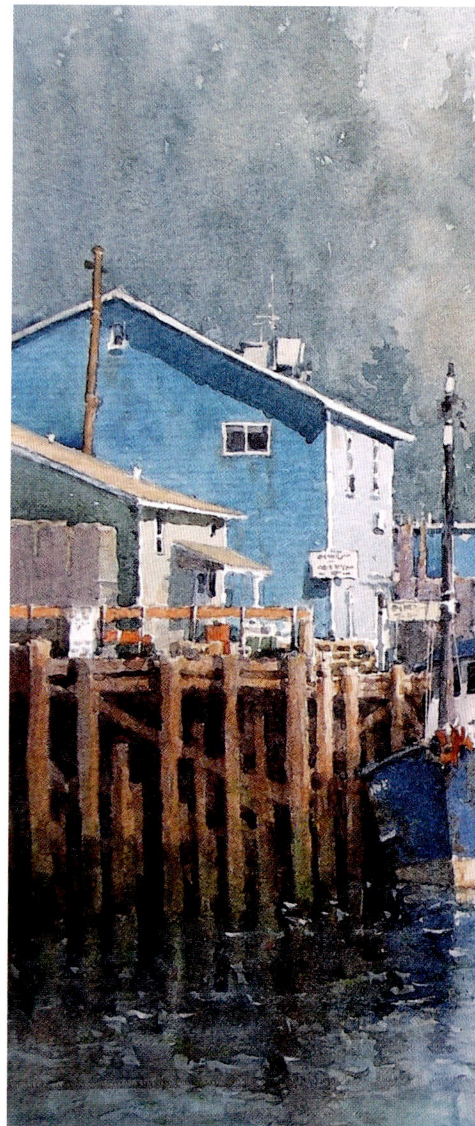

■ Bringing it together

In order to make your painting a composition containing boats, and not a portrait of a boat or boats, look for ways to keep the scene connected. Make sure that the boats, dock, and structures connect and flow into each other where possible. Think about the setting, using a backdrop to contain the different elements, and blending each area into another to maintain a flow through the composition.

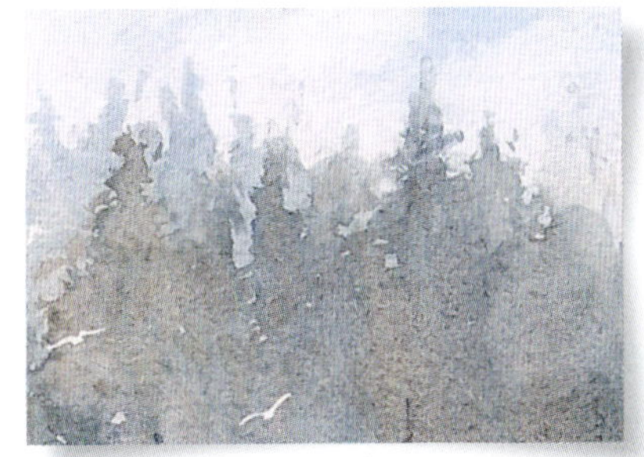

Background silhouette
By eliminating some of the buildings from the background the area is simplified and becomes a silhouette, adding atmosphere and depth.

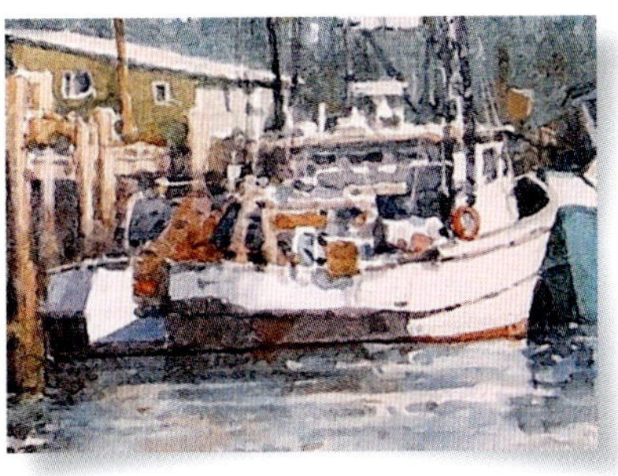

Realistic forms
Painting the harbour structures and boats in detail attracts the eye through the painting. Carry colours and merge edges to keep the elements connected.

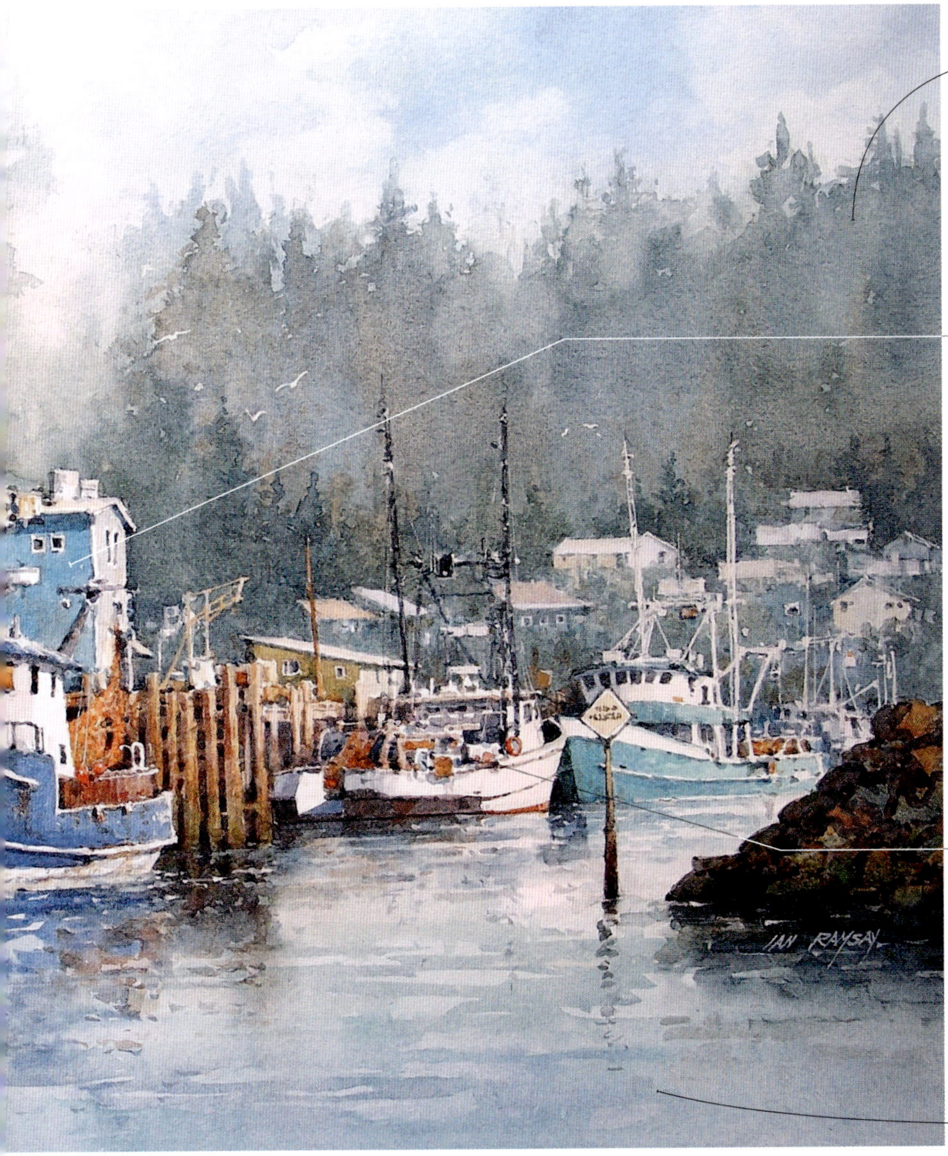

Layers of blue and green added with a fan brush introduce texture to the wooded hills

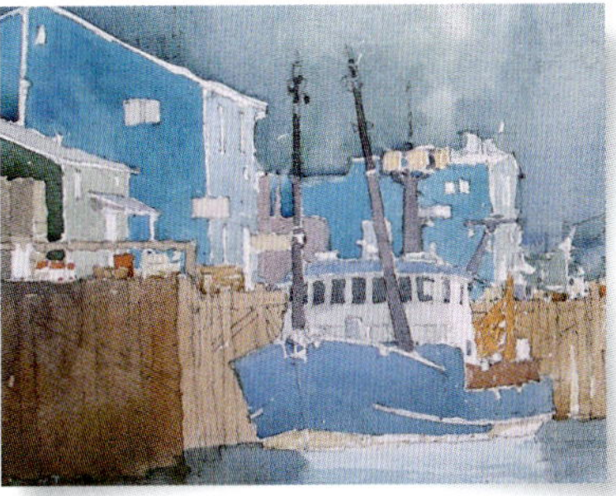

3 Introduce colour
Start to fill in the boats and harbour scene with colour, using large round brushes in order to avoid becoming too involved with detail. Lift out (see pp.82–83) and soften some areas to suggest mist.

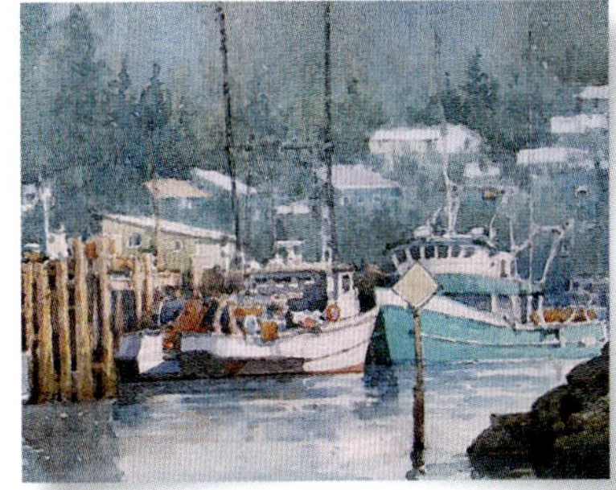

4 Define forms
Solidify the three-dimensional objects and create areas of contrast. Add line detail, accented colour, and some white gouache for sparkle.

Layer movement in the water with a light touch and a large round brush with a sharp point

Colours in snow

PAINTING WHITE USING COLOUR

Like other white subjects, snow reflects the colours around it. The key is to identify the light and shadow patterns, breaking the scene down into light, medium, and dark tonal values, and looking for colours to convey the snowy atmosphere.

◼ Using colour and tone

The appearance of snow is influenced by the colours of the surrounding objects and light sources. Look for tonal colour changes in shadows to describe snowy shapes, and observe the effects of perceived temperature where cool shadows are contrasted against a patch of warm sunlight.

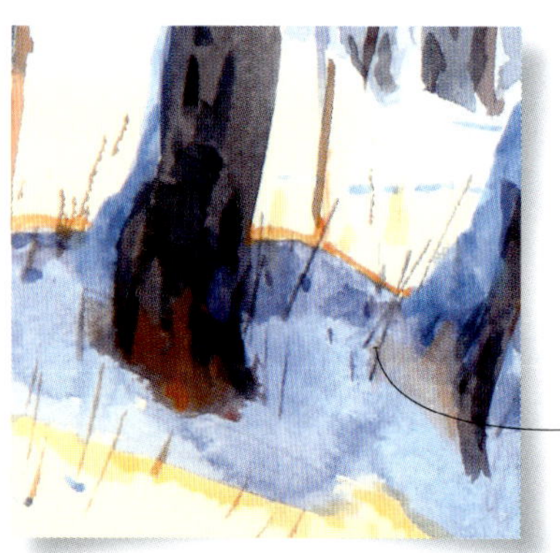

Shadow colours

In general, shadows on snow will reflect the sky. A clear sky will produce blue snow shadows, compared to dull tones of an overcast scene.

Use tonal variations of blue for shadows on sunlit snow

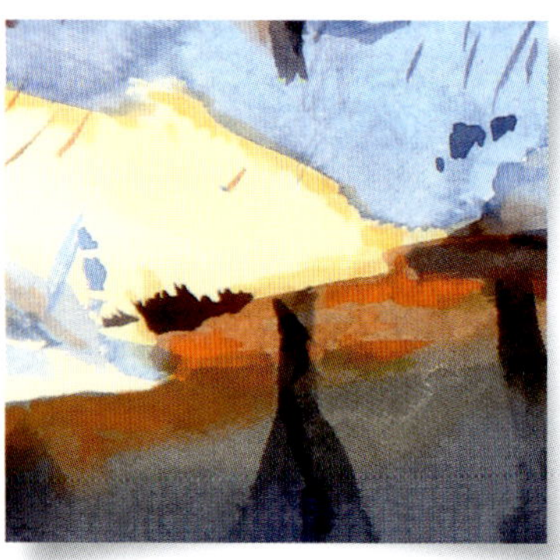

Temperature contrasts

Use contrasts in colour temperature (see pp.34–35) to convey the literal chill of the shadows, where large areas of cool blue are juxtaposed against patches of warm orange or yellow.

PUTTING IT INTO PRACTICE

The feeling of light in the snowy scene is created through the dramatic contrast between the dark creek and the white snow. The warm, late afternoon sunlight and cool shadows enhance the drama.

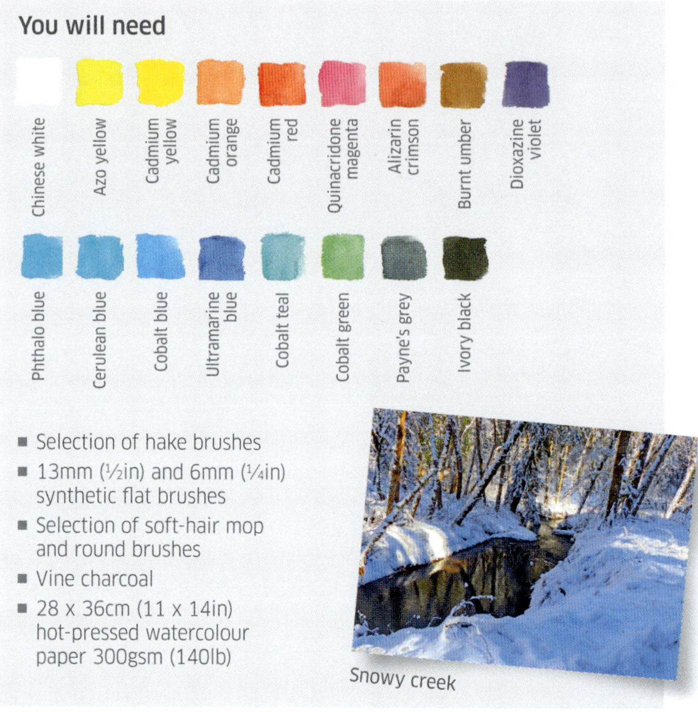

- Selection of hake brushes
- 13mm (½in) and 6mm (¼in) synthetic flat brushes
- Selection of soft-hair mop and round brushes
- Vine charcoal
- 28 x 36cm (11 x 14in) hot-pressed watercolour paper 300gsm (140lb)

Snowy creek

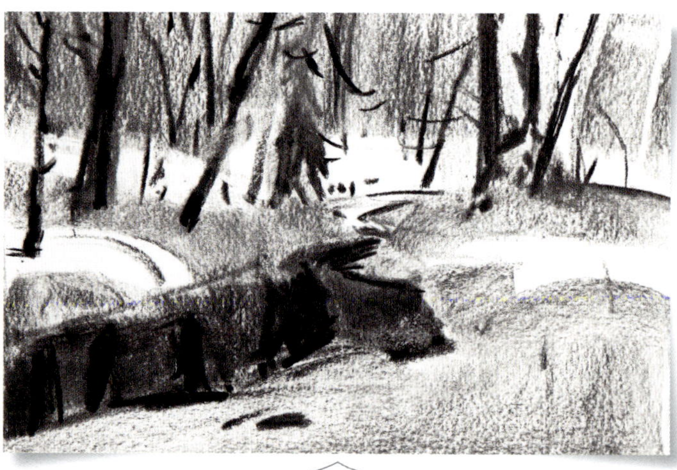

1 Tonal study
Simplify your scene into a tonal study using charcoal. Note the shapes created by the areas of light, mid, and dark tone. Transfer these areas to your paper in a pencil sketch to guide your washes.

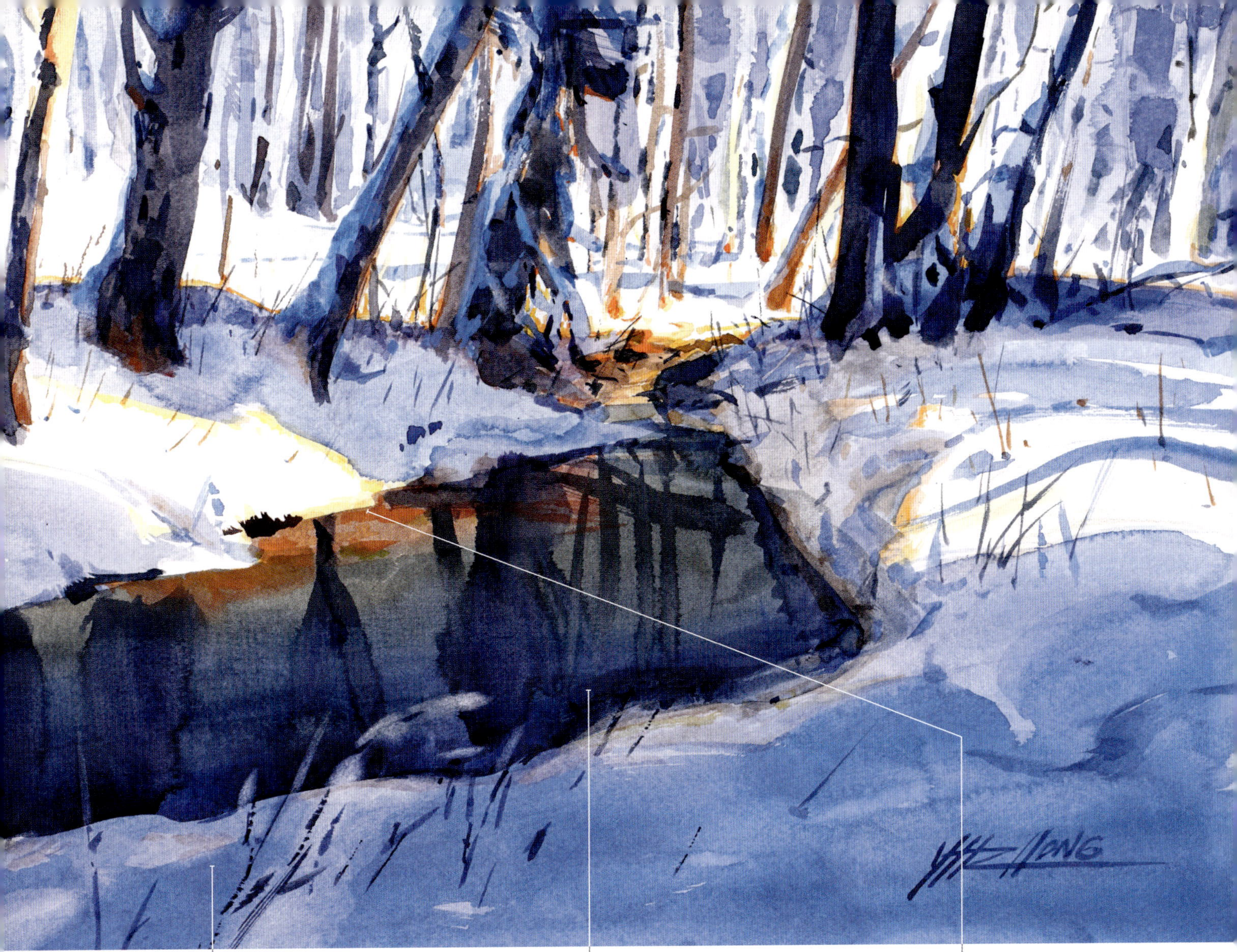

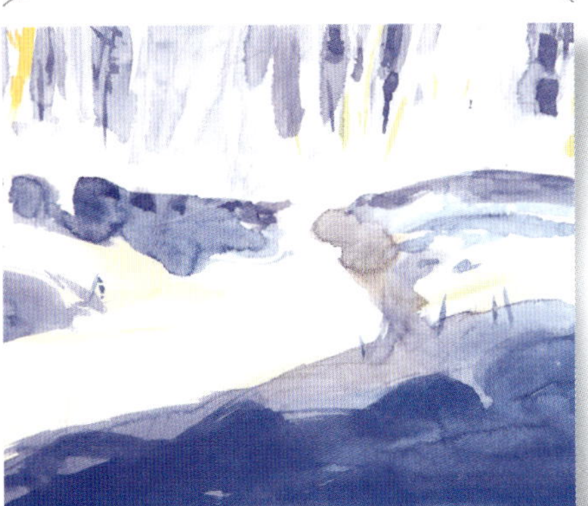

2 Light and mid tones

Start with the light tones, adding the warm yellow of the sunlit snow to wet paper to give soft edges. Block in the mid values of the shadows and background, with varied tones.

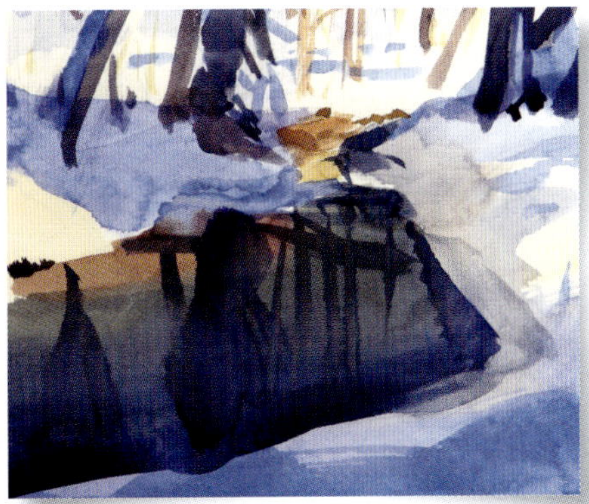

3 Dark tones

Next, fill the areas of darkest tone in the creek and the distant tree trunks. The stark contrast between dark and light edges helps to throw the snowy bank forward.

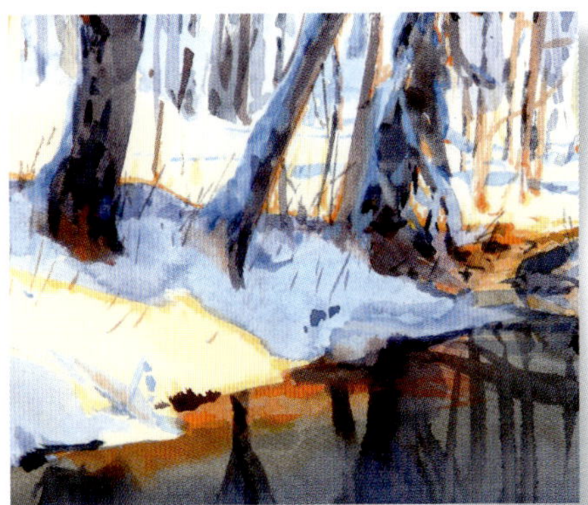

4 Warm and cool contrasts

Add warm yellows and orange where the sun breaks through and hits the snow. Outline the blue shadow edges with yellow; the stark contrast makes the shadows appear colder.

Bright snow

WAYS WITH WHITE

Using pure white to depict snow can give a graphic, illustrative feel to a painting. The purest white you have in watercolour is the white of the unpainted paper, but using opaque gouache is another option. Painting white with a combination of techniques creates layers and textures that make the single colour more interesting.

▇ Creating effects in a snowy landscape

A very minimal colour palette suited to a wintry scene can produce an image that has considerable depth as well as textural interest. Combining techniques and tools offers the artist plenty of choice.

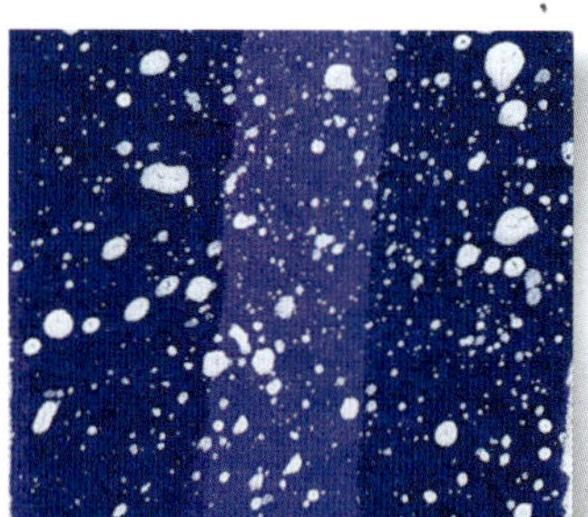

Snow texture
Using a toothbrush and white gouache, spatter falling snow to create natural-looking flakes of random size and shape. You need to use a strong dilution for them to show up well.

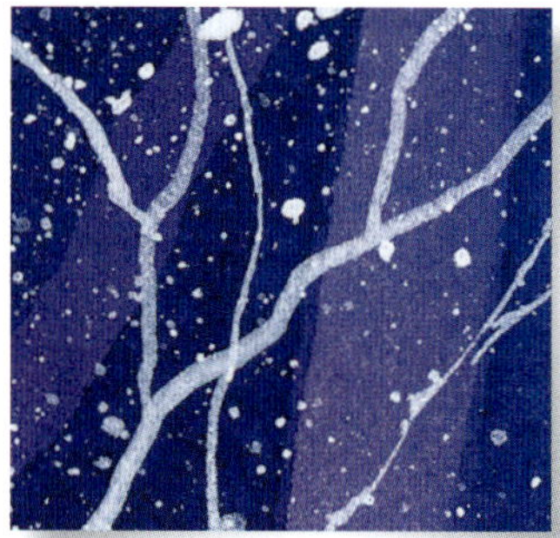

White details
A rigger is a very slender and expressive brush and is ideal for suggesting smaller branches that narrow to elegant tips.

Negative reflections
Unless water is very still, edges of objects will not exactly match the reality. Paint ripples to enhance the impression of water.

PUTTING IT INTO PRACTICE

Negative spaces between the trees give a sense of depth which is enhanced by the overlapping slender white branches. A spattering of snow over the scene gives a more natural effect.

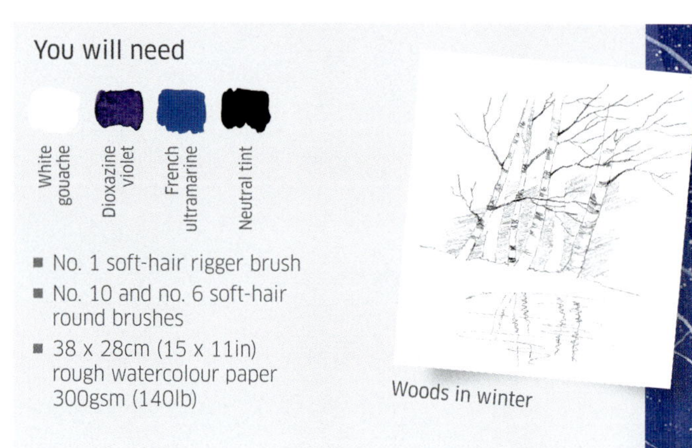

- No. 1 soft-hair rigger brush
- No. 10 and no. 6 soft-hair round brushes
- 38 x 28cm (15 x 11in) rough watercolour paper 300gsm (140lb)

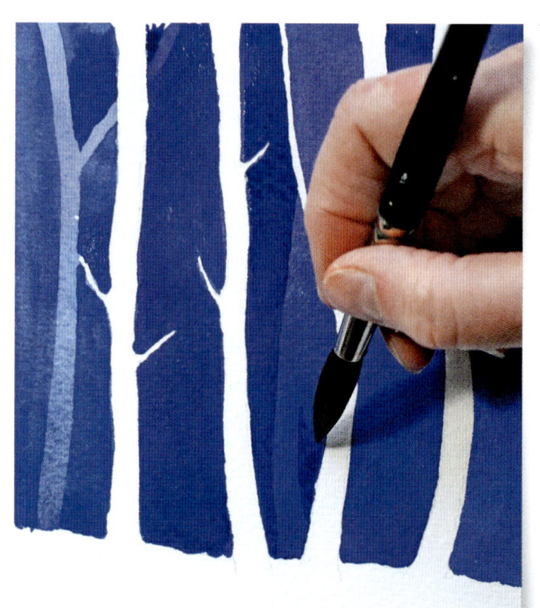

1 The background
After making a sketch, mix blue and violet and lay a wash, reserving white paper for four trees and the ground. When this wash is dry, lay a second wash, this time leaving the first wash visible in the shapes of more tree trunks. Repeat this wash to darken it further.

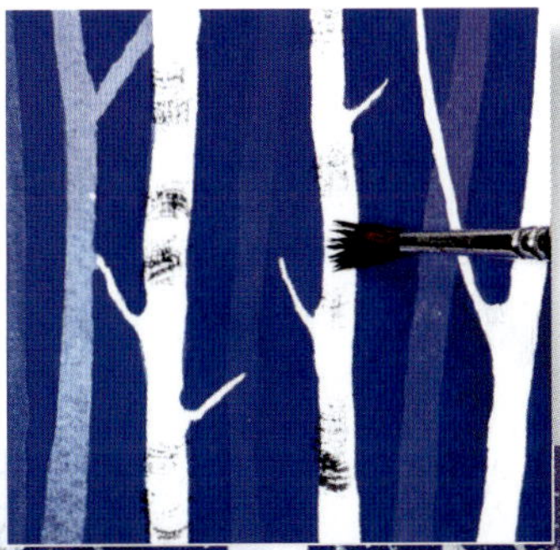

2 Tree bark effect
Make a creamy mix of some neutral tint. Squeeze most of the water out of a no. 6 round brush and splay the hairs. Pick up a little neutral tint with the brush and drag across the trunks in a slightly curved stroke.

"**Combining several ways** with white makes a lively snow scene."

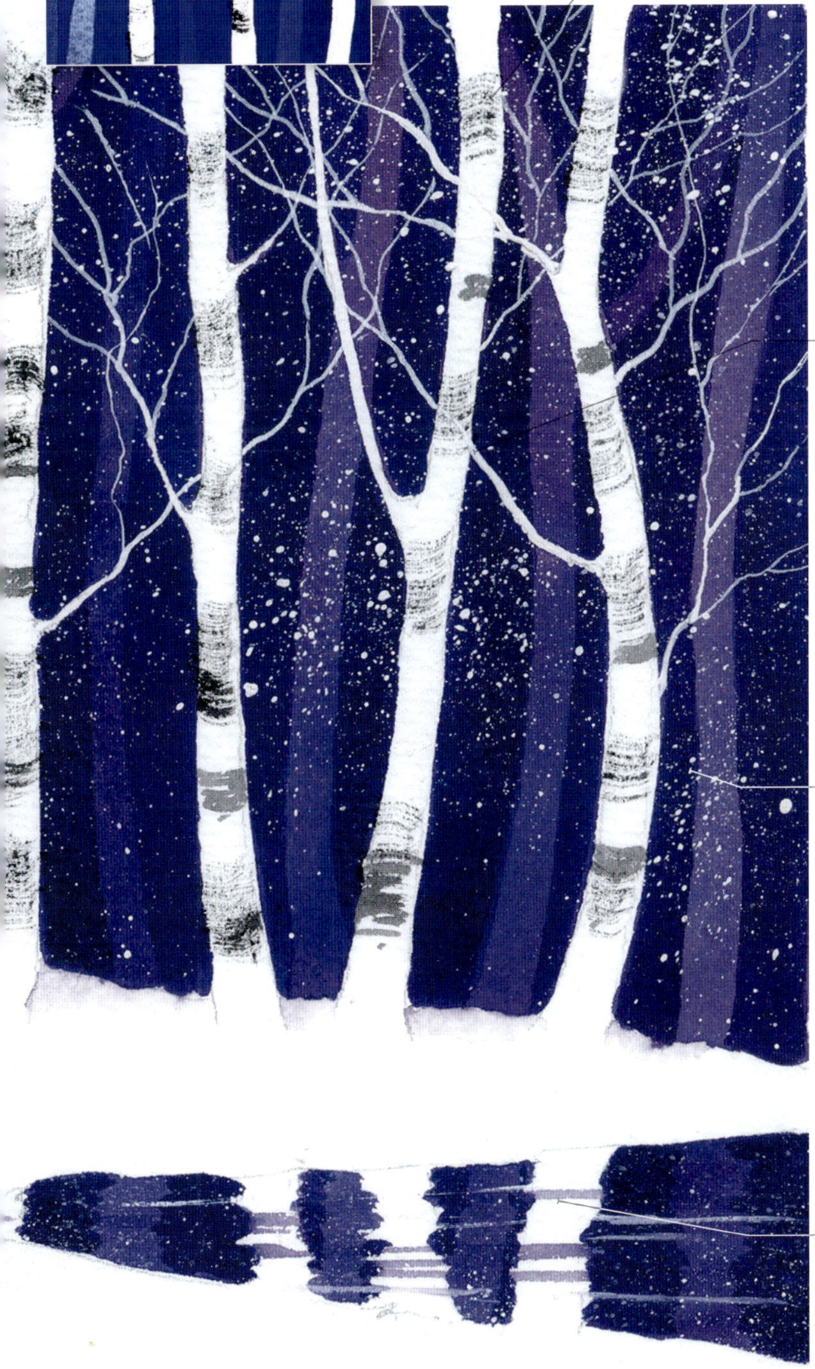

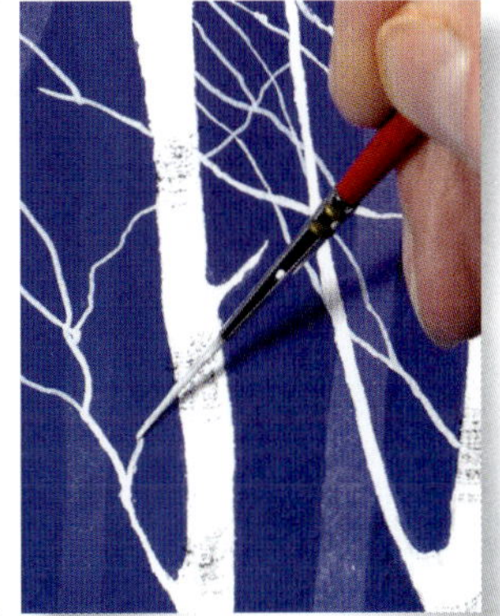

3 Fine branches
Check that all the paint is dry then, using white gouache and a rigger brush, paint the fine white branches. Pull the brush rather than push it, and hold it with a light touch away from the ferrule. Let the branches overlap.

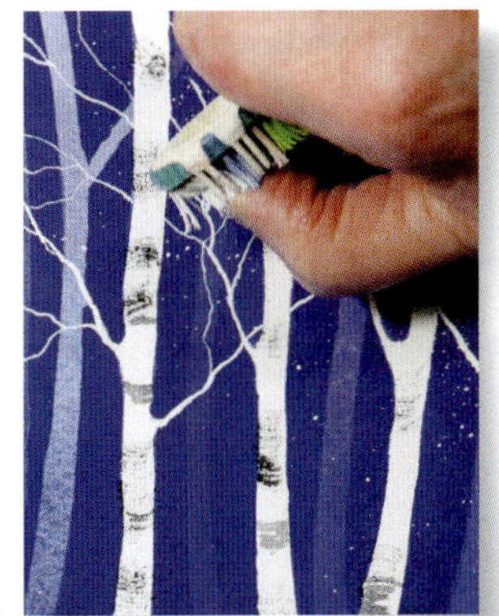

4 Falling snow
With an old toothbrush dipped in more white gouache, spatter fine snow falling. Point the bristles downwards and then pull your thumb backwards across the brush.

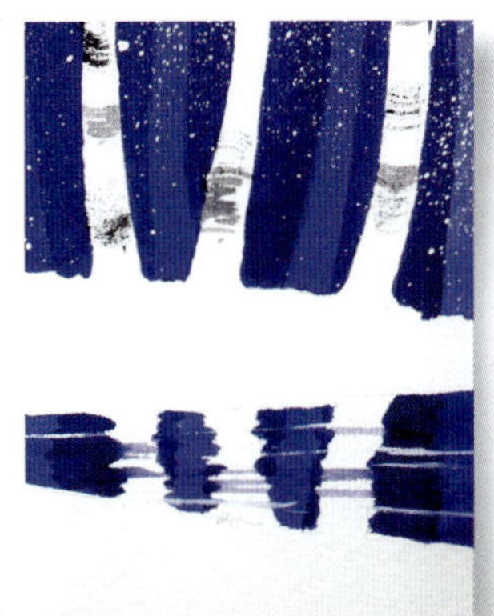

5 Water
Use the method in step 1 to paint the water and reflections of the trees. With the point of your brush, paint horizontal ripples in blue across the water and reflected trees.

Urban cityscapes

CAPTURING STREET SCENES

With so much variety of shape, activity, movement, and colour on offer in a vibrant city scene, you must plan your painting carefully to include a focus of attention. Capture the city atmosphere by rendering buildings in a recognizable way, and use the street-level bustle of people and cars to draw the viewer into the scene.

◼ Balancing cityscape components

A street scene comprises many elements: people, vehicles, street furniture, windows, buildings. These can all be used to create interest and shape your composition, with people adding focus and buildings and signs used to direct the eye to the street-level activity. When choosing what to include, make the scene look as natural as possible.

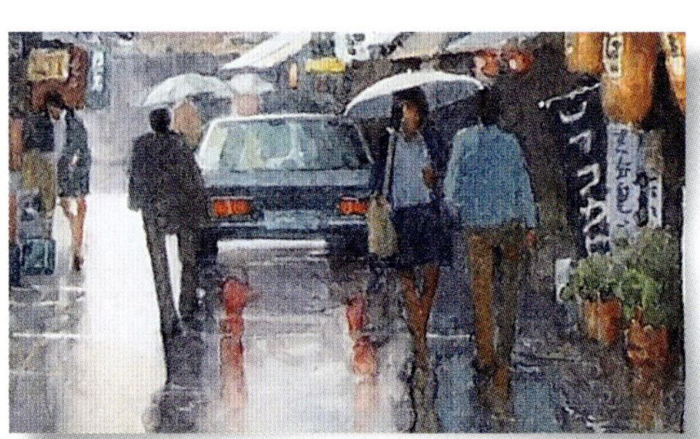

People

Including figures will give life to your painting. Ensure that there is variety in clothing and poses, with men and women moving in different directions. If you are combining references, overlap rather than isolate figures, to connect the scene.

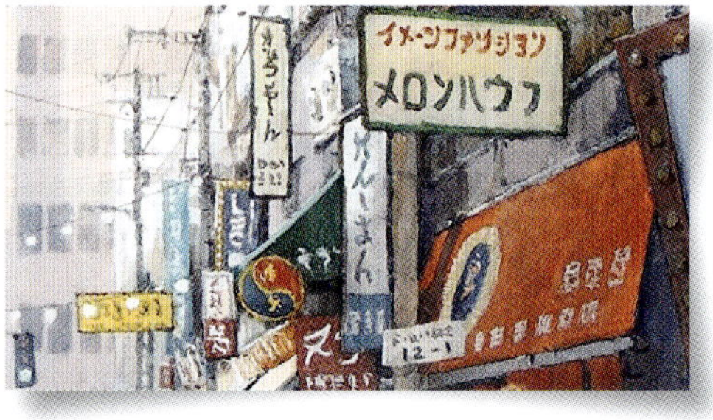

Street furniture

The visual variety of street furniture can be used to aid the composition by directing the eye along the street and down to street level. Edit out detailed signage from the top of an image that might detract from the foreground focus.

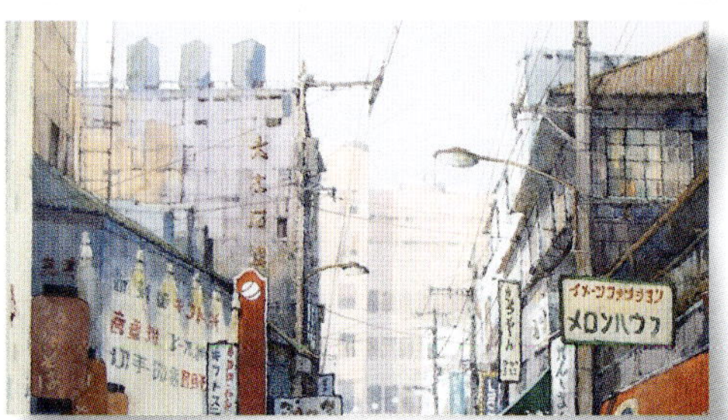

Buildings

Including buildings provides a quiet setting for the real stars of the show – the people, signs, and shop fronts. Paint buildings as generalized shapes, with correct proportions and perspective, and placed logically along the street plan.

PUTTING IT INTO PRACTICE

Multiple references were used to compose this engaging painting. Dark values draw you in, signage and moving figures add foreground interest, and the wet road surface connects both sides of the street.

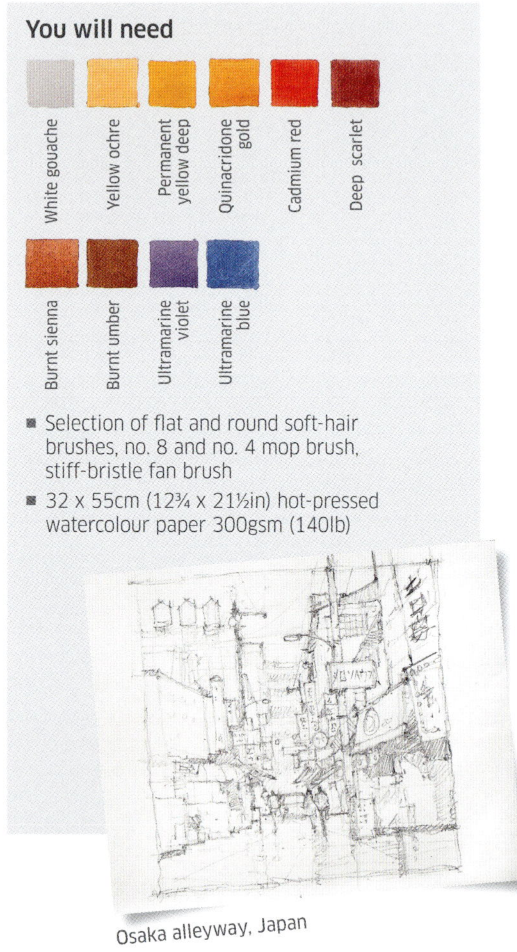

- ◼ Selection of flat and round soft-hair brushes, no. 8 and no. 4 mop brush, stiff-bristle fan brush
- ◼ 32 x 55cm (12¾ x 21½in) hot-pressed watercolour paper 300gsm (140lb)

Osaka alleyway, Japan

"In an urban scene **few surfaces are parallel** but the horizon remains **constant.**"

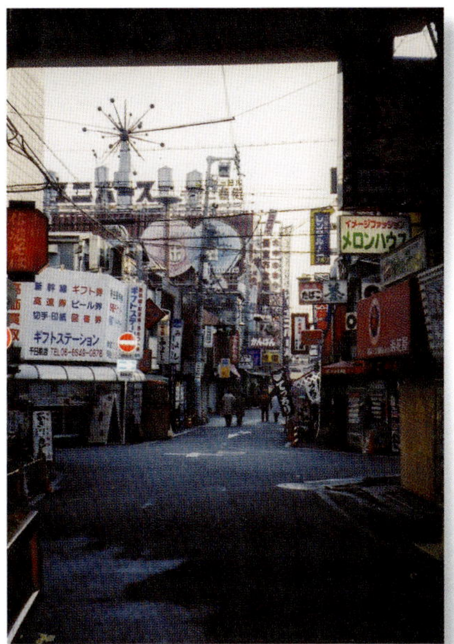

Reference photo 1

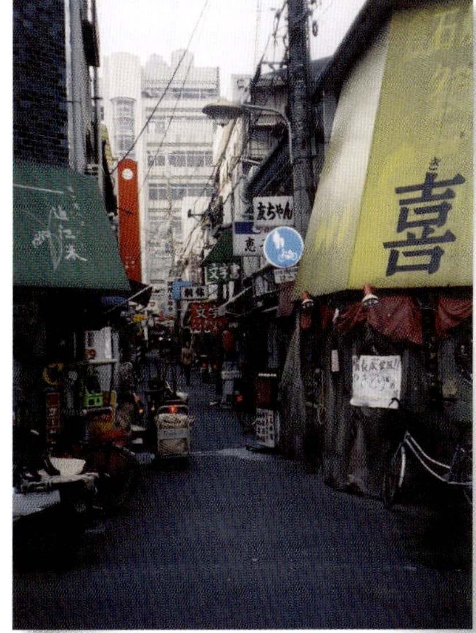

Reference photo 2

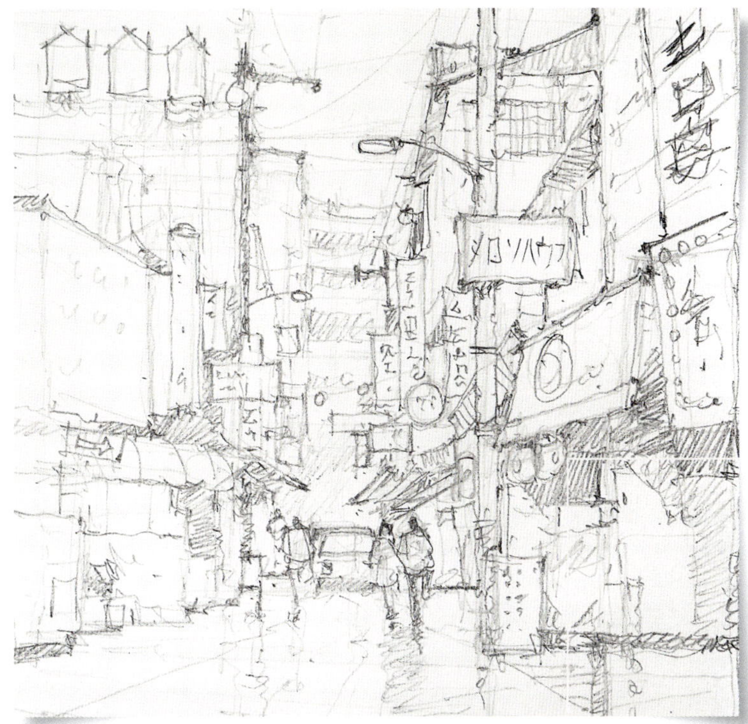

Rough placement and perspective

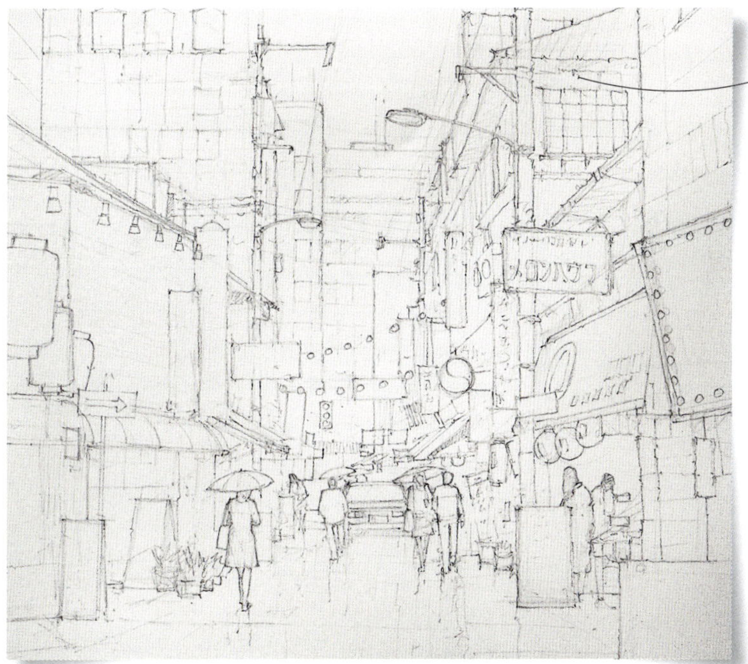

Buildings add scale

Additional details, figures, and corrected perspective

1 Choose which elements to include

Using more than one reference image means that you can select and combine different components. Both of these scenes are dark and interesting but the yellow awning in Photo 2 was too dominant. The signs and street furniture in both images add interest and the foreground of Photo 1 shows the contrast of light and dark.

2 Develop a composition

Taking the photographs as a starting point, work up your composition in sketches, combining different elements to create a scene that is convincing in perspective and proportion. Pay close attention to the interaction of people and check that all of the objects are the right size in relation to the height of the people in the street.

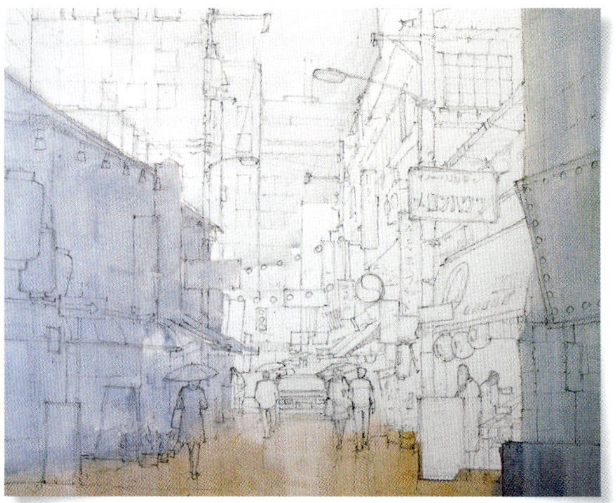

3 First washes

Apply a watery yellow ochre wash to the sky with a flat brush, working quickly and adding ultramarine for the shadows to establish the light and dark areas of the painting. Paint the road in two layers, using no. 4 and no. 8 mop brushes with washes of quinacridone gold and burnt sienna.

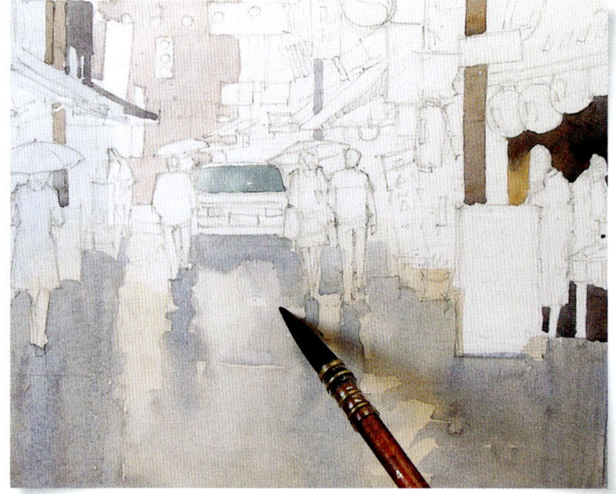

4 Initial reflections

Working wet-in-wet with a mop brush, quickly paint a loose rendition of a rainy street surface, leaving bright light on the street that contrasts with the beginnings of reflections in the wet pavement.

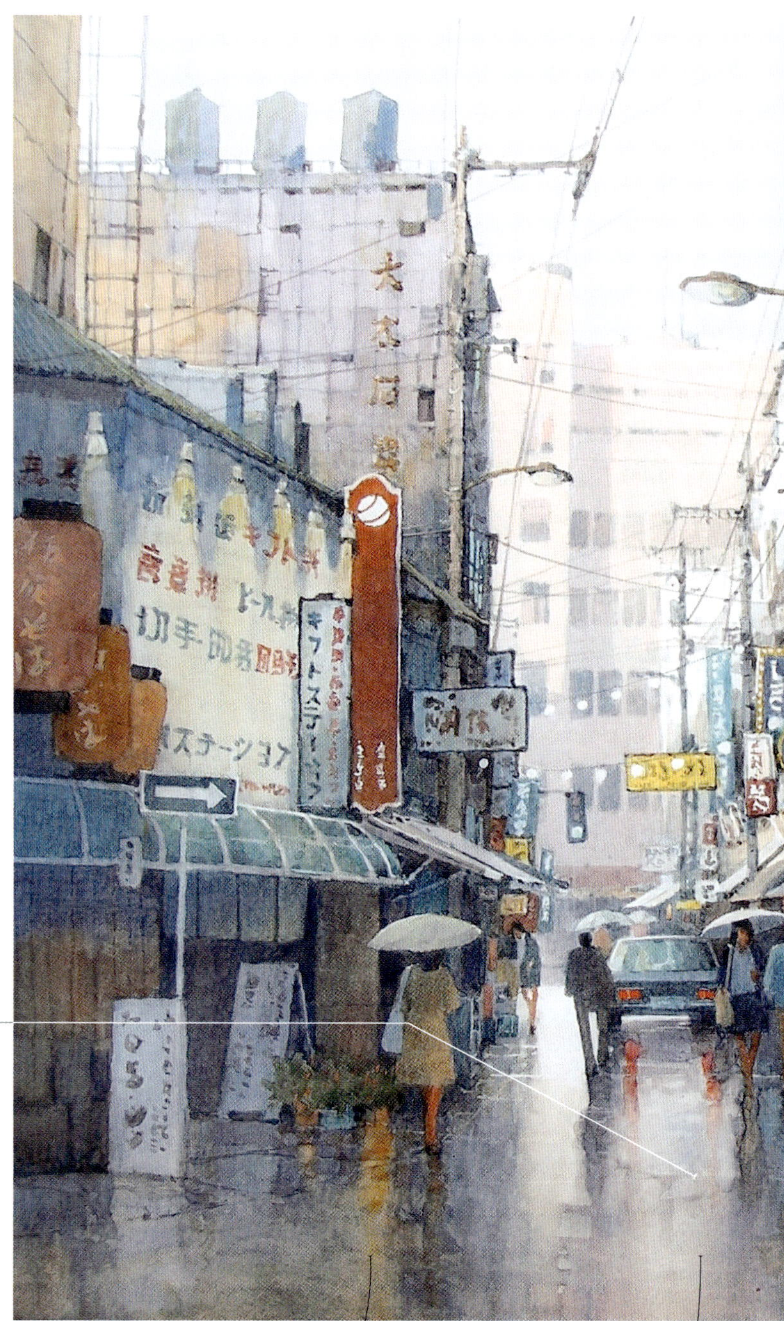

Yellow ochre added to the initial wash suggests reflections

Cool values in the foreground

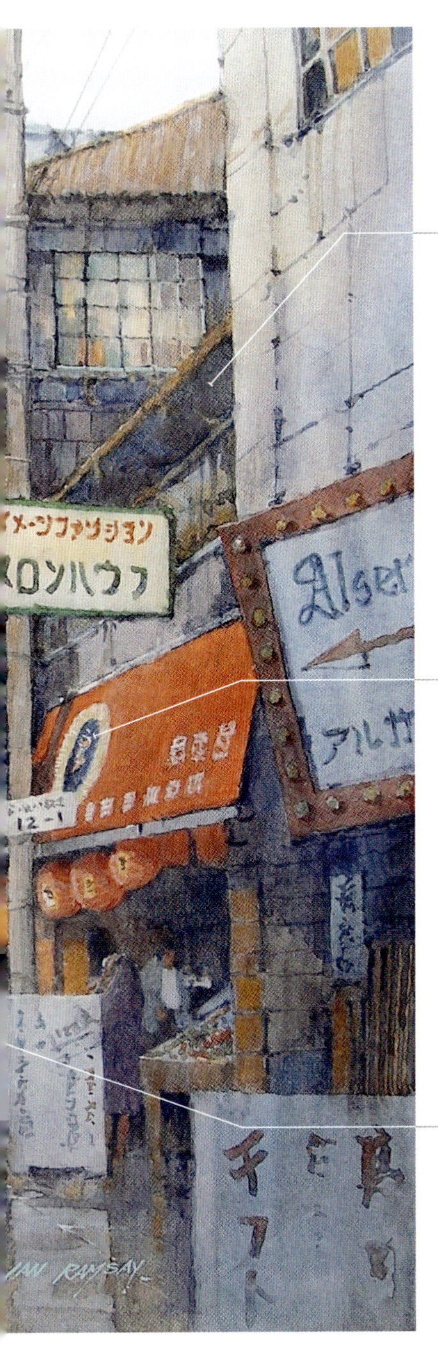

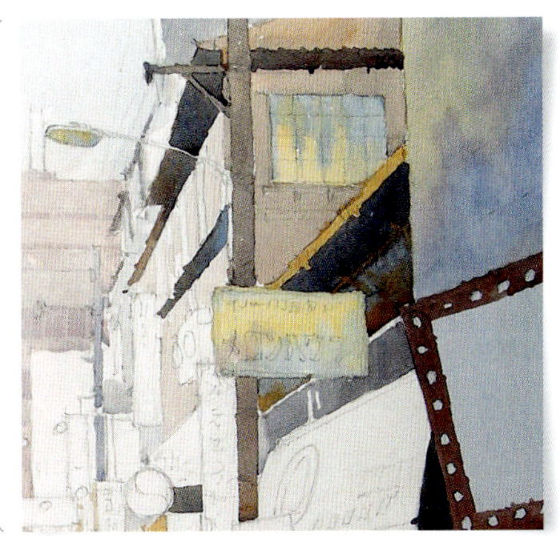

5 Add dark values

Start to add colour to some of the forms. Develop an overall warm colour scheme with cadmium red and deep scarlet for the background buildings, in contrast to cooler tones mixed with ultramarine used in the foreground. Introduce darker values to give depth and perspective, defining the buildings and some street furniture and foreground figures.

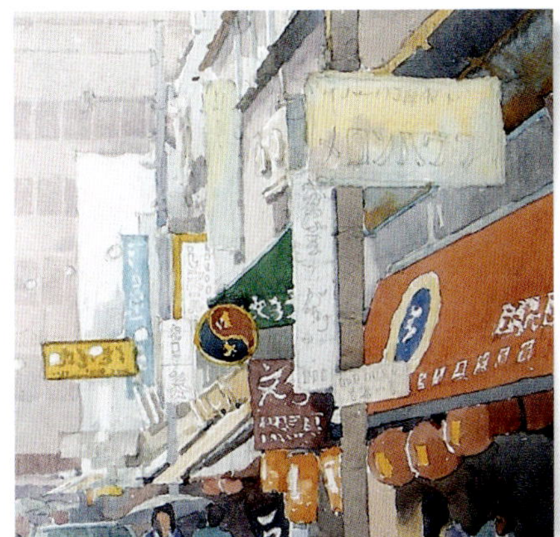

6 Define different elements

Signs, awnings, people, telephone poles, and cars are the elements that make a city scene interesting. Begin to define them, taking care to make sure they work together as a whole instead of being individual elements; carry similar colours, such as the warm tones used in the lanterns, through the painting, using round soft-hair brushes to blend the colours and bring the painting together.

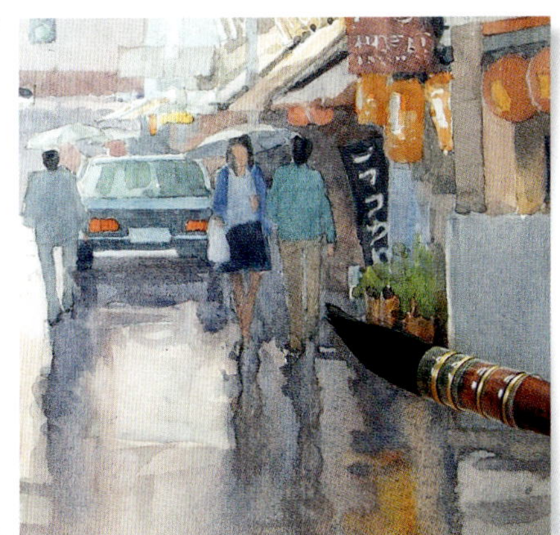

7 Final details

Add colour to all surfaces, blending the edges together with a loaded mop brush to avoid any hardness between the various features. Finish with line detail to define elements such as signage, using dark values for depth and a rigger brush for fine lines such as the electric wires. Add a little white gouache mixed with transparent watercolour to add accent and sparkle.

"Contrasts of shape and value draw the viewer into a scene. Exploit shadows cast from buildings on a sunny day or reflections on a wet street."

Buildings

RECORDING LANDMARKS AND VIEWS

Using a pared-back style to record an urban scene encourages you to simplify the view and make a feature of a particular building that may have caught your eye. Record surrounding details that provide a setting, using a simplified style filled with strong colour and outlining features for impact.

■ Sketching guidelines

Approach the scene by simplifying the elements to a shorthand, using loosely drawn and coloured local elements to provide a setting, suggesting perspective with simple lines, and sketching in details and features with a pen to add focus at the end.

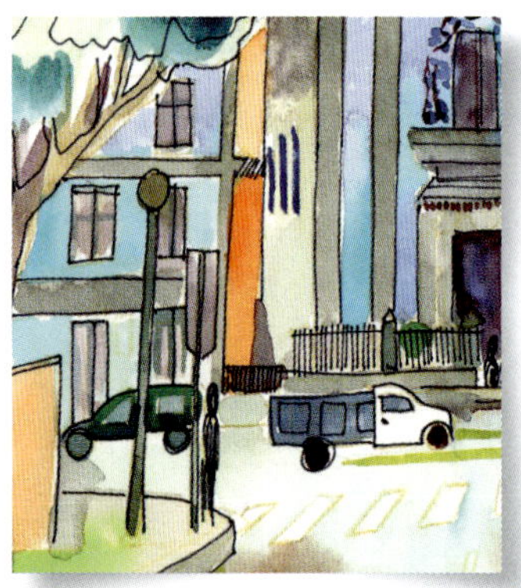

Local elements
Simply drawn figures, cars, trees, and street furniture give quick reference points for proportion and scale when setting the scene.

Perspective lines
Observe linear perspective on buildings with simple lines without being too accurate; enough to give a sense of depth.

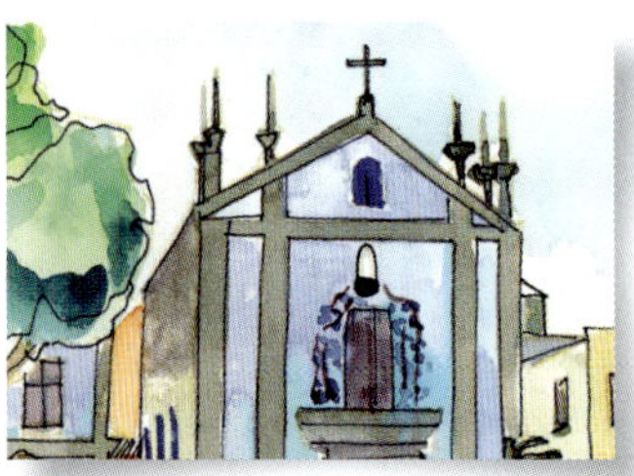

Drawn detail
To focus on your main areas of interest, render architectural features in a little more detail on top of flat washes by outlining or drawing them with a fine brush or ink pen.

PUTTING IT INTO PRACTICE

Here simple washes provide a neutral background for adding more intense tones that draw attention to the central building, where ink lines focus on details. Loosely sketched local detail sets the scene.

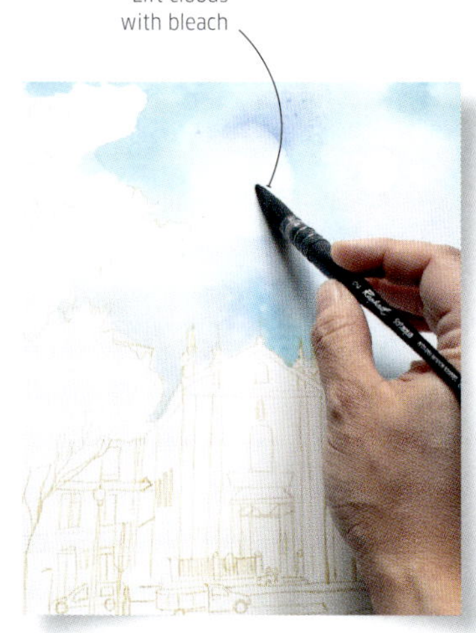

1 Neutral backdrop
Make a quick sketch of the main elements to note solid shapes, with the foreground tree framing the edge. Paint graduated washes for the sky to create a neutral backdrop.

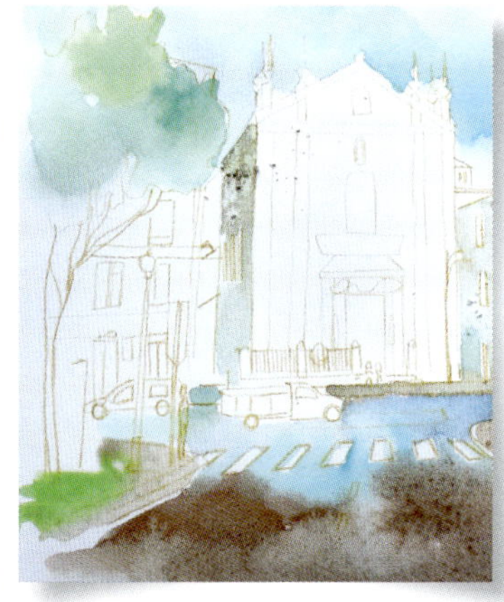

2 Initial tones
Continue to add lighter tones, keeping the same colours but adjusting the tone on each one while the painting is still wet. A warm foreground helps lead the eye down the road to the cooler blue.

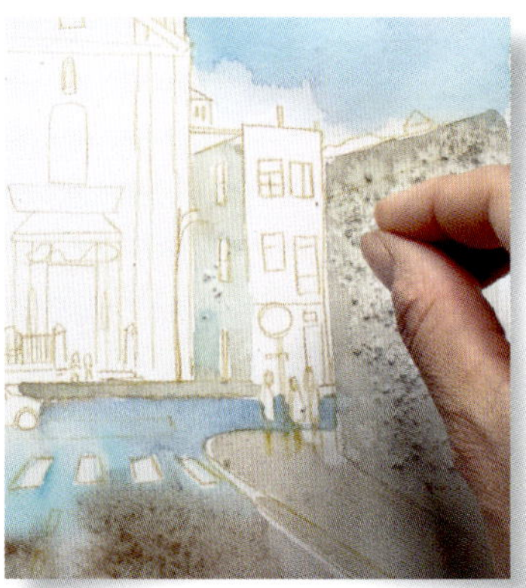

3 Urban textures
Apply grains of salt to the wet, flat wash on the side wall and road, to create the effect of urban textures of concrete and stone. Leave to dry completely before removing.

You will need

Watercolour
- Transparent orange
- Perylene violet
- Light brown
- Ultramarine blue
- Aqua green

Liquid watercolour
- Turquoise blue
- Pastel green

- No. 2 soft-hair mop brush
- No. 1 and no. 0 soft-hair round brushes
- Fineliner pen
- Bleach

- Table salt
- 30 x 20cm (12 x 8in) NOT watercolour paper 300gsm (140lb)

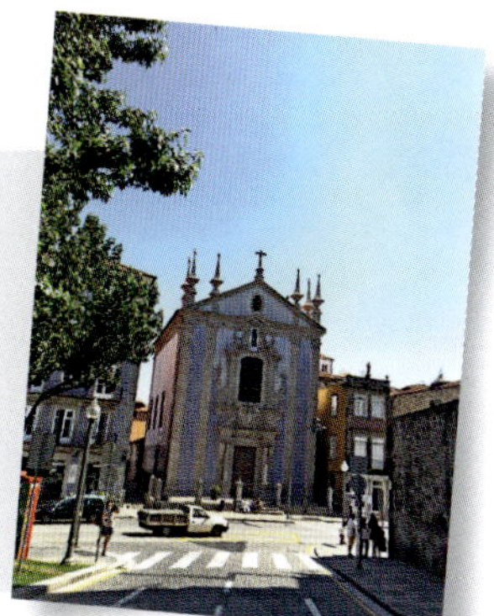

Porto, Portugal

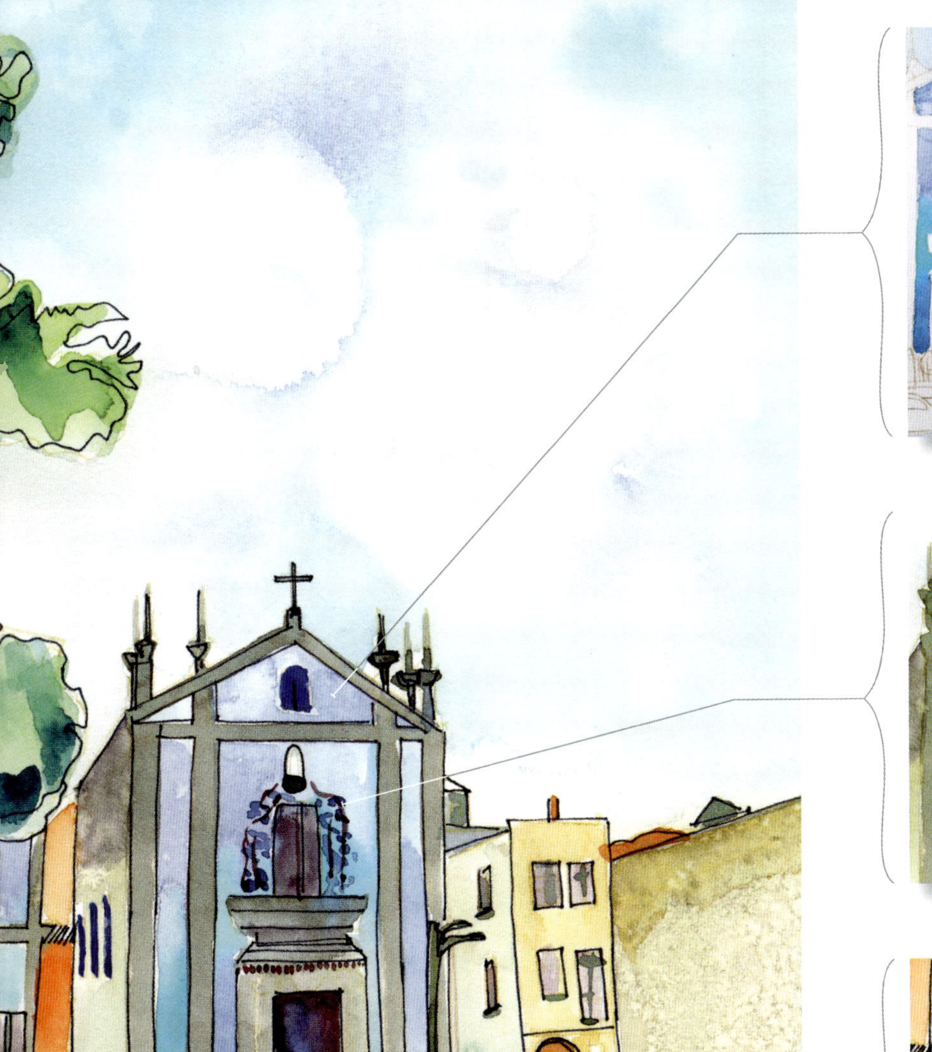

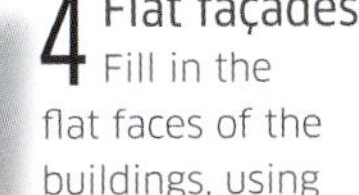

4 Flat façades

Fill in the flat faces of the buildings, using different tones for shadowed sides and overlapping some colourful washes of turquoise and ultramarine to bring interest to the main features.

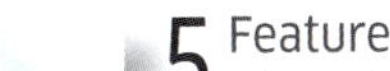

5 Features

Mix darker tones and add details over the flat washes. Use a neutral grey for stonework and rich mixes for shadows of doors and windows. Loosely suggest the ornamental surround on the church.

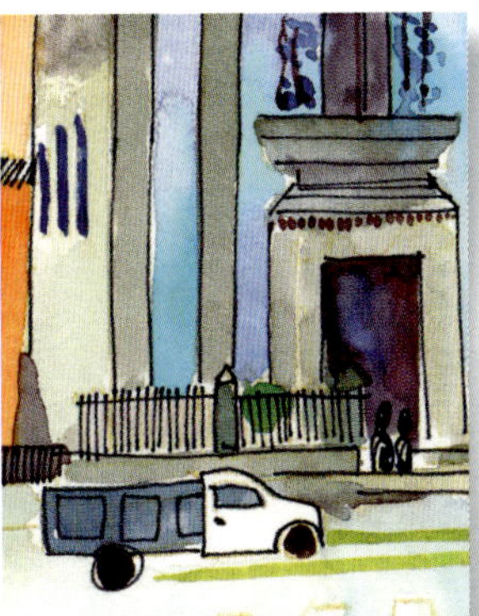

6 Final detail

Use a pen to outline architectural details and street furniture. Include local details, such as passing cars and figures, adding a sketchy, loose line to bring the tree into focus.

Urban abstract

EVOKING A LOCATION AND ATMOSPHERE

A complicated urban scene can be daunting for an inexperienced artist, but simplifying it to the point of abstraction can be an accessible and exciting approach. Working quickly and not getting drawn into too much detail will keep your painting looking dramatic. The aim is to create a sense of place that will engage the viewer without making a very representational painting.

PUTTING IT INTO PRACTICE

The essence of a moody urban landscape drawn from the imagination can be captured quickly with the use of hard-edged shapes, strong, darker colours, bold gestures, and emphatic contrasts.

You will need

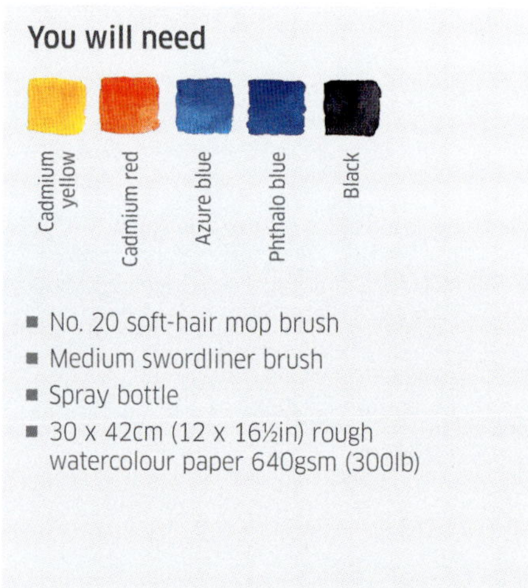

- No. 20 soft-hair mop brush
- Medium swordliner brush
- Spray bottle
- 30 x 42cm (12 x 16½in) rough watercolour paper 640gsm (300lb)

"**Dark colours and angular shapes suggest industrial areas.**"

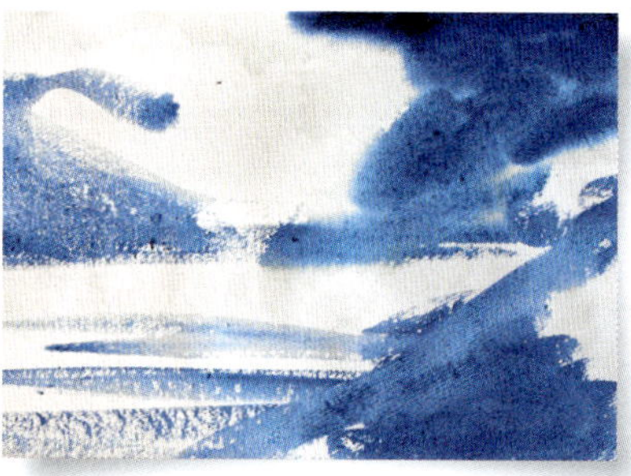

1 Block in the basics
Dampen the paper with a water spray. Decide where your horizon line will be and block in strong compositional marks with the mop brush. Trust your instincts and make some exciting marks. Use a concentrated mix of blue as it will become lighter when it dries.

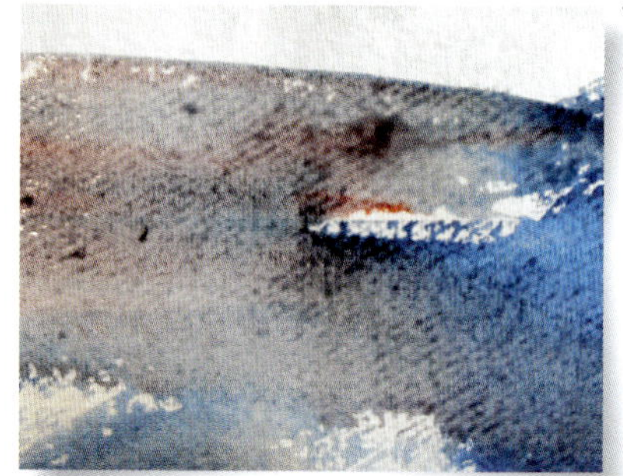

2 Let colours bleed together
Add a hint of diluted red to the blue areas, applying it loosely and keeping your brushmarks simple. Let the colours bleed together, but be sure to leave some areas of white paper.

Minimizing details

To make an abstract painting of an urban setting, reduce the amount of detail that gives definite information to the viewer. Instead, aim for ambiguity, allowing for the interpretation of the scene as the viewer wishes. Combine the basics of strong composition with diffuse edges, angular shapes that indicate buildings, and a play of lights and darks, emphasizing the latter as a way to evoke an industrial area.

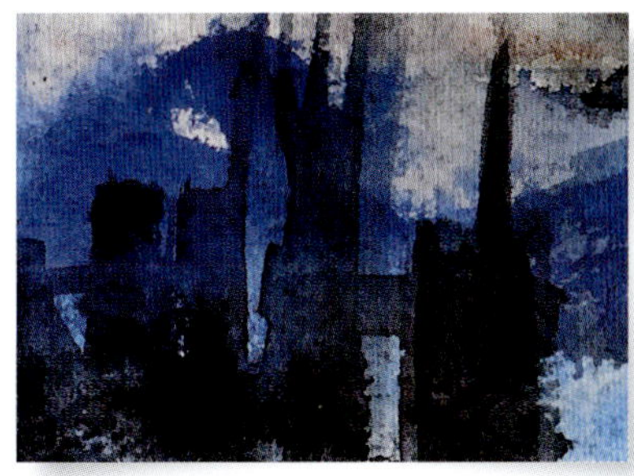

Ambiguous shapes
These shapes could be read as wooden posts, clumps of reeds, rocks, or distorted reflections of buildings; the spattering might be birds, pebbles, or water spray.

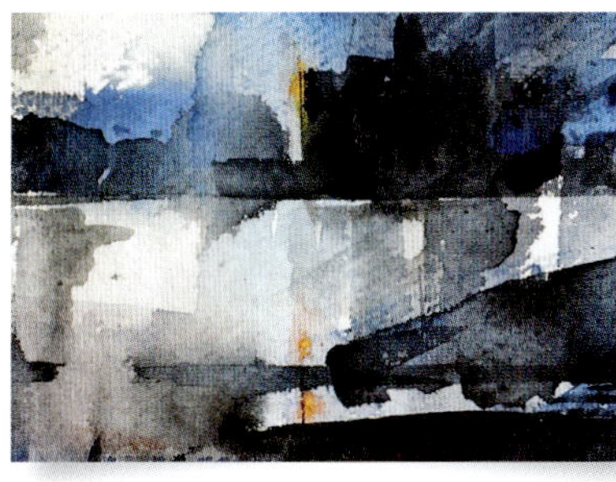

Leading the eye
Strong diagonals in the sky and buildings and the linear shapes in the foreground lead the eye to the patch of light on the water that is the focal point.

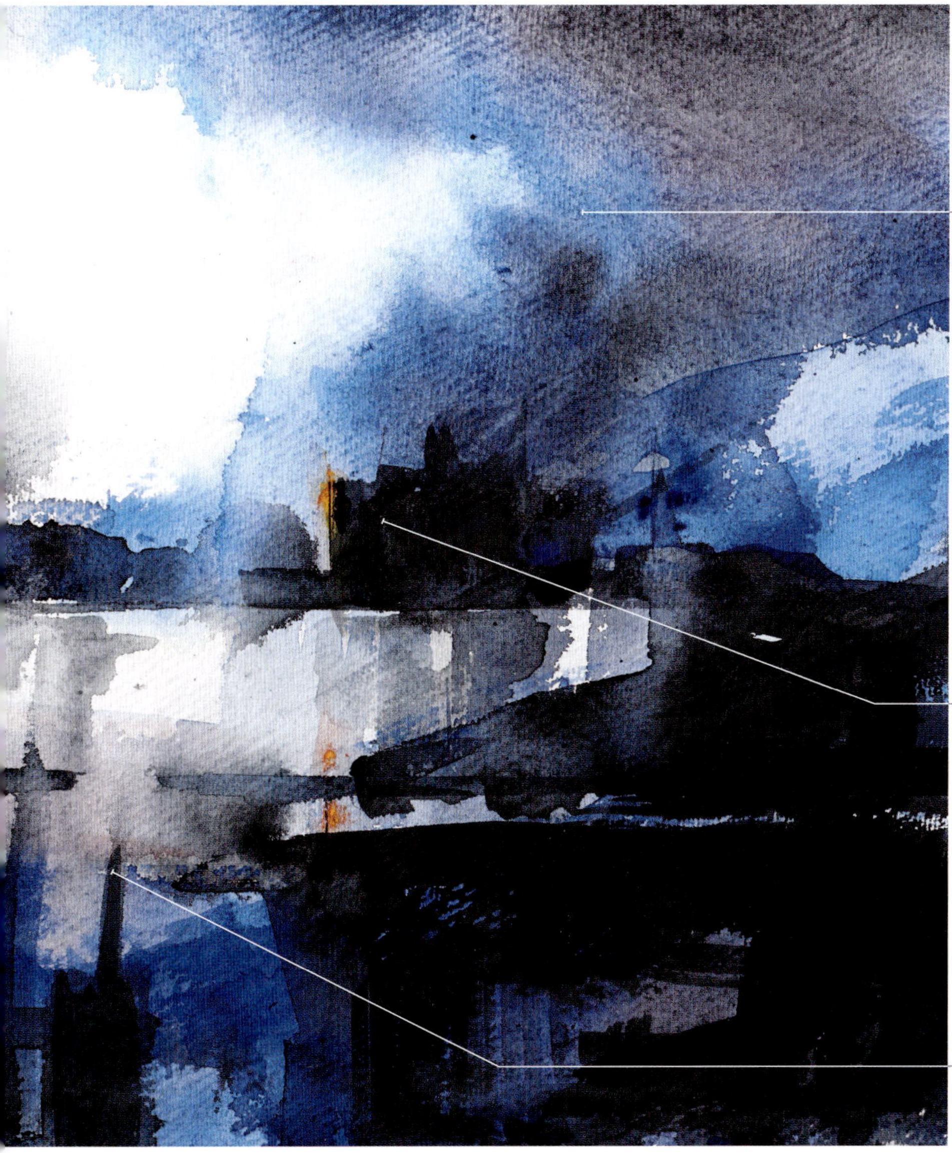

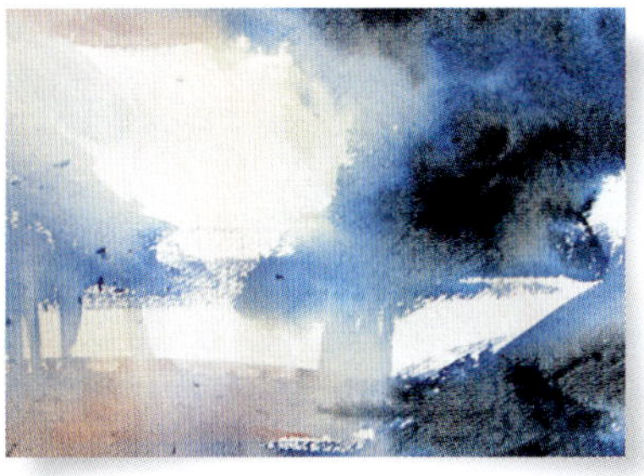

3 Add the sky
Angle your board and give the paper a spray of water from the top. Let the colours merge. Blend black into the blue, suggesting a stormy or polluted sky.

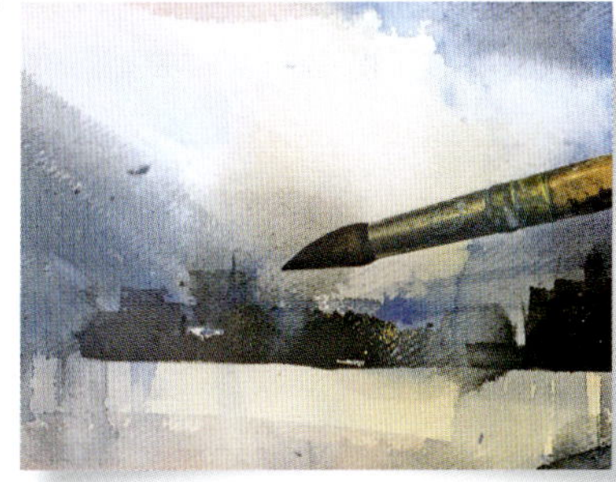

4 Indicate the buildings
When the paint has dried, suggest the buildings with strong black marks to indicate warehouses and dockland.

5 Add foreground interest
Once the paint is dry, paint a few strong blue brushstrokes over the foreground black shapes to form a more solid area. Finally, add a couple of small orange highlights.

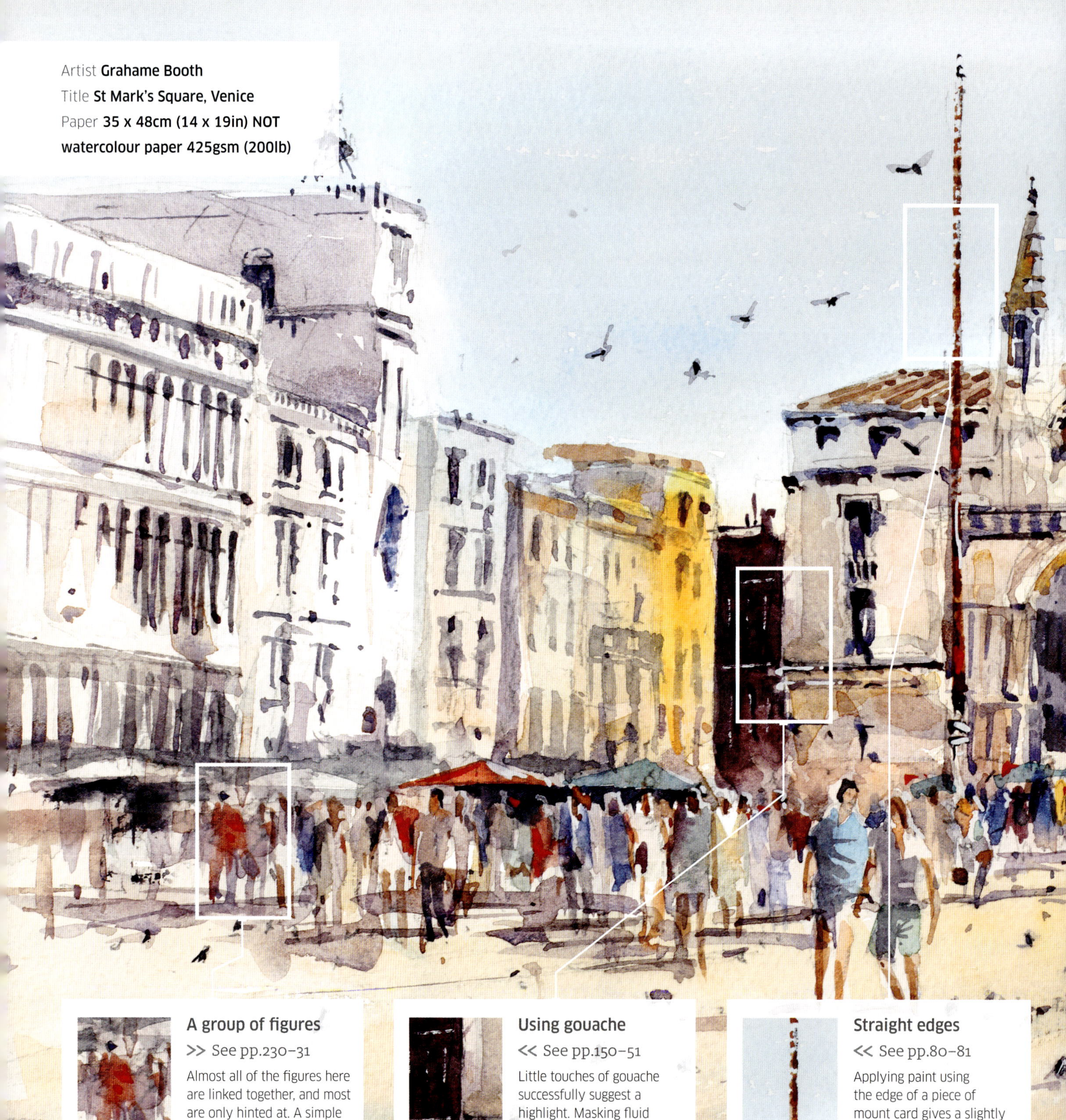

Artist **Grahame Booth**
Title **St Mark's Square, Venice**
Paper **35 x 48cm (14 x 19in) NOT**
watercolour paper 425gsm (200lb)

A group of figures

>> See pp.230–31

Almost all of the figures here are linked together, and most are only hinted at. A simple approach is always best, but the proportions must be correct for the effect to work.

Using gouache

<< See pp.150–51

Little touches of gouache successfully suggest a highlight. Masking fluid would also work, but it must be applied at the very beginning, before painting.

Straight edges

<< See pp.80–81

Applying paint using the edge of a piece of mount card gives a slightly broken straight edge, ideal for the flagpoles in this scene.

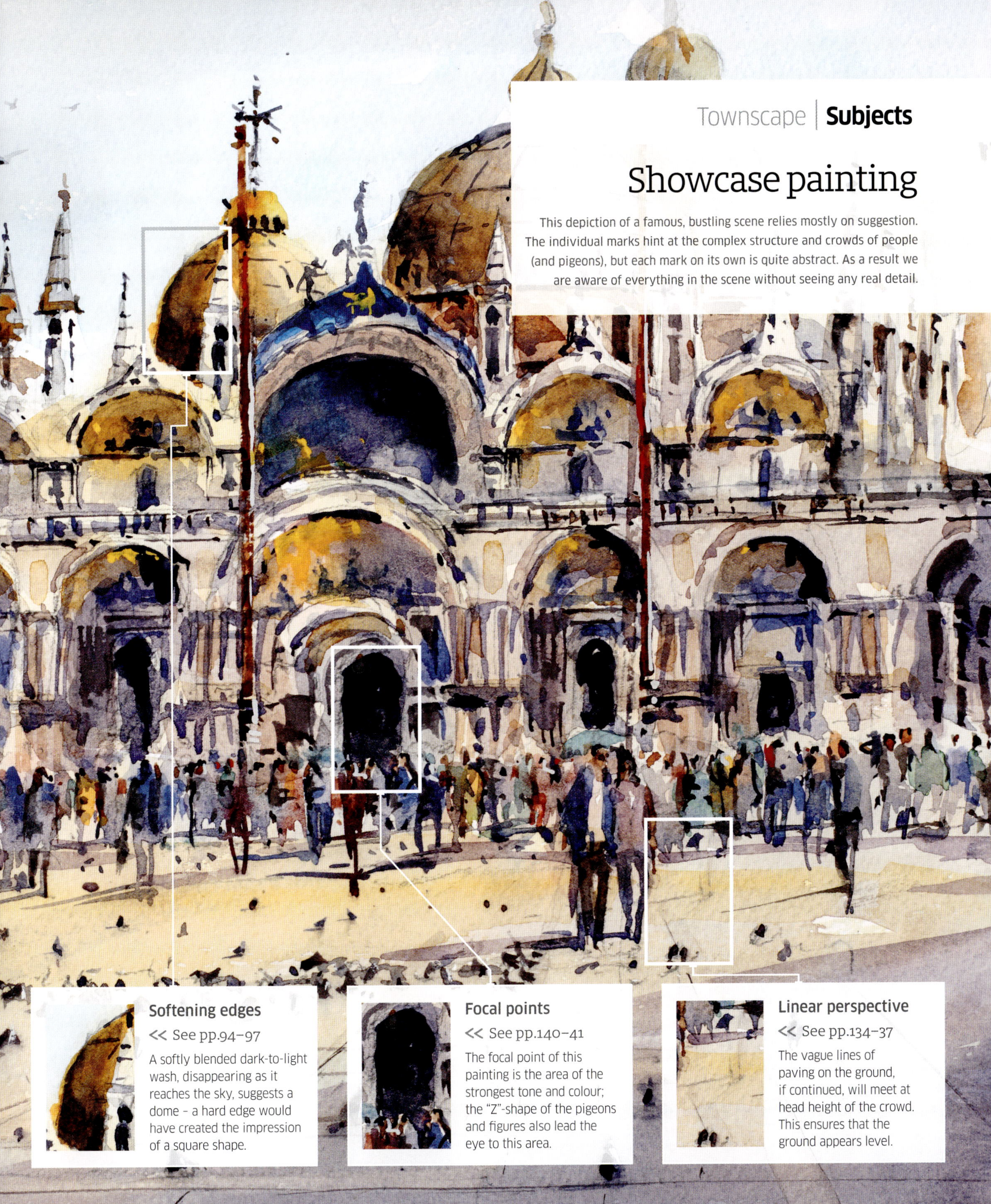

Showcase painting

This depiction of a famous, bustling scene relies mostly on suggestion. The individual marks hint at the complex structure and crowds of people (and pigeons), but each mark on its own is quite abstract. As a result we are aware of everything in the scene without seeing any real detail.

Softening edges

≪ See pp.94–97

A softly blended dark-to-light wash, disappearing as it reaches the sky, suggests a dome – a hard edge would have created the impression of a square shape.

Focal points

≪ See pp.140–41

The focal point of this painting is the area of the strongest tone and colour; the "Z"-shape of the pigeons and figures also lead the eye to this area.

Linear perspective

≪ See pp.134–37

The vague lines of paving on the ground, if continued, will meet at head height of the crowd. This ensures that the ground appears level.

Creating patterns

BUILDING A FLORAL DESIGN

A successful pattern design is one that has a continuous, seamless repetition that will flow and extend endlessly without obvious variations. Use similar shapes and colours to create fluid connections on your base tile pattern, which will become the foundation for extended repeats.

Repeating designs

To extend your watercolour tile pattern, scan or copy your artwork as many times as required, cropping the edges as close as you can so that there are no borders or empty spaces. How you position the copies will affect the repeat. Orientate each copy the same way for a simple repeat, use a half-drop position, or try a mirrored effect.

PUTTING IT INTO PRACTICE

This base tile builds in successive layers, using organic elements that are linked together with repeated shapes and colours, to create a balanced pattern that can be used in repeated designs.

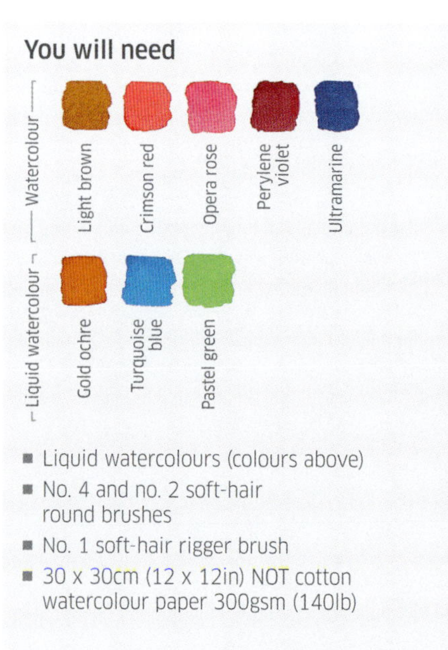

- Liquid watercolours (colours above)
- No. 4 and no. 2 soft-hair round brushes
- No. 1 soft-hair rigger brush
- 30 x 30cm (12 x 12in) NOT cotton watercolour paper 300gsm (140lb)

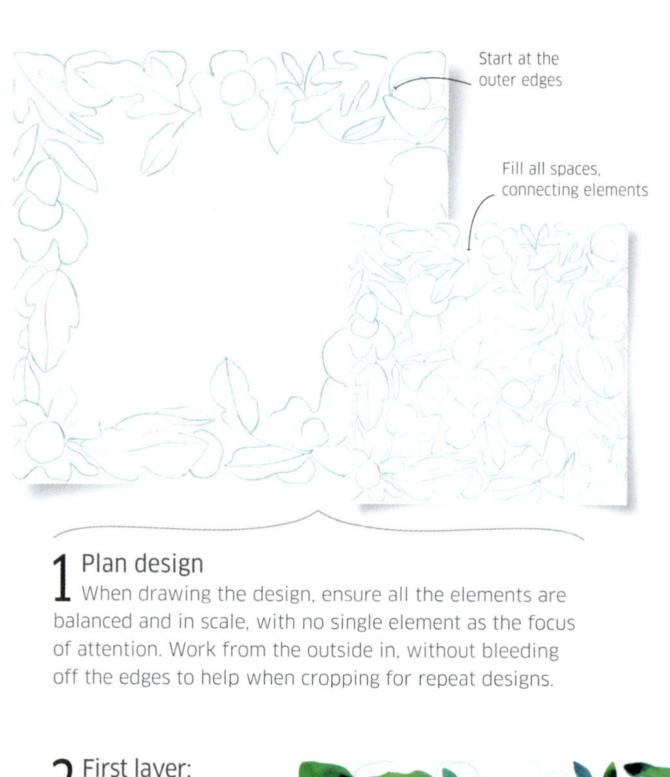

1 Plan design
When drawing the design, ensure all the elements are balanced and in scale, with no single element as the focus of attention. Work from the outside in, without bleeding off the edges to help when cropping for repeat designs.

2 First layer: foundation shapes
Start painting groups of elements by colour. Here, three tones of green are used for the first colour layer of leaves, mixing on the surface wet-in-wet. Ensure that the colours and shapes are evenly distributed across the whole tile.

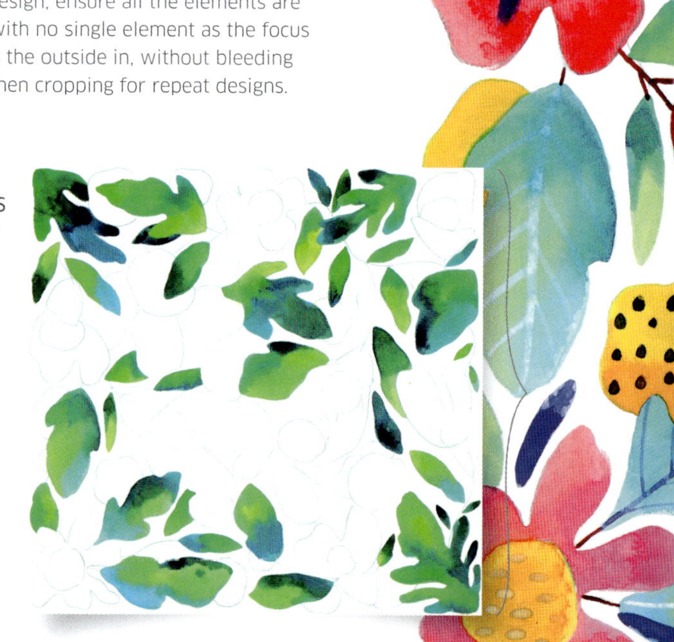

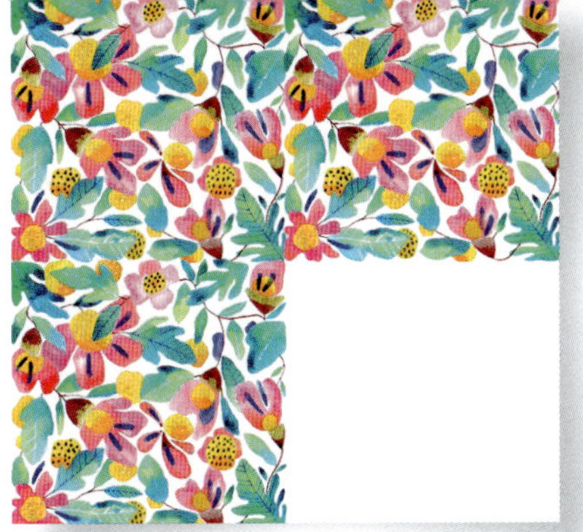

Simple repeat
Place your copies in pairs in the same orientation without any spaces in between. Work in rows, ensuring corners meet neatly.

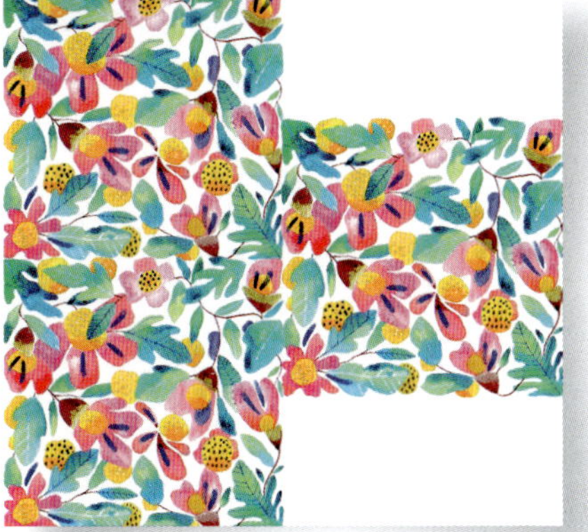

Half-drop repeat
Position two copies together vertically, align the mid-point of the third copy at the horizontal join. Add copies above and below.

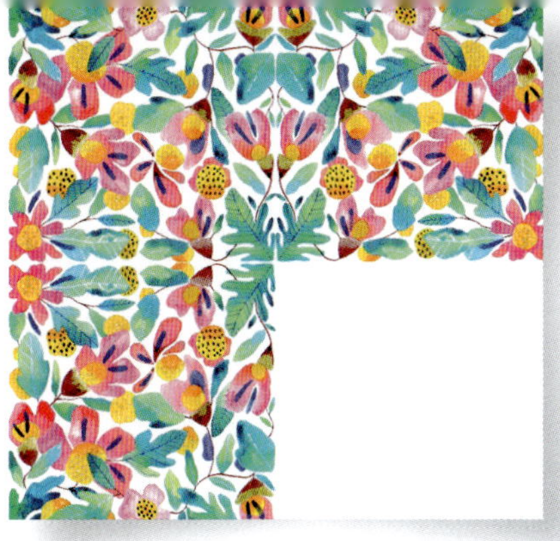

Mirrored repeat
This is similar to a simple repeat but turn each copy so that the same corner meets in the centre, creating a symmetrical design.

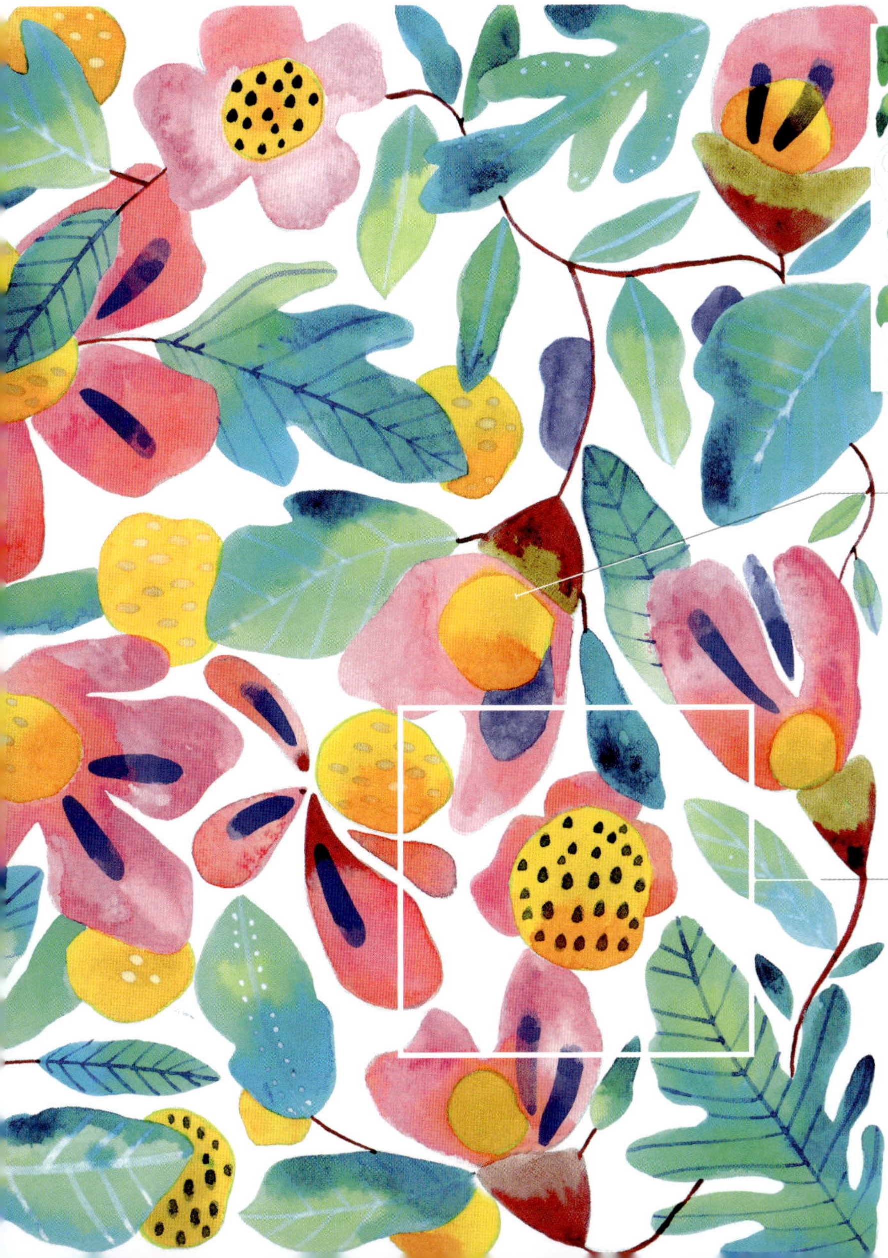

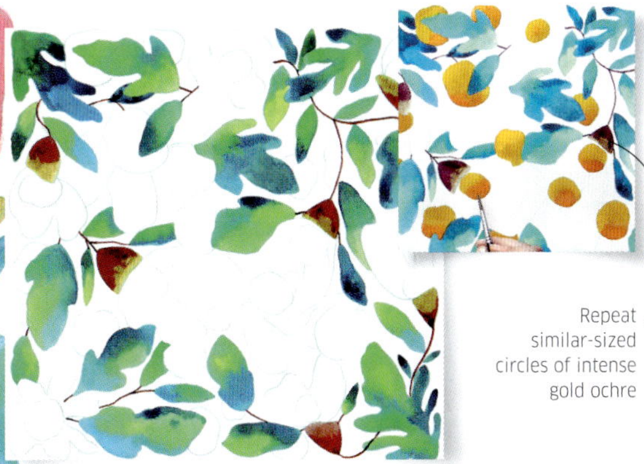

Repeat similar-sized circles of intense gold ochre

3 Second layer: connections
Mix two tones of brown from light brown and perylene violet for the tendrils that connect the flowers and help create harmony between the elements. Don't vary shapes too much; repetition is key to pattern making.

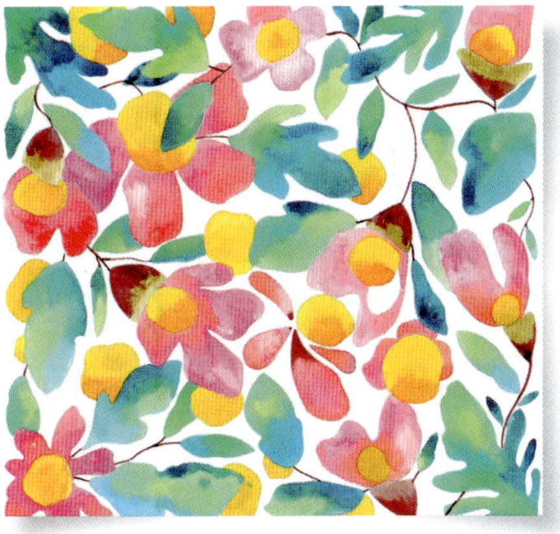

4 Third layer: balance colour
Use intense mixes of pink and red for the petals and carry the colour across the pattern to maintain the balance. Add details with lines and dots and overlap some new elements.

Still life shadows

USING LIGHT AND TRANSPARENCY

When composing a still life, think about the effect of lighting; the strength, direction, and brightness of a light source will create shadows that help to give a sense of space and realism. The transparent nature of watercolour lends itself to delicate shadows, blending fleeting edges of light with colours and tones from the solid objects.

■ Working with shadow effects

In most still life set-ups you will need to consider not only the balance of solid objects but also the effects of shadows in the overall composition. Shadows add depth and help to anchor objects to the surface. Look at shadows carefully, thinking about their placement, shape, and colour.

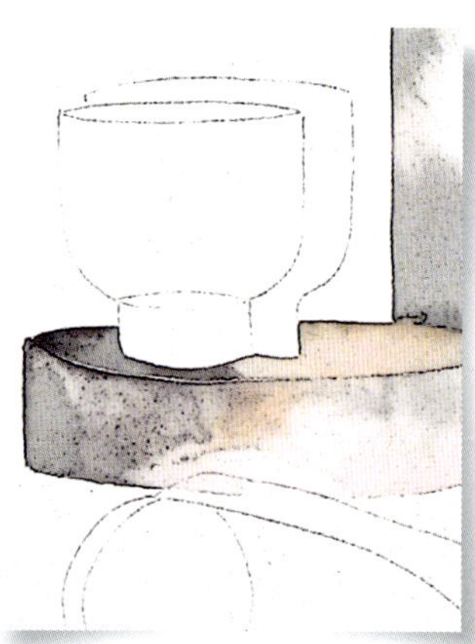

Plan ahead

Establish areas of darker tone or shade to give shape to solid objects, ensuring that you leave highlights. Sketch in the outlines of cast shadows, mirroring the shape of the object and checking that the angle of the shadow is consistent.

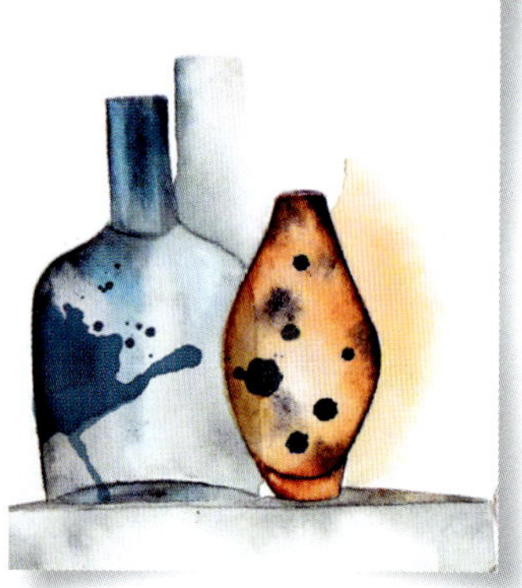

Shadow colour and shape

Observe shadow colours, as they often contain muted tones of the main object. Use a diluted wash to reflect the shape of the object in its cast shadow, noting the direction and source of light. If lit from the side, shadows will fall at oblique angles; overhead light creates short shadows. The vertical shadows seen here suggest a flat backdrop.

PUTTING IT INTO PRACTICE

By keeping the shadows consistent you can create a convincing still life from a fabricated set-up. In this still life, coloured glass creates shadows in muted shades that are reflected onto a white backdrop, mirroring the varied shapes of the vases.

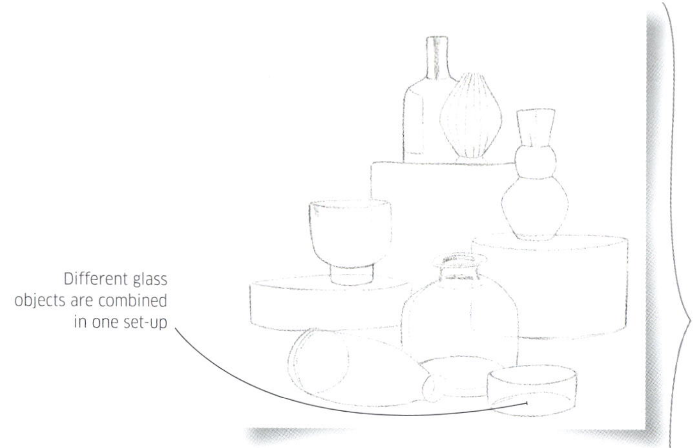

Different glass objects are combined in one set-up

1 Plan the composition

You can create a still-life composition using found images. Here, the two pink vases inspired a still life that was set up as a photo montage of glass objects. Transfer the outlines of the composition to your watercolour paper.

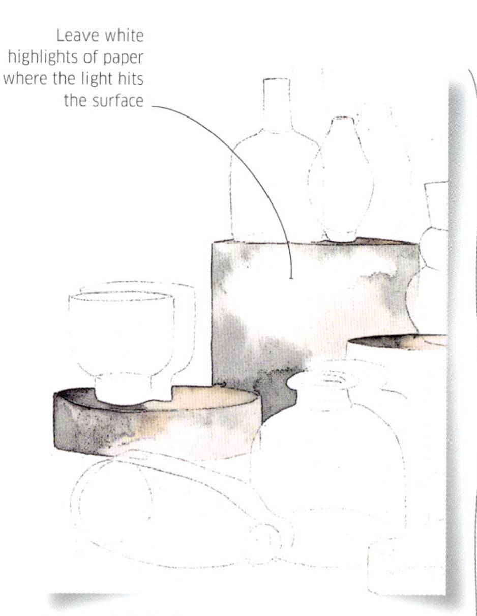

Leave white highlights of paper where the light hits the surface

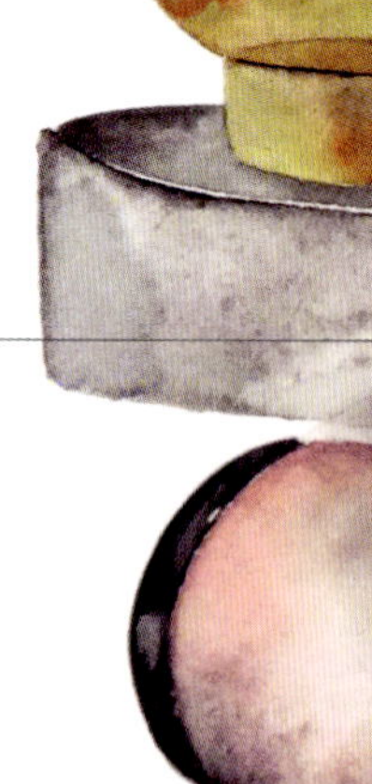

2 Establish background shapes

Establish the solid shapes that are the background for the glass objects. Wet the areas of the plinths and fill them with a light, medium grey tone with a no. 6 brush.

You will need

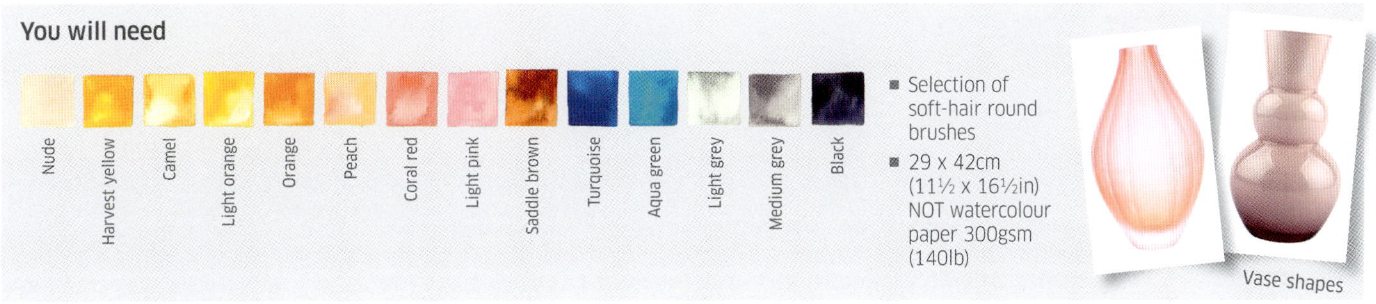

Nude · Harvest yellow · Camel · Light orange · Orange · Peach · Coral red · Light pink · Saddle brown · Turquoise · Aqua green · Light grey · Medium grey · Black

- Selection of soft-hair round brushes
- 29 x 42cm (11½ x 16½in) NOT watercolour paper 300gsm (140lb)

Vase shapes

Splattered colour adds visual interest to the solid forms of the vases

Transparent wash bleeds at the edges into wet paper for muted tones

3 Transparent colour

Fill the shapes of the vases in different colours, using transparent washes to vary the tones and represent the translucent surface. Where objects overlap, ensure one wash is dry to maintain crisp edges.

4 Add shadows

Using a lighter, transparent tone of the coloured glass, apply the shapes of the shadows, keeping the wash darker close to the object and letting it soften and lighten towards the outside.

Aged surfaces

FOCUSSING ON TEXTURE

The appeal of painting still lifes is that you can select your subject matter, bringing together objects that have a common theme. When focussing on texture, draw on different techniques to produce a painting that is visually exciting, with sedimentary pigments, granulation medium, and salt to convey your subject without painstakingly painting every detail. Use these methods for many subjects, from metal to fur.

PUTTING IT INTO PRACTICE

For this still life of rusty and mossy objects, grainy pigment represents the aged surface, with saturated salt applied to add real surface texture. Dry brush marks contrast with smooth blends.

You will need

Lemon yellow · Cadmium red · Burnt sienna · Cerulean blue · Cobalt turquoise light · Ultramarine blue

Granulating — Piemontite genuine · Shadow violet · Cobalt blue · Lunar blue · Green apatite genuine

- No. 18, no. 10, and no. 6 soft-hair round brushes
- Granulation medium
- Salt wash of 50:50 salt to water
- 26 x 38cm (10½ x 15in) rough watercolour paper 300gsm (140lb)

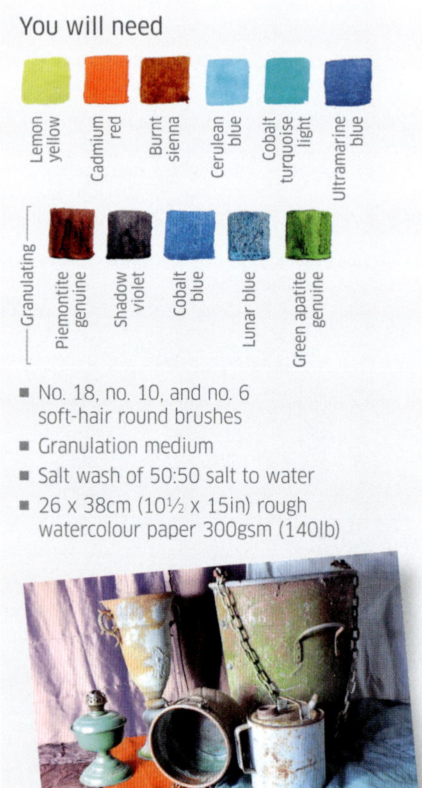
Patinated textures

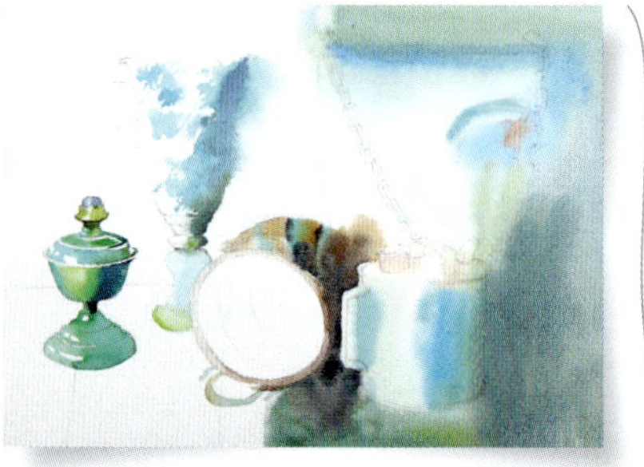

1 Highlight underpainting

Paint the highlights that you want to retain, using large, transparent, overlapping washes for the brightest surfaces. For the rusted edges, use dry brush marks (see pp.56–57) and granulating pigments such as cobalt to introduce texture. Mix green and violet granulating pigments for the algae effect.

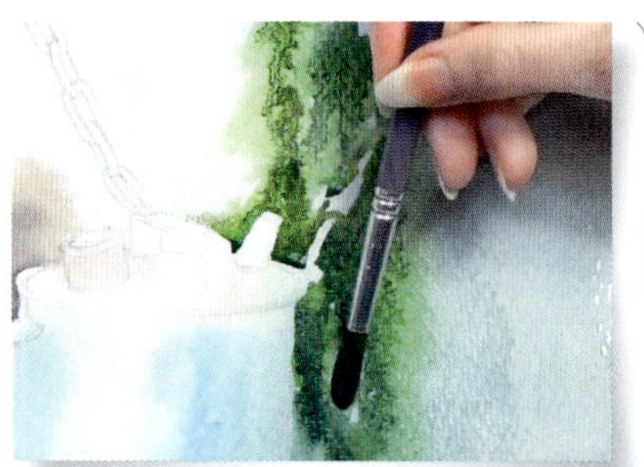

2 Encourage granulation

When the underpainting is dry, apply a wash of clear granulation medium over the areas of algae. While still wet, add granulating pigments with more medium, painting with a loaded brush at a vertical angle. Encourage rivulets to run freely.

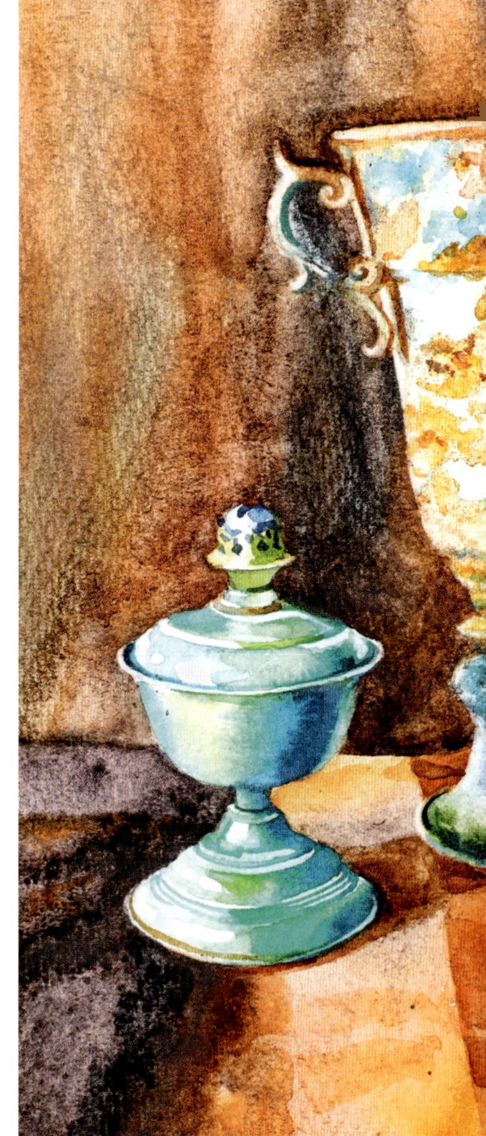

Controlling textures

By combining granulating pigments (see pp.90–91) with granulation medium or salt, you can intensify or manipulate the effects to create some unique patterns, such as free flowing rivulets. Plan your palette to include pigments that separate, and match them to your subject and the textures that you wish to convey. A salt wash attracts pigment to look grainy, which differs from the light, mottled effects of using dry salt (see p.148).

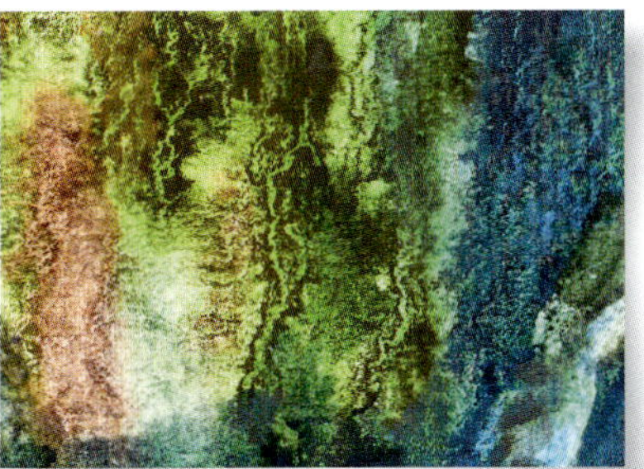

Rivulets and runs
Apply granulation medium to the underpainting. Then slowly dribble granulation medium and granulating pigments down the surface for rivulets.

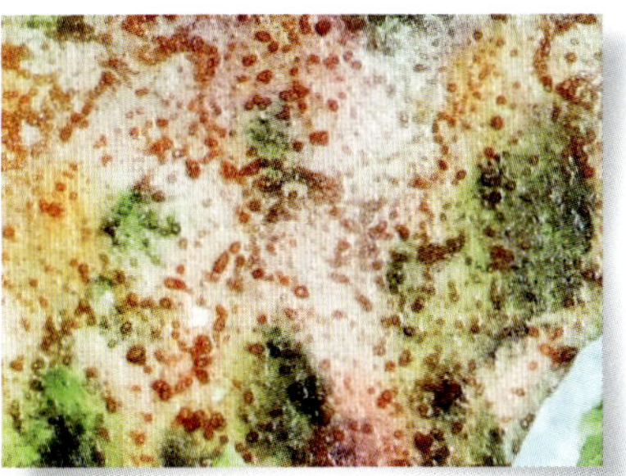

Salt wash
Mix 50:50 salt and water and apply as a clear wash. Drop strong pigment into the wash before it dries. The pigment and salt combine for a textured effect.

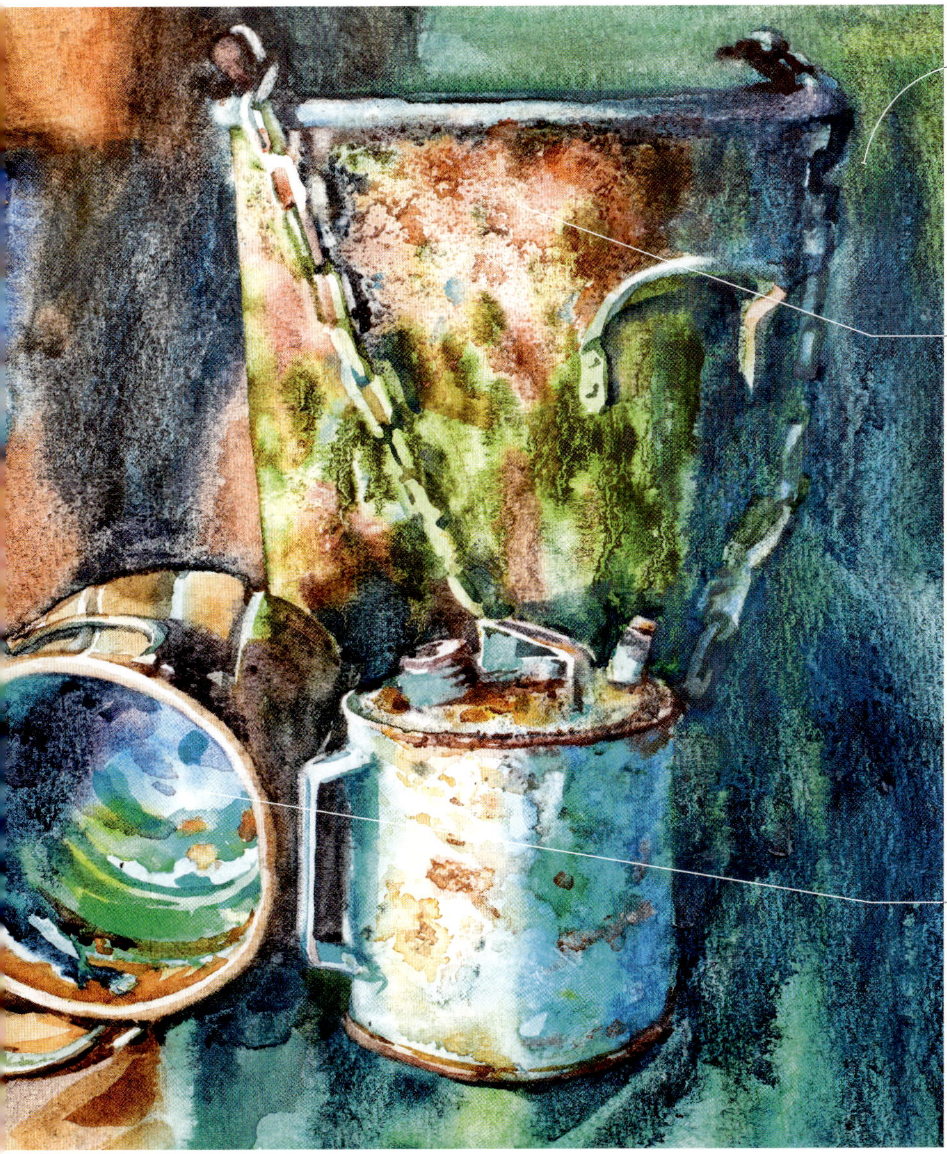

The texture of the rough paper holds pigment that adds to the overall effect

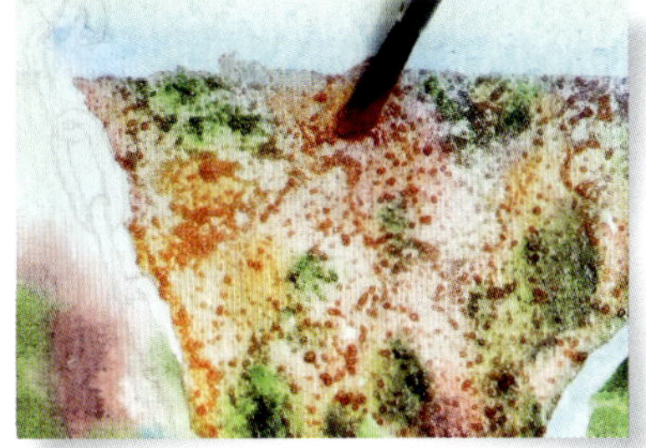

3 Apply salt wash
Once your rivulets have dried, scoop up a thick quantity of saturated salt onto your brush and apply it with the salt water to the rusty areas. Quickly add plenty of burnt sienna in blobs to this area; it will appear lighter as the pigment is drawn to the salt grains.

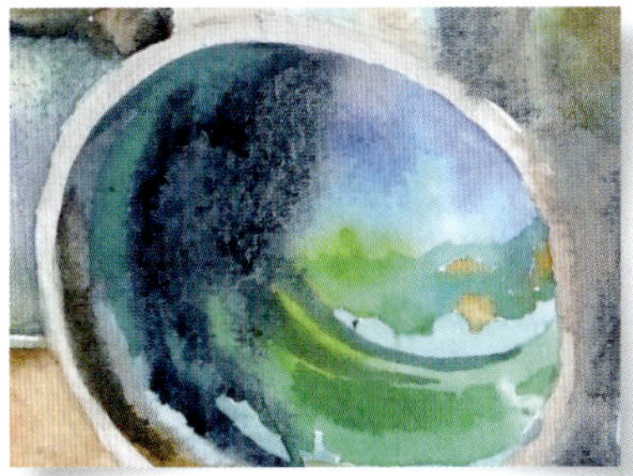

4 Smooth contrasts
While working on the rusty texture, keep other parts smooth for contrast, working wet-on-dry for the lamp base. Add the background, keeping the textures simple in order not to detract from the main focal points.

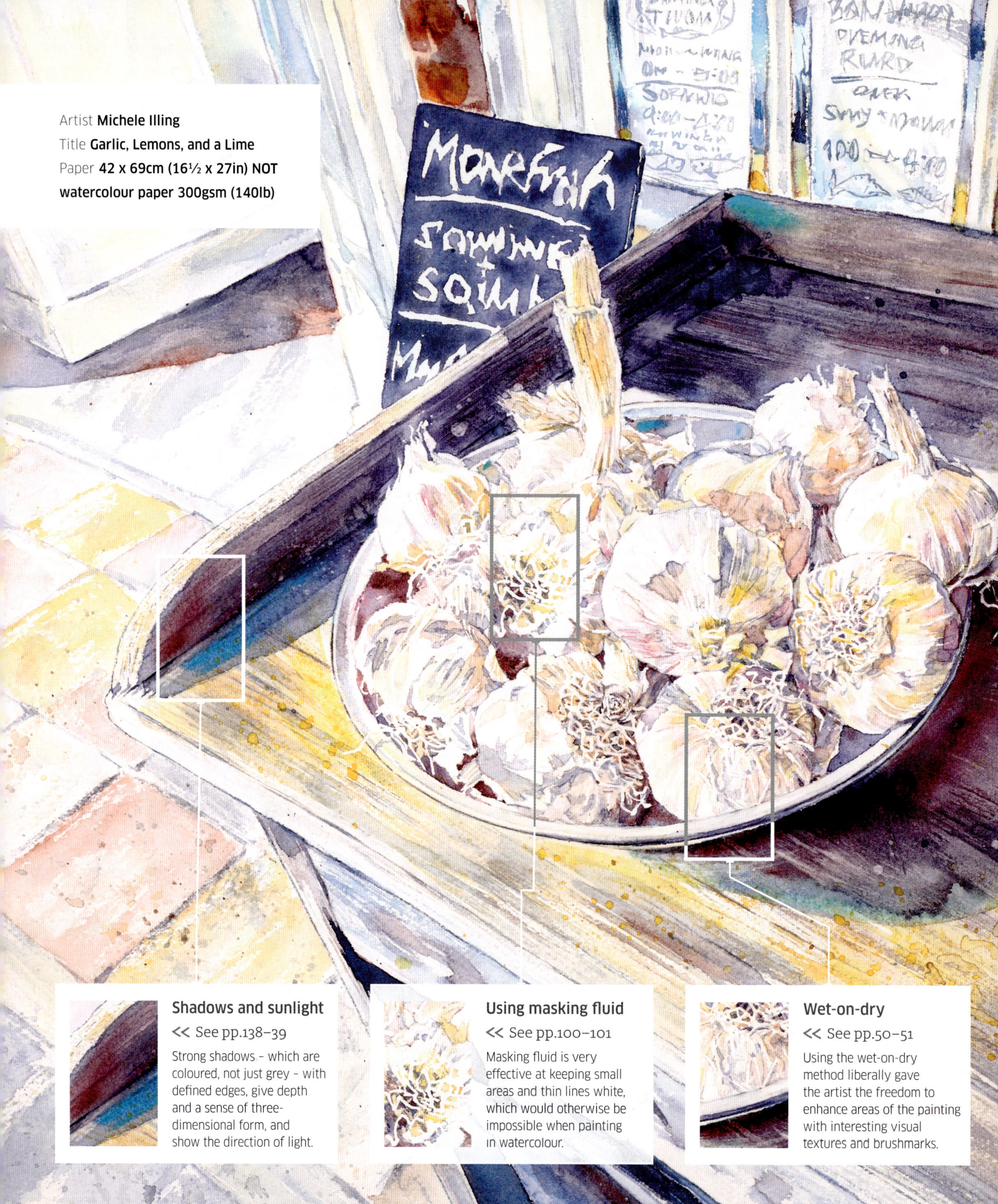

Artist **Michele Illing**
Title **Garlic, Lemons, and a Lime**
Paper **42 x 69cm (16½ x 27in) NOT**
watercolour paper 300gsm (140lb)

Shadows and sunlight
<< See pp.138–39
Strong shadows – which are coloured, not just grey – with defined edges, give depth and a sense of three-dimensional form, and show the direction of light.

Using masking fluid
<< See pp.100–101
Masking fluid is very effective at keeping small areas and thin lines white, which would otherwise be impossible when painting in watercolour.

Wet-on-dry
<< See pp.50–51
Using the wet-on-dry method liberally gave the artist the freedom to enhance areas of the painting with interesting visual textures and brushmarks.

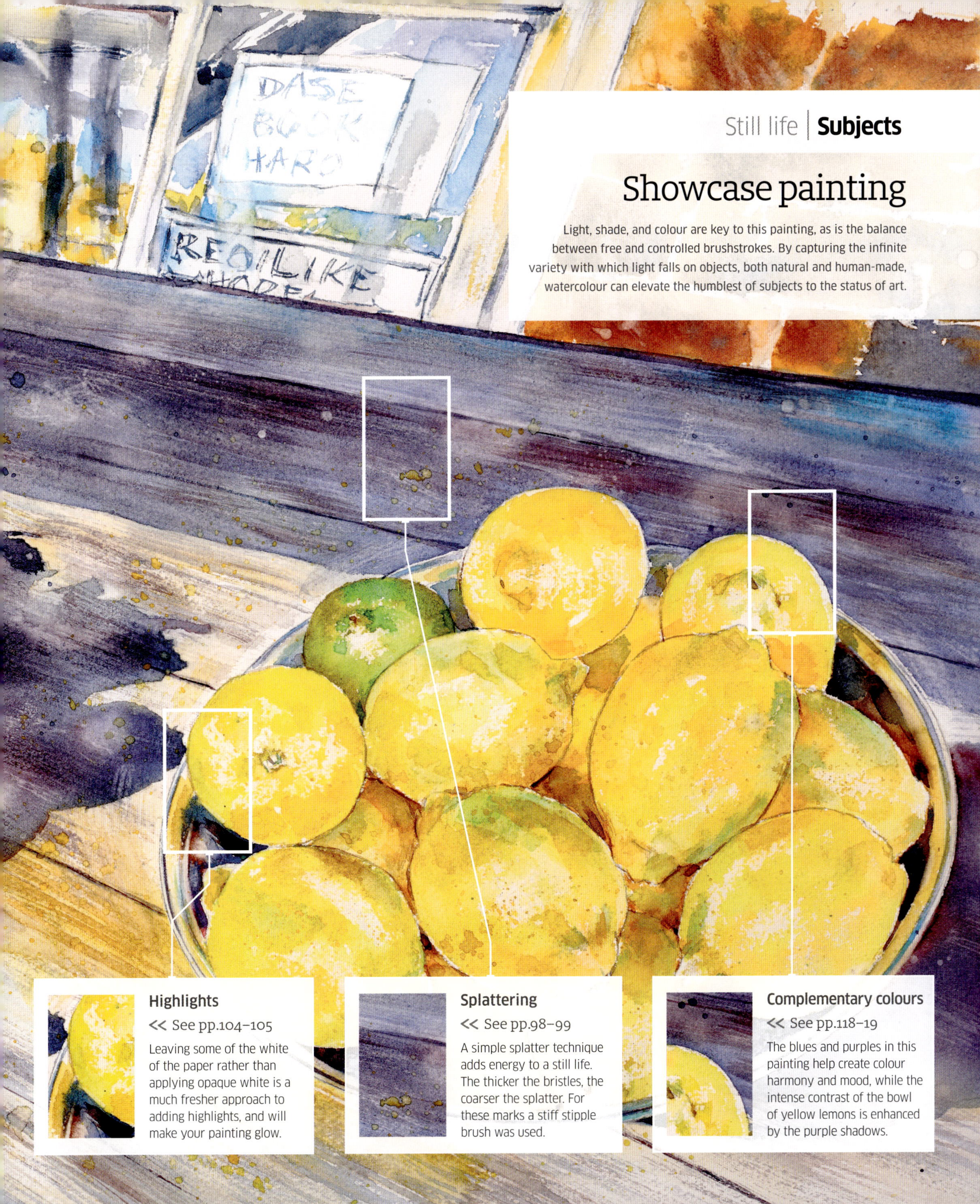

Showcase painting

Light, shade, and colour are key to this painting, as is the balance between free and controlled brushstrokes. By capturing the infinite variety with which light falls on objects, both natural and human-made, watercolour can elevate the humblest of subjects to the status of art.

Highlights

« See pp.104–105

Leaving some of the white of the paper rather than applying opaque white is a much fresher approach to adding highlights, and will make your painting glow.

Splattering

« See pp.98–99

A simple splatter technique adds energy to a still life. The thicker the bristles, the coarser the splatter. For these marks a stiff stipple brush was used.

Complementary colours

« See pp.118–19

The blues and purples in this painting help create colour harmony and mood, while the intense contrast of the bowl of yellow lemons is enhanced by the purple shadows.

Botanical painting

DEPICTING PLANT LIFE ACCURATELY

Sitting somewhere between art and science, botanical art serves both faculties. The botanical illustrator not only depicts the form, colour, and botanical structure of a plant as accurately as possible, but also paints with artistic expression.

▨ Beautifully accurate

Build up layers gradually, starting with the lighter tones and working to darker ones. Successive washes help to create the form of the flower and give a luminosity to the piece. As well as using delicate wet-in-wet brushwork, a drier brush technique (little paint, little water) is best for adding details and darker shadows.

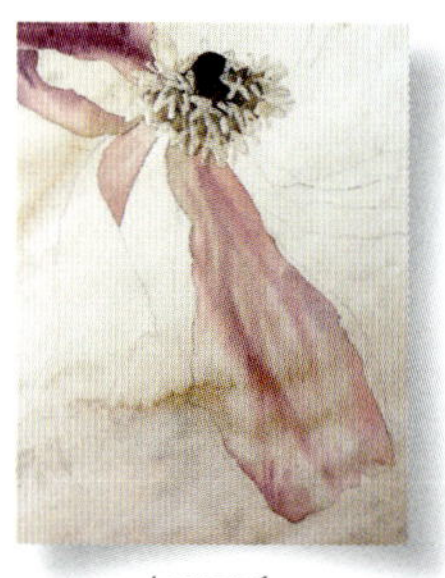

Layer 1

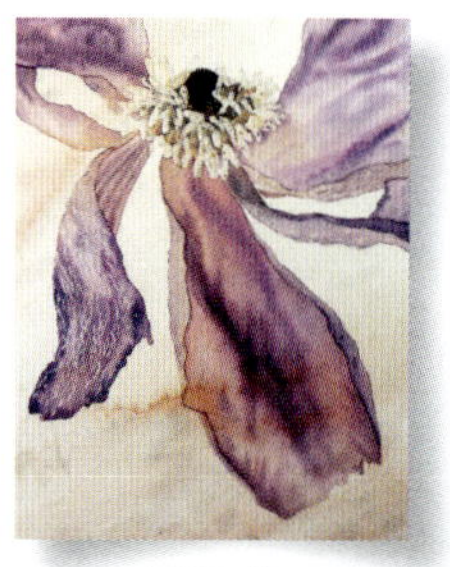

Layer 2

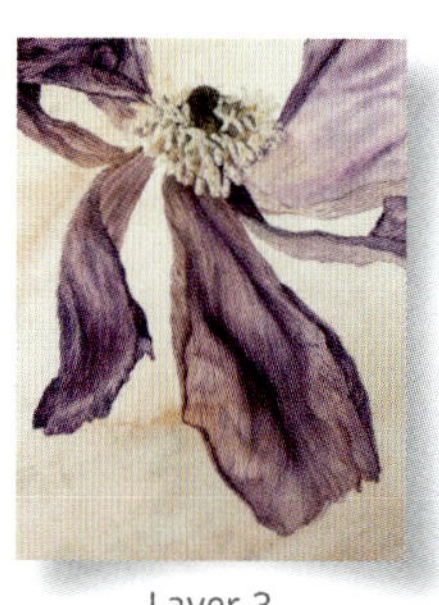

Layer 3

Layer upon layer

Build up rich colours over several carefully applied layers of wet-in-wet washes. Allow each layer to dry completely before applying the next one. This repeated sequence creates form and strengthens colour.

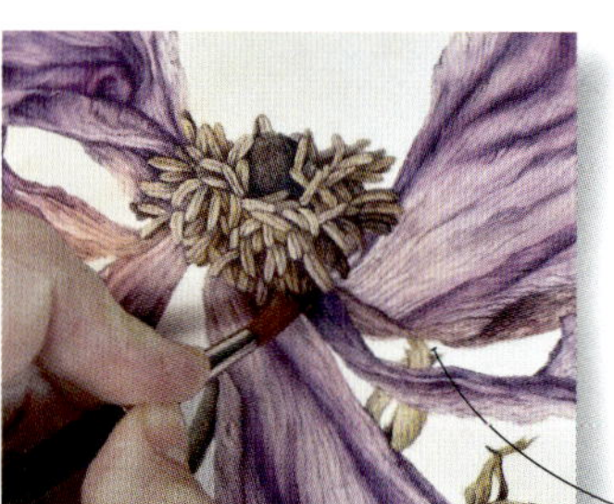

A drier brush works best for details

Darker details

Highlight detail or deepen shadows with a drier brush. Pick up small amounts of drying paint on the tip of your brush or switch to a smaller brush.

PUTTING IT INTO PRACTICE

A moment in time is captured in this study of a fading anemone flower. Such detailed work demands a smooth surface, so a hot-pressed watercolour paper works better than a more textured paper.

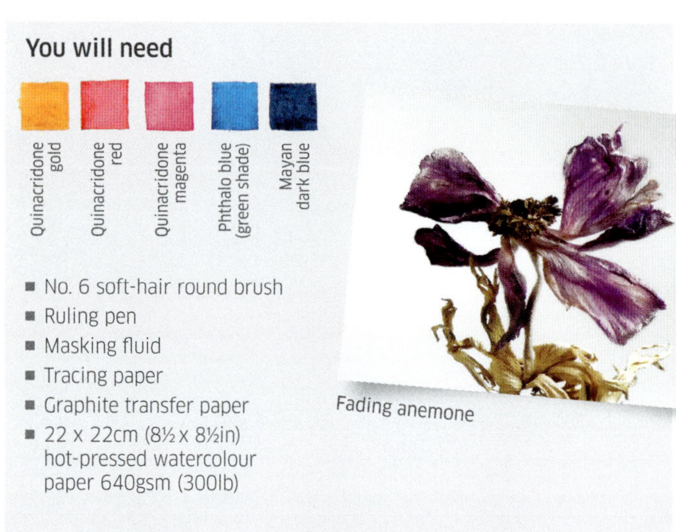

You will need

Quinacridone gold

Quinacridone red

Quinacridone magenta

Phthalo blue (green shade)

Mayan dark blue

- No. 6 soft-hair round brush
- Ruling pen
- Masking fluid
- Tracing paper
- Graphite transfer paper
- 22 x 22cm (8½ x 8½in) hot-pressed watercolour paper 640gsm (300lb)

Fading anemone

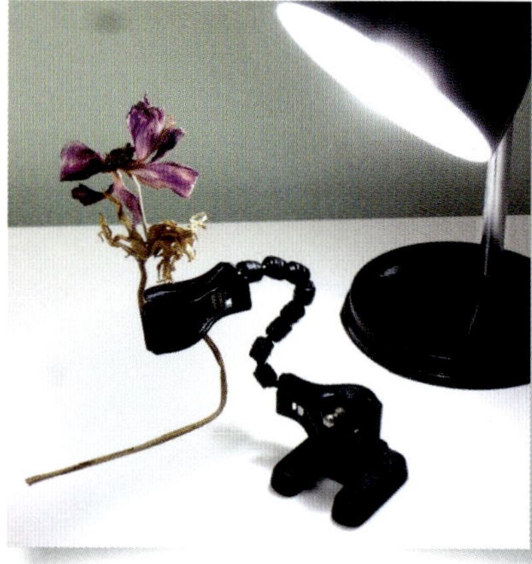

1 Posing the subject

Position the main light source in front of the subject but to one side. A secondary light on the other side will act as a back light to enhance the translucence of the papery petals.

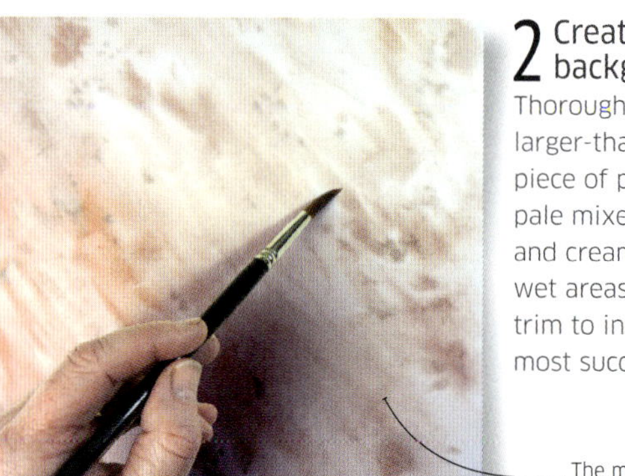

2 Creating the background

Thoroughly wet a larger-than-needed piece of paper. Dab pale mixes of browns and creams into the wet areas. Once dry, trim to include the most successful area.

The mottled appearance echoes fading book pages

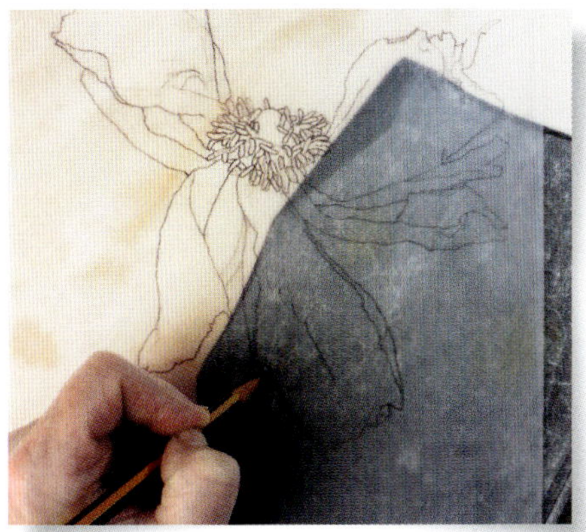

3 Transfer the drawing
Working alongside the specimen, draw the flower larger than life size onto tracing paper. Transfer using graphite transfer paper.

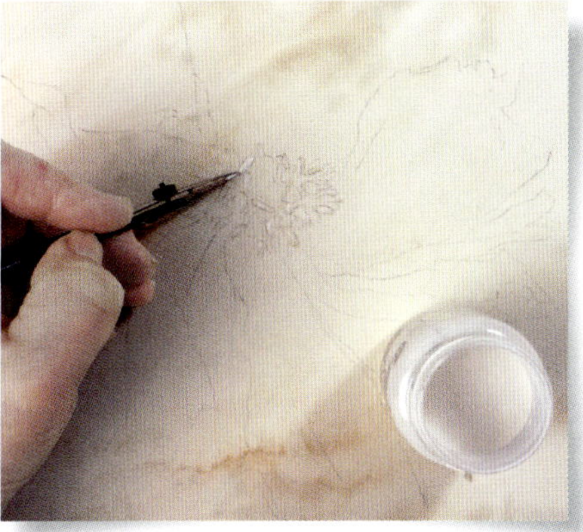

4 Protect lighter areas
Apply masking fluid to the central stamens with a ruling pen. Once dry, you can safely wash over the masked shapes to create depth.

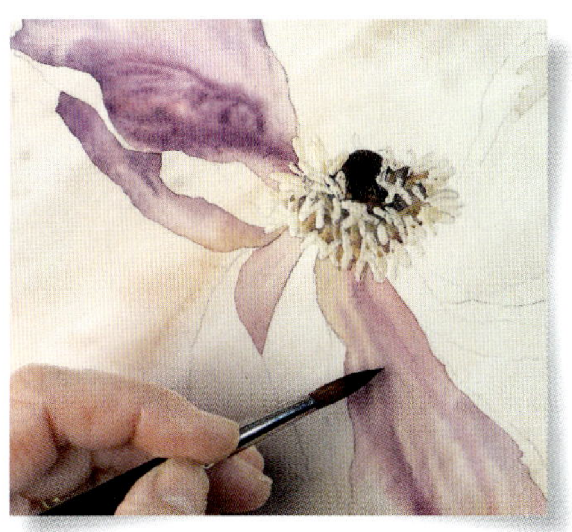

5 The wet-in-wet washes
Wet the whole shape then dab colour to create the underlying undulations and forms on one petal at a time. Watch out for dryness.

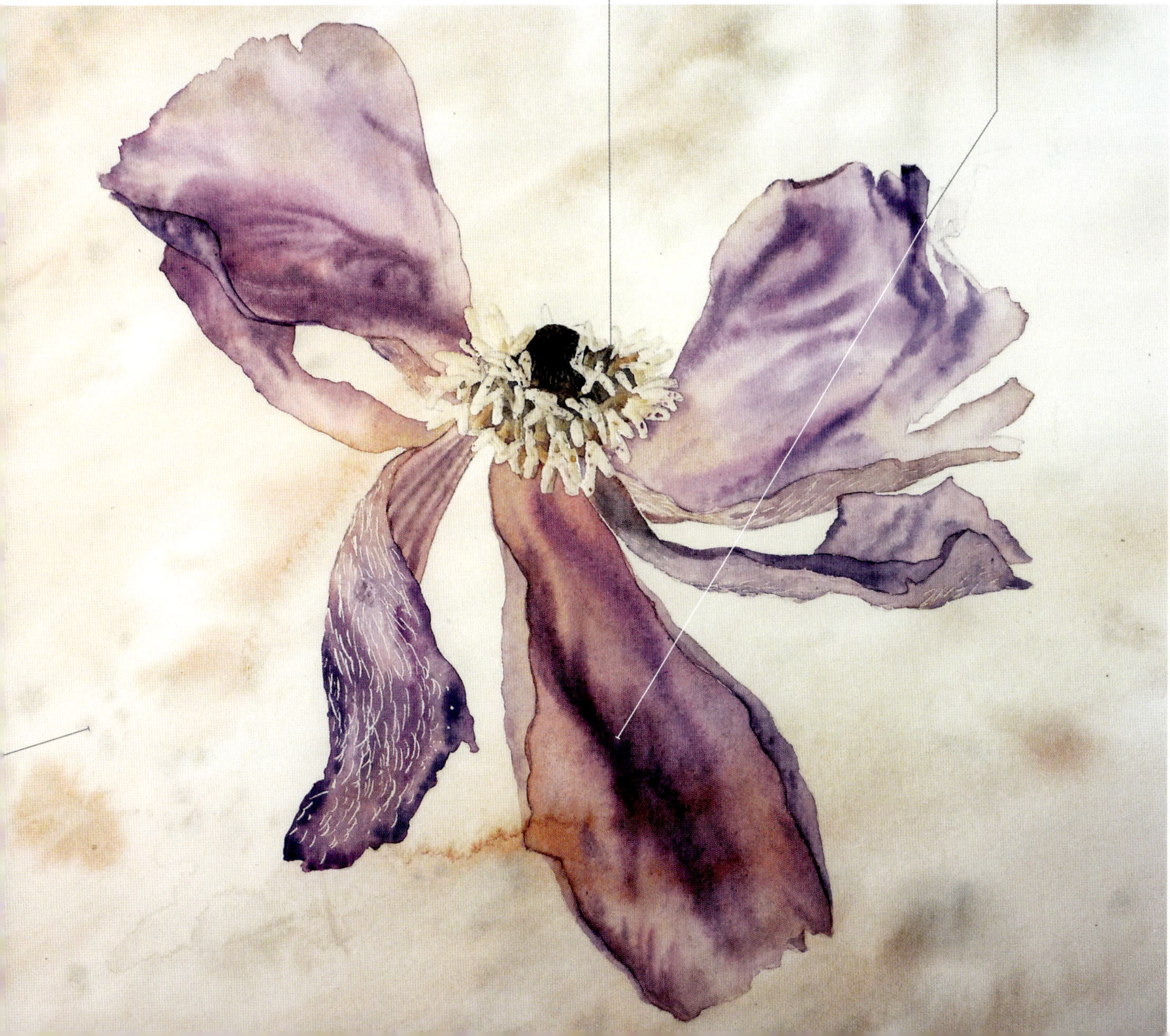

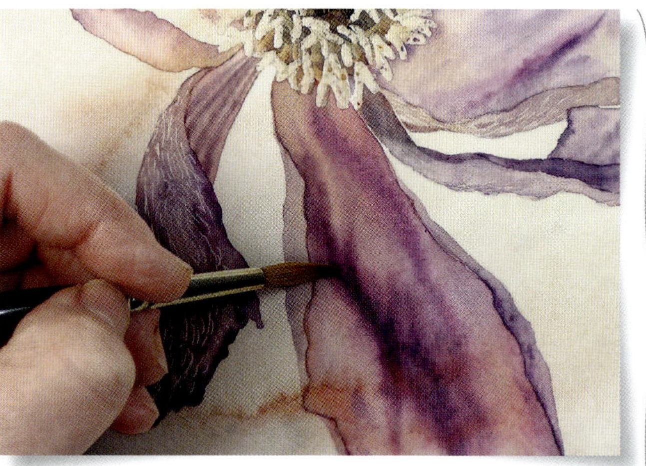

6 Successive layers

Repeat the wet-in-wet washes, as needed, to build up the form or colour. It is not unusual to have to apply several layers at this stage as colours tend to dry paler than when first applied. The golden rule is to not fiddle once the paint starts to dry, then leave to dry completely before working on subsequent layers.

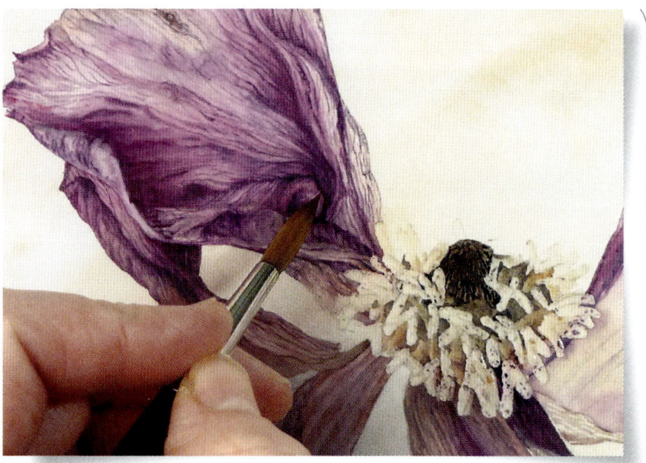

7 Detail on petals

Once you're happy that the petals are looking three-dimensional, switch to a drier brush technique for veining detail and to deepen shadows. "Draw" the detail using small amounts of dried paint colour. Make these veins irregular and uneven to reflect the dried, papery feel of the petals.

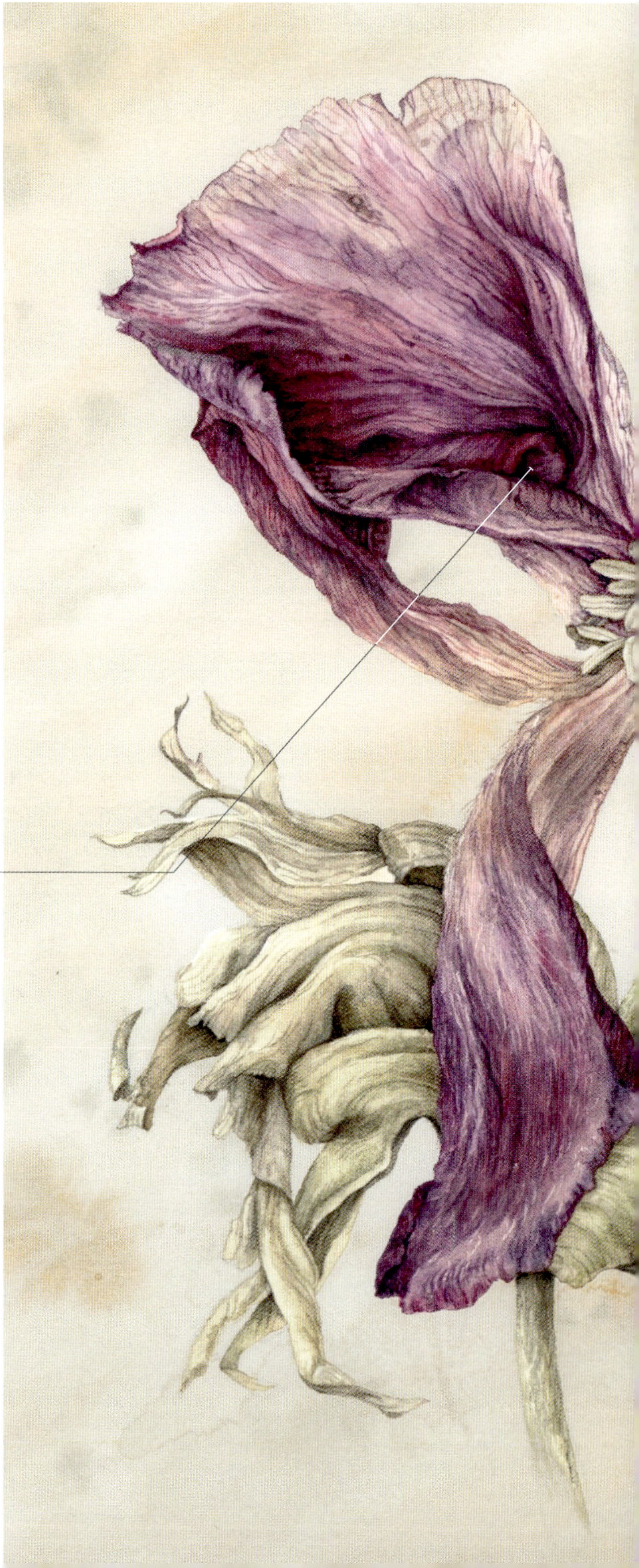

"Fading flowers **shrink as they dry,** so are easier to depict if **painted larger than life.**"

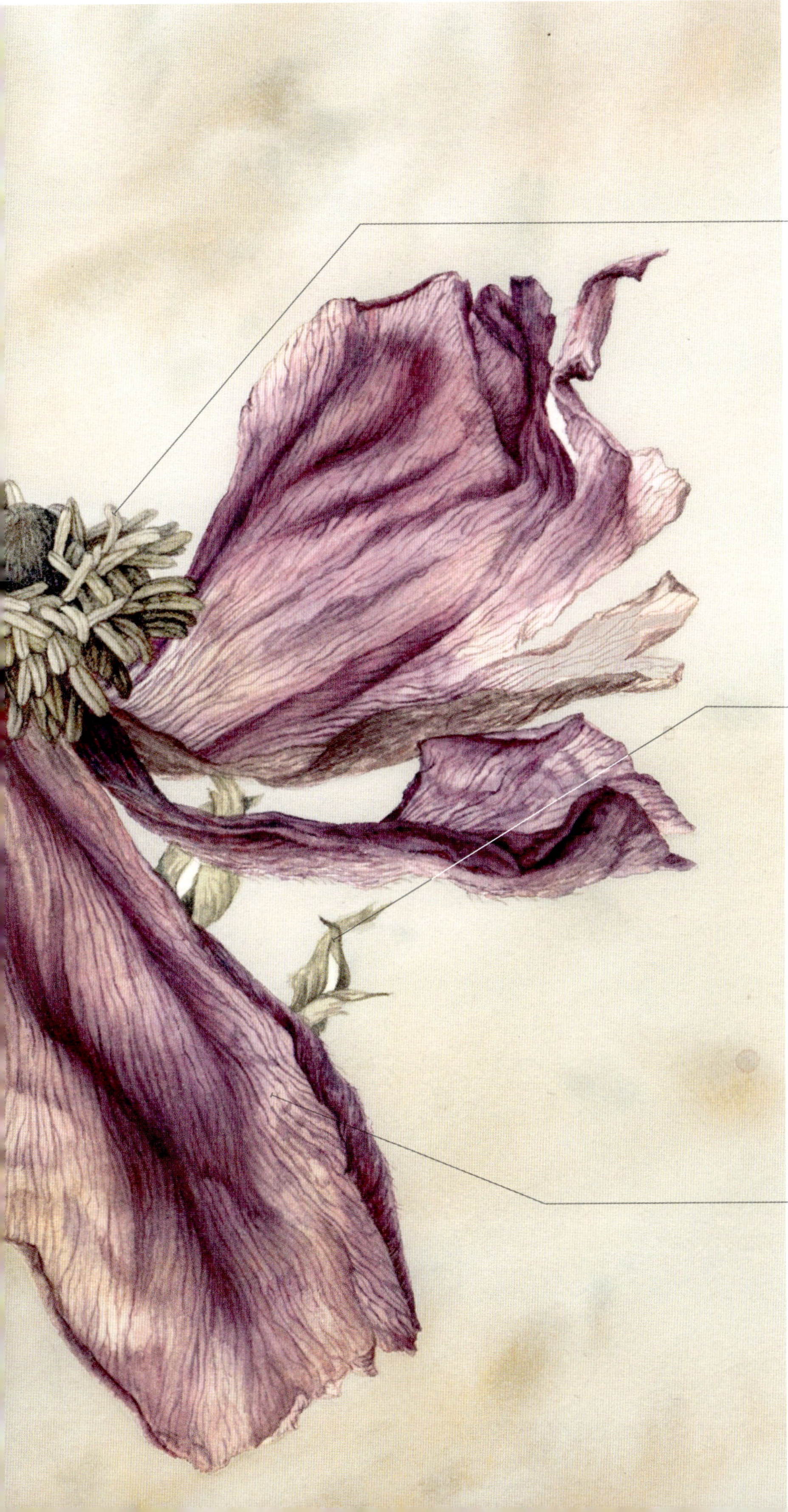

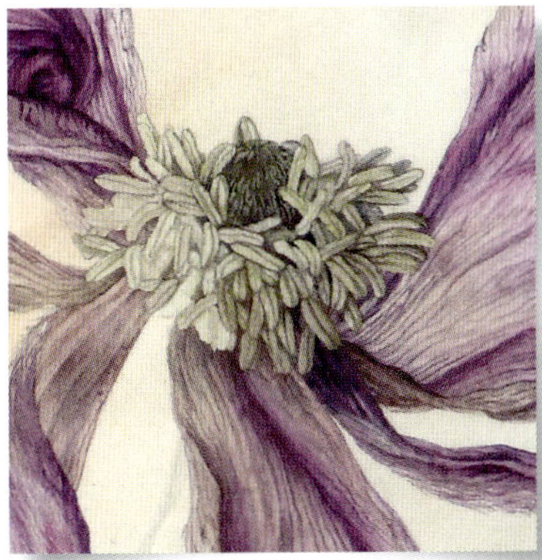

8 Revisit the centre

Once you are happy with the depth of colour and the paint is dry, rub off the masking fluid with clean fingers to reveal and paint the individual stamens.

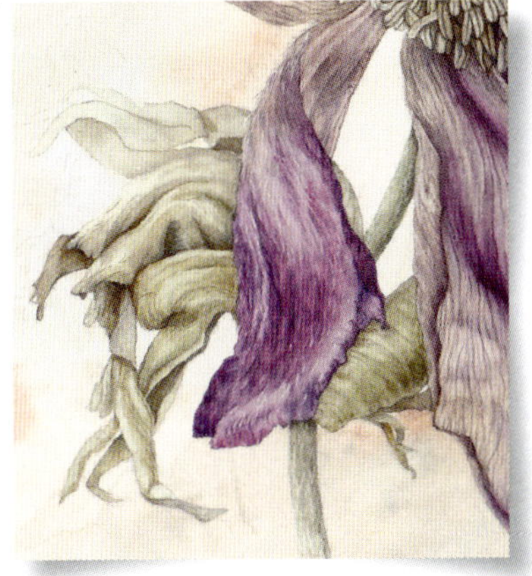

9 Leaves next

Experiment with the arrangement of the leafy collar on your tracing paper drawing. Then, transfer this drawing over your painted image.

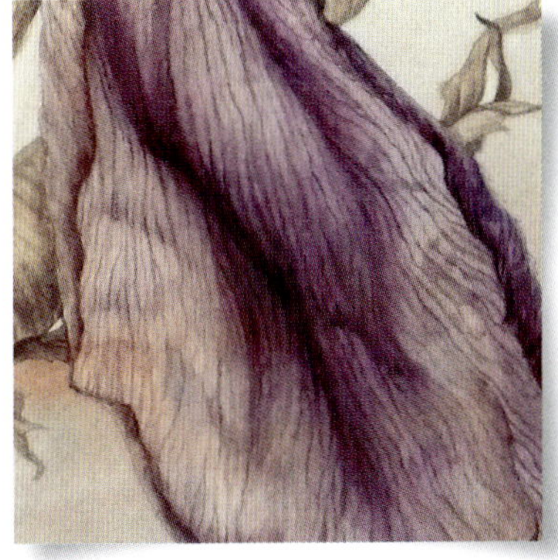

10 Finishing touches

Assess the whole range of tones from dark to light and adjust. Even tiny areas of dark, where a petal turns over, for instance, can bring a painting to life.

Loose flowers

SUGGESTING FLOWERS SIMPLY

When painting flowers in a loose, fluid style, it is important to be selective about how wet you choose your paper to be. Broad washes of colour that flow across the paper provide exciting effects that allow the viewer's imagination to fill in the petals further, but some detail is also needed to give structure and variety.

■ Suggesting depth and detail

Using a mixture of soft and harder edges conveys the three-dimensionality of the flowers, while also stimulating the eye of the viewer with different textures and lines. Strong colours and harder lines advance in the painting, while diffuse washes of similar colours for the background give the idea of a larger number of flowers that cannot be clearly discerned.

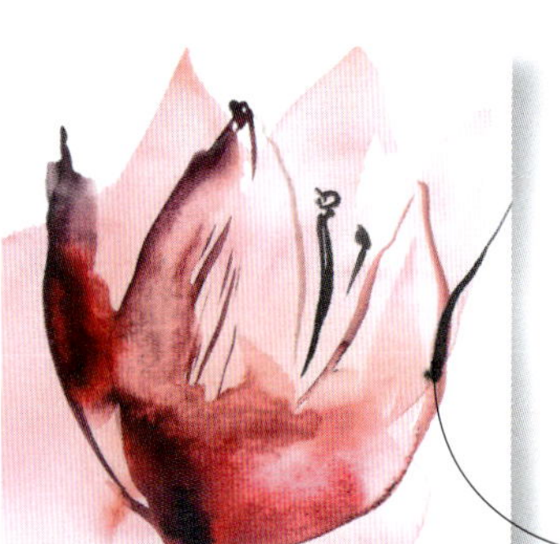

Hard and soft edges

A combination of hard and soft edges describes the flowers yet also invites the viewer to lend their imagination. A detailed botanical approach is not necessary to explain the flowers – suggesting their essence is sufficient.

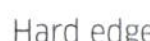
Hard edge

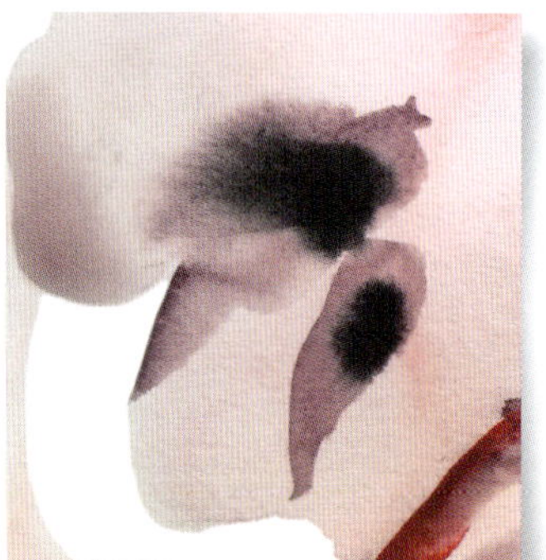

Suggestive background

A background that is not clearly explained suggests depth to the viewer and invites the sense that there is more to be revealed. Diffuse shapes and diluted colours mean that the background enhances rather than competes.

PUTTING IT INTO PRACTICE

The energy of the strokes in saturated colour adds vibrancy to this still life. The random effect of one colour flowing into another brings dynamism.

You will need

Madder lake red light · Red ochre · Hooker's green · Rose · Phthalo blue (green shade) · Neutral black

- No. 18 and no. 12 soft-hair mop brushes
- No. 5 synthetic and no. 3 soft-hair round brushes
- 21 x 15cm (8¼ x 6in) hot-pressed watercolour paper 300gsm (140lb)

Pink lilies

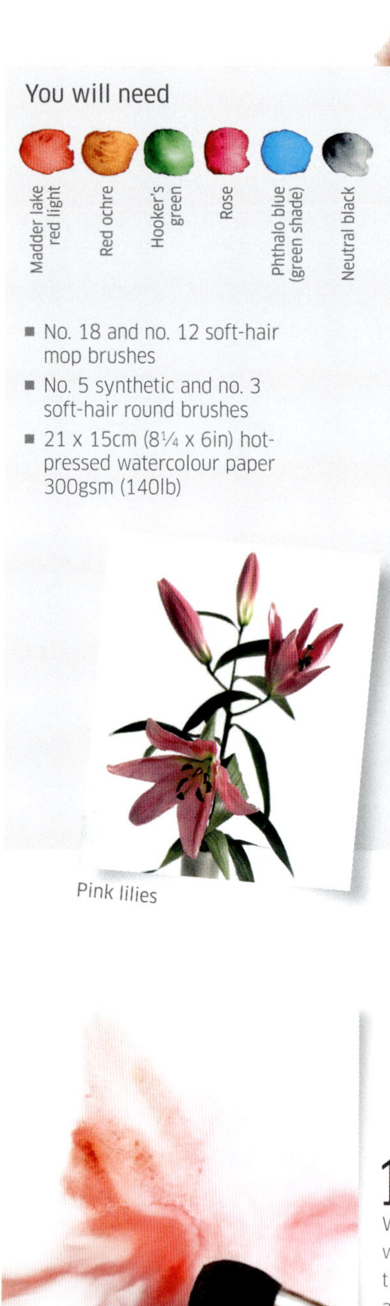

1 First hints at form

Wet the whole sheet with a thick brush, then loosely apply a mix of ochre and madder lake red light where the flowers are. If needed, you can tilt the paper to allow the paint to flow freely.

"Fluid washes of colour evoke the freshness of living flowers while defined marks give structure."

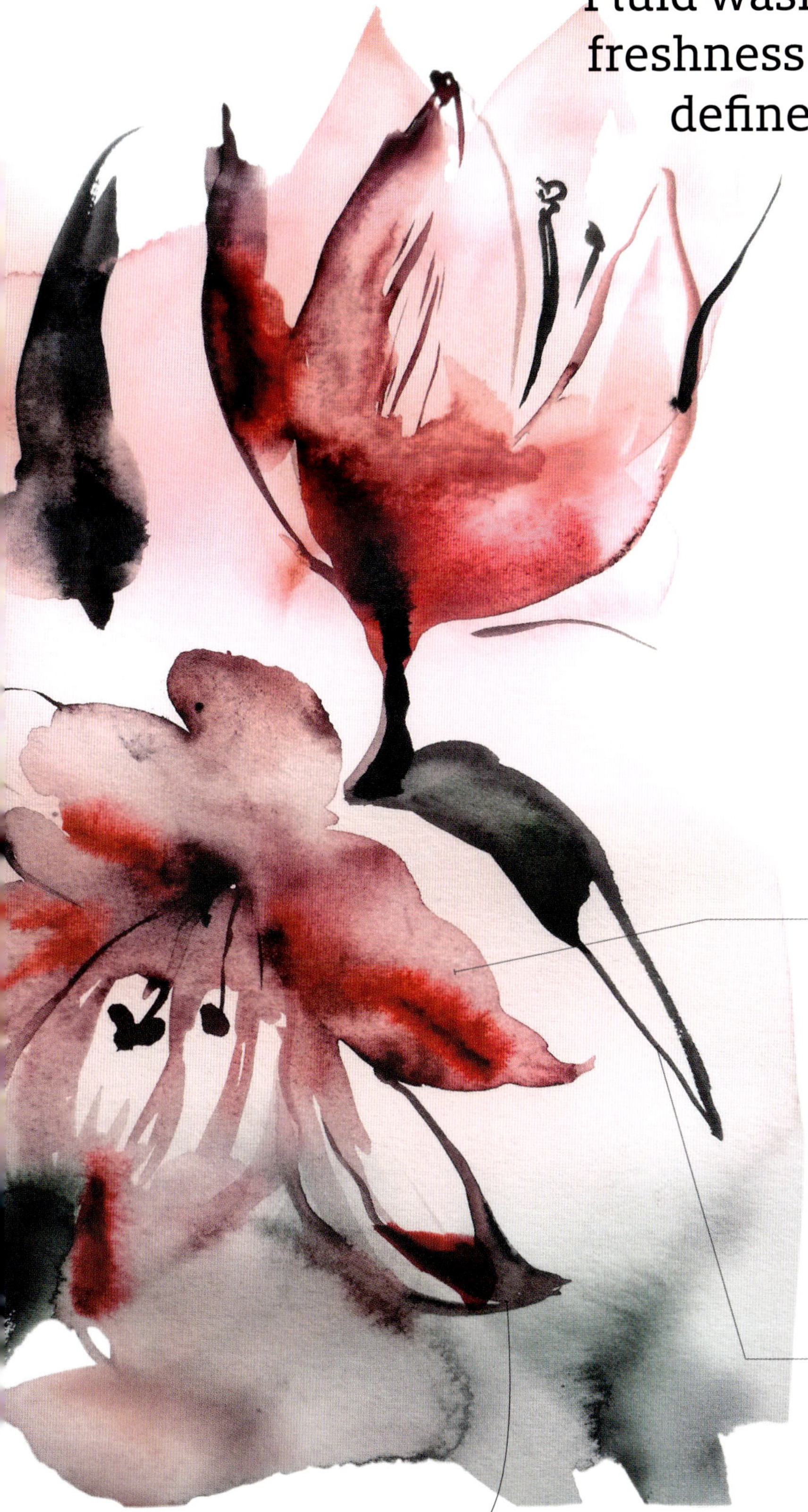

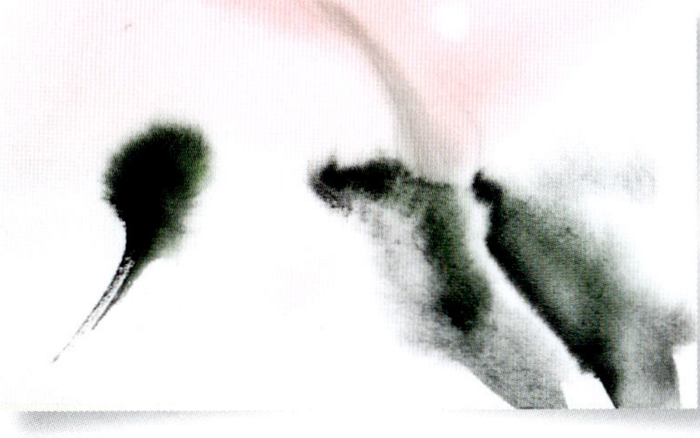

2 Leaves and stem structure

When the paper dries out a little but is mostly wet, add structure. For leaves and stems, mix green with black and madder. Where the paper is drier, the strokes will be clearer and where it is wet, they will be blurry.

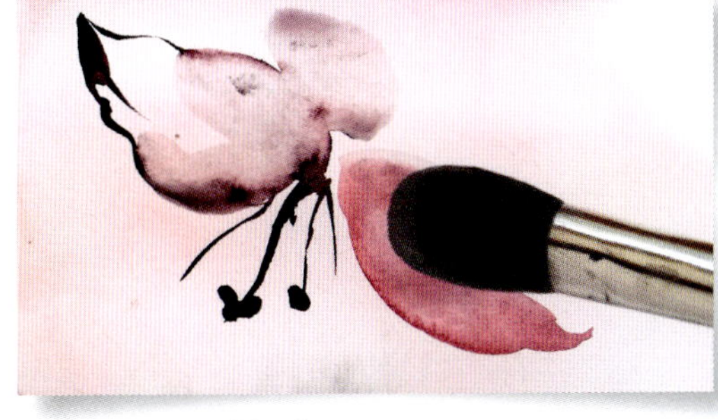

3 Flowers and buds

When the paper dries a little more, indicate flowers and buds with free strokes, mixing colours as you choose. Use intense colours for line details and less saturated ones for more general colour.

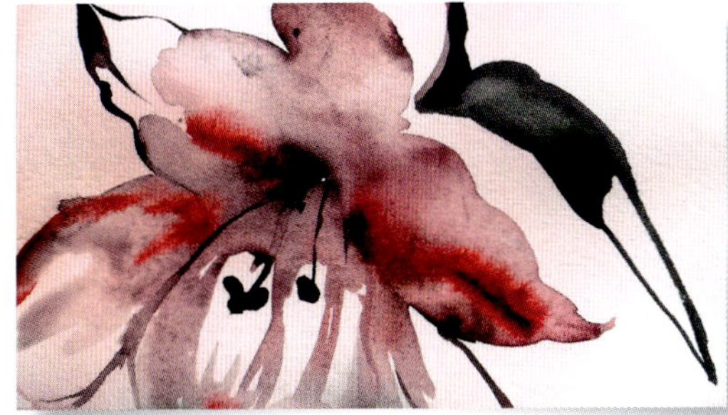

4 Finishing touches

When the paper is completely dry, add details with a fine brush. As well as lines, you can apply water and dot on some paint, allowing it to spread slightly.

Add leaves where you like to enhance the composition

Painting faces

CAPTURING A LIKENESS

The first step is to choose a pose that is interesting and relatively easy until you have gained some experience; a slightly turned profile is attractive and you need to paint only one eye rather than trying to match the exact gaze of a full-face portrait. Use natural lighting so the colouring of your subject will be more true to reality.

Making a lively portrait

What you leave out of a portrait is as important as what you include. Hair and clothing can be merely suggested; your colours and technique can add more vitality to the subject than painting everything will achieve. Save your finer detail for the focal point, often the eyes.

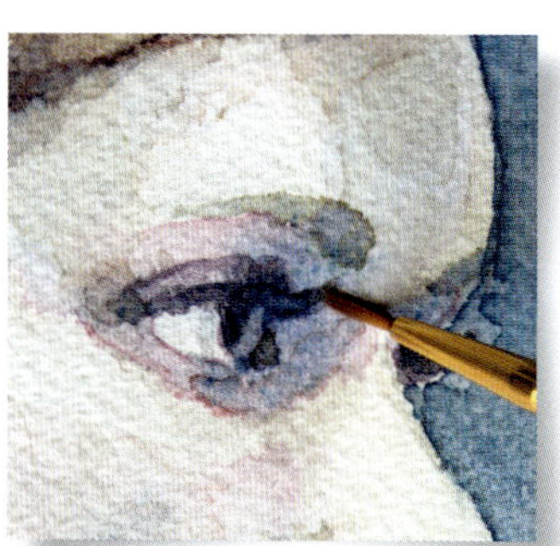

The eyes

Render the eyes with more controlled strokes, using a thin brush to build shadows on the eyelid, adding fine marks for eyelashes, and leaving crisp, wet-on-dry edges for the pupil.

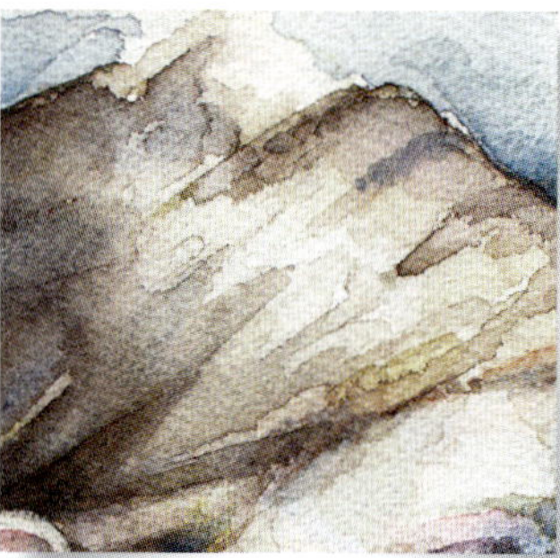

The hair

Whatever the style, hair can be minimally suggested using just blocks of colour with a few strokes painted to describe its general direction.

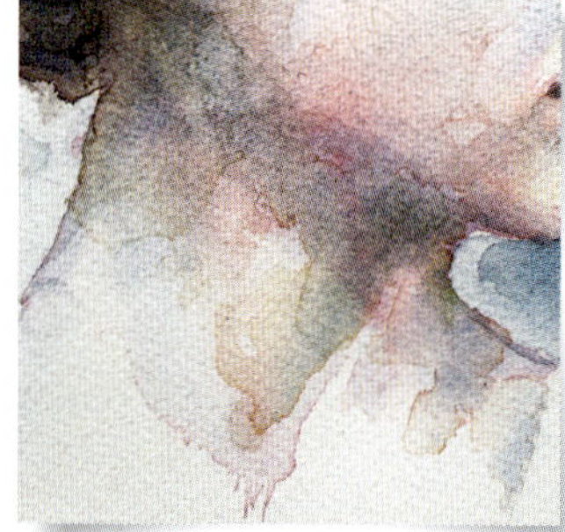

Shading with colour

A successful rendition of skin tone (see pp.220–23) is integral to a good portrait. Try less literal colour mixes such as blue with pink, for a lively effect.

PUTTING IT INTO PRACTICE

Breaking the tones down into shapes makes portraits easier to paint as you can more easily see the placing of the features. You need to be decisive early on about what you will paint and what you will omit.

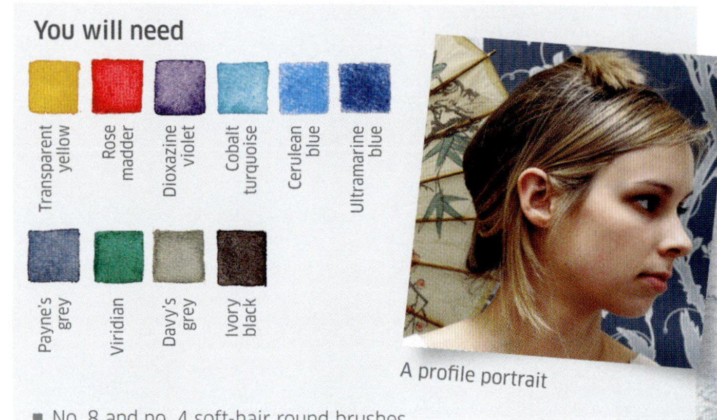

A profile portrait

- No. 8 and no. 4 soft-hair round brushes
- No. 0 synthetic round brush
- 20 x 20cm (8 x 8in) NOT watercolour paper 300gsm (140lb)

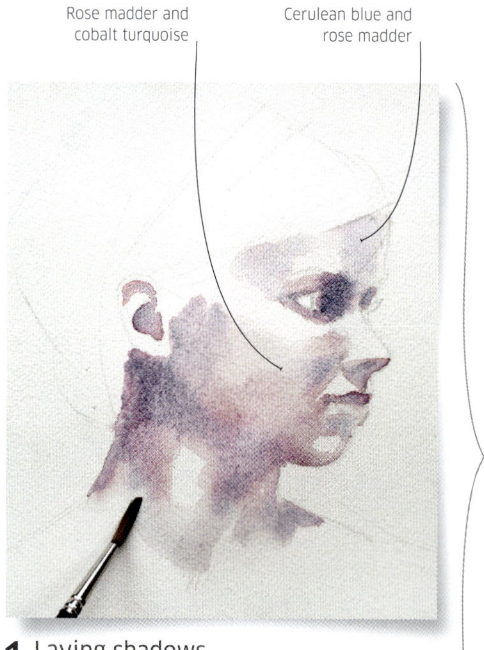

1 Laying shadows

Using the no. 8 round brush, lightly lay pools of rose and turquoise where the shadows on the face are present. Use a slightly cooler mix of cerulean and rose on the forehead, which is on a different plane to the cheek in relation to the light.

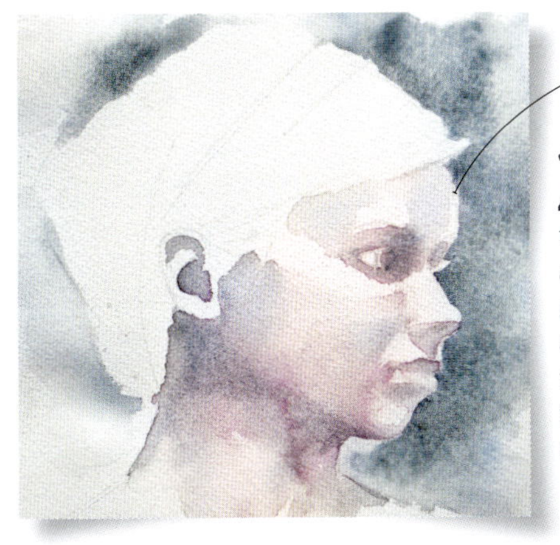

Painted negative space emphasizes the shape of the face

2 Framing the face

Use the no. 8 brush to paint the negative space of the face, neck, and hair with Payne's and Davy's grey mixed together. Carefully work around the edges, causing the face to emerge. Allow plenty of space for the hair – remember that the eyes are halfway down the head.

> "Natural lighting will give you the truest skin tones in a portrait."

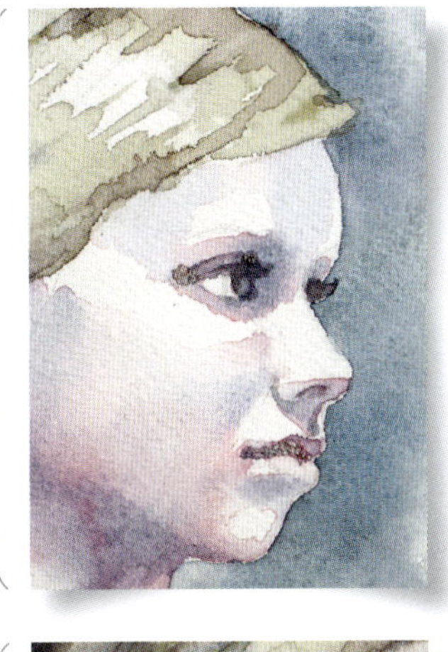

3 Defining the features

Mix yellow, violet, and ultramarine for the hair and build up with the no. 4 brush. Mix viridian and rose with the no. 0 brush to define the darkest areas of the features. Use a touch of black for the pupil and rose for the lips.

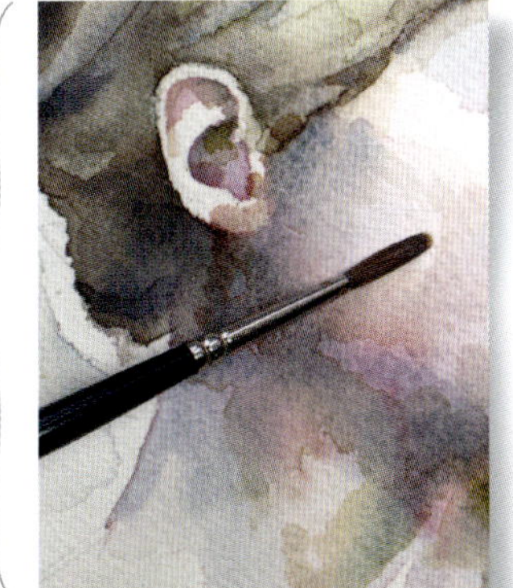

4 Shadows and highlights

With the no. 4 brush, mix cerulean, rose, and yellow. Paint the shadows on the skin to create more depth. Add a very dilute wash of yellow to create warmth on the highlights.

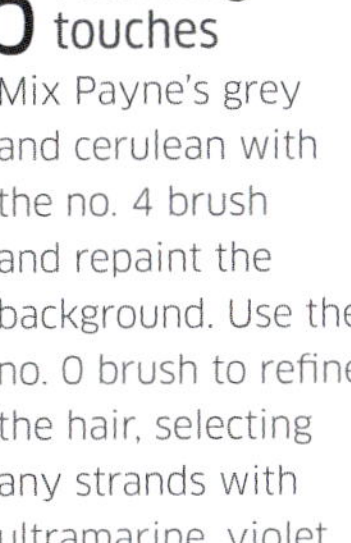

5 Finishing touches

Mix Payne's grey and cerulean with the no. 4 brush and repaint the background. Use the no. 0 brush to refine the hair, selecting any strands with ultramarine, violet, and yellow.

Skin tones

PAINTING THE COLOURS IN SKIN

Realistic skin tones are best painted with just a few basic colours, since this results in tones that harmonize with each other and provide a natural appearance. All skin tones, from the lightest to the darkest, can be painted with a limited palette of just three colours, with reserved paper providing white for the highlights.

Light and shade

Look for the high, mid, and dark tones in your subject's skin, which depend on the direction and strength of the light source. When close to light, the skin may look paler, cooler, or yellower. Using a cool green or purple mix is an effective way to depict shadows, as they will complement the warm reds and yellows in the skin.

Flesh tones

Using a basic palette will give you a good starting point for mixing skin tones. Earth colours such as sienna, umber, and ochre often provide a good foundation for flesh tones; you can mix them with primary colours to create warmer or cooler hues according to the high, mid, and dark tones you have identified.

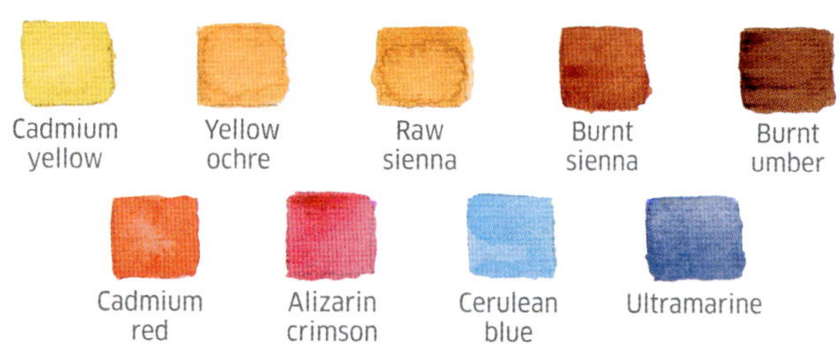

Limited palette

Mixing skin tones from a limited palette of colours will help unify your painting. Choosing a warm and cool version of each primary colour will ensure that you can create a wide variety of convincing skin tones, no matter the complexion of the subject.

Dark skin tones

Dark skin uses burnt sienna in the high tone. Mixing it with cool crimson prevents the skin tone being too orange. Burnt umber in the mid tone gives a warm brown which can make a mauve in darker mid tones.

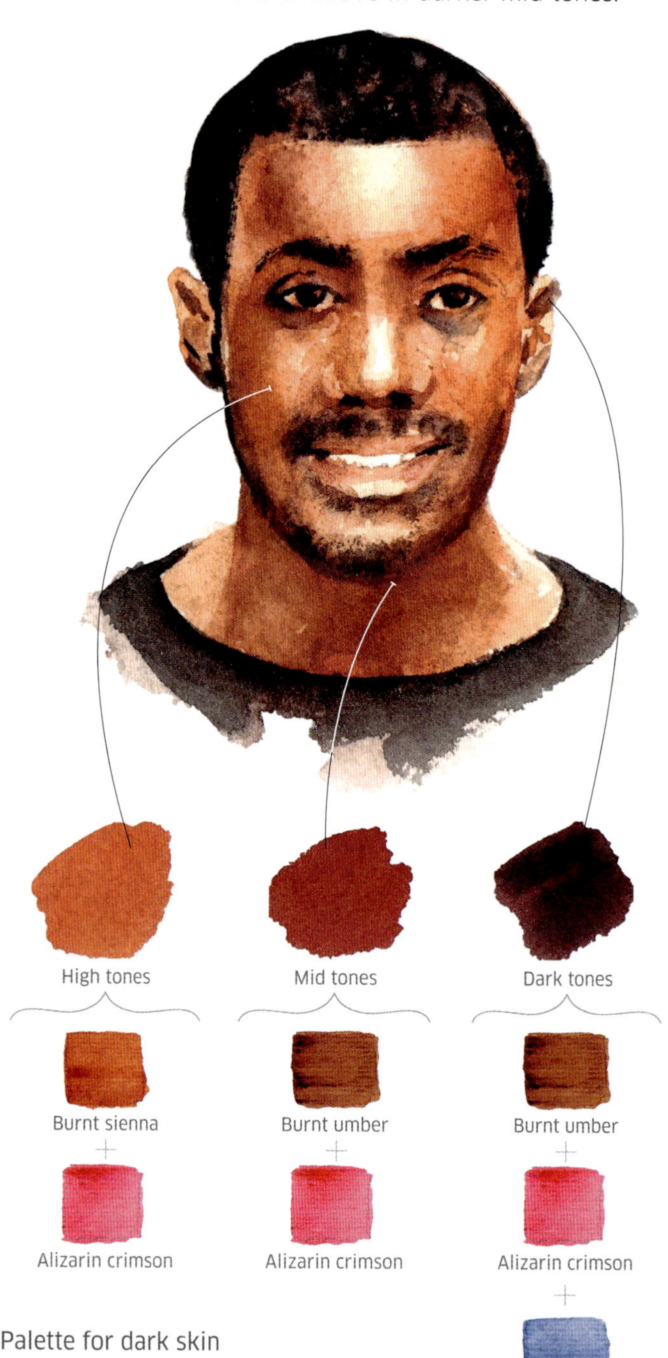

Palette for dark skin

Use burnt sienna with crimson for the high tones, substituting burnt umber for the sienna in the mid tones. For very dark skin, make strong mixes and add ultramarine to cool the colour a little so that the crimson does not dominate.

Olive skin tones

Olive skin has raw sienna instead of burnt sienna in the first mix for the high tone. Raw sienna is a yellower colour, which is also used in the mid tone to keep the olive complexion from looking too brown.

Light skin tones

Light skin can be painted from pink through to yellow tones by varying the balance of alizarin crimson to yellow ochre in the first mix for the high tone. Use darker tones of the mixes for shadowed areas.

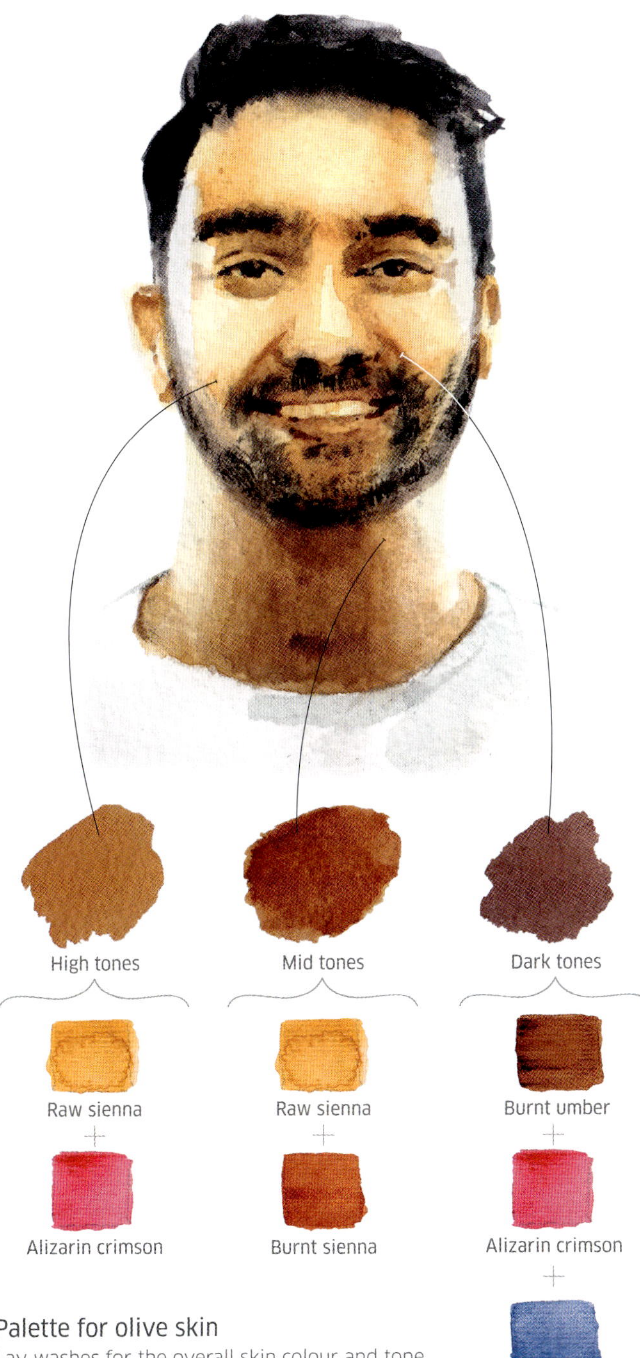

High tones

Mid tones

Dark tones

Raw sienna
+
Alizarin crimson

Raw sienna
+
Burnt sienna

Burnt umber
+
Alizarin crimson
+
Ultramarine

Palette for olive skin

Lay washes for the overall skin colour and tone then use darker tones for shadow areas. For olive skin, use only subtle variations of colour and tone to give a convincing effect. Allow washes to dry then build up gradually.

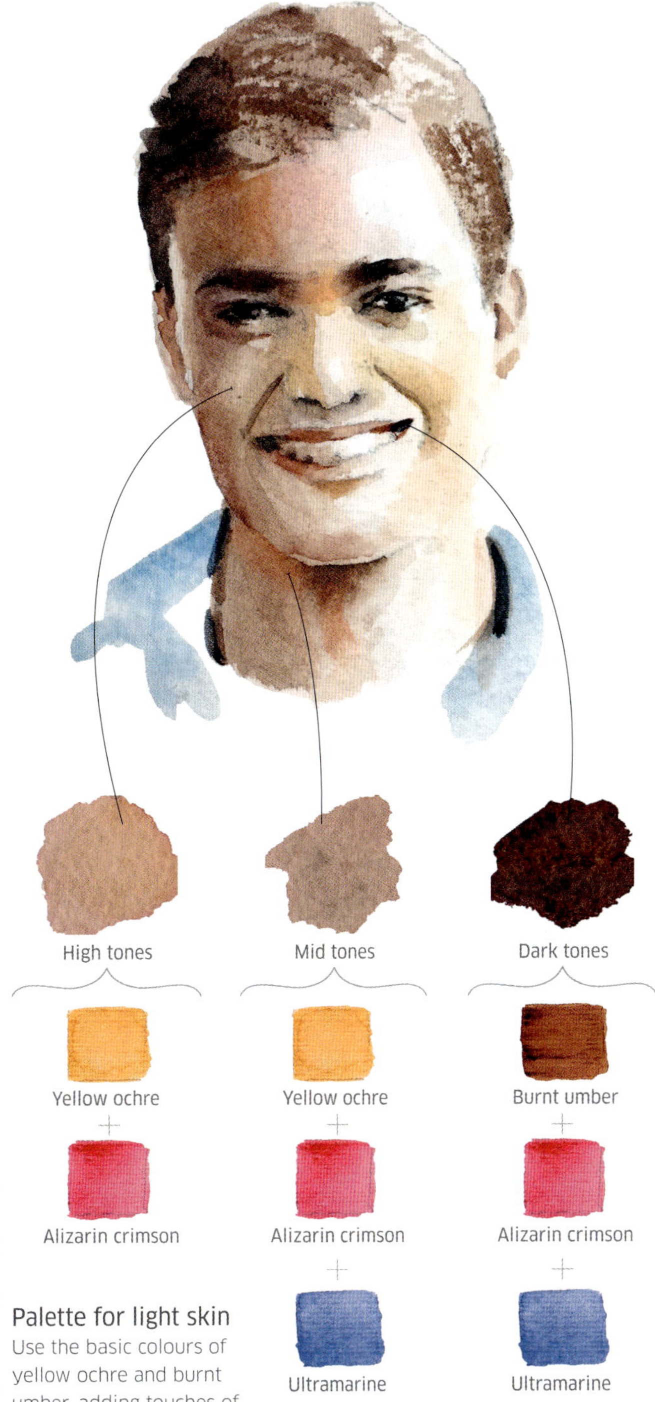

High tones

Mid tones

Dark tones

Yellow ochre
+
Alizarin crimson

Yellow ochre
+
Alizarin crimson
+
Ultramarine

Burnt umber
+
Alizarin crimson
+
Ultramarine

Palette for light skin

Use the basic colours of yellow ochre and burnt umber, adding touches of crimson or ultramarine for warm or cool areas.

PUTTING IT INTO PRACTICE

Portraits rely on a slow build up of washes, for it is easy to add extra paint but undesirable to lift out unwanted edges and marks, since it leaves the skin looking too shiny. Secondary colours are best mixed rather than using manufactured colours.

Cerulean blue and alizarin crimson create a cool lilac shadow

You will need

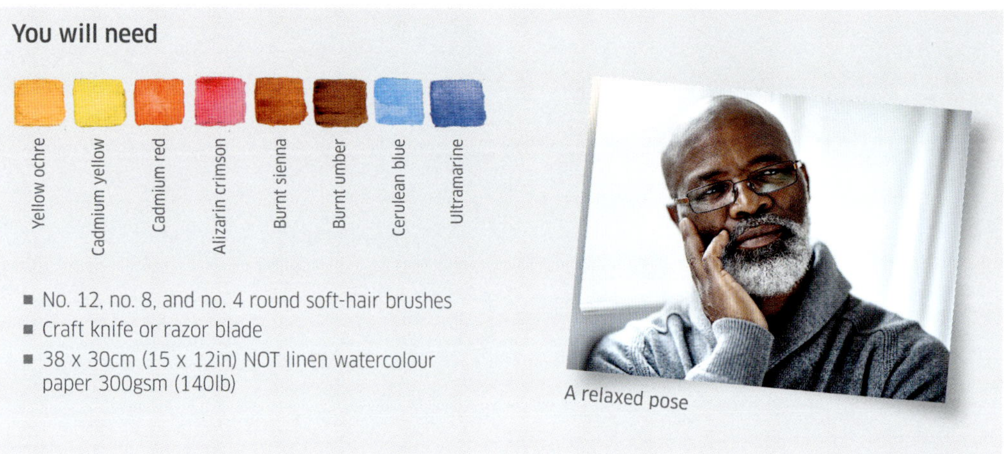

- Yellow ochre
- Cadmium yellow
- Cadmium red
- Alizarin crimson
- Burnt sienna
- Burnt umber
- Cerulean blue
- Ultramarine

- No. 12, no. 8, and no. 4 round soft-hair brushes
- Craft knife or razor blade
- 38 x 30cm (15 x 12in) NOT linen watercolour paper 300gsm (140lb)

A relaxed pose

1 Laying a base colour

Paint a mix of crimson and ochre over the face, leaving reserved highlights on the top and side of the head and the beard area. Dilute the wash where the moustache will be. When this wash is dry, use the colour again to darken some areas, in particular around the eye sockets, sides of the nose, and under the chin.

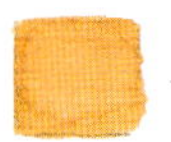 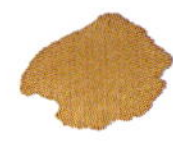

Yellow ochre + Alizarin crimson = First wash colour

2 Modelling the head

Mix a wash of crimson, ochre, and cerulean with which to create a three-dimensional tonal image, paying attention to the bone structure of the head. Form the eye sockets, define the nose, and shape the cheek bones. When this is dry, use the same wash a second time to darken the features.

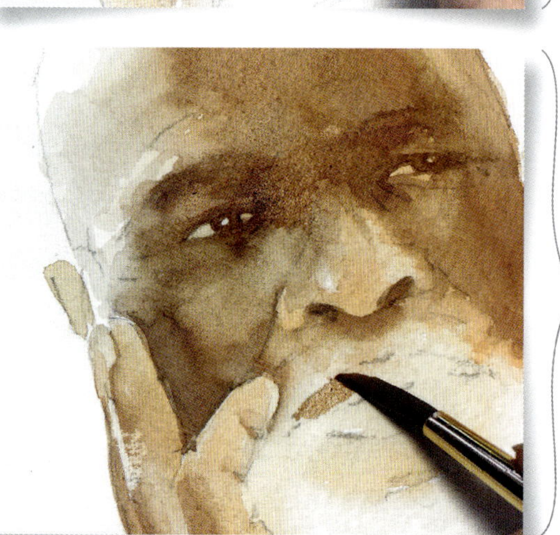

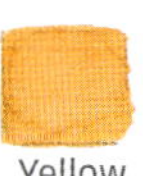 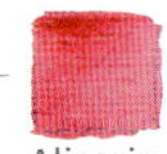 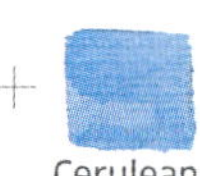

Yellow ochre + Alizarin crimson + Cerulean blue = Second wash colour

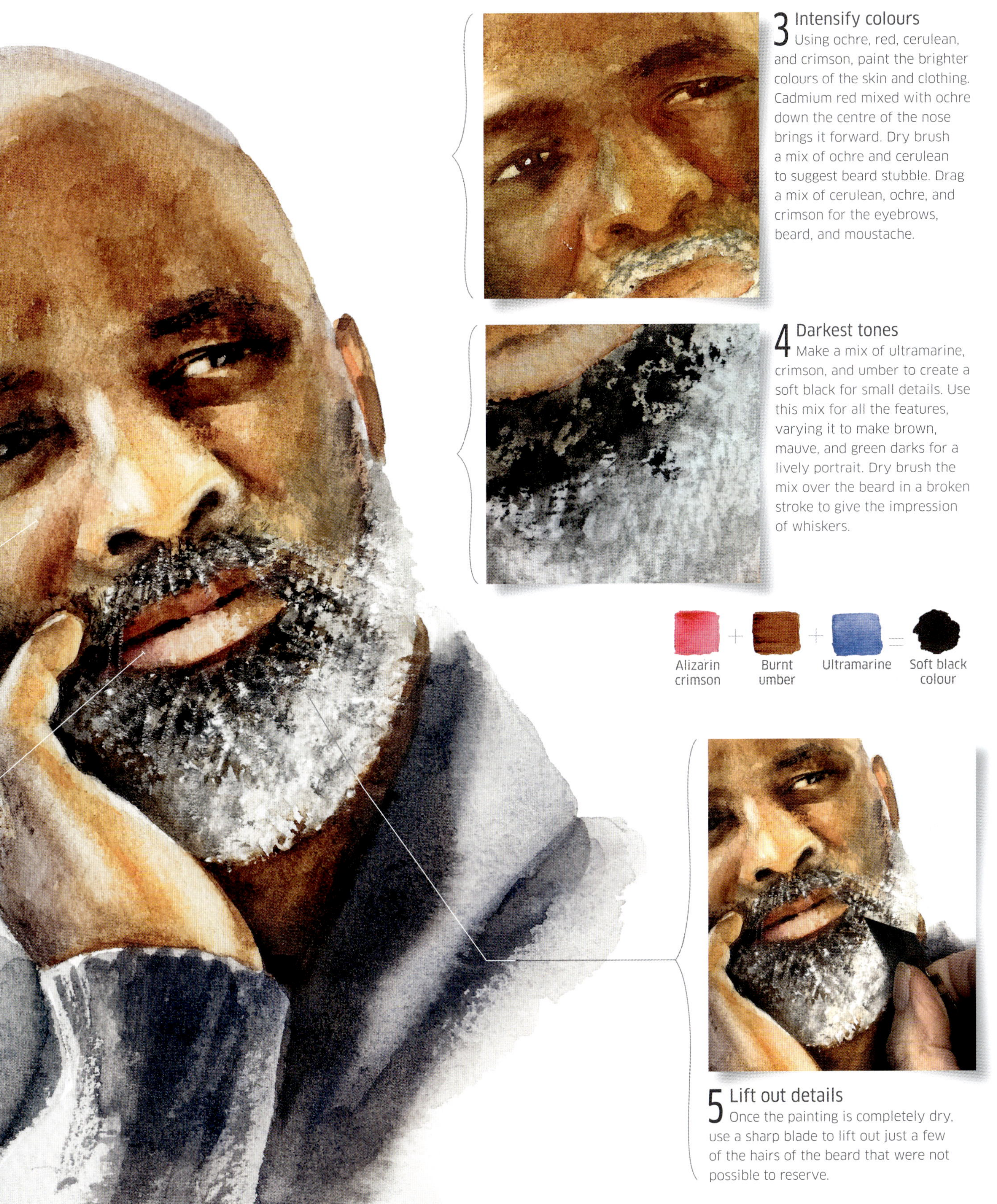

3 Intensify colours
Using ochre, red, cerulean, and crimson, paint the brighter colours of the skin and clothing. Cadmium red mixed with ochre down the centre of the nose brings it forward. Dry brush a mix of ochre and cerulean to suggest beard stubble. Drag a mix of cerulean, ochre, and crimson for the eyebrows, beard, and moustache.

4 Darkest tones
Make a mix of ultramarine, crimson, and umber to create a soft black for small details. Use this mix for all the features, varying it to make brown, mauve, and green darks for a lively portrait. Dry brush the mix over the beard in a broken stroke to give the impression of whiskers.

5 Lift out details
Once the painting is completely dry, use a sharp blade to lift out just a few of the hairs of the beard that were not possible to reserve.

Expressive portrait

CONTRASTING BOLD AND SUBTLE COLOURS

Vibrant colour blocks, quick strokes, and subtle layers combine here to create an expressive style of portrait. The skin tones on the face are created from layers of warmer or cooler transparent colour.

■ Creative colour

The multiple layers of colour on the face, the vibrant multi-coloured blocks of colour flowing into each other on the hair, and the quick free lines on the clothes and hair give the effect of expressive realism. The colours may spread beyond the pencil lines to give the effect of additional dynamism.

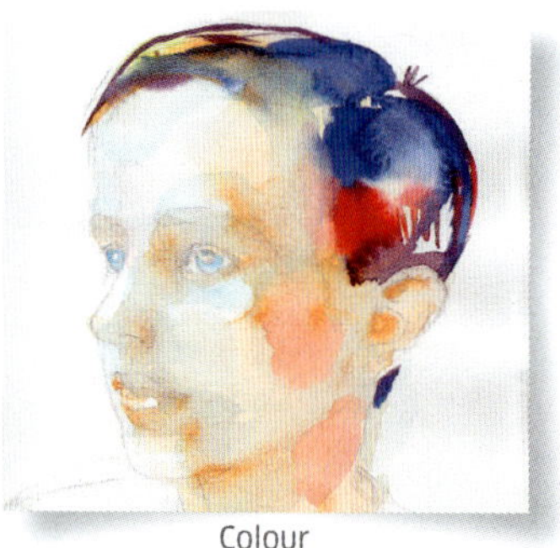
Colour

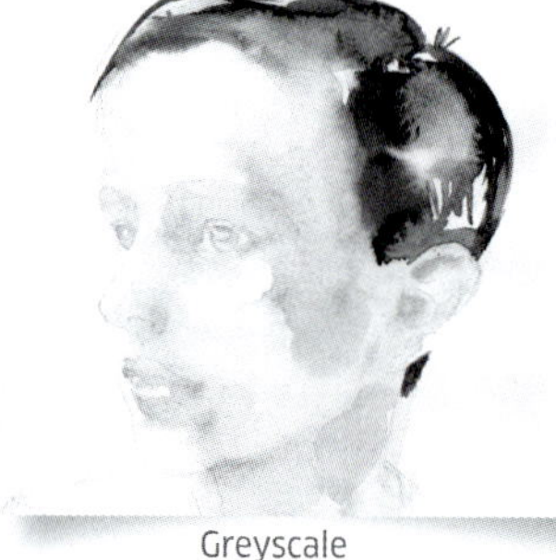
Greyscale

Colourful tonal range
The hair colours may seem unconventional, but converted to greyscale they can be seen to follow a tonal range: yellow for high tones, red for mid tones, and blue for the darkest tones.

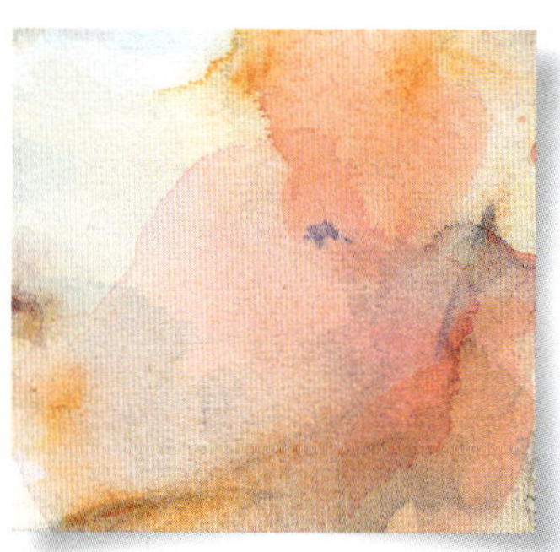

Glazing the skin
Several layers of delicate, transparent washes create a multi-dimensional effect on the skin. They are especially suitable to convey the youth and sensitivity of the subject.

PUTTING IT INTO PRACTICE

In this technique, the effect of inventive colours, strokes, and lines is important. In contrast, the face and eyes are clearly drawn, giving structure and a focal point respectively.

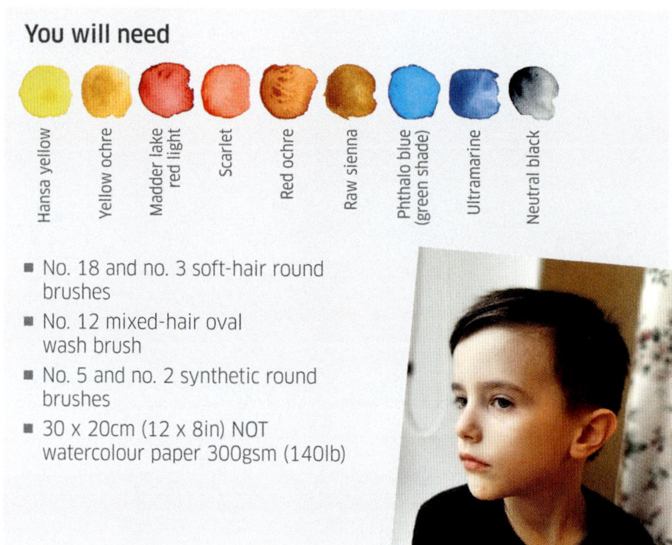

- No. 18 and no. 3 soft-hair round brushes
- No. 12 mixed-hair oval wash brush
- No. 5 and no. 2 synthetic round brushes
- 30 x 20cm (12 x 8in) NOT watercolour paper 300gsm (140lb)

Three-quarter profile

1 Mark highlights and shadows

In your pencil sketch, mark circles where there will be highlights or dark tones. Leave fine lines, but erase excess ones. You can erase some after applying the first layer once it has dried.

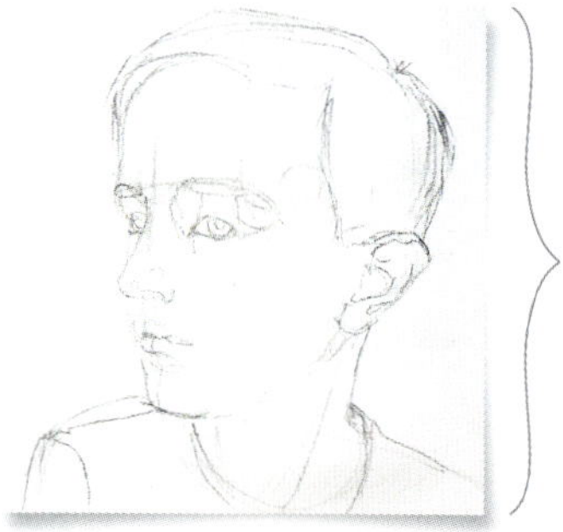

2 Apply a base wash

With a thick brush, lay a dilute wash of sienna, leaving white paper for highlights. Lay more paint for dark tones with a mixed oval wash brush. Apply water to lighter areas, blot it, then lift off colour with a clean thick brush.

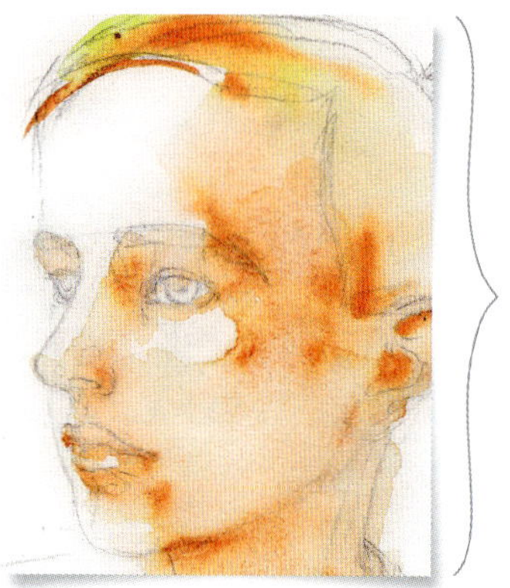

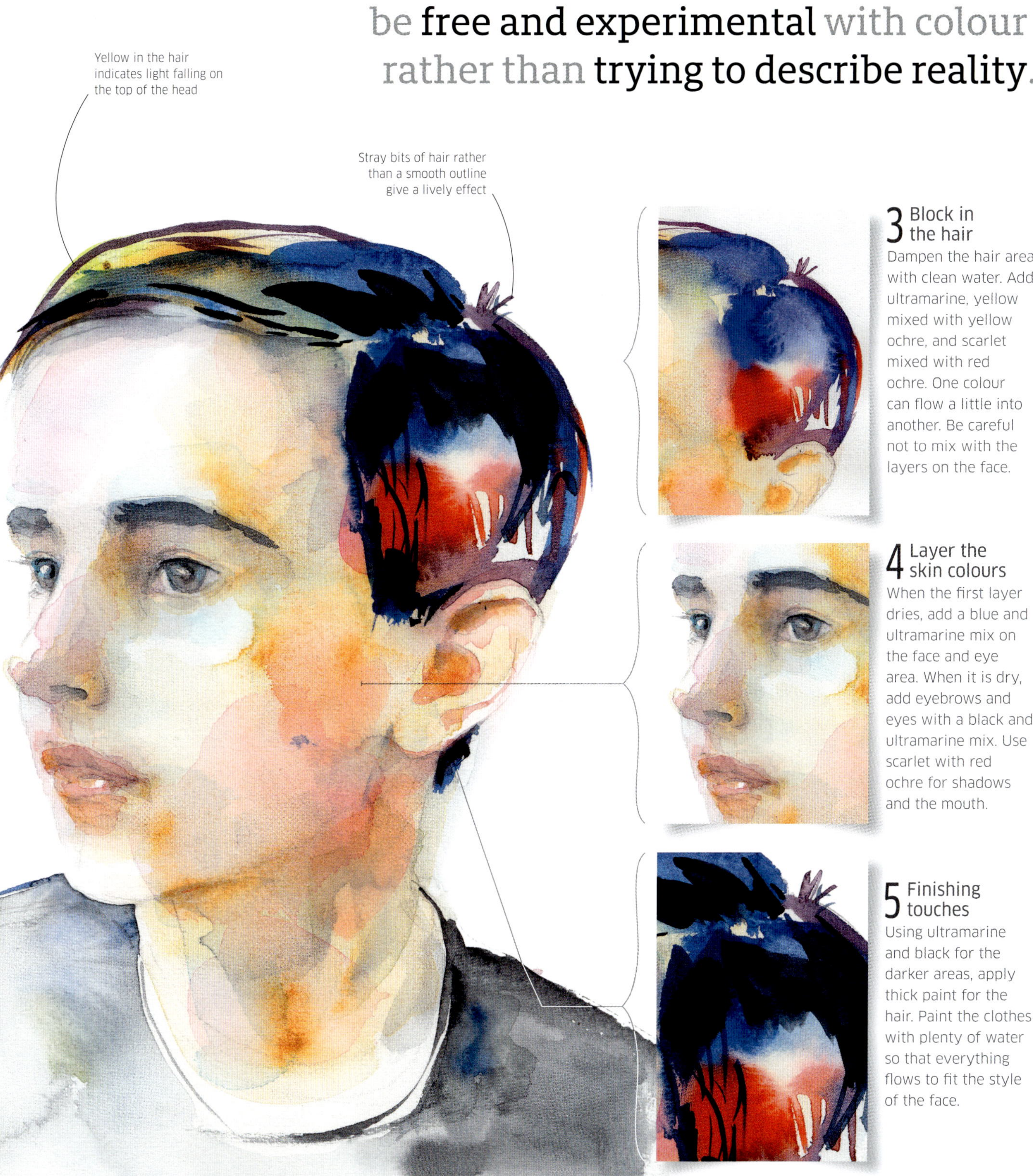

> "An expressive portrait allows you to be free and experimental with colour rather than trying to describe reality."

3 Block in the hair
Dampen the hair area with clean water. Add ultramarine, yellow mixed with yellow ochre, and scarlet mixed with red ochre. One colour can flow a little into another. Be careful not to mix with the layers on the face.

4 Layer the skin colours
When the first layer dries, add a blue and ultramarine mix on the face and eye area. When it is dry, add eyebrows and eyes with a black and ultramarine mix. Use scarlet with red ochre for shadows and the mouth.

5 Finishing touches
Using ultramarine and black for the darker areas, apply thick paint for the hair. Paint the clothes with plenty of water so that everything flows to fit the style of the face.

Artist **Denise Findlay**
Title **Balanced**
Paper **28 x 45cm (11 x 17½in) NOT watercolour paper 300gsm (140lb)**

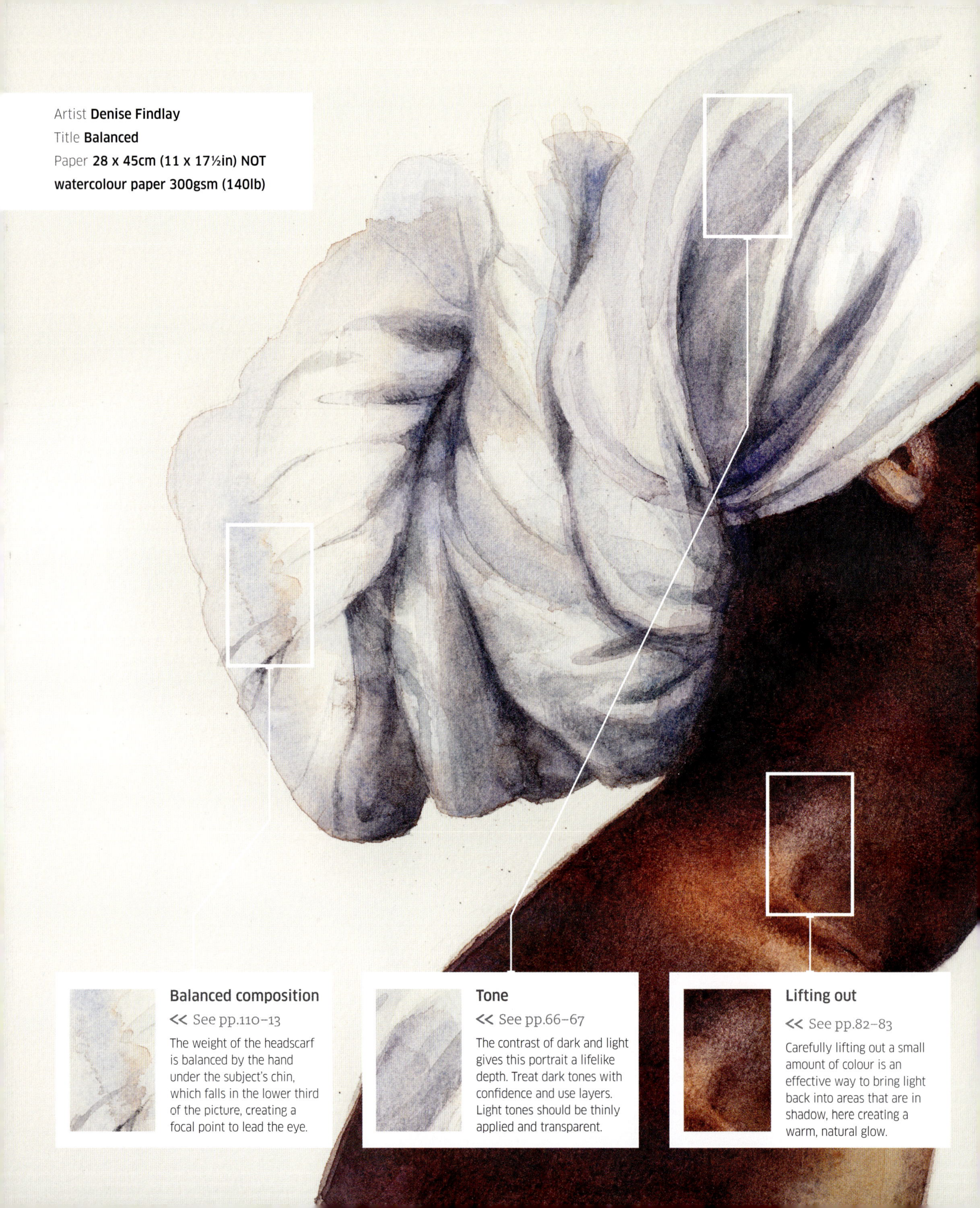

Balanced composition

≪ See pp.110–13

The weight of the headscarf is balanced by the hand under the subject's chin, which falls in the lower third of the picture, creating a focal point to lead the eye.

Tone

≪ See pp.66–67

The contrast of dark and light gives this portrait a lifelike depth. Treat dark tones with confidence and use layers. Light tones should be thinly applied and transparent.

Lifting out

≪ See pp.82–83

Carefully lifting out a small amount of colour is an effective way to bring light back into areas that are in shadow, here creating a warm, natural glow.

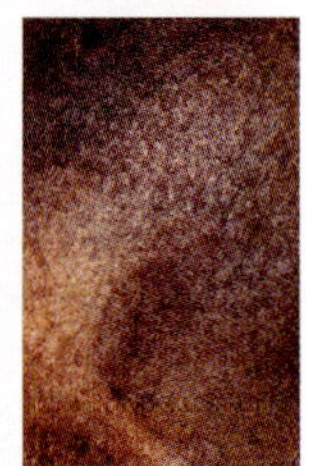

Showcase painting

This luminous portrait combines a striking composition with a soft, delicate approach to conveying the subtleties of skin tone, light, and shade. Painting a person in profile emphasizes the contours of the face, especially effective against the minimalistic background used here.

Negative spaces

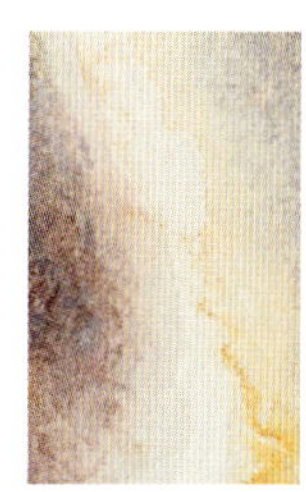

« See pp.114–15

The silhouette of the subject's head and hand create interesting background shapes in the space between and around the form.

Softening edges

« See pp.94–97

A seamless transition between light and dark areas was created by adding water to the edge of a coloured wash, then blending with a dry brush.

Single figures

POSE, SETTING, AND COMPOSITION

Successful figure paintings usually create a sense of scale, proportion, and perspective. The best way to achieve this is to think of the figure as part of a setting. Pay attention to the overall composition and spatial relationships between the figure and the other elements in your painting.

Scale and relationships

Figures are enhanced when painted in relation to another point of interest. The comparative sizes of the horse and farrier need to be judged to create harmony between the two shapes. The sense of space between them is produced by using warm and cool colours.

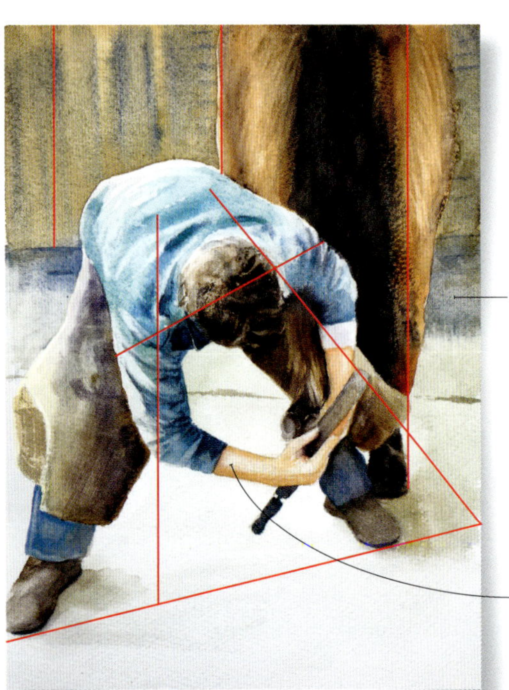

Cool colours push the background away from the viewer

Warm colours help the foreground advance and create a sense of depth

Identifying key shapes
The upright shape of the horse gives structure to the top of the painting. Impact comes from the diagonal of the farrier's feet and shoulders, while shadows in the sleeves show the stretch of the arms.

PUTTING IT INTO PRACTICE

Tonal contrast is important in this painting, for the focal point is where the lightest and darkest tones touch each other. The defined edge of the horse's flank against the blurred background gives perspective to the scene.

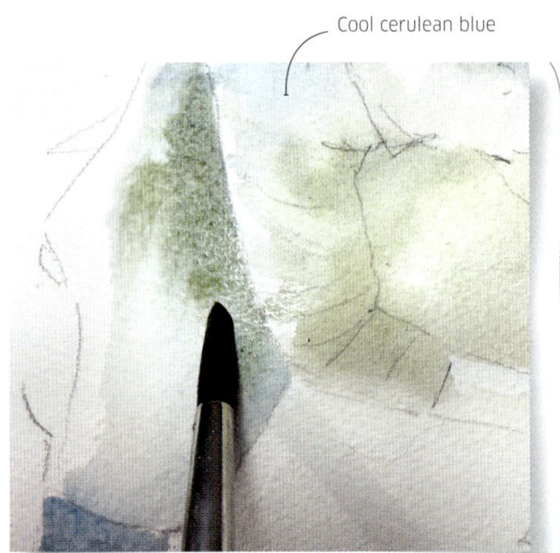

Cool cerulean blue

1 Cool background tones
Using cool cerulean blue on the back of the sweatshirt, and a mix of cerulean and ochre behind the forearm, pushes back these areas to create distance. The white of the forearm is reserved to bring it forward.

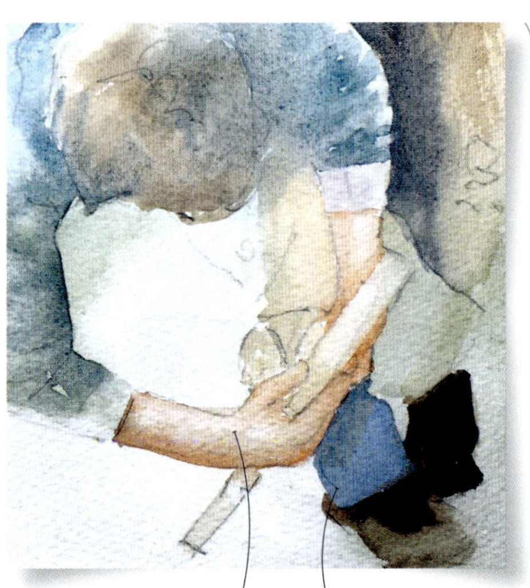

Warm cadmium orange

Warm ultramarine

2 Warm foreground tones
Warm ultramarine is used for the jeans to bring the front leg forward. Allowing the cerulean and ochre mix to bleed into it gives granulation that suggests denim.

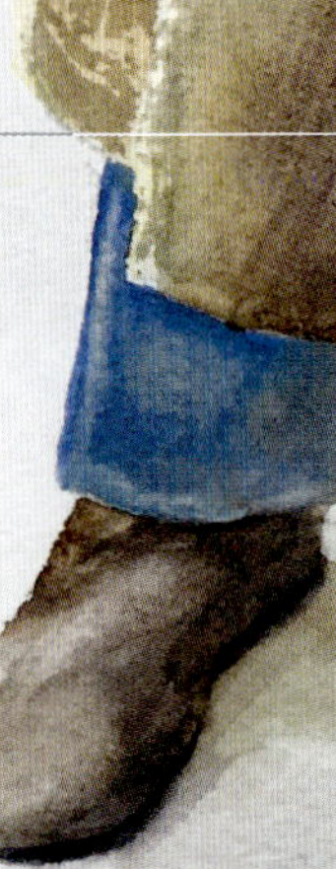

You will need

- Cadmium yellow
- Yellow ochre
- Cadmium red
- Alizarin crimson
- Burnt sienna
- Burnt umber
- Cerulean blue
- Ultramarine

- No. 14 and no. 8 soft-hair round brushes
- 38 x 28cm (15 x 11in) NOT linen watercolour paper 300gsm (140lb)

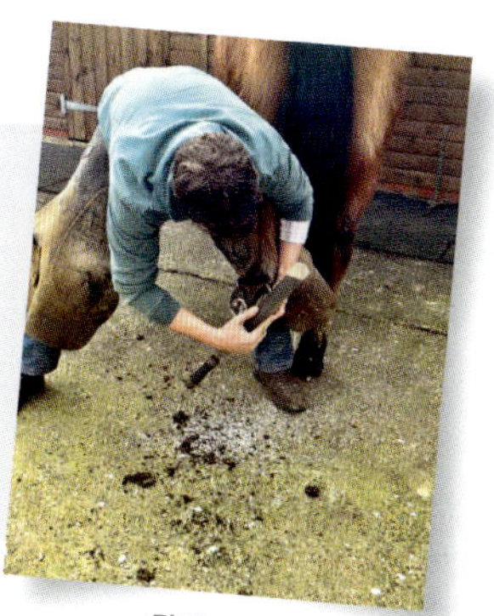
Fitting a horseshoe

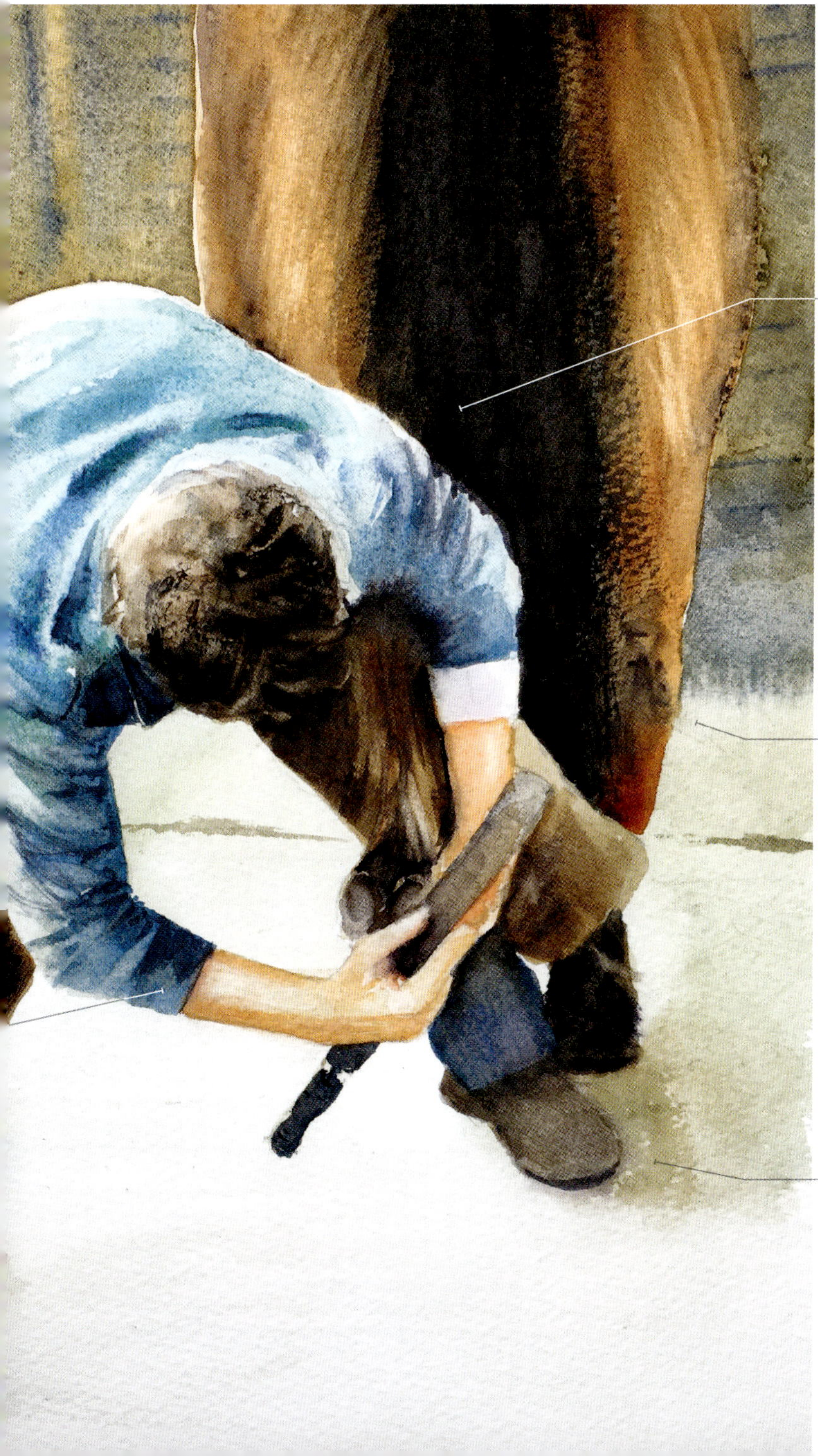

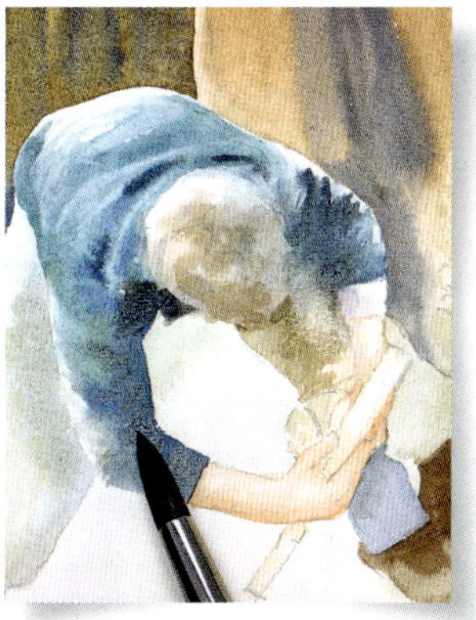

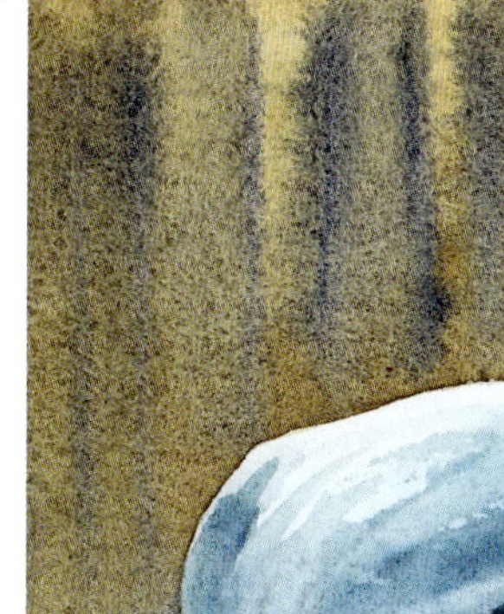

3 Hard and soft marks

Scale and balance are emphasized by using hard edges towards the front of the farrier and keeping the mark-making soft for painting the horse behind him.

4 Wet-in-wet backdrop

Wet-in-wet painting using cool tones gives some interest in the background while at the same time keeping it visually soft to maintain the sense of distance.

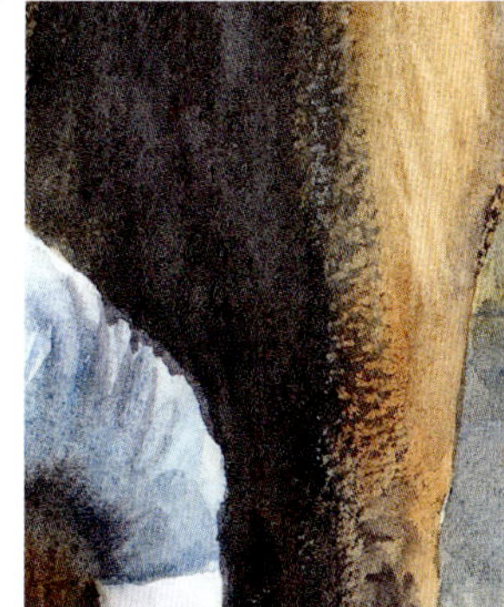

5 Dry-brush texture

A dry-brush technique is used to paint the tail of the horse, giving the impression of movement and the texture of the hairs.

A group of figures

PUTTING PEOPLE IN THE PICTURE

Many artists avoid putting people in their paintings, but a few figures can make your painting come alive. They needn't be detailed; often a suggestion of a figure is enough. The key to bring unity to the piece is capturing the proportions of figures within the perspective of the scene.

▪ Capturing people

Focus on the proportions, gesture, and pose of the figures: the way they walk, swing their arms, and lift their legs. Always consider the scale – you don't want figures taller than doorways, for instance. Unless the person is up-close, there is no need to worry about facial features or details of the hands and feet.

PUTTING IT INTO PRACTICE

This painting is more about the figures than the landscape. If you concentrate on the proportions and get the gestures right, you can use surprisingly loose brushwork to convey the sense of a bustling crowd.

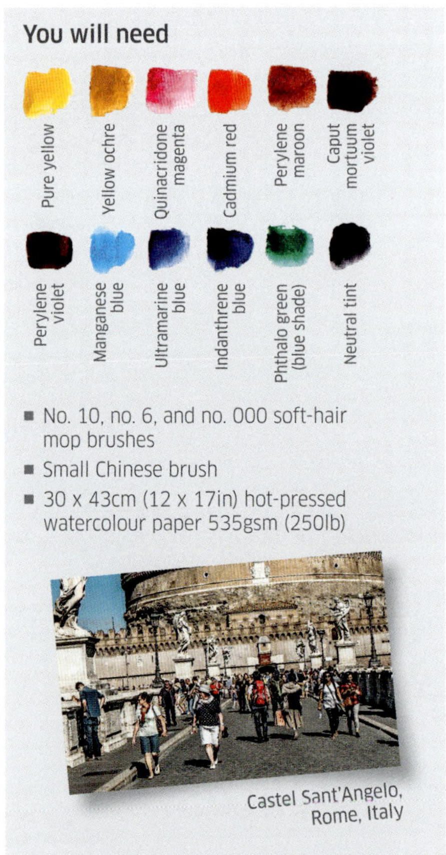

You will need

- Pure yellow
- Yellow ochre
- Quinacridone magenta
- Cadmium red
- Perylene maroon
- Caput mortuum violet
- Perylene violet
- Manganese blue
- Ultramarine blue
- Indanthrene blue
- Phthalo green (blue shade)
- Neutral tint

- No. 10, no. 6, and no. 000 soft-hair mop brushes
- Small Chinese brush
- 30 x 43cm (12 x 17in) hot-pressed watercolour paper 535gsm (250lb)

Castel Sant'Angelo, Rome, Italy

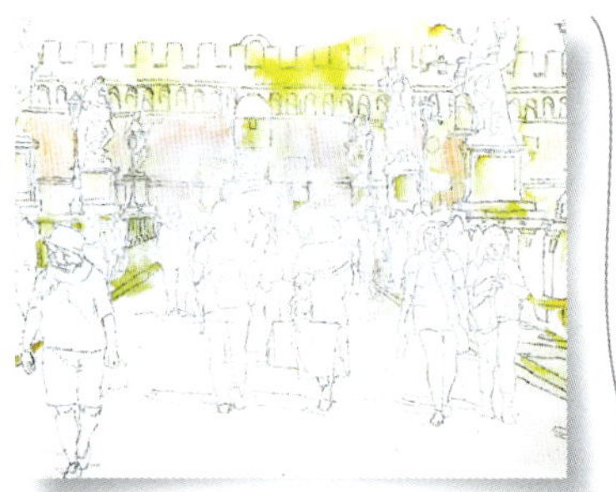

1 Prepare the paper
Using a large mop brush, dampen the paper around the foreground figures and statues. Lay wet-in-wet washes for the background, being careful to leave some light in the foreground. Think about colour as it will set the mood of the painting.

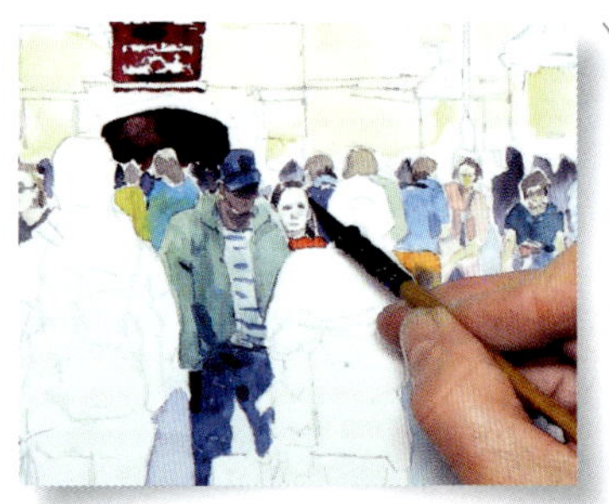

2 Background figures
Build up the background figures using a wet-on-dry technique, thoroughly drying each layer as you go. Separate light and dark tones as figures recede; very distant figures can just be silhouetted shapes.

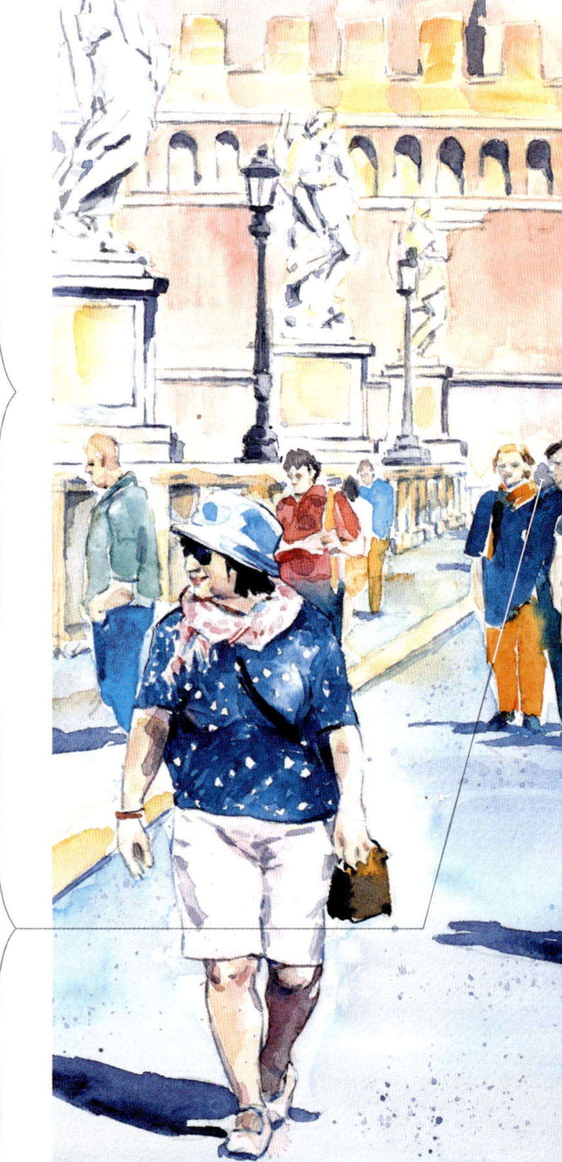

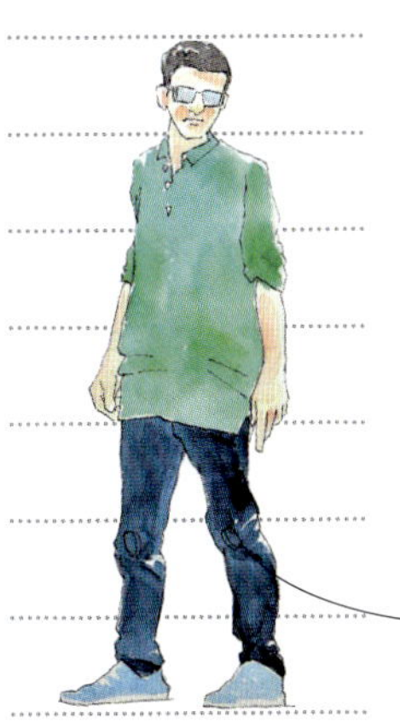

Proportions

A person is generally 7 to 8 "heads" tall. The belly button sits 3 heads down; wrists, crotch, and hips are halfway down; 4 heads down for fingertips; 5 for knee caps. Make sure the head sits on, and does not float above, the shoulders.

Bottom of knee cap is 5 "heads" down

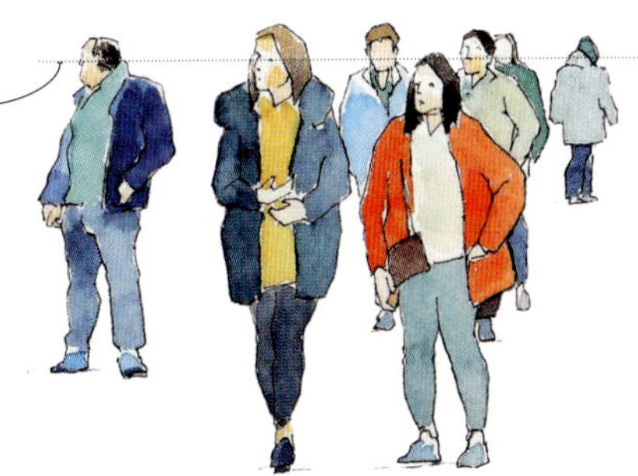

Standing perspective

On level ground, a crowd of people's heads appear at the same height but their leg-length decreases as they gain distance.

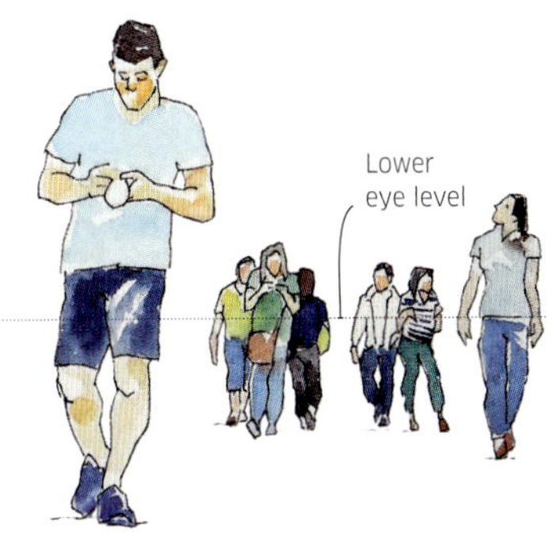

Seated perspective

If you are sitting, the eye line would be lower and run through the same part of each figure, probably around the chest.

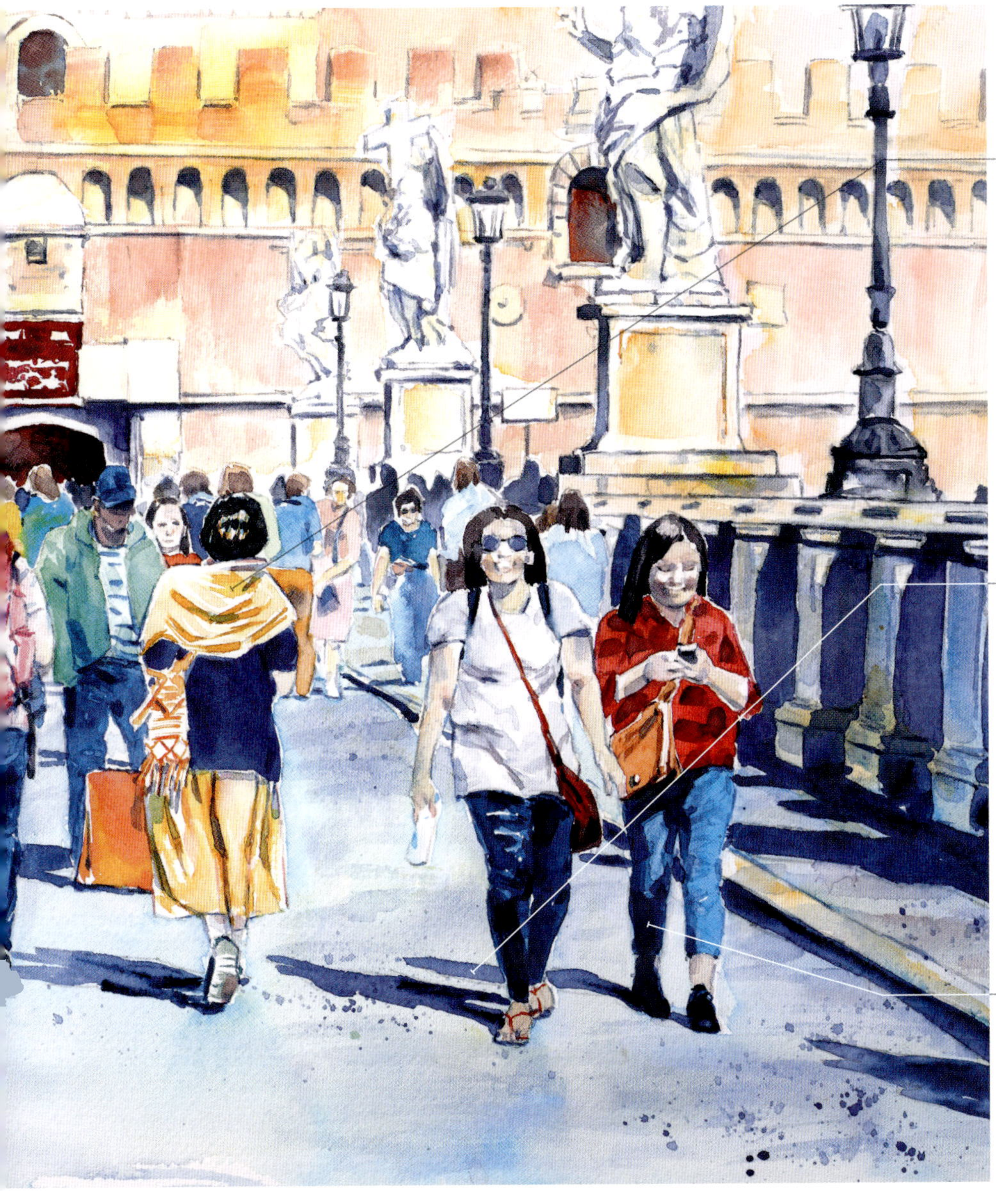

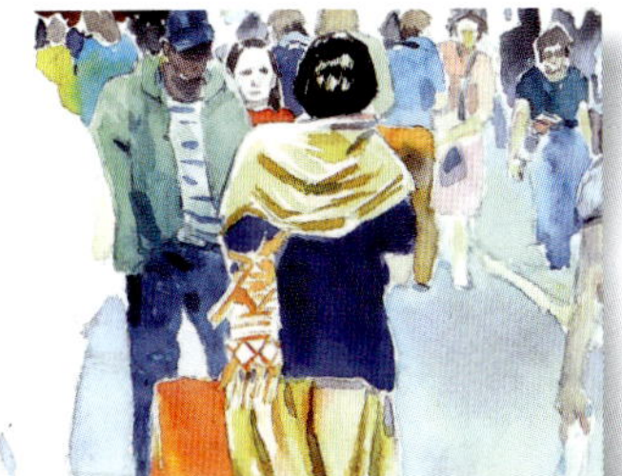

3 Foreground figures

Gently define features of the foreground figures as you build up tone, without being over-fussy with detail – just hint at features.

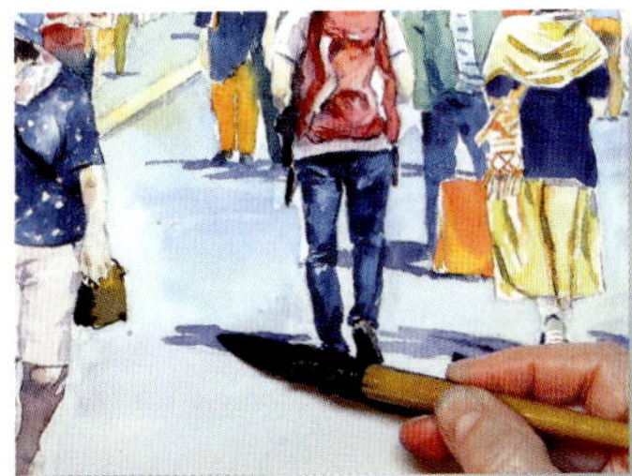

4 Add shadows and detail

Once each layer is dry, paint in shadows and detail, focussing on ever-smaller shapes every layer.

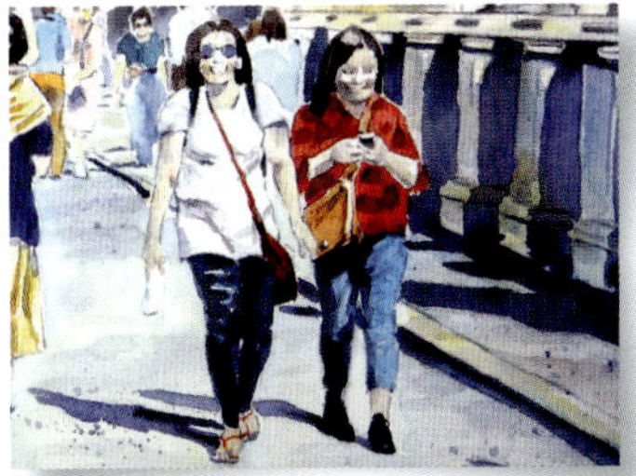

5 Finishing touches

Add more local colour and splatter the foreground for interest. Darker tonal accents will give depth.

Fashion illustration

EXPRESSING CREATIVE IDEAS

Compared to traditional figure painting, fashion illustration allows you to develop a more abstract, simplified approach to a pose. Any medium is suitable but watercolour is especially expressive.

■ Taking a graphic approach

Your choice of materials is endless, and this is a great opportunity to use mixed media and many expressive watercolour techniques to convey the originality of your designs. Using graphic materials, such as liquid watercolour, fineliner pens, technical pencils, gouache, and collage, will add extra drama to the clothes.

PUTTING IT INTO PRACTICE

Inspired by catwalk images, this illustration combines bold, simple colours with added pattern and fine detail to showcase the clothes, using varied tones and blends to add depth and texture.

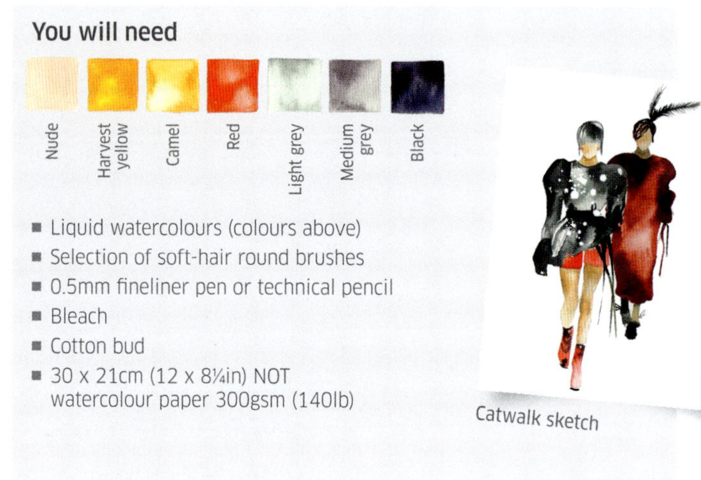

- Liquid watercolours (colours above)
- Selection of soft-hair round brushes
- 0.5mm fineliner pen or technical pencil
- Bleach
- Cotton bud
- 30 x 21cm (12 x 8¼in) NOT watercolour paper 300gsm (140lb)

Catwalk sketch

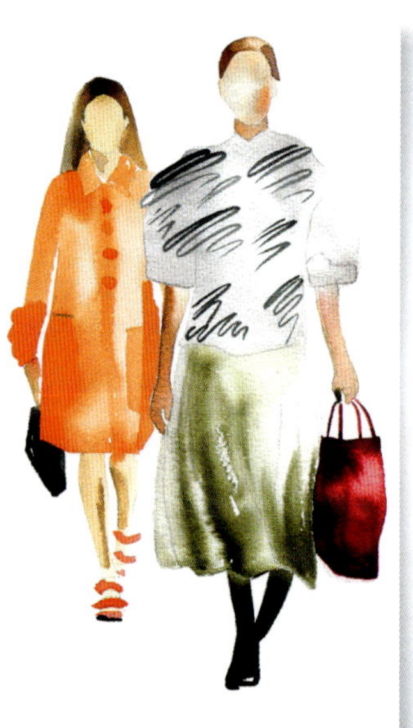

Pen and ink
Technical pens and fine marker pens can be used to either outline an image, or add detail over a dry wash. Scribbles, hatching, and shading can all be used to suggest pattern or fabric sheen.

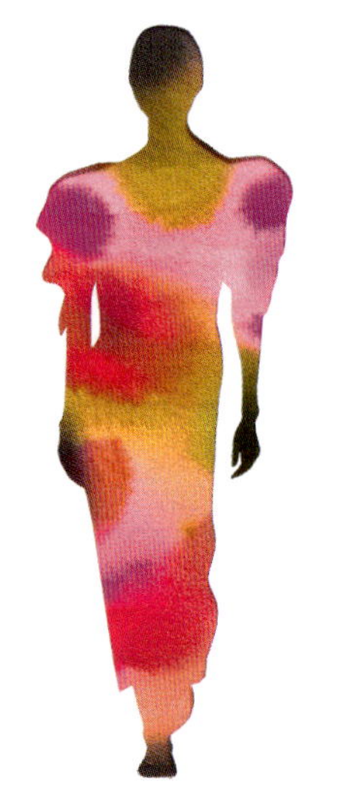

Watercolour effects
Fluid wet-in-wet blends within a simplified outline, or silhouette, suggest both movement and pattern in fabric. Manipulate blends to suggest garment components, such as sleeves.

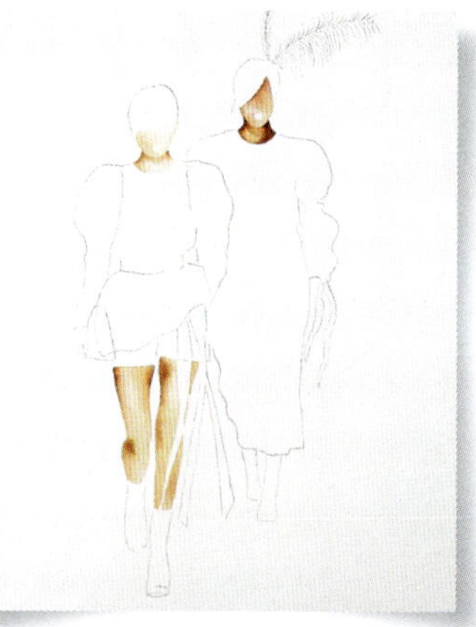

1 Draw outlines and add skin tones
Use a fine pen or pencil to develop your ideas. Include details and outline any areas of different colours. Facial features are kept to a minimum but add hair shape and lips. Start by painting the skin with two or three natural tones and no. 2 and no. 4 brushes, keeping just inside the pencil line.

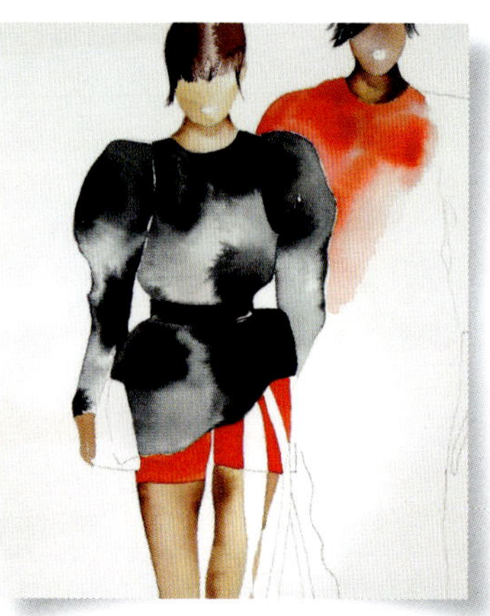

2 Build colour
Fill the coloured areas, using undiluted colour for solid features, such as the shorts, and ensuring each area dries before adding the next. Use dilutions of black to fill the top.

> "**Combine** graphic drawing skills **with painterly** effects to develop ideas."

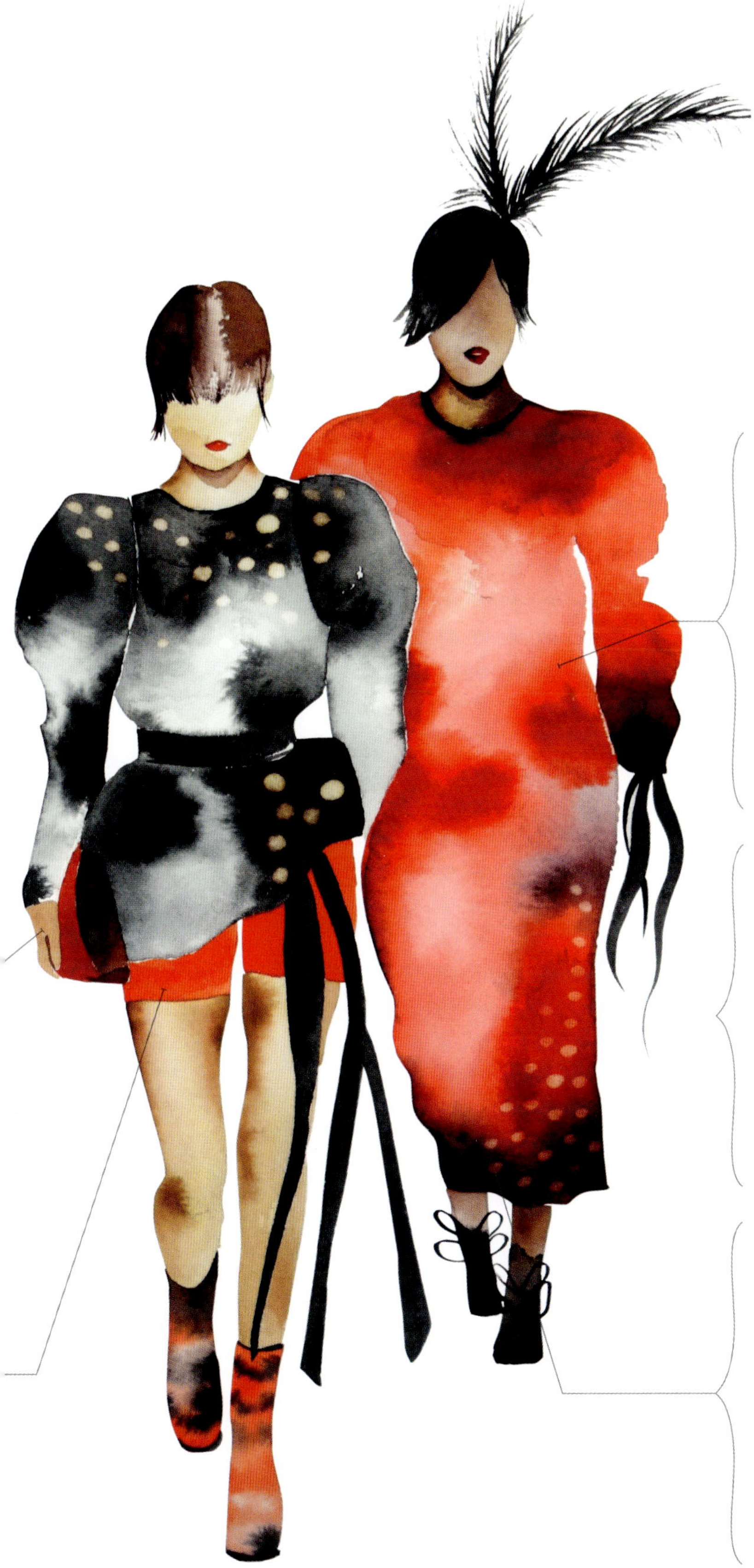

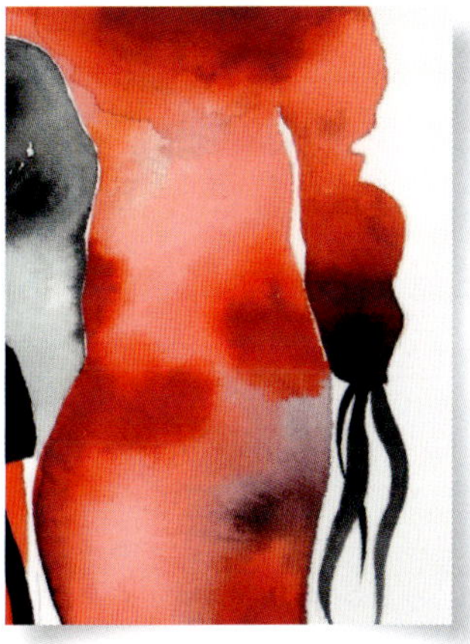

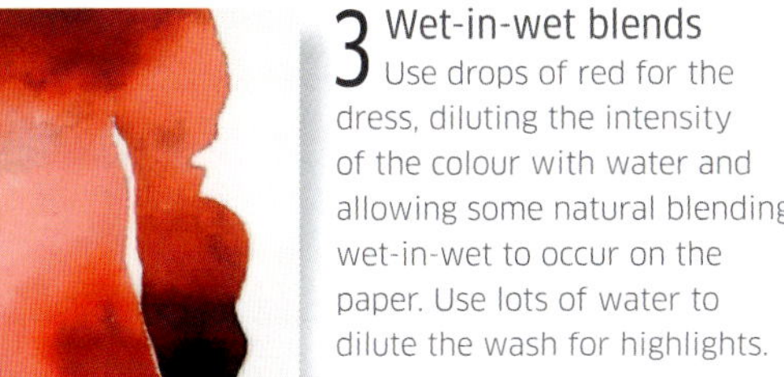

3 Wet-in-wet blends
Use drops of red for the dress, diluting the intensity of the colour with water and allowing some natural blending wet-in-wet to occur on the paper. Use lots of water to dilute the wash for highlights.

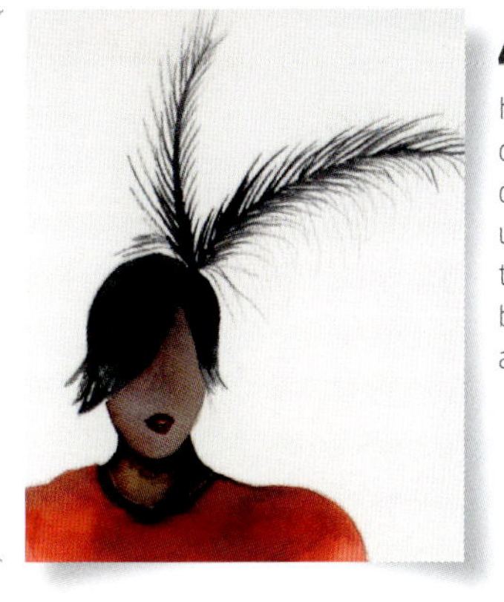

4 Fine details
Once the main clothes have been added and have dried, continue to add the finer details and the accessories, using a thin no. 1 brush. Paint the feathers with undiluted black. Alternatively, use a fineliner pen.

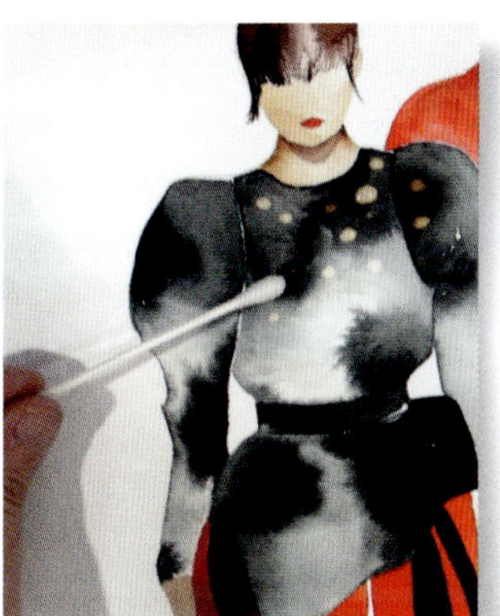

5 Fabric patterns
To add a dot pattern to both figures, carefully apply drops of bleach with a cotton bud over the watercolour, re-applying the cotton bud each time and using the tip to vary the size of the dots. Some pigments will leave a lighter tone rather than a bright white.

Incidental figures

PORTRAYING FIGURES IN A LANDSCAPE

Figures naturally tend to demand our attention and can dominate a scene. For landscapes, all elements should blend to a harmonious whole. Through careful planning and colour choices, you can subdue the impact of figures in various ways to create a balanced composition.

PUTTING IT INTO PRACTICE

In this view, the figures are part of the landscape, adding incidental detail to the overall composition. Similar colours and tones from the sea and land help the figures to blend with other elements without distraction.

You will need

- Azo yellow
- Cadmium yellow
- Burnt sienna
- Quinacridone magenta
- Cadmium red
- French ultramarine
- Phthalo blue (green shade)

- No. 14 soft-hair round brush
- No. 10 soft-hair mop brush
- 25 x 35cm (10 x 14in) NOT watercolour paper 300gsm (140lb)

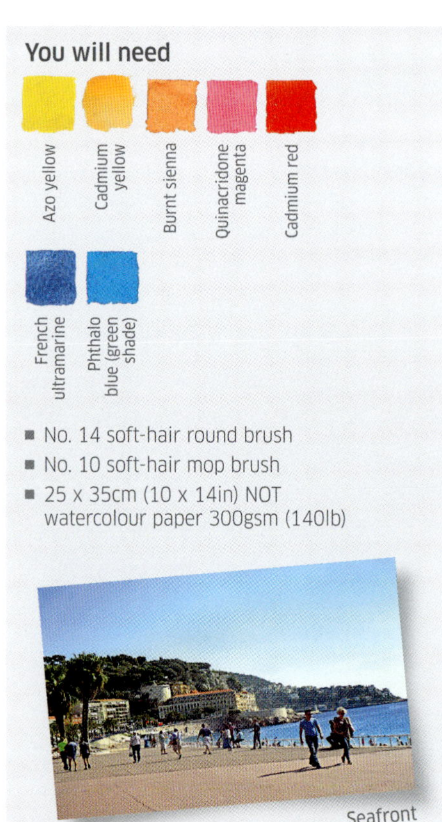
Seafront

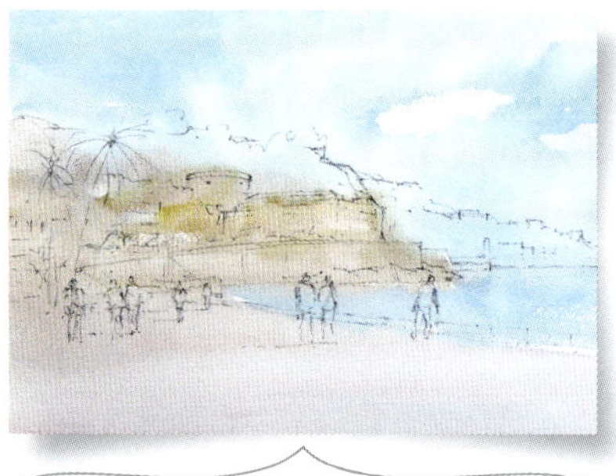

1 All-over wash
Paint a blending background wash from top to bottom. Use a mix of phthalo blue with a touch of quinacridone magenta for the sky and sea, and a warm mix of quinacridone magenta and azo yellow for the land. Do not leave space for the figures; nothing is more isolating than a hard edge around every figure.

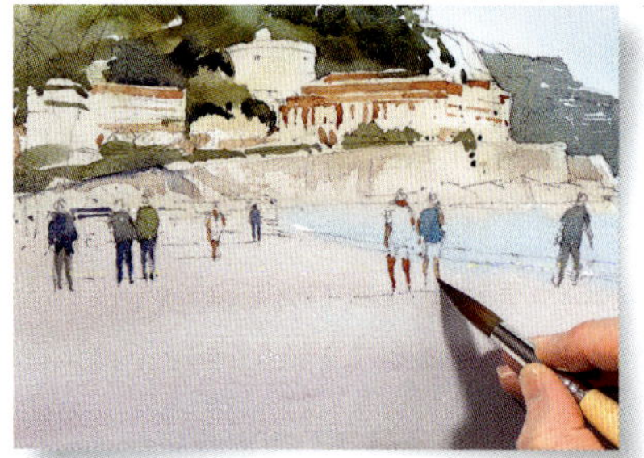

2 Blend figures to background
Start to gradually define the elements with the second wash, warming the middle ground with cadmium yellow. Use similar tonal values for the figures, carrying touches of burnt sienna in the landscape to create visual connections.

◼ Integrating figures
It is easy to make figures in a landscape too prominent. Remember you are painting a landscape that happens to have figures, not a figure study with a landscape; the figures must blend with the other elements. Try to connect and harmonize the figure with the landscape by merging edges and repeating colours.

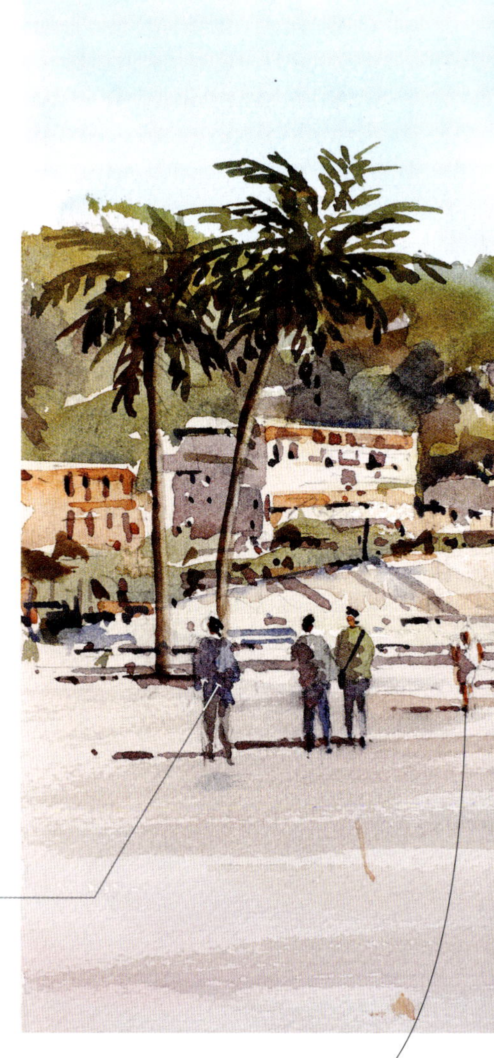

Allow some of the figures to partly blend with the background

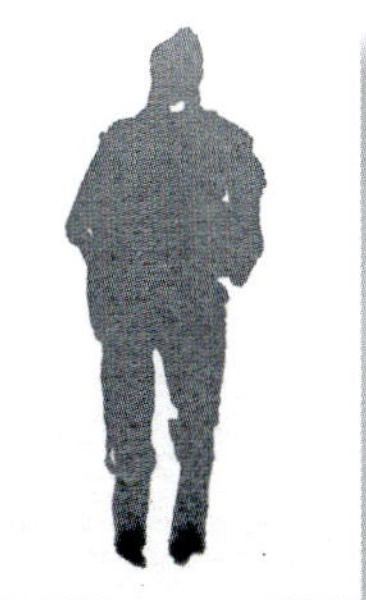 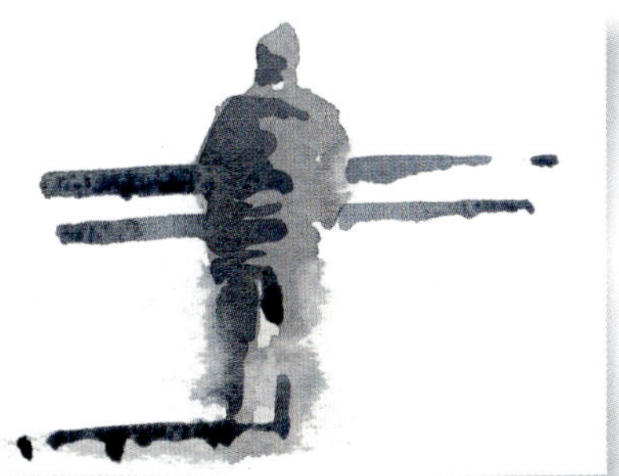

Blending in

White space or painting a hard edge around a figure will immediately isolate them, as if spotlit. To avoid this, soften edges and partly blend the figure with the background, linking it to other features.

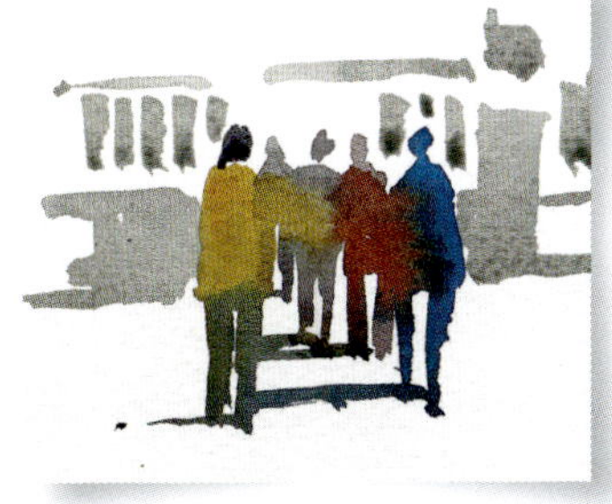 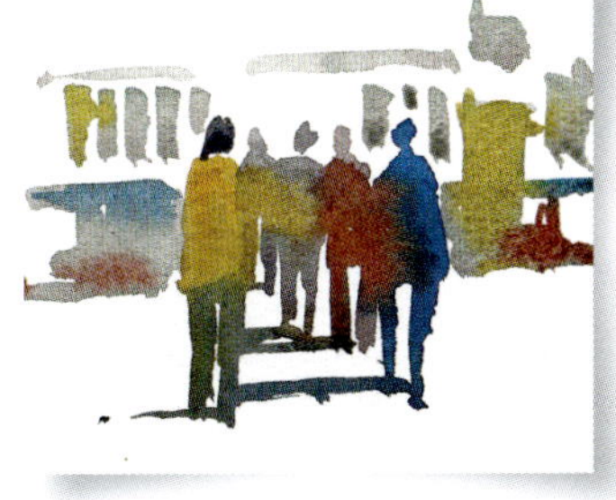

Repeating colours

Try to integrate figures into the rest of the landscape by using the local colour for both, and if you must use a strong colour such as red in your figure, include it in the landscape, too, to lessen the visual effect.

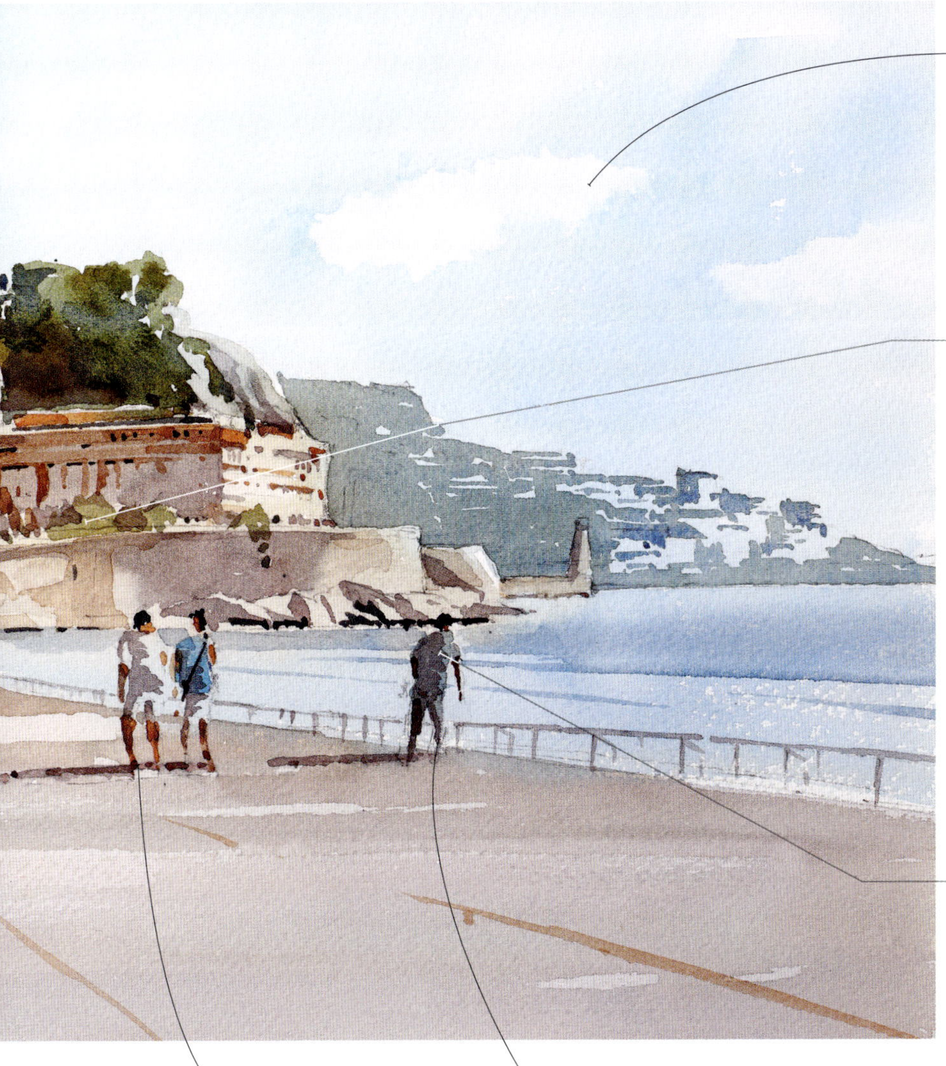

A few light clouds break up the sky wash and balance the composition

The same mix of phthalo blue and cadmium red is used to link all mid and foreground shadows

Blend the lower legs with the shadows to anchor the figure to the ground

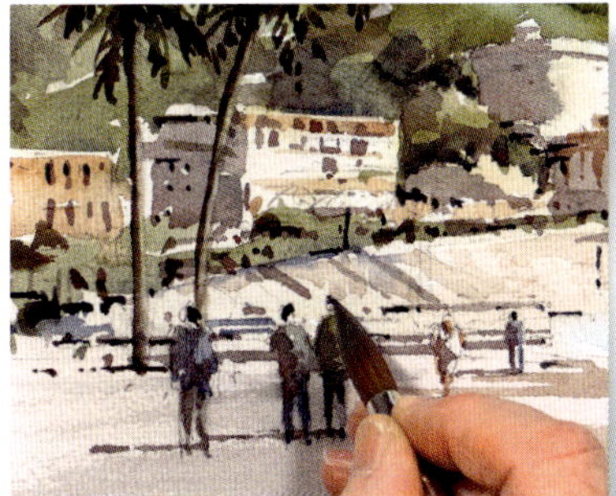

3 Connect colours

Repeat every colour in the landscape in the figures (and vice versa) to create harmony. Here, the stronger greens and browns of the palm trees link to the clothing in the figures beneath.

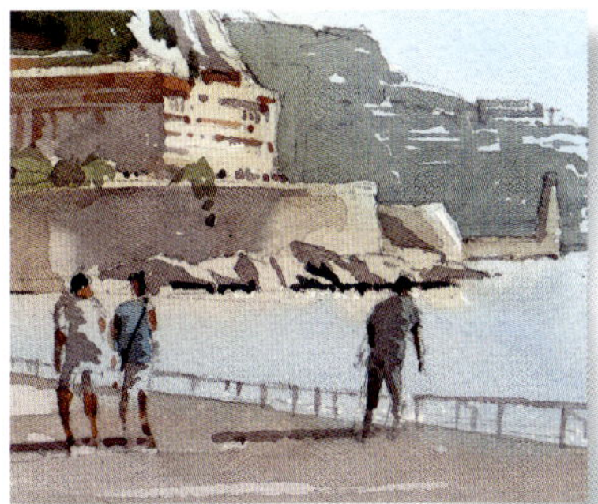

4 Tonal balance

Continue to strengthen all colours, adding darks here and there with dots and dashes to create tonal interest. Treat the figures with no more importance than the trees or buildings, using similar tones and colour.

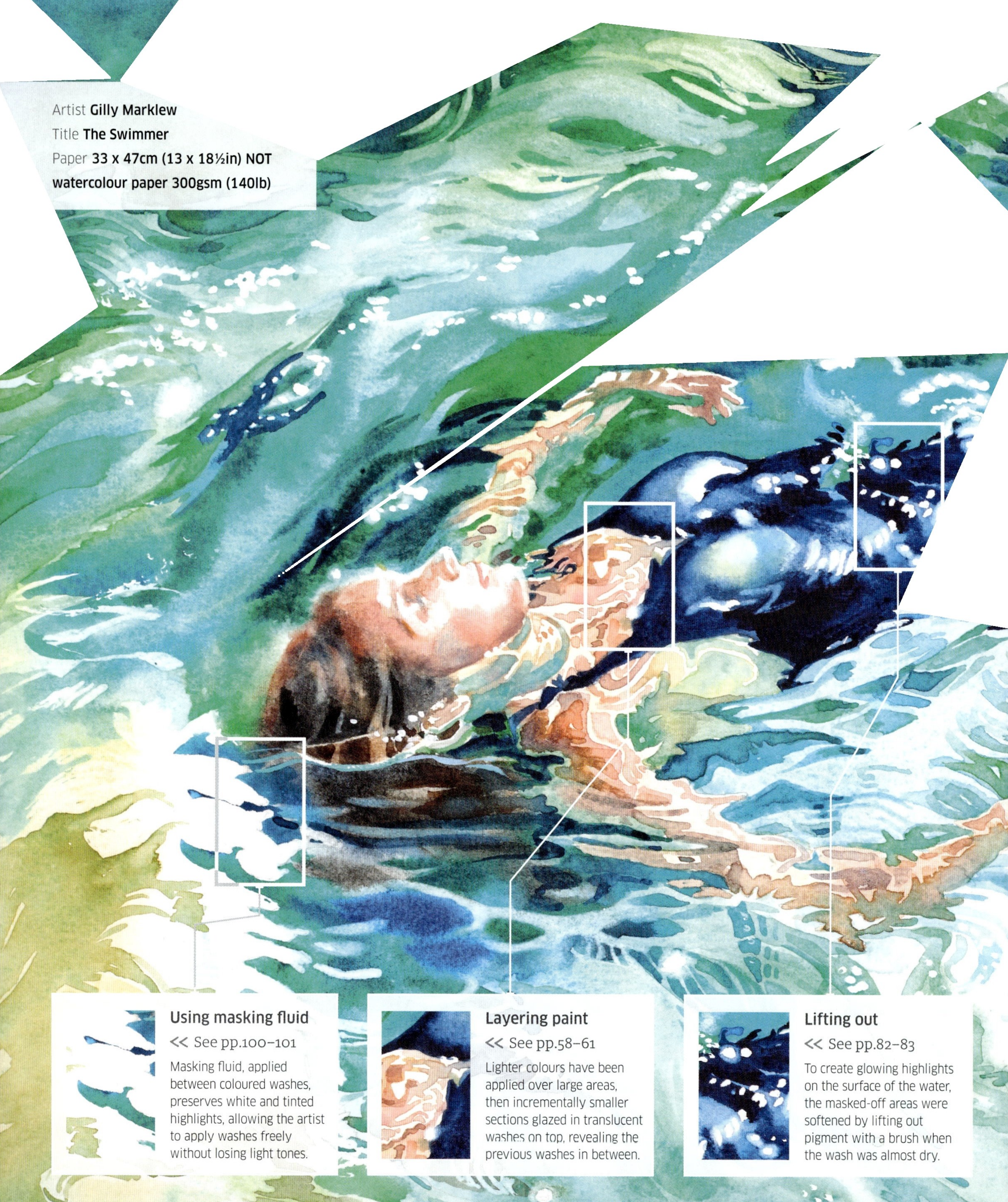

Using masking fluid
<< See pp.100–101

Masking fluid, applied
between coloured washes,
preserves white and tinted
highlights, allowing the artist
to apply washes freely
without losing light tones.

Layering paint
<< See pp.58–61

Lighter colours have been
applied over large areas,
then incrementally smaller
sections glazed in translucent
washes on top, revealing the
previous washes in between.

Lifting out
<< See pp.82–83

To create glowing highlights
on the surface of the water,
the masked-off areas were
softened by lifting out
pigment with a brush when
the wash was almost dry.

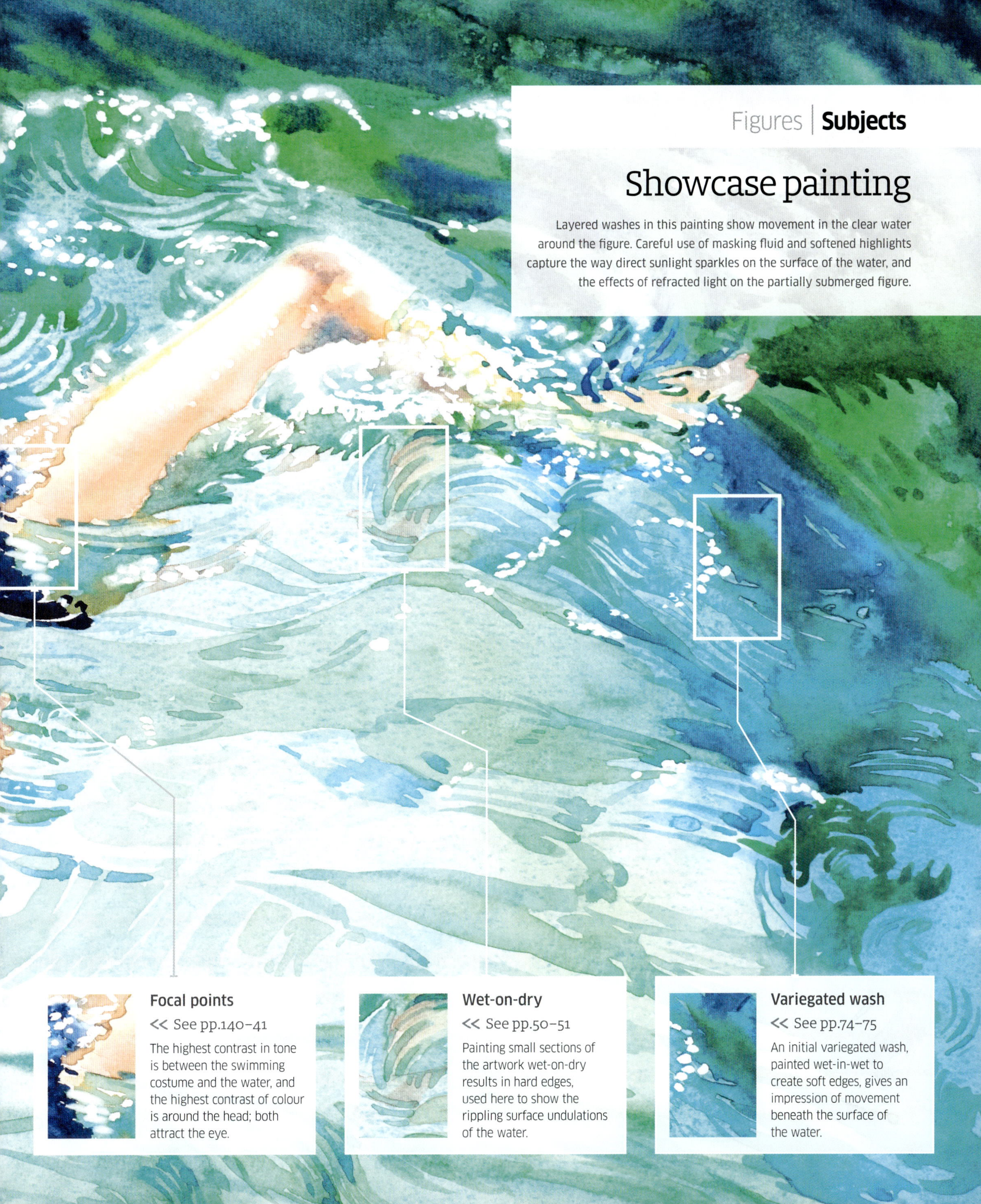

Showcase painting

Layered washes in this painting show movement in the clear water around the figure. Careful use of masking fluid and softened highlights capture the way direct sunlight sparkles on the surface of the water, and the effects of refracted light on the partially submerged figure.

Focal points
<< See pp.140–41

The highest contrast in tone is between the swimming costume and the water, and the highest contrast of colour is around the head; both attract the eye.

Wet-on-dry
<< See pp.50–51

Painting small sections of the artwork wet-on-dry results in hard edges, used here to show the rippling surface undulations of the water.

Variegated wash
<< See pp.74–75

An initial variegated wash, painted wet-in-wet to create soft edges, gives an impression of movement beneath the surface of the water.

Pet portraits

PAINTING ANIMAL COMPANIONS

Capturing your pet's unique character in watercolour is a challenge, but with a subject that is familiar and a medium that is particularly suited to the soft nature of fur and whiskers, you will soon master pet portraiture. Sketch from life and take lots of reference photos to help choose a pose.

■ Conveying highlights and textures

A common characteristic of most pets is their fur. Utilize different brushstrokes for fur textures, layering your strokes wet-on-dry to build a sense of density and direction, helping to give your pet form. Highlights found in eyes, wet noses, and shiny fur can be incorporated with resist techniques (see pp.100–103).

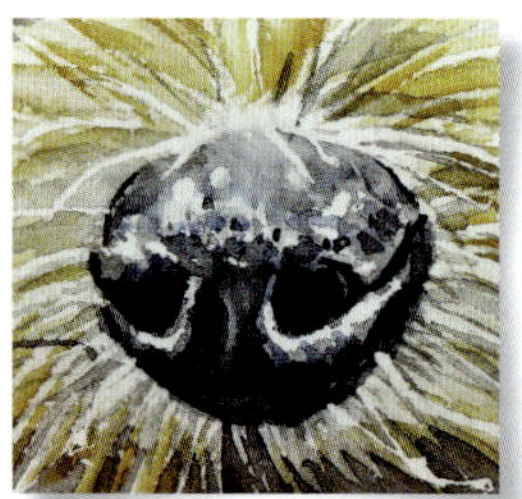

White highlights
For contrasts in markings you can leave some of the white of the paper showing, or use masking fluid in the early stages to preserve the highlights. Once removed, the masked area will have a defined, crisp edge that can be softened if required.

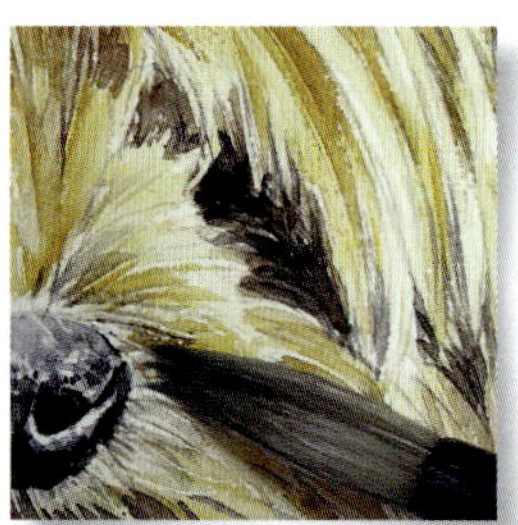

Fur texture
Chinese brushes are ideal for painting fur as they hold their shape when spread, and you can paint several hairs at the same time. These brushes are very absorbent and will hold a lot of paint, creating fluid strokes.

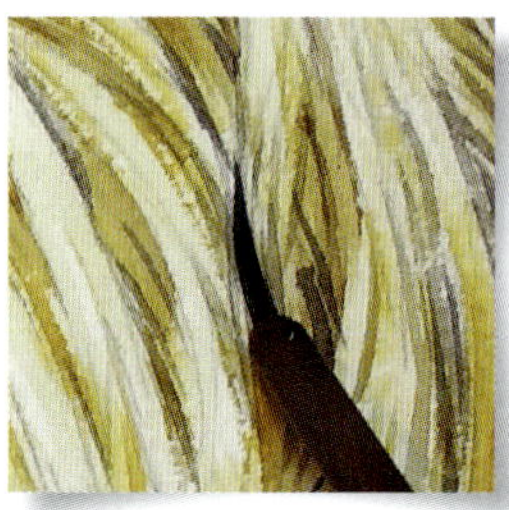

Wet-on-dry strands
Load a small brush with wet paint and paint on dry paper to achieve strokes with hard edges; ideal for defining strands of fur. This wet-on-dry technique tends to give you more control when working in small areas.

PUTTING IT INTO PRACTICE

In this pose the face is painted in detail, making the spaniel's doleful eyes the focus with his direct gaze. The form of the body is conveyed using different brushes, set against a loosely defined background.

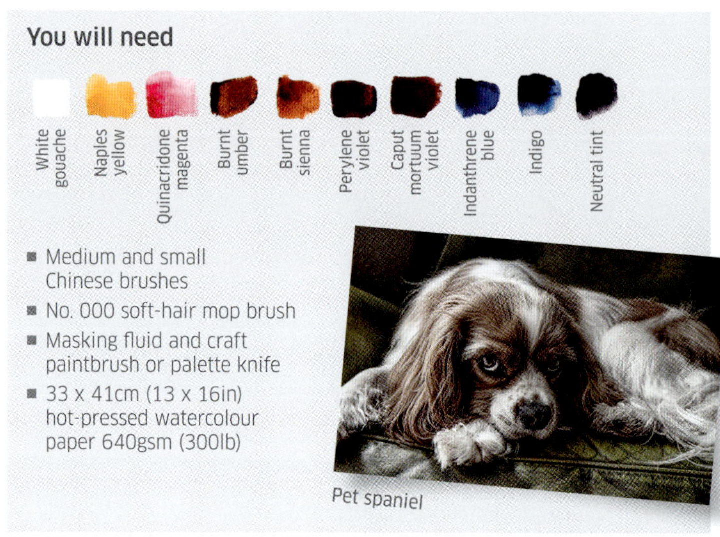

- Medium and small Chinese brushes
- No. 000 soft-hair mop brush
- Masking fluid and craft paintbrush or palette knife
- 33 x 41cm (13 x 16in) hot-pressed watercolour paper 640gsm (300lb)

Pet spaniel

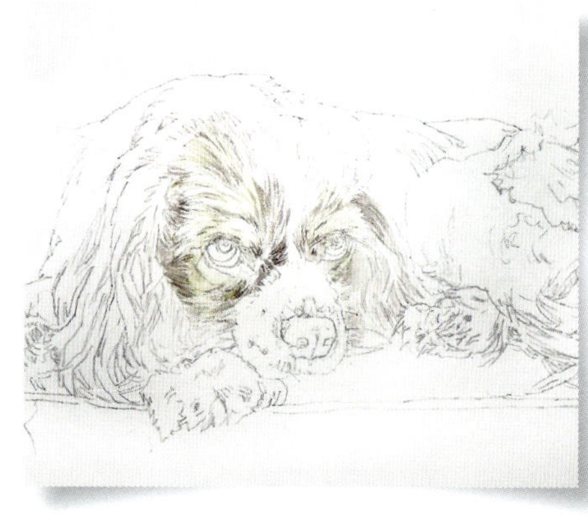

1 Establish basic proportions
Check the relationship between eyes, nose, and ears to make sure your drawing is accurate. Mask highlights such as the whiskers and eyes, and lay in lightest colour areas with a splayed Chinese brush.

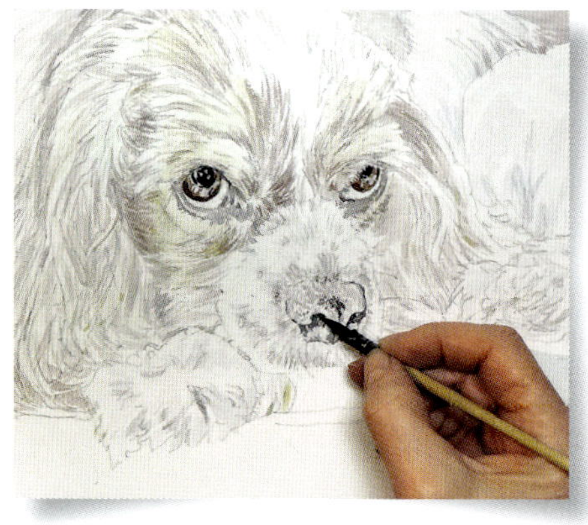

2 Underlying form
Notice how the fur follows the underlying form, parting over the muzzle, for example. Mask to keep the areas of lightest paint. Think of masking fluid like paint and consider the marks you're making. Start to build up glazes for the eyes and nose.

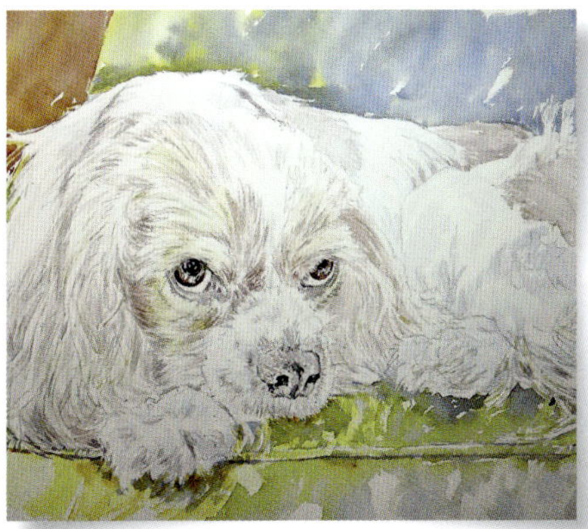

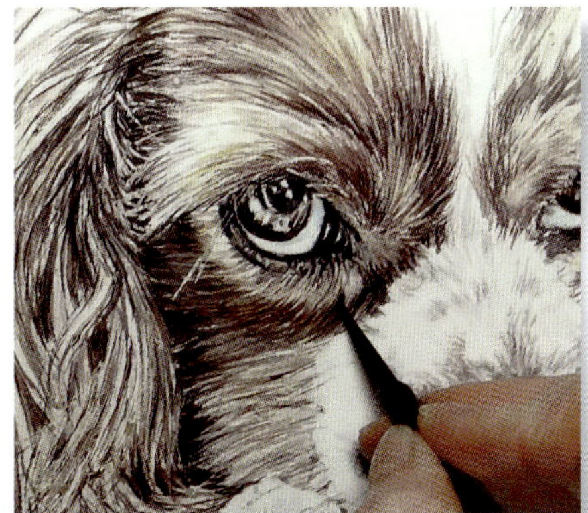

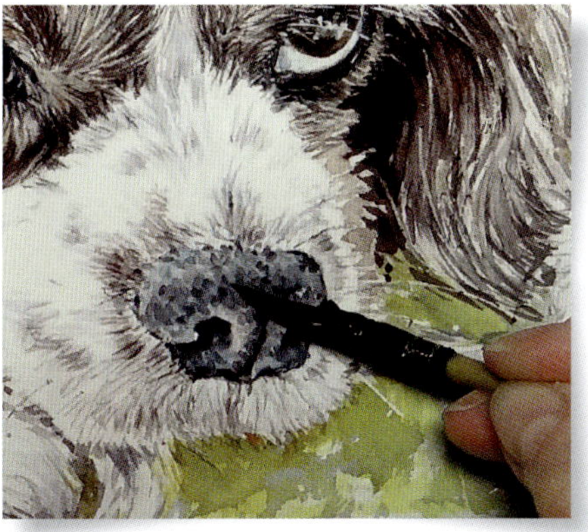

3 Background washes

Paint in a loose background with large variegated washes. Mix your colours on the paper not on the palette; they will be much fresher. Use the side and tip of a medium Chinese brush for different, loose marks.

4 Build layers

Add fur colour and when dry define the area, following the direction of the fur with your brush. Use a small Chinese brush to build detail wet-on-dry (see left), giving the illusion of layers of fur without overworking.

5 Soften edges

When you feel you have built enough depth in your painting, remove the masking fluid. Use a damp mop brush to soften and blend hard edges as needed. Add final details with a few strokes of white gouache.

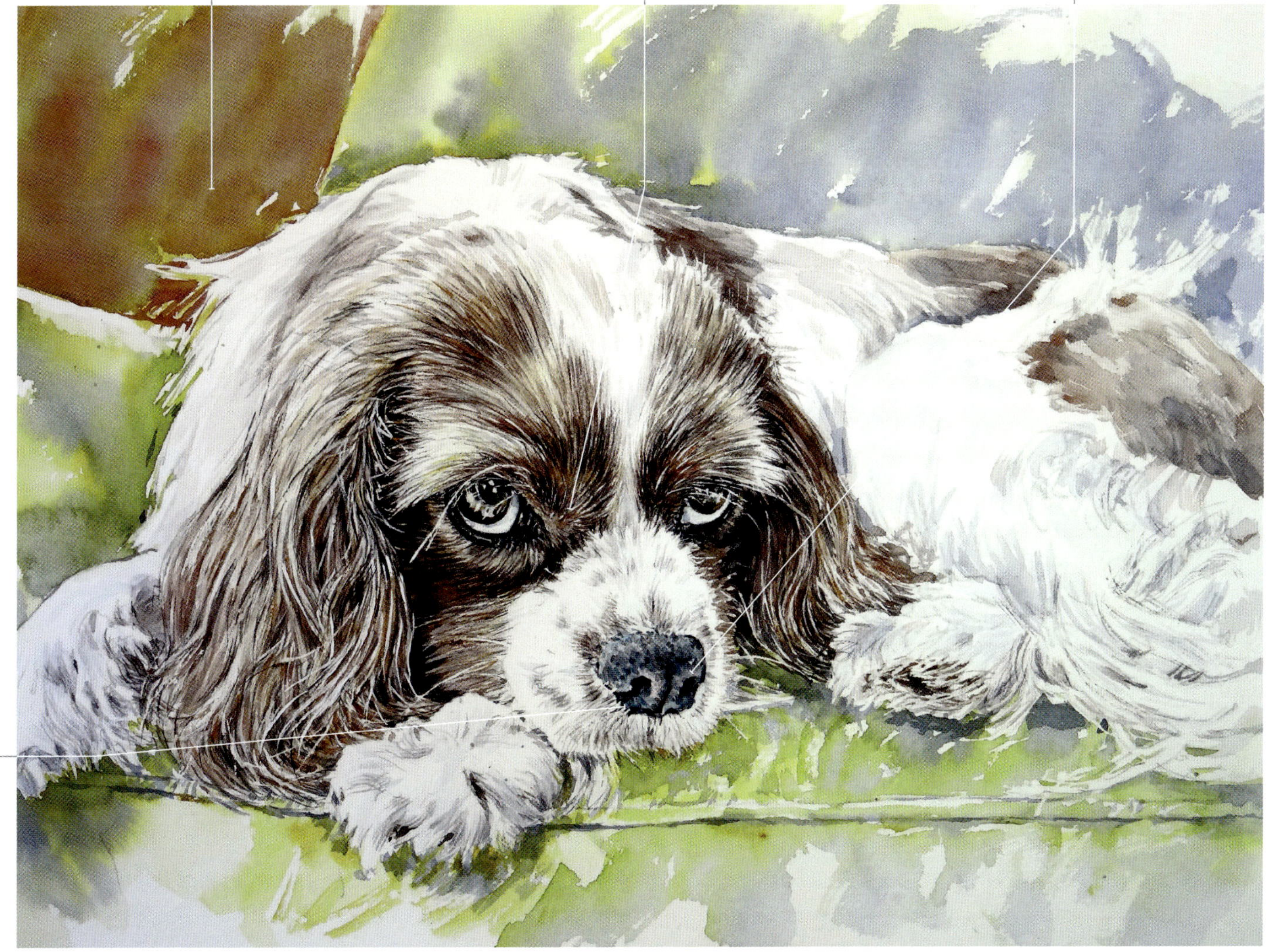

Creatures in motion

CAPTURING WILDLIFE CHARACTERISTICS

Careful observation is key to painting animals since you need to capture their essence in nature in just a few brushstrokes. Understanding their anatomy is useful, too, as proportion and balance are equally important for an authentic portrayal.

◼ Defining features and form

Experiment with the best techniques to use to express the key features, such as eyes, ears, nose, mouth or beak, feathers or fur. Certain techniques lend themselves perfectly to describe fur, where you want to give the impression of both texture and density. Layering techniques help to build colours that not only describe an animal's pelt but also help to suggest the form of the body beneath.

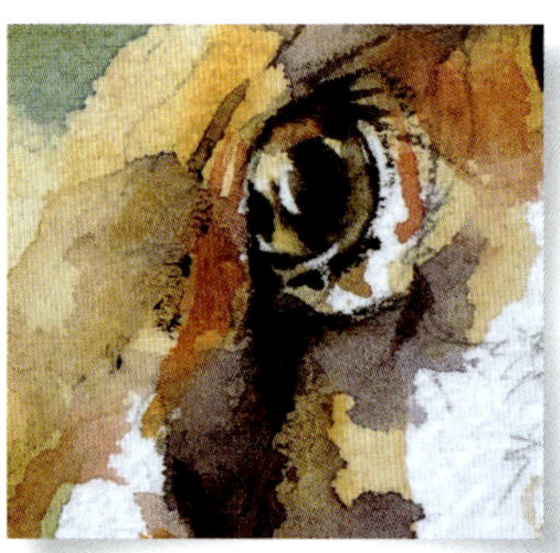

Dry-in-wet

Single, brisk strokes or dabs of dry paint into wet washes produce very effective results for fur, hair, or animal markings. The drier the paint, the more it will hold its form in the wet layer, blurring just enough to give credible effects of fur. Be aware that if paint is not dry enough it might cause runbacks.

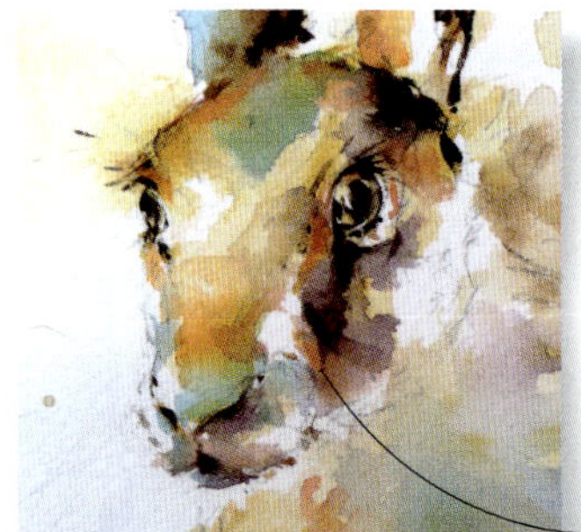

Stretching out

Mix a loose wash and paint it lightly over the dried layer. With a slightly damp brush, drag and "stretch" the wet paint into the areas where you want crisp shapes of tone, shadow, or fur. Such "stretching out" allows you to control the sharp edges.

PUTTING IT INTO PRACTICE

The interplay of cooler tones contrasting with the warmer tones in this painting aims to thrust the hare forward, emphasizing a sense of urgency and its speed. Loose impressions of fur add vitality.

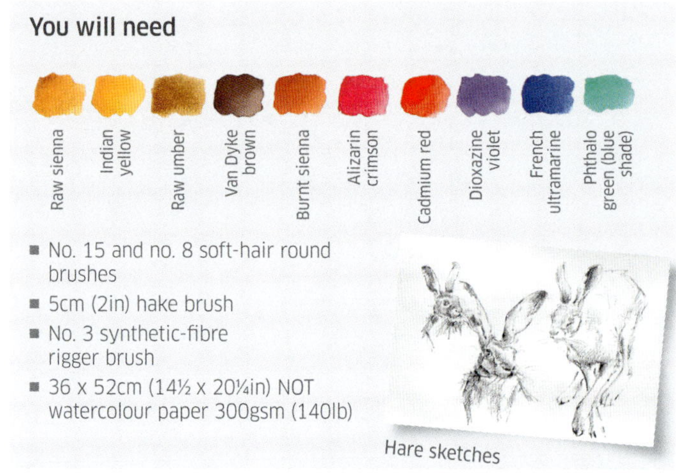

You will need

- No. 15 and no. 8 soft-hair round brushes
- 5cm (2in) hake brush
- No. 3 synthetic-fibre rigger brush
- 36 x 52cm (14½ x 20¼in) NOT watercolour paper 300gsm (140lb)

Hare sketches

1 Initial sketch
Sketch the pose, noting the angle and length of the ears (the ears of a hare are surprisingly long). The setting of the ears dictates the pitch of the head. Take care to get the balance right so that the shift of weight on the downward leg would convincingly propel the hare forwards. Correct proportion is key.

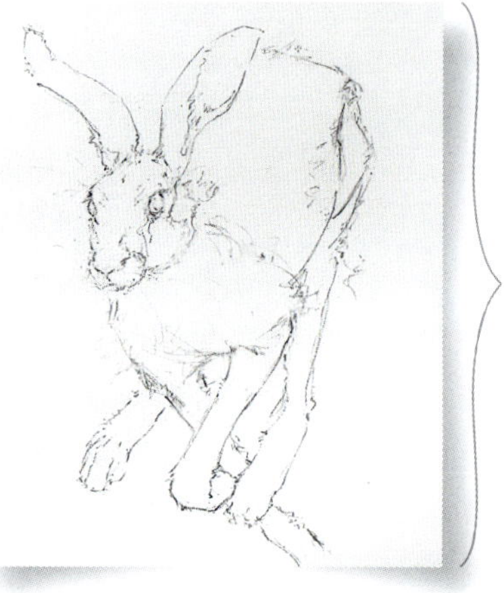

Sharper edges add definition

"**Use rapid strokes** and loose wet-in-wet mixes **to reflect the immediacy** of a moving subject."

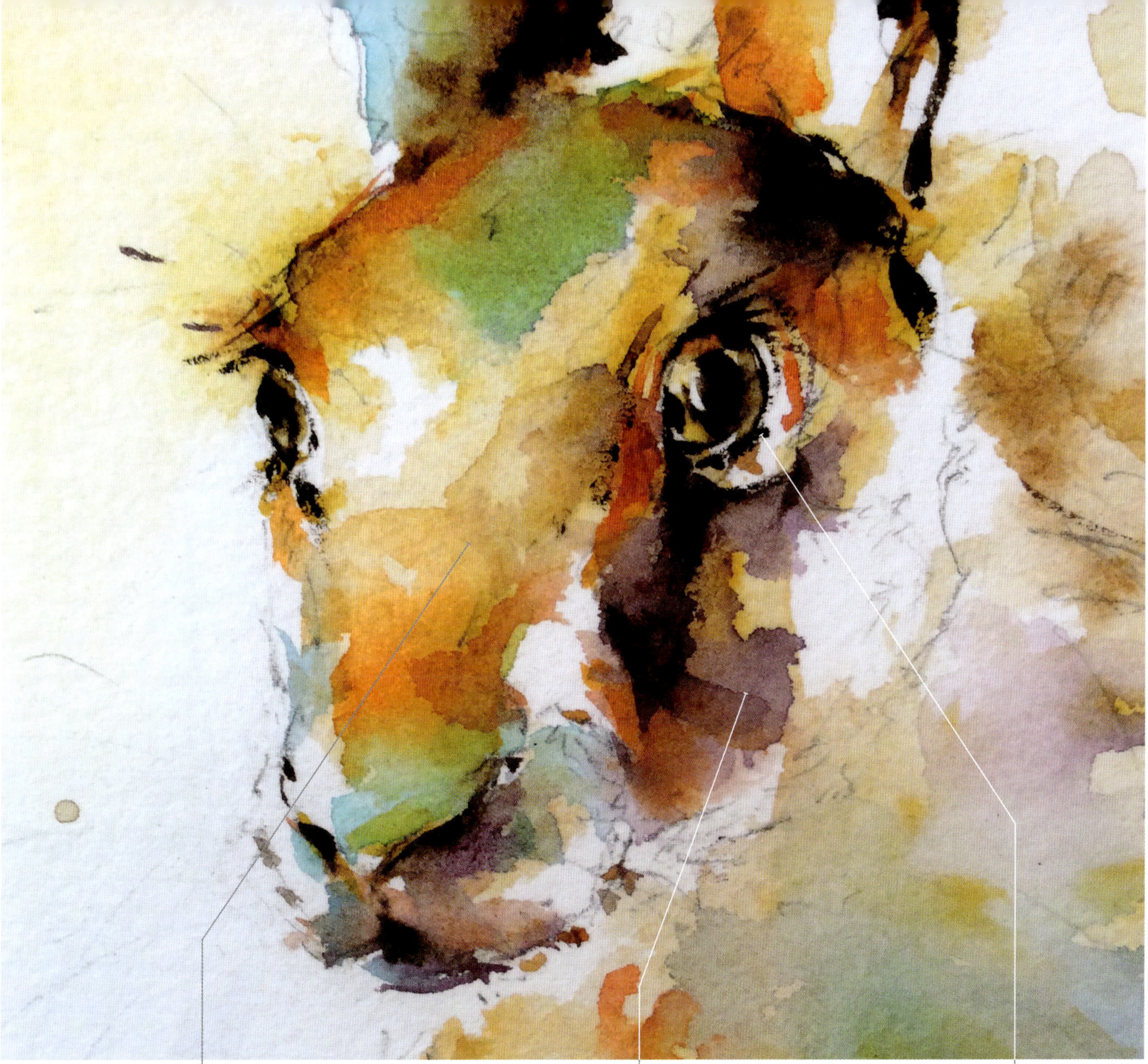

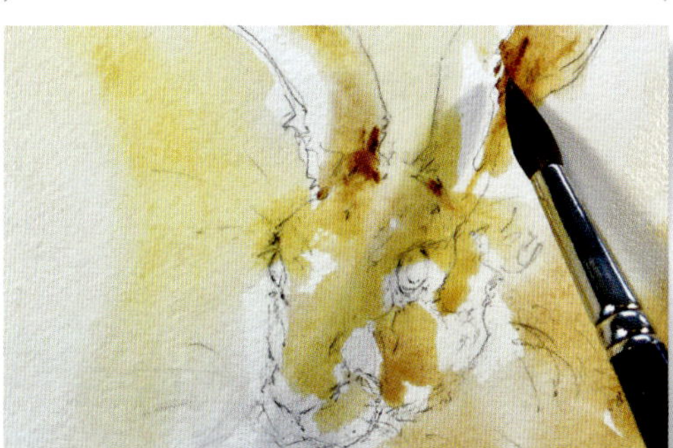

2 Wet-in-wet variegated wash
Generously wet the paper, leaving some areas dry as highlights. Drop in raw sienna, burnt sienna, and raw umber, alternating the quantities and strengths to establish the initial form and depth.

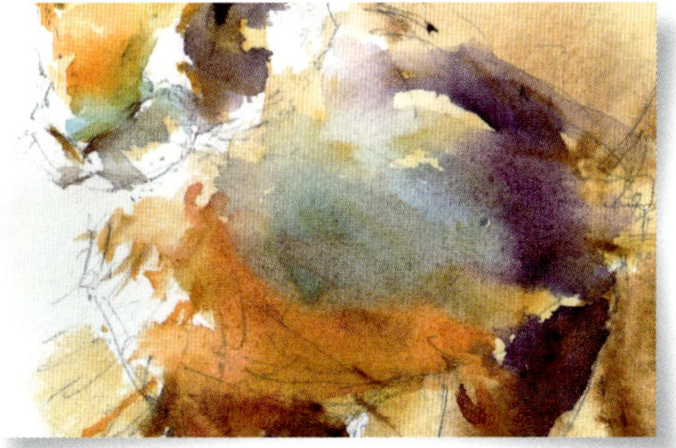

3 Darker tones
Once the initial glaze layer is dry, re-wet areas to establish stronger darker tones using a wet-in-wet wash of Dioxazine violet and Van Dyke brown for the darks, and warmer oranges for the highlights.

4 Dry-in-wet detail
Beginning with a wet-in-wet wash, drop a mix of raw sienna with a hint of Indian yellow into the eye area, leaving a chink unpainted for the highlight. Using the dry-in-wet method (see left), add the pupil with Van Dyke brown and a touch of French ultramarine to deepen the hue.

5 Stretch out

When the second glaze is dry, use the purple mix to stretch out and form the deeper tone of the cheek below the eye. Do the same for the shadow inside the ear and the top of the head, using a cooler tone of the phthalo green. The sharp edges help to define the anatomy.

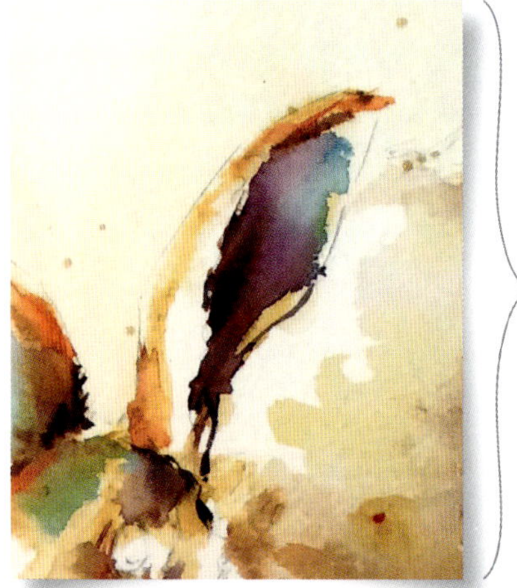

6 Dry brush detail

With Van Dyke brown and a dry brush, indicate the nose, taking care not to make it too strong nor to drag attention away from the eye.

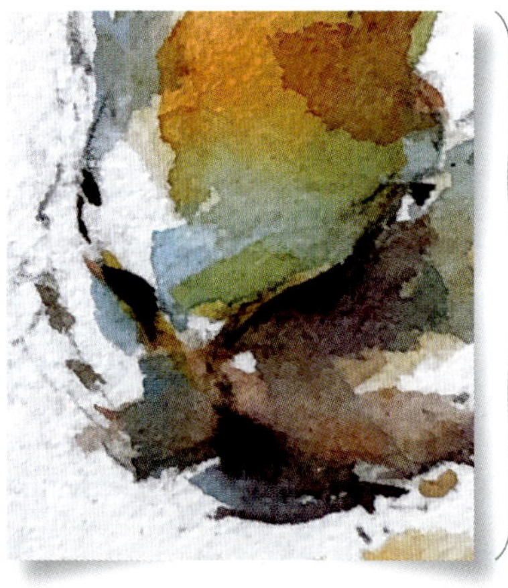

7 Fur effects

Suggest the shape of the body through a combination of stretching out and dry-in-wet techniques to create the effect of fur and form. Use a wet-on-dry glaze layer on the body with thicker paint in wetted areas to suggest dense fur.

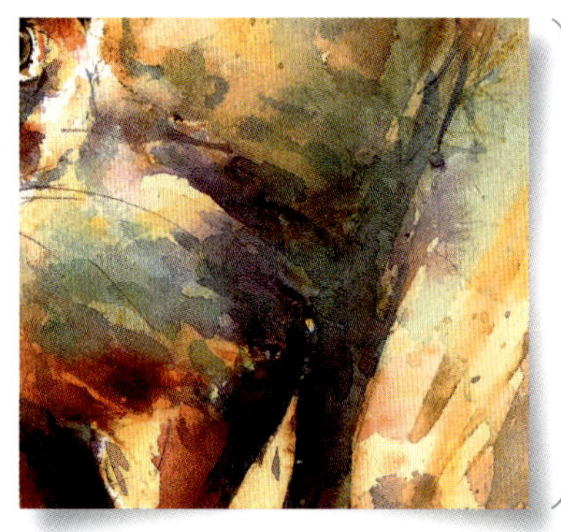

"When working **dry-in-wet,** test **how dry the paint is** on your brush **before applying it** to the wet paint."

8 Defined details

With a rigger brush, paint the whiskers with dry Van Dyke brown in one swift stroke per whisker, to keep it light and immediate.

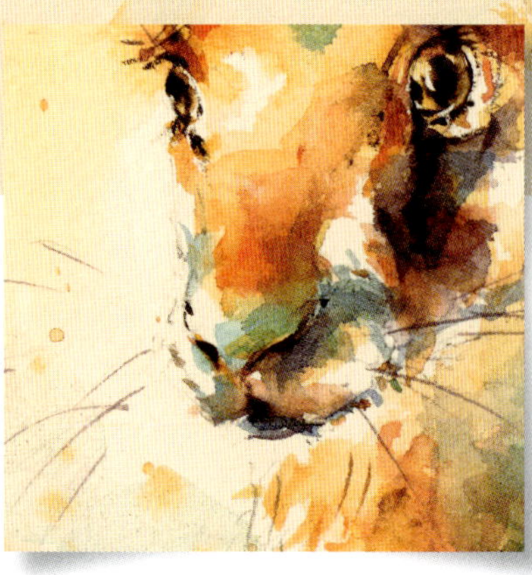

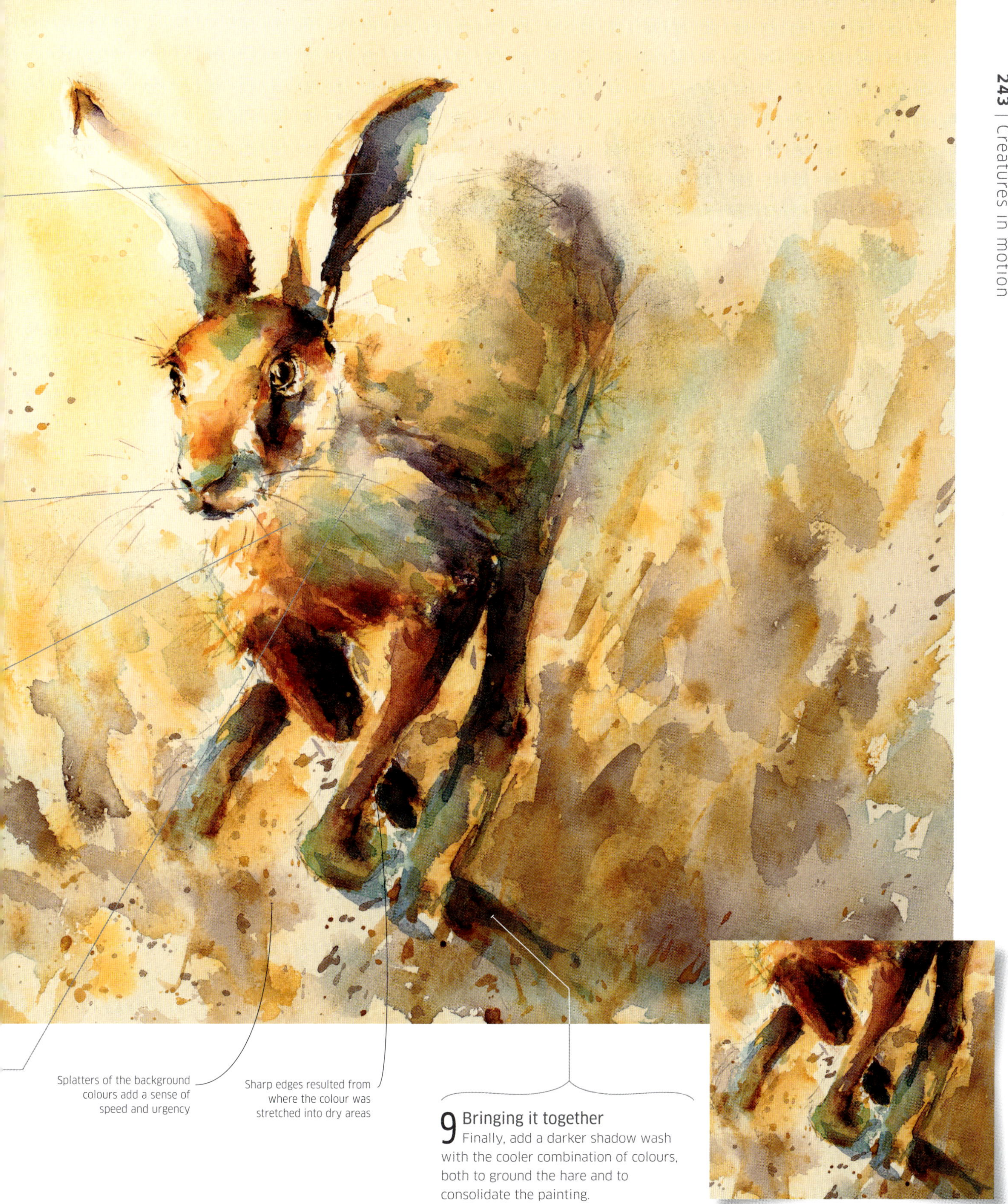

Splatters of the background colours add a sense of speed and urgency

Sharp edges resulted from where the colour was stretched into dry areas

9 Bringing it together

Finally, add a darker shadow wash with the cooler combination of colours, both to ground the hare and to consolidate the painting.

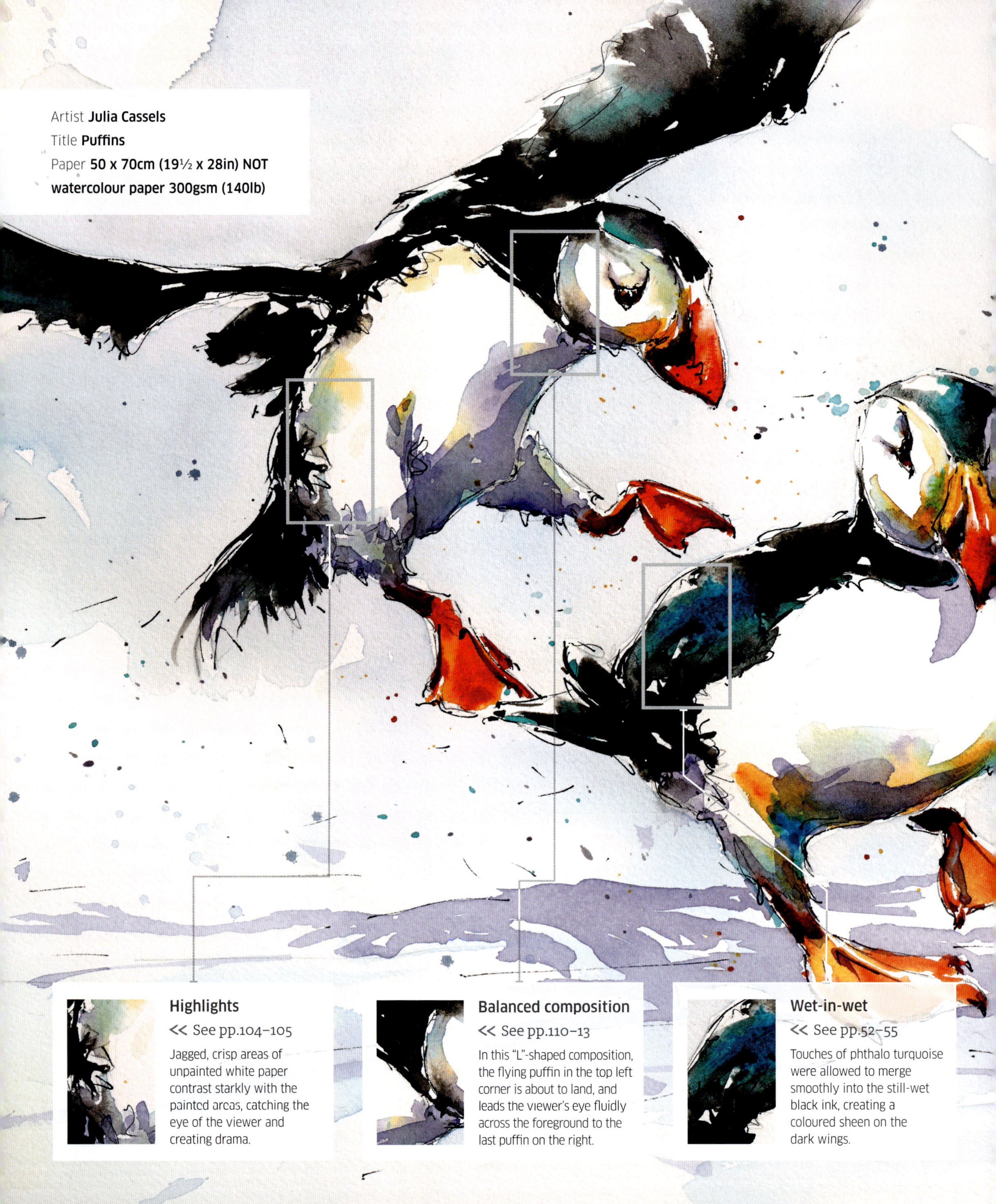

Highlights

≪ See pp.104–105

Jagged, crisp areas of unpainted white paper contrast starkly with the painted areas, catching the eye of the viewer and creating drama.

Balanced composition

≪ See pp.110–13

In this "L"-shaped composition, the flying puffin in the top left corner is about to land, and leads the viewer's eye fluidly across the foreground to the last puffin on the right.

Wet-in-wet

≪ See pp.52–55

Touches of phthalo turquoise were allowed to merge smoothly into the still-wet black ink, creating a coloured sheen on the dark wings.

Showcase painting

Fluid lines, loose washes, and areas of bright colour create a sense of
liveliness in this painting. The intense contrast between the black ink and
crisp white highlights brings the subject to life, while the composition
guides the eye smoothly from the flying puffin to those on the ground.

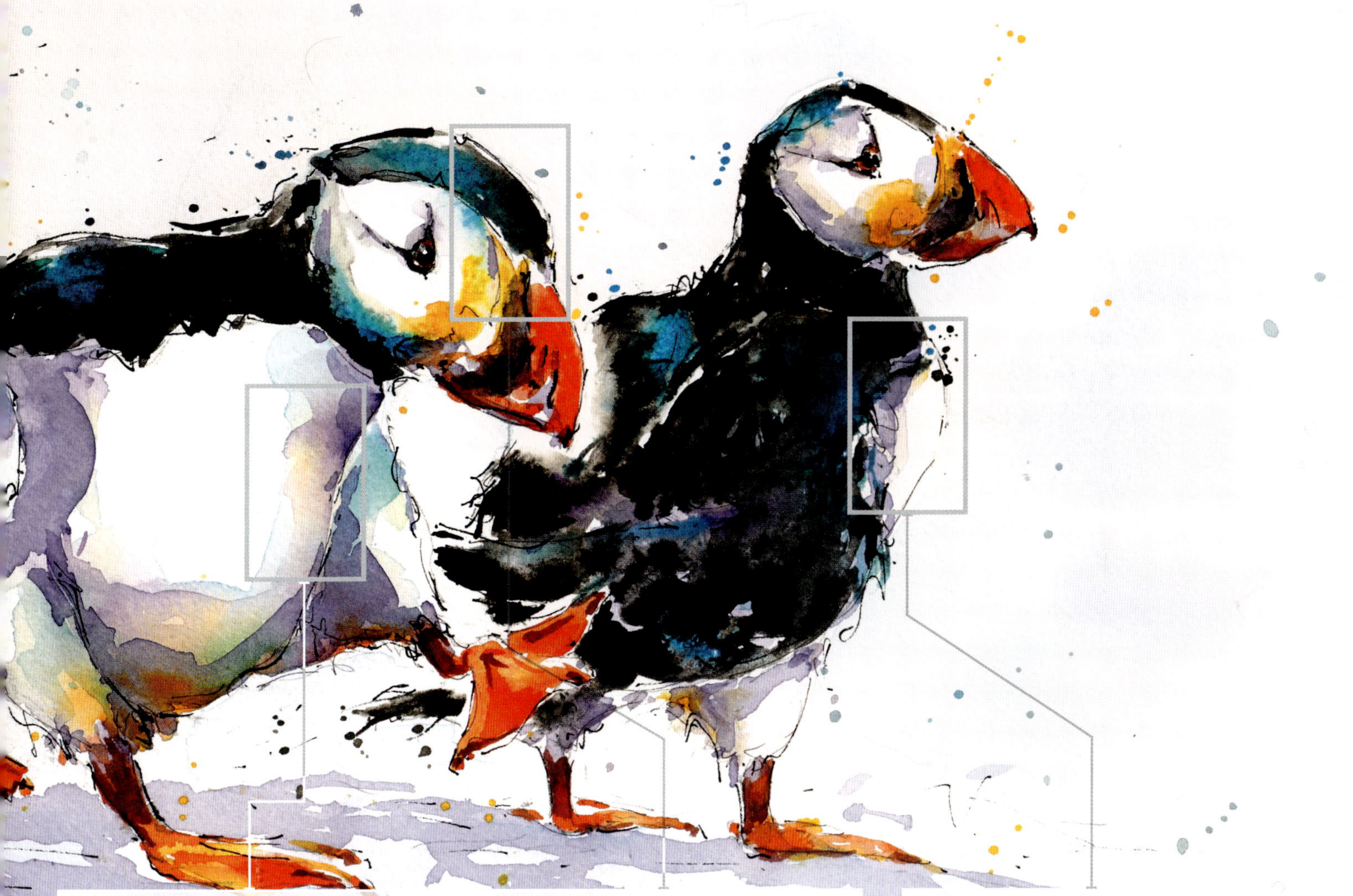

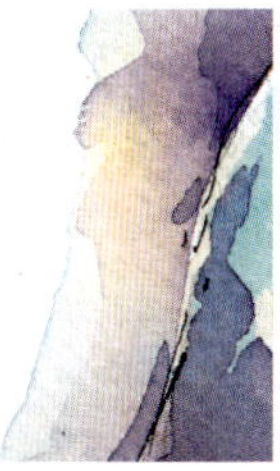

Glazing

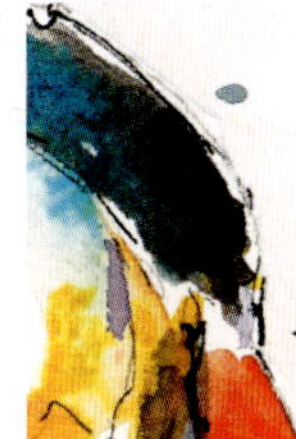

≪ See pp.124–25

A glaze of transparent
pigment, such as the purple
shadow on this bird's front,
allows the richer, warmer
tones of body colour beneath
to glow through.

Line and wash

≪ See pp.76–79

The washes of colour
deliberately do not quite
meet the sketched lines of
ink around them, producing
a sense of life and movement
in the painting.

Using inks

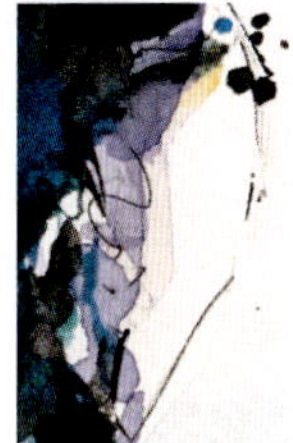

≪ See pp.154–55

Indian ink is water-based, so
works well with watercolour;
it is useful for intense tone,
as seen here in the contrast
between the black and white
areas of the puffins.

Glossary

Terms with their own entry are given in bold type.

Aerial perspective
Portraying the illusion of depth, especially in landscapes, by painting distant objects lighter and cooler in tone compared to warmer, brighter, and more detailed foreground objects. Also called atmospheric perspective.

Alla prima
Italian for "at first attempt", this term describes a painting finished in one sitting.

Analogous colours
Groups of colours that are next to each other on the **colour wheel** – such as red, orange, and yellow.

Blending
A painting method in which two colours gradually merge together.

Body colour
Opaque paint, such as gouache, which will obscure underlying areas of paint.

Bristle brush
A brush made from stiff fibres, such as hog hair. Can be used damp in watercolour painting for removing dry paint.

Cockling
Wrinkling or buckling in lightweight papers, caused by the paper expanding when wet. Can be prevented by **stretching**.

Colour wheel
A visual device for showing the relationship between **primary**, **secondary**, **tertiary**, and **complementary colours**.

Complementary colours
Colours located directly opposite each other on the **colour wheel**: yellow and purple, red and green, blue and orange. They brighten each other when used together.

Composition
The way in which the various components of a painting, including the main area of focus, are arranged to create a harmonious whole.

Cool colours
Colours with a bluish tint. They tend to appear to recede in a picture, so can be used to create **aerial perspective**.

Crosshatching
A drawing technique in which criss-crossing parallel lines create **tone**. The closer the lines, the denser the tone.

Dry brushwork
Applying paint with a sparsely loaded brush. The almost dry paintbrush is dragged across the paper to produce textured marks.

Flat wash
A wash of a single uniform colour. Produced by painting overlapping bands of consistent **hue** and dilution strength to create an even layer of colour.

Focal points
Points of interest that the eye is drawn to immediately, whether because of the **perspective**, the colour, or an intricate shape.

Form
The solid, three-dimensional shape of an object.

Glazing
The application of a **transparent** layer of paint over a layer of paint that has completely dried. Used for adjusting the **hue** or **tone** of layers underneath.

Graduated wash
A wash that fades smoothly between light and dark. Created by laying down bands of progressively diluted paint. Also known as a graded wash.

Granulated wash
A wash in which watercolour **pigments** separate from the binder and water, creating a grainy texture when dry.

Granulating pigments
Pigments with heavy particles that can form a grainy texture on the paper. Examples include French ultramarine, cerulean blue, and Mars black. Also known as sedimentary pigments.

Highlight
The lightest **tone** in a **composition**, occurring on the most brightly lit parts of a subject.

Hot-pressed paper
Paper with a very smooth surface that has been pressed between hot rollers.

Hue
Another word for colour.

Key
The overall **tone** of a painting: a predominantly light painting is said to have a high key, while a dark one has a low key.

Layering
Painting one colour over another colour that is dry.

Lifting out
Removing paint from the surface of the paper, using a damp brush or paper towel, often in order to create soft **highlights**.

Linear perspective
Portraying three dimensions in a painting by ensuring that parallel lines appear to converge in the distance on a horizon.

Masking fluid
A latex fluid that is painted onto paper and resists any watercolour paint put over it. Used to create **highlights**.

Medium
A substance used to modify the fluidity, thickness, or finish of paint. Also describes the materials used to paint, such as watercolour, gouache, or ink.

Mid tones
All variations of **tone** between the darkest and the lightest.

Modelling
Using light and dark **tone** to create a three-dimensional impression of an object.

Monochrome
Working in any single colour.

Negative space
The gaps between objects. Negative space is as important as **positive shape** in creating a satisfying **composition**.

NOT paper
Meaning "not **hot-pressed**", this is paper with a slightly textured surface that has been pressed by cold rollers during its manufacture. It is sometimes called cold-pressed paper.

Opaque colour
Colour that is impervious to light and which obscures anything underneath; the opposite of **transparent**.

Palette
Any suitable mixing surface for paint. Also means the range of colours used for a painting, or an artist's preferred colours.

Pan
A small block of solid watercolour paint that can be slotted into a **palette** or paintbox.

Perspective
The method of creating a sense of depth on a flat surface through the use of **modelling**, **linear**, and **aerial perspective**.

Pigment
Particles with inherent colour that can be used in paints.

Plein air
Meaning "open air" in French. Describes painting outdoors.

Positive shape
The outline shape of an object.

Primary colours
There are three primary colours – yellow, red, and blue – that cannot be made by mixing any other colours. Any two primaries can be mixed together to make a **secondary colour**.

Recession
Moving from the foreground to the background. Colour recession is the use of **warm** and **cool colours** to create a sense of depth.

Repelling pigments
Pigments that can prevent **blending** and **merging**, often because of their opacity. Examples include cadmium yellow, orange, and red, and Naples yellow. **Lifting out** these pigments is usually easy.

Reserving whites
Leaving areas of paper unpainted to show the colour white. This allows the paper to form the lightest **tones** and **highlights** in the painting, instead of paint.

Resist
A method of preserving **highlights** by applying a material that repels paint, such as **masking fluid**.

Rigger
A long, fine brush used for detailed work.

Rough paper
Paper with a highly textured surface that has been left to dry naturally, without pressing.

Rule of thirds
An aid to **composition** that divides a picture into thirds, horizontally and vertically, to make a grid of nine squares. Points of interest are placed on the "thirds" lines, and **focal points** on the intersections.

Runbacks
Irregular shapes, sometimes called blooms or cauliflowers, caused when a weak wash (less pigment) is added to a strong wash (more pigment).

Sable
Sable fur is used in the finest quality paintbrushes. The long, dark brown hairs have a great capacity for holding paint and create a fine point.

Scraping back
Using a blade or other tool to remove layers of dry paint in order to reveal the white paper below and create **highlights**.

Scumbling
Applying a thin, irregular layer of paint over a previously painted surface, allowing patches of the colour underneath to show.

Secondary colours
Colours made by mixing two **primary colours** together. They are: green (mixed from blue and yellow), orange (mixed from red and yellow), and purple (mixed from blue and red).

Separating pigments
Combinations of **pigments** that do not mix fully and separate on the paper, for example cadmium red and phthalo blue. Also describes **granulating pigments** that can separate on drying.

Shadow
The darkness cast when light is obscured, either on an object or by it.

Soft-hair brush
A brush made from soft-textured animal hair, such as **sable**, squirrel, or goat.

Softening
Blending the edges of a paint stroke with a brush dampened with clean water to prevent paint from drying with a hard edge.

Spattering
Flicking paint from a loaded toothbrush to produce a fine spray of dots.

Splattering
Flicking paint from a loaded paintbrush to produce texture.

Staining pigments
Pigments that leave behind some colour when **lifted out**, and cannot be fully removed. Examples include phthalo blue, Prussian blue, and azo yellow.

Stippling
The application of relatively neat dots to form a colour field, or to create shading.

Stretching
A method of wetting paper, taping it to a board, and allowing it to dry flat. Stretching paper helps to prevent it from **cockling**.

Support
Any surface onto which paint is laid, such as paper or canvas.

Tertiary colours
The colours between the **primary** and **secondary colours** on a **colour wheel**. They are created by mixing an equal proportion of the primary colour into the secondary colour.

Tone
The relative lightness or darkness of a colour. In watercolour, the tone of a paint can be lightened by diluting it with water.

Transparent colour
Colour that light will shine through easily. When layered, it will not obscure anything underneath. Transparent pigments are ideal for **glazing**.

Underpainting
An initial layer of paint that serves as a base for **composition**.

Value
The **tonal** position of colours on a scale from light to dark.

Variegated wash
A wash that changes from one colour to another. A variegated wash may be laid in bands of progressively changing colour so that the colours **blend** smoothly, or in random dots and dabs so that the colours mingle.

Warm colours
Colours with a reddish or orange tint. Warm colours appear to come forward in a picture and can be used to create **aerial perspective**.

Wax resist
A method of using candle wax or oil pastel to prevent the surface of the paper from accepting paint. Once applied, the wax or pastel cannot be removed.

Wet-in-wet
Applying paint onto wet paper or onto paint that is still wet.

Wet-on-dry
Adding layers of paint on top of colour that has already dried. Painting in this way produces vivid colours with strong edges.

Index

About the artists

Grahame Booth has won numerous exhibition awards throughout his successful career as a watercolour artist. He now teaches, passing on over 25 years of experience to master the challenges of learning watercolour. Grahame has produced two DVDs and has written three books on watercolour techniques, as well as contributing to many others. He writes regularly for *Artists & Illustrators* magazine and has a popular YouTube painting channel. Grahame is the consultant artist for this book; he wrote "The basics" chapter and his work features on pages 80-81, 122-23, 128-29, 138-39, 172-73, 202-203, and 234-35. www.grahamebooth.com

Alisa Adamsone is a watercolour artist and illustrator, having earned her degree in printmaking from the Art Academy of Latvia. Her work is inspired by the fluidity of nature – flowers and animals being some of her best-preferred subjects. Alisa's paintings are included in private collections all over the world and she has exhibited both in the UK and in Latvia. Alisa's work features on pages 74-75, 216-17, and 224-25. www.saatchiart.com/alisaadamsone

Veronica Ballart Lilja has been a full-time illustrator since 2007, with a number of high-profile clients mainly in the fields of fashion, packaging, editorial, magazines, advertising, and textiles. Originally from Sweden, she earned her degree in graphic design in Barcelona and spent 15 years in Spain before moving to New York. Her art has been published in several magazines, books, advertising campaigns, and on postage stamps. Veronica's work features on pages 152-53, 156-57, 206-207, and 232-33. www.veronicaballart.com

Glynis Barnes-Mellish has painted since childhood and was particularly drawn to the exciting and fresh approach that watercolour could bring to portraiture. Experimentation with various weights and weaves of paper, and the detailed study of anatomy and physiology, have contributed to Glynis's

rise as one of the UK's leading portrait painters. Glynis has won the Daler Rowney Watercolour Award and has been a major contributor to many books on watercolour painting. Glynis's work features on pages 58-61, 220-23, and 228-29. www.barnesmellish.co.uk

Julia Cassels is a well-known wildlife artist, with her work found in collections worldwide. A decade living in Zambia and Tanzania has provided a deep understanding of her artistic subjects to capture the flowing style that is characteristic of her work. Julia has illustrated, written, and contributed to several books, and has been successfully shortlisted for the David Shepherd 'Wildlife Artist of The Year' award for four years running. Julia also runs courses and workshops from her Hampshire studio, and leads painting holidays to Zambia, Spain, and the Camargue. Julia's work features on pages 52-55, 92-93, 240-43, and 244-45. www.juliacassels.com

Rod Craig trained at the West of England College of Art and ran a graphic design consultancy for over 30 years. He now paints full-time, with watercolour being his preferred medium to create the fluid and energetic abstract landscapes that are his trademark. Rod exhibits widely in the UK and has had a solo exhibit in New York. Also a performing musician, he enjoys combining his passions for art and music and names most of his paintings after the music that helped to inspire them. Rod's work features on pages 64-65, 104-105, 162-65, 178-79, and 200-201. www.rodcraig.com

Denise Findlay graduated from the Glasgow School of Art in 1996 and went on to produce solo exhibitions throughout Scotland and England. She has won many awards including the Elizabeth Greenshields Award three times. Denise's work features in many private collections and she has appeared on Sky TV's *Portrait Artist of the Year.* She believes that "painting is a purely visual experience where the viewer should not be left unsure of its

meaning". Denise's work features on pages 66-67, 94-95, 218-19, and 226-27. www.denisefindlay.com

Eleanor Hardiman works on commercial projects around the world, using watercolour illustration for children's books, magazine covers, packaging, and stationery. She uses a mix of traditional and unconventional watercolour techniques to achieve her distinctive style, and she is particularly inspired by the patterns and prints of William Morris, specimen drawings, and Japanese woodcuts. Eleanor's work features on pages 112-13, 126-27, and 130-31. www.eleanorhardiman.co.uk

Michele Illing is an award-winning artist, with a background in illustration in advertising and publishing. She has shared her passion for art in her classes and workshops for over 17 years and now tutors painting groups abroad in France and Italy. Michele has created several online art video courses in collaboration with ArtTutor.com and has been a featured artist in a number of art magazines. Michele's work features on pages 50-51, 84-85, 86-87, 144-45, 210-11, 230-31, and 238-39. www.micheleilling.co.uk

Gilly Marklew studied graphic design and illustration, going on to work in advertising and for all the major publishing houses in London, as well as the Arkwright museum in Derbyshire, before embarking on a career as a children's book illustrator. Gilly has been exhibiting watercolour paintings since 2003 and teaches watercolour classes at her studio in Norfolk. Gilly's work features on pages 56-57, 68-69, 82-83, 102-103, 208-209, and 236-37. www.goodworks.myzen.co.uk/GillyMarklew/Site/Home.html

Rachel McNaughton has enjoyed drawing and painting from an early age; her interest in art eventually took on a life of its own and she now spends much of her time in her studio, creating watercolours of flowers, landscapes, and animals. Watercolour is Rachel's preferred medium – she enjoys allowing the paint to run and mix on the paper for the unpredictable effects that result in her loose and expressive style. Rachel's work features on pages 98–99, 116–17, 146–47, 174–75, and 192–93. www.artbyrachel.co.uk

Maria Montiel is a Venezuelan illustrator and graphic designer with a degree from the Instituto Europeo de Diseño, Madrid. Her passion for art is inspired by her family, her childhood in the Caribbean, and her travels. Now based in Barcelona, Maria uses watercolour to create imaginative worlds full of warmth and magic – in particular, her memories of the Latin American jungle, with its vivid colours and rich textures, bloom in her vibrant illustrations. Maria's work features on pages 76, 78–79, 120–21, 148–49, 166–67, 198–99, and 204–205. www.mariamontielstudio.com

Paul O'Kane is a retired architect and now a *plein air* painter. He spends the summer months on painting holidays in Europe where he tutors and runs workshops in all art mediums. Paul is also a multi-award-winning article writer, a keen urban sketcher, and a regular watercolour tutor to the annual international *plein air* art fair, Art in the Open, in Wexford. Paul's work features on pages 62–63, 76–77, 150–51, 158–61, and 186–87. www.paulokane.co.uk

Ian Ramsay is an internationally recognized watercolour artist and workshop instructor. His work is representational and selectively detailed, reflecting his earlier training and vocation as an architect. Ian's paintings are included in collections around the world and he has been represented by galleries in the USA, UK, and Japan. Many of his watercolour images have featured in books and magazine articles on the subject. Ian's work features on pages 134–37, 142–43, 188–89, and 194–97. www.ianramsay.blogspot.com

Chris Robinson is an architect and a painter. He enjoys the spontaneity of working *en plein air* and expressing his love of light and atmosphere in his work. He has featured in international art magazines, has exhibited at the Royal Academy Summer Exhibition and the Royal West of England Academy, and has been awarded 'The Most Innovative Use of Watercolour' by the Royal Institute of Painters in Watercolour. Chris's work features on pages 72–73, 96–97, 106–107, 110–11, 132–33, 140–41, and 176–77. www.chrisrobinsonwatercolours.com

Ingrid Sanchez is a Mexican-British artist and designer best known for her vibrant, nature-inspired watercolours. After working in the graphics industry, she founded CreativeIngrid to focus on developing her signature style for product and surface design, leading to numerous brand partnerships. Ingrid teaches creative workshops around the globe, showcasing her unique style of watercolour and mixed media, and has also developed tailored corporate classes for clients such as Target, Harrods, and Cass Art. Ingrid's work features on pages 100–101, 108–109, and 154–55. www.ingridsanchez.com

Julia Trickey loves to capture the beauty and detail of nature in watercolour, and is particularly drawn to the imperfections in specimens such as autumnal leaves, seed heads, and fading flowers. Exhibiting regularly, Julia has been awarded four RHS gold medals, among other awards. She tutors art and runs botanical art workshops around the UK and beyond, teaching as far afield as Transylvania and New York. She has written articles for national art magazines and has produced many resources for aspiring botanical artists. Julia's work features on pages 88–89 and 212–15. www.juliatrickey.co.uk

James Willis is best known for his paintings of architecture and cityscapes. The way that colour and light play on buildings and landscapes are essential elements in his paintings. James gathers inspiration for his work through sketching and painting during his travels around Europe. He has exhibited throughout the UK and his work features in both public and private collections around the country. James's work features on pages 70–71, 90–91, 114–15, 118–19, and 182–85. www.jameswillisart.co.uk

Yong Hong Zhong was born in Canton, China and immigrated to the United States when he was 12 years old. He developed a keen interest in drawing at an early age, and attended LaGuardia High School of Music and Arts in New York, followed by a degree in illustration and art history from Pratt Institute. Yong worked for Disney Animation Studios from 1995 to 2008 before taking a different direction to focus on his passion for traditional fine art painting. Yong's work features on pages 124–25, 152, 180–81, and 190–91. www.yonghongzhong.com

Acknowledgments

The publisher would like to thank Nigel Wright at XAB for additional photography; William Collins at the DK Picture Library; Geetika Bhandari, Assistant Picture Researcher; John Friend and Katie Hewett for proofreading; and Vanessa Bird for creating the index.

We are also grateful to the following for their kind permission to reproduce their photographs. (Key: a-above; b-below/bottom; c-centre; f-far; l-left; r-right; t-top)

Picture credits: 4 123RF.com: Andrey Guryanov (br/Reference). 5 iStockphoto.com: PeopleImages / E+ (tr/Reference). 25 iStockphoto.com: PeopleImages / E+ (bc, br/Reference). 98 Dreamstime.com: Nuli (cra). 99 Dreamstime.com: Nuli (Reference for all 3). 102 123RF.com: Andrey Guryanov (cra). 103 123RF.com: Andrey Guryanov (l/Reference). 170 iStockphoto.com: PeopleImages / E+ (br/Reference). 220 123RF.com: Volodymyr Melnyk (cr/Reference). 221 123RF.com: dolgachov (cl/Reference). Dreamstime.com: Gstockstudio1 (cr/Reference). 222 iStockphoto.com: PeopleImages / E+ (cra). 222–223 iStockphoto.com: PeopleImages / E+ (Reference for all 6). 226–227 iStockphoto.com: PeopleImages / E+ (Reference for all 6). 238 Pixabay: Fran__ (cra). 238–239 Pixabay: Fran__ (Reference for all 9)

All other images © Dorling Kindersley www.dkimages.com

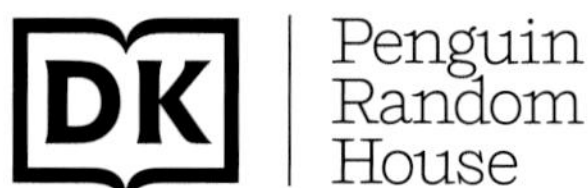

SECOND EDITION

DK LONDON
Editorial Manager Clare Double
Senior Designer Glenda Fisher
Editor Jasmin Lennie
Production Controller Celine MacLeod
Jacket and Sales Material Co-ordinator Emily Cannings
Art Director Maxine Pedliham
Publishing Director Katie Cowan

Jacket Design and Styling Eleanor Ridsdale

DK DELHI
Managing Editor Saloni Singh
Editor Ankita Gupta
Managing Art Editor Neha Ahuja Chowdhry
DTP Designers Satish Chandra Gaur, Raman Panwar
DTP Coordinator Pushpak Tyagi
Pre-production Manager Balwant Singh
Creative Head Malavika Talukder

FIRST EDITION

Managing Editor Dawn Henderson
Managing Art Editor Marianne Markham
Consultant Artist Grahame Booth
Senior Editor Alastair Laing
Senior Art Editor Emma Forge
Project Editor Shashwati Tia Sarkar
Editors Katie Hardwicke, Megan Lea, Nikki Sims, Diana Vowles
Designers Tom Forge, Karen Constanti
DTP Designers Rajdeep Singh, Satish Gaur, Anurag Trivedi
Editorial Assistant Kiron Gill
Senior Jackets Creative Nicola Powling
Senior Producer Tony Phipps
Producer Rebecca Parton
Pre-production Manager Sunil Sharma
Art Director Maxine Pedliham
Publishing Director Mary-Clare Jerram

This edition published in 2024
First published in Great Britain in 2020 by
Dorling Kindersley Limited
DK, 20 Vauxhall Bridge Road,
London, SW1V 2SA.

The authorised representative in the EEA is
Dorling Kindersley Verlag GmbH. Arnulfstr. 124,
80636 Munich, Germany

Copyright © 2024, 2020 Dorling Kindersley Limited
A Penguin Random House Company
10 9 8 7 6 5 4 3 2
003–338908–Aug/2024

A CIP catalogue record for this book
is available from the British Library.
ISBN: 978-0-2416-5359-3

Printed and bound in China

www.dk.com

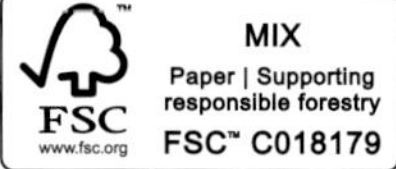

This book was made with Forest
Stewardship Council™ certified
paper – one small step in DK's
commitment to a sustainable future.
Learn more at
www.dk.com/uk/information/sustainability